Edgar Allan Poe

A to Z

EDGAR ALLAN POE

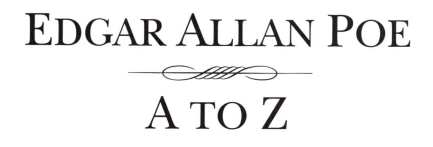

A TO Z

The Essential Reference to His Life and Work

DAWN B. SOVA

Checkmark Books®

An imprint of Facts On File, Inc.

Edgar Allan Poe A to Z

Checkmark Books
An imprint of Facts On File, Inc.
11 Penn Plaza
New York NY 10001

Library of Congress Cataloging-in-Publication Data

Sova, Dawn B.
Edgar Allan Poe, A to Z: the essential reference to his life and work / Dawn B. Sova.
p. cm.
Includes bibliographical references and index.
ISBN 0-8160-3850-3 (alk. paper)—ISBN 0-8160-4161-X (pbk.: alk. paper)
1. Poe, Edgar Allan, 1809–1849—Encyclopedias. 2. Authors, American—19th century—
Biography—Encyclopedias. I. Title.

PS2630.S68   2001
818'.309—dc21   [B]   00-061039

Checkmark Books are available at special discounts when purchased in bulk quantities for businesses, associations, institutions, or sales promotions. Please call our Special Sales Department in New York at 212/967-8800 or 800/322-8755.

Paper cover design by Nora Wertz
Jacket design by Cathy Rincon

Printed in the United States of America

VB FOF 10 9 8 7 6 5 4 3 2 1
(pbk) 10 9 8 7 6 5 4 3 2 1

This book is printed on acid-free paper.

CONTENTS

ACKNOWLEDGMENTS

To examine comprehensively the life and works of an author such as Edgar Allan Poe requires tenacity of the individual and tolerance of all with whom she makes contact in the years that such a work is in progress. In writing *Edgar Allan Poe A to Z*, I have tried to exhibit the necessary tenacity as one source after another led to a dead end, while other unexpected sources emerged unannounced. I gratefully acknowledge that those personally closest to me, as well as professional contacts whose names appear here or whose names are omitted by their choice, have shown a remarkable tolerance over the years during which this guide acquired form and moved to completion. Unlike my subject, who lived many of his 40 years with feelings of loss, abandonment, and personal as well as professional frustration generated by others, I have enjoyed willing assistance and personal support, for which I am grateful.

Bert Holtje of James Peter Associates, Inc., is a remarkable individual who is both literary agent and caring voice of reason. I have appreciated his confidence in my dedication to the project and his support, despite difficulties that threatened to derail my progress. I am also heartily grateful for his extensive knowledge of many subjects, which makes his problem-solving efforts that much more meaningful.

Anne Savarese, my editor at Facts On File, Inc., who inherited this project already formed and was charged with bringing it to fruition, has shown admirable grace and tenacity in assisting me to produce a comprehensive and valuable work of which we can both feel proud.

I very much appreciate her professional insight, her willingness to work with me, and her encouragement in the writing of *Edgar Allan Poe A to Z*. Such dedication by an editor should not be taken for granted.

I. Macarthur Nickles, director of the Garfield [New Jersey] Public Library, has made me view every new book project as a cause for celebration because each brings a renewed opportunity to enjoy the continuing innovation he has brought to my hometown library. His professional expertise, his knowledge of people and resources, his understanding of the multitude of possibilities in research, and his graciousness in sharing that knowledge have been invaluable in this and other projects.

Robert Gregor, whose professional world is one of web-based researching and information technology, provided valuable technical and resources management assistance that enabled me to harness the power of my computer and my time. For his patience and expertise I am grateful.

My appreciation also goes to the University of Virginia libraries and special collections; the Edgar Allan Poe Society of Baltimore, Maryland; the Edgar Allan Poe Library of Richmond, Virginia; the library of Montclair State University, New Jersey; and the people who have dedicated themselves to maintaining sites both large and small dedicated to Poe.

Last and most important are the debts that I owe to my family, especially my parents, Violet and Emil J. Sova, who instilled in me a love of learning and the desire to know.

INTRODUCTION

The popular view of Edgar Allan Poe as a writer has depended largely on only a few of his works. The larger part of his extensive writings remain unknown to all but a small number of readers. Poems such as "The Raven," "The Bells," and "Annabel Lee," and such short stories as "The Black Cat," "The Cask of Amontillado," "The Pit and the Pendulum," and "The Tell-Tale Heart" have provided source material for television dramas and comedies—some with a nod to the author, but more often not. Everyone recognizes the plot or certain famous lines, but few know the full range of Poe's work in science fiction, literary criticism and theory, and philosophy. *Edgar Allan Poe A to Z* seeks to fill that void with more than 3,400 entries on Poe's writings and his life.

Readers whose knowledge of Poe is limited to entries in high school anthologies or college textbooks might be amazed to learn that Poe published more than 350 stories, poems, essays, and critical articles under his own name, and is the likely author of many more. He popularized the American short story, and he is credited with inventing the modern detective story with an investigator who uses reasoning instead of legwork to solve crimes. Poe also served as editor of several periodicals at different times in Richmond, Virginia; Philadelphia, Pennsylvania; New York, New York; and Baltimore, Maryland. His correspondence with the other leading writers of his day was extensive, and he was praised in print by many other literary figures who never met him but admired his work. He also had the critical status and the credibility in his day to savagely attack in print the works of other writers who today enjoy stronger reputations than his. Such critical assessments appeared in leading literary and popular periodicals of the time, as did his stories and poems.

A large body of Poe's work is no longer in print, leaving only the well-known and frequently creatively recycled stories and poems to perpetuate his fame. Most libraries long ago cleared their shelves of his literary criticism and decimated sets of his collected works, retaining the best-known tales and poems and winnowing out the rest. The reasons for such decisions are varied, of course, but most have to do with the low regard in which Poe was held during the first half of the 20th century. As biographers who have taken the time to consult the correspondence, journals, and criticism of Poe's day have found, his loss of status was largely undeserved and easily traced to the successful efforts of Rufus Wilmot Griswold at defaming Poe's character. Griswold, nominally a friend, claimed after Poe's death that he had been designated the author's literary executor. He manipulated Poe's mother-in-law, Maria Clemm, into supporting his handling of Poe's writings, and went on to destroy Poe's character in the author's own obituary, a piece of writing that under most circumstances is truthful—or, if untrue, errs on the side of praise. On October 9, 1849, Griswold avenged an old grudge against Poe by publishing a defamatory obituary—to which Griswold signed the name "Ludwig"—that cast aspersions on Poe's moral character. Griswold suggested that the necrophiliac behavior, the madness of the narrators, and the excesses of Poe's fiction were renderings of Poe's own experiences and life. While many of Poe's contemporaries tried to correct this image by publishing defenses of Poe in the decades that followed, Griswold's charges remained in the public mind for many years and led to the decline of Poe's literary reputation.

Edgar Allan Poe A to Z is a comprehensive examination of Poe's writings that presents a complete portrait of a complicated and brilliant thinker and writer. Other studies have examined all of the known stories or some of the best-known poems, and a few have identified and discussed several of the essays that gained prominence, such as "A Rationale of Verse," "Eureka," or "The Poetic Principle." No single work, however, has covered all of these works along with Poe's extensive literary criticism.

The reader who picks up *Edgar Allan Poe A to Z* to obtain information about one of Poe's well-known works will discover many other important writings by the author, along with essential facts about his short and difficult life.

Abel-Phittim Character in "A TALE OF JERUSALEM." He is one of the Gizbarim, the three collectors of the offerings in the Holy City, and the one who carries the shekels to the Romans in trade for lambs that the conquered Jewish faithful will sacrifice on the altar. When the story first appeared in the June 9, 1832, issue of the *Philadelphia Saturday Courier,* the character was named Abel-Shittem. In Hebrew, "shittem" refers to the camping place on the Plain of Moab where the people of Israel began to mix freely with the nonbelievers and to reject their Jewish faith, giving up dietary laws and worshipping the gods of the Moabs. To avoid the obvious scatological references, Poe changed the name for later publication of the story in the April 1836 issue of the SOUTHERN LITERARY MESSENGER.

Abernethy, Dr. John (1764–1831) Well-known, eccentric British physician to whom C. Auguste DUPIN refers in "THE PURLOINED LETTER" when suggesting that the prefect of police employ counsel in the matter. Dupin relates that a miserly rich patient, hoping to receive free medical advice by posing a hypothetical question, asked Abernethy what one should take in a particular situation. The physician replied, "Take advice."

"About Critics and Criticism: By the Late Edgar A. Poe" Essay written by Poe in 1849. It appeared posthumously in the January 1850 issue of GRAHAM'S MAGAZINE. The piece reviews the diverse approaches of criticism, praising critics of greater "candor and more discriminating taste" while condemning those who shut their "eyes tightly to all autorial [*sic*] blemishes, and open them, like owls, to all autorial merits." In this analysis of the role played by critics, Poe asserts that the true literary critic has the obligation to do more than to merely offer readers a summary of the work with all of its positive qualities. Instead, "his legitimate task is still, in pointing out and analyzing defects and showing how the work might have been improved to aid the general cause of Letters, without undue heed of the individual literary men." Poe cautions would-be critics that the merits of beauty in a literary work should not have to be explained, and that to do so is to admit that they are not merits altogether. He offers the example of the English historian and essayist Thomas Babington MACAULAY, whom he sees as able "to accomplish the extremes of unquestionable excellences—the extreme of clearness, of vigor (depending upon clearness), of grace, and very especially of thoroughness." Although he praises the Macaulay for "rhetoric which has its basis in common sense," Poe recommends that other critics not to attempt to merely imitate him "but to outstrip him in his own path—a path not so much his as Nature's." Poe presents this advice as an antidote to the propensity of American critics to exaggerate the merits of British authors and to "extol without discrimination work that would be surely condemned if credited to American authors."

"Achilles' Wrath" Poe's response in the BROADWAY JOURNAL of April 19, 1845, to an angry letter from Mr. W. Dinneford, a theater manager who strongly condemned Poe's scathing review of "THE ANTIGONE AT PALMO'S" and threatened that Poe would no longer receive free theater tickets in New York. In his rebuttal, Poe reprinted Dinneford's original letter, which first accused Poe of having solicited free tickets for the play, then of writing a critique "characterized much more by ill nature and an illiberal spirit, than by fair and candid, or even just criticism." Poe mocks what he perceives to be the "gross discourtesy" of the manager and claims that not only did Dinneford not answer his request for tickets, but also that none were left for him at the box office. In a condescending manner, Poe details the words Dinneford wrote in capital letters and itemizes the number of times Dinneford underlined words for emphasis. Asserting that he had asked for free tickets only because he had been led to believe that "it was usual in New York, among editors newly established, to apply (by note) for the customary free admission to the theatres," Poe calls the custom "a wretched one" and the task of asking for tickets "a dirty one." The nature of Poe's attacks on Dinneford suggest that the negative tone of the play review were, at least in part, colored by the desire to avenge a humiliation. He makes this clear in stating: "And the blatherskite who could behave in so indecent a manner, as to fail first in answering our note, and secondly in paying attention to the request it contained, has the audacity to find fault with us because we dared to express an unbiased opinion of his stupidity—that is to say, of the stupidity of a play gotten up by himself, Mr. Dinneford."

"An Acrostic"   Unpublished nine-line poem written by Poe sometime around 1829 for his cousin Elizabeth Rebecca HERRING. Thomas Ollive Mabbott included it among the unsigned works in his definitive *Collected Works of Edgar Allan Poe* (1969). Critics have noted the influence of John Keats in the poem's mention of Endymion (Keats's poem "Endymion" was published in 1818) and the way it connects love, pride, and death.

Ada   Character who appears in the first version of "TAMERLANE," a Byronic poem published in 1827 by the 19-year-old Poe, who signed it merely "by a Bostonian." The character was inspired by Sarah Elmira ROYSTER, the first of Poe's loves, a neighbor's daughter whom he had met four years earlier. Dark and brooding, the poem was written while Poe was reading works by the English romantic poets, most pointedly George Gordon, Lord BYRON, whose daughter Augusta Ada Gordon was popularly known as Ada. The 20th-century Russian emigré author Vladimir Nabokov, who acknowledged his own fascination with Poe, adopted the name as the title of his novel *Ada, or Ardor* (1969). When Poe revised the original 403-line poem to 243 lines for publication in 1845, he removed the name of Ada, much as her model has disappeared from his life, thus creating a lament for all lost love rather than only one specifically named.

Adams, John (1773–1825)   Mayor of Richmond, Virginia. He gave weapons to the young Poe, who was then a member of the paramilitary Junior Volunteers, and instructed him to use them in forming a bodyguard when the French general Lafayette visited the city in 1824.

"Addendum to 'A Few Words on Secret Writing'"   An article that appeared in the August 1841 issue of *GRAHAM'S MAGAZINE* that contained a cryptographic challenge to Poe—a message written in a complex code—which he published for his readers after he deciphered the message. Poe also includes several letters from the challenger and others familiar with his interest in cryptography who express surprise at his speed in translating the passage and praise his skill in doing so. He offers the cryptogram to his readers and assures them that the solution will appear in the next issue of the publication.

Addison, Joseph (1672–1719)   English essayist whose work appeared frequently in the *Spectator* and the *Tatler*. Poe admired Addison for his original and natural style. In his sketch of Nathaniel Parker WILLIS in "THE LITERATI OF NEW YORK," Poe equates Willis's command of language with Addison's "easy brilliance."

"Address Delivered at the Annual Commencement of Dickinson College, July 21, 1836, by S. A. Roszel"   Poe's review in the *SOUTHERN LITERARY MESSENGER* of October 1836 of a speech given by S. A. Roszel, principal of Dickinson's grammar school. Poe takes the opportunity both to praise the educator as "a scholar, of classical knowledge more extensive, and far more accurate than usual" and to condemn him for inventing words "at will, to suit the purpose of the moment." The review observes that Roszel's "Address on Education" is confined to a defense of "tutorial instruction as embraced under the divisions of the subjects to be taught, and the manner of teaching them." Noting that the greater emphasis of the address is on the "the loftier prospective benefits, and true spiritual uses of classical attainments," Poe praises Roszel's "defence of the learned tongues from the encroachments of a misconceived utilitarianism, and in urging their suitableness as a study for young." He also observes that the educator is "not only forcible, but has contrived to be in a great measure, original," and claims that the speaker's remarks regarding the duties of a teacher and "stern sense of the elevated moral standing of the tutor" are deserving of admiration and respect. Despite this, Poe is highly critical of the wording of the address. He finds fault with the speaker's "too frequent use of primitive meanings" and accuses Roszel of inventing word origins, "some few of Mr. Roszel's inventions are certainly not English." In ending the review, Poe magnanimously suggests that the fervor and the beauty of the address outweigh its faults: "But to these sins (for the world will have them such) a fellow-feeling has taught us to be lenient."

"Address Delivered before the Baltimore Lyceum. Athenaeum Society, William Wirt Society, Washington Lyceum, Philo-Nomian Society and Franklin Association, Literary and Scientific Societies of Baltimore, on the 4th of July, 1836. By Z. Collins Lee, Esq."   A brief review in the *SOUTHERN LITERARY MESSENGER* of November 1836 of a speech by Zaccheus Collins LEE, in which Poe praises its "impassioned and scholar-like performance" and claims that nothing less was expected, because he was "well aware of Mr. Lee's oratorical powers . . . and from the deep attention with which, we are told its delivery was received." In a rare moment of restraint in critiquing a public address, Poe states that he has no intention of examining the text in detail "at this late date" [six months after the fact] a presentation that "must have depended so largely upon anniversary recollections." Instead, Poe claims that he alludes to the speech "now with the sole purpose of recording, in brief, our opinion of its merits, and of quoting one of its passages without comment."

"**Address Delivered before the Goethean and Diagnothian Societies of Marshall College, at Their Annual Celebration, September 24, 1839. By Joseph O. Chandler**" A review in BURTON'S GENTLEMAN'S MAGAZINE for December 1839 of an address given by Joseph R. CHANDLER on September 24, 1839, on the subject of ancient versus modern oratory. Poe praises the speech, asserting that it stands apart from most addresses, which, "in general, are very ordinary matters, and we dislike to say anything about them, because we seldom have anything more to say than a few brief words of utter condemnation." Characterizing most addresses of the day as composed of "stale wisdom, overdone sentiment, schoolboy classicalities, bad English, worse Latin, and wholesale rhodomontade," Poe states that "Mr. Chandler has given us a good Address, and done an original thing." The originality lies largely in the speaker's willingness to deviate from the usual emphasis upon classical models and to profess, instead, "the vast superiority which modern intellect and its results maintain over the boasted civilization and proudest mental efforts of even the golden Heathen ages." Labeling Chandler a genius, and his address as "just such a turn as the man of genius might be led to give to a discourse upon an occasion of the kind, and such as only the man of genius would have given," Poe bases his praise on the speaker's "elevated knowledge of a futurity of existence—and through the glowing and burning hopes to which that knowledge of futurity gives rise." In typical fashion, the review is not wholly complimentary: it finds fault with Chandler's willingness to concede that ancient rhetoricians were more eloquent than his contemporaries, a concession that Poe views as "weakening his own position." Rather than agree with Chandler that the eloquence of the oratory of a speaker such as Demosthenes was greater than that of any modern speaker, Poe asserts that the difference lies in the effects upon the listeners because "the circumstances of the audience make the important difference in the reception of the oration." Describing the Greeks as "a highly excitable and an unread race" who had no printed books and to whom everything was new, he observes that "the incitements of the ancient rhetorician, were, when compared with those of the modern, absolutely novel, and therefore possessed an immense adventitious force." In contrast, the modern orator has a difficult task to convince listeners who have often heard the same exhortations many times. In short, "Demosthenes appealed to the passions of a populace; the modern orator struggles to sway the intellect of a deliberative assembly."

"**An Address Delivered before the Students of William and Mary at the Opening of the College on Monday, October 10, 1835. By Thomas R. Dew, President, and Professor of Moral and Political Philosophy. Pub[lished] by Request of the Students. Richmond: T. W. Wh...**" An article in the SOUTHERN LITERARY MESSENGER for Oc[to]ber 1836, in which Poe uses the address by Thomas R. DEW, the president of William and Mary, as a basis for describing the curriculum and degrees granted by the college. After providing preliminary words of praise for Dew, whom Poe singles out for "the influence of his character, and unusual energy," the article turns attention to the "brilliant prospects" of "this institution [which] has given the world more useful men than any other—more truly great statesmen." Poe characterizes the college as respected and venerated, and asserts that it offers an efficient education and a rigid discipline that "relies strongly on the chivalry and honor of the Southern student." Poe's detailed description of the courses of study provides insight regarding the programs, which include the "A.B., B.L., and A.M." in classical studies, law, and civil engineering. In conclusion, Poe claims that space limitations have prevented him from making "long extracts from the excellent Address now before us." He reassures his readers that "it is, as usual with every thing from that same source, comprehensive and eloquent, and full of every species of encouragement to the searcher after knowledge."

"**Address of the Carriers of the Cincinnati Daily American Republican to Its Patrons, for January, 1845**" The review of a poem written by the Cincinnati poet Mrs. Rebecca Shepard Reed Nichols, which appeared in the March 22, 1845, issue of the BROADWAY JOURNAL. Highly complimentary of the work, Poe writes that "although we should scarcely look for anything original in a News Address, still there is a great deal of originality and other high merit here." The review quotes "at random" four five-line verses, which Poe assures his readers are scarcely sufficient "to convey any just idea of the skill manifested in the general conduct of the poem." The stanzas describe the human life cycle metaphorically as seasons of the year, from "Bride of my youthful days, gentle and fair" through "Winter approached and enshrouded the dead!" Even as Poe acknowledges that all of the stanzas contain lapses, "except the second one quoted which is rhythmically perfect," he defends these flaws as "variations, [which] are strictly defensible, and show that Mrs. Nichols has, at all events, a well-cultivated ear."

"**An Address on Education, as Connected with the Permanence of Our Republican Institutions. Delivered before the Institute of Education of Hampden Sidney College, at Its Anniversary Meeting, September the 24th, 1835, on the Invitation of the Body. By Lucian Minor, Esq., of Louisa. Published by Request of the Institute**" A review of a speech delivered by Lucian e *SOUTHERN LITERARY MESSEN-* which Poe praises Minor's ...esting the establishment of ...Characterizing the text as ...loquence, and impressive energy ...he has enforced them," Poe expresses the ...pe that the state legislature will create school districts similar to those in New England as a means of reversing the fading glory of Virginia: "Her once great name is becoming, in the North, a bye-word for imbecility—all over the South, a type for 'the things that have been'." The review expresses the hope that Minor's words "may succeed in stirring up something akin to action in the legislative halls of the land," in order to reverse the "dying condition" of the state.

"Address on the Subject of a Surveying and Exploring Expedition to the Pacific Ocean and South Seas. Delivered In the Hall of Representatives on the Evening of April 3, 1836. By J. N. Reynolds. With Correspondence and Documents. New York: Published by Harper & Row" A review of explorer Jeremiah REYNOLDS's address that appeared in the *SOUTHERN LITERARY MESSENGER* of January 1837. Poe developed a lifelong admiration for Reynolds's exploits and used the address as his main source in writing *THE NARRATIVE OF ARTHUR GORDON PYM*. The review supports the move by Congress to authorize an expedition to explore the Pacific Ocean and the South Seas after "ten years in litigation," and credits Reynolds as "the originator, the persevering and indomitable advocate, the soul of the design." Poe praises Reynolds's eloquent address and professes that the review is meant to give "an outline of the history, object, and nature of the project" in order to tempt readers to read the original in its entirety. With an eye to the profits that can be made, Poe cites details regarding the large number of seamen and ships already engaged in the maritime industry and suggests that extending the reach of the United States through "a special national expedition could accomplish everything desired." He states that the scientific world will also benefit and that "the people demand it, and, thus there is a multiplicity of reasons why it should immediately be set on foot." The review, for the most part, devotes more space to the efforts that Reynolds made to successfully obtain government backing for the expedition than to revising the actual text of the address.

"The Adventures of a Gentleman in Search of a Horse. By Caveat Emptor, Gent. One, Etc. Philadelphia: Republished by Carey, Lea and Blanchard" A review of a guide to buying a horse that appeared in the *SOUTHERN LITERARY MESSENGER* for August 1836, in which Poe advises all amateurs "to look well, and look quickly into the pages of Caveat Emptor." The term *caveat emptor* is Latin for "let the buyer beware," and the book is a guide to the legal aspects of horse-buying, "serviceable law, too, intended as a matter of reference." The review states that "the first 180 pages are occupied with what the title implies, the adventures of a gentleman in search of a horse—the remaining 100 pages embrace, in all its details, difficulties, and intricacies, a profound treatise on the English law of horse-dealing warranty!" Poe expresses surprise that this is the first such work of its kind, given the great interest of most English gentry. He recommends the book highly to "all amateurs" and finds in it "much fine humor, good advice and useful information in all matters touching the nature, the management, and especially the purchase of a horse."

Aeschylus (525–456 B.C.) Greek dramatist and author of 90 plays, including *Seven Against Thebes, The Persians, Prometheus Bound, The Suppliant Woman,* and the *Oresteia* (a trilogy), who Poe ranks above SOPHOCLES and Euripides in dramatic ability. He claims in "MARGINALIA" that "Euripides and Sophocles were merely echoes of Aeschylus," and in "PINAKIDIA" calls *The Persians* one of the "only historical tragedies by Grecian authors."

Agathos Character in the short story "THE POWER OF WORDS." Dead for 300 years, he is one of two "angelic intelligences" engaged in a dialogue in the story and speaks lyrically of the divine power of words. In contrast to his counterpart OINOS, who is "a spirit newfledged with immortality," Agathos has learned through experience that "happiness lies in the acquisition of knowledge." He also proclaims "the physical power of words" and instructs his companion that every word is "an impulse on the air."

Ainsworth, William Harrison (1805–1882) Prolific English novelist whose work was strongly criticized by Poe for being boring and pandering to the lowest of popular tastes. The author of 41 novels, among them "THE TOWER OF LONDON," "GUY FAWKES," and *Jack Sheppard,* he became popular among Victorian readers, but Poe asserted in his review of *The Tower of London* that such "popularity of this work in London is no proof of its merit." In "MARGINALIA," Poe further denigrated the author's work by noting, "I cannot imagine why it is that Harrison Ainsworth so be-peppers his books with his own dog Latin and pig Greek—unless he agrees with Encyclopedia Chambers, that nonsense sounds worse in English than in any other language." Poe includes the author in "THE BALLOON-HOAX" as a passenger on the transatlantic voyage.

Al Aaraaf The name of the region between heaven and hell, or limbo, in the Koran, as well as the name that the astronomer Tycho Brahe gave to a star he discovered in 1572. Poe applied this name to a star that suddenly appears, then disappears, when he uses a metaphor for the concept of idealized fantasy in the poem "AL AARAAF."

"Al Aaraaf" An early poem, the longest Poe wrote, which he first self-published in May 1827 in the collection titled TAMERLANE AND OTHER POEMS. The poem received little notice in its first publication because of distribution difficulties. Poe submitted the poem to literary critic John NEAL, who mentioned the work in his column in the September 1829 issue of *Yankee*. Although Neal called "Al Aaraaf" in the main "nonsense, rather exquisite nonsense," he also expressed hope that the young poet "would but do himself justice." In December 1829, the poem appeared in *AL AARAAF, TAMERLANE, AND MINOR POEMS*, published commercially by the firm of Hatch and Dunning. When Poe chose on October 16, 1845, to read the poem at the Odeon in Boston, as part of his lecture before the Lyceum, he identified it as "The Messenger Star." The length of the poem and its abstract imagery dismayed listeners, many of whom walked out during Poe's lecture. The press severely criticized Poe for making a poor choice of reading and provided new ammunition to his enemies. The poem mingles science with poetry and creates a dream world of ravishing sights while it emphasizes the ideal of absolute beauty. In part one of the poem, the maiden NESACE, who symbolizes ideal beauty, lives in perfect happiness on the star. In her paradise, the inhabitants, all superior to humans but inferior to God, are free of the needs and conflicts that plague ordinary people. Nesace is God's favorite, a superior intelligence and the ruling presence on Al Aaraaf, and she alone in the universe can hear God's voice directly. She begs him to restore the lower beings on Al Aaraaf to their former high spiritual plane. In part two, she calls together all of her subjects and commands the angel of harmony LIGEIA, who also exists in a nonmaterial state, to awaken the spirits of those who lie dormant. Nesace then instructs those assembled to devote their time to the contemplation of beauty and purify their natures so that their corporeal state will be transformed into pure idea. To those who do not, the godly realm of perfect knowledge will always remain closed.

Al Aaraaf, Tamerlane, and Minor Poems Poe's second collection of poetry and the first to be commercially published. Two hundred and fifty copies of the 71-page work were published by Hatch and Dunning of Baltimore in December 1829. The publication of the collection drew harsh criticism from early reviewers who could not understand it, and many echoed the words of the critic J. H. Hewitt, who stated, "no man has been more shamefully overestimated." To attract readers, Poe included as an advertisement the claim that the

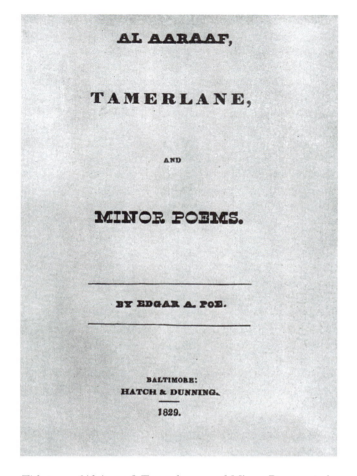

Title page of Al Aaraaf, Tamerlane, and Minor Poems, *published in 1829.* (Robert Gregor)

poems had earlier been printed in Boston in 1827 "but suppressed through circumstances of a private nature." The truth was more mundane than the mysterious words suggested, because the self-published Poe had simply run out of money to publish more than a few copies of the work.

Albermarle, County of The site of the University of Virginia, which Poe attended from February 1, 1826, through December 15, 1826. The county had a distinguished history, as well as the distinction of having produced many prominent Americans, including President Thomas JEFFERSON and the explorers Merriwether LEWIS and William CLARK.

"Alciphron: A Poem. By Thomas Moore, Esq., Author of 'Lalla Rookh,' Etc., Etc. Carey and Hart, Philadelphia" A review of Moore's poem that appeared in *BURTON'S GENTLEMAN'S MAGAZINE* in January 1840. After describing the construction and content of the poem in detail, Poe proceeds to a lengthy discussion of the difficulties between imagination and fancy. He labels

Moore "a poet of fancy," after quoting British Romantic poet Samuel Taylor COLERIDGE on the definition of the two terms: "the fancy combines, the imagination creates." Although he labels "Alciphron" a work of fancy and says the poet's "English is now and then objectionable," Poe praises the ease with which the poet "recounts a poetical story in a prosaic way." The review expresses disapproval of Moore's penchant for recounting details and points specifically to the manner in which "the minute and conflicting incidents of the descent into the pyramid are detailed with absolutely more precision than we have ever known a similar relation detailed with in prose." Poe ascribes such facility to the mathematician, not the poet, and he also criticizes the frequency with which Moore "draws out the word Heaven into two syllables—a protraction which it never will support." The reviewer also disparages the poet's seeming learnedness, as he points out that Moore has "stolen his 'woven snow' from the ventum textilem [woven wind] of Apuleius" and "either himself has misunderstood the tenets of Epicurus, or wilfully misrepresents them through the voice of Alciphron." In spite of the many flaws which Poe identifies, he credits Moore with a "vivid fancy, an epigrammatic spirit, a fine taste, vivacity, dexterity, and a musical ear."

Aldrich, James (1810–1856)   American poet and editor whom Poe accused of plagiarism. In a review of another poet's work in the January 13–14, 1845, issue of the New York *Evening Mirror*, Poe charged that Aldrich's poem "A Death-Bed" was a close imitation of the subject and the meter of Thomas Hood's poem of the same name. He repeated the charge in "MARGINALIA," but conceded that such imitation did not mean that Aldrich was incapable of writing poetry. Poe also repeated the charge of plagiarism in "THE LITERATI OF NEW YORK CITY," then praised Aldrich's poem "Molly Gray."

Alessandra   Character in Poe's unfinished drama *POLITIAN*. She is the niece of Duc di BROGLIO and betrothed to his son, CASTIGLIONE.

Alexander, Charles W. (1796–1866)   Printer working for several newspapers and magazines in Philadelphia in which Poe's work appeared, including *BURTON'S GENTLEMAN'S MAGAZINE*, *ALEXANDER'S WEEKLY MESSENGER* (of which he was publisher), and the *Daily Chronicle*.

Alexander's Weekly Messenger   Philadelphia journal owned and published by Charles W. ALEXANDER and edited by John Frost. From 1839 to 1842, Poe published several articles on cryptograms and cryptography in this magazine.

"Alice Ray: A Romance In Rhyme. By Mrs. Sarah Josepha Hale. Author of 'Northwood' Etc., Etc. Philadelphia"   A favorable review of a poetic romance that appeared in the *BROADWAY JOURNAL* for November 1, 1845. Poe claims to be pleasantly surprised by its "fancy of conception and the truthful simplicity and grace of its manner." He admits to having read many of Sarah Josepha HALE's poetic works, but "nothing so good" as the poem reviewed, which he suggests will add to her "well-earned reputation—providing always the unpretending form in which it comes before the public, does not injure it in that most worldly public's estimation." Poe quotes whole passages from the poem and makes particular note of the long *a* sound ("a constantly recurring in ay"), which he calls "one of the very happiest we have known in poetical art."

Allamistakeo, Count   Character in "SOME WORDS WITH A MUMMY." He is mistakenly embalmed while still alive, and the hieroglyphic cartouche on the sarcophagus indicates that Allamistakeo is the mummy's name. Dead and buried 5,000 years before, he comes to life when members of a museum team apply electrical current to the corpse in a "Voltaic experiment."

Frances Keeling Valentine Allan, the first wife of John Allan and Poe's foster mother. (Edgar Allan Poe Society)

Allan, Frances Keeling Valentine (1785–1829) Poe's foster mother and the first wife of John ALLAN, she also became one of the languishing women in Poe's life. She and her husband were unable to have children, although John Allan would later have children with his second wife. Mrs. Allan and other "ladies of the most respectable families" thought it to be their charitable duty to visit sick, impoverished families and to take them food and whatever other comfort they could. The manager of the last theater in which Elizabeth POE, Edgar Allan Poe's mother, worked inserted an advertisement in the November 25, 1811, edition of the *Richmond Enquirer,* a statement in appeal on the Poe family's behalf "to the kindhearted of the city." Mrs. Allan and Mrs. W. MacKenzie answered it. When Elizabeth Poe died less than two months later, the two women took the children. Edgar went with Mrs. Allan and his sister Rosalie went with Mrs. Mackenzie. Childless for eight years of marriage, Frances Allan welcomed the experience. As Poe's foster mother, the tender and unassertive woman gave young Edgar the maternal security and love that he craved, and during his childhood she protected him against her husband's anger. After Poe left the Allan household in 1827, he continued his contact with her and wrote her affectionate letters. She was chronically ill and died of tuberculosis at the age of 44. In letters written to Sarah Elmira ROYSTER, Poe revealed that he felt guilty about her death, feeling that he somehow might have been able to prevent it had he remained on good terms with John Allan and continued to live with the family. His grief was increased because he could not be with her in her final hours due to a bureaucratic delay in processing his military papers. He arrived in Richmond the day after her funeral.

Allan, John (1779–1834) Poe's foster father and the husband of Frances Keeling Valentine ALLAN. A Scottish immigrant and Richmond tobacco mercantiler, Allan at his wife's urging took Edgar into their home after the death of Elizabeth Arnold POE in 1811. Although Allan reared the orphaned child as the seeming heir to his fortune, he never legally adopted Edgar. Instead, Allan, who with his partner Charles Ellis eventually became a wealthy merchandiser of tobacco commodities and also inherited a great deal of money from his uncle William GALT, provided Edgar with only minimal support. He sent Edgar to the University of Virginia, but failed to provide him sufficient funds to buy furniture, clothes, meals, or books. When Edgar dropped out of the college and later won an appointment to the United States Military Academy at West Point, Allan refused to provide any of the financial support that would raise Edgar's military life from its meager, rigid, and difficult existence of bare survival. Edgar

John Allan, Poe's foster father. (Edgar Allan Poe Society)

might have tolerated the frugal coldness that Allan showed him, but he was intensely protective of his foster mother. The greatest cause for the deep rift between the two men most likely resulted from Edgar's discovery that Allan had had extramarital affairs and fathered several children by different women. Intensely loyal to Frances Allan, Edgar resented John Allan's treatment of her. Although Allan had been relatively tolerant toward the child Edgar, he became increasingly impatient and abrupt as Edgar entered adolescence, and their relationship continued to deteriorate until Allan's death. The two were civil to each other after the funeral of Frances Allan in February 1829, but no true reconciliation ensued. Upon his death, Allan provided one more insult to his foster son by omitting all mention of Edgar from his will. He provided inheritances, however, for illegitimate twin sons born in 1830, only a year after the death of Frances. John Allan continued to exert a negative influence on Edgar's life, and this showed in Poe's tales. Critics have suggested that the condemnatory inquisitors of "THE PIT AND THE PENDULUM" are inspired by the grown Poe's memories of his rigidly authoritarian foster father, and that he ridiculed Allan's rigid materialism in "THE BUSINESS MAN."

Allan, Louisa Gabriella Patterson (1800–1881) John ALLAN's second wife, with whom he had three sons. They married on October 5, 1830, while Poe was a cadet at the United States Military Academy. Unlike Frances ALLAN, Louisa had no interest in Poe's well-being and offered no hope of reconciliation for him. Soon after the marriage, Poe wrote to his foster father for help in obtaining a discharge from the Academy. When Allan failed to answer, Poe became derelict in duty to earn a court-martial and dishonorable discharge. Several biographers have suggested that Poe felt hostile toward Louisa because he feared she would increase Allan's animosity toward him and eliminate all possibility of an inheritance.

Allen, William Character in the novel THE NARRATIVE OF ARTHUR GORDON PYM. A member of the cook's party aboard the ship *Jane Guy,* he joins the mutineers and is later tossed over the bulwarks.

Allston, Washington (1779–1843) American painter and the author of a little-read novel *Monaldi.* In an analysis of Allston's signature in "AUTOGRAPHY," Poe describes his paintings without explanation as "not to our taste." Poe also describes the faults of Allston's pencil and pen as identical. He criticizes Allston's poetry as "not all of a high order of merit," but praises without explanation his "Spanish Maid" as a poem every reader will remember "with pleasure."

"Alnwick Castle, with Other Poems. By Fitz-Greene Halleck. New York: George Dearborn" A collection of poems reviewed in the SOUTHERN LITERARY MESSENGER for April 1836. Because Poe compares Halleck's work to that of Joseph Rodman Drake, the review generally is referred to as "The Drake-Halleck Review." Poe especially criticizes "Alnwick Castle" for its mix of ideality with low burlesque at the conclusion of the poem because it destroys "unity of effect." In his review, Poe notes that the poem "is sadly disfigured by efforts at the farcical introduced among passages of real beauty" and accuses Halleck of "profanation" for creating verses that are "odd, and nothing more." Not totally unfavorable, the review also points out several passages of "remarkable beauty" and suggests that Halleck is possessed of "an ideality of far loftier character than that which is usually ascribed to our poet." Poe bestows moderate praise on Halleck's verse, but declares that Drake is the superior poet. In June 1836, Poe received a letter from Washington IRVING that declared his review to be "one of the finest pieces of criticism ever published in this country."

"Alone" Written by Poe in 1829, this poem, originally untitled, was not published until September 1875, when it appeared in *Scribner's Monthly* as "Alone." The persona of the poem expresses a sense of isolation from everyone and exhibits an awareness of his great difference from the way others think and feel. The poem states quite clearly what seems to have been Poe's plight: "From childhood's hour I have not been as others were—I have not seen as others saw—I could not bring my passions from a common spring."

Ambler, Richard Carey (1810–1877) A physician and Virginia gentleman farmer who was also one of Poe's boyhood friends, Ambler lived across the street from the Allan family in Richmond. He enjoyed swimming with Poe in Shochoe Creek and laughed with him as Poe wrote and recited verses that satirized members of a Richmond debating society. With several other schoolmates, Ambler and Poe presented dramatic productions under a tent in a vacant lot near their homes, for which they charged admission fees of one cent.

"Amelia Welby" Poe's review of Amelia Ball Welby's poem "Musings" that appeared in the *Democratic Review* of December 1844. Welby was a minor poet who published one volume of poetry—a collection of already published verse—in 1846. Poe says the "great demerit" of the poem is that "the subject has nothing of originality," but he praises its purity and naturalness. Impressed by the minor poet's tone of "a gentle and melancholy regret," he notes that her efforts to interweave them with a "pleasant sense of the natural loveliness surrounding the lost in the tomb" reflect his own poem "LENORE." Poe's conclusion is mixed: He characterizes her line endings as "grossly objectionable," yet praises her "novel, rich and accurate combination of the ancient musical expressions."

"America and the American People. By Frederick von Raumer, Professor of History in the University of Berlin, Etc., Etc. Translated from the German by William W. Turner. New York; J. & G. H. Langley" The review of a translation of Frederick von Raumer's book that appeared in the BROADWAY JOURNAL for November 29, 1845. The review opens with an excerpt from the translator's preface, which praises profusely the German author's thoroughness in researching the subject. Poe concurs, and adds that the commendable features of the work also include its "candor, evident desire for truth, freedom from prejudice, comprehensiveness, and masterly breadth of generalization." Despite a stated intention to make allowance "for the foreigner's imperfect means of information in detail," Poe roundly criticizes von Raumer, who "has set forth with accuracy not one fact in relation to American letters." Citing as an example the praise that von Raumer gives to American publishing for paying a Mr. Prescott

$6,000 as an advance for his book *The Conquest of Mexico,* Poe points out that the author had spent many years and much of his own money in researching the book. Poe reserves more virulent criticism for von Raumer's praise of "POETS AND POETRY OF AMERICA," written by Poe's bitter rival Rufus Wilmot GRISWOLD. Poe claims that if Griswold's book were accepted as accurately representing American poetry, then American literature is "in a very ridiculous condition indeed."

"The American Almanac, and Repository of Useful Knowledge for the Year 1837. Boston: Published by Charles Bowen"   The eighth in a series of yearbooks, Poe reviewed the volume in the *SOUTHERN LITERARY MESSENGER* of October 1836. Poe praises the editor J. E. Worcester for having the "acute judgment" necessary to select "the most needful topics" and to exclude those which are of only "a comparative value." He recommends the book for its "perspicuity and brevity." After listing the range of topics covered in the volume, including state-by-state statistics on population, public facilities, and commerce, Poe states that the next volume will contain an account of "Pauperism in the United States" and greater information about the interaction between the United States and other nations. The review ends with praise for the "mechanical execution" of the books which are "worthy of the highest recommendation."

"The American Drama"   A critical essay published in the August 1845 issue of *American Whig Review* in which Poe proposes to write a series of papers that would take "a somewhat deliberate survey of some few of the most noticeable American plays." Motivated by what he sees as an "ever recurring topic, the decline of drama," Poe first makes a cursory examination of engineering, sculpture, painting, and architecture to determine the extent to which these arts have suffered decline. He concludes that engineering and architecture, in which "the Reason, which never retrogrades, or reposes, is called into play," has not declined. In contrast, "the arts of Sculpture, Painting and the Drama have not advanced" because they depend more upon feeling or taste. Poe asserts that "all seem to have declined, because they have remained stationary while the multitudinous other arts (of reason) have flitted so rapidly by them." The review places the blame for the lack of public support, and states that it is unsupported "because it does not deserve support." Poe proposes to rectify this situation by examining examples of successful and unsuccessful drama and to "speak with absolute frankness both of merits and defects." Poe cites Nathaniel Parker WILLIS's *Tortesa, the Usurer* as an example of the former and lambastes Henry Wadsworth LONGFELLOW's *The Spanish Student* as a failure, because it

is a "hybrid and paradoxical composition." After accusing Longfellow of "borrowing" from his own play *POLITIAN* in writing *The Spanish Student,* Poe asserts that Longfellow should "Let a poem be a poem only; let a play be a play and nothing more."

"The American in England. By the Author of 'A Year in Spain.' 2 vols. New York. Harper and Brothers"   A review written by Poe of Lieutenant Alexander Slidell MACKENZIE's book and published in the *SOUTHERN LITERARY MESSENGER* of February 1836. Poe both praises and finds serious fault with the book. The review at one point commends the author's literary skill for having "a fine eye for the picturesque" and describes his depictions of scenes as having "all the spirit, vigor, raciness and illusion of a panorama," yet only paragraphs later points out "the simplicity of its modus operandi." In an apparent paradox, Poe compliments the author for taking a surface approach to his topic: "It appears to us that Mr. Slidell has written a wiser book than his neighbors by not disdaining to write a more superficial one." The review meticulously recounts the details of a journey, from embarkation through experiences on board the ship, which "are told with the gusto of a seaman," to the eventual arrival and adventures in England. After his high praise of the work in the first half of the review, Poe heartily attacks the writing style of the work and tells readers that "upon Mr. Slidell's mechanical style we cannot bring ourselves to look with favor." He expresses astonishment over "a few of his singularly ill-constructed sentences" and suggests that only "great tedium and utter weariness with his labor" could be responsible for a sentence that Poe claims to have read more than once before he "could fathom its meaning." In quick succession, the grammatical faults are delineated, from incorrect pronoun references to repetition of words such as "how" and "only," proclaimed by Poe to be "disagreeable." Poe saves his most severe criticism for Slidell's wordiness, pointing in example to one sentence that he abridged to 18 words from its original 54. Yet another sentence is denounced as being "one of the most ludicrously ill-arranged, and altogether ungainly pieces of composition which it has ever been our ill fortune to encounter." The review concludes with significantly fainter praise than it began, as Poe pronounces, "The Lieutenant's book is an excellent book—but then it is excellent in spite of its style. So great are the triumphs of genius."

The American Museum of Science, Literature, and the Arts   Baltimore journal, originally named *North American Quarterly Magazine of Baltimore,* which Poe's Baltimore friend Nathan C. Brooks purchased in 1838. He changed it to a monthly and gave it a new name. The new publication carried several of Poe's works from

1838 through 1840, including "HOW TO WRITE A BLACK-WOOD ARTICLE" and "LIGEIA."

"The American Parnassus" A literary project that Poe proposed but never completed for publication. He had intended to create a comprehensive study of American writers and their works and, to this end, he wrote a letter on June 26, 1845, to solicit an advance of $50 from Wiley and Putnam's editor Evert A. DUYCKINCK, promising to finish the work "as soon as possible." Poe selected the term "Parnassus" as a reference to the mountain in Greece, which the ancient Greeks believed to be sacred to the god Apollo as well to the Muses; by Poe's time the word had come to mean poets or poetry collectively or any center of artistic activity.

"American Prose Writers. No. 2. N.P. Willis. New Views—Imagination—Fancy—Fantasy—Humor—Wit—Sarcasm—The Prose Style of Mr. Willis" A critical evaluation of the work of Nathaniel Parker WILLIS published in the BROADWAY JOURNAL for January 18, 1845. Poe distinguishes between "fancy" and "imagination," using as his foundation the definitions devised by Samuel Taylor COLERIDGE that "fancy combines—Imagination creates." In assessing Willis's work, Poe identifies "innumerable merits" that are fanciful rather than imaginative, and he concedes that "they are merits which he shares with other writers." The review soon abandons consideration of Willis's work and turns to a consideration of the manner in which imagination, fancy, fantasy, and humor interact, and what they have in common with combination and novelty. Declaring that "the range of Imagination is therefore, unlimited," Poe asserts that the interaction, two at a time, of the four determines whether a work will exhibit harmony or novelty. The review concedes that "when either Fancy or Humor is expressed to gain an end—is pointed at a purpose—whenever either becomes either objective in place of subjective—then it becomes, also, pure Wit and Sarcasm, just as the purpose is well-intentioned or malevolent." Poe returns to a consideration of Willis's work in the closing paragraph of the review and traces its charm "to the brilliant FANCY [sic] with which it perpetually scintillates or glows."

American Quarterly Review A Philadelphia periodical edited by Robert Walsh, to whom Poe once appealed for advice regarding poetry. Mention of the publication appears briefly in the SOUTHERN LITERARY MESSENGER of June 1835.

American Whig Review A New York City periodical originated and edited by George H. COLTON, to whom James Russell LOWELL recommended Poe as an editorial assistant in December 1844. Poe had pronounced Colton's poem "Tecumseh" as "insufferably tedious" as part of his profile of the editor in THE LITERATI OF NEW YORK CITY series that appeared in *GODEY'S MAGAZINE AND LADY'S BOOK* in May 1846, and Colton had not forgotten the slight. In the same profile, Poe characterized the *Review* as "by far the best of its order in this country" and characterized it as "a Whig magazine of the higher (that is to say, of the five dollar) class." Despite Colton's hostility toward Poe, the *Review* published an advance proof copy of "THE RAVEN" in the February 1845, but Colton accepted the poem with its anonymous author from John A. SHEA, who acted as Poe's intermediary in that and other attempts to place work. Poe's "ULALUME" also appeared anonymously in the December 1847 issue of the *Review*. In 1849 the periodical suspended publication, no longer able to pay for contributions.

Anacreon of Teos (sixth century B.C.) An ancient Greek poet whose poems celebrate hedonistic virtues. In the poem "ROMANCE," Poe alludes to Anacreon's emphasis upon wine, women, and song and ruefully recalls his early reading of Anacreon: "For, being an idle boy lang syne, / Who read Anacreon, and drank wine, / I early found Anacreon rhymes / Were almost passionate sometimes."

Ana-Pest, Her Serene Highness the Arch Duchess A character in the short story "KING PEST" and one of the five rotting relatives of King Pest's family court. She is "a diminutive young lady" whose trembling "wasted fingers," "livid hue of her lips," and "the slight hectic spot that tinged her otherwise leaden complexion" signal that she is dying of consumption (tuberculosis). Poe mixes beauty with the grotesque in describing her appearance as one of high tone, for she wears her shroud in a "graceful and *dégagé* manner," and "her hair hung in ringlets over her neck; a soft smile played around her mouth." At the same time exists the horror of her long thin nose, "flexible and pimpled," which hangs down far below her lower lip, forcing her to move it to one side or the other with her tongue in a "delicate manner."

"Anastatic Printing" An essay by Poe that appeared in the *BROADWAY JOURNAL* for April 12, 1845. Poe describes the potential value and consequences of a printing process using zinc plates that could inexpensively and quickly produce multiple copies of magazines or books, thus increasing the value of their literary content while decreasing their worth as mere material objects. He states that with this discovery, "anything written, drawn, or printed, can be made to stereotype itself, with absolute accuracy, in five minutes." The rather lengthy essay provides readers with a detailed description of the process, which Poe predicts will revolutionize the production of printed matter and allow publishers to release more cheaply many works that they would formerly have ignored. Moreover, the author also views the process as creating a new perception of books that will result in "the ascendancy to the literary value, and thus by their literary values will books come to be estimated among men." He warns, however, that this process of printing will increase the need for strong national and international copyright laws: "The necessity of the protection will be only the more urgent and more obvious than ever."

Anaxagoras (born ca. 500 B.C.)   A Greek philosopher who wrote about the cosmos and expressed thoughts of uniting and integrating the spiritual and material universes. His writings, especially "On Nature," appear to have influenced Poe's concept of negative creation in "EUREKA." Anaxagoras also receives mention in "LOSS OF BREATH" and in "PINAKIDIA," in which Poe states that "Anaxagoras of Clazomenae is said to have prophesied that a stone would fall from the sun."

Andreini, Giovanni Battista (1579–1654)   An actor, composer of opera, and dramatist mentioned in "PINAKIDIA." Poe credits Andreini with providing the source for John MILTON's *Paradise Lost* (1637) in his religious play *L'Adamo* (1613), which tells the Creation story and provides in its character of Adamo the source of Milton's Adam.

Angel of the Odd   A character in Poe's tale "THE ANGEL OF THE ODD" whose mission is to force the unnamed narrator to drink to excess and to acknowledge the existence of the odd, the unexplained, and the absurd. The insulting and offensive angel speaks with a pronounced German accent. Its body is constructed of a rum cask, with wine bottles for arms and kegs for legs. The head is a Hessian canteen with a funnel on its top "like a cavalier cap slouched over the eyes." This ridiculous personage appears to the narrator and plies him with so much liquor that the man forgets the need to renew the fire insurance on his home. He falls asleep and does not awaken until the fire insurance has expired and his house is on fire. Not satisfied with leaving the narrator homeless, the angel continues to stalk the man and create disaster at every turn until the man finally nods his head in assent to the angel's demand, "You pelief, ten, in te possibility of te odd?"

"The Angel of the Odd: An Extravaganza"   Short story. This tale appears to be Poe's satire on the philosophy of human perfectibility. The story was highly popular when it first appeared because of the strong public interest in spiritualism and spiritual manifestations of the time.

PUBLISHING AND DRAMATIZATION HISTORY

The story first appeared in print in the October 1844 issue of *Columbian Magazine*. No films have been made of the tale.

CHARACTERS

ANGEL OF THE ODD, unnamed narrator.

PLOT SYNOPSIS

The plot relates the story of an unnamed narrator, a heavy drinker of alcohol who professes to be a rationalist. As the story begins, he concludes his dinner with "some apologies to dessert, with some miscellaneous bottles of wine, spirit and *liquer*." After attempting to read a newspaper and "reading it from beginning to end without understanding a syllable, conceived the possibility of its being Chinese," one paragraph catches his attention. The improbable story about a man who accidentally inhales rather than blows a long needle while playing a game called "puff-the-dart" angers the narrator, who pronounces the story "a contrived falsehood—a poor hoax." He asserts that the gullibility of the age has encouraged the publication of "improbable possibilities—of odd accidents, as they term them." Commending himself for having a "reflecting intellect," the narrator declares he will "believe nothing henceforward that has anything of the 'singular' about it." He has hardly uttered these words when a heavily accented voice intrudes on his thoughts, telling him, "Mein Gott, den vat a fool you bees for dat!" After frustrating the narrator's attempts to ignore him, the speaker identifies himself as "te *Angel ov te Odd*." The odd-looking being claims that he is "the genius who presided over the *contretemps* of mankind, and whose business it was to bring about the *odd accidents* which are continually astonishing to the skeptics."

The narrator's skepticism is tested after he drives the angel away, then falls asleep because he has drunk too much. His intended nap of 25 minutes stretches into two hours, making him late for an appointment during which he had intended to renew his fire insurance on the house. The house burns down, and the narrator breaks his arm when a hog rubs up against the escape ladder he is descending. The narrator loses his hair, then finds his attempts to marry a rich widow blocked by the antics of the angel. When the narrator attempts suicide by leaping into the river, the angel drops a guide rope from a balloon and demands, "'Ave you pe got zober yet and come to your zenzes?'" When the narrator still refuses to admit to the reality of the absurd, the angel cuts the rope and the narrator falls down through the chimney of his house, which has been miraculously rebuilt while he wandered. He awakens sober at four in the morning, surrounded by shattered bottles and overturned jugs. Whether or not his experiences were a dream, he is forced to revise his narrow philosophy of a reasonable universe and to admit that accident, unreason, and absurd probability are real.

WRITER'S NOTES

The inspiration for this story may lie in three sources: the article "It's Very Odd," which appeared in the January 1829 issue of BLACKWOOD'S MAGAZINE; "Progress of Social Questions," published on June 8, 1844, in the New York *Tribune*; and a novel titled *The Man About Town*, written by Cornelius Webbe and published in 1839. All three show minor resemblances to the story, and Webbe's novel also includes a character who speaks in a German dialect similar to that of the Angel of the Odd. This story has not attracted significant critical attention, but psychoanalyst Marie Bonaparte suggests that Poe uses it to acknowledge his demons, even if he is unable to avoid them. The addictions to alcohol and drugs, his feelings of lacking control over his destiny, and the memories of his abuse at the hands of John ALLAN are all contained within the treatment that the unnamed narrator undergoes at the hands of the Angel of the Odd.

Angelo   Character in the poem "AL AARAAF." He is an angelic creature, the spirit of a man who was the world's greatest lover and creator of beauty. He leaves the earth after dying during a catastrophe and seeks to enjoy a life of sensuality and passion with the angelic creature IANTHE, who inhabits the fantasy star AL AARAAF, rather than a spiritualized love that would have led to perfect knowledge. His downfall is that he chooses the world of passion over the world of the mind.

"Animal and Vegetable Physiology Considered with Reference to Natural Theology. By Peter Mark Roget, M.D. Secretary to the Royal Society, &C., &C. Two vols. Large octavo, Philadelphia: Published by Carey, Lea, and Blanchard"   A review of a scientific study that appeared in the SOUTHERN LITERARY MESSENGER of January 1836. Fifth in a series of texts commissioned by the Royal Society, the work earned Poe's praise for the appropriateness of the selection made by Roget "from an exuberance of materials." Poe begins the review by introducing readers to the Bridgewater Treatises, created by a bequest of 8,000 pounds made by Francis Henry, Earl of Bridgewater, to the Royal Society of London, which was empowered to appoint their choice of individuals to "'write, print, and publish, one thousand copies of a work, *On the Power, Wisdom and Goodness of God, as manifested in the Creation; illustrating such work by all reasonable arguments, as, for instance, the variety and for-*

mation of God's creatures, in the animal, vegetable, and mineral kingdoms; the effect of digestion, and thereby of conversion; the construction of the hand of man and an infinite variety of other arguments; as also by discoveries ancient and modern, in arts, sciences and the whole extent of literature'." Poe asserts that Henry did not intend to divide the bequest among eight writers, and he judges that the resulting works and their writers have suffered from the arrangement: "Treatises now published might have been readily discussed in one connected work of no greater bulk than the *Physiology*, whose title forms the heading of this article." The final fifth of Poe's review offers a specific description of Roget's difficulties that are detailed in the preface to the work and delineated in the contents of the work.

"Annabel Lee"   One of Poe's final finished poems. Composed in May 1849, the poem first appeared as part of Poe's obituary published in the New York *Tribune* on October 9, 1849, and was later published in the November 1849 issue of the SOUTHERN LITERARY MESSENGER and the January 1850 issue of *Sartain's Union Magazine*, which also posthumously published "THE BELLS" and "THE POETIC PRINCIPLE." The poem contains themes that appear in many of Poe's works, such as the death and burial of a beautiful woman, undying love, and deification of her memory—although the specific influence on its composition appears to have been Poe's loss of Virginia CLEMM. Despite strong contemporary sentiment that Poe composed the poem to memorialize his love and loss of Virginia, after his death other women in his life, including Sarah Anna LEWIS, Helen WHITMAN, and Sarah Elmira ROYSTER, claimed that they had been immortalized in this poem. The poem recounts a love so powerful that even the angels feel envious of the bond, which transcends death and overcomes both human and cosmic forces that seek to "dissever my soul from the soul of the beautiful Annabel Lee." Poe's words also exhibit his resentment for the years of poverty that often left him powerless: "So that her highborn kinsmen came and bore her away from me."

Annie (1)   Central figure in "FOR ANNIE," a poem written during the last year of Poe's life. Annie is a nurturing figure who lovingly cares for the dying narrator, a maternal figure who "tenderly kissed" him, "fondly caressed" him, then allowed him "gently / To sleep on her breast." She helps him to rest contentedly and provides him the security of her love.

Annie (2)   Character in the sketch "LANDOR'S COTTAGE" whom some have identified with Annie RICHMOND. The hostess of the cottage, she is "a young woman of about twenty-eight years of age—slender, or rather slight, and somewhat above the medium

> Annabel Lee.
> By Edgar A. Poe.
>
> It was many and many a year ago,
>   In a kingdom by the sea,
> That a maiden there lived whom you may know
>   By the name of Annabel Lee; —
> And this maiden she lived with no other thought
>   Than to love and be loved by me.
>
> She was a child and I was a child,
>   In this kingdom by the sea,
> But we loved with a love that was more than love —
>   I and my Annabel Lee —
> With a love that the wingéd seraphs of Heaven
>   Coveted her and me.
>
> And this was the reason that, long ago
>   In this kingdom by the sea,
> A wind blew out of a cloud by night
>   Chilling my Annabel Lee;
> So that her high-born kinsmen came
>   And bore her away from me,
> To shut her up in a sepulchre
>   In this kingdom by the sea.

Poe's handwritten version of his poem "Annabel Lee." (Robert Gregor)

height." What most attracts the narrator is the "*modest decision* of her step" and her "unworldliness," which he sees in her eyes of "'spiritual gray'" and her light chestnut hair. He finds that "peculiar expression" of her eyes "is the most powerful, if not absolutely the *sole* spell" that rivets his attention in a woman.

"The Antediluvians, or the World Destroyed: A Narrative Poem, In Ten Books. By James McHenry, M.D., Author of the 'Pleasures of Friendship,' ETC. One Volume. J. B. Lippincott and Co., Philadelphia" A review by Poe that appeared in the February 1841 issue of GRAHAM'S MAGAZINE and skewered James MCHENRY's pretentious epic. Poe criticized the numerous melodramatic elements in the poem that he saw as excessive and attacked what he saw as Dr. James McHenry's arrogance in presuming to associate his work with that of John MILTON. The review begins with the statement,

"There are two species of poetry known to mankind,— that which the gods love and that which men abhor. The poetry of the doctor belongs to the latter class, though he seems lamentably ignorant of this." Poe attacks the poet's pretentiousness in connecting his name with that of Milton and likens McHenry in esteem to "a tom-tit twittering on an eagle's back." The review then methodically examines the contents of each of the 10 books and points out McHenry's contention that in the Deluge he had found a theme "exalted and extensive enough for the exercise of poetic talents of the highest order." Poe counters that the extensive catalogue of minor incidents contains, instead, "the materials of a half a dozen bad novels woven into a worse poem." As Poe quotes liberally from the epic, he identifies the flaws of each section and accuses the poet of plagiarizing whole passages from Milton's *Paradise Lost,* with the intention of "showing at once the grandeur of the model and the feebleness of the imitation." In a sarcasm-filled conclusion, Poe advises McHenry to give up poetry and states, "We are satisfied that, if he should be arraigned for writing poetry, no sane jury would ever convict him; and if, as most likely, he would plead guilty at once, it would be as quickly disallowed, on that rule of law which forbids the judges to decide against the plain evidence of their senses."

Anthon, Charles (1797–1867) A professor of Greek and Latin classics at Columbia College and an early supporter of the SOUTHERN LITERARY MESSENGER. Poe noticed Anthon's "Sallust's Jurgathine War" in the May 1836 issue of the *Southern Literary Messenger* and asked him by letter to translate several Hebrew phrases while preparing his review of John L. STEPHENS's monograph "Incidents of Travel in Egypt, Arabia Petraea, and the Holy Land." Poe also profiled Anthon in "THE LITERATI OF NEW YORK CITY," calling him "the best classicist in America" and complimenting him on the "extensive erudition of his *Classical Dictionary.*" In an analysis of Anthon's signature in "AUTOGRAPHY," Poe attributed to him "the love of elegance—together with the scorn of all superfluous embellishment, which so greatly distinguish the compilations of the writer."

"The Antigone at Palmo's" An extremely negative review of a revival of *Antigone,* the tragic drama by SOPHOCLES, that appeared in the April 12, 1845, issue of the *BROADWAY JOURNAL.* Poe calls the production at Palmo's Theatre "an unintentional burlesque," as well as "a piece of folly," and relates that the full house of the opening night performance had dwindled to an audience of fewer than 100 by the second night. Poe first condemns the play itself, labeling Antigone "vastly inferior to any one of the dramas by Aeschylus" and consigning to it "an insufferable baldness, or platitude, the inevitable result of inexperience in Art." Decrying Sophocles's lack of skill in writing *Antigone,* Poe asserts that the attempt to present a Greek play before a modern audience "is the idea of the pedant and nothing beyond." He warns his readers that they will be disappointed if they expect to learn from this performance how the Greeks wrote and performed drama. He suggests that people attend the play only if they want others to assume that "they have a scholastic taste, and could discourse learnedly on certain classical themes . . . [or] enjoy a good joke." The review also finds fault with the music, which Poe characterizes as "Greek thought adapted into German." "The only excuse that can be offered for the miserable way in which the choruses were executed," he continues, "is the want of sufficient time to study them." Poe's harsh review motivated angry letters to the editor, several of which he responded to, most notably one identified as "ACHILLES' WRATH."

Antiochus Epiphanes   A character known as Antiochus the Illustrious, who is also the king of Syria in "FOUR BEASTS IN ONE; THE HOMO-CAMELEOPARD." He is a man of gigantic height who dons animal hides when he and his army march triumphantly into Antioch after defeating the Hebrew army. Also referred to as Antiochus Epimanes, or Antiochus the Madman, he is hailed by his people as "The Prince of Poets," "Glory of the Earth," and "most remarkable of Cameleopards." The wild animals domesticated in his kingdom view him differently and take offense at his wearing of animal hides. In the middle of his triumphant march, they attack him and attempt to devour him, thus forcing him to rapidly run away.

"An Appendix of Autographs"   Poe's supplement to the "AUTOGRAPHY" articles that appeared in the *SOUTHERN LITERARY MESSENGER* in the February and August issues of 1836. The 19 additional analyses of signatures that appeared in the December 1841 and January 1842 issues of *GRAHAM'S MAGAZINE* included those of Ralph Waldo EMERSON, Oliver Wendell HOLMES, and Washington ALLSTON.

Apuleius, Lucius (born ca. A.D. 125)   Roman author who wrote *Asino Aureo* (*The Golden Ass*), a satirical romance about magic and transformation. The story is narrated in the first person by an immoral young man named Lucius who steals a potion from a sorceress, thinking that it will turn him into an owl. Instead, he is turned into an ass and must wander through Greece in this form, becoming the property of a variety of owners. He is finally restored to human form through the intervention of the goddess Isis, after the narrative has produced a series of lively and risqué stories. Poe

appears to have known the story well in its original Latin form, for he mentions one of its lines, *"ventum textilum"* (woven wind), in "THE SPECTACLES." In his review of "ALCIPHRON," Poe also accuses the poet Thomas Moore of stealing the line "woven snow" from Apuleius.

Arago, Dominique François Jean (1786–1853)   French astronomer and chemist. He appeared in a book of biographies that Poe reviewed, "SKETCHES OF CONSPICUOUS LIVING CHARACTERS OF FRANCE. TRANSLATED BY R. M. WALSH." Poe selects the biography of Arago to illustrate Walsh's skill in creating verisimilitude, noting that the "genius of Arago is finely painted, and the character of his quackery put in a true light."

Archer, Robert (1794–1877)   An army surgeon at the military hospital at Fortress Monroe, Virginia, who also had relatives living near John ALLAN in Richmond. Archer attended to Poe during a serious bout with fever in January 1829, during which the young soldier confided in Dr. Archer that he was the foster son of John Allan and that the name under which he had enlisted, Edgar A. PERRY, was an alias.

Archimedes (287–212 B.C.)   Greek scientist and author of scientific works that interested Poe. In *Incidentibus in Fluido,* Archimedes provides an explanation of hydraulic law through his description of the manner in which a cylinder in a vortex offers resistance to suction, and Poe refers to it in "THE DESCENT INTO THE MAELSTROM."

Aristarchus (died 153 B.C.)   Greek scholar associated with the great library at Alexandria. Poe mentions in "PINAKIDIA" his efforts to standardize the *Iliad,* and observes that Aristarchus used all of the copies of the epic then in existence to create the definitive version, "a new edition, the text of which has finally prevailed."

Aristophanes (ca. 446–385 B.C.)   Greek comic dramatist, social satirist, and the author of many plays, including *The Birds, The Frogs, Dionysus,* and *The Clouds,* to whom Poe refers in several works. In "MARGINALIA," Poe honors him for having invented rhyme, despite what he sees as a common belief that rhyme is "of modern invention," and recommends that readers "but see *The Clouds* of Aristophanes." In the short story "BON-BON," the devil stated that he had had occasion to consume the soul of Aristophanes and found that it tastes "racy."

Aristotle (384–322 B.C.)   Greek philosopher and writer whose ideas on psychology, nature, logic, physics, metaphysics, and ethics appear to have been well known to Poe. In "MARGINALIA," Poe identifies Aristotle's didactic and moral sense as the enemy of art and beauty, and observes disparagingly that "Aristotle's Treatise on Morals is next in succession to his Book on Physics, and this he supposes the rational order of study." In the short story "BON-BON," the devil dismisses Aristotle's philosophy as mere deductive and didactic nonsense, claiming that he provided the "one solid truth" voiced by the philosopher: "'Why it was I who told Aristotle that, by sneezing, men expelled superfluous ideas through the proboscis.'"

Arnay, Jean-Rodolphe d' (fl. ca. 1757) French historian. In "MARGINALIA," Poe identifies d' Arnay's social study *De la Vie privée des Romains* [Private life of the Romans] (1764) as a major source used by Edward George Earle BULWER-LYTTON in writing *The Last Days of Pompeii*. He criticizes Lytton for failing to acknowledge this source "which he had so little scruple about incurring."

Arnold, Benedict (1741–1801) American Revolutionary War general who betrayed the Americans' fort at West Point to the British after General George Washington gave him the command in 1780. Until well into adulthood, Poe knew nothing about his parents except their names, but he did know that his mother's maiden name was Arnold. He may have encouraged or even begun the rumor, rampant during his years at the United States Military Academy at West Point, that he was the grandson of the traitor, which added to the air of mystery that he cultivated.

Arnold, Elizabeth (?–1798?) Poe's maternal grandmother. Once an actress at the Covent Garden Theatre in London, she immigrated to Boston, Massachusetts, in January 1796 with her daughter Elizabeth, who became Poe's mother.

Arnold, William Henry (died 1790) Poe's maternal great-grandfather and a professional actor at Covent Garden Theatre in London.

Arthur, Timothy Shea (1809–1885) American novelist and editor of the *Baltimore Athenaeum* and *Young Men's Paper*. He is also the author of the famous temperance tale, which later became a play, "Ten Nights in a Barroom and What I Saw There" (1854), about an alcoholic whose drinking ruins his family. Poe condemned Arthur's efforts at social reform as melodramatic moralizing. In his analysis of Arthur's signature in "AUTOGRAPHY," Poe observed that Arthur may have "a rich talent for description of scenes in low life, but is uneducated, and too fond of mere vulgarities to please a refined taste." Poe asserts in a condescending manner that Arthur's "hand is a commonplace clerk's hand, such as we might expect him to write."

Timothy Shea Arthur, author of the temperance tale "Ten Nights in a Barroom," drew Poe's criticism for his efforts at social reform. (Library of Congress, Stills Division)

"The Assignation" Short story. This tale, one of Poe's most romantic, is a story of passion that relates a clandestine love affair and its tragic consequences. It is the only one of Poe's tales in which any character commits suicide.

PUBLISHING AND DRAMATIZATION HISTORY

The story was first published under the title of "The Visionary" in the January 1834 issue of *GODEY'S MAGAZINE AND LADY'S BOOK*. The early version contained both a 30-line poem titled "To One in Paradise" and two introductory paragraphs in which the unnamed narrator claims to know the identity of the mysterious stranger of the story, one "devoutly admired by the few who read." The name is also one that the narrator is "determined to conceal," and he vows not to dishonor the man by creating a fictional name for him, "whose melancholy end is a tissue of malevolent blasphemies." The early version of the story began with the following two epigraphs:

Ich habe gelebt, und geliebet.

—Schiller's *Wallenstein*

I have lived, and I have loved.

*Und Sterbich denn, so sterbich doch
Durch sie—durch sie.*

—Goethe

And if I die, at least I die
With her—*with* her.

The final version of the story, published in the June 7, 1845, issue of the *BROADWAY JOURNAL,* contains only one epigram, taken from the Exequy by Henry King, Bishop of Chichester, written on the death of his wife:

Stay for me there! I will not fail
To meet thee in that hollow vale.

No film has been made of "The Assignation" to date.

CHARACTERS

Marques di MENTONI, Marquesa di MENTONI, unnamed narrator, unnamed young Byronic stranger.

PLOT SYNOPSIS

The plot relates the story of the young and beautiful Marquesa di Mentoni, "the adoration of all Venice—the gayest of the gay—the most lovely where all were beautiful," who is married to the "old and intriguing Mentoni." The story takes place in Venice and opens on "a night of unusual gloom." Shrieks fill the air as the unnamed narrator learns that the Marquesa has accidentally dropped her baby into the canal. As she stands watching swimmers try to find her child in the water, her husband, the Marques, stands in the shadows, looking bored and strumming a guitar while sporadically giving directions to the searchers. Just when all hope seems lost, a dark and mysterious figure steps from the shadows of the old Republic prison, linked to the ducal palace by the Bridge of Sighs. His cloak is heavy with water, and in his arms lies "the still living and breathing child." The stranger hands the child to its mother. As a servant quickly snatches the child and takes it into the

palace, the Marquesa touches the stranger's hand and the narrator hears her whisper, "Thou has conquered . . . thou has conquered—one hour after sunrise—we shall meet—so let it be!" As the stranger leaves the palace, the narrator offers to share his gondola with the man whom he has recognized as one "with whose name the greater part of Europe was then ringing."

Invited to visit the stranger's lavishly decorated palazzo the following day, the narrator sees there a full-length portrait of the Marquesa that contains a scroll with these words: "I am waiting but for thee." The two men drink several glasses of wine, then the stranger lies down on a chaise lounge to sleep while the narrator prepares to leave. Before he can exit, a page from the ducal palace bursts in and cries out, "My mistress!—Bianca! ["Aphrodite" in the final version]—poison! Horrible! Horrible!" The startled narrator tries to awaken his host but finds him dead, having deliberately drunk poisoned wine. The ending strongly suggests that an illicit affair between Bianca, the beautiful, young Marquesa di Mentoni, and the mysterious Byronic stranger has overwhelmed both with hopelessness, leading them to keep their final assignation with each other through suicide.

WRITER'S NOTES

The inspirations for this story appear to include accounts of an affair between the English poet Lord BYRON and Contessa Teresa Guiccioli, who, like the Marquesa di Mentoni, was married to an older Venetian nobleman. The likelihood of this source is strengthened by Poe's familiarity with Thomas Moore's notorious biography *Byron,* which recounts the affair in detail. The incident of the baby falling into a canal resembles an incident that appears in chapter 23 of *The Vicar of Wakefield* (1776), a novel written by Oliver GOLDSMITH. In that account, a young woman married to an older Neopolitan nobleman holds her infant son as she stands at an open window that overlooks the river Volturna. The child wriggles out of her arms, falls into the water below, and disappears. A third possible influence is the tale titled "Doge and Dogaressa" by E. T. A. Hoffman, in which a young man rescues the husband of the woman he loves from drowning.

With its mysterious stranger, dark surroundings, and suicides by two characters at the same hour, the story appears to have begun as a parody of the type of Gothic tale popular at the time. This perception prevented critics from seriously appraising the inherent artistry of the piece, and, for too long, they viewed "The Assignation" as one of Poe's minor tales. It has attained status as a major tale since critics have recognized its significance as the first of Poe's tales to appear in a nationally prominent magazine and also the first to focus on the death of a beautiful woman, a theme that dominates his later work.

Astor, John Jacob (1763–1848) German-born businessman and fur trader. Soon after Astor arrived in the United States in 1784, he opened a fur store in New York City, bought real estate, organized trading posts in the West, and used his wealth to become a national and international power. He also encouraged Washington IRVING to write the travelogue ASTORIA; OR, ANECDOTES OF AN ENTERPRISE BEYOND THE ROCKY MOUNTAINS, an account of his fur trade in the Northwest, which Poe reviewed. Poe also used material from descriptions of Astor's trading expeditions on the Columbia River as the basis for the unfinished novel THE JOURNAL OF JULIUS RODMAN.

"Astoria; or, Anecdotes of an Enterprise beyond the Rocky Mountains. By Washington Irving. Philadelphia: Carey, Lea & Blanchard." Lengthy favorable review that appeared in the January 1837 issue of the SOUTHERN LITERARY MESSENGER. Poe describes Washington IRVING's account of John Jacob ASTOR's fur trading enterprises beyond the Rocky Mountains and the founding of Astoria, Oregon, as written in a "masterly manner." He asserts that the detailed work contains "fullness, comprehensiveness, and beauty, with which a long and entangled series of details, collected, necessarily, from a mass of vague and imperfect data, has been wrought into completeness and unity." The review reveals the genesis of the work as well, and describes the first meeting of Irving and Astor to propose the book as well as the subsequent means by which Irving gathered material for the book. Poe weaves direct summary of the work and quoted material with comments upon Irving's skill in recounting Astor's adventures and the challenges to his endeavor. In careful detail, Poe also identifies the many individuals who collaborated with Astor, as well as the details of their expedition. Despite Poe's assertion of Irving's "masterly manner" in writing *Astoria,* he points out several discrepancies in names as well as in dates, afterward stating that "these errors are of little importance in themselves but may as well be rectified in a future edition."

Auden, W[ystan] H[ugh] (1907–1973) English-born poet and literary critic. Auden created a renaissance in Poe studies in the United States when he edited *Edgar Allan Poe: Selected Prose and Poetry* (1950), which led to Poe's recognition as a major international influence. The edition includes THE NARRATIVE OF ARTHUR GORDON PYM, which Auden called "one of the finest adventure stories ever written." In Auden's estimation, Poe provided inspiration to a range of writers from diverse backgrounds, and by creating "portraits of abnormal or self-destructive states contributed to Dostoyevsky; his ratiocinating hero is the ancestor of Sherlock Holmes and his many successors, his tales of the future lead to H. G. Wells, his adventure stories to Jules Verne and Stevenson."

"Autography" A series of articles that appeared in the February and August 1836 issues of the SOUTHERN LITERARY MESSENGER and the December 1841 and January 1842 issues of GRAHAM'S MAGAZINE in which Poe purports to analyze the actual signatures of writers and other public figures to determine their true personalities. Rather than solicit actual correspondence, Poe wrote a series of fictional letters and claimed that they were written by contemporary figures, including 38 American writers. Poe then created fake signatures for each writer and proceeded to impute specific personality characteristics to the presumed writer on the basis of the penmanship of the signature. In essence, he used the series as a means of praising people whom he favored and to condemn and criticize those who had offended him or whose work he disliked.

Ayres, Frederic (1876–1926) Pseudonym of the American composer Frederic Ayres Johnson, who lectured and wrote on musical subjects. His musical compositions, animated by his love for the Rocky Mountains, include the overture *From the Plains,* the song cycle *The Seeonee Wolves,* and piano pieces including *The Open Road, Moonlight,* and *The Voice of the City.* In 1909, Ayres composed music for Poe's poem "The Sleeper," a vocal work in three parts that the magazine *Musical America* called "an ultra modern work of great interest."

Azrael The angel who separates the soul from the body in Jewish and Moslem legend. In describing the agony of death suffered by LIGEIA, the narrator asserts, "I saw that she must die—and I struggled desperately in spirit with the grim Azrael."

Baal-Zebub Character in the short story "THE DUC DE L'OMELETTE." He is the devil who, with haughty disdain for the self-important aristocrat, takes de l'Omelette from his rosewood coffin to hell, then orders him to strip off his clothing and meet his fate. Referring to himself at one point as the Prince of the Fly, Baal-Zebub insults, goads, and torments de l'Omelette. When his victim suggests a game of cards to wager for his soul, Baal-Zebub agrees to a game of double or nothing, but the overly confident devil fails to give the game his full attention. When de l'Omelette draws a king from the deck, the devil loses both the game and his claim on the aristocrat's soul.

Bacon, Sir Francis [Lord Verulam] (1561–1626) English essayist and the proponent of a new approach to science. In "LIGEIA," Poe refers to Bacon's concept of beauty stated in "Of Beauty" but misquotes him slightly by altering Bacon's statement "There is no excellent beauty that hath not some strangeness in the proportion" to read "There is no exquisite beauty without some strangeness in the proportions." Poe makes other references to Bacon's inductive scientific method in reviews, critical essays, and the tale "MELLONTA TAUTA." In these references, Poe characterizes as too restrictive both the inductive and deductive methods of seeking objective truth. He labels as faulty Bacon's methodology for attaining scientific truth because it "cultivated the natural sciences to the exclusion of Metaphysics, the Mathematics, and Logic."

Bag Character in the short story "THE BUSINESS MAN." He is Peter PROFFIT's lawyer, who seems to have more integrity than his client. When Proffit demands that Bag bring a suit against an associate who "doubled his fist" and knocked Proffit down, and that he demand $1,000 in damages, Bag cautions him that for so simple a knockdown any amount over five hundred dollars is excessive. Proffit considers such common sense unacceptable and determines to fire Bag for having "no *system* at all."

Balan, Joan (1892–?) Romanian composer whose symphonic works were published in Berlin and Vienna and performed in Germany, France, England, Holland, Belgium, Czechoslovakia, and the Baltic countries.

Among these works are the symphonic poem *Fatum* as well as the orchestral pieces *Humoreske, Praludium, Suite Fantastique,* and others. Balan was fascinated by the emotional rhythms of Poe's poetry and tales and in 1934 composed piano scores for "THE RAVEN," (*Der Rabe*), "ULALUME," and "METZENGERSTEIN" (*Das Feurpferd*). Further inspired by "TO ONE IN PARADISE," the composer also wrote in 1934 *Elegie,* Op. 17, a vocal and piano score for soprano and orchestra that uses the first two stanzas of the poem. In 1938, Balan wrote *Elegie II,* Op. 70, a voice and piano score for soprano or tenor and orchestra, based on Poe's "THE HAUNTED PALACE."

Baldazzar, Duke of Surrey Character in Poe's drama *POLITIAN*. He is a close friend and attendant of the Earl of Politian and travels with him from Great Britain to Rome. Baldazzar not only rouses the earl from his deep melancholy but also sternly reminds him of his responsibility to exhibit a pleasant demeanor as a guest and visitor. Although he disagrees with the reason, Baldazzar also acts as a go-between when Politian challenges the host's son CASTIGLIONE to a dual after falling in love with the younger man's betrothed.

Balfe, Michael W. (1808–1870) Irish composer best known for the lighthearted opera *The Bohemian Girl,* among approximately 30 operas and operettas that include *The Rose of Castile, Il Talismano,* and *Satanella.* In 1865, Balfe wrote melancholy music to accompany the words of Poe's poem "ANNABEL LEE" and later that year composed a song, made up of a full score for a band, to accompany the first stanza of "THE BELLS."

"Ballads and Other Poems. By Henry Wadsworth Longfellow, Author of 'Voices of the Night,' 'Hyperion,' & c. Second Edition. John Owen, Cambridge" A two-part review of Henry Wadsworth Longfellow's poetry that appeared in the March and April 1842 issues of *GRAHAM'S MAGAZINE*. In the first part, Poe disputes the validity of public taste in determining what constitutes good poetry, for "it has been yielded to the clamor of the majority." While he professes to admire Longfellow's "genius," Poe maintains that "we are fully sensible of his many errors of affectation and imitation." In example, the reviewer asserts that "his didactics are all *out of place*," and contends that Longfellow "has written brilliant poems—by accident." Poe finds fault with the poet's overt didacticism, a theme that he pursues in great detail in the lengthy second part of the review. The reviewer claims that Longfellow's "conception of the *aims* of poesy is erroneous" and his "inculcation of a *moral* as essential" detract from the artistic quality of the poetry. This observation leads Poe into a lengthy digression to consider the true aim of poetry. He insists that art must serve the imagination first and states that the premier purpose of poetry is "the *Rhythmical Creation of Beauty.*" In particular, Poe strongly denounces any purpose of poetry beyond the following:

> Beyond the limits of Beauty its province does not extend. Its sole arbiter is taste. With the Intellect or with the Conscience it has only collateral relations. It has no dependence, unless incidentally, upon either Duty or *Truth.*

After espousing his theory of poetic principles at length, Poe methodically applies that theory to Longfellow's poems, such as "The Village Blacksmith," "The Wreck of the Hesperus," and "The Skeleton in Armor," finding faults with all. Poe is particularly disdainful of the poet's translations of German poems into English, and feels that "*His* time might be better employed in original conception."

"The Balloon-Hoax" Short story. This tale was conceived as an attempt to fool newspaper readers into believing that a manned balloon flight across the Atlantic Ocean was completed in 75 hours.

PUBLISHING AND DRAMATIZATION HISTORY

The story was first published as a newspaper article in the *Extra Sun* on April 13, 1844, under the following headline: "Astounding Intelligence by Private Express from Charleston via Norfolk!—The Atlantic Ocean crossed in three days!! Arrival at Sullivan's Island of a Steering Balloon invented by Mr. Monck Mason." The article was reprinted the following day in the New York *Sunday Times*. To strengthen the image of verisimilitude, Poe used the names of real individuals who had already published accounts of their aeronautical expeditions. As an aid to convincing readers that the voyage actually had occurred, he named the popular novelist William Harrison AINSWORTH as having been among the crew. Once the story was revealed to be a hoax, the *Sun* printed the following retraction on April 15, 1844:

> BALLOON — The mails from the South last Saturday night not having brought a confirmation of the arrival of the Balloon from England, the particulars of which from our correspondent we detailed in our Extra, we are inclined to believe that the intelligence is erro-

neous. The description of the Balloon, and the voyage was written with a minuteness and scientific ability calculated to obtain credit everywhere, and was read with great pleasure and satisfaction. We by no means think such a project impossible.

No film has been made of "The Balloon-Hoax" to date.

CHARACTERS

William Harrison AINSWORTH, Sir Eveard Bringhurst, Charles GREEN, William HENSON, Robert Holland, Monck MASON, Mr. Obsorne, two seamen from Woolwich.

PLOT SYNOPSIS

The tale is written in the journalistic style of the big scoop and provides readers with convincing details, including a technical description of the balloon, and aerodynamics of transatlantic travel, and journal entries presumably written by Mason. After establishing the credentials of his travelers, Poe reports to his readers that "the particulars furnished below may be relied upon as authentic and accurate in every respect, as, with a slight exception, they are copied *verbatim* from the joint diaries of Mr. Monck Mason and Mr. Harrison Ainsworth, to whose politeness our agent is also indebted for much verbal information respecting the balloon itself, its construction, and other matters of interest." The account is divided into two parts: "The Balloon" and "The Journal." In the first section, Poe draws upon nonfiction descriptions of balloons and their functioning to methodically delineate the size, shape, and working details of the balloon. Readers are informed in clear language of the many intricate parts that make up the balloon and its basket, and they are warned of the consequences should damage occur to any one of these parts. The account also provides a careful delineation of the steps required to raise the balloon and to keep it afloat. The second part of the account purports to contain daily journal entries about the voyage, written by Mason and appended with postscripts by Ainsworth, from Saturday, April 6, through Tuesday, April 9. Each entry recreates the fictional activities of the balloon crew and recounts their thoughts and apprehensions regarding the journey. The story ends with the safe descent of the balloon at Fort Moultrie and Sullivan's Island, in South Carolina, and the statement by the "reporter" that "we can safely promise our readers some additional information either on Monday or in the course of the next day, at farthest."

WRITER'S NOTES

The inspiration for the story lies in the high interest that the public of the 1830s and 1840s had in manned balloon flights. Balloonists competed for records in height, speed, and distance, and many magazines carried articles that described the latest model balloons and their capabilities. Poe earned $50 for what the *Sun* believed to be an exclusive story, but he may have experienced even greater satisfaction for having fooled many people who had not appreciated his writing previously. He was proud of the stir that his account caused and described his pleasure in an article in the *Columbian Spy,* published in May 1944, a month after the hoax was revealed:

'The Balloon-Hoax' made a far more intense sensation than anything of that character since the 'Moon-Story' of Locke. On the morning (Saturday) of its announcement, the whole square surrounding the 'Sun' building was literally besieged, blocked up—ingress and egress being alike impossible, from a period soon after sunrise until about two o'clock P.M. In Saturday's regular issue, it was stated that the news had been just received, and that an 'Extra' was then in preparation, which would be ready at ten. It was not delivered, however, until nearly noon. In the meantime I never witnessed more intense excitement to get possession of a newspaper. As soon as the first few copies made their way into the streets, they were bought up, at almost any price, from the news-boys, who made a profitable speculation beyond doubt. I saw a half-dollar given, in one instance, for a single paper, and a shilling was a frequent price. I tried, in vain, during the whole day, to get possession of a copy. It was excessively amusing, however, to hear the comments of those who had read the 'Extra.'

Despite Poe's self-satisfaction in having fooled 50,000 people, the success of the hoax had a negative effect on his career. Publishers viewed the incident as reinforcing their suspicions that Poe was not quite trustworthy and led to concern that he might, if hired, play jokes on them and their readers. This led to a hesitance among editors to approach Poe, and demand for his work decreased.

Baltimore, Maryland   Poe's association with the city of Baltimore began in late March 1831, after he left the United States Military Academy at West Point. He lived for a time with his older brother Henry in the attic of a home owned by his paternal aunt, Mrs. Maria Clemm, later his mother-in-law, who also cared for his paternal grandmother and who was the mother of nine-year-old Virginia, Poe's future wife. The city also contained other Poe relatives, some of whom shared their contacts with the young author in attempts to help him to find work. Poe first received literary recognition during his years in Baltimore, from 1831 to 1835. He wrote many of his early tales in the attic of Mrs. Clemm's home and began to see his work published in Baltimore publications. Poe left Baltimore for Richmond,

Virginia, in 1835, but he returned to Baltimore and died there at three o'clock in the morning on October 7, 1849.

Baltimore Sunday Visiter   Periodical edited by Lambert A. WILMER. In July 1833, the *Visiter* offered monetary prizes of $25 for the best poem and $50 for the best short story, which prompted Poe to submit his work. The author's short story "A DESCENT INTO THE MAELSTROM" won, and his poem "THE COLISEUM" also was selected to win. The judges felt that awarding both prizes to the same person would be unfair, so they gave the poetry prize, instead, to John H. HEWITT for "The Song of the Winds." After Wilmer was replaced as the *Visiter*'s editor in 1834, mentions of Poe in the paper were far less favorable.

Barbour, John Strode (1790–1855)   Virginia politician. He endorsed Poe's appointment to the United States Military Academy at West Point.

"The Bargain Lost"   First title and draft version of the short story "BON-BON." The work appeared in the *Philadelphia Saturday Courier* on December 1, 1832.

Barker, George (n.d.)   Arranger of four-part recitative chant that uses stanzas 1, 2, 3, 7, 15, 16, 17, and 18 of "THE RAVEN." Composed in 1866, this now out-of-print work was published by J. L. Peters & Bro. The only known copy exists in the library archives of Johns Hopkins University in Baltimore, Maryland.

"Barnaby Rudge. By Charles Dickens (Boz), Author of 'The Old Curiosity Shop,' 'Pickwick,' 'Oliver Twist,' & c., & c. With Numerous Illustrations, By Cattermole, Browne & Sibson. Lea & Blanchard: Philadelphia"   A long and laudatory review of Charles Dickens's novel that appeared in both the *Philadelphia Saturday Evening Post,* on May 1, 1841, and *GRAHAM'S MAGAZINE,* in February 1842. When Dickens was on tour in the United States in March 1842, Poe sent him a copy of the review and requested an interview, which was not granted. Poe begins the review by denouncing the "literary Titmice" who judge works merely by the number of books sold and who sneer at critical excellence. He mocks their "little opinions" and states that "if the popularity of a book be in fact the measure of its worth," most scientific tomes must be judged inferior to the popular novels. Poe specifically contests "the fallacy of one of their favorite dogmas; we mean the dogma that no work of fiction can fully suit, at the same time, the critical and the popular taste; in fact, that the disregarding or contravening of Critical Rule is absolutely essential to success, beyond a certain and very limited extent, with the public at large." In evidence of his position, Poe

Downtown Baltimore as it looked in 1849, the year Poe died there. (National Archives—Stills Division)

offers Dickens's *Barnaby Rudge,* which he characterizes as "the legitimate and inevitable result of certain well-understood critical propositions reduced by genius into practice." He claims that his intention is not to enter into "any wholesale *laudation*." Before offering a critique, Poe first provides a detailed summary of the novel, which he characterizes as "a very meagre outline of the story," then points out the structural weaknesses of the novel and the inconsistencies that emerge because the novel was published in installments rather than as a whole. These flaws aside, Poe turns to the strengths that he finds in the novel, particularly Dickens's skill "as a delineator of character." Examining each character in the novel, Poe points out Dickens's originality in handling even such stock figures as Sir John Chester, "a vast improvement upon all his predecessors." In the final analysis, the review asserts that *Barnaby Rudge* is not Dickens's finest, "but there are few—very few others to which we consider it

inferior." Poe feels that Dickens "has done this thing well—he would do anything well in comparison with the herd of his contemporaries—but he has not done it so thoroughly well as his high and just reputation would demand."

Barnard, Augustus   Character in the novel THE NARRA-TIVE OF ARTHUR GORDON PYM. The son of Captain BARNARD, he joins Pym in becoming drunk and reveling aboard the sailboat *Ariel,* then sails with him on the *Grampus.* When the two become stranded, Barnard reluctantly joins Pym in becoming a cannibal as the two are forced by starvation to eat the corpse of seaman Richard Parker. Barnard later dies at sea, and his body is thrown to the sharks.

Barnard, Captain   Character in the novel THE NARRA-TIVE OF ARTHUR GORDON PYM. He is the captain of the

Grampus, the ship on which Pym stows away, and he is also the father of Augustus BARNARD.

Barnum's Hotel   Famous Baltimore hotel at the intersection of Fayette and Calvert Streets, built in 1827 and known for its "canvas-back ducks done rare," where Poe frequently joined other former West Point cadets for supper. Maria CLEMM's lawyer had his offices in the basement of the building.

Barrett, Elizabeth [Browning] (1806–1861)   English poet and the wife of Robert BROWNING. Poe greatly admired her poem "Lady Geraldine's Courtship," of which he stated in "FIFTY SUGGESTIONS": "I have never known a poem combining so much of the fiercest passion with so much of the most delicate imagination." Poe dedicated his edition of THE RAVEN AND OTHER POEMS to her. He also contributed a long, double review of her poetry to the BROADWAY JOURNAL of January 4, 1845, and January 12, 1845 (see "DRAMA OF EXILE AND OTHER POEMS").

Barry, Lyttleton   A pen name used by Poe and created from two pseudonyms: the name "Barry Cornwall," used by the songwriter Bryan Waller Procter, and "Mack Littleton," the named used by J. P. Kennedy in writing the 1835 novel *Horse-Shoe Robinson.* Poe published five stories under this pseudonym: "DUC L'OMELETTE" (1832), "LOSS OF BREATH" (1832), "KING PEST" (1835), "WHY THE LITTLE FRENCHMAN WEARS HIS HAND IN A SLING" (1837), and "MYSTIFICATION" (1837).

Bartlett, Honorable John R. (fl. 1840)   Judge in whose New York City home Poe was a frequent visitor during the winter of 1845–46. In letters, Poe observed that he joined "the best intellectual society of the city" at the judge's home.

Bas-Bleu, Big Miss   Character in the short story "LIONIZING." She is a pseudoliterary bluestocking who welcomes the author of a pamphlet on the science of noses with the delighted exclamation: "What can he be?"

Bas-Bleu, Little Miss   Character in the short story "LIONIZING." She is a literary bluestocking who welcomes the author of a pamphlet on the science of noses with the delighted exclamation. "Where can he be?"

Bas-Bleu, Miss   Character in the short story "THE MAN THAT WAS USED UP" and one of the guests at Mrs. Kathleen O'TRUMP's party. Miss Bas-Bleu (French for "bluestocking") is a shrill-voiced "little feminine interloper" and literary know-it-all who appeals to the narrator to settle a dispute with another guest who has identified Lord BYRON's poetical drama as *Man Friday.* Stuck with "a very bitter animosity against the whole race of Bas-Bleus," the narrator sides with her opponent in the dispute.

Bas-Bleu, Mrs.   Character in the short story "LIONIZING." She is a literary bluestocking who welcomes the author of a pamphlet on the science of noses with the delighted exclamation: "Who can he be?"

Bashan   The place in the short story "A TALE OF JERUSALEM" from which the sub-collectors believe that the sacred offering has come: "It is a fatted calf from the pastures of Bashan." The term refers to a region east of Jordan and north of Arnon in the Bible, characterized by smooth, fertile land and distinguished for its fine cattle.

Baudelaire, Charles (1821–1867)   French poet and early critical defender of Poe's work whose translations remain the best in any language. Baudelaire is responsible for establishing Poe's reputation in France through his translations, which were published over 16 years from 1848 to 1864 and that now occupy five books of the 12-volume set of Baudelaire's standard works. Baudelaire also published three well-received critical essays about Poe's work. The French poet identified closely with the tortured artist in Poe, referring to him as *le pauvre Eddie* (the poor Eddie) and *mon semblable, mon frère* (my likeness, my brother). Writers have found numerous similarities between the two men. Photographs of Baudelaire show him to have had a large head with a prominent forehead like that of Poe. Both men revolted against the father figures in their lives—Baudelaire against his stepfather General Aupich, and Poe against his foster father John Allan. As literary critics, both were vicious in their estimation of the works of their peers, and the result was that Baudelaire made numerous enemies, as did his idol. Baudelaire's personal life contained the same self-destructive behavior as Poe's, and his opium use and alcohol abuse are widely documented. Decrying that Poe "isn't much in America," Baudelaire vowed to make Poe a great man in France. In the preface to his work *Nouvelles histoires extraordinaires,* published in 1857, Baudelaire examines the psychological aspects of Poe's work and analyzes the distinct personality traits that led to such creations, declaring Poe one of America's major poets. Baudelaire's writings show that he reserved his greatest admiration for Poe's portrayal of extreme mental states, from nightmares through subconscious fears and insanity that permeate the stories. In "Spleen," Baudelaire lightly rephrased the opening sentence of "THE FALL OF THE HOUSE OF USHER" and paraphrased Poe's conclusion of "TO HELEN" in "The Living Flame."

The French poet and critic Charles Baudelaire made Poe famous in France. (Library of Congress)

In "Voyage to Cythera," Baudelaire rephrases in verse Poe's narrative description of seabirds devouring a man's flesh that appears in THE NARRATIVE OF ARTHUR GORDON PYM. In his 1863 critical essay "The Painter of Modern Life," in which he praises Poe as "the most powerful pen of our age," Baudelaire also labels "THE MAN OF THE CROWD" as the best of Poe's stories. This story also strongly influenced Baudelaire's poem "The Seven Old Men," as it recounts a similarly obsessive relationship between the narrator and a filthy old man in ragged clothing, with dire consequences for the narrator. Poe's influence can be seen both throughout the psychological states created by Baudelaire and in his stated poetic principle that poetry should exist for its sake alone and not to teach.

Beachcroft, Richard O. (n.d.) English musician and Musical Doctor (an academic rank) from Oxford University and member of the Royal College of Organists. His composition, a unison chorus with piano accompa-

niment to Poe's poem "ELDORADO," was published in 1925.

Beale, Upton (fl. 1826) Close friend of Poe's at the University of Virginia who later became an Episcopal minister.

Beardsley, Aubrey (1872–1898) English fin-de-siècle artist and illustrator whose work is characterized by a highly imaginative and hedonistic style that gave him a reputation as one of England's most innovative illustrators. Beardsley's black-on-white fantastic images, especially the female and hermaphroditic figures, aroused controversy. Beardsley designed posters and wrote fiction, as well as illustrating *The Works of Edgar Allan Poe* (1894–95).

Beauchamp-Sharp Murder Case A celebrated crime of passion, known as "The Kentucky Tragedy," that occurred in 1825 and furnished Poe with a real-life source for his drama POLITAN, set in 16th-century Rome. The case involved Ann Cook of Frankfort, Kentucky, who was seduced by Solomon P. Sharp, the state solicitor general. Cook gave birth to Sharp's child, then agreed to marry Jeroboam O. Beauchamp in 1824 on the condition that he promise to kill Sharp. Beauchamp kept his promise and stabbed Sharp to death on November 5, 1825. Beauchamp was arrested and subjected to a long and sensational trial, during which he pleaded not guilty. After the judge convicted Beauchamp for murder and ordered his execution, Ann Cook joined him in his cell on the eve of his execution. The two attempted suicide. Ann Cook died of a laudanum overdose and stab wounds, while Beauchamp survived to be hanged on July 7, 1826. Poe was not the only author inspired by the real-life tragedy. The authors William Gilmore Simms and Thomas Holley Chivers incorporated details of the tragedy into their respective novels, *Beauchampe* (1842) and *Conrad and Eudora* (1834).

Beauvais, Monsieur Character in the short story "THE MYSTERY OF MARIE ROGÊT." He makes inquiries for Marie Rogêt and is present when fishermen retrieve her corpse from the Seine River in Paris, where it is found floating. Beauvais is asked to identify the body and does so after some hesitation. His contention that he recognized the body because of the hair on the arm raises doubts of his veracity. Despite this, he later takes control of the family and brings suspicion on himself: "For some reason, he determined that nobody should have anything to do with the proceedings but himself and he has elbowed all of the male relatives out of the way, according to their representations, in a very singular manner."

Bedloe, Augustus   Character in the short story "A TALE OF THE RAGGED MOUNTAINS." He is an apparently young gentleman, "remarkable in every respect," who excites in the narrator "a profound interest and curiosity." A tall and thin man, Bedloe appears cadaverous: "He stopped much. His limbs were exceedingly long and emaciated. His forehead was broad and long. His complexion was absolutely bloodless. His mouth was large and flexible, and his teeth were more wildly uneven . . . than I had ever before seen teeth in a human head." Bedloe is also highly excitable, with a vigorous imagination that the narrator attributes to his habitual use of morphine. The character usually takes a very large dose of morphine after breakfast each morning, then goes for his morning walk into the Ragged Mountains. Upon his return from one of these walks, Bedloe tells an extraordinary story of having seen a battle and being wounded, then feeling the sensation of dying. His attending physician shows the narrator a portrait of a British officer named Oldeb, who resembles Bedloe and who actually died 50 years earlier in such a battle with the doctor present. Within a week after his vision, Bedloe is dead. The newspaper obituary reports that he died while being bled with "a venomous vermicular sangsues," a poisonous leech. His name is nearly the opposite spelling of the long-dead soldier.

Belial   Character in the short story "DUC DE L'OMELETTE." He is one of the devil's assistants, his "Inspector of Cemeteries," who conveys the Duc to hell.

"The Bells"   Poem by Poe written in May 1848 and published posthumously in *SARTAIN'S UNION MAGAZINE* in November 1849. Biographers have credited inspiration for the poem to Marie Louise SHEW, who helped to care for the dying Virginia CLEMM in the little Fordham cottage. In the month after Virginia's death, Poe became emotionally attached to Mrs. Shew and often spent time at her home, which was close to Grace Church in New York City. On one evening, Poe claimed that he had to write a poem but devoid of inspiration. Church bells in the background encouraged his companion to write playfully, "The bells, the little silver bells," and Poe finished the stanza. He then contemplated other types of bells, and created stanzas for each. The poem went through three major revisions and was submitted to *Sartain's Union Magazine* three times before being published in November 1849. Divided into four major movements, the poem deals with different types of bells that mark the four ages of human beings: silver for youth and merriment, golden for happiness and harmony in love and marriage, brass for maturity, and iron for old age and death. Appropriate sound devices such as onomatopoeia and repetition produce sonority

and rhythm in the poem. Sounds are alternately harsh, mellifluous, jarring, loving and cajoling. The poem was published with editor John Sartain's note that "There is a curious piece of literary history connected with this poem. . . . It illustrates the gradual development of an idea in the mind of a man of original genius." The poem has since been assessed by critics as belonging to "the finest order of his works."

Bemans, Samuel (1785–1871)   New York composer and editor of the monthly musical magazine *The Nightengale or the Jenny Lind Songster,* devoted to the publication of the choicest songs sung by Jenny Lind and other celebrated vocalists." Bemans composed an unaccompanied melody to "THE RAVEN," probably intended for group singing, which appeared in the June 1850 issue of the *Nightengale.*

Benevenuta, The Improvisatore of Florence   An allusion created by Poe in "BON-BON" whose lines the author uses to comment upon the colorful and highly decorative clothing of Pierre Bon-Bon: "it was difficult to say whether Pierre Bon-Bon was indeed a bird of Paradise, or the rather a very Paradise of perfection."

Benjamin, Park (1809–1864)   Editor at different times of *American Monthly Magazine, New Yorker, Signal,* and *New World.* He defended Poe's writing in the June 4, 1842, issue of *New World,* stating that Poe was "one of the best writers now living. . . . [I]n whatever sphere he moves, he will surely be distinguished." Poe appears to have held mixed feelings toward Benjamin, whom he both praised and reprimanded in "AUTOGRAPHY." He characterized Benjamin as independent and critical of all classes without reservation, ". . . let the consequences fall where they may. He is no respecter of persons, and his vituperance as often assails the powerful as the powerless—indeed the latter rarely fall under his censure." Poe tempered such praise by stating that Benjamin's independence was less a matter of principle than of personal feelings, "now of friendship, and again of vindictiveness." Poe judged his writing to be "lucid, terse, and pungent," and he found the man to be "witty, often cuttingly sarcastic, but seldom humorous." Poe pronounced Benjamin's poetry to be "not very dissimilar to Mr. [Washington] Irving's" and devotes the article "SATIRICAL POEMS" to its analysis.

Bennet   Part-owner of the schooner sailed by Captain GUY in *THE NARRATIVE OF ARTHUR GORDON PYM.* He never appears in the story and nothing is told about his life, but Guy gives Bennet's name to an islet situated at 82° 50' South latitude, 42° 20' West longitude.

"Berenice" Short story. The story is one of Poe's most morbid and gruesome, and he admitted in a letter to the editor of the SOUTHERN LITERARY MESSENGER on April 30, 1835, "I allow that it approaches the very verge of bad taste—but I will not sin quite so egregiously again."

PUBLISHING AND DRAMATIZATION HISTORY

The story was first published in the March 1835 issue of the *Southern Literary Messenger*. After its publication, readers wrote letters to the editor to complain about the subject matter, which deals with grave robbing and corpse mutilation. Poe claimed that the story originated in a bet with an unnamed editor after both read an article in the February 23, 1833, issue of the BALTIMORE SUNDAY VISITER on the subject of graves being robbed to obtain teeth for dentists. In his defense of "Berenice," Poe stated that the story was very similar in content to other tales found in magazines of his day, "in the ludicrous heightened into the grotesque; the fearful coloured into the horrible; the witty exaggerated into the burlesque; the singular wrought out into the strange and the mystical."

The story opens with the following epigraph:

Dicebant mihi sodales, si sepulchrum amicae visitarem, curas meas aliquantulum fore levatus. [My companion told me I might find some little alleviation of my misery in visiting the grave of my beloved.]

— Ebn Zaiat (c. A.D. 218)

CHARACTERS

BERENICE, EGAEUS.

PLOT SYNOPSIS

The plot is the story of an aborted attempt at marriage between Egaeus, the "gloomy" and "ill" last descendant of an ancient family that "has been called a race of visionaries," and his "graceful and energetic" cousin Berenice. Self-described as suffering from "monomania . . . a morbid irritability," Egaeus engages in meditations that were "*never* pleasurable." As the wedding approaches, Egaeus's monomania becomes more intense, and the once-vibrant Berenice becomes ill and begins to waste away. As he views his changed bride-to-be, the narrator can focus only the "white and ghastly *spectrum* of her teeth." He obsesses over their perfection: "The teeth!—the teeth!—they were here and there, and everywhere, and visibly and palpably before me; long, narrow, and excessively white, with the pale lips writhing above them." The emaciated Berenice soon dies early one morning, after what the narrator describes as an epileptic seizure, and she is buried "at the closing in of the night." At midnight, the narrator awakens from "a confused and exciting dream" with no recollection of how he has spent the hours since interring Berenice at sundown. He is plagued by a great feeling of unease but has no explanation until a servant enters and tells him that Berenice's grave has been violated, and that other servants had searched and found "a disfigured body, enshrouded, yet still breathing, still palpitating, still alive!" As the mud-covered Egaeus shrieks and bounds out of his seat, a box falls from the table and out fall "some instruments of dental surgery, intermingled with thirty-two small, white and ivory-looking substances."

WRITER'S NOTES

The public outcry against the story led Poe to remove four paragraphs that contained detailed, gory descriptions of the coffin and the body of the dead Berenice. Poe had specifically depicted "the peculiar smell of the coffin" and "the deleterious odor [that] was already exhaling from the body." The graphic description of Berenice's mouth, whose "livid lips were wreathed into a species of smiles" and similar descriptions were considered to be in bad taste. The edited version was published in the *Southern Literary Messenger* in 1840.

Berenice Character in the short story "BERENICE" who is buried alive by the cousin to whom she is betrothed. At the outset of the story, Berenice is vital and healthy, but her health deteriorates as her wedding day approaches, until she becomes frail and wraithlike. After suffering an epileptic seizure, Berenice is buried by her gloomy bridegroom, EGAEUS, who believes that she is dead. Late that same night, a servant reports that the grave has been violated and that Berenice's enshrouded body has been found "yet still breathing, still palpitating, still alive!" Someone or something has ripped out all 32 of her teeth, disfiguring her. Berenice is one of the many frail and dying Poe heroines who experience death in life.

Bergen, Alfred Hiles (1884–?) American composer, conductor, and singer born in Milwaukee, Wisconsin, who made extensive song recital tours in the United States and Canada. In 1911, Bergen composed musical accompaniment to Poe's poem "TO F———." In 1926 he composed his Op. 15, No. 1, to accompany Poe's poem "ANNABEL LEE." He also composed music for male voices with piano or orchestra accompaniment to Poe's poem "ELDORADO" in 1938 and to "THE BELLS" in 1968.

Bergh, Arthur (1882–1962) American composer, conductor, and director of recording at the Emerson Phonograph Company from 1915 through 1922 and at the Columbia Phonograph Company from 1922 through 1930. In addition to composing such melodramas as *The Pied Piper of Hamelin* and *The Intruder*, the song cycle to *The Congo*, and numerous piano and violin pieces, Bergh composed a musical melodrama for Poe's "THE RAVEN" to be accompanied by piano or orchestra. The first public performance of the work took place at the Hall of Fame of New York University on January 19, 1909, with Bergh at the piano.

Berlifitzing, Count Wilhelm Character in the short story "METZENGERSTEIN." An "infirm and doting old man," he is "loftily descended" and "remarkable for nothing but an inordinate and inveterate personal antipathy to the family of his rival" Metzengerstein. He participates daily in the chase, despite his age and the danger of the sport. After he dies in a stable fire, his spirit returns to earth and inhabits the body of a horse to become an agent of supernatural revenge against the rival family.

Bernard, P. D. (fl. 1840) Prominent Philadelphia publisher, printer, and author connected with the *SOUTHERN LITERARY MESSENGER*. Poe wrote to him on March 24, 1843, "to ascertain if the list of 'The South: Lit: Messenger' is to be disposed of" and to express his desire "to purchase the list and unite it with that of the Stylus." (See *STYLUS*.)

"Big Abel and the Little Manhattan" Review by Poe that appeared in the *BROADWAY JOURNAL* of September 27, 1845. A lengthened version of the review of Cornelius Mathews's historical fantasy appeared in *GODEY'S MAGAZINE AND LADY'S BOOK* for November 1845. Poe characterized the novel, which concerns two claimants to the island of Manhattan, as "an emblematical romance of homely life" that functions as an allegory contrasting the present with "the true values of the savage and uncivilized state." The rivals are "a houseless vagabond, the great-grandson of Henry Hudson the navigator, and the descendant from the last Indian chief of the Maunahatta" who have proposed to lay claim to various areas of Manhattan based on papers that they assert sustain their claims. In their rovings throughout the city, "these two being a little demented, or whimsical or ignorant" divide what they believe to be their holdings, naming as they go such landmarks as Trinity Church and Delmonico's. Poe calls it "an ingenious, an original, and altogether, an excellent book," but he also points out that the casual reader will probably be confused by it, for "Its chief defect is a very gross indefiniteness, not of conception, but of execution." In conclusion, he asserts that popularity must not be Mathews's intention, because "out of ten readers nine will be totally at a loss to comprehend the meaning of the author."

"Binney's Eulogism" Poe's review of a eulogy delivered by Horace Binney on the death of Chief Justice Marshall; the review appeared in the *SOUTHERN LITERARY MESSENGER* in December 1835. Poe asserts that "Mr. Binney speaks with no less truth than modesty, in making it the consolation alike of the humblest, and of the most gifted eulogist" when he states in the eulogy that "'to give with simplicity the record of his life' is most nearly to copy 'the great original'."

"The Biography and Poetical Remains of the Late Margaret Miller Davidson. By Washington Irving. Philadelphia, Lea and Blanchard" Review of Irving's biography of the child poet Margaret Miller Davidson, in *GRAHAM'S MAGAZINE* for August 1841. Similar to her sister Lucretia, whose work is reviewed in "POETICAL REMAINS OF THE LATE LUCRETIA MARIA DAVIDSON," Margaret "perished (of consumption) in her sixteenth year" and left poetry that her mother compiled, arranging the material chronologically and inserting observations on her daughter's life as well as a letter detailing the last moments of the girl's life. Poe commended Irving for conveying "a just idea of the exquisite loveliness of the picture here presented to view," but he also criticizes Irving for overestimating the artistry of the works and states that "his words, however, in their hyperbole, do wrong to his subject, and would be hyperbole still, if applied to the most exalted poets of all time." Nonetheless, Poe pays particular attention to her 2,000-line poem "Lenore" and credits her with "occasional bursts of the truest poetic fire." He further singled out two other poems for high praise: "To Mamma" and "My Native Lake."

Bird, Robert Montgomery (1806–1854) American novelist, author of *Nick of the Woods; or The Jibbenainosay* (1837). Poe reviewed several of Bird's books for the *SOUTHERN LITERARY MESSENGER*, including *Calavar*, "by far the best of them, and beyond doubt one of the best of American novels." Poe included Bird in "AUTOGRAPHY" and noted that the "degree of nervousness" in his signature exhibited that "a restless and vivid imagination might be deduced from this MS."

Bird, William Character in the short story "THE MURDERS IN THE RUE MORGUE." He is an English tailor who first suggests that the voice that he believes to belong to the murderer was speaking German. His erroneous interpretation of what he has heard delays the solution to the crime and mistakenly leads the authorities away from the true perpetrator.

Bisco, John (fl. 1840) Cofounder with Charles BRIGGS of the *BROADWAY JOURNAL* and Poe's partner for a brief period in 1845. After Briggs left, Bisco continued to publish with Poe, allowing Poe a one-third interest in the publication for several months. In October 1845, he sold his interest in the magazine for $50 to Poe, who paid him with a personal note endorsed by Horace GREELEY.

"The Black Cat" Short story. Critics generally view the tale as among Poe's finest works, and they have especially praised his handling of the mentally ill protagonist. Poe drew upon superstitions about cats as sacred and as having special powers, as well as upon medieval belief that black cats were Satan's favorite disguise when he roamed the earth.

PUBLISHING AND DRAMATIZATION HISTORY

The story was first published in the *United States Saturday Post* on August 19, 1843. Public reaction was immediately favorable, and the story became so great a success that it spawned a parody the following year, "The Ghost of the Grey Tadpole," written by Thomas Dunn ENGLISH.

The name recognition of Poe's popular short story has led to its use as the title of films that have not always reflected the content of the original. The title has attracted audiences, but the plots of these films have been far different from Poe's story. Both the 1934 film *The Black Cat,* starring Boris Karloff and Bela Lugosi, and the 1941 film of the same name, starring Lugosi and Basil Rathbone, share only the title of the original; neither contains plot characteristics that reflect the short story. The 1968 Japanese film *Kuroneko* ("The Black Cat") is a story of two women, raped and murdered by samurai, who return to haunt their attackers, while the 1990 American film *The Black Cat* places its action in a haunted house, without a hint of the original plot. Critics have described the 1981 film *The Black Cat,* starring Patrick Magee and Mimsy Farmer, as "vaguely Poe-ish": the film does contain a cat, but the cat is possessed by an evil spirit. The most faithful rendering of the story appears in the 1962 *Tales of Terror,* directed by Roger Corman, who presented three of Poe's short stories—"MORELLA," "THE FACTS IN THE CASE OF M. VALDEMAR," and "The Black Cat"—starring Vincent Price, Peter Lorre, Basil Rathbone, and Debra Paget.

CHARACTERS

PLUTO, an unnamed male narrator, the unnamed wife of the narrator.

PLOT SYNOPSIS

The story relates the gradual mental deterioration of a man whose early kindly temperament becomes warped, leading to irrational, violent acts against what he loves most at the outset of the story. He blames his changed and newly violent personality on "that Fiend Intemperance," which he views as a disease over which he has no control. The protagonist begins his reign of cruelty as he "made no scruple of maltreating the rabbits, the monkey, or even the dog, when by accident, or through affection, they came in my way." For a while his black cat Pluto escapes this treatment, until one night when the narrator returns home and, in an act of "evil malevolence," uses his penknife to pry the cat's eye from its socket. As the cat heals in the weeks that follow, the narrator experiences moments of remorse, but "the spirit of perverseness" soon overtakes him and he hangs Pluto in the garden, experiencing a mixture of pleasure with "the bitterest remorse at heart" and terrible self-loathing. The narrator's wife replaces Pluto with a second cat, also entirely black except for a single splotch of white on its breast, and her husband's aggression becomes greater, making him want to perform acts of even greater cruelty. Imagining that the white splotch on the cat's breast is in the shape of a gallows, the narrator seeks to kill this second cat. He axes his wife to death when she tries to protect the cat, and then inters her in a false chimney in the cellar with "a glee at heart [that] was too strong to be restrained." However, the cat escapes him. When the police arrive unexpectedly four days later, the overly confident narrator invites them to search the cellar, but his crime is revealed when the police hear inhuman shrieks and howls coming from behind the wall. After the police tear down the wall, the narrator sees the hated cat, sitting on the gore-clotted corpse's head and seeming to grin at the murderer.

WRITER'S NOTES

Critics have suggested that Poe found inspiration for the story in a passage that appears in Sir Walter SCOTT's *Letters on Demonology* (1830), in which a lawyer explains to his doctor that he has been plagued by a cat which may or may not be real: "I found myself . . . embarrassed by the presence of a large cat, which came and disappeared I could not exactly tell how. . . . I was compelled to regard it . . . [as having] no existence save in my deranged visual organs, or depraved imagination." The story influenced several scenes in Richard Wright's *Native Son* (1940), in which the main character Bigger has a cat that seems to stare at him in an accusatory manner at one point. Later, after Bigger has committed a particularly violent murder, the cat howls and races past him, then turns and leaps onto his shoulders, digging its claws deeply into his shoulders as newspaper reporters search the premises.

Blackwood, William (1776–1834) The founder and editor of *BLACKWOOD'S MAGAZINE,* which abounded in sto-

ries of garish psychological states and tales of solitary victims in lethal predicaments. Poe included him as a character in several short stories. In "HOW TO WRITE A BLACKWOOD ARTICLE," the character named Blackwood interviews Signora Psyche ZENOBIA, who wishes to be published, and tells her the way to do so is to use real experiences and embellish them with foreign phrases.

Blackwood's Magazine   Scottish literary periodical founded by William BLACKWOOD. The material published in the magazine was often gothic and sensational, and it influenced Poe, who sometimes imitated the writing style.

Blaettermann, George (fl. 1826)   Professor of modern languages at the University of Virginia during Poe's residency. Poe's proficiency in Italian earned Blaettermann's praise for his translation from Tasso. Poe and other young men at the university were also welcomed in the home of the young German-born professor and his English wife.

Bless-My-Soul, Duchess of   Character in the short story "LIONIZING." She is sitting for her portrait when Robert JONES enters the artist's studio. Enthralled by Jones's newly gained celebrity following the publication of his monograph on "nosology," the duchess later invites him to accompany her to an exclusive gathering at Almack's, where being admitted is as great a distinction as being presented at court.

Bliss, Elam (fl. 1830)   A New York publisher, Bliss seems to have visited Poe at West Point at the end of 1830 and made arrangements to bring out a volume of his poetry entitled POEMS. The second edition, published in 1831, is dedicated to the West Point cadets who supplied money for its printing. Mr. Bliss had editorial offices at 111 Broadway, where Poe, who left West Point early in 1831, edited the proof pages of his book. Biographers suggest that Bliss was a kind man who probably took pity on the nearly penniless Poe and invited him to dine at the publisher's home at 28 Dey Street.

Block, Captain E. T. V.   Character in the novel THE NARRATIVE OF ARTHUR GORDON PYM. He is the captain of the *Penguin*, the whaling ship that runs down the sailboat *Ariel*.

The Blood Demon   A 1967 German-produced film that is loosely based on Poe's "THE PIT AND THE PENDULUM." The bloody film tells the tale of an aristocrat who is resurrected from the dead and who seeks revenge on the two men whom he blames for his demise. He lures them to his castle, where he subjects them to a range of mental and physical torture, distributed as *The Torture Chamber of ___* on video as *Castle of the Walking Dead*.

Bluddennuff, Elector of   Character in the "LIONIZING." His name translates from the German "blood enough," but in slang also means "sufficient stupid." He insults the great authority on "nosology," Robert JONES by shouting at his appearance *"Tousand teufels"* (thousand devils). This initiates a duel between the two, during which Bluddennuff's nose is shot off, and this turn of events makes him the most revered of the inhabitants of Fum-Fudge, replacing Jones.

Blunderbuzzard   Character mentioned in the short story "THE DEVIL IN THE BELFRY." He is cited as the author of a make-believe scholarly work entitled *De Derivationibus* that is identified by the narrator as a source for the name of the fictional Dutch borough of Vondervotteimittiss, the setting of the story.

Boanerges, the Son of Thunder   In the first publication of "A TALE OF JERUSALEM," the story ended with the Pharisee, who has been tricked by the heathens, drawing his cloak tightly about himself and leaving the city as he utters these words: "Let me no longer be called Simeon, which signifieth 'he who listens'—but rather Boanerges, 'the Son of Thunder.'"

Bob, the devil   Printer's devil (i.e., an apprentice) and errand boy for the newspaper the *Tea-Pot* in the short story "X-ING A PARAGRAB." Twelve years old and only four feet tall, "he was equal to any amount of fight, in a small way." He is pressed to typeset a paragraph of copy that must be run off for the next morning's edition, but he finds that all of the *O* letters, both capital and lower case, have disappeared. Unable to find the needed vowel, Bob substitutes the letter *X* wherever an *O* is needed, which places the town in an uproar.

Bob, Thingum   Character in the short story "THE LITERARY LIFE OF THINGUM BOB, ESQ." He is a mysterious author who explains how he attained literary success. Eager to avoid his father's profession of merchant-barber, he resolved to be a great man "and to commence by becoming a great poet." With his father's approval, Thingum then buys numerous ancient editions of poems, recopies them in his own hand, and signs them with his pseudonym, Oppodeldoc. He then sends his plagiarized poetry to the editors of four principal magazines, "with a request for speedy insertion and prompt pay," but they are not fooled and they criticize him broadly in print. Now convinced that "honesty is the best policy," Thingum sends out his original efforts under his own name and the proud satisfaction of seeing my poem printed ength." As his fame increases, he becomes the darng of the literary set, eventually managing to inherit one famous literary magazine, then to buy the three remaining rivals and combine them into one. With great pride, Thingum becomes the quotable Mr. Bob: "You cannot take up a common newspaper in which you shall not see some allusion to the immortal THINGUM BOB. It is Mr. Thingum Bob said so, and Mr. Thingum Bob wrote this, and Mr. Thingum Bob did that."

Bob, Thomas, Esq. Character in the short story "THE LITERARY LIFE OF THINGUM BOB, ESQ." He is the father of the narrator of the story, Thingum Bob, and a merchant-barber who stands "at the summit of his profession" in the city of Smug. When his son approaches him about becoming an editor and a poet, Thomas encourages him and offers to provide Thingum with "a garret; pen, ink, and paper; a rhyming dictionary . . . you would scarcely demand any more." He collaborates with his son on a two-line poem that catapults Thingum to literary fame, but the ungrateful son soon views his father as an "old bore" who must be removed if he is to achieve his full potential.

Bobby Character in the short story "THREE SUNDAYS IN A WEEK." He is the narrator and the nephew of the curmudgeonly granduncle RUMGUDGEON, whom he thrashes and argues with in his imagination but to whom he shows the utmost respect in person, because he is dependent upon the uncle for his living. Eager to marry his beloved KATE, he asks his uncle to name a time when it would be most convenient for the wedding to occur, and Rumgudgeon responds "when three Sundays come together in a week." Bobby is used to being abused by his granduncle, for he tells readers that "it was a dog's existence that he led me, after all. From my first year until my fifth, he obliged me with very regular floggings. From five to fifteen, he threatened me, hourly, with the House of Correction. From fifteen to twenty, not a day passed in which he did not promise to cut me off with a shilling." In the end, because of Kate's acuity, Bobby is finally granted permission to marry her.

Bogart, Elizabeth (1806– ?) Minor poet reviewed briefly by Poe in "THE LITERATI OF NEW YORK CITY." Poe relates that she is a member of "one of the oldest families in the state" and provides a detailed physical description, as well as information regarding her ability to converse. He notes further that she "has a keen appreciation of genius and of natural scenery; is cheerful and fond of society." As to her poetry, "Miss Bogart has not yet collected her writings in volume form. Her fugitive pieces have usually been signed 'Estelle.' They are noticeable for nerve, dignity, and finish."

Bonaparte, Marie (1882–1962) Poe biographer, student of Freud, and literary psychoanalyst. She was a great-niece of Napoleon I and wife of Prince George of Greece. The author of *The Life and Works of Edgar Allan Poe: A Psychoanalytic Interpretation* (1933), with a foreword by Sigmund Freud, she initiated a new approach to Poe criticism that used Freudian psychobiography to interpret his works. In particular, she examined the effects on his fiction and poetry of his obsession with dying women and with mother surrogates. Her readings of the works produce overwhelming evidence of sexual maladjustment: she finds symbols of impotence, sexual inadequacy, incestuous desire, and necrophiliac longing throughout. In "THE BLACK CAT," Bonaparte interprets the hanged cat as a specific symbol of the penis of the impotent Poe. The closeness of Roderick and Madeline USHER in "THE FALL OF THE HOUSE OF USHER" signals the incestuous feelings that Bonaparte believed Poe had for his child bride Virginia CLEMM. She also identified the husband/narrator of "LIGEIA" as Poe himself, with LIGEIA as his dead mother, Elizabeth Arnold POE, and the second wife Poe's bride Virginia. Bonaparte interprets falls into an abyss to be Poe's terror of encountering the female genitals. She determines, based on her case studies of the poetry and fiction, that Poe was "psychotically disturbed" and "maternally ambivalent," and that he also felt deep guilt because of his sexual inadequacy. Bonaparte's work initiated a new approach to Poe criticism that used Freudian psychobiography to interpret his works.

"Bon-Bon" Short story. The tale is considered by critics to be one of his successes in the comic vein, and it is typical of Poe's tales of comic encounters with demons.

PUBLISHING AND DRAMATIZATION HISTORY

Poe first published the story under the title "The Bargain Lost" in the Philadelphia *Saturday Courier* for December 1, 1832, then revised it for later publication under the title "Bon-Bon—A Tale" in the SOUTHERN LITERARY MESSENGER for August 1835. Each version of the story has its own epigraph. Preceding the first published version of the story is this quote taken from William SHAKESPEARE's play *As You Like It:* "The heathen philosopher, when he had a mind to eat a grape, would open his lips when he put it into his mouth, meaning thereby that grapes were made to eat and lips to open." Poe attached the following more lengthy epigram from *Les Premiers Traits de l'érudition universelle (The Most Important Characteristics of Universal Wisdom)*, published in 1767 by Baron Bielfeld, to his final version of the story:

Quand un bon vin meuble mon estomac,
Je suis plus savant que Balzac—
Plus sage qu Pibrac;
Mon bras seul faisant L'attaque
De la nation Cosaque,
La mettroit au sac:
De Charon je passerois le lac
En dormant dans son bac;
J'irois au fier Eac,
Sans que mon coeur fit tic ni tac,
Presenter du tabac.

[When a good wine fills my stomach
I am more learned than Balzac—
Wiser than Pibrac;
My lone arm attacking
The Cossack nation,
Plunders it;
I cross Charon's lake
Asleep in his ferry;
I would go to proud Aeacus,
Without my heart beating hard
To offer him some snuff.]

The tale has not been dramatized for the screen, but it was rewritten for the stage and enjoyed a brief off-Broadway run in 1920.

CHARACTERS

Pierre BON-BON; the devil.

PLOT SYNOPSIS

The tale centers on Pierre Bon-Bon, a superb chef and masterful philosopher, who receives a visit from the devil one snowy winter evening. Known both for his superb omelettes and for being "a man of genius," Bon-Bon also has "an inclination for the bottle." As he drinks his wine and ponders a volume that he is soon going to submit for publication, Bon-Bon is startled by Satan's sudden appearance in his apartments. The guest is a vampire-like figure who wears "garments [that] had evidently been intended for a much shorter person than their present owner. His ankles and wrists were left naked for several inches. . . . His head was bare, and entirely bald, with the exception of the hinder part, from which depended a *queue* of considerable length." Bon-Bon plays the perfect host to the devil, placing on the table several more bottles of Chambertin, drawing chairs comfortably near the fire, and waiting until his guest speaks first. Bon-Bon is not fearful, but instead looks forward to a lively philosophical exchange with the devil, and "to elicit some important ethical ideas, which might, in obtaining a place in his contemplated publication, enlighten the human race, and at the same time immortalize himself—ideas which . . . his visitor's great age, and well-

known proficiency in the science of morals, might very well have enabled him to afford." As Bon-Bon listens, his guest lists the names of numerous intellectual giants of the past whom he claims have been roasted, fricasseed, parboiled, sauteed, and souffleed down in hell. When Bon-Bon proposes to discuss the soul as being insubstantial and a shadow, the devil counters by describing the souls of the great intellectuals that he has tasted: "I found that Horace tasted very much like Aristotle,—you know that I am fond of variety. Terentius I could not have told from Menander. Naso, to my astonishment, was Nicander in disguise. Virgilius had a strong twang of Theocritus." Running through an extensive list of thinkers, the devil points out their foibles and the false ideals that people hold of them. He also lists for Bon-Bon numerous individuals, such as Cain, Nero, and Caligula, "who never knew what it was to have a soul during the latter part of their lives." As Bon-Bon becomes increasingly drunk, he offers the devil his soul "'—a bargain.'" The devil calmly refuses the offer, claiming that he cannot take advantage of someone in this "'present disgusting and ungentlemanly situation.'" As the devil leaves, Bon-Bon throws an empty bottle that severs the chain on the lamp above him, hitting him on the head and knocking him out.

WRITER'S NOTES

Under the earlier name of "The Bargain Lost," the story was originally a shorter piece about a Venetian metaphysician named Pedro Garcia who has a strange encounter with a messenger of the devil. When he revised the story and renamed it "Bon-Bon," Poe moved the setting from Venice, Italy, to France, and made the protagonist a chef-philosopher to increase the possibilities for comic commentary.

Bon-Bon, Pierre Character in the short story "BON-BON." Renowned in his town as a master chef and a brilliant metaphysician, there is much in "the *restaurateur* calculated to impress the imagination of the quadruped," and his cat and dog show appropriate respect for him. Barely three feet tall, he has a "diminutively small" head and a rotund stomach that carries with it "a sense of magnificence nearly bordering upon the sublime." In dress, Bon-Bon cuts quite a figure, from his conical-shaped white flannel cap through his yellow-satin breeches, sky-blue cloak, and his bright purple slippers with their "exquisite pointing of the toes." Proud of his erudition, Bon-Bon welcomes a visit from the devil, with whom he hopes to discuss the ancient philosophers and the knowledge of the ages. Instead, he drinks too much wine and offers his soul to the devil as "a bargain."

Bonfanti's   A provider of the unusual in the short story "THE MAN THAT WAS USED UP" where Brevet Brigadier General John A. B. C. SMITH claims to have purchased a palate, for "there isn't Bonfanti's equal, however, in America, for really good articles of this description."

Bonner, Jim   Character in the novel *THE NARRATIVE OF ARTHUR GORDON PYM*. A sailor aboard the *Grampus,* he is thrown off the deck during an argument.

Bonneville, Captain Benjamin Louis Eulalie de (1796–1878)   American army officer who explored the Rocky Mountain region extensively and inspired Washington IRVING's *Adventures of Captain Bonneville, U.S.A.* Poe mentions Bonneville's expeditions in "THE JOURNAL OF JULIUS RODMAN."

"The Book of Gems. The Poets and Artists of Great Britain. Edited by S. C. Hall. London and New York: Saunders and Otley"   Poe's review of an anthology edited by S. C. Hall. The review appeared in the *SOUTHERN LITERARY MESSENGER* for August 1836. Poe lists the English poets included in the anthology and notes that the skill and artistry attributed to them is misplaced: "Verses which affect us to-day with a vivid delight, and which in some instances, may be traced to this one source of grotesqueness and to none other, must have worn in the days of their construction an air of a very commonplace nature." Instead, he protests that "better extracts might be made" and provides harsh criticism: "There are long passages now before us, of the most despicable trash, with no merit whatsoever, beyond that of their antiquity." He also takes issue with the critiques by the editor, claiming that they "do not please us in a great degree" and observing that "he seems to have fallen into the common cant in such cases." Of the choices in the anthology, Poe finds Andrew Marvell's "Maiden Lamenting for Her Fawn" an example of the type of poetry that he would "prefer not only as a specimen of the elder poets, but, in itself, as a beautiful poem, abounding in the sweetest pathos, in soft and gentle images, in the most exquisitely delicate imagination, and in *truth*—to any thing of its species."

Bornschein, Franz (fl. 1936)   American composer and conductor born in Baltimore who wrote in 1935 a three-part chorus for women's voices, with orchestra or piano accompaniment, to Poe's "THE CONQUEROR WORM."

Boston, Massachusetts   Poe had a long and not always happy association with Boston, where he was born on January 19, 1809, and lived for the first six months of his life while his parents were appearing there in a production at the Federal Street Theatre. This early association did not make Poe a Bostonian, for the Virginia influence prevailed, but he did hold strong feelings—largely negative—about the city of his birth. Poe traveled to the city in April 1827, because it was a literary center and because he planned to look up friends of his parents in an effort to reconnect with his early years, now that he was estranged from his foster father John ALLAN. In Boston, Poe arranged to have *TAMERLANE AND OTHER POEMS* printed without his name, only "By a Bostonian," on the title page. For the most part, Poe viewed the Boston literary scene with contempt. In "BOSTON AND THE BOSTONIANS" he satirizes Boston inhabitants as Frogpondians, who "have no soul" and who "have always evinced toward us individually, the basest ingratitude."

"Boston and the Bostonians. Editorial Miscellany"   Two essays by Poe that appeared in the November 1, 1845, and November 22, 1845, issues of the *BROADWAY JOURNAL* in which he responded to the attacks on his work by specific critics. In the first essay, he defended himself against the criticism of Cornelia Walter, whom he viewed as seeking vengeance because he had written unflattering critiques of works by Henry Wadsworth LONGFELLOW and called Walters "a pretty little witch" in one of his reviews. Poe also defended his choice of "AL AARAAF" for a reading at the Boston Lyceum and criticized the Boston audience "who evinced characteristic discrimination in under-standing, and especially applauding, all those knotty passages which we ourselves have not yet been able to understand." In the November 1 piece, Poe cites a review of his Boston Lyceum reading of "The Messenger Star" (the name that the press assigned to "Al Aaraaf" when Poe did not identify the poem by name) from the *Sunday Times and Messenger* of October 26, 1845, and accuses the Boston audience of lacking soul: "They have always evinced towards us individually the basest ingratitude for the services we rendered them in enlightening them about the originality of Mr. Longfellow." Poe opens the second piece by quoting extensively from a review of his poetry from the *Charleston Patriot,* after which he responds methodically and vituperatively to disparaging remarks about his Lyceum lectures by the Bostonians, whom he calls Frogpondians: "We knew that write what we would they would swear it to be worthless. . . . The Frogpondians may as well spare us their abuse. We despise them and defy them (the transcendental vagabonds!) and they may all go to the devil together." In response to the insinuation that he must have been "'intoxicated' to have become possessed of sufficient audacity to 'deliver' such a poem to the Frogpondians," Poe sinks to adolescent rhetoric. While he neither confirms nor denies that he may have been intoxicated—"We shall get drunk when we please"—he attacks his critic Cornelia Walter, stating that "we advise her to get drunk, too, as soon as possible—for when sober she is a disgrace to her sex—on account of being so awfully stupid."

Bouffon, Le Grand   A character spoken of in "THE SYSTEM OF DOCTOR TARR AND PROFESSOR FETHER" and provided as one example of the type of inmates with which the superintendent of an asylum dealt. Deemed an "extraordinary personage in his way," he becomes deranged after a failed love affair and imagines that he has two heads. The first is the head of Cicero, but the second is far more complicated. He imagines that his second head is a composite of "Demosthenes' from the top of the forehead to the mouth, and Lord Brougham from the mouth to the chin." The narrator states that Le Grand Bouffon is a man of great eloquence, with "an absolute passion for oratory" who could not refrain from displaying ability.

Boullard, Monsieur   Character in the short story "THE SYSTEM OF DOCTOR TARR AND PROFESSOR FETHER." One of the inmates in an asylum for the mentally ill, he is called a "tee-totum" because "he was seized with the droll, but not altogether irrational crotchet, that he had been converted into a tee-totum." He spends hours at a time turning around and around upon one heel, an action that earns him the title of "a madman, and a very silly madman at best; for who, allow me to ask you, ever heard of a human tee-totum?"

Braine, Robert (1896–1940)   American composer who in 1924 wrote a full score for baritone and orchestra for Poe's poem "THE RAVEN" and in 1930 wrote the symphonic poem *The House of Usher,* based on Poe's tale "THE FALL OF THE HOUSE OF USHER."

Bransby, Reverend Dr.   Character in the short story "WILLIAM WILSON." He is young William Wilson's schoolmaster, as well as the principal of the gloomy school. Possessed of a "sour visage" and wearing "snuffy habiliments," Bransby regularly administers corporal punishment with a cane to enforce "the Draconian laws of the academy." He is also the pastor of the church, who ascended the pulpit "with step solemn and slow . . . with countenance so demurely benign, with robes so glossy and so clerically flowing" that the young William Wilson found his behavior to be a "giant paradox, too monstrous for solution!"

Bransby, Reverend John (1784–1857)   Principal of the Manor House School at Stoke Newington, England, where Poe was a student from 1818 to 1820. The recipient of an M.A. degree from St. John's College, Cambridge, Bransby was a Tory clergyman with a large

family and cheerful habits. His passion for hunting was well known to the boys in his school, and when he cleaned his gun they knew that he would be gone for the day. Popular with his students, Bransby was something of a classical scholar as well, and he was known for his literary and scientific writing as well as for his political pamphlets. He regarded the young Edgar Allan as "a quick and clever boy" but decried that his parents had spoiled him by giving him too much pocket money. His view of Poe was that he was "intelligent, wayward, and wilful." Poe included a character of the same name but of a decidedly different disposition in the tale "WILLIAM WILSON."

Brennan, Mr. and Mrs. Patrick   A kind married couple who welcomed Poe, Maria CLEMM and Virginia CLEMM into their home as boarders during the summer of 1844. Their old farmhouse, known as "the house where 'THE RAVEN' was written," was located on a rocky knoll that was a few hundred feet from the northeast corner of the present 84th Street and Broadway in New York City. The couple had a 15-year-old daughter named Martha, as well as five younger children, and their farm consisted of 216 acres on which they raised produce and flowers that were sold at the city markets. Their home provided Poe, Virginia, and Mrs. Clemm with a beautiful view, excellent food, and pleasant surroundings. After the summer ended, the Poe family moved back to town but kept close contact with the Brennans. Mrs. Brennan seemed to find Mrs. Clemm an amiable companion, and her later recollections of Poe are all pleasant. Only once did she feel the need to speak sharply to him, when he absentmindedly scratched his name into the well-cared-for mantelpiece in his room. In early 1846, when Virginia's illness had deepened and her death appeared near, Poe made arrangements for Virginia and her mother to return to the farm to provide Virginia with "the bracing help of country breezes and the soothing quiet of country air" for a few weeks.

Brennan, Thomas   Son of a kindly farm couple in whose home Poe lived with his family during the summer of 1844. Years after Poe's death, Thomas recalled watching Poe draw designs in the dust with his cane, and he spoke of how Poe would wander off to nearby Mount Tom and sit on the banks of the Hudson River, gazing and daydreaming.

Brewster, Sir David   British scientist who dabbled in natural magic, i.e., harnessing the powers of the earth, and deduced that the Pole of the Equator is not the Pole of maximum cold, among other discoveries. Poe refers to Brewster in the unpublished notes to

"Eureka," "MAELZEL'S CHESS-PLAYER," and "THE UNPARALLELED ADVENTURE OF ONE HANS PFAALL."

"Bridal Ballad" Poem by Poe that was first published under the title "Ballad" in the January 1837 issue of the SOUTHERN LITERARY MESSENGER. Poe revised the poem and retitled it "Bridal Ballad," then submitted it for publication in the July 31, 1831, issue of the *Saturday Evening Post*. Under this title, it was also one of the selections Poe included in THE RAVEN AND OTHER POEMS in 1845. Told from the point of view of the bride just after her marriage, the poem recounts her regrets for a lover "who fell / In the battle down the dell, / And who is happy now." As she lies in the arms of her new husband, she feels obliged to remain faithfully married to him even though she feels that doing so will probably disrupt the eternal peace of her dead lover to whom she has broken her vow to love him eternally: "For I dream I know not how, / And my soul is sorely shaken / Lest an evil step be taken,— / Lest the dead who is forsaken / May not be happy now."

Briggs, Charles F. (1804–1877) Author and, with Poe, coeditor of the BROADWAY JOURNAL. Briggs, who wrote under the pseudonym of Harry Franco, admired Poe's work strongly but criticized Poe's tendency toward drink. When he left the *Broadway Journal* in July 1845, Briggs told friends that he felt Poe had betrayed him professionally, and he charged that Poe was unable to conceive of anyone doing anything except for personal advantage. Briggs caricatured Poe in his novel *The Trippings of Tom Pepper* (1847), and he published an unsigned article that appeared in the May 26, 1846, issue of the EVENING MIRROR in which he broadly criticized Poe, pointing out "One of the strange parts of his strange nature was to entertain a spirit of revenge towards all who did him service." Poe also had little good to say about Briggs, whom he profiled in "THE LITERATI OF NEW YORK CITY." He characterizes Briggs's simplicity of writing as "insipidity," and notes that "his picturesque low-life is made to degenerate into sheer vulgarity." Moreover, Poe claims that Briggs "has some humor, but nothing of an original character." Still, Poe concedes, "He has much warmth of feeling, and is not a person to be disliked, although very apt to irritate and annoy."

Briscoe, Captain John American whaling captain and navigator mentioned in chapter 16 of THE NARRATIVE OF ARTHUR GORDON PYM. In 1831, he set sail from London for the South Seas, where he discovered an island and "took possession of it in the name of William IV, calling it Adelaide's Island, in honour of the English queen."

Broad-Street Theatre The theater in Richmond, Virginia, where Elizabeth Arnold POE performed as part of a company called the Virginia Comedians in the months before she became ill. On the day after Christmas, 1811, two weeks and two days after Elizabeth was buried, the theater burned to the ground. The governor of Virginia and 72 other socially prominent Virginians died in the fire. The Monumental Church was built as a memorial on the theater site.

Broadway Journal Periodical in whose publication Poe acted as a partner with Charles BRIGGS and John BISCO. It republished many revised versions of Poe's tales, including "LIGEIA," "WILLIAM WILSON," and "THE TELL-TALE HEART." Poe began his association with the periodical early in 1845 as a writer and editor, earning $1 a column for his contributions. After a financially struggling Briggs left the journal, Poe bought out Bisco and became sole owner and editor on October 24, 1845. He paid Bisco $50, in the form of a personal note endorsed by Horace GREELEY. Poe used the columns of the journal to promote his own writing, and the publication provided both the poet and his work with a larger and more important audience than he might have other attained. Poe also used his columns to continue attacks upon other writers and to respond to negative reviews of his works. Poe's management of the *Broadway Journal* was fraught with problems. He was unable to raise the $140 needed to preserve the publication, and the magazine was defunct by December 1845. In the final issue, which appeared on January 3, 1846, Poe published the following farewell:

VALEDICTORY

Unexpected engagements demanding my whole attention, and the objects being unfulfilled so far as regards myself personally, for which the *Broadway Journal* was established, I now, as its editor, bid farewell—as cordially to foes as to friends.

Edgar A. Poe

Broglio, Duc di Character in Poe's play POLITIAN. The patriarch of an old and distinguished family in 16th-century Rome, he is the uncle of Alessandra, who is betrothed to his son, CASTIGLIONE. He is eager to gain favor with Earl of Leicester, who is visiting from England; he is unaware that the earl had met his ward LALAGE earlier and has fallen in love with her. Although he assumes that he knows and controls everything that occurs in his palazzo, he is also ignorant of his son's recent erratic behavior and unrestrained drinking.

The Broad Street Theatre in Richmond, Virginia, where Elizabeth Arnold Poe last performed, burned down shortly after her death in December 1811. (Edgar Allan Poe Library)

"The Broken Vow and Other Poems. By Amanda M. Edmond. Boston: Gould, Kendall & Lincoln" A review of a volume of verse appearing in the October 11, 1845, issue of the BROADWAY JOURNAL. Poe lambasted the poet, labeling the poems "by no means impressive" and characterizing them as containing subjects that generally "find favor in boarding schools." In assessing the collection, Poe stated that some of the poems were "mere doggerel" and said that they "have no right to the title of poem, and should not be included in the volume." Although he judges Edmond's versification and imagery to be "at least respectable," Poe notes that "in the loftier and distinctive attributes, we are pained

to say that she is totally wanting. We look in vain throughout her volume for one spark of poetic fire."

"Brook Farm" A review that appeared in the December 13, 1845, issue of the BROADWAY JOURNAL in which Poe claims to "sincerely respect" the Brook Farm weekly magazine *Harbinger* while calling it "the most reputable organ of the Crazyites." (Brook Farm was a utopian community founded by a group of New England Transcendentalist writers and thinkers.) He indicates that the publication is "conducted by an assemblage of well-read persons who mean no harm— and who, perhaps, can do less" and asks what he has done that "should stop the ordinary operations at Brook-Farm for the purpose of abusing us." Poe includes in his review of the magazine a negative and condescending review of THE RAVEN AND OTHER POEMS that was written by John S. Dwight and published in the December 6, 1845, issue of the *Harbinger*. Following the reprint, Poe methodically selects phrases and sentences from the review to refute and to ridicule, responding, as he says, "like a Dutch uncle." In concluding his attack, Poe observes that "it shocks us to hear a set of respectable Crazyites talking in so disingenuous a manner." He expresses the hope that "in the future, 'The Snook Farm Phalanx' will never have any opinion of us at all."

Brooks, James Gordon (1801–1841) Minor American poet and editor of *Minerva; or Literary Entertaining and Scientific Journal.* Poe said of him in "AUTOGRAPHY" that he enjoyed "a private rather than public literary reputation; but his talents are unquestionably great." Poe also noted that Brooks possessed "nervous common sense, without tinsel or artificiality, and a straightforward directness of composition" and that this is "precisely true of his literary style."

Brown, Gould (1791–1857) American writer and author of *Institutes of English Grammar* (1823), cited by Poe in "THE RATIONALE OF VERSE" for his definition of versification as "the art of arranging words into lines of correspondent length, so as to produce harmony by the regular alternation of syllables differing in quantity."

Brown, Thomas Dunn Poe's name for his enemy Dr. Thomas Dunn ENGLISH in "THE LITERATI OF NEW YORK CITY."

Browne, Doctor William Hand (1828–1912) American physician, critic, and early defender of Poe's personal and artistic reputation. He assisted John H. INGRAM in his work on Poe's life and reviewed Ingram's corrective biography of Poe in the June 1875 issue of the *Southern Monthly-New Eclectic Magazine.* He also became acquainted with the widow of Poe's friend Dr. Joseph Evans SNODGRASS, to whom Poe had directed that a note be sent when he became ill during his final days of life. Browne made an exact copy of the note "from the original in the possession of Mrs. Snodgrass, widow of Poe's friend" and supplied it to biographers.

Browne, Sir Thomas (1605–1682) English author whose "Hydriotaphia [Urn Burial]" appealed to Poe's morbid nature. In his review "THE QUACKS OF HELICON: A SATIRE," Poe attempts to explain the nature and guidelines of criticism. He quotes Browne as saying, "What

song the Syrens sang . . . or what name Achilles assumed when he hid himself among women, though puzzling questions, are not beyond all conjecture." Poe adds, "but it would puzzle Sir Thomas, backed by Achilles and all the Syrens in Heathendom, to say, in nine cases out of ten, what is the object of a thorough-going Quarterly Reviewer?"

Browning, Robert (1812–1889) English poet. The husband of Elizabeth BARRETT Browning, he became aware of Poe's work through his wife. Critics have found similarities in the theme of loss and the atmosphere of melancholy that appear in Poe's tales and such works of Robert Browning as the "Madhouse Cell" poems, "Porphyria's Lover," and "Johannes Agricola in Meditation" in *Dramatic Lyrics.* Critics have also noted that Browning's word *losel,* used in referring to the lost selves of his dramatic monologues, fits many of the first-person narrators in Poe's tales, who themselves are lost selves or displaced and disoriented humans.

Brownson, Orestes Augustus (1803–1876) American clergyman and editor of the *Boston Quarterly Review* who was also associated with transcendentalism and liberal causes. He is mentioned in Poe's "MESMERIC REVELATION," where the narrator studies closely Brownson's moralistic novel *Charles Elwood; or, The Infidel Converted* (1840) and states that it is "logical, but the portions which were not merely logical were unhappily the initial arguments of the disbelieving hero of the book." In examining the novel in "AUTOGRAPHY," Poe declares that the book shows "the writer has not altogether succeeded in convincing himself of those important truths which he is so anxious to impress upon his readers." Still, Poe concedes that Brownson is "in every respect, an extraordinary man, and with the more extensive resources which would have been afforded him by early education, could not have failed to bring about important results."

Bruenner, Leopold (1869–?) German-American composer, conductor, and organist whose op. 1, no. 5, is a song setting of Poe's poem "ELDORADO."

Bryan, Daniel (1790–1866) A poet and the postmaster at Alexandria with whom Poe exchanged letters in the summer of 1842. Poe stated that Bryan had "written some very excellent poetry and is appreciated by all admirers of 'the good old Goldsmith school.'" In an entry in "AUTOGRAPHY," Poe claimed that Bryan's habit of underscoring his sentences is "exactly parallel with the augmentative nature of some of his best poems."

Bryant, William Cullen (1794–1878) American poet and editor of the *New York Evening Post* whom Poe met once in 1845 and whose work he reviewed in an essay published in the April 1846 issue of GODEY'S MAGAZINE AND LADY'S BOOK. Poe used the review to spend considerable space discussing the issue of editorial forthrightness, stating at one point, "We put on paper with a grave air what we could not for our lives assert personally to a friend without either blushing or laughing outright. That the opinion of the press is not an honest opinion, that necessarily it is impossible that it should be an honest opinion, is never denied by the member of the press themselves." The reviewer admits that he previously has joined others in underestimating Bryant's creative abilities. Although "it will never do to claim for Bryant a genius of the loftiest order," Poe says the time has come to reverse what he sees as "a growing disposition to deny him *genius* in *any* respect." In his analyses of Bryant's best-known poems, Poe asserts that while they do not exhibit signs of genius, their "completeness and pointed termination" make them successful, for Bryant is "the most generally correct of our poets." Poe also quotes a portion of Bryant's poem "June" in "THE POETIC PRINCIPLE," which he praises highly: "The rhythmical flow, here, is even voluptuous—nothing could be more melodious. The intense melancholy which seems to well up, perforce, to the surface of all the poet's cheerful sayings about his grave, we find thrilling us to the soul—while there is the truest poetic elevation in the thrill. . . . The impression left is one of a pleasurable sadness." Yet, despite such praise, Poe asserts in "AUTOGRAPHY" that Bryant's handwriting is that of "the most commonplace clerk's hands which we have ever encountered, and has no character about it beyond that of the daybook and ledger."

Bubastis   The name of the moon in Egypt, according to the pseudo-learned president of Fum Fudge University in Poe's short story "LIONIZING."

"Bubbles from the Brunnens of Nassau. By An Old Man. New York: Harper and Brothers"   Poe's review of travel sketches and stories written by "an old man," whom Poe identified as "the present Governor of Canada." The review appeared in the April 1836 issue of the SOUTHERN LITERARY MESSENGER. Poe explains that the "bubbles" of the title are "hasty sketches of whatever chanced for the moment to please either the eyes or the mind" of the writer, who had been sent to drink the mineral waters of Nassau for his health. The "old man" author pronounces his book to be "empty, light, vain, hollow and superficial: 'but then,' says he, 'it is the nature of 'bubbles' to be so.'" In his evaluation, Poe suggests that the sketches should be called "whimsical" rather than "facetious," as others have commonly labeled them. He observes that the manner of the

sketches are "an agreeable mixture of *Charles Lamb's* and *Washington Irving's*" containing the "same covert conceit, the same hidden humor, the same piquant allusion."

Buchanan, Reverend John   The clergyman who in 1812 baptized Edgar Allan and Rose MacKenzie POE at the residence of Mr. John Richard in Richmond, Virginia.

Buck, Dudley (1839–1909)   American composer, conductor, and organist who composed "Sleigh Bells," his op. 19, no. 2, for the piano, to accompany Poe's poem "THE BELLS."

Buckingham, Mr. Silk   Character in Poe's short story "SOME WORDS WITH A MUMMY." He hides under the table when the mummy's eyelids move.

Bugaboo and Kickapoo Indians   Names of tribes coined by Poe to identify the opponents of Brevet Brigadier General John A. B. C. SMITH in "THE MAN THAT WAS USED UP" in a military campaign, a "tremendous swamp-fight away down South."

Buhrman, Albert J. (1915–)   American musician who wrote a score for the piano to accompany Poe's poem "ELDORADO."

Bullet-head, Mr. Touch-and-Go   Character in "X-ING A PARAGRAB." He serves as the temperamental editor of the Alexander-the-Great-o-nopolis publication, *Tea-Pot.*

Bulwer-Lytton, Edward George Earle (first Baron Lytton) (1803–1873)   English novelist, dramatist, and politician, born Edward Lytton. Poe refers to him as both "Bulwer" and "Lytton" in numerous mentions of the author, who added his mother's family name in 1843. In several reviews, Poe denigrates Lytton's intellect but praises the writing produced by that intellect. In a November 1841 review of Lytton's critical writings that appeared in GRAHAM'S MAGAZINE, Poe wrote that Lytton "is never lucid and seldom profound. His intellect seems to be rather well balanced than lofty; rather comprehensive than penetrative." In the same review, Poe states, "Apart from his intellect, however,—or rather as a portion of that intellect,—we recognize in his every written word the keenest appreciation of the right, the beautiful, and the true." In a review of Lytton's ZANONI, A NOVEL," Poe is similarly ambivalent: he praises the idea of the novel as "simply grand," having "unity that overpowers us," yet he also finds that the "glaring defects in his former novels, are perceptible." Assessing Lytton's artistic strengths and weaknesses in "MARGINALIA," Poe criticizes his tendency to sentimentalize even death, as in *Ernest Maltravers,* which speaks of "that sweet smile and serene—that smile never seen but upon the face of the dying and the dead." Such quotations lead Poe to assert that "Bulwer is not the man to look a stern fact in the face. He would rather sentimentalize upon a vulgar although picturesque error." In a very lengthy review of "NIGHT AND MORN-ING," Poe accuses Lytton of "excessive elaborations, all tending to one point" and states, "His mere English is grossly defective—turgid, involved, and ungrammatical." Although Poe both attacked and praised Lytton in reviews of his many works, he apparently believed his assessment of the man was exceedingly accurate at each point because the author's extensive writings provide adequate room for such inconsistent quality. In the entry for Sarah Margaret FULLER in "THE LITERATI OF NEW YORK CITY," Poe speaks of the author's work as an extension of the author's self and uses Lytton as an example: "Of such a person we get, from his books, not merely a just, but the most just representation. Bulwer, the individual, personal man, in a green velvet waistcoat and amber gloves, is not by any means the veritable Sir Edward Lytton, who is discoverable only in 'Ernest Maltravers,' where his soul is deliberately and nakedly set forth."

Burke, William (fl. 1823)   Master of the Richmond boys' seminary where Poe studied classical subjects and languages in the spring of 1823. Biographers have characterized Burke as a man of "sound learning" and "rigid discipline." He took a personal interest in the 14-year-old Edgar, and he joined other supporters who went along in a rowboat should they be needed when Poe undertook a six-mile swim against what he later boasted was "one of the strongest tides ever known in the James River." Poe's purpose was to duplicate a similar feat by Lord BYRON, who swam from Abydos to Sestos in Turkey.

Buried Alive   A 1990 made-for-television film directed by Frank Darabont, that claims to be "based upon stories by Edgar Allan Poe." The script uses elements from such Poe short stories as "THE PREMATURE BURIAL," "LIGEIA," and "BERENICE," but the added excesses of sex and gore make the main plot depart substantially from the originals.

Burling, Ebenezer (1808–1832)   Childhood friend whom Poe met during weekly services at the Monumental Church, where the Allan family had pew 80. With Burling, Poe read *Robinson Crusoe.* The two often would take a boat onto the James River, which seems to provide a possible model for the little pleasure yacht that appears at the beginning of THE NARRATIVE OF ARTHUR GORDON PYM. An inebriated Burling accompa-

nied Poe when he left Richmond and the Allan house after a quarrel in March 1826, but he changed his mind as soon as the two boarded a ship. Burling returned to Richmond with the story that Poe had gone abroad. A weak and dissipated man, Burling died in 1832 of cholera.

Burns, Joe (fl. 1935)   American organist who wrote musical accompaniment to "SONNET—SILENCE."

Burr, Charles Chauncey (1815–1883)   A Philadelphia author who provided Poe with financial assistance during his July 1849 visit to Philadelphia and later defended Poe's character in an article in the *Nineteenth Century* for February 1852.

Burton, William Evans (1802–1860)   English-born owner and editor of BURTON'S GENTLEMAN'S MAGAZINE, which began publication in July 1837. In April 1839, Burton reviewed THE NARRATIVE OF ARTHUR GORDON PYM in an essay that was heavy with sarcasm, yet the following

William Burton, founder of Burton's Gentleman's Magazine.   (Library of Congress)

month he hired Poe as an all-purpose assistant editor who was expected to edit articles, to proofread, and to contribute occasional reviews. Burton reserved the right to censor his writers and refused in several instances to publish inflammatory reviews by Poe. Poe's drinking and difficult behavior eventually led to his dismissal. Burton soon became bored with publishing, and he returned to his former profession of comic actor and manager, spending more time in the theater than in the editorial offices. When he needed to raise money to erect his own theater, Burton placed the magazine up for sale. He offered it first to George R. GRAHAM, who bought it outright for $3,500. Burton used the money to purchase Cook's Olympic Circus, between Eighth and Ninth Streets in Philadelphia, where he appeared as both manager and chief clown. Perhaps at the urging of Maria CLEMM or from a sense of duty, he told Graham that as part of the sale, he wanted the new owner to rehire and "take care of my young editor," who happened to be Poe.

Burton's Gentleman's Magazine   A literary publication founded in 1837 in Philadelphia by the English-born comedian William Evans BURTON as a magazine that would be "worthy of a place upon every parlour table of every gentleman in the United States." Poe was hired as the magazine's all-purpose assistant editor in May 1839, and although the magazine published many of his works, Poe never identified as closely with this publication as he had with the *SOUTHERN LITERARY MESSENGER*. The following Poe short stories were published in the magazine: "THE MAN THAT WAS USED UP" in August 1839, in September "THE FALL OF THE HOUSE OF USHER," in October "WILLIAM WILSON," in November "MORELLA," in December "CONVERSATIONS OF EIROS AND CHARMION," and in February 1840 "Peter Pendulum" (later "THE BUSINESS MAN"). In 1841, Burton sold the magazine to George R. GRAHAM, who merged the subscription list of 3,500 with the subscription list of 1,500 of his own publication, *Atkinson's Casket*. The new publication created by merging *Burton's Gentleman's Magazine* with *Atkinson's Casket* was named *GRAHAM'S MAGAZINE*, which began with a healthy subscription list of 5,000 and grew to more than 37,000 in only a few months under Poe's editorship.

Burwell, William Mecreery (1809–1888)   A constant companion of Poe's during their days as students at the University of Virginia, and later the renowned editor of *De Bow's Review*. Burwell published his reminiscences of Poe in an article titled "Edgar A. Poe, and his College Contemporaries" that appeared in the May 18, 1884, issue of the *New Orleans Times-Democrat*. The account provides a vivid account of life at the university, where many wealthy sons of landowners lived extravagantly—

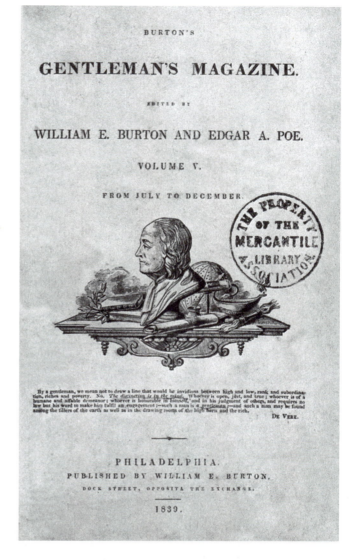

Poe began work as an editor at Burton's Gentleman's Magazine *in 1839.*   (Library of Congress)

gambling, drinking, hunting, and rarely attending class. Of Poe, however, Burwell observed "he was certainly not habitually intemperate, but he may occasionally have entered into a frolic. I often saw him in the lecture-room and in the library, but never in the slightest degree under the influence of intoxicating liquors. . . . [U]nder no time during the session did he fall under the censure of the faculty."

Bush, George (1796–1859)   A professor of Hebrew at the University of New York who was "long distinguished for the extent and variety of his attainments in oriental literature." Poe includes his profile in "THE LITERATI OF NEW YORK CITY" and describes him as "a Mesmerist and a Swedenborgian" whose work "Anastasia, or the Doctrine of the Resurrection: in which it is shown that the

Doctrine of Resurrection of the Body is not sanctioned by Reason or Revelation" had caused "a singular commotion in the realm of theology." The review compliments Bush for a "lucidly, succinctly, vigorously and logically written" work.

"The Business Man" Short story. Critics have determined that this story reflects Poe's often-strained relationship with his foster father John ALLAN, as well as his own ambivalence over the desire to write for art's sake and the need to write to survive.

PUBLISHING AND DRAMATIZATION HISTORY

An early version of the story appeared under the title of "Peter Pendulum, the Business Man" in the February 1840 issue of BURTON'S GENTLEMAN'S MAGAZINE. The story was published with a new title in the August 2, 1845, issue of the BROADWAY JOURNAL, preceded by the following epigraph:

"Method is the soul of business."

—Old Saying

The story has not been dramatized to date.

CHARACTERS

BAG, Mr. Gruff, Peter PROFFIT, Mr. SNAP.

PLOT SYNOPSIS

The story is narrated by Peter Proffit, a man who alerts readers at the outset: "I am a business man. I am a methodical man." He prides himself on his "general habits of accuracy and punctuality," and he provides readers with a smug self-evaluation of his rise that reveals his egotistical satisfaction at achieving commercial success. The story contains accounts of his eight business "speculations" on the road to success. He begins his career by running away from home at the age of 16, although "the most of boys run away from home at ten or twelve years of age." His delay would have been even longer had he not overheard his mother planning to set him up in grocery business. The horror of this line of work sends him into the world where he first works as a "Tailor's Walking-Advertisement," "the onerous duties of this profession" that he survives only by concentrating on "a scrupulous *method*." When his employers, Mssrs. Cut and Comeagain, Merchant Tailors, refuse to honor his meticulously detailed bill, reproduced in the story, he leaves the job. As he moves into other businesses, the reader sees that the businessman Proffit uses marginally legal tactics, as indicated in his description of profits gained in "the Eye-Sore trade," a slum building scheme to drive down real estate prices, and the

"Assault and Battery Business," which is insurance fraud. Proffit engages in similarly shady dealings such as Mud-Dabbling, Cur-Spattering, and Organ-Grinding. The latter, however legal, is not profitable enough, so Proffit gives it up and takes up Sham-Posting, which involves collecting postage for counterfeit letters. Proffit finally devises a "cat-growing" scheme that brings him the financial success that he desires. This, coupled with Poe's use of names such as Peter Proffit, makes the story a harsh satire on the values of the American businessman.

WRITER'S NOTES

Poe took the name "Peter Pendulum" for his hero in the early version of the story from sketches that appeared in *Farmer's Museum*, written by Joseph Dennie published in 1795–99. Critics also identify "The Business Man" as a parody of Joseph C. Neal's characterizations of "honest loafers," lazy men and women, that appeared in *Charcoal Sketches* (1838), a collection of character sketches, with a hero who is exactly the opposite in all areas.

Buzi-Ben-Levi Character in the short story "A TALE OF JERUSALEM." He is one of the three Gizbarim, subcollectors of the offering in the holy city of Jerusalem. Of the three, he is the most optimistic that the Ammonites will be fair and sell for 30 silver shekels each the lambs that the Hebrews need for their religious sacrifice. He is "read in the laws of the Gentiles, and has sojourned among them who dabble with the Teraphim" [ancient household idols of the Jews used for divination, mentioned in the old Testaments books of Judges, Hosea, and Genesis].

"Byron and Miss Chaworth" An article written by Poe and published with an engraving of Lord BYRON and his youthful sweetheart Mary Chaworth in the December 1844 issue of the *Columbian Magazine*. The article emphasizes the idealized vision of Byron's passion for Mary, as Poe observes that every allusion to her in Byron's work contains "a vein of almost spiritual tenderness and purity, strangely in contrast with the gross earthliness pervading and disfiguring his ordinary love poems." Poe points out that "a hundred evidences of fact" exist in Byron's poems and letters and in memoirs of his relatives to prove that the love was "earnest and abiding." At the same time, Poe asserts that this was also a passion "of the most thoroughly romantic, shadowy, and imaginative character . . . born of the hour, and of the youthful necessity to love. . . . It had no peculiar regard to the person, or to the character, or to the reciprocating affection of Mary Chaworth. . . . The result was not merely natural or merely probable, it was as inevitable as destiny itself."

Byron, George Gordon, Lord (1788–1824) English Romantic poet and notorious hedonistic socialite whom Poe admired both for his poetry and his rebelliousness. John ALLAN made clear his hatred for the cult that had grown up around Byron, and blamed Poe's attention to Byron for his foster son's profligate ways. Although Poe reassured Allan in a letter dated May 29, 1829, that he had long before given up Byron as a model, this statement appears in a letter in which he also asked his guardian to write to the publishers of AL AARAAF to guarantee the book to the extent of $100. For years afterward, Poe was fond of reciting Byron's poetry during his public recitations. In one lecture, presented in Lowell, Massachusetts, on July 10, 1848, his recitation of Byron's "Bride of Abydos" was rendered so affectingly that one onlooker wrote, "His manner of rendering some of the selections constitutes my only remembrance of the evening which so fascinated me." The influence of the Byronic personality and attitudes on Poe's work is found in his manner of dress in dramatic black, as well as in letters, poems, and several tales. A few Poe characters are thinly veiled examples of the Byronic physiognomy and personality. The unnamed suicidal stranger in Poe's story "THE ASSIGNATION" has "the mouth and chin of a deity—singular, wild, full liquid eyes—and a profusion of curling black hair, from which a forehead of unusual breadth gleamed forth at intervals all light and ivory." The face of Roderick USHER is also reminiscent of the countenance of Byron. To the end, Poe cultivated a dark, shadowy self that projected a sense of mystery to acquaintances.

Cabell, Robert G. (1802–1890) Boyhood friend of Poe's who, with their schoolmaster, William BURKE, went together in a rowboat to rescue Poe when he took the daring six-mile swim down the James River. Cabell and Poe, with Robert C. STANARD, spent their adolescence continually in each other's company and all attended the same school. Although Poe appears not to have kept contact with his old friend after leaving John ALLAN's household, Cabell's father, Robert L. Cabell, served as witness for John Allan's will.

Cadet Poe's name for an imagined country. The DUC DE L'OMELETTE in the story of the same name is said to be reclining "languidly on that ottoman for which he sacrificed his loyalty in outbidding his king,—the notorious ottoman of Cadet" when he expires.

Cain Allusion in Poe's short story "BON-BON" to the biblical figure who committed the first murder. In Poe's story, the devil relates the "innumerable purchases" he has made, including Cain and "a thousand others, who never knew what it was to have a soul during the latter part of their lives."

Calhoun, John C. (1782–1850) Vice president of the United States from 1825 to 1832 (first under President John Quincy Adams and then under Andrew Jackson), and later a U.S. Senator representing South Carolina. He and Daniel Webster engaged in a historic debate in the Senate over slavery and slaves' rights. Calhoun accompanied General Lafayette, the French-born hero of the American Revolutionary War, when he visited Richmond, Virginia, in 1824. The Richmond Junior Volunteers, a company containing sons of some of the best families in Richmond, was armed to serve as a bodyguard for Lafayette. The 15-year-old Poe was a lieutenant in the Volunteers and proudly met both Lafayette and Calhoun.

Calvert, George H. (1803–1899) An editor of the *Baltimore American* and a would-be poet. Poe repaid him for unfavorable reviews by crediting him in "AUTOGRAPHY" with having written "some good paragraphs on the commonplace topics of the day" but denouncing him for being "a feeble and common-place writer of poetry." Poe also observes that Calvert had written "one or two original poems . . . which did him no credit."

Calvin, John (1509–1564) French religious reformer, to whom Poe makes a satiric reference in "NEVER BET THE DEVIL YOUR HEAD," which he repeats in "PINAKIDIA," that "Jacobus Hugo [Jacques Hughes, author of *True History of Rome* (1655)] has satisfied himself that by Euenis, Homer meant to insinuate John Calvin." The statement is a paraphrase of a statement that appeared in *Introductions to the Study of the Classic Poets* (1831), written by H. N. Coleridge, who asserted that Hughes probably meant Eumaios, the swineherd whom Odysseus meets while disguised as a beggar in Homer's *Odyssey*. This represents still another of Poe's jabs at erudition.

Campanella, Tommaso (1568–1639) Pseudonym of the Italian philosopher Giovanni Domenico Campanella. In 1599, he was arrested on charges of heresy and of conspiring against the Spanish government in Naples. During his 27 years in prison, he wrote *Civitas Solis* [City of the Sun], published in 1623. After his release from prison in 1626, he experienced continued persecution for his ideas and he sought refuge in France. In "THE FALL OF THE HOUSE OF USHER," Poe includes "The City of the Sun of Campanella" among the reading materials of Roderick USHER, "the books which, for years had formed no small portion of the mental existence of the invalid." In "THE PURLOINED LETTER," detective C. Auguste DUPIN identifies the method of an eight-year-old boy whose success at guessing in the game of "even and odd" is based on having "effected the *thorough* identification" with the emotions of his opponents as lying "at the bottom of all the spurious profundity which has been attributed to Rochefoucauld, to La Bougive, and to Campanella." In "Usher," the mention appears to mirror Roderick's distrust of accepted thought and his embracing of the unusual and the occult. In "The Purloined Letter," the opposite seems true.

Campbell, Major John (fl. 1829) Influential Virginian who wrote one of the four letters of recommendation to West Point for Poe in April 1829. Campbell was not personally acquainted with the young adult Poe and remembered having seen him only at the resort "The Spring" in 1812.

"Camperdown; or, News from Our Neighborhood—Being a Series of Sketches, by the Author of 'Our Neighborhood,' &c. Philadelphia: Carey, Lea & Blanchard" Review that appeared in the July 1836 issue of the SOUTHERN LITERARY MESSENGER and favorably recommended Mary Griffith's collection of six short stories. The review contains a brief summary of the content of the collection, and Poe observes that this is the second volume in a series which "will be followed up by others—in continuation." Poe found the stories "The Little Couple" and "The Thread and Needle Store" to be "skilfully told, and [to] have much spirit and freshness," while the remaining four stories are full of "originality of thought and manner" and "sufficiently outre" to make the collection a success.

Canning, Sir Launcelot Mentioned in the short story "THE FALL OF THE HOUSE OF USHER" as the author of a book titled *The Mad Trist*. The narrator seeks to calm the agitated Roderick USHER by reading "the antique volume" which he calls "a favourite of Usher's more in sad jest than in earnest." The romance, "the only book immediately at hand," tells the stirring story of the brave Ethelred, and the passage that the narrator chooses to read to Usher ends with a large brass shield falling noisily on a silver floor. As soon as the narrator reads this passage, he and Usher hear a sound "as if a shield of brass had indeed, at that moment, fallen heavily upon a floor of silver," which unnerves them both.

"The Canons of Good Breeding, or the Handbook of the Man of Fashion. By the Author of the 'Laws of Etiquette.' Lea and Blanchard, Philadelphia" Review of a handbook to good manners that appeared in the November 1839 issue of BURTON'S GENTLEMAN'S MAGAZINE. The handbook's author also wrote an earlier volume titled *Advice to a Young Gentleman*. Poe warns that those who casually peruse the volume "will, of course, be included to throw it aside with contempt upon perceiving its title"; however, he assures the reader that "the volume abounds in good things," among them its "grouping together of fine things from the greatest multiplicity of the rarest works." Praising the author for having a "radiancy of fine wit, so commingled with scholar-like observation and profound thought," Poe highlights some of the advice with a tongue-in-cheek approach, as in the following example: "'The inferior classes of men, as you may see if you think fit to take notice of them, only press the rim of the hat when they speak to women of their acquaintance, you should be careful, when you salute a lady or gentleman, to take your own entirely off, and cause it to describe *a circle of at least ninety degrees.*'"

Canova, Antonio (1757–1822) Italian sculptor whose Venus is mentioned in Poe's short story "THE ASSIGNATION" and in his literary criticism "THE AMERICAN DRAMA." The Byronic stranger in "The Assignation" prefers Canova's Venus to the Venus di Medici, stating, "'Give *me* the Canova!'" In comparing modern sculpture to that of the ancients, Poe states in "The American Drama" that "the Venus of Canova is worth any time two of that of Cleomenes." The modern Venus is more fully realized and physically complete.

Cant Mentioned in "MELLONTA TAUTA" and referring to the philosopher Immanuel Kant as one of the two "greatest disciples" of "a Turkish philosopher (or Hindoo possibly) called Aries Tottle," the other great disciple being "Neuclid." The story is a satire, thus Poe satirizes erudition by distorting names.

Caplet, Andre (1879–1925) French composer, conductor, and critic who wrote an arrangement in four parts for the harp or the piano inspired by Poe's story "THE MASQUE OF THE RED DEATH."

Capricornutti, Count Character in the short story "LIONIZING." One of the guests at Almack's, apparently the center of social/intellectual activity of London in the 19th century, he jealously mutters "*Diavolo!*" when the revered nosologist Robert JONES enters the salon and witnesses Jones's challenge to the Elector of BLUDDENNUFF.

Caravaggio (1573–1610) Italian Baroque painter, born Michelangelo Merisi, whose use of models from the lower levels of society played a pivotal role in the development of a naturalistic style in 17th-century painting. In Poe's short story "LIONIZING," Signor TINTONTINOTINO from Florence pretentiously speaks "of the gloom of Caravaggio, of the amenity of Albano, of the colors of Titian, of the frows of Rubens, and of the waggeries of Jan STEEN."

Carey, Mathew (1760–1839) Philadelphia economist, bookseller, and publisher who founded Carey, Lea & Carey, the publishing house to which Poe first submitted AL AARAAF, TAMERLANE, AND OTHER MINOR POEMS, and TALES OF THE FOLIO CLUB without success. Poe includes an analysis of Carey's signature in "AUTOGRAPHY," noting only that "Mr. Carey does not write a legible hand."

Carlyle, Thomas (1795–1881) English literary critic and social historian whose attacks on sham, hypocrisy, and excessive materialism echoed Transcendental thought and led Poe to view his work in a negative light. Poe found significant faults in Carlyle's work. In "MARGINALIA," he wrote, "I have not the slightest faith in Carlyle. In ten years—possible only five—he will be remembered only as a butt for sarcasm." In contrast to other critics who praised conciseness in writing, Poe asked, "What, then, should be said of the concision of Carlyle—that those are mad who admire a brevity which squanders our time for the purpose of economizing our printing-ink and paper." Regarding one of Carlyle's works, he wrote, "The book about 'Hero-Worship'—is it possible that it ever excited a feeling beyond contempt?" After scourging the concept, Poe concludes, "Carlyle, however, has rendered an important service (to posterity, at least) in pushing rant and cant to that degree of excess which inevitably induces reaction." In a review of the work of William Ellery CHANNING, titled "OUR AMATEUR POETS, NO. III," Poe suggests that negative qualities of Channing's work suggest the influence of Carlyle, whose work he finds too obscure to understand: "Either a man intends to be understood, or he does not. If he write a book which he intends not to be understood, we shall be very happy indeed not to understand it; but if he write a book which he means to be understood, and, in this book, be at all possible pains to prevent us from understanding it, we can only say he is an ass—and this, to be brief, is our private opinion of Mr. Carlyle, which we now take the liberty of making public."

Carpaccio, Vittorre (1455?–1526?) Italian painter who created four cycles of narrative paintings, one of which is the well-known *St. George Slaying the Dragon*. In Poe's short story "LIONIZING," the pretentious Signor TINTONTINOTINO from Florence shows off his knowledge of painting as "he discoursed of Cimabué, Arpino, Carpaccio, and Argostino."

Carson, John Character in *THE NARRATIVE OF ARTHUR GORDON PYM*. A member of the *Jane Guy* crew and a native of London, he is one of three men who volunteer their services to stay on the island and to complete the building of structures in which to dry the *beche de mer*, an unusual mollusk that the crew finds in the waters surrounding the uncharted island on which they land. He is killed by savages.

Carter, Doctor John (fl. 1849–1884) A physician in whose company with friends Poe spent the last evening of his life in Richmond, Virginia, before boarding a boat bound for Baltimore, where he would die. Biographers report that Poe left Carter's office to go to supper at a fashionable Richmond restaurant named Saddler, taking the doctor's cane and leaving his own as a sign that he intended to return. Carter never saw his own cane nor his friend again, for Poe met other friends at the restaurant who kept him there until the time for departure was near, then accompanied him to the boat.

Carter, Doctor William Gibbon (fl. 1849–1884) Brother of Doctor John CARTER and a physician who spent the final day in Richmond, Virginia, with Poe. After Poe's death, he revealed that in the months before dying in Baltimore, the poet had experienced several serious attacks of delirium, and that his body had become so weak that only one drink of hard liquor would trigger such an attack. After an especially serious bout in August 1849, Carter had warned Poe that further indulgence would be fatal, and through his influence Poe joined the SONS OF TEMPERANCE in early September 1849.

Carver, Captain Jonathan (1710–1780) A member of the British provincial army and explorer of the Great Lakes, Carver wrote *Travels Through the Interior Part of North America* (1778). In *THE JOURNAL OF JULIUS RODMAN*, Poe devotes several passages to Carver to add verisimilitude to the story. Poe also identifies Carver's contributions to finding a northwest passage in his review of Washington IRVING's "ASTORIA": "In 1763, shortly after acquisition of the Canadas by Great Britain, this gentleman projected a journey across the continent, between the forty-third and forty-sixth degrees of northern latitude, to the shores of the Pacific." Poe notes that Carver failed in two individual attempts to accomplish the journey.

Cary, Henry (1804–1870) American poet and translator of Dante. Cary, Poe stated in "MARGINALIA," is "best entitled to distinction" as an essayist and not as a poet; but, adds Poe in "THE LITERATI OF NEW YORK CITY," he is "a fifth or sixth rate one [essayist]." Poe condescendingly says of Cary that "for a long time he was President of the Phoenix Bank of New York, and the principal part of his life has been devoted to business." Seemingly as a result of this background, he notes that "Mr. Cary, in fact, abounds very especially in superfluities . . . and, to speak the truth, is continually guilty of all kinds of grammatical improprieties. I repeat that, in this respect, he is decent, and no more."

"The Cask of Amontillado" Short story. The tale, one of Poe's most popular short stories, is considered a masterpiece because of its blend of horror at the protagonist's actions with the ironic humor of the situation.

PUBLISHING AND DRAMATIZATION HISTORY

The story was first published in the November 1846 issue of *GODEY'S MAGAZINE AND LADY'S BOOK*, where New York publishing insiders recognized it as Poe's fictional response to libelous attacks written by Thomas Dunn ENGLISH that appeared first in the May 1846 issue of the New York *EVENING MIRROR* and continued in ensuing months. The initial article spoke harshly of Poe's drinking and criticized his physical appearance, creating a verbal caricature that proclaimed he had "a chin narrow and pointed, which gives his head upon the whole, a balloonish appearance which may account for his supposed lightedness."

Several film productions have made use of the plot of this tale, although no production carries its name. In 1931, the German film *Funf Unheimliche Geschichten* (released in the U.S. as *The Living Dead*) included the plot in its story line, as did the 1948 French remake *Histoires Extraordinaires* (*Extraordinary Tales*). *Master of Horror,* a 1961 film made in Argentina, also included the story within the larger plot but did not give specific attention to Poe or to his protagonist.

CHARACTERS

FORTUNATO, LUCHESI, MONTRESOR.

PLOT SYNOPSIS

Set in Italy and told 50 years after the events have occurred, the story is one of revenge, which the vindictive narrator Montresor has plotted with the careful planning required of a military campaign. He begins by telling readers why he seeks revenge: "The thousand injuries of Fortunato I had borne as I best could; but when he ventured upon insult, I vowed revenge." Neither the reader nor Fortunato is made aware of the exact nature of these injuries, and one can only assume that the "insult" of which Montresor speaks is the failure of the inebriated Fortunato to remember the motto that appears on the Montresor family arms: *Nemo me impune lacessit* ("No one provokes me with impunity"). The arms evidently stand as a warning to all enemies of the Montresors: the design depicts a huge golden foot in an azure field, and "the foot crushes a serpent rampant whose fangs are imbedded in the heel." Montresor takes advantage of Fortunato's careless mood during "the supreme madness of the carnival season," while the motley-wearing partygoer is celebrating Mardi Gras. Aware that Fortunato is "a man to be respected and even feared," Montresor takes advantage of his one weak point, his pride on his connoisseurship of wine. He suggests that another wine connoisseur, Luchesi, has aided him in obtaining a bargain on a pipe (about 130 gallons) of amontillado, an aged dry, light sherry. Unable to ignore the implied challenge, Fortunato insists that Montresor let him sample the amontillado, so that he might ascertain if it is genuine. To do so, the two must leave the carnival festivities and crowds and venture to Montresor's deserted villa, devoid even of the servants, who are also away and celebrating. The two descend into the catacombs that house both Montresor's stock of wine and a large crypt, of which the niche in one wall has been cleared. As the two walk through the catacombs, Montresor offers his guest wines at several intervals so that Fortunato is completely inebriated when they reach the exposed crypt wall. Within moments, Montresor has chained Fortunato to the granite walls of the niche and proceeds to apply stone and mortar to seal the niche. After completing all but one stone of eleven tiers, Montresor hears his prisoner's low laugh and the nervous words ". . . a very good joke indeed—an excellent jest. We will have many a rich laugh about it at the palazzo." When Montresor fails to confirm that the action is a joke, Fortunato panics and cries out, "For the love of God, Montresor." When no more words emerge, Montresor throws his torch into the opening, then places the final stone in the wall and seals it with mortar. Montresor's final words, uttered 50 years after the crime—"*In pace requiescat!*"—seem to reflect both a blessing upon the dead Fortunato and a hope that he can someday overcome his guilt.

Cass, Lewis (1782–1866)   Secretary of war under President Jackson and literary scholar whose signature Poe included in "AUTOGRAPHY." In his analysis, Poe praises Cass as "one of the finest *belles-lettres* scholars of America" and mentions that he had recently contributed "one or two very excellent papers" to the *SOUTHERN LITERARY MESSENGER,* while Poe was editor.

Castiglione   Character in Poe's drama *POLITIAN.* He is the heir and cowardly son of the Due di BROGLIO, who seems ignorant of Castiglione's drinking and carousing. In a short time, his character appears to deteriorate from being "A very nobleman in heart and deed" to being a habitual drunk whom the family servants must pull "from under the table where he lay / And tumbled him into bed." His "low debaucheries—his gambling habits / And all his numerous vices" seem to date from the time that he seduced his father's orphaned ward Lady LALAGE, and the servants surmise that "the sin sits heavy on his soul."

Castle Island   The site of Fort Independence, a United States Army military installation in Boston Harbor, where Poe entered the army as Edgar A. PERRY in May 1827 and spent the first six months of his service with Battery H of the First Artillery. At this site, he carried out the duties of a company clerk in the peacetime army, preparing the routine battery papers, writing letters dictated by officers, preparing the payrolls and muster rolls, and serving as messenger between the company and regimental headquarters.

Catalini, Angelica (1786–1849)   Italian opera singer mentioned by C. Auguste DUPIN in "THE PURLOINED LETTER."

Catarina Referred to in letters written by Poe as both "Catarina" and "Catterina," a large tortoiseshell cat loved by Virginia CLEMM and owned by Poe, first in Philadelphia and then at their Fordham cottage in New York. When Poe and his wife hurriedly left Philadelphia on April 6, 1844, they left behind Mrs. CLEMM and Catarina. In a letter to Mrs. Clemm, Poe writes that their first night away, Virginia "had a hearty cry because you and Catterina weren't there." A week later, due to his success in publishing "THE BALLOON-HOAX," Poe sent for Mrs. Clemm, who arrived "with tears of joy in her eyes, and a basket containing Catarina." Catarina/Catterina paraded around the Poe home, serving as a companion and a source of physical warmth to the frail and often-shivering Virginia. After Virginia's death, Poe wrote a letter of response to Mrs. Louise SHEW, who had written that she had to stop visits with Poe because of gossip. In the letter, Poe writes, "I heard you greet my cat Catarina but it was only as a memory."

Caus, Solomon de When the unnamed narrator of "SOME WORDS WITH A MUMMY" deplores the Egyptian ignorance of steam, Count ALLAMISTAKEO demands to know if he is "really such a fool as not to know that the modern steam engine is derived from the invention of Hero, through Solomon de Caus," a Norman engineer.

Cayley, George (1774–1857) British scientist and aeronautical pioneer known as the father of British aeronautics. Poe refers to his early-19th-century experiments with ellipsoid balloons in "THE BALLOON-HOAX." The balloon in the story is similar in several details to the one invented by Cayley.

Chamberlayne, William (1619–1689) Minor British playwright active in the time of William SHAKESPEARE. Poe uses a garbled version of a quotation from Chamberlayne's play *Love's Victory* (1615) as an epigraph to the short story "WILLIAM WILSON."

Chambers, Robert (1802–1871) British cosmologist and author. Many of Poe's contemporaries suggested that Chambers's work *The Vestiges of Creation* was a strong influence on Poe's "EUREKA." Epes SARGENT openly stated in an article published in the July 20, 1848, issue of the *Boston Evening Transcript* that "Eureka" reminded him "of that remarkable work 'The Vestiges of Creation' by the character and tendency of the author's scientific romancing." Both works deal with the attempt to construct a synthesis based in mathematics, poetics, and intuition as well as to create meta-physic-cosmic theories that identified all life as a part of God.

Chandler, Joseph R. (1792–1880) Editor of the *Philadelphia United States Gazette*. Poe reviewed his "ADDRESS, DELIVERED BEFORE THE GOETHIAN AND DIAGNOTHIAN SOCIETIES OF MARSHALL COLLEGE, AT THEIR ANNUAL CELEBRATION, SEPTEMBER 24, 1839," stating that "it assuredly does its accomplished author much credit." He also praises Chandler in "AUTOGRAPHY": "Mr. Chandler's reputation as the editor of one of the best daily papers in the country, and as one of our finest *belles lettres* scholars, is deservedly high." Citing Chandler's numerous published writings, especially prose tales, Poe observes that "these latter evince imaginative powers of a superior order."

Channing, William Ellery (1818–1901) Minor poet and essayist whose writing Poe lampooned in "OUR AMATEUR POETS, NO. III. WILLIAM ELLERY CHANNING." Noting that he is only "*the son* of the great essayist deceased," the eminent clergyman poet William Ellery Channing, Poe states "the necessity of employing the indefinite rather than the definite article. He is *a,* and by no means *the,* William Ellery Channing." Taking the mockery further, Poe observes, "It may be said in his favor that nobody ever heard of him. Like an honest woman, he has always succeeded in keeping himself from being made the subject of gossip." Channing was popular in literary circles and numbered among his friends Emerson, Hawthorne, and Thoreau, but Poe found him to be a fertile source of material. Channing's poetry is mentioned in a satiric context in Poe's short story "HOW TO WRITE A BLACKWOOD ARTICLE."

Chantilly Character mentioned in the short story "THE MURDERS IN THE RUE MORGUE." C. Auguste DUPIN describes him as a delicate-featured man whose "diminutive figure unfitted him for tragedy." A one-time cobbler in the Rue St. Denis, he had become "stage-mad, had attempted the role of Xerxes, in Crebillon's tragedy" and was severely lampooned for his efforts. Dupin sees him as an early link in the chain that leads to the solution of the murders.

Chapman, George (1559–1634) English translator, poet, and dramatist. His 1607 tragedy *Bussy D'Ambois* is inaccurately quoted by the narrator in the short story "THE ASSIGNATION" as follows: "He is up / There like a Roman statue! He will stand / Till death hath made him marble." Although Poe's narrator distinctly identifies Chapman and the play, the actual lines are: "I am up, / Here, like a Roman statue I will stand / Till death hath made me marble."

"A Chapter of Suggestions" An essay written by Poe and published in the November 1845 issue of the New York annual *The Opal,* edited by Nathaniel Parker

WILLIS. The writing deals with the exercise of intuition and contains eleven paragraphs, each dealing with a different area of intuitive life. Among the areas of discussion are the steps by which a work of art goes from conception to formal realization; an examination of the reliability of intuition; suggestions about the metaphysical life; analyses of the power of the imagination and the nature of true genius; and a defense of the necessity of precision and clarity in matters of logic. The essay presents Poe's strong belief in the power of intuition, and he sums up its intellectual value by stating: "Great intellects guess well. The laws of Kepler were, professedly, guesses."

German astronomer Johannes Kepler helped to establish the validity of the Copernican system by using an empirical formulation of the laws of planetary motion as well as the precise data of the Danish astronomer Tycho Brahe, yet Poe believes that intuition played a bigger role and that Kepler only guessed.

"A Chapter on Autography" Alternate name for Poe's analyses of the fabricated handwriting and signatures of more literary personalities. These appeared in a three-part series in GRAHAM'S MAGAZINE in issues published in November 1841, December 1841, and January 1842. *See* "AUTOGRAPHY."

"The Characters of Shakespeare. By William Hazlitt. Wiley & Putnam's Library of Choice Reading. No. XVII" A review of the volume that appeared in the August 16, 1845, issue of the BROADWAY JOURNAL. Generally complimentary to Hazlitt's efforts, Poe notes that "with his hackneyed theme he has done wonders, and those wonders well." Stating that only seeing Hazlitt's name affixed to the commentary "*could* induce us to read anything more in the way of commentary on Shakespeare," he declares the author to be "emphatically a critic, brilliant, epigrammatic, startling, paradoxical, and suggestive, rather than accurate, luminous, or profound." In typical fashion, Poe devotes more than half of the review to expounding upon his own theories. In this case, he takes issue with all who have commented on Shakespeare, faulting them for dealing with the characters as if they were "actual existences upon earth." Taking Hamlet as his example, Poe writes that if Hamlet had really lived, then critics could "reconcile his inconsistencies and settle to our satisfaction his true character. But the task becomes pure absurdity when we deal only with a phantom." Poe views it as "little less than a miracle, that this obvious point should have been overlooked."

"Charles O'Malley, the Irish Dragoon. By Harry Lorrequer. With Forty Illustrations by Phiz. Complete in One Volume. Carey & Hart: Philadelphia" Review appearing in the March 1842 issue of GRAHAM'S MAGAZINE. Poe opens his review by noting that the first point to be observed regarding the novel "is the great *popularity*" of the work. . . . At all events it has met with a most extensive sale." He is quick, however, to point out that he would not insult readers "by supposing any one of them unaware of the fact, that a book may be exceedingly *popular* without *any* legitimate literary merit." To emphasize his point, Poe states that "so long as the world retains its present point of civilization, so long will it be almost an axiom that no extensively *popular* book, in the right application of the term, can be a work of high merit, *as regards those particulars of the work which are popular*." In this largely negative review, Poe provides only a brief summary of the plot, which he disparages as having "more absurdities than we have patience to enumerate." He notes that "in the story proper are repetitions without end. . . . It would be difficult to convey to one who has not examined this production for himself, any idea of the exceedingly rough, clumsy, and irrational manner in which even this bald conception is carried out." Using a series of excerpts from the novel, Poe condemns the plot as "exceedingly meagre" and methodically identifies by page number the errors and "vulgarisms" that he anticipates would be offensive to readers. In the final analysis, Poe concludes that the novel has been written by an author who is "aping the airs of intellect" and who has done "violence to the feelings and judgment even of the populace."

Charmion Character in the short story "THE CONVERSATION OF EIROS AND CHARMION." A celestial specter who converses with EIROS, both of whom have experienced the dissolution of their earthly existences and who have "passed into Night through the grave," she eagerly questions him to learn the details of the "stupendous event" of the fiery catastrophe that has consumed the earth. She urges him to "converse of familiar things, in the old familiar language of the world which has so fearfully perished."

"A Chaunt of Life and Other Poems, With Sketches and Essays. By Rev. Ralph Hoyt. In Six Parts. Part II. New York: Le Roy & Hoyt" Review that appeared in the July 26, 1845, issue of the BROADWAY JOURNAL. Poe expressed admiration for the collection of poetry and incidental writings, and quoted extensively from "The Chaunt of Life," which he declared to be itself "quite fine." He argued, however, that some of the other poems were marred by missing feet or "peculiarities of metre." The reviews also contains the full text of a poem titled "Old," which Poe included because it "has so many rare and peculiar excellences," as well as "some exquisite passages of pathos and of imagination."

Cheever, George B. (1807–1890) American religious writer whose profile Poe included in "THE LITERATI OF

NEW YORK CITY." Poe identifies Cheever as the editor of *The Commonplace Book of American Poetry,* "a work which has at least the merit of not belying its title, and *is* exceedingly commonplace." The review expresses regret that the publication was for years the only compilation to provide material by which Europeans would "form an estimate of the poetical ability of Americans," because the selections appeared to him to be "exceedingly injudicious, and have all a marked leaning to the didactic." Poe is no more charitable in his estimations of Cheever's "Defence of Capital Punishment," a work in which the author does not offer "one novel argument."

Child, Lydia Maria (1802–1880) Abolitionist and crusader for the rights of women whose novel PHILOTHEA Poe reviewed and whom he profiled as one of "THE LITERATI OF NEW YORK CITY." Poe describes her as of "a fervid and fanciful nature" and quotes her poem "Marius amid the Ruins of Carthage" to illustrate the excellence of her shorter compositions. He asserts that "some of her magazine papers are distinguished for graceful and brilliant *imagination*—a quality rarely noticed in our countrywomen."

"The Child of the Sea, and Other Poems. By S. Anna Lewis, Author of 'Records of the Heart,' Etc., Etc." A review that appeared in the September 1848 issue of the SOUTHERN LITERARY MESSENGER. Poe's praise for Sara Anna LEWIS's poetry collection was one way of repaying her for the financial and emotional assistance she gave him after Virginia's death. Citing various poems that she had published, Poe asserts, "All critical opinion must agree in assigning her a high, if not the very highest rank among the poetesses of her land." The review identifies by name several of the poems in the collection, and copies stanzas to support his praise that "the versification, while in full keeping with the general character of simplicity, has in certain passages a vigorous, trenchant euphony which would confer honor on the most accomplished masters of the art." In conclusion, he predicts that the collection "will confer immortality on its author."

Childs, George W. (1829–1894) Newspaper publisher who owned both the *Philadelphia Public Ledger* and the *Dollar Newspaper,* which awarded Poe a $100 prize for "THE GOLD-BUG" as the best short story submitted in its 1843 contest.

Chiponchipino Character briefly mentioned in the short story "THE MAN THAT WAS USED UP." He is a sculptor and friend whom the narrator wishes might see the properly proportioned calf and the leg of Brevet Brigadier General John A. B. C. SMITH.

Chivers, Thomas Holley (1809–1858) Georgia poet and author of the 1852 biography *Life of Poe.* His novel *Conrad and Eudora* (1834) is based on the same material that Poe used in writing the drama POLITIAN. Although he found Poe's alcoholism repulsive, he offered Poe a permanent home in Georgia in 1845. Poe refused, but the two remained strong friends. In his biography, Chivers attributed to Poe an independence of spirit, yet pointed out that "no man living loved the praises of others better than he did."

Poe was generous in praising his friend's work and wrote a positive review of Chivers's poem "THE LOST PLEIAD" in 1845. In "AUTOGRAPHY," he called Chivers "one of the best and one of the worst poets in America" and wrote that "his productions affect one as a wild dream-strange, incongruous, full of images of more than arabesque monstrosity, and snatches of sweet unsustained song."

Thomas Holley Chivers, a writer and friend of Poe. (Edgar Allan Poe Society)

"The Christian Florist; Containing the English Botanical Names of Different Plants, with Their Properties Delineated and Explained. Illustrated by Texts From Various Authors. First American From the Second London Edition. Philadelphia: Carey, Lea & Blanchard" A book review by Poe that appeared in the January 1836 issue of the SOUTHERN LITERARY MESSENGER. Poe praises the book for being "well adapted for a Christmas present" and for the richly colored illustrations, which he describes. The review praises the poetical selections as having been, for the most part, excellently chosen, and the prose commentaries on each article in good taste." Poe concludes that the work "deserves the good will of all sensible persons."

"The City in the Sea" Poem written by Poe that appeared first in the April 1845 issue of the *American Review*. The poem, thus titled, was also included in Poe's collection THE RAVEN AND OTHER POEMS, published late in 1845 by Wiley & Putnam and believed to be "the most important volume of poetry that had been issued up to that time in America." Under the title "THE DOMED CITY," an earlier version of the poem had appeared in Poe's third book, POEMS, published by Elam Bliss in 1831. Included by critics as one of Poe's most romantic works, the poem attracted the admiration of the English Pre-Raphaelite poets, particularly Swinburne, to whom such lines as "Whose wreathed friezes intertwine / The viol, the violet, and the vine" embodied the view that poetry should possess a lyrical, unified structure that combines sensual sound with sensuous imagery. The poem is a meditation that centers on an underwater necropolis illuminated from an infernal energy below its surface rather than from "rays from holy heaven," and where the buildings and streets "[r]esemble nothing that is ours." This is a city without people, sound, or movement, devoid of spiritual hope, over which Death presides and surveys with satisfaction his authority and handiwork: "while from a proud tower in the town / Death looks gigantically down."

Claflin, Avery (1898–1979) American composer who in 1921 wrote *The Fall of Usher,* an opera in one act with orchestral accompaniment, based on Poe's "THE FALL OF THE HOUSE OF USHER." Claflin also wrote *Hester Prynne,* a libretto derived from Nathaniel Hawthorne's novel *The Scarlet Letter,* and *Moby Dick Suite,* an arrangement for orchestra based on Herman Melville's novel *Moby Dick.*

Clark, Captain William (1770–1838) American soldier and explorer who shared command of the Lewis and Clark expedition. Poe included references to Clark's explorations in THE JOURNAL OF JULIUS RODMAN and his review of Washington IRVING's "ASTORIA: OR, ANECDOTES OF AN ENTERPRISE BEYOND THE ROCKY MOUNTAINS."

Clark, Lewis Gaylord (1808–1873) One of the editors of the KNICKERBOCKER MAGAZINE and a frequent opponent of Poe. Clark used his column "Editors' Table" to attack Poe's writing, printing one particularly virulent attack on THE NARRATIVE OF ARTHUR GORDON PYM. Clark's attacks combined with Poe's rebuttals to create a highly public feud in print that led in 1845 to physical violence when Poe attacked Clark on a New York street. Thomas Holley CHIVERS restrained Poe, and neither man was injured. As revenge, Poe printed a negative portrait of Clark in "THE LITERATI OF NEW YORK CITY," claiming that Clark's magazine "is deficient in that absolutely indispensable element, individuality," and, "as the editor has no precise character, the magazine, as a matter of course, can have none." Poe further attacked Clark for having "no determinateness, no distinctiveness, no saliency of point." In a clever turn of phrase, Poe charges that "he is noticeable for nothing in the world except for the markedness by which he is noticeable for nothing."

Clarke, Joseph Hanson (1790–1885) A pedantic Dublin-born classical scholar in whose Richmond academy Poe began an in-depth study of Greek and Latin classical literature after returning from England in the fall of 1820. Clarke considered the young Poe to be "a born artist," and many years later he remembered Poe as a man whose "imaginative powers seemed to take precedence over all his other faculties." He feared, however, that the young Poe suffered from inordinate vanity and did not want to encourage this. Therefore, when John ALLAN showed Clarke a sheaf of papers containing the 11-year-old Poe's poetry and asked if they were worthy of publication, Clarke suggested that Allan encourage the young poet to give up writing of verses.

Clarke, Thomas Cottrell (1801–1874) Publisher, gentleman, and the first editor of the PHILADELPHIA SATURDAY EVENING POST. Clarke joined other backers in early 1843 to provide support for Poe's proposed magazine, the STYLUS. He provided Poe with money to travel to Washington to secure endorsements and subscriptions of prominent men and government clerks. After Poe arrived in Washington, Clarke received a letter from another backer, J. E. Dow, informing him that "on the first evening [Poe] seemed somewhat excited, having been over-persuaded to take some port wine. . . . I cannot bear that he should be the sport of senseless creatures." By May 1843, Clarke withdrew support probably because of Poe's drinking. In a letter to James Russell LOWELL, Poe reported the destruction of his dream: "My magazine scheme has exploded, or, at least, I have been deprived, through the imbecility, or rather through the idiocy of my partner, of all means of prosecuting it for the present."

Clay, Cassius (1810–1903)   American abolitionist and statesman who in 1845 founded the antislavery weekly *True American*. He met Poe during the winter of 1845–46 when the author resided in New York City and often joined "the best intellectual society of the city."

Cleef, Augustus Van   Author of an article titled "Poe's Mary" that appeared in *Harper's New Monthly Magazine* for March 1889. The article contained an account of Poe's love for a Baltimore girl named Mary DEVEREAUX in the year following his dismissal from West Point. Van Cleef interviewed Mary and most of the article is told in her words and from her point of view.

Clemm, Maria Poe (1790–1871)   Poe's paternal aunt, the sister of his father David Poe, and his mother-in-law, as the mother of Virginia CLEMM. At the age of 27, Maria married William Clemm, Jr., a widower with five children and a little property, and whose late wife was Maria's first cousin. They had three children by this marriage: Henry, Virginia Maria, and Eliza, who died in infancy. Nine years after her marriage, Mrs. Clemm was a penniless widow with two children to raise. Nicknamed "Muddy," she was a strong-willed woman who seems to have provided a dependable home to more than just Edgar, who first went to live with her in Baltimore in 1829 when she had been a widow for two years. When he arrived, he joined her seven-year-old daughter Virginia and son Henry, an intermittent drinker; his paralytic grandmother, old Mrs. David Poe, who had been bedridden for two years; and his alcoholic older brother William Henry Leonard POE, who suffered from advanced tuberculosis. The household was poverty-stricken and survived only on the money that Henry Clemm made as a mason's apprentice, Poe's allowance from John ALLAN, and Mrs. Clemm's sewing; yet Mrs. Clemm enthusiastically welcomed this new member of her household.

At this time, she also began a means of survival that she would use repeatedly in the years ahead, when Poe, Virginia, and she would move repeatedly as her dear "Eddie" chased his dream of literary fame. She would take her large wicker market basket and call upon the Baltimore Poes and anyone else who was slightly connected with the family. Hervey Allen recounts in *Israfel* that "Mrs. Clemm in her widow's cap and large motherly person, her broad benign face troubled with an eleemosynary woe, was wont to appear at irregular but disconcerting intervals, the basket upon her arm, her fine gray eyes yearning with stark anxiety, and a tale of dole upon her lips that would have drawn tears from

Maria Poe Clemm, Poe's aunt and mother-in-law. (Edgar Allan Poe Society)

the mask of Comedy." She would tell of her latest family catastrophe then wait stolidly until she received a contribution to the basket—sometimes a chicken, clothing for Virginia, potatoes, turnips, or bread.

From the first, Maria Clemm gave her emotional and financial support to Poe's literary genius and backed his efforts to publish his early stories, and she offered him physical and mental support as well as emotional assistance throughout his career. When Poe died in 1849, she was devastated by the loss, writing to her friend Mrs. Annie RICHMOND, "my Eddie is *dead*. He died in Baltimore yesterday. Annie! pray for me, your desolate friend. My senses *will leave me*." Weeks before his death, Poe had unexplained asked Rufus GRISWOLD to edit his works in the case of his sudden death, a request to which Griswold had agreed. Griswold also acquired the copyright to the works at that time and later refused to turn it over to Mrs. Clemm when Poe died. Instead, in order to publish the material with an appearance of credibility, he asked that she endorse him as executor of Poe's literary estate and as editor of the works, which she did in a Preface to the first volume of Griswold's 1850 edition. For her efforts, she received several sets of the published works, which she tried to sell to raise money on which to survive. Left without a home at Poe's death, she lived with friends at different times in Richmond and Fordham before returning to Baltimore in 1858. On February 16, 1871, she died in the Church Home and Infirmary, formerly named the Baltimore City Marine Hospital, where Poe himself had died in 1849.

Clemm, Reverend William T. D. (1816–1892) Minister of the Methodist Episcopal Church and Virginia CLEMM's first cousin. Described as "cold-blooded and unchristianlike" by one observer, he read the three-minute burial service at Poe's funeral on October 8, 1849.

Clemm, Virginia (1822–1847) Poe's first cousin and child bride. Born on August 22, 1822, Virginia was seven years old when Poe moved into the household of her widowed mother Maria CLEMM in August 1829, four months after his discharge from the army. For six years, Poe used the Clemm household—which also included Maria's son Henry, an intermittent drinker; Poe's paralytic grandmother (and Maria's mother) old Mrs. David Poe, who had been bedridden for two years; and his alcoholic older brother William Henry Leonard POE, who suffered from advanced tuberculosis—as his home base while he traveled to Richmond and elsewhere to publish his writing and to secure a living. During most of that time, he treated Virginia simply as his young cousin whom he called "Sis" or "Sissie." Accounts of the very young Virginia describe her as having brown hair and violet eyes and being a lively and somewhat plump child who exuded good health and vitality. In 1832, when Poe fell in love with Mary DEVEREAUX, a young woman who lived near the Clemms, then-ten-year-old Virginia played the role of messenger, carrying love letters between the two. After his grandmother and brother died and Maria's son went to sea, Poe felt a responsibility for the security of Maria and Virginia, with whom he had formed the first happy family unit in his life. In 1834, Poe expressed his love for the intelligent and beautiful 12-year-old Virginia, 13 years his junior, and proposed marriage. He tried to obtain a teaching position at Richmond Academy to provide a stable income for his new life, and while he was in Richmond, his second cousin Neilson POE, who had married Virginia's half-sister, offered to take Virginia into his household and to care for her until she was of what he considered to be a more suitable age for marriage. Virginia and her mother took pity on Edgar, who had written desperate letters to them in which he had expressed his passionate love for Virginia and begged her to reject Neilson's offer. In a threatening and agonizing letter sent on August 29, 1835, Poe wrote, "Virginia, My love, my own sweetest Sissy, my darling little wifey, think well before you break the heart of your cousin."

In October, when Poe was rehired by the *SOUTHERN LITERARY MESSENGER*, Virginia and Maria joined him in Richmond. After seven months, on May 16, 1836, the 13-and-a-half-year-old Virginia and the 27-year-old Poe were married. A witness swore that Virginia was 21. Poe made every effort to develop Virginia's intellectual and social abilities, tutoring her in the classics, algebra, and other academic subjects, and he stretched his meager income to provide her with singing and piano lessons. Her sweet disposition and complete adoration of her "Eddie" made the first six years of marriage a time of emotional peace for the little household. Witnesses have stated that for the first two years, Poe continued to sleep apart from Virginia, but they began a normal married life when she turned 16, which continued until she experienced her first hemorrhage from tuberculosis when she was 20. From all accounts, the young wife remained childlike, plump and sweet-tempered throughout most of these six years. In 1842, after a period of severe financial strain, Virginia lost considerable weight and became ill. On January 20, 1842, while

This likeness of Virginia Clemm, the only one in existence, was painted a few hours after she died. (Edgar Allan Poe Society)

she was playing the piano and singing to amuse her husband, a blood vessel in her throat broke and blood began to gush from her mouth. Little more than five years later, on January 30, 1847, Virginia died. In the intervening years from the first serious evidence of her illness, Virginia had become an invalid, and her increasingly fragile health and the destruction of her body by tuberculosis sent Poe into deep depression. He lived in daily fear of her death, and the pain of watching her body waste away stayed with him until his own death. In a letter to John INGRAM, dated January 4, 1848, Poe wrote:

> This "evil" was the greatest that can befall a man. Six years ago, a wife, whom I loved as no man ever loved before, ruptured a blood-vessel in singing. Her life was despaired of. I took leave of her forever, and underwent all the agonies of her death. She recovered partially, and I again hoped. At the end of a year, the vessel broke again. I went through precisely the same scene. . . . Then again—again—and even once again, at varying intervals. Each time I felt all the agonies of her death—and at each accession of the disorder I loved her more dearly and clung to her life with more desperate pertinacity. But I am constitutionally sensitive—nervous in a very unusual degree. I became insane, with long intervals of horrible insanity. During these fits of absolute unconsciousness, I drank—God only know how often or how much. As a matter of course, my enemies referred the insanity to the drink, rather than the drink to the insanity. I had, indeed, nearly abandoned all hope of a permanent cure, when I found one in the *death* of my wife. This I can and do endure as becomes a man. It was the horrible, never-ending oscillation between hope and despair which I could *not* longer have endured, without total loss of reason. In the death of what was my life, then, I received a new but—Oh God!—how melancholy existence.

Many critics have seen the influence of Virginia's five years of dying in Poe's work during those years, especially in works that focus upon death in life, such as "ELEONORA," "BERENICE," "LIGEIA," and "THE FALL OF THE HOUSE OF USHER." The madness of which Poe speaks in this letter and in other communications becomes the madness of the narrators of "THE CASK OF AMONTILLADO," "THE TELL-TALE HEART," and "THE BLACK CAT." Although "ANNABEL LEE" may reflect their relationship, it is "ULALUME," published in December 1847, that was inspired by Virginia's death and which Poe made clear was a memorial to his late wife.

Clemm, William, Jr. (1779–1826)   Husband of Maria CLEMM. William, a Baltimore widower with five children and a little property when he married Maria, had previously been married to her first cousin, Harriet Poe.

When he died, his property was left to the children of his first marriage.

"Clinton Bradshaw; or the Adventures of a Lawyer. Philadelphia: Carey, Lea & Blanchard"   Review of F. W. Thomas's novel published in the December 1835 issue of the SOUTHERN LITERARY MESSENGER. Poe states that he has "no doubt that this book will be a favorite with many readers," but he finds the novel "the very worst species of imitation, *the paraphrasical.*" The review compares the work with *Henry Pelham, or the Adventures of a Gentleman,* a 1828 novel by Edward BULWER-LYTTON, and finds Thomas's work lacking. Although Poe claims to "dislike the novel, considered *as a novel,*" he admits that "some detached passages are very good" and identifies that "the chief excellence of the book consists in a certain Flemish caricaturing of vulgar habitudes and action."

Cloud, C. F.   Owner and publisher of the BALTIMORE SUNDAY VISITER. His move in 1834 to replace Lambert WILMER with John H. HEWITT as editor of the publication deprived Poe of a friendly home for his writing.

Cocke, John Hartwell (1780–1866)   An acquaintance of John ALLAN who served as host to the Allans and two-year-old Poe during the 1811 Christmas holidays. The Virginia planter and planner worked with Thomas JEFFERSON in creating the University of Virginia.

Cock-neighs   The "men-vermin" or "man-animals" in Poe's "THE THOUSAND-AND-SECOND TALE OF SCHEHERAZADE." They have the size and shape of men, "altogether resembling them, except they wore no garments (as men do)." They attach themselves to the back of a "sea-beast" and goad it through "their nibblings and stingings" into "that degree of wrath which was requisite to make it roar and commit ill." The narrator of the tale presumes that they are called Cock-neighs, "because their language formed the connecting link between that of the horse and that of the rooster."

Cognoscenti, Arabella   Character in the short story "THE MAN THAT WAS USED UP," her last name means "one in the know." She is one of two "exquisite specimens of affability and omniscience" with whom the narrator of the story converses when he visits the box overlooking the stage during a play at the Rantipole Theatre. Asked about General John A. B. C. SMITH, she calls him "a great man!—perfect desperado—immortal renown—prodigies of valor!" Her short attention span and failure to make sense in her conversation frustrates the narrator, who abruptly leaves her company.

Cognoscenti, Miranda   Character in the short story "THE MAN THAT WAS USED UP," her last name means "one in the know." The narrator of the story describes her and her sister Arabella COGNOSCENTI as "those exquisite specimens of affability and omniscience." When he questions them about General A. B. C. SMITH, Miranda asks, "Did you ever behold a finer figure?" She expresses her adoration of the general and tells the narrator of Smith's "inimitable grace," "just appreciation of stage effect," and "delicate sense of the true beauties of Shakespeare."

Coleridge, Samuel Taylor (1772–1834)   English Romantic poet and literary critic to whom Poe owed most of his theory of poetry. Poe was highly familiar with Coleridge's "Rime of the Ancient Mariner," "Christabel," "Kubla Khan," and *Biographia Literaria,* which he described in the review "LETTERS, CONVERSATIONS AND RECOLLECTIONS OF S. T. COLERIDGE" as "the most deeply interesting of the prose writings of Coleridge." He expresses surprise that American publishers have not published the work in America and states that it "affords a clearer view into his mental constitution than any of his other works." Poe extracted substantial material from chapter 14 of the work and used it to develop and elaborate his own canons for both writing and critiquing verse, including some of it verbatim in his famous lecture on "THE POETIC PRINCIPLE."

"The Coliseum"   Poem by Poe that first appeared in the October 26, 1833, issue of the *BALTIMORE SUNDAY VISITER* and which he also included in the drama *POLITIAN.* The poem is a dark meditation in which the poet speaks of Rome's shadowy past and present of "grandeur, gloom, and glory." He speaks of the doomed fame of ancient Rome, now with "these crumbling walls; these tottering arcades / These mouldering plinths—these sad and blacken'd shafts." The destroyed surroundings of the poet contain "shattered cornices—this wreck—this ruin—these stones," as the poet hears sounds emerging "from all ruin" that still speak of hope. The stones of the Coliseum speak of their past glory and insist, "We are not impotent—we pallid stones / Not all our power is gone—not all our fame." The poet insists that the essence of ancient Rome's greatness still lives in his imagination and in the visions of those who retain the memories that "clothe us in a robe of more than glory."

Collyer, Robert   A druggist from Stonehaven, Scotland, who assured Poe in a letter dated December 16, 1845, and published in the *BROADWAY JOURNAL* that the account of reanimation appearing in "THE FACTS IN THE CASE OF M. VALDEMAR" was entirely plausible. Collyer claimed that he "did actually restore to active animation a person who died from excessive drinking of ardent spirits." He promised Poe that, upon receiving a reply to his letter, he would give a detailed account of his own experiences "in order to put at rest the growing impression that your account is merely a *splendid creation* of your own brain, not having any truth in fact."

"The Colloquy of Monos and Una"   Short story. The tale is an allegorical fantasy in the form of a celestial dialogue between two lovers, reunited centuries after their death. Critic have noted the similarity of thought between this tale and Poe's "CONVERSATIONS BETWEEN EIROS AND CHARMION," both of which examine the nature of existence after earthly death.

PUBLISHING AND DRAMATIZATION HISTORY

First published in the August 1841 issue of *GRAHAM'S MAGAZINE,* the story was later collected with eleven other tales in *TALES BY EDGAR A. POE,* published by Wiley & Putnam in 1845.

The story is preceded with an epigraph taken from SOPHOCLES' *Antigone* and translated by Poe as "These things are in the future."

No film to date has been made of the tale.

CHARACTERS

MONOS, UNA.

PLOT SYNOPSIS

The tale consists entirely of a dialogue between two characters, Monos ("the single one") and Una ("the one") on the nature of death. In the opening lines, Una poses the question "Born again?" to Monos, who answers that Death has resolved for him the meaning of those words. The exchange consists largely of Una posing questions and Monos providing profound explanations; yet it is Una who states, "in Death we have both learned the propensity of man to define the indefinable." To this, Monos provides a lengthy philosophical discussion on the nature of humankind's self-destructive nature, which has meant the "widest ruin as the price of highest civilization." The speakers recall their own deaths a century earlier, and Monos describes in painful detail his dying and death, the funeral preparations, the grieving by those left behind, and the bodily sensations remaining after death, including the ability to feel Una being buried above him in the grave. Monos describes the sensations of dying, including the hyperexcitation of his senses and his eerie awareness, as exhibiting more of life than he experienced while fully living. He disparages passion as "the affliction of an impure nature" that marks one who is not sufficiently devoted to transcending the earthly state to become worthy of inhabiting the paradise where pure spirits dwell. The tale ends with Monos expressing the peace that he felt when, at last, all form and sentience had left him and "for all this nothingness, yet for all this immortality, the grave was still a home, and the corrosive hours, co-mates."

Colquhon, Captain Character in THE NARRATIVE OF ARTHUR GORDON PYM. One of the many sea captains who have visited Tristan d'Acunha, he is the skipper of the American brig *Betsey,* which "touched at the largest of the islands for the purpose of refreshment." While there, he and his men planted onions, cabbages, potatoes, and numerous other vegetables, "an abundance of all which are now to be met with."

Colton, George Hooker (1818–1847) Editor of the AMERICAN WHIG REVIEW. In February 1845, he bought Poe's poem "THE RAVEN" for less than $20. Colton described the poem in an editorial as "one of the most felicitous specimens of unique rhyming which has for some time met our eye." In his profile of Colton in "THE LITERATI OF NEW YORK CITY," Poe described him as "a man of genius in his successful establishment of the magazine within so brief a period [one year]," yet stated that he could not "conscientiously call Mr. Colton a good editor. . . . His taste is rather unexceptionable than positively good. He has not, perhaps, sufficient fire within himself to appreciate it in others."

Colton, Walter A correspondent who wrote to Rufus GRISWOLD and praised his October 9, 1849, obituary that appeared in the NEW YORK TRIBUNE and slandered Poe. Colton wrote, "[I]t is terrific. . . . In literary execution it rivals the best passages in Macauley." He also claims to have known "something of Poe—something of the unfathomed gulfs of darkness out of which the lightning of his genius sent its scorching flashes," although Colton's name does not appear in Poe biographical materials.

"The Coming of the Mammoth—The Funeral of Time and Other Poems. By Henry B. Hirst, Boston: Philips & Sampson" Review of a poetry collection by the young Philadelphia lawyer Henry B. HIRST that appeared in the July 12, 1845, issue of the BROADWAY JOURNAL. Although Poe praised extravagantly Hirst's "commendable poems," stating that "his versification is superior to that of any American poet" and claiming that "'Isabelle' is the finest ballad ever written in this country," he also observes that the poet "is apt to *overdo* a good thing." Poe identifies Hirst's defects as including "a want of constructive ability, occasional extravagance of expression, and a far more than occasional imitativeness," and he asserts that "there is nothing in the book which is fairly entitled to be called original,

either in its conception, execution, or manner, as a whole." The title poem "The Coming of the Mammoth" attracts Poe's harshest criticism. He observes that it is one of Hirst's earliest literary efforts, and that the author "began to write at a very immature age." After quoting from two passages in which a mammoth pursued by aborigines first leaps across the Mississippi River in one bound, then ascends a summit of the Rocky Mountains, from which it leaps to the Pacific Ocean, Poe mocks the author and notes that "from the summit of the Rocky Mountains to the Pacific is a tolerably long leap even for a Mammoth—although he had had some previous practice in jumping the Mississippi." He states that this work is "the most preposterous of all the preposterous poems ever deliberately printed by a gentleman arrived at the years of discretion. Nor has it one individual point of redeeming merit. Had Mr. Hirst written only this we should have thrown his book to the pigs without comment."

Commodus, Emperor Lucius Aelius Aurelius (A.D. 161–192) Emperor of Rome from 180 to 192. His reign was marked by personal extravagance, violence, and license. He gloried in his strength and participated in gladitorial combat. He also demanded to be worshiped as a god and became the object of numerous assassination attempts. He was murdered in 192. In "THE ASSIGNATION," Poe compares the appearance of the mysterious Byronic stranger to those of the emperor: "his were features than which I have seen none more classically regular, except, perhaps, the marble ones of the Emperor Commodus."

The Conchologist's First Book See PREFACE AND INTRODUCTION TO *THE CONCHOLOGIST'S FIRST BOOK,* 1839.

"Confessions of a Poet, 2 vols. Carey, Lea, and Blanchard" Review of an unsigned novel that appeared in the April 1835 issue of the SOUTHERN LITERARY MESSENGER. The author was first assumed to be John NEAL because of the colloquial tone and the flighty and irregular manner of the narrative, but Laughton OSBORN was identified as the author after the newspapers "unscrupulously misrepresented and abused" the work. Osborn retaliated by publishing what Poe described as "a bulky satirical poem, leveled at critics in general." Poe was unmerciful in his estimation of the work and began his review by stating, "The most remarkable feature in this production is the bad paper on which it is printed, and the typographical ingenuity with which matter barely enough for one volume has been spread over the pages of two." Although he concedes that there is "some merit in this book, and not a little satisfaction," he determines that "the author has very few claims to the sacred name [poet] he has thought proper to assume" and declares that "none but *le vulgaire* [the common or low individual], to speak poetically, will ever think of getting through with the confessions."

"The Confessions of Emilia Harrington. By Lambert A. Wilmer. Baltimore"　Review of Lambert A. Wilmer's novel that appeared in the February 1836 issue of the SOUTHERN LITERARY MESSENGER. Poe praises "the simple verisimilitude of his narrative" and claims that the novel, which is written as the memoir of a young woman who goes morally astray, "will render essential services to virtue in the unveiling of the deformities of vice," for it supports the viewpoint that "ignorance of wrong is not security for the right." Although he finds the work highly believable and praises. Wilmer's style as both good itself and well adapted to his subject, Poe maintains, "Yet, unhappily, books thus written are not the books by which men acquire a contemporaneous reputation."

"The Conqueror Worm"　Poem first published in the January 1843 issue of GRAHAM'S MAGAZINE and later included in Poe's THE RAVEN AND OTHER POEMS, published in 1845 by Wiley & Putnam. The poem was also incorporated into the text of "LIGEIA" when the story was reprinted in the September 27, 1845, issue of the BROADWAY JOURNAL. Poe made the poem the dying words of the doomed LIGEIA to correct the impression that Ligeia's return suggested too strongly that she has successfully escaped death. The poem characterizes life as a struggle between mankind and the inevitable death, a "play is the tragedy, Man / And its hero, the conqueror Worm." The Worm, which is death, achieves its end amid ". . . much of Madness, and more of Sin / And Horror, the soul of the plot!" As mankind engages in this battle of horror, the "pallid and wan" angels fail to act on behalf of humans and, instead, seem amused by the struggle. Although originally published separately from the tale, the poem is represented as the creation of Ligeia, and it functions to reveal her anxiety about the decay of the body and her desire to escape death. The death envisioned in the poem is violent: "And the seraph sob at vermin fangs / In human gore imbued."

"The Conquest of Florida by Hernando De Soto. By Theodore Irving. Philadelphia: Carey, Lea & Blanchard"　Review appearing in the July 1835 issue of the SOUTHERN LITERARY MESSENGER. Poe declares the work "one of great interest . . . which Mr. Irving has presented in a most attractive form." Praising the conquests and explorations of the Spanish adventurers, Poe declares them to be suitably represented in Irving's work, which "abounds with thrilling passages." The review contains brief descriptions of the conquest of Florida by Hernando de Soto, as well as the adventures of Ponce de Leon, who sought the Fountain of Youth in what is now Florida; Vasquest de Ayllon, the ruthless kidnapper; Pamphilo de Narvaez, the well-known rival and opponent of Hernando Cortez, conqueror of Mexico. Poe claims that once someone begins to read the book, it is impossible to "lay it aside until its perusal is concluded," but refuses to attribute this fascination to "the merit of the writer or his subject (probably it is a combination of both)."

"Conti the Discarded: with Other Tales and Fancies, by Henry F. Chorley. 2 vols. New York: Published by Harper and Brothers"　Review by Poe that appeared in the February 1836 in the SOUTHERN LITERARY MESSENGER. Poe identifies the author of the work as a man from whose pen "evidences of rare genius have been perceptible," and claims that in the current work of eight tales and essays "these evidences are more distinct, more brilliant, and more openly developed." Discussion of the tales leads Poe to undertake a lengthy digression on the stature of the artist, and to ask, "When *shall* the artist assume his proper situation in society—in a society of thinking beings? How long shall he be enslaved? How long shall mind succumb to the grossest materiality?" To his own questions, Poe optimistically responds, "Not long. Not long will such rank injustice be committed or permitted." He proceeds to identify the superior qualities in Chorley's stories. He bestows the highest praise upon the collection of tales, that "it bears no little resemblance to that purest, and most enthralling of fictions, the Bride of Lammermuir [sic]; and we have once before expressed our opinion of this, the master novel of Scott."

"A Continuation of the Voluminous History of the Little Longfellow War—Mr. Poe's Further Reply to the Letter of Outis"　The subtitle of a series of five articles written by Poe and published in the BROADWAY JOURNAL in response to a letter published in the New York EVENING MIRROR on March 1, 1845, and signed "Outis," the Greek word for "Nobody." The writer claims to have written the letter "from no personal motives, but simply because, from my earliest reading of reviews and critical notices, I have been disgusted with this wholesale mangling of victims without rhyme or reason." "Outis" castigates Poe both for his recent attack on Henry Wadsworth LONGFELLOW in a February 28, 1845, lecture before the Society Library and for earlier negative comments regarding and charges of plagiarism in Longfellow's works in reviews published from 1838 to 1842. (*See* "HYPERION: A ROMANCE," "VOICES OF THE NIGHT," "BALLADS AND OTHER POEMS," and "THE AMERICAN DRAMA.") Moreover, the anonymous "Outis" points out similarities between "THE RAVEN" and an anonymously published poem titled "The Bird of the Dream," but the writer states, "I shall not charge Mr. Poe with plagiarism—for, as I have said, such charges are perfectly absurd. Ten to one, he never saw this before." Yet, the letter lists 15 "identities" of similar content in the two poems, "without a word of *rhythm, metre or stanza, which should never form a part of such a comparison."

In reviews of Longfellow's work, Poe had written that the poet plagiarized liberally in producing much of his writing, most markedly in "The Spanish Student," which Poe claimed was stolen from his drama POLITIAN, and "The Beleaguered City," which Poe asserted bore an undeniable resemblance to "THE HAUNTED PALACE." Poe had also charged that Longfellow's "Midnight Mass for the Dying Year" was plagiarized from Alfred, Lord Tennyson's "Death of the Old Year" and that several of his collected ballads, significantly "The Good George Campbell," were plagiarized from William Motherwell's *Minstrelsy Ancient and Modern,* published in Glasgow in 1827.

Each of the five replies to "Outis" presents a different focus in the rebuttal. In "Imitation—Plagiarism—Mr. Poe's Reply to the Letter of Outis," which appeared in the March 8, 1845, issue of the *Broadway Journal,* Poe quotes liberally from the letter by "Outis" and lists the 15 "identities" of similarity between "The Raven" and the anonymous "The Bird of the Dream," mocking their validity without further discussion.

In the second reply, published in the March 15, 1845, issue of the *Broadway Journal,* Poe focuses directly on the issue of plagiarism. He claims to afford "Outis" the opportunity of "fair play," as he admits "not only the possibility of the class of coincidences for which he contends, but even the impossibility of there not existing just as many of these coincidences as he may consider necessary to make out his case." Poe ends this section of the reply with the promise "that there will be some 'interesting developments' before I have done."

The third reply to the letter from "Outis," published in the March 22, 1845, issue of the *Broadway Journal,* consists largely of Poe's methodical refutation of the similarities cited in the charge that he plagiarized "The Raven." He claims that "Outis" forced a similarity between the two poems, and that so lengthy a poem would naturally call to mind myriad similarities to others. Poe ends the article with the promise, not to be kept, that "in the next number of the Journal, I shall endeavour to bring this subject to an end."

The article appearing in the March 29, 1845, issue of the *Broadway Journal* opens with a virulent attack on "the Outises who practise this species of bullyism" who are guilty of "insufferable cant and shameless misrepresentation practised by just such persons." To counter the charge by "Outis" that Poe's "wholesale mangling

of the victims without rhyme and reason" was unpopular, Poe points out the increases in circulation in one year for the SOUTHERN LITERARY MESSENGER from 700 to nearly 5,000 and, "in little more than twice the same time," for GRAHAM'S MAGAZINE from "five to fifty-two thousand subscribers." He then reprints and methodically compares Longfellow's "Midnight Mass for the Dying Year" with Tennyson's "The Death of the Old Year," Longfellow's "The Good George Campbell" with Motherwell's "The Bonnie George Campbell," and Longfellow's "The Spanish Student" with sections from his own *Politian* to reaffirm his charge that Longfellow is a plagiarist. Poe ends the article with a suggestion that he would have no difficulty in citing numerous other instances of Longfellow's "imitation" and that he should be admired "for great moderation in charging him with imitation alone."

The final installment in the replies to "Outis" was published on April 5, 1845. Poe claims to have brought the issue to a close in the previous article and now feels "at liberty to add a few words of postscript, by way of freeing myself of any suspicion of malevolence or discourtesy." He discourses on the nature of "the poetic sentiment," which results in a rather strong defense of perceived borrowing by poets: "What the poet intensely admires, becomes thus, in fact, a portion of his own intellect. It has a secondary origination within his own soul—an origination altogether apart, although springing from its primary origination from without. The poet is thus possessed by another's thought, and cannot be said to take of it, possession . . . he thoroughly feels it as *his own."* Lest readers think that he is condoning plagiarism, Poe cautions that "the liability to accidents of this character is in the direct ratio of the poetic sentiment . . . for the most frequent and palpable plagiarisms, we must search the works of the most eminent poets."

"Contributions to the Ecclesiastical History of the United States of America—Virginia. A Narrative of Events Connected with the Rise and Progress of the Protestant Episcopal Church in Virginia. To Which Is Added an Appendix, Containing the Journals of the Conventions in Virginia, from the Commencement to the Present Time. By the Reverend Francis, L. Hawks, D.D., Rector of St. Thomas's Church, New York. New York: Published by Harper and Brothers" Review of a historical study published in the March 1836 issue of the SOUTHERN LITERARY MESSENGER. Poe praised the "large and handsome" appearance of the volume, but protests that his very cursory examination of the work "will not warrant us in speaking of the work in other than general terms." After his disclaimer, Poe cites specific pages of the work on which appear "a few of the most striking points of the History before us."

Although the review is generally positive, Poe criticizes references in the work to the historian George Bancroft, who had intimated in his own history of the United States that the Virginia colony had exhibited disloyalty during the protectorate of Oliver Cromwell. Poe answers the charges of disloyalty point by point, and in defense of Virginia he enjoins readers, "that through faith alone it remained a slave—and that its love of monarchy was a mere necessary consequence of its attachment to the Church of England." Poe later wrote in the April 1836 issue of the Southern Literary Messenger that an "injustice" had been done to Mr. Bancroft, "not only by ourselves, but by Dr. Hawks and others."

"The Conversation of Eiros and Charmion" Short story. The tale reflects the apocalyptic visions that obsessed many Americans in 1839. Four years earlier, Halley's Comet had appeared and many people were gripped in a frenzy that the end of the world was imminent. Poe's tale, with its vision of the earth being consumed in a fiery ball, suited the taste of the times.

PUBLISHING AND DRAMATIZATION HISTORY

The story appeared in the December 1839 issue of BURTON'S GENTLEMAN'S MAGAZINE, and it was simultaneously published in Poe's short story collection TALES OF THE GROTESQUE AND ARABESQUE in December 1839, although the title page read 1840.

The epigraph accompanying the story is taken from Euripides's drama Andromache: "I will bring fire to thee."

The tale has not been dramatized nor made into a film.

CHARACTERS

CHARMION, EIROS.

PLOT SYNOPSIS

The brief story consists solely of a dialogue between two characters, one dead 10 years and the other newly arrived on Aidenn. Their earthly names have been sloughed off with their earthly existences, and the two disembodied entities now must forget both as they begin to experience "the full joys and wonders" of this new existence. Charmion has preceded Eiros in death, and she cautions him that he will need time to adjust: "It is now ten earthly years since I underwent what you have undergone—yet the remembrance of it hangs by me still." Before enlightening Eiros about the adjustments they must make in "their perception of the new," however, Charmion asks for a detailed description of "that stupendous event which threw you among us." Most of the tale is devoted to Eiros's description of

events preceding the earth's destruction by collision with a comet. Their exchange reveals that the survival of the soul is not dependent upon moral, pious, or good behavior while alive on earth. Instead, the survival of the soul means the survival of the mind capable of pure thought. The explanation of "that last hour" that Eiros gives to Charmion is a lengthy and detailed mix of astronomy, philosophy, religion, chemistry, and human behavioral science. The combination of these studies leads earth's inhabitants into a false security, "As if by some sudden convulsive exertion, reason had at once hurled superstition from her throne. The feeblest understanding had derived vigor from excessive interest." Soon, as Eiros states, mankind was overtaken by "the bitterness of despair," as they realized their danger and understood that the scientists and not the theoreticians had been correct in their predictions. The world was destroyed in an instant. "For a short moment there was a wild lurid light alone, . . . then there came a great pervading sound, as if from the very mouth of HIM" before the world exploded into "a species of intense flame."

Converse, Reverend Amasa Clergyman who performed the wedding ceremony for Poe and Virginia CLEMM in Richmond, Virginia, on May 16, 1836. He was a Presbyterian minister who also edited the Southern Religious Telegraph. An account given years later by Jane Foster, then a child visiting the owner of the boarding house where the wedding took place, indicates that Converse remarked that the bride had a pleasing air, "'but did seem young.'" He described Mrs. Maria CLEMM, as "'polished, dignified, and agreeable in her bearing'" and as giving away Virginia "'freely.'"

Cook, Captain James (1728–1779) English navigator, marine explorer, and author to whose voyages Poe refers in THE NARRATIVE OF ARTHUR GORDON PYM and THE JOURNAL OF JULIUS RODMAN. Cook circumnavigated the South Pole with his ship Resolution and reached 70°10' latitude. The account of Cook's polar voyage appears at the beginning of chapter sixteen of The Narrative of Arthur Gordon Pym. In "Julius Rodman," Cook is mentioned in chapter one as a former associate of John LEDYARD, one of the earliest explorers of the northern United States.

Cools, Eugene (1877–1936) French composer of symphonic and dramatic music. In 1926, he wrote Hop-Frog: Poème symphonique d'après un conte d'Edgard Poe [Hop Frog: Symphonic Poem Based on a Tale by Edgar Poe], a symphony for dual piano accompaniment.

Corinnos Mentioned in "Shadow—A Parable" as "the artizan Corinnos" who has fashioned "a lofty door of brass . . . being of rare workmanship" that was fastened from within and which safeguards seven people "in a dim city called Ptolemais" who have locked themselves away during a "Pestilence" sometime in the distant past. The historical Corinnos is actually a poet who flourished during the Trojan War, but the reference might be an allusion to Corinth, where brassmaking was an art and the artisans included gold and silver in their brass.

Corman, Roger (1926–)   Hollywood producer-director who achieved his greatest fame as a director in the 1960s for the movies based on Edgar Allan Poe's stories, many of them starring Vincent PRICE. A graduate of Stanford University with an engineering degree, began his Hollywood career as a messenger at Twentieth Century–Fox, then rose to story analyst, after which he moved in 1955 to the newly formed American International Pictures. Corman's work includes science fiction, gangster melodramas, and biker movies, but his successful and stylish Poe-based horror films, created for American International Pictures, have drawn the greatest attention. In 1960, Corman had a box-office hit with his first Poe story, a version of "THE FALL OF THE HOUSE OF USHER." Eleven Poe-related stories followed, although most were loosely based on the works, sometimes associated only by title or the recitation of the relevant poem at the beginning or end of the movie. The following Corman-directed films starred Vincent Pirce: *The Pit and the Pendulum* (1961), *Tales of Terror* (1962), *The Raven* (1963), *The Masque of the Red Death* (1964), *The Haunted Palace* (1964), *The Tomb of Ligeia* (1965), *The City Under the Sea* (1965), *The Conqueror Worm* (1968), *The Oblong Box* (1969), and *Cry of the Banshee* (1970). Corman cast Ray Milland as the star of *The Premature Burial* (1962).

"Corse de Leon: Or the Brigand. A Romance, by G. P. R. James. Two Volumes. Harper and Brothers"   Review by Poe that appeared in the June 1841 issue of *GRAHAM'S MAGAZINE.* Poe provides readers with a fairly lengthy plot synopsis of this historical novel that is set in the time of the French king Henry II, then informs them that the novel is "largely of the common-place, and marred by the conclusion . . . which was introduced only for the purpose of introducing the famous death of Henry the Second, at a tournament." Poe exhibits even greater contempt for the characters, which he decrees to be "still more common-place." While two may be identified as "beneficent spirits" and two "are the evil geniuses," the remaining characters are condemned as "lifeless, common, and uncharacteristic. They make no impression, and you almost forget their names." Poe states that the principal character, Corse de Leon, mimics the characters of Edward BULWER-LYTTON in speaking philosophically, "and is altogether a plagiarism from that bombastic, unnatural,

cut-throat school." In Poe's final assessment, "this is but a readable novel, and a mere repetition of the author's former works."

Cowles, Walter Ruel (1881–1976)   American composer whose musical accompaniment for men's voices to Poe's poem "ELDORADO" was published in 1929 and part-song accompaniment for men's voices to Poe's poem "HYMN" was written for the University Glee Club in 1928.

Cowper, William (1731–1800)   English pre-Romantic poet who suffered from bouts of religious mania and intermittent attacks of insanity. His best-known work is "The Task," and its glorification of life in rural England is considered a precursor to the works of the English Romantic poet William Wordsworth. Poe used Cowper's lines from "Tirocinium" as an epigraph for *TAMERLANE AND OTHER POEMS* and praised Cowper's style in "MARGINALIA."

"Coxe's Saul"   A brief review of the Reverend Arthur Coxe's lengthy poem *Saul, A Mystery* that appeared in the September 6, 1845, issue of the *BROADWAY JOURNAL.* Poe reprints "The Retort," an unsigned poem that originally appeared in the *Hartford Columbian,* and defends Coxe's poem, after first stating that it had "been condemned in no measured terms by Poe of the Broadway Journal, and Green of the Emporium." Following the poem, Poe expresses his hope that "no one will think the worse of the one above when we say that we have expressed *no opinion whatsoever* of 'Saul'." Rather, he admits that "as yet we have not found time to read the poem—which, to say the truth, is an unconscionably long one."

Crab, Mr.   Character in the short story "THE LITERARY LIFE OF THINGUM BOB, ESQ." The editor of the magazine *Lollipop,* he appears to be involved in a heated professional and personal rivalry with another editor. After a lengthy discourse upon the unsavory characteristics of his rival publication, Crab shows his miserly nature when the young Thingum asks about remuneration for his work. Crab takes on the appearance of "a highly agitated elderly duck in the act of quacking." Speechless in his astonishment, Crab takes several minutes to recover, then informs the young writer that his magazine never pays for a first effort: "For the most part, we are *paid* for the insertion of a maiden attempt." Crab exhibits the same reaction whenever Thingum makes future attempts to be paid.

Cranch, Christopher Pearse (1813–1892)   American poet and minister whom Poe included among his "LITERATI OF NEW YORK CITY." Poe identified him as "one of the least intolerable of the school of Boston transcendalists" and commended his move to New York as having "reformed his habits of thought and speech." The review begins with an expression of sympathy for the poet, whose volume *Poems by Christopher Pearse Cranch* "was most unmercifully treated by the critics, and much injustice, in my [Poe's] opinion, was done to the poet." Poe states that "he seems to me to possess unusual vivacity of fancy and dexterity of expression, while his versification is remarkable for its accuracy, vigor, and even for its originality of effect," but he is also guilty of a "preference for Imagination's half sister, the Cinderella, Fancy. . . . There must always be, to afford him perfect satisfaction, a certain amount of the odd, of the whimsical, of the affected, of the *bizarre*." The reviewer finds such intentionally manufactured constructions to be artificial and declares of Cranch that "he has been at uncommon *pains* to make a fool of himself." The review ends with a discussion of "Niagara," which Poe declares to be one of his best poems but which also fails to please, for "it is difficult to conceive anything more ludicrously out of keeping."

"The Crayon Miscellany. By the Author of the Sketch Book No. 3—Containing Legends of the Conquest of Spain. Philadelphia: Carey, Lea & Blanchard"　Review that appeared in the December 1835 issue of the SOUTHERN LITERARY MESSENGER. Poe praises Washington Irving's collections of legends for their "beauty of style," and he singles out "The Story of the Marvelous and Portentous Tower" as supreme in the collection. Despite such praise, Poe acknowledges that Irving has simply taken "a few striking and picturesque legends possessing, at the same time, some absolute portion of verity, and to adorn them in his own magical language."

"The Crayon Miscellany, No.II. Containing Abbotsford and Newstead Abbey. Philadelphia: Carey, Lea & Blanchard. 1835"　Review that appeared in the July 1835 issue of the SOUTHERN LITERARY MESSENGER. Poe hails Washington Irving's descriptions of the homes of Sir Walter SCOTT and Lord BYRON as "the tribute of genius to its kindred spirits, and it breathes a sanctifying influence over the graves of the departed." The review relates that Irving provides a complete image of the surroundings within which Scott created the works that thrilled thousands of readers, while his descriptions also "give a melancholy interest to the early misfortunes of Byron." Unlike the earlier *Crayon Miscellany*, which dealt in legends, this work is based upon personal observation of the surroundings of two individuals who lived. Poe's assessment is that Irving manages to illuminate fully the characters of the two individuals in his sketches.

Crebillon, Prosper Jolyot de (1674–1762)　French dramatist. At the end of Poe's story "THE PURLOINED LETTER," detective C. Auguste DUPIN quotes the following lines from Crebillon's 1707 tragedy *Atrée et Thyeste*: "— Un dessein si funeste, / S'il n'est digne d'Atrée, est digne de Thyeste" [A design so deadly, even if not worthy of Atreus, is worthy of Thyestes]. The revenge tragedy is taken from Greek mythology and concerns the story of king Atreus of Mycenae who took revenge on his brother Thyestes for seducing his wife by murdering his nephews, Thyestes's sons, and serving them to Thyestes for dinner. After the meal, Thyestes pronounced a curse on the house of Atreus. Poe also refers to Crebillon in "MARGINALIA" and calls his work *The Age of Reason* "the half-profound, half-silly, and wholly irrational composition of a very clever, very ignorant, and laughably impudent fellow."

"Critical and Miscellaneous Essays. By T. Babington Macaulay. Carey and Hart, Philadelphia"　Review that appeared in the June 1841 issue of GRAHAM'S MAGAZINE. Poe began the review by declaring that Macauley's "deservedly great" reputation was "yet in a remarkable measure undeserved" and stated that those who viewed him as "a comprehensive and profound thinker, little prone to error, err essentially themselves." The misperception, Poe suggests, lay in "a tendency in the public mind toward logic for logic's sake" that leads people to "be so dazzled by the luminousness with which an idea is set forth as to mistake it for the luminousness of the idea itself." Although he approves of the terse style and "simple vigour" with which Macauley writes, Poe objects to the minutiae of detail contained within the writings that fail to address the subject of each essay as a whole. Poe concludes that "Mr. Macauley, in short, has forgotten that he frequently forgets, or neglects, the very gist of his subject."

"The Critical and Miscellaneous Writings of Henry Lord Brougham, to Which Is Prefixed a Sketch of His Character. Two Vols. Lea & Blanchard"　Review that appeared in the March 1842 issue of GRAHAM'S MAGAZINE in which Poe derided miscellaneous selections from the writings of Henry, Lord Brougham. The review praises "Discourse on the Objects, Pleasures and Advantages of Science" as a well-written essay but condemns it as abounding in misstatements and contestable facts and containing "the strangest grammatical errors." Poe scoffs at a statement in the preface to the work that decrees "there was only one individual living by whom it could have been produced" and professes to know "at least a dozen individuals who could have written this treatise *as well* as the Lord Chancellor has written it." The most severe criticism in the review appears near the end, as Poe examines Brougham's success with an article that considers the authorship of Junius. Poe's sharp criticism of the piece, which appeared in a recent issue of the *Edinburgh Quarterly,* as having made "no attempt at analysis—no new fact is adduced—no novel argument is urged—and yet the thing is called a criticism and liberally paid for as such" suggests envy for his own circumstances, which often were financially strained. He ends the review by declaring Brougham's work to be among "the ordinary character of the English review-system," which is "that of mystifying the reader by an artful substitution of the interest appertaining to the text for the interest aroused by the commentator."

Croissart, Mademoiselle Character in the short story "THE SPECTACLES." The eldest daughter of a banker, she marries at age 15 and becomes the mother of the protagonist of the story, Napoleon Bonaparte FROISSART.

Cross, Henry (1895–1978) American composer, organist and conductor who wrote musical accompaniment to Poe's poem "DREAM WITHIN A DREAM." Published in 1936, the piece is written for a full chorus of mixed voices in eight parts *a cappella* with pianoforte accompaniment for rehearsal only.

cryptography Poe established his reputation as a cryptographer by creating and solving cryptographs in *ALEXANDER'S WEEKLY MESSENGER.* In December 1839, Poe issued a challenge to readers to solve cryptograms that appeared in the publication, motivating a strong reader response and increasing circulation. When Poe moved to *GRAHAM'S MAGAZINE,* he took the interest with him. In July 1841, Poe's article "A Few Words about Secret Writing" presented his cryptographic principles and motivated letters from readers and attempted solutions to the puzzles that he included in the article and in three supplements that were added to the August, October, and December issues. Poe's interest in cryptographs was confined to his nonfiction and appears in his fiction only in "THE GOLD-BUG," in which he included a simple cryptograph. Modern cryptographic experts rank very highly Poe's skills in decoding.

Cullum, George Washington Fellow cadet with Poe at West Point. He rose to the rank of general and later recalled Poe as "slovenly, heedless, and eccentric, and more inclined to the making of verses than the solving of equations."

"The Culprit Fay, and Other Poems, By Joseph Rodman Drake. New York: George Dearborn" A review, known as the Drake-Halleck review, which appeared in the April 1836 issue of the *SOUTHERN LITERARY MESSENGER.* In the same article, Poe also reviewed "ALNWICK CASTLE"

by Fitz Greene HALLECK. Before dealing directly with the works, the review considers the "present state of American criticism" that has become "boisterous and arrogant in the pride of a too speedily assumed literary freedom." He decries the tendency of those who choose to encourage native writers at the expense of writing quality and condemns the "misapplied patriotism" that leads his contemporaries to "the gross paradox of liking a stupid book the better, because, sure enough, its stupidity is American." The review also dedicates significant space to examining the nature of imagination and the "the sentiment of Poesy," which Poe asserts to be "the sentiment of Intellectual Happiness here, and the Hope of a higher Intellectual Happiness hereafter." One-third of the way through the article, Poe discusses *The Culprit Fay and Other Poems,* a poem of 640 lines divided into 36 stanzas. The review ridicules the premise of the poem, which relates the tribulations of an Ouphe, one member of a race of fairies living in the vicinity of West Point on the Hudson River in New York State. He has broken fairy law by falling in love with a mortal and, after suffering for his sin, is eventually redeemed by the love of his "sinless mistress." Poe states that the greater part of the poem "is utterly destitute of any evidence of imagination whatever" and pleads "guilty to a predominant sense of the ludicrous while occupied in the perusal of the poem." This disdain for the poem remained with Poe, who referred to the poem as Drake's "puerile abortion" in a review of "ALCIPHRON" in 1840.

Curtis, Mrs. Adelaide Character mentioned in the short story "THE OBLONG BOX." She is the artist's mother-in-law living in Albany, New York, to whom the mysterious box is addressed.

Cushing, Caleb (1800–1879) American statesman and Boston orator who served in the U.S. House of Representatives from 1835 to 1843, then became U.S. commissioner to China under President John Tyler. He preceded Poe on the program at the Lyceum's Odeon Theater lecture series on October 16, 1845. Cushing delivered a long lecture on Great Britain before Poe's reading of "AL AARAAF." When Poe wrote of the occasion in "BOSTON AND THE BOSTONIANS," he wrote of himself in the third person and stated that "Mr. Poe committed another error in consenting to address an audience in verse, who, for three mortal hours, had been compelled to sit and hear Mr. Caleb Cushing in prose. The attempt to speak after this, in poetry, and fanciful poetry, too, was sheer madness."

Cuvier, Baron Georges Léopold Chrétien Frédéric Dagobert (1769–1832) French naturalist and a founder of the studies of comparative anatomy and

D——, Minister Character in the short story "THE PURLOINED LETTER." He steals a letter from "the royal apartments" with the intent of blackmailing "a personage of most exalted station" in the hope of political gain. Described as a man "who dares all things, those unbecoming as well as those becoming a man," he acquires the incriminating letter by exchanging it for a worthless one of his own. To fool the police, who are thorough in their search of his premises and person, he places the letter in an obvious place in plain sight, knowing that it will be overlooked during a search.

Dagon God of fertility worshipped by the Philistines and throughout the ancient Middle East, whose name with others the Pharisee calls out in trying to understand the nature of the pagan gods mentioned by the Roman soldier in "A TALE OF JERUSALEM."

Daguerre, Louis (1789–1851) French painter and inventor of the daguerreotype process, the art of photography on metal plates that is the precursor to modern photography. Poe refers to Daguerre in "THE THOUSAND-AND-SECOND TALE OF SCHEHERAZADE" as having "directed the sun to paint his portrait, and the sun did."

Dammit, Toby Character in "NEVER BET THE DEVIL YOUR HEAD." He begins life as a child precocious in vice: "At five months of age, he used to get into such passions that he was unable to articulate. At six months, I caught him gnawing a pack of cards. At seven months he was in the constant habit of catching and kissing the female babies. At eight months he peremptorily refused to put his signature to the Temperance pledge." By the age of one, he not only insists upon wearing "moustaches" but also he contracts "a propensity for cursing and swearing, and for backing his assertions by bets." As a man, his favorite wager is "I'll bet the Devil my head." When he wagers that he can jump a bridge turnstile and his head collides with a bridge support, he loses both the bet and his head.

Daniel, John Moncure (1825–1865) Editor of the RICHMOND EXAMINER whom Poe challenged to a duel in August 1848, after he had questioned the motive of Poe's attentions to Sarah Helen WHITMAN. Daniel refused to take the challenge seriously, and, after a meeting in which he offered Poe use of his pistols to duel in the newspaper office, the two men reconciled and no duel took place. His article in the March 1850 issue of the SOUTHERN LITERARY MESSENGER praised Poe for being "all times passionately genuine" and whose "complexity of his intellect, its incalculable resources" marked Poe's literary brilliance.

Daphne The little village in "FOUR BEASTS IN ONE" that contains a temple to the goddess of the same name. It is situated next to Antiochia Epidaphne, the actual site of the story.

"Dashes At Life with a Free Pencil. By N. P. Willis. Part III. Loiterings of Travel. New York. J. S. Redfield" A review that appeared in the August 23, 1845, issue of the BROADWAY JOURNAL. Poe was highly complimentary of the author's skills and spoke of Willis as "one of the *truest* men of letters in America" whose works "show his fine genius as *it is*." He finds Willis and the work to be free of the "unoriginal mediocrity" that marks most literary men and their endeavors in his day.

Davidson, Lucretia Maria (1808–1825) American child poet whose poem "Amir Khan" (1829) contains a reference to "Israfil." Critics suggest that the reference may have provided inspiration to Poe for his poem "ISRAFEL." He reviewed her work in the "POETICAL REMAINS OF THE LATE LUCRETIA MARIA DAVIDSON," published in the December 1841 issue of GRAHAM'S MAGAZINE. The cause of death is distinctly vague in the few accounts that exist of her life. Writing in 1869, Caroline May asserted that her health was "always, very feeble." One month before her 17th birthday, "the strength of affection and the skill of physicians, however, failed to restore it."

Davis, Dr. Hugh Wythe Nephew of Dr. Creed THOMAS, Poe's deskmate at Burke's School in Richmond, Virginia. When Thomas died in 1899, Davis wrote his obituary. It included numerous details about the friends that Poe and his uncle held in common and about their early adventures. The obituary helped to dispel other accounts including that by Rufus W. GRISWOLD that Poe as a boy was a loner or that "no one knew him."

Davy, Sir Humphry (1778–1829) English chemist and inventor. His experiments with gases led him to discover the anesthetic effects of nitrous oxide (laughing gas). He also conducted experiments with electrical current. In "VON KEMPELEN AND HIS DISCOVERY," the narrator makes reference to the "Diary" of Sir Humphry Davy and demonstrates von Kempelen's debt to the British scientist for his discovery.

Dawes, Rufus (1803–1859) Baltimore poet and editor of the *Minerva and Emerald*, which in 1829 printed an unfavorable review of Poe's "AL AARAAF" that unmercifully poked fun at the new poet. Poe's anger simmered for seven years, then erupted in a scathing denunciation of Dawes's abilities in "AUTOGRAPHY" in 1836. Poe asserted that Dawes was in style "the most inflated, involved, and falsely-figurative of any of our more noted poets. . . . His apparent erudition is mere verbiage, and, were it real, would be lamentably out of place where we see it." Fourteen years after the initial insult, Poe wrote a devastating critique of Dawes's poetry titled "THE POETRY OF RUFUS DAWES—A RETROSPECTIVE," which appeared in the October 1842 issue of *GRAHAM'S MAGAZINE.*

Day, Frederic Lansing (1890–1975) American dramatist and composer who created music to accompany Poe's "THE FALL OF THE HOUSE OF USHER," which he also dramatized. The music consists of a song for solo voice, a chant for solo voice, and a group dance as the setting for the poem "THE HAUNTED PALACE," which Poe included in "The Fall of the House of Usher." The play appears in seven short scenes, with brief entr'actes that occur in darkness, during which strains of the music are heard.

Debussy, Claude-Achille (1862–1918) Master French impressionist composer whose best-known works are the symphonic poem *Prélude à l'après-midi d'un faune* (*Prelude to the Afternoon of a Faun;* 1892) and his masterwork lyric drama *Pelléas et Mélisande,* completed in 1903, among numerous other compositions. At his death in 1918, Debussy left two unfinished operas on Poe themes, *Le Diable dans le Beffroi* ["THE DEVIL IN THE BELFRY"] and *La Chute de la Maison Usher* ["THE FALL OF THE HOUSE OF USHER"], on which he had been at work for years and which obsessed him. In a 1902 letter to André Messager, Debussy stated: "Don't mention this to anyone; I am very much taken. . . . I have got into the way of thinking of nothing else but 'Roderick Usher' and 'The Devil in the Belfry.' . . . I fall asleep with them, and I awake either to the gloomy sadness of the former or to the sneers of the latter." He viewed the potential play based on "The Devil in the Belfry" as "a happy blending of the real and the fantastic." Rather than to use traditional staging to present the devil, he sought to create one which would be "cynical and cruel—much more devilish than the red, brimstone-breathing clown that has, so illogically, become a tradition with us. I should also like to put an end to the idea that the devil is the spirit of evil. He is simply the spirit of contradiction." The devil would also remain silent throughout the play and only whistle, and the one singing part would be that of the crowd. The composer also told friends that he had become obsessed with the "'heir of the Usher family'" and had nearly finished a long monologue of "poor Roderick's. It is sad enough to draw tears from a stone."

Had Debussy completed the two operas, their first performances would have been at the Metropolitan Opera in New York, which had secured the rights to the works in progress. Signor Guilio Gatti-Casazza, the former impresario of the opera house, insisted that Debussy sign the agreement and pressed upon him a modest advance despite the composer's warning that he was a lazy writer who took weeks to write a few bars of music. Prophetically, Debussy also told Gatti-Casazza, "Remember also that you are the one who insisted on making this agreement and that probably you will not receive anything."

"Dedication to Poe's Poems, Edition of 1845" Originally titled *THE RAVEN AND OTHER POEMS* but commonly referred to "The Edition of 1845," the volume contained 30 poems that had been printed previously in such publications of Poe's time as the *SOUTHERN LITERARY MESSENGER, GRAHAM'S MAGAZINE,* and the *BROADWAY JOURNAL.* Published by Wiley & Putnam in New York, the volume contained Poe's glowing dedication to the English poet Elizabeth BARRETT Browning:

> To the Noblest of her Sex—To the Author of 'The Drama of Exlie'—To Miss Elizabeth Barrett Barrett, of England, I Dedicate this Volume, with the most Enthusiastic Admiration, and with the most Sincere Esteem.—E. A. P.

Dee, Doctor Dubble L. Character in the short story "THREE SUNDAYS IN A WEEK." He does not appear directly in the story but is cited as an authority on "the extraordinary concurrence of events."

Defoe, Daniel (1659–1731) English novelist whom Poe admired for his power of verisimilitude in writing. In his 1836 review of Defoe's *The Life and Surprising Adventures of Robinson Crusoe* (1719), Poe praises the author for having "the faculty of *identification*—that dominion exercised by volition over imagination which enables the mind to lose its own, in a fictitious, individuality."

De Kock, Monsieur Character in the short story "THE SYSTEM OF DOCTOR TARR AND PROFESSOR FETHER." He pretends to be one of the caretakers of an asylum for the insane, but he is actually a patient who believes that he is a donkey. At intervals, he kicks violently to demonstrate his mania.

D'elormie Character in Poe's poem "BRIDAL BALLAD." He is the female narrator's first love, who dies in battle. Because her memory of him is strong, she is unable to give herself completely to a new husband.

De Hart, John The maternal grandfather of Miss Louisa Gabriella PATTERSON, the second wife of John ALLAN. De Hart was a member of the Continental Congress of 1774–76 from New Jersey and later attorney general of that state, as well as a wealthy and influential lawyer. In short, De Hart was the father of Poe's step-foster mother and a source of family prominence.

Delos In Greek mythology, the birthplace of the deities Apollo and Artemis. In "LIGEIA," Poe compares the maiden LIGEIA's beauty to that of the radiance of "the phantasies which hovered about the slumbering souls of the daughters of Delos."

Del Rio, Antonio Mentioned in "LIONIZING: A TALE" as one of several scientists whose works the narrator has read on the subject of noses.

Deluc, Madame Character in the short story "THE MYSTERY OF MARIE ROGÊT." She is the proprietor of a roadside inn not far from the bank of the river in which Marie ROGÊT's body is found floating. She tells investigators that Marie visited her inn in the company of a young man with a dark complexion and recalls that, after they left, "a gang of miscreants made their appearance, behaved boisterously, ate and drank without making payment, followed in the route of the young man and girl, returned to the inn about dusk, and re-crossed the river as if in great haste." She claims to have heard a woman screaming soon after dark and asserts that she recognizes a scarf found in the thicket and the dress on the corpse as belonging to the girl. Marie's relatives later identify the articles as hers.

Demon, the Character in Poe's short story "SILENCE— A FABLE." He is the demon of imagination who demands that the narrator of the tale listen to his story. The demon tells of finding a large gray rock into which is carved the word *desolation* and recounts a tale of having hidden and watched the actions of man who stands upon the summit of that rock and "who trembled in the solitude" as the demon creates chaos in the world around. When the demon has done his worst, the man remains steadfast, but the letters in the rock have transformed to form the word *silence*, leading the man to react in terror. The demon finishes his story then laughs at human frailty and becomes angry when the narrator does not join him in laughing.

De Quincey, Thomas (1785–1859) English writer, author of *Confessions of an English Opium Eater.* Critics have suggested that his influence is to be found in Poe's tales such as "THE ISLAND OF THE FAY" and poems such as "DREAM-LAND," as well as in "THE FALL OF THE HOUSE OF USHER," in which the narrator makes a blatant reference "to the after-dream of the reveller upon opium" in the opening paragraph of the story. Poe's sole direct reference to De Quincey appears in "HOW TO WRITE A BLACKWOOD ARTICLE," in which his Mr. BLACKWOOD names *Confessions of an Opium-eater* as one of the articles to be used as a "model or study." The assessment is decidedly unfavorable, as the speaker characterizes the article as "fine, very fine!—glorious imagination—deep philosophy—acute speculation— plenty of fire and fury, and a good spicing of the decidedly unintelligible. . . . It was composed by my pet baboon, Juniper, over a rummer of Hollands and water, 'hot, without sugar.' (This I scarcely would have believed had it been anybody but Mr. Blackwood, who assured me of it.)"

"A Descent Into the Maelstrom" Short story. The tale is one of Poe's most fantastic efforts of ratiocination, yet it remains believable in its methodical and logical account of the sole survivor of a shipwreck who is hurtled into a whirlpool and survives. In a review published in the January 1848 issue of the SOUTHERN LITERARY MESSENGER, the critic P. Pendleton Cooke observed that in the story "you are made fairly to feel yourself on the descending round of the vortex, convoying fleets of drift timber, and fragments of wrecks; the terrible whirl makes you giddy as you read."

PUBLISHING AND DRAMATIZATION HISTORY

The story was first published in the April 1841 issue of *GRAHAM'S MAGAZINE.* The story is preceded by Poe's paraphrase of an epigraph taken from Joseph Glanvill's essay "Against Confidence in Philosophy and Matters of Speculation," collected in *Essays on Several Important Subjects* (1676):

> The ways of God in Nature, as in Providence, are not as our ways; nor are the models that we frame any way commensurate to the vastness, profundity, and unsearchableness of His works, *which have a depth in them greater than the well of Democritis.*

The original is as follows:

The *ways* of God in *Nature* (as in *Providence*) are not as *ours* are: Nor are the models we frame any way commensurate to the vastness and profundity of his Works, which have a *Depth* in them greater than the *Well of Democritus.*

Democritus (born 460 B.C.) said that truth lies at the bottom of a well.

No film has been made of "Descent into the Maelstrom" to date, although elements of the tale appear in the silent film *The Raven* (1912) and in *War Gods of the Deep* (1965; also released as *City Under the Sea*).

CHARACTERS

Old man (survivor of the maelstrom), unnamed narrator.

PLOT SYNOPSIS

The story opens with a striking similarity to Samuel Taylor COLERIDGE's *Rime of the Ancient Mariner* (1798), in which a wild-eyed old man accosts wedding guests and seeks to tell them his horrendous story of shipwreck and survival. At the outset, the seemingly old man assures the narrator that he is not very old, and protests that "the six hours of deadly terror which I then endured have broken me up body and soul." He informs the narrator that his presumptions are incorrect. "You suppose me a *very* old man—but I am not. It took less than a single day to change these hairs from a jetty black to white, to weaken my limbs, and to unstring my nerves, so that I tremble at the least exertion, and am frightened at a shadow." The old man takes the narrator to the pinnacle of a cliff where they both gaze over the ocean and, as the mountain trembles, the narrator sees and feels a series of whirlpools that lead to the "the great whirlpool of the Maelstrom." Once the old man is certain the the narrator fully appreciates the power and mysteries of the maelstrom, he tells the story of how he and his two brothers, with their "schooner-rigged smack of about seventy tons of burthen" on which they fished, were pulled into the whirlpool. One brother grasped the mast in the effort to survive, while the second brother took hold of a ringbolt fastened to the ship, but their "sensible" efforts were in vain. The old man describes the descent of the ship and all its contents into the vortex. He explains that he used his powers of ratiocination and observed the movement of the objects around him before deciding to lash himself to a watercask rather than wait to go down with the ship. His action, which shows a remarkably detached self-control, is based on the observation that "the larger the bodies, the more rapid their descent." After several wild gyrations, the barrel "sunk very little than half the distance between the bottom of the gulf and the spot at which I leaped overboard," then the gyrations begin to lessen and finally cease. When a ship picks up the sole survivor, his hair has turned white in only one day and he is fatigued and speechless. Despite the change in his physical appearance, even those fishermen who knew him refused to believe his story.

Desoulières, Jules Character in "THE SYSTEM OF DOCTOR TARR AND PROFESSOR FETHER." An inmate of an insane asylum, "a very singular genius, indeed," who believes that he is a pumpkin. He persecutes the cook to make him up into pies—"a thing which the cook indignantly refused to do."

detective story Edgar Allan Poe is widely credited for having invented the modern detective story, a form of narrative fiction that focuses on a crime and its solution, and for establishing in C. Auguste DUPIN the model for the detective—either amateur or professional, a member of the official police force or a private investigator—who uses his intellectual powers to solve crime. In Poe's stories, as in those of his successors in the genre, the detective is the main protagonist, who must interrogate all suspects, elicit and identify clues, and ultimately track down the perpetrator, usually a murderer. Although the detective reveals all clues to the reader in a range of ways, the significance of the clues is not revealed until the end of the story. Poe's detective stories made the reader a witness who looked over the detective's shoulder. Poe's Dupin, a French detective hero, appeared in "THE MURDERS IN THE RUE MORGUE" (1841), "THE MYSTERY OF MARIE ROGET" (published over 1842 and 1843), and "THE PURLOINED LETTER" (1845). Dupin's remarkable powers of deduction and his idiosyncrasies—such as the desire to sequester himself from society and his procedure of entering the mind of the murderer—as well as the dual national association of a French detective created by an American writer, led to a range of successors both in the United States and abroad, the most famous of which was Sir Arthur Conan DOYLE's Sherlock Holmes. Doyle used Poe's technique of narrating his detective's exploits through the viewpoint of a companion, and he gave Holmes intellectual capabilities as well as bizarre habits similar to those of Dupin. Critics have also suggested that Agatha Christie had Poe's Dupin in mind in creating her Belgian detective Hercule Poirot, who insists that his powers of detection reside in his use of "the little gray cells" and whose idiosyncrasies are abundant.

De Vere, Guy Character in the poem "LENORE." He is Lenore's grieving lover. Although he fails to weep when he looks at her beautiful form lying on the funeral bier, the conflicting views that he expresses about her death as he rants throughout the poem show his deep devotion to her. De Vere accuses Lenore's family and friends of treating her in a cold and unfeeling manner while she was alive, and he states that in his love for her "No dirge will I upraise." Instead of mourning, he will sing a song of triumph as "her sweet soul" leaves the earth that caused her so many tears.

Devereaux, Mary   A neighbor of Maria CLEMM's in Baltimore who gave an extensive interview 40 years after Poe's death in which she claimed to have been his sweetheart during the first year after he moved to Baltimore. Her story was related in an article by Augustus Van CLEEF, titled "Poe's Mary," that appeared in the March 1889 issue of *Harper's New Monthly Magazine*. She relates that Poe often sent Virginia CLEMM to carry messages between the two, and that before Devereaux had actually met Poe, Virginia had appeared with his request for a lock of her bright auburn hair, a favor that she granted. Most of what she states simply confirms what is known about Poe's personality, especially that "he was passionate in his love" and that "his feelings were intense and he had but little control over them."

Her story of their breakup adds a sexual dimension to Poe that is absent from other accounts. Mary states that Poe failed to appear one evening until late, then appeared smelling of liquor. He excused himself by stating that he had met several cadets from West Point, and the group had gone to a local hotel for supper and champagne. He claimed that he had rushed to meet her as soon as he could, but their meeting soon erupted into a quarrel, and Mary ran into her house. She claims that Poe followed her and tried to go upstairs with her to her bedroom, but her mother blocked his way and told him to leave. A passionate Poe insisted that he would talk with Mary, shouting, "I have a right. She is my wife now in the sight of Heaven!" Mary broke off all contact with Poe and concluded the following: "He didn't value the laws of God or man. He was an atheist. He would just as lief have lived with a woman without being married to her as not. . . . I made a narrow escape in not marrying him." Unwilling to let the relationship end, Poe harassed Mary, and her uncle wrote a severe letter telling the Poe to desist. In that same article, Mary relates that the indignant poet confronted her uncle, "a man of over fifty at the time," at his store and "cowhided him" but became the worse for wear when Mary's aunts and two sons joined the struggle and tore Poe's frock coat before chasing him off.

Ten years later, in 1842, while Virginia lay on her deathbed, Poe went on a spree and tracked Mary to her home in Jersey City, New Jersey, where he demanded to know why she had married and if she had married for love.

devil, the (1)   Character in the short story "BON-BON." The devil visits Pierre BON-BON with the intention of snaring his soul, but later rejects it. This devil speaks in "a whining voice" that has "a shrill undertone." Possessed of an "exceedingly lean" figure, he is poorly dressed in clothing that is not only old-fashioned but also apparently made for "a much shorter person than their present owner," which leaves his ankles and wrists bare for several inches. In his too-tight suit of faded black cloth, he has the physical appearance of a poorly paid accounting clerk. Only his shoes, adorned with "a pair of very brilliant buckles gave the lie to the extreme poverty implied by the other portions of his dress." In the breast pocket of his coat, he carries a small black book bearing the words *Rituel Catholique* in white letters, and the precision with which he has tied his dirty white cravat ironically gives him the appearance of an ecclesiastic, an idea that Poe extends through physical description: "The forehead was lofty, and deeply furrowed with the ridges of contemplation. The corners of the mouth were drawn down into an expression of the most submissive humility. There was also a clasping of the hands, as he stepped toward our hero—a deep sigh—and altogether a look of such untter sanctity as could not have failed to be unequivocally prepossessing." When he removes the green spectacles, Bon-Bon sees that "simply a dead level of flesh" exists where eyes should have been. When his host becomes disgustingly drunk and offers his soul as "a bargain," this devil declines, protesting that he is "supplied at present" and would not want to take advantage of Bon-Bon's "present disgusting and ungentlemanly situation."

devil, the (2)   Character in the short story "THE DEVIL IN THE BELFRY." He disrupts the happy ignorance of the residents of a village who run their lives according to their seven-faced steeple clock. The devil, something of a dandy, is "a very diminutive foreign-looking man" with a snuff-colored countenance, "and he had a long hooked nose, pea eyes, a wide mouth, and an excellent set of teeth." His "audacious and sinister kind of face" is covered with "mustachios and whiskers" and his hair is "neatly done up in *papillotes* [curling papers]." His clothing is well-cut and elegant, consisting of "a tight-fitting swallow-tailed black coat, . . . black kerseymere kneebreeches, black stockings, and stumpy-looking black pumps, with huge bunches of black satin ribbon for bows." He carries a huge silk three-cornered hat under one arm and a fiddle "nearly five times himself" under the other. His appearance is disconcerting to the townspeople, but more upsetting is his "cutting all manner of fantastic steps . . . a fandango here, and a whirligig there" without having the "remotest idea in the world of such a thing as *keeping time* in his steps."

"The Devil in the Belfry" Short story. The tale is by Poe's admission a true grotesque that deals comically with the German intellectualism of his day and which also satirizes the credulity and conventionality of the mob. In the first publications of the story, Poe provided a footnote to the name "Vondervotteimittiss" to pronounce the town name as "Vonder vaat time it is," to make certain that his readers understood the target of his satire. The tale might be seen as a comic variation of the theme of too much timekeeping and reliance on rationality, which Poe also handles in "A PREDICAMENT" and "THE PIT AND THE PENDULUM."

PUBLISHING AND DRAMATIZATION HISTORY

The story was first published on May 18, 1839, in the Philadelphia *Saturday Chronicle and Mirror of the Times.* The satiric sketch brought to mind for readers of Poe's time Washington IRVING's *A History of New-York,* written under the pseudonym of Diedrich Knickerbocker, in the creation of the Dutch borough of Vondervotteimittiss.

The French composer Claude DEBUSSY obsessed about turning the tale into an opera; he began writing it in 1902, but the opera remained unfinished at his death in 1918. Debussy sought to make the work "a happy blending of the real and the fantastic" and to create a devil that would "put an end to the idea that the devil is the spirit of evil. He is simply the spirit of contradiction." The devil also would remain silent throughout the play and only whistle, and the one singing part would be that of the crowd.

In keeping with his efforts throughout the story to mock the pretentiousness of the pseudo-learned, Poe precedes the tale with the following epigraph: "What o'clock is it?—*Old Saying.*"

No film has been made of "The Devil in the Belfry" to date.

CHARACTERS

Unnamed narrator, the belfry-man, the devil.

PLOT SYNOPSIS

The story opens as an unnamed narrator in the persona of a historian expresses the desire to "give a history of the calamitous events which have so lately occurred within the limits" of the Dutch borough of Vondervotteimittiss. In the manner of many learned treatises, the story contains mock attempts to provide readers with an etymology of such people and place names as "Kroutaplenttey" ["kraut-a-plenty," suggesting German origins as it obviously refers to the well-known German cabbage dish sauerkraut], and *"Vonder, lege Donder—Votteimittis, quasi und Bleitziz—Bleitziz obsol: pro Blitzen."* The stuffy and erudite narrator further refers

Illustration by D. Wagel for "The Devil in the Belfry" in The Collected Works of Edgar Allan Poe *(1902).*

"the reader desirous of information" to the invented *"Oratiunculae de Rebus Praeter-Veteris,* of Dundergutz [Little Discussions of the Most Ancient Things by Dunderhead]" and additional learned works complete with marginal notes and folio numbers for verification. After admitting that the date of founding of the borough is unknown, the narrator relates that "it has always existed as we find it in this epoch. The oldest man in the borough can remember not the slightest difference in any portion of it; and, indeed, the very suggestion of such a possibility is considered an insult." Vondervotteimittiss is a place of precision, order, neatness, uniformity, and punctuality where "[t]he buildings themselves are so precisely alike that one can in no manner be distinguished from the other." Every house is decorated with the same carvings of cabbages and timepieces, and all are exactly alike, as are the citizens. The pride of the borough—and its source of precision and harmony—is the seven-faced town clock, which strikes the hours regularly and which "was never yet known to have any thing the matter with it."

As is the custom in the borough, "people who hold sinecure offices are held in more or less respect" and the reliability of the town clock has made the position of belfry-man "the most perfect of sinecures, [so] he is the most perfectly respected of any man in the world. He is the chief dignitary of the borough, and the very pigs look up to him with a sentiment of reverence." When the "very diminutive foreign-looking man" enters the town and disrupts the clockwork paradise by overpowering the belfry-man and making the town clock chime 13 strokes at noon, "all Vondervotteimittis flew at once into a lamentable state of uproar." Mealtimes are off schedule, food is overcooked, pipes run out of tobacco, and the population is nearly unable to function as every clock in town also strikes 13. The devil disorders their mechanical reality, which can only be restored in one way. As the narrator importunes readers, "Let us proceed in a body to the borough, and restore the ancient order of things in Vondervotteimittiss by ejecting the little fellow from the steeple." Until the little devil in the belfry can be evicted, the borough of Vondervotteimittiss will never know the correct time again.

Dian   *See* DIANA (1).

Diana (1)   Deity in Roman mythology; called Artemis in Greek mythology. She is the hunter goddess and the guardian of springs and streams, as well as the protector of wild animals. Typically shown as a young hunter, she usually is depicted carrying bow and arrows. References to the goddess appear in "LIONIZING," in which the pretentious President of Fum Fudge University pontificates that "the moon was called Bendis in Thrace, Bubastis in Egypt, Dian in Rome, and Artemis in Greece"; and in "FOUR BEASTS IN ONE" and "MARGINALIA," which makes references to the Temple of Diana. In reviews of the poetry of Henry HIRST and Richard H. HORNE's "ORION: AN EPIC POEM IN THREE BOOKS," Poe refers to the goddess who plays prominent role in both works.

Diana (2)   A lapdog owned by Signora Psyche ZENOBIA in the satiric "HOW TO WRITE A BLACKWOOD ARTICLE" and "A PREDICAMENT: THE SCYTHE OF TIME." In the first tale, the narrator Zenobia professes to take Mr. Blackwood's advice to wander around Edinburgh, and while doing so is "attended by one negro-servant Pompey, and my little lap-dog Diana, whom I had brought with me from Philadelphia." In "A Predicament," Zenobia is "attended at a respectful distance" by Diana as they walk through the city that Poe now calls Edina. Readers learn that Diana is a poodle with "a quantity of hair over one eye, and a blue riband tied fashionably around her neck." She is not more than five inches tall

with a head that appears to be somewhat bigger than her body, "and her tail being cut off exceedingly close, gave an air of injured innocence to the interesting animal which rendered her a favorite to all." So obedient is the dog to her master that she continues to sit in the corner as ordered even when attacked by a rat that picks her bones clean, leaving the trapped Zenobia to see only "the departed spirit, the shade, the ghost of my beloved puppy, which I perceive sitting with a grace so melancholy in the corner." In grief, Zenobia hears the dog speak, "and heavens! is in the German of Schiller: *Unt stubby duk, so stubby dun / Duk she! duk she!*" [And if I died at least I died / For thee—for thee.] The poodle has sacrificed itself for Zenobia.

Di Broglio   *See* BROGLIO, DUC DI.

Dickens,   Charles (1812–1870)   English novelist whom Poe admired greatly to the point of labeling him "the greatest British novelist." Poe's favorable reviews of three of Dickens's works appeared in various publications (the first in 1836, the latter two in 1841) before the two met. (*See* "THE POSTHUMOUS PAPERS OF THE PICKWICK CLUB," "THE OLD CURIOSITY SHOP," and "BARNABY RUDGE.") When Poe learned that Dickens was to make an American tour in 1842, he wrote the novelist a highly complimentary letter and asked for a meeting. Poe conducted two interviews with Dickens at the United States Hotel in Philadelphia in March 1842, during Dickens's first American visit. When Dickens returned to England in 1842, he tried to obtain a London publisher for Poe's short stories, without success; this failure led to some bitterness on Poe's part. In an 1846 letter, Poe asked Dickens to aid him in becoming the American correspondent for the London *Daily News,* but Dickens replied that he was no longer connected with the journal as he had been in the early 1840s. The influence of Dickens on Poe appears to have gone beyond mere correspondence. In Dickens's *Barnaby Rudge,* which Poe reviewed in 1842, the raven appears to have supplied the germ of thought and the artistic philosophy for Poe's later poem. Poe noted that "the raven, too, intensely amusing as it is, might have been made, more than we now see it, a portion of the conception of the fantastic Barnaby. Its croakings might have been *prophetically* heard in the course of the drama." In 1851, when Dickens again returned to the United States to tour and to give readings, he visited Maria CLEMM, now bereft of her dear "Sissy" and "Eddie," and left the financially impoverished woman $150 at the close of his visit.

"A Dictionary of Greek and Roman Antiquities. Edited by William Smith, Ph.D., and Illustrated by Numerous Engravings on Wood. Third American Edition, Care-

fully Revised, and Containing Numerous Additional Articles Relative to the Botany, Mineralogy, and Zoology of the Ancients. By Charles Anthon, LLD. New York: Harper and Brothers" Favorable review of the third American edition of the classical compendium that appeared in the April 12, 1845, issue of the BROADWAY JOURNAL. The review praises both the work and its compiler, whom Poe designates "not only the best scholar in America—but perhaps the most absolutely accurate one in the world." Poe writes that the work is "the most valuable of its class—or rather it is a class by itself," partly because it contains "all the recent discoveries of the Germans, and has all the fulness and accuracy for which the German scholars are noted."

Dictu, Mr. Horribile One of the 10 men, "as ill-looking as they are stupid," who form Poe's fictional FOLIO CLUB. Dictu, a man with white eyelashes, has graduated from the pompous-sounding university at Göttingen and thus, matches the collective intelligence of which Poe is clearly disdainful.

"Didactics—Social, Literary, and Political. By Robert Walsh. Philadelphia: Carey, Lea, and Blanchard" Review published in the Nay 1836 issue of the SOUTHERN LITERARY MESSENGER. Poe generally praises Walsh as "one of the finest writers, one of the most accomplished scholars, and when not in too great a hurry, one of the most accurate thinkers in the country." He discusses several of the essays at length, giving particular attention to "a very excellent Essay on the acting of Kean," published anonymously, in which Poe finds ideas that echo his own. This recognition motivates the statement, "We read it with that thrill of pleasure with which we always welcome our own long-cherished opinions, when we meet them unexpectedly in the language of another." Poe expresses similar delight and approval of essays in the collection, objecting only to a paper on phrenology that fails to treat the subject as a legitimate metaphysical science. Charging Walsh with being "evidently ignorant," Poe asserts that "Mr. Walsh is either ashamed of this article now, or he will have plentiful reason to be ashamed of it hereafter."

"Diddling Considered as One of the Exact Sciences" Short story. The tale is constructed as parody of serious treatises, most notably of the sort published by the British philosopher and economist Jeremy Bentham, whose doctrine of utilitarianism and treatises on law and morality were lauded by Poe's contemporaries and had great influence on early 19th-century thought. Poe makes his intentions clear in the opening lines of the work:

Since the world began there have been two Jeremys. The one wrote a Jeremiad about usury, and was called

Jeremy Bentham. He has been much admired by Mr. John Neal, and was a great man in a small way. The other gave name to the most important of the Exact Sciences, and was entitled Jeremy Diddler. He was a great man in a *great* way—I may say, indeed, in the very greatest of ways.

PUBLISHING AND DRAMATIZATION HISTORY

The story was first published under the title "Raising the Wind; or, Diddling Considered as One of the Exact Sciences" in the October 14, 1843 issue of the *Philadelphia Saturday Courier* and reprinted under the present title in BROADWAY JOURNAL on September 13, 1845.

Poe appends to the story an epigraph of lines from a Mother Goose nursery rhyme, but he identifies the source as a lofty epic written by the pseudonymous "Flaccus," actually the amateur poet Thomas WARD, whom Poe had dubbed "a ninety-ninth-rate poetaster" in a March 1843 review: "'Hey, diddle, diddle, / The cat and the fiddle.'—From an Epic by 'Flaccus'."

CHARACTERS

The diddler.

PLOT SYNOPSIS

Classified as a tale, the piece is actually a mock scientific study that discusses in a methodical and serious manner the numerous ways of diddling—stealing, swindling, and committing petty larceny. Poe contends that "the principle of diddling is, in fact, peculiar to the class of creatures that wear coats and pantaloons" and asserts that man "was made to diddle. This is his aim—his object—his *end*." He identifies the elements of successful diddling as "minuteness, interest, perseverance, ingenuity, audacity, nonchalance, originality, impertinence, and grin" and explains each aspect in detail before offering a range of instructive examples. Among the confidence games identified are means of obtaining free tobacco by confusing the shopkeeper about the change; cheating greedy reward seekers of money for turning in what seem to be valuable finds; skipping out on rent due; and bilking gullible job seekers of fees for jobs that do not exist. Poe shows the "diddlers" to be a clever and enterprising group. He shows little sympathy for their victims, whose greed and stupidity lead to their downfall. The work reveals Poe's fascination with hoaxes of every kind.

Didier, Eugene (1838–1913) Early Poe biographer and editor. With the use of information gained from interviews with Maria CLEMM, he wrote "The Life of Edgar Poe," a preface to *The Life and Poems of Edgar Allan Poe*, published by W. J. Widdleton in 1876. In approaching his subject, Didier stated his ideal: "The only way to examine an author is with the enthusiasm of a lover and the intelligence of a scholar." He also defended Poe's character in an article titled "Poe: Real and Reputed," published in the April 1894 issue of *Godey's Magazine and Lady's Book.*

Diodorus Siculus (fl. first century B.C.) Greek author of the Bibliotheca Historica, a history of the world in 40 books from the creation through the Gallic Wars and up to the first years of the Roman Empire. Poe mentions his work as a historical source in "LOSS OF BREATH," and the unnamed narrator in "SOME WORDS WITH A MUMMY" relates that after his queries to the mummy, "the silent member again touched me quietly on the elbow, and begged me for God's sake to take a peep at Diodorus Siculus." Poe seems to have respected the authenticity of Diodorus, for he ends "SOME ACCOUNT OF STONEHENGE, THE GIANT'S DANCE, A DRUIDICAL RUIN IN ENGLAND" with a passage from Diodorus and also remarks in "PINAKIDIA" that "the fullest account of the Amazons is to be found in Diodorus Siculus."

"A Dissertation on the Importance of Physical Signs in the Various Diseases of the Abdomen and Thorax. By Robert W. Haxall, M.D. of Richmond, Va. Boston: Perkins and Marvin" Poe's review of a medical pamphlet. The review appeared in the October 1836 issue of the SOUTHERN LITERARY MESSENGER. Poe asserts that Haxall "evinced too more than ordinary powers of analysis" and expects that the work would command "the entire respect of every well-educated man, as a literary composition in its own peculiar character." Despite Poe's praise of the writing, he finds fault with the content because it "does not respond, in the fullest extent, to the category proposed." Instead of focusing solely on diseases of the abdomen and thorax, Poe writes, "the most important and altogether the most original portion of the Essay, is that relating to the fever called *Typhoid."*

"The Doctor, &c. New York: Republished by Harper and Brothers" A critical review that appeared in the July 1836 issue of the SOUTHERN LITERARY MESSENGER. Poe states that the work "professes to be a Life of one Doctor Daniel Dove and his horse Nobs—but we should put no very great faith in this biography." Although the review observes that "the wit and humor of the *Doctor* have seldom been equalled," it also points out the inconsistencies of the work, and suggests it was "written with the sole view (or nearly with the sole view) of exciting inquiry and comment." The review relates that the book appeared to have achieved this goal in England and was expected to do so in America as well, where, Poe says, its publication already "has given rise to every variety of conjecture and opinion." Poe also debates

the nature of the book and writes that he has read it "with attention" but "can make nothing of it," and therefore is of the opinion "that the *Doctor* is precisely—nothing. We mean to say that it is nothing better than *a hoax."* Poe was a good judge of such matters, given his own efforts in the area in such published work as "THE BALLOON-HOAX," "THE UNPARALLELED ADVENTURE OF ONE HANS PFAALL," "VON KEMPELEN AND HIS DISCOVERY," and "MAELZEL'S CHESS-PLAYER."

Doellner, Robert (1899–1977) American composer and violinist. He wrote a musical recitation to Poe's poem "ANNABEL LEE" and an orchestral score to "A TALE OF THE RAGGED MOUNTAINS."

"The Domain of Arnheim, or the Landscape Garden" Short story. This short story combines the essay form with that of the tale in an effort to improve on nature. Critics have praised the story as a marvelous prose poem that contains a musical element similar to that which Poe attempted to achieve in his poetry.

PUBLISHING AND DRAMATIZATION HISTORY

The story was first published in its present form in the March 1847 issue of *Columbian Lady's and Gentleman's Magazine.* An early, briefer version of the story appeared as "THE LANDSCAPE GARDEN" in the October 1842 issue of *Snowden's Ladies' Companion.* Poe enlarged the story, incorporating most of "The Landscape Garden" in the first 15 paragraphs of the present story.

An epigraph from "Christ's Victorie and Triumphe in Heaven and Earth" (1610) by Giles Fletcher (1588–1623) precedes the story:

> The garden like a lady fair was cut,
> That lay as if she slumbered in delight,
> And to the open skies her eyes did shut.
> The azure fields of Heaven were 'sembled right
> In a large round set with the flowers of light.
> The flowers de luce and the round sparks of dew
> That hung from their azure leaves did shew
> Like twinkling stars that sparkle in the evening blue.

CHARACTERS

ELLISON, unnamed narrator.

PLOT SYNOPSIS

Ellison inherits "four hundred and fifty millions [sic] of dollars" from an ancestor who died a century before and "bequeathed the aggregate amount to the nearest of blood, bearing the name of Ellison, who should be alive at the end of the hundred years." A man "profoundly enamored of music and poetry," despite the importuning of friends and family and the applications of others, he decides to use his wealth to construct a picturesque and private paradise "which still is nature in the sense of the handiwork of the angels that hover between man and God." Ellison searches "for several years" for a spot that is suitable for his garden, rejecting "a thousand spots" in that time. When he finally settles on a suitable locale, he names his romantic domain Arnheim. The garden is a physical and sensuous Eden "upspringing confusedly from amid all, a mass of semi-Gothic, semi-Saracenic architecture, sustaining itself by miracle in mid-air."

"The Domed City" *See* "THE CITY IN THE SEA."

Doyle, Sir Arthur Conan (1859–1930) British physician, novelist, and writer of detective stories. He is best known as the creator of Sherlock Holmes, the master sleuth whom many view as an immediate descendant of Poe's C. Auguste DUPIN. Holmes first appeared in the novel *A Study in Scarlet* (1887). Doyle acknowledged Poe's influence on his creation and on the genre, noting of the stories that "each is a root from which a whole literature has developed. . . . Where was the detective story until Poe breathed the breath of life into it?" Both Holmes and Dupin possess eccentric and solitary personalities and rely on ratiocination for success in their investigations.

"The Drake-Halleck Review" *See* "THE CULPRIT FAY."

"The Drama" (1) A review of the acting debut at Niblo's Theatre of Mrs. Anna Cora MOWATT, who had already achieved a reputation as a playwright. The review appeared in the July 19, 1845, issue of the *BROADWAY JOURNAL*. Although her appearance on stage as Pauline in Edward BULWER-LYTTON's *The Lady of Lyons* "has been very successful, [and] drew large and fashionable as well as intellectual audiences," the review states that she has "somewhat injured the *prestige* of her name" by appearing on stage in the United States and "she would have *gained* much by first appearing in London." Quick to make clear that it is not the acting profession that he criticizes, Poe reminds readers that "the writer of this article is himself the son of an actress—has invariably made it his boast—and no earl was ever prouder of his earldom than he of the descent from a woman who, although well-born, hesitated not to consecrate to the drama her brief career of genius and beauty." Instead, Poe criticizes the venue, but he gives high praise to Mrs. Mowatt's acting ability and predicts for her a successful stage career.

"The Drama" (2) A review of Mrs. Anna Cora MOWATT's second week of stage roles at Niblo's Theatre, appearing in the July 26, 1845, issue of *BROADWAY JOURNAL*. Poe writes that Mowatt has charmed audiences

with her role as Lucy Ashton in Sir Walter SCOTT's *The Bride of Lammermoor,* a role "for which Mrs. Mowatt is peculiarly adapted." The review states that she should confine herself to "the more gentle sentiments and the most profound passions. Her sympathy with the latter is evidently intense." So effective does the audience find her acting that they "grew pale, and were betrayed into silence and tears—and if anyone went away sneering that night, it is at least quite certain that he felt ashamed of the sneer."

"The Drama of Exile and Other Poems: By Elizabeth Barrett Barrett [*sic*], Author of 'The Seraphim,' and Other Poems" Poe's lengthy and enthusiastic review of Elizabeth BARRETT's collected poems, which include "The Drama of Exile," a poem on the subject of the fall of Adam and Eve. The review was published in two installments in the January 4 and 11, 1845, issues of the *BROADWAY JOURNAL*. Poe provides a detailed discussion of the contents and quotes liberally from the poems, in addition to assessing their technical and aesthetic quality. Poe attributed "Homeric force" to her story of Adam and Eve, but he objected to what he termed "a continuous mystical strain of ill-fitting and exaggerated allegory." The review provides details regarding other poems in the collection. Of "The Vision of Poets," Poe objected to its length and "the didacticism of its design." He also reviewed in general the 28 sonnets in the collection and asserted that her poems confirm that "[h]er sense of art is pure in itself." In the collection, Poe finds "The Lady Geraldine" to be "the only poem of its author which is not deficient, considered as an artistical whole." In his summation of Barrett's work, Poe concludes that her sense of art "has been contaminated by pedantic study of false models" and suggests that her ill health has "diverted her from proper individuality of purpose—and seduced her into the sin of imitation."

Drayton, William (1776–1846) Philadelphia judge and casual acquaintance who occasionally financially aided and encouraged Poe. Poe's *TALES OF THE GROTESQUE AND ARABESQUE* are dedicated to Drayton.

"A Dream" Lyric poem in four quatrains that first appeared in *TAMERLANE AND OTHER POEMS* (1827) and was republished in the collection *AL AARAAF, TAMERLANE, AND MINOR POEMS* (1829). The poet expresses his inability to distinguish between the dream and the reality, because he is haunted by memories of "a dream of joy departed." Entangled within his reverie, the speaker finds his faculties clouded "with a ray / Turned back upon the past." The poet and critic Richard Wilbur identified the source of Poe's poem as Byron's lyric "I Would I Were a Careless Child."

"Dream-Land" Lyric poem in five stanzas that first appeared in the June 1844 issue of GRAHAM'S MAGAZINE and was republished in the June 28, 1845, issue of the BROADWAY JOURNAL. The poem contains identical opening and closing stanzas to indicate the dream-voyager's arrival in and decision to remain in the extraterrestrial place "[w]here an Eidolon named Night" reigns over a realm somewhere beyond time and space. The destination is a forsaken landscape of "mountains toppling evermore / Into seas without a shore" and filled with gothic images of ghouls dwelling by dismal tarns and pools, shapes of dark memory, and a general sense of loss and anguish. Yet the dream-voyager perceives the beauty within the horror, "a peaceful, soothing region . . . an Eldorado" that can never be apprehended by the rational restraints of the waking state: "Never its mysteries are exposed / To the weak human eye unclosed."

"A Dream within a Dream" Poem that first appeared in the March 31, 1849, issue of the FLAG OF OUR UNION. The poet questions what is needed to distinguish between the dream and the reality and states firmly at the end of the first stanza, "All that we see or seem / Is but a dream within a dream." In the second stanza, the poet expresses the torment of not being able to grasp the grains of sand within his hand and asks "can I not grasp / them with a tighter clasp?" The realization that he cannot save one grain of sand from "the pitiless wave" leads to his final question of doubt: "Is all that we see or seem / But a dream within a dream?"

"Dreams" Poem published by Poe's brother, William Henry Leonard POE, in the May 19, 1827, issue of the *North American, or, Weekly Journal of Politics, Science, and Literature.* The poem mourns the great distance between reality and the pleasures of the dream world and expresses the desire to remain forever in a dream life. The ability of the dreamscape to endow reality with a "vivid coloring of life" and to, thus, transform it, promises happiness to the poet, who concludes that he can only be happy when he enters into the dream world where "I have been happy, though in a dream. / I have been happy—and I love the theme."

Drummummupp, Rev. Doctor Character in the short story "THE MAN THAT WAS USED UP." The minister of the church where the narrator encounters Miss Tabitha T., he delivers a "very capital discourse" at the top of his voice, and with a thump that came near knocking the pulpit about our ears."

Dubourg, Pauline Character in the short story "THE MURDERS IN THE RUE MORGUE." Her name in French means "of the borough or market town," appropriate for a laundress of low social class. A newspaper article published the day after the murders reports that Dubourg "deposes that she has known both the deceased for three years, having washed for them during that period." She provides little insight regarding the personal habits of the murdered mother and daughter, aside from reporting that they "seemed on good terms" and paid her well.

"The Duc de l'Omelette" Short story. This tale was conceived as a humorous assessment of the career of Nathaniel Parker WILLIS, whose critics had long predicted the end of his popularity as a writer. The same florid literary style that elicited disdain from most literary reviewers, however, attracted readers to his work. Critics generally agree that this short, simple story is one of Poe's most successful comic tales, providing as it does a sympathetic main character whose antagonist is the devil. In its link between gourmet dining and the horrors of damnation, the story is closely related to another of Poe's stories, "BON-BON."

PUBLISHING AND DRAMATIZATION HISTORY

The story was first published under the title "The Duke of l'Omelette" in the March 3, 1832, issue of the Philadelphia *Saturday Courier.*

The epigraph preceding the story is taken from *The Task* (1785) by William COWPER, a long poem in which the descriptions of country life foretell the 19th-century Romantic movement: "And stepped into a cooler clime."

The story has not been adapted for stage or screen.

CHARACTERS

The devil (*see* BAAL-ZEBUB), Duc de l'Omelette.

PLOT SYNOPSIS

The story opens as the Duc de l'Omelette is about to dine on an ortolan, "the most delicate of birds." When dinner is served, "the door gently opens to the sound of soft music" and the duc is confronted by the incorrectly prepared dish, "this little bird which you have stripped the feathers from and which you have served without paper" [the sign of a well-dressed bird is that it is served with the paper cuffs on the ends of legs]. Shocked by the impropriety of the situation, "the Duc expired in a paroxysm of disgust." Three days later, he finds himself in hell, where the devil tells him, "I took thee now from a rose-wood coffin inlaid with ivory. Thou wast curiously scented, and labelled as per invoice." For the duc, hell is a lavish apartment filled with statuary and sumptuous paintings, but a single uncurtained window that gives him full view of the hell-fires just beyond the pleasure chamber. The devil, who has haughty disdain for the self-important aristocrat, orders de l'Omelette to strip off his clothing and to meet his fate. When his victim suggests a game of cards to wager for his soul, Baal-Zebub agrees to a game of double or nothing, but the overly confident devil fails to give the game his full attention. When de l'Omelette draws a king from the deck, the devil loses both the game and his claim on the aristocrat's soul.

Dumas, Paul Character in the short story "THE MURDERS IN THE RUE MORGUE." He is the physician who is first called to give medical evidence as to the cause of death in the double murder. He states his opinion that Mademoiselle L'ESPANAYE "had been throttled to death by some person or persons unknown" and describes at length the injuries to both victims.

Duncan Lodge The Richmond home of the Mr. and Mrs. William MACKENZIE, who adopted Rosalie POE, Edgar's sister. Contemporaries of Poe reported that he was always welcome at the home and the family always treated him well. He made more frequent visits there after the death of Virginia CLEMM. As Poe neared the end of his life, when drink made him incoherent he was often taken to Duncan Lodge, where Dr. John CARTER attended him.

Dundergutz Character mentioned in the short story "THE DEVIL IN THE BELFRY." The narrator of the story cites the treatise *Oratiunculae de Rebus Praeter Veteris* ["Little Discussion of the Most Ancient Things"] of this fictional scholar as a source for the derivation of the town's name. The name is intended to evoke a relationship to the term "dunderhead."

Dunderheads Members of the FOLIO CLUB who are contributing authors to a collection of 16 tales titled *Tales of the Folio Club*. Poe labeled his imaginary authors "a mere Junto of Dunderheadism. I think too the members are quite as ill-looking as they are stupid. I also believe it is their settled intention to abolish literature, subvert the Press, and overturn the Government of Nouns and Pronouns." Among the members of this imaginary literary society are Mr. Snap, the President, and nine other members: Mr. Convolvulus Gondola; De Rerum Natura, Esqr.; Mr. Solomon Seadrift; Mr. Horribile DICTU; Mr. Blackwood Blackwood; Mr. Rouge-et-Noir; Chronologos Chronology; and two unnamed Dunderheads, "a very little man in a black coat with very black eyes" and "a stout gentleman who admired Sir Walter Scott."

Dunn, James Philip (1884–1936) American composer who wrote a tone poem for voice and orchestra as accompaniment to Poe's poem "ANNABEL LEE" in January 1909 in honor of the 100th anniversary of the poet's birth. He also wrote instrumental music to Poe's poem "TO HELEN" in 1916.

Dupin, Andre Marie Jean-Jacques (1783–1865) French orator described by Poe in "MARGINALIA" as one who "'spoke, as nobody else, the language of everybody.'" Poe contrasts Dupin's manner of speech with the belabored approach of the Bostonian transcendentalists, "the Frogpondian Euphuists." Poe appears to have taken the name of the clear-headed French orator for his lucid detective, Monsieur C. Auguste DUPIN.

Dupin, C. Auguste Poe's amateur detective who is the major character in three short stories: "THE PURLOINED LETTER," "THE MURDERS IN THE RUE MORGUE," and the "THE MYSTERY OF MARIE ROGÊT." The detective, who resides at No. 33 Rue Dunot, Faubourg St. Germain, uses his unofficial status and his superior mental powers to identify with the criminal mind and to help the police in solving crimes. His personality, his use of clues, his employment of postulation, and his use of logic in revealing the criminal are traits that later writers incorporated into their fictional detectives, especially Sir Arthur Conan DOYLE in his creation of Sherlock Holmes. Despite Dupin's peculiar and solitary personality, his consciousness allows him to understand the mundane and the practical to crack cases that baffle everyone else, including the police. His sharpest mental weapon is "ratiocination," a higher form of reasoning that permits Dupin to detect what others have overlooked or dismissed as unimportant. Dupin's remarkable powers of deduction and his idiosyncrasies, as well as the dual national association of a French detective created by an American writer, led to a range of successors both in the United States and abroad. Doyle used Poe's technique of narrating his detective's exploits through the viewpoint of a less-talented, often bumbling companion. He also gave Holmes not only intellectual capabilities similar to those of Dupin, but bizarre habits as well. Critics have also suggested that Agatha Christie had Poe's Dupin in mind in creating her Belgian detective Hercule Poirot, who insists that his powers of detection reside in his use of "the little gray cells" and whose idiosyncrasies are abundant.

Duval, Henry Character in the short story "THE MURDERS IN THE RUE MORGUE." A silversmith, he is a neighbor of the murder victims and "one of the party who first entered the house." He testifies that even though he "was not acquainted with the Italian language," he "was convinced by the intonation that the speaker was Italian." He also tells investigators that he was sure that the voice did not belong to either of the victims, for he had spoken with both frequently.

Duyckinck, Evert Augustus (1816–1878) Editor at Wiley & Putnam's publishing house in New York, to whom Poe made appeals for money and publication several times during the 1840s. In 1845, the editor selected the entries for *TALES BY EDGAR A. POE,* which became a critical success. Poe expressed dissatisfaction with Duyckinck's selections, which he thought emphasized the ratiocinative works and failed to represent the full range of his abilities. Nonetheless, in portraying the editor in "THE LITERATI OF NEW YORK CITY," Poe described him as "one of the most influential of the New York *littérateurs,* [and someone who] has done a great deal for the interests of American letters." Of Duyckinck's personal characteristics, Poe stated: "In character he is remarkable, distinguished for the bonhomie of his manner, his simplicity, and single-mindedness, his active beneficence, his hatred of wrong done even to any enemy, and especially for an almost Quixotic fidelity to his friends."

E———, Mrs. *See* ELLET, Elizabeth Fries.

"Early Naval History of England by Robert Southey, LL.D., Poet Laureate. Philadelphia: Carey, Lea & Blanchard" Poe's review of Southey's historical study, published in September 1835 issue of the SOUTHERN LITERARY MESSENGER. Poe expresses a high opinion of Southey, calling him "a writer who has few equals anywhere, either in purity of English prose, or in melody of immortal verse" and the history "a work of no common merit." The review observes that, even though the reviewer might want to temper some of the enthusiasm of Southey's "too zealous friends for overrating his merely poetical abilities, we could not find it in our hearts to place him second to any one." Poe also heartily approves of the subject of the history, for "in no national characteristic do we bear closer analogy to our progenitors in Great Britain than in the magnificence and glory of our many triumphs both over and upon the sea." He ends the review with a reaffirmation of the mastery of Southey as a prose writer, asserted despite what readers might deem to be "a deficiency of patriotic feeling."

Eaton, Major John Henry (1790–1856) Secretary of war under President Andrew Jackson. John ALLAN wrote to Eaton on May 6, 1829, and asked him to expedite an appointment to the United States Military Academy (West Point) for Poe, noting "I declare that he is no relation to me whatever." In July, Poe, to show his guardian that he was serious in his desire for a West Point appointment, walked from Baltimore to Washington, D.C., for a personal interview with Eaton. Once there, Poe learned that 10 more cadets than the quota allowed had been appointed, but Eaton promised that Poe would receive the next appointment once 10 resigned, or that he would be the first appointed the following year.

"Editorial Miscellany" A brief note that appeared in August 9, 1845, issue of the BROADWAY JOURNAL. Poe reprinted a brief column that had appeared in the New York *Morning Express,* which had credited its source to "the New York Correspondent" of the *Cincinnati Gazette.* The column claimed to have information about a "flare-up in the Broadway Journal, which prevented the appearance of one number of a week or two since." The correspondent also criticized the publication, claiming that it "needs more catholicity—more liberality, and a little less attempt at severity," and suggested that greater success would result "with its flashy name exchanged for something more dignified, and its main plan retained." Poe responded with a complete denial that any "flare-up" had occurred and stated of the writer that "he is right only in the proportion of one word in ten."

Edmunds Character mentioned in THE NARRATIVE OF ARTHUR GORDON PYM. The young Arthur Gordon PYM accidentally encounters his grandfather near Edmunds's well just before going to sea.

Egaeus Character in and narrator of the short story "BERENICE." A self-described monomaniac, Egaeus is engaged to marry his cousin BERENICE, with whose teeth he becomes obsessed. The emaciated Berenice dies early one morning, and she is buried "at the closing in of the night." At midnight, Egaeus awakens from "a confused and exciting dream" with no recollection of how he has spent the hours since interring Berenice at sundown—until a servant tells him that Berenice's grave has been violated. As the mud-covered Egaeus shrieks and bounds out of his seat, a box falls from the table and out fall "some instruments of dental surgery, intermingled with thirty-two small, white and ivory-looking substances."

Eiros Character in the short story "THE CONVERSATION OF EIROS AND CHARMION." Eiros gives CHARMION an account of the end of the world, which he has observed to end in a fiery blast.

Eisler, Paul (1878–1972) Austrian conductor and pianist who wrote *Hymn to the Virgin,* a musical composition in four-part chorus for mixed voices with organ accompaniment, inspired by Poe's poem "HYMN."

Elah Gabalah Character in the short story "FOUR BEASTS IN ONE." Referred to in the story as "his Sunship," this is the name given in Syria to the sun god, correctly spelled "Ela Gabal" or "Elagabalus," who is represented in the form of a huge, cone-shaped stone.

"Eldorado" Poem first published in the April 21, 1849, issue of the FLAG OF OUR UNION. Critics suggest that the poem was Poe's response to the excitement of the great gold rush to California that occurred in 1849. The ballad is constructed of four six-line stanzas, with short lines replicating a journey on horseback. The poem reflects the Arthurian tradition in the questing knight, the pilgrim shadow, and the unfinished search and task to which the now-old knight has dedicated himself. Instead of a holy grail or a maiden in distress, however, the knight of the poem seeks the mythical Eldorado, which means "gilded one," and hopes to find the golden man in his city of gold. The heroic striving of the knight to find Eldorado has dominated his life since his youth, and now he has little hope of completing his quest before mortality takes its toll. The knight meets the "pilgrim shadow," which encourages him to travel "Over the Mountains of the Moon, / Down the Valley of the Shadow, / Ride, boldly, ride" beyond all earthly limits. This was one of the last poems written by Poe. Rather than the idealistic quest of Arthur, Poe's knight seeks material enrichment, yet he, too, must accept that the only lasting reward is the spiritual reward.

"Eleonora" Short story. This tale is Poe's most romantic, and it is written in the style of his prose poems "SILENCE," "SHADOW," and "THE ISLAND OF THE FAY." This is one of Poe's only stories that contains a romantic male-female relationship without a multitude of morbid details.

PUBLISHING AND DRAMATIZATION HISTORY

The story was first published in *The Gift: A Christmas and New Year's Present* (1842), an annual published by Carey and Hart, then republished in the May 24, 1845, issue of the BROADWAY JOURNAL.

The story begins with an epigraph that appears in Victor Hugo's *Notre-Dame de Paris,* in chapter six of book seven: *Sub conservatione forme specificae salva anima.* ["Under the protection of a specific form the soul is safe."]

No film has been made of "Eleonora."

CHARACTERS

ELEONORA, ERMENGARDE, unnamed narrator.

PLOT SYNOPSIS

The first-person narrator of the tale is obsessed with the strange beauty of his cousin Eleonora, with whom he lives innocently for 15 years with her mother, the narrator's aunt, "beneath a tropical sun in the Valley of Many-Colored Grass." The narrator never explains why the three live so solitary an existence, although critics have found the relationship similar to Poe's living arrangement with Maria CLEMM and her daughter Virginia, who later became his wife. The characters' surroundings are paradisiacal, where "no unguided footsteps ever came upon that vale. . . . No path was trodden in its vicinity." They live in solitary bliss, "knowing nothing of the world." Once the narrator and Eleonora become aware of their love, the world changes and becomes even more lush to mirror "the passions which had for centuries distinguished our race, came thronging with the fancies for which they had been equally noted."

One day, Eleonora cries uncontrollably and tells the narrator that "she had seen that the finger of Death was upon her bosom," but her fears are not of death. Instead, she fears that after she is dead the narrator will leave the valley and fall in love with a woman in the outside world. Prostrate with grief, the narrator pledges undying devotion and vows to never marry anyone else. After Eleonora dies, the narrator remains in the valley for several years, but changes eventually force him to leave. He journeys to a strange city where he finds work at the court of a king, and where he also begins to experience "burning thoughts" and "terrible temptations." He falls in love with Ermengarde, "with the fervor, and the delirium, and the spirit-lifting ecstasy of adoration" that leads him to marry her without a thought of his promise to Eleonora. One night, he believes he hears Eleonora's "sweet voice" reassure him that he is absolved from his vows to her "in taking to thy passionate heart her who is Ermengarde." Thus, the narrator is inexplicably released from his earlier vow of devotion to find happiness in a second, passionate marriage with a woman from the outside world. Although Poe's wife, Virginia Clemm, would not die for five more years, she experienced her first hemoptysis (expectoration of blood from the lungs) in 1842, which undoubtedly made Poe consider the seriousness of her condition and the possibility of her death. Critics have also linked the death of Eleonora to that of Poe's mother, Elizabeth Arnold POE. In both cases, a spiritual, nonphysical relationship ends, leaving the poet to hope for a later, adult, passionate relationship.

Eleonora Character in the short story "ELEONORA." She is a young and beautiful woman who was born and has been raised in the secluded Valley of the Many-Colored Grass, apart from the corrupting outside world. With the narrator of the story, she experiences the freedom of their paradise: she falls in love with him, and he returns her love. Her happiness is short-lived, however, and she soon sees that "the finger of Death was upon her bosom." Similar to other Poe heroines, "she had been made perfect in loveliness only to die."

Elfrida, A Dramatic Poem in Five Acts   A composition by Frances OSGOOD. Poe included a lengthy summary and criticism of the work in his article on Osgood that appeared in "THE LITERATI OF NEW YORK." The plot involves deception and ambition. King Edgar hears of Elfrida's extraordinary beauty and sends his favorite, Athelwood, to determine if the reports are true. Athelwood falls in love with her and lies to the king, telling him that she is neither beautiful nor agreeable, then woos her himself. After telling the king that he merely want Elfrida for her money, Athelwood marries her. When another man later tells the king of this deception, he resolves to visit Athelwood's castle to see for himself, and the panic-stricken Athelwood begs his wife to make herself look plain for the king's visit. Although she agrees, the devious Elfrida is ambitious and makes herself look exceedingly beautiful for the king's visit. Athelwood is destroyed and Elfrida becomes King Edgar's queen. Poe praised Osgood's artistry, stating that "the hand of the genius is evinced throughout," and he was particularly complimentary of "the passionate expression of particular portions, to delineation of character, and to occasional scenic effect." He was less impressed with her technical talents and noted that although she had "unquestionably failed in writing a good play, has, even in failing, given indication of dramatic power."

"The Elk"   Travel essay and landscape sketch published in the annual *The Opal* for 1844. Poe first titled the work "Morning on the Wissahiccon," because it describes the beauties of the Wissahiccon, a brook that runs into the Schuylkill River near Philadelphia: "Flowing in England, it would be the theme of every bard." The work is highly critical of "our own most deliberate tourists," from whom "the Edens of the land lie far away from the track." He notes that foreign tourists, as well, see only "the most beaten thoroughfares of the country," not the area to which he has become privy through his own explorations of "the truest, the richest, and most unspeakable glories of the land." Poe describes the wild beauties of his surroundings, especially the meandering Wissahiccon. On one excursion, he sees upon a cliff a magnificent elk, standing "with neck outstretched, with ears erect . . . one of the oldest and boldest of those identical elks which had been coupled with the red men in my vision." Visions of the wild pass through Poe's mind until he sees a man holding "a quantity of salt" advance toward the elk, which does not attempt to escape. The man attaches a halter to the animal and leads it away, thus ruining Poe's romantic vision, for he realizes that "it was a *pet* of great age and very domestic habits, and belonged to an English family occupying a villa in the vicinity."

"Elkswatawa; or the Prophet of the West. A Tale of the Frontier. New York: Harper and Brothers"   Critical review by Poe that appeared in the August 1836 issue of the *SOUTHERN LITERARY MESSENGER*. Poe gives what he calls "a dry compendium" of the novel, which he claims does "little more than afford some idea of the *plan* of the novel," a romance of Tecumseh and his brother Elkswatawa. The novel relates a tale of the abduction of a young white woman by the Indians and of the search for her by the young man who loves her. Although Poe acknowledges that the characters of Tecumseh and Elkswatawa "appear to us well drawn," he criticizes the novel as a whole as too imitative of James Fenimore Cooper and Sir Walter SCOTT, and warns that the mannerisms of Scott should be avoided "as a little too much of a good thing." He also finds the heroine to have no character whatsoever: "Miss Foreman we dislike, because we cannot comprehend her." In sum, Poe concludes that the author has done "just nothing at all" to advance his reputation.

Ellet, Elizabeth Fries (1818–1877)   Poet, translator, and New York bluestocking socialite. Poe said that she was "the most malignant and pertinacious of all fiends—a woman whose loathsome love I could do nothing but repel with scorn." She wrote anonymous passionate love letters to Poe while he lived in the cottage at Fordham, New York, with Virginia and Maria CLEMM, but he returned her letters and rejected all of her advances. Poe claimed that her gossiping cast doubts on his fidelity and hastened Virginia's death by creating stress, and labeled Ellet as part of "a heartless, unnatural, venomous, dishonorable set." In her entry in "AUTOGRAPHY," Poe wrote that she acquired "an enviable reputation" as a translator, but that those "often known as translators, but seldom evince high originality or very eminent talent of any kind."

Elline   Character in the short story "FOUR BEASTS IN ONE." One of the "two principal concubines" of ANTIOCHUS EPIMANES who holds the ruler's giant fake tail aloft when he is dressed as the "cameleopard."

Ellis, Colonel Thomas H. (1812–1888)   Childhood friend of Poe and the son of the senior member of Ellis and Allan, the firm in which John ALLAN was a partner. In May 1881, Ellis published an article of reminiscences of Poe, later reprinted in the September 1900 in the New York *Independent,* in which he corrected errors regarding Poe's early years and the activities of the Allan family. Of Poe, he stated: "[H]e was very beautiful, yet brave and manly for one so young. No boy ever had a greater influence over me than he had." The account characterizes the young Poe as an adventurous boy whose daring led him into trouble as a child, but it also admits to the brilliance of the young adult who "was sent to the best schools, he was taught every accomplishment that a boy could acquire, he was trained to all the habits of the most polished society."

Ellis, Powbatan (1790–1863) Brother of Charles Ellis, John ALLAN's business partner. The United States Senator from Mississippi recommended Poe's appointment to the U.S. Military Academy on March 13, 1830, thus providing evidence of a powerful association to ensure Poe's success in acquiring the appointment.

Ellison Character in the short story "THE DOMAIN OF ARNHEIM." A friend of the narrator, he is a wealthy aesthete who has devoted himself to creating the ideal landscape plot as his private domain of beauty. Profoundly enamored of music and poetry, he ignores the advice of friends and family and the applications of others and decides to use his wealth to construct a picturesque and private paradise "which still is nature in the sense of the handiwork of the angels that hover between man and God."

Ellison, Mr. Seabright Character mentioned in the short story "THE DOMAIN OF ARNHEIM." He is the rich ancestor of Ellison, the narrator's friend. Through various modes of investment, he "minutely and sagaciously" amasses a fortune, but he has no immediate relatives to whom he may leave it. As an alternative, he directs that the fortune should be left to accumulate for a full century, and he bequeathed it to "the nearest of blood, bearing the name of Ellison, who should be alive at the end of the hundred years."

Embury, Emma C. (1806–1863) Minor New York poet and novelist who wrote under the nom de plume "Ianthe." In "THE LITERATI OF NEW YORK CITY," Poe praised her for having "a poetic capacity of no common order" and noted that her reputation as a poet had been overshadowed by her renown as a writer of short stories: "In this latter capacity she has, upon the whole, no equal of her sex in America—certainly no superior." Poe also praised the freshness of her subjects and noted that "she has also much imagination and sensibility, while her style is pure, earnest, and devoid of verbiage and exaggeration."

Enderby, Messieurs Characters in Poe's novella THE NARRATIVE OF ARTHUR GORDON PYM. They are the London-based owners of a whale ship who employ Captain BRISCOE.

Engelsburg, Eduard Schon (1825–1879) Viennese composer of voice and instrumental compositions who wrote a musical setting of Poe's "ANNABEL LEE."

"England in 1835. Being a Series of Letters Written to Friends in Germany. During a Residence in London and Excursions Into the Provinces. By Frederick Von Raumer, Professor of History at the University of Berlin, Author of the 'History of the Hohenstaufen,' of the 'History of Europe from the End of the Fifteenth Century,' of 'Illustrations of the History of the Sixteenth and Seventeenth Centuries,' &c. &c. Translated from the German by Sarah Austin and H. E. Lloyd. Philadelphia: Carey, Lea & Blanchard" A review that appeared in the July 1836 issue of the SOUTHERN LITERARY MESSENGER. Poe evaluates the content of the work, the ability of the translator, and the manner of the translation. He praises Von Raumer as "a man of unquestionable and lofty integrity . . . profoundly versed in moral and political science" and reports that the work contains discussion of diverse topics, including political issues of the day and the current state and future prospects of England. Poe observes that Von Raumer portrays honestly the state of affairs in England and "presents a vivid picture of the miseries of Ireland." For these reasons, he "has the honor of being called by the English organ of the High Church and Ultra Tory Party, 'a vagrant blackguard unfit for the company of a decent servant's hall.'" Of the translator Sarah Austin, Poe notes that she "has taken some liberties in the way of omission, which cannot easily be justified." In particular, Austin appears to have removed passages that are unfavorable to her friend Jeremy Bentham: "We learn this as well by her own acknowledgment as by ominous breaks in particular passages concerning the great Utilitaran."

English, Thomas Dunn (1819–1902) Physician and amateur poet who was first Poe's close friend and strong defender, then later became as strong an enemy. As editor of the New York monthly the *Aristidean*, he reviewed Poe's work. Mutual animosity began in 1843 when Poe mocked English's poems in public. English took his revenge by featuring a Poe-like character in his novels *Walter Woolfe* (1843), *The Doom of the Drinker* (1844), and *The Power of the S.F.* (1846). The attack in the latter novel was even more vehement than in the first, for English's character "Marmaduke Hammerhead" closely resembles Poe and is credited with writing "The Black Crow" and "The Humbug, and Other Tales." This publication caused Poe and English to quarrel violently and to come to blows, followed by a violent literary war. Poe ridiculed English in "THE LITERATI OF NEW YORK CITY," stating that nothing is "more pitiable than that of a man without the commonest school education busying himself in attempts to instruct mankind on topics of polite literature." English retaliated with a fiery letter to the editor that appeared in the July 23, 1846, issue of the NEW YORK

Thomas Dunn English, whom Poe sued for libel. (Edgar Allan Poe Society)

MIRROR, in response to which Poe sued English for libel and defamation of character. English printed unflattering material about his nemesis until Poe's death, then tarnished his reputation further by giving accounts of Poe's uncontrolled drinking and drug use.

"An Enigma" A lighthearted riddle poem that was first published in the March 1848 issue of the *Union Magazine of Literature and Art* under the title "Sonnet." The poem was retitled "An Enigma" by Rufus Wilmot GRISWOLD, Poe's literary executor. Originally written as a gift to Sarah Anna LEWIS, a poet and friend of Poe's during his days living at the Fordham cottage, the sonnet was presented to her in a letter dated November 27, 1847. The light and humorous sonnet contains an odd rhyme scheme (*ababbccb cddbdd*), which combines the two-part octave-sestet construction of the Petrarchan (or Italian) sonnet form with the final couplet of the Shakespearean (or English) sonnet. Also a name puzzle, the sonnet contains a concealed anagram of

Sarah Anna Lewis. The light mood and the wordplay of the poem make a mocking reference to "Petrarchan stuff," and the subject is a comic lament over the superficiality of periodical poetry, using such lines as "Trash of all trash!" and "The Owl-downy nonsense that the faintest puff / Twirls into trunk-paper the while you con it," to sustain the mood.

epigraphs Poe began most of his short stories and two of his poems, "IN YOUTH I HAVE KNOWN ONE" and "ISRAFEL," with epigraphs drawn from diverse sources, from nursery rhymes to the Greek and Roman classics to the obscure or spurious. In some cases, Poe cited an author but not the specific source in an author's works, while in others he completely fabricated an epigraph and simply attached a name, as with the fictitious epigraph to "LIGEIA" from Joseph Glanvill.

Epimanes, Antiochus Character in the short story "FOUR BEASTS IN ONE." (*See* ANTIOCHUS EPIPHANES.)

Epimenides Obscure Greek philosopher in "A LOSS OF BREATH." The narrator states that when a great plague raged at Athens and every means to eradicate the plague had been exhausted, the philosopher "advised the erection of a shrine and temple 'to the proper God.'"

"Erato. By William D. Gallagher. No. 1, Cincinnati, Josiah Drake—No. 11, Cincinnati, Alexander Flash" Review by Poe that appeared in the July 1836 issue of the *SOUTHERN LITERARY MESSENGER*. Poe begins the review with moderate praise for this first volume of poetry, pointing out that Gallagher "is fully a poet in the abstract sense of the word and will be so hereafter in the popular meaning of the term." Although the review describes the poet as having "a far more stable basis for solid and extensive reputation than we have seen in more than a few of our countrymen," the reviewer finds considerable fault with Gallagher's execution of his work: "Long passages of the merest burlesque, and in horribly bad taste, are intermingled with those of the loftiest beauty." As evidence of the poet's failings, Poe reprints lines from one of the poems, "The Penitent," which he describes as "ill-conceived, ill-written, and disfigured by almost every possible blemish of manner."

Ermengarde Character in the short story "ELEONORA." She is the narrator's second wife, "the ethereal Ermengarde . . . the seraph Ermengarde . . . the angel Ermengarde," whose beauty and "memorial eyes" make him forget his vow to his first wife to never marry again after her death. Ermengarde inspires in the narrator "the fervor, the delirium, and the spirit-lifting ecstasy of adoration."

Ethix, Aestheticus Character in the short story "LION-IZING." "He spoke of fire, unity, and atoms; bipart and pre-existent soul; affinity and discord; primitive intelligence and homoomeria," Poe wrote. "Homoomeria" refers to homoeomery, the belief of the Greek philosopher ANAXAGORAS that the ultimate particles of matter are all of the same kind. In this reference to Newtonian theory, Poe mocks the scientists who pretended to have comprehensive knowledge of the natural and the spiritual worlds.

Etienne, Alexandre Character in the short story "THE MURDERS IN THE RUE MORGUE." A Parisian surgeon, he is called in with Doctor Paul DUMAS and corroborates the testimony as to the cause of death. Poe may have named his character after Alexander Stephens, a Georgia state legislator and member of Congress from 1843 through 1859 who later served as the vice-president of the Confederacy; *Etienne* is Stephen in French.

"Ettore Fleramosca, or the Challenge of Barletta, An Historical Romance of the Times of the Medici, by Massimo D'Azeglio. Translated from the Italian by C. Edwards Lester, U.S. Consul at Genoa, Author of 'The Glory and Shame of England,' Member of the Ateneo Italiano at Florence, Etc. New York: Paine & Burgess" Review by Poe that appeared in the August 9, 1845, issue of the *BROADWAY JOURNAL*. Poe welcomes the translation, stating that the literature "of Italy has been of late altogether, or nearly altogether neglected." Although he grants that the work "is certainly a vivacious work," he condemns the work as being "feeble, too frequently, from its excess of simplicity in form and tone" because it lacks "the 'autorial comment'—that which adds so deep a charm to the novels of Scott, of Bulwer, or of D'Israeli." According to Poe the most grievous fault of the work is that the author merely narrates, and "the interest of mere incident, is all."

"Eulalie—A Song" Poem that first appeared in the July 1845 issue of the *American Review,* as well as in the August 9, 1845, issue of the *BROADWAY JOURNAL*. The poem also appeared in *THE RAVEN AND OTHER POEMS,* published by Wiley & Putnam in October 1845, a collection deemed by critics of the period as the most important volume of poetry that had been issued up to that time in America. Written in February 1844, "Eulalie" is a bridal song that describes the speaker's salvation from loneliness, despair, and "a world of moan" through marriage to "the yellow-haired young Eulalie." The speaker feels secure in his love for "Now Doubt—now Pain / Come never again," for he has found a soulmate who derives her strength from the celestial goddess Astarte.

Eulalie The "blushing bride" of Poe's poem "EULALIE—A SONG." She is "fair and gentle," a "smiling bride" whose eyes are far brighter than "the stars of the night." In Eulalie's radiance, her "most unregarded curl" and "most humble and careless curl" exceed in beauty and wonder "the morn-tints of purple and pearl." The speaker's "yellow-haired young Eulalie" with "her violet eye" is beautiful within, as well, "for her soul gives me sigh for sigh." She draws her beauty and strength from the goddess Astarte, the Semitic goddess of fertility and sexual love: "ever to her dear Eulalie upturns her matron eye— / And ever to her young Eulalie upturns her violet eye."

"Eureka: An Essay on the Material and Spiritual Universe" Poe's 10th published volume, the last published in his lifetime, appeared in March 1848. A small hardcover book, this cosmological treatise is Poe's longest nonfiction work at nearly 40,000 words, and was published by the firm of Wiley & Putnam as *Eureka: A Prose Poem.* Poe dedicated the work "With profound Respect" to Friedrich Heinrich Alexander Baron von Humboldt (1769–1859), author of *The Cosmos,* whose work inspired Poe to construct a cosmological synthesis based on mathematics, poetics, and intuition. Despite the depth of spiritual exploration contained in *Eureka,* Poe states in the Preface, "Nevertheless it is as a Poem only that I wish this work to be judged after I am dead." He addresses his work "to the dreamers and those who put faith in dreams as in the only realities— I offer this Book of Truths, not in its character of Truth-Teller, but for the Beauty that abounds in its Truth; constituting it true."

The work, in which Poe created metaphysic-cosmic theories intended to identify all life as being a part of God, originated as a lecture called "On the Cosmogony of the Universe," which Poe delivered on February 3, 1848, at the Society Library in New York. He had hoped to raise funds to resuscitate the *STYLUS,* but the cold and stormy weather on the night of the lecture brought an audience of only 60—who, nonetheless, listened to Poe read for about two and a half hours what would become nearly the whole text of *Eureka,* in which he unveiled the mysteries of God and Nature. The lecture did not make the expected money to resuscitate the *Stylus.* His audience left confused, and newspaper reports the following day painted the lecture as ludicrous. One reviewer called it "hyperbolic nonsense." Poe's friend Evert DUYCKINCK, an editor at Wiley & Putnam who was usually sympathetic to Poe's work, he wrote to his brother that the lecture had bored him to death and that it was "full of a ludicrous dryness of scientific phrase—a mountainous piece of absurdity for a popular lecture." Undeterred, Poe offered the renamed lecture to the publisher George P. Putnam with enthusiasm, expressing his faith in the importance of the "discoveries" in the work and suggesting that Wiley & Putnam publish an edition of 50,000. The more levelheaded Putnam published an edition of 500, which sold very slowly and provided only small financial returns.

Eureka was both a financial and a critical failure that reviewers condemned as filled with wild speculations and scientific errors. In particular, critics pointed out that Poe's statements violated Newtonian principles in their representation of the rotation and density of the planets. As his General Proposition, Poe states: "Because Nothing was, therefore All Things are." He attempts to connect the individual soul and the mind of God, identifying the universe itself as a cosmic masterpiece and "a plot of God." Poe sought to transcend the limits of death and to "reach these lands but newly from some ultimate dim Thule." Various passages in *Eureka* echo segments of Poe's poems and short stories that speak of penetrating death's barrier to find the beautiful truth of some great beyond: "Guiding our imaginations by that omniprevalent law of laws, the law of periodicity, are we not, indeed, indulging a hope— that the process we have ventured to contemplate will be renewed forever, and forever, and forever?" With this pseudoscientific explanation of the creation and destruction of the universe, Poe attempted to unite his concept of highest beauty in final and highest form. Critics do not suggest that he succeeded.

"Euripides Translated by the Reverend R. Potter, Prebendiary of Norwich. Harper & Brothers, New York. [The Classical Family Library. Numbers XV, XVI, and XVII.]" Review by Poe that appeared in the September 1835 issue of the SOUTHERN LITERARY MESSENGER. The three volumes appearing in the Classical Family Library series are said to contain "the whole of Euripides," for whom Poe claims to hold "no passion." After quickly dismissing any discussion of the translator's skills by noting that "a hasty glance at the work will not enable us to speak positively in regard to the value of these translations," the review becomes a critique of the techniques employed by Euripides. From the charge that "we behold only the decline and fall of that drama" in Euripides to his charge that the playwright misinterpreted the role of the chorus in his plays, Poe finds Euripides wanting. Unlike SOPHOCLES and Aeschylus, Euripides introduces his heroes "familiarly to the spectators" and "his Divinities are very generally lowered to the most degrading and filthy common-places of an earthly existence." In concluding the review, Poe quotes August Wilhelm von Schlegel (1767–1845), the German critic, translator, and scholar, who stated that Euripides had "destroyed the internal essence of tragedy, and sinned against the laws of beauty and proportion in its external structure."

Eusebius of Caesarea (260–340) Theologian, church historian, and scholar. Also called Eusebius Pamphili, he was probably born in Palestine. He became bishop of Caesarea in 314 and was said to be one of the most learned men of his time. Poe refers to him in "LIONIZING" as one of the thinkers of whom Theologus THEOLOGY speaks. In Poe's short story "BON-BON," "a toasting fork might be discovered by the side of Eusebius" in Hell, thus making it convenient for the devil to toast him at will.

Evening Mirror New York City newspaper edited first by Nathaniel Parker WILLIS and later by Hiram FULLER. Poe began work at the paper as a "mechanical paragraphist"—a columnist, in modern parlance—in 1844. In January 1845, the paper was the first to publish Poe's "THE RAVEN," for which it is chiefly remembered. Despite Poe's sober efforts to increase subscriber interest in the paper, and Willis's testimony that Poe complied with his editor's requests to decrease the acridness of his criticisms and to modify his irony, the paper betrayed Poe after Willis left. In the May 26, 1846, issue, the *Evening Mirror* printed Charles F. BRIGGS's excoriation of Poe's character, which insinuated that Poe was insane.

"Evening Star" Lyric poem by Poe that first appeared in the collection TAMERLANE AND OTHER POEMS, published by Calvin F. S. Thomas, Printer, in 1827. The speaker stares at the stars and "the brighter, cold moon," finding them "Too cold—too cold for me." Gazing into the distance, he spies the "Proud Evening Star, In thy glory afar," which exudes a warmth and attraction that the nearer stars do not. His contemplation brings joy when he comes to recognize that the "distant fire" of the star is far more admirable than "the colder, lowly light." Critics suggest that the poem bears some comparison with John Keats's sonnet "Bright Star" and Thomas Moore's "While Gazing on the Moon's Light."

Everett, Edward (1794–1865) Distinguished American orator and editor of the *North American Review,* a New England publication whose solid position Poe undermined with the success of the SOUTHERN LITERARY MESSENGER. In "AUTOGRAPHY," Poe wrote that Everett's handwriting "has about it an air of deliberate precision emblematic of the statesman, and a grace and solidity betokening the scholar." Contemptuous of all connected with the *Review,* Poe stated further: "The man who writes thus will never grossly err in judgment or otherwise. We may venture to say, however, that he will not attain the loftiest pinnacles of renown."

Ezekiel Old Testament prophet and Hebrew leader. Ezekiel was the first of the major Hebrew prophets to

"The Facts in the Case of M. Valdemar" Short story. The realistic tone of the narrative and the popular belief in the powers of "mesmerism" in the United States in the 1840s led many readers to believe that Poe's tale was fact rather than fiction. The publication in December 27, 1845, issue of the BROADWAY JOURNAL of a letter from the Scottish druggist Robert COLLYER, who claimed to have restored "to active animation" someone who had died "from excessive drinking of ardent spirits," further blurred the line between fiction and fact. Poe is said to have sought technical data from Andrew Jackson Davis, whose lectures on mesmerism he had attended.

PUBLISHING AND DRAMATIZATION HISTORY

The story appeared simultaneously in the December 1845 issue of the *American Review,* and in the December 20, 1845, issue of the BROADWAY JOURNAL. The story also appeared in the first issue of *Amazing Stories* in 1926 as a work of "scientification."

The tale has appeared as one segment of a 1960 Argentinian film *Masterpieces of Horror,* which was shown in the United States in 1965. Roger CORMAN also included the story as one of the three short films that made up the 1962 film *Tales of Terror.*

CHARACTERS

Dr. D———, Dr. F———, M. P———, Mr. Theodore L——l, M. Ernest VALDEMAR.

PLOT SYNOPSIS

P———, a professional mesmerist, narrates the story, which tells of a hypnotic experiment that he has conducted on a dying friend, M. Ernest Valdemar, to determine if the mesmeric process can forestall death and decomposition. When physicians determine that Valdemar has only 24 hours to live, Valdemar sends P—— a note summoning the mesmerist to his bedside. Together, they relieve the attending physicians, Dr. D—— and Dr. F——, of his care and ask only that one or the other look in on him during the course of P—'s intended experiment. In the presence of Mr. Theodore L——l, a medical student who will take notes on the proceedings, the mesmerist places the immobile Valde-

mar into a trance when he is just about to expire—a state in which he remains for seven months, during which nurses attend him. Although Valdemar seems to be technically alive, the mesmerist also realizes that to bring Valdemar out of the trance "would be merely to insure his instant, or at least, his speedy dissolution." Sensing that no progress can be made, the narrator, with the agreement of Dr. F——, decides to awaken Valdemar, whatever the consequences. After making "the customary passes," P—— asks, "'M. Valdemar, can you explain to us what are your feelings or wishes now?'" The response comes quickly, as Valdemar's "hideous voice" intones, "'For God's sake!—quick! —quick!—put me to sleep—or, quick!—waken me! —quick!—*I say to you that I am dead!*'" As P—— "made the mesmeric passes, amid ejaculations of 'dead! dead!'" the body of M. Valdemar "absolutely rotted away beneath my hands. Upon the bed, before that whole company, there lay a nearly liquid mass of loathsome—of detestable putridity."

The story expresses Poe's ambivalence toward the mesmeric science that preoccupied the thinking of his time. On the one hand, the process fascinates and offers to Poe the possibility of prolonging life, yet the truly scientific side of his nature admits the impossibility of anything but the ultimate decomposition of the human body, despite all efforts at maintaining life. Thus, the adventure ends in even greater loathsomeness than simple death and decomposition as Valdemar is reduced to "detestable putridity."

"Fairy-Land" Poem, originally called "Heaven," written while Poe lived in the barracks at the United States Military Academy at West Point. It first appeared in AL AARAAF, TAMERLANE, AND MINOR POEMS, published by Hatch & Dunning in December 1829. Fourteen lines were excerpted from the poem and appeared in the *Yankee and Boston Literary Gazette* for November 1829. Like other poems Poe wrote during this time, such as "TO HELEN," "THE SLEEPER," "A PAEAN," and "THE VALLEY OF UNREST," "Fairy-Land" hints of the dim northern twilight of Scotland and the Celtic folk tales that Poe had heard from the old people at Irvine, Scotland where John Allan had taken his family and the young Poe in 1815, as well as the mystic landscapes of South Carolina and exotic influence of his "Oriental" readings. The lyric contrasts the eerie beauty of a moonlit landscape, where "Huge moons there wax and wane," with the daylight, when "They use that moon no more / For the same end as before-." / The fairy beings have "forms we can't discover" and "they put out the star-light / With the breath from their pale faces." The daylight breaks the spell is broken and provides only a mundane version of the magical fairy wings that populate the moonlit fairyland of night.

"The Fall of the House of Usher" Short story. The most popular of Poe's stories, and one that attracted considerable attention when it first appeared, the tale has inspired numerous interpretations. Multiple layers of meaning spring from the Gothic trappings of the plot and the mysterious relationship of the brother and sister characters. Many critics believe this tale reveals the most about Poe's life—from one critic's assertion that the description of Roderick USHER is "the most perfect pen-portrait of Poe which is known" to another's suggestion that references to "the morbid condition of the auditory nerve" and the shifting visual imagery in the mansion unmistakably reflect a familiarity with the effects of opium. Certainly, the wasting away of Madeline USHER strongly calls to mind the sufferings of Poe's child-bride Virginia CLEMM.

The complex nature of the story has led scholars to disagree over its exact meaning. While some prefer to see "Usher" as simply a story of the supernatural, others see in the events and characters the workings of the human mind on the brink of insanity, with Madeline and Roderick each representing the unconscious and the conscious, respectively. When the conscious (Roderick) strives to deny the existence of the unconscious (Madeline), the human mind (the house encompassing both) must fall into destruction. A third approach moves the meaning of the story into the realm of creativity and the role of the romantic artist in achieving an ideal creative plane. The dilemma faced by the romantic artist is represented by Roderick, who effectively plunges into madness when he leaves the real world behind in his search for the sublime.

PUBLISHING AND DRAMATIZATION HISTORY

The story was first published in the September 1839 issue of BURTON'S GENTLEMAN'S MAGAZINE and was later collected among the 12 tales appearing in TALES BY EDGAR A. POE, published by Wiley & Putnam in 1845. The publication of the story brought positive critical attention to Poe as a serious writer, who was by that time considered respectable enough for publisher Lea & Blanchard to publish his first collection of short stories, TALES OF THE GROTESQUE AND ARABESQUE, which appeared in December 1839 and contained 25 of Poe's works.

The story opens with the following epigraph: *Son coeur est un luth suspendu; / Sitot qu'on le touche il resonne* [His heart is a suspended lute; / Whenever one touches it, it resounds]. The lines are take from the poem "Le Refus" by Pierre-Jean de Beranger (1780–1857). The story also includes the first appearance of Poe's poem "THE HAUNTED PALACE" spoken by Roderick as he contemplates mortality.

The visually graphic content of the story has made it the subject of several film versions. The earliest film of the story appeared in France in 1929 as *Le Chute de la Maison Usher* [The Fall of the House of Usher], directed by Jean Epstein and Luis Bunuel. This impressionistic version, which features flying drapery, low-lying mists, sudden gusts of wind, and artistically flickering candle flames, earned critical acclaim. Television movie versions appeared in England in 1950; in the United States in 1958, as part of the NBC-TV *Matinee Theater;* and in 1982, as an amateurish production with cardboard sets. Roger CORMAN's low-budget 1960 version, titled *House of Usher* in the United States and *The Fall of the House of Usher* in Great Britain, is considered by many film critics to be the best film adaptation of the story, despite the liberties it takes in making the narrator Madeline's fiancé and in having the house first burn, then sink into the ground. This film was the first of eight Poe adaptations by Corman.

The story also became an obsession of the French composer Claude DEBUSSY, who worked sporadically from 1890 through his death in 1918 on an opera based on the story, yet left it unfinished. The composer told friends that he had become obsessed with the "heir of the Usher family" and had nearly finished a long monologue of "poor Roderick's. It is sad enough to draw tears from a stone," he said.

CHARACTERS

Madeline USHER, Roderick USHER, unnamed narrator.

PLOT SYNOPSIS

The plot of the story was familiar to readers of gothic romances in Poe's time. A young man is mysteriously summoned to an ancient home that holds long-hidden secrets imbued with power over life and death. The decaying Usher mansion has vacant, staring windows and a nearly invisible crack that scars the façade. While visiting, the narrator is involved in a series of bizarre and supernatural events for which he can provide no scientific explanation, and he is called upon to take part in a strange task—in this case, to assist Roderick Usher in providing Madeline with "temporary entombment" after her apparent death. Later, while a violent storm rages outside, the narrator reads aloud to Usher from a medieval romance. Madeline rises from her coffin and then appears to them, as Usher informs the narrator that Madeline was buried alive. The enshrouded Madeline falls onto her brother, dragging him "to the floor a corpse, and a victim to the terrors he had anticipated." As brother and sister fall dead, the house begins to collapse, and the narrator runs out to avoid being killed. Having barely escaped with his life, the narrator gapes in horror as "the deep and dank tarn at [his] feet closed sullenly and silently over the fragments of the House of Usher," and he is left to tell the tragic story of the Ushers.

The story departs from the usual gothic fare in its emphasis upon introspection rather than action and incident. Aside from the entombment of Madeline, none of the standard elements, such as mysterious appearances and disappearances, hidden rooms, or ghosts and visions, exist. The focus is placed on the narrator's perceptions and observations of a disintegrating intellect—of a crumbling Roderick Usher rather than a crumbling castle or abbey. The effect produced is not one of physical terror but of the psychological, which requires the reader to enter Roderick's mind and to join him in fearing the onslaught of insanity. The end of the standard gothic tale brings resolution through revelations of familial relationships, old vendettas, and interpersonal debts. The end of "The Fall of the House of Usher" serves no such purpose. Instead, it raises questions that can never be answered as the characters who may possess vital knowledge perish.

Fashion   *See* "THE NEW COMEDY. BY MRS. MOWATT"; MOWATT, Anna Cora.

Fatquack, Mr.   Character mentioned in the short story "THE LITERARY LIFE OF THINGUM BOB, ESQ." Decreed one of the "galaxy of genius," he received 62-and-a-half cents for his domestic novelette, *Dish-Clout*. The character is associated with James Fenimore Cooper, whose writing abilities Poe viewed with contempt. In "A FEW WORDS ABOUT BRAINARD," Poe reviews the works of various "native writers" and states, "It is not because we have *no* Mr. Coopers but because it has been demonstrated that we might, at any moment, have as many Mr. Coopers as we please."

Fay, Theodore Sedgwick (1807–1898)   Author of the novel *Norman Leslie: A Tale of the Present Times,* a book that exemplified popular taste and that the NEW YORK MIRROR praised heavily and Poe condemned. In "AUTOGRAPHY," Poe describes Fay's signature as having "an air of swagger about it. There are too many dashes—and the tails of the long letters are too long." Moreover, he finds the writing to have a "wavering, finicky, and overdelicate air, without pretension to either grace or

force." *See* "NORMAN LESLIE: A TALE OF THE PRESENT TIMES."

Feltspar, Ferdinand Fitz Fossillus   Character in the short story "LIONIZING." He is one of the many pseudointellectual guests at the Prince of Wales's literary banquet and an expert on obscure facts regarding rocks.

Female Poets of America   A large volume edited and compiled by Rufus W. GRISWOLD containing representative poetry of 95 women poets, beginning with Anne Bradstreet and ending with the now-forgotten Anna H. Phillips, who wrote under the pseudonym Helen Irving, published in 1842 by Carey & Hart. Poe's review of the work appeared in the November 1842 issue of the *Boston Miscellany*. The review praises Griswold for introducing many of the "lady-poets" to the public for the first time, as well as for having "been at the pains of doing what Northern critics seem to be at great pains *never* to do—that is to say, he has been at the trouble of doing justice, in great measure, to several poetesses who have not had the good fortune to be born in the North." Aside from such praise, Poe also finds fault with the volume and contends that Griswold has not done one or two of the poets justice and that he has left out several whom Poe would have included. In the final analysis, he praises the courage shown by Griswold for going against "the four or five different *cliques* who control our whole literature in controlling the larger portion of our critical journals" and for recognizing "the poetical claims of the ladies mentioned above."

Fergusson, John W.   Printer with the SOUTHERN LITERARY MESSENGER in the mid-1830s who attended Poe's wedding to Virginia CLEMM. In years after Poe's death, Fergusson was interviewed about the author and provided the following characterization: "There never was a more perfect gentleman than Mr. Poe when he was sober, [but at other times] he would just as soon lie down in the gutter as anywhere else."

"Festus: A Poem by Philip James Bailey, Barrister at Law. First American Edition. Boston: Benjamin P. Mussey. For Sale in New York by Redfield & Company"   Review by Poe that appeared in the September 6, 1845, issue of the *BROADWAY JOURNAL*. In this review, Poe calls the narrative poem one "of the most remarkable power" and finds it strange that the poem, published six years earlier in Britain, has only appeared in the United States within the previous eight or nine months. Although he admits "we have read it only in snatches," Poe characterizes the poem as "a Vesuvius-cone at least—if not an Aetna—in the literary cosmos." He expresses approval of the swagger that pervades the poem, "its imperiousness—its egoitism—its energy—its daring—its ruggedness—its contempt of law in great things and small," and commends the poet for issuing this American edition.

Fether, Professor   Character referred to in Poe's short comic tale "THE SYSTEM OF DOCTOR TARR AND PROFESSOR FETHER." He is credited with having discovered, with Doctor TARR, a novel and effective medical treatment system of "rigorous severity" in place of the "soothing system" in dealing with "the caprices of madmen."

"A Few Words About Brainard"   Review by Poe that appeared in the February 1842 issue of *GRAHAM'S MAGA-ZINE.* Although ostensibly a review of *The Poems of John G. C. Brainard. A New and Authentic Collection, with an original Memoir of his Life,"* published by Edward Hopkins in Hartford, Connecticut, it also comments on the state of American literature. In particular, Poe questions the dubious poetical standing of Joseph Rodman Drake's "THE CULPRIT FAY" and expresses the view that "the general merit of our national Muse has been estimated too highly, and that the author of 'The Connecticut River' has, individually, shared in the exaggeration." Poe reviews Brainard's "The Fall of Niagara" with disdain and questions whether he actually had seen the great falls before writing about them: "[N]o poet could have looked upon Niagara, in the substance, and written thus about it. If he saw it at all, it must have been in fancy—'at a distance'." Examining the poem line by line, Poe finds that the poem "does not deserve all the unmeaning commendation it has received." He does, however, cite "The Tree Toad," a brief, humorous composition as imaginative and "one of the *truest poems* ever written by Brainard."

"A Few Words on Secret Writing"   *See* CRYPTOGRAPHY.

Fibalittle, Mrs.   Character mentioned in the short story "THE LITERARY LIFE OF THINGUM BOB, ESQ." She is one of the writers who provide "numerous magnificent contributions" to the *Lollipop,* a literary magazine, a part of the "galaxy of genius."

Fichte, Johann Gottlieb (1762–1814)   German philosopher, educator, and proponent of an idealist theory of reality and moral action. His theories defined consciousness as an interaction between the ego, the "I", and otherness, the "not-I." Poe speaks in "MORELLA" of "the wild Pantheism of Fichte"; and in "LOSS OF BREATH," the imminence of death brings "like a flood" a remembrance of Fichte. In "HOW TO WRITE A BLACK-WOOD ARTICLE," Poe recommends that would-be authors "Talk of the academy and the lyceum, and say something about Ionic, and Italic schools, or about

Bossarian, and Kant, and Schelling, and Fichte." Poe also makes reference to Fichte's theories in the discussion of "Geraldine" in a review of the work of Rufus DAWES.

"Fifty Suggestions"   A collection of 50 sometimes brief, often cynical observations by Poe that were published in the May 1845 and June 1845 issues of *GRAHAM'S MAGAZINE.* The statements range from observations on politics to observations on human nature. They are often vitriolic and include the names of philosophers or other figures from history, as well as hints of the names of contemporary authors.

Fitzgerald, Bishop O. P.   Virginia clergyman who in 1899 spoke at commencement exercises at the University of Virginia and recounted his experiences in hearing Poe read and lecture in 1848 and 1849. Although some of what Fitzgerald said has since been found to be inaccurate, his remarks have been used by numerous pseudobiographers to create a composite of Poe's last days. Fitzgerald claimed that Poe, in a final lecture on September 24, 1849, raised as much as $1,500 speaking about The Poetic Principle. If true, then Maria Clemm's continued poverty at the time would be due to a cruel Poe who wouldn't share his fortune with her. Later accounts correct this and assert that the amount was much smaller, so low that Poe was forced to borrow $5 to go north that day. Bishop also professed to have inside knowledge of Poe's final days and speaks of parties and toasts that remain uncorroborated.

Fitzwilliam, Edward Francis (1824–1857)   English composer of songs and dramatic music who composed "Hear the Sledges with the Bells," a musical setting of the first stanza of Poe's poem "THE BELLS."

Flag of Our Union   Boston weekly journal, owned by Frederick Gleason. Although it did not have a large subscriber list, the Boston sheet did, for a time, pay Poe promptly and fairly well. Among other pieces, it printed Poe's short story "HOP-FROG" on March 17, 1849; the poem "TO MY MOTHER" on July 7, 1849; and "For Annie" on April 28, 1849. The newspaper announced in late April 1849 that it could no longer pay for whatever articles and poetry it published, and Poe stopped submitting his work.

Flavius Vospiscus (c. A. D. 172)   Second-century poet, born in ancient Syracuse. He is mentioned in Poe's short story "FOUR BEASTS IN ONE." Poe cites Latin verses from Vospiscus's "Divius Aurelianus," part of *Scriptores Historiae Augustae,* for the crowd to use in celebrating the valor of their king ANTIOCHUS EPIPHANES.

Fletcher the Younger, Giles (1588–1623) English poet. Poe used one stanza from Fletcher's "Christ's Victorie and Triumph in Heaven and Earth" as an epigraph to his short story "THE DOMAIN OF ARNHEIM." Fletcher is mentioned as one of "the principal poets and artists of Great Britain" in Poe's review "THE BOOK OF GEMS. THE POETS AND ARTISTS OF GREAT BRITAIN," in the August 1836 issue of the *SOUTHERN LITERARY MESSENGER.*

"Flora and Thalia; Or Gems of Flowers and Poetry: Being an Alphabetical Arrangement of Flowers, with Appropriate Poetical Illustrations, Embellished with Colored Plates. By a Lady. To Which Is Added a Botanical Description of the Various Parts of a Flower and the Dial of Flowers. Philadelphia: Carey, Lea, & Blanchard" Review by Poe that appeared in the June 1836 issue of the *SOUTHERN LITERARY MESSENGER.* Poe begins the review by calling the work "a very pretty and very convenient volume, on a subject which, since the world began, has never failed to excite curiosity and sympathy in all who have a proper sense of the beautiful." He compliments the choice of engravings and asserts that the poems accompanying the floral illustrations are all "above mediocrity." Poe also compliments the author for her clever instructions for a *"Dial of Flowers,"* in which flowers are planted according to their properties for opening and shutting at various times of the day "to indicate the succession of the hours, and to make them supply the place of a watch or clock."

Flud, Robert (1574–1637) British Rosicrucian, a member of an international fraternity of religious mystics devoted to applying esoteric religions in daily life, who dealt in the occult art of palmistry. Among Roderick USHER's favorite volumes in his library is *The Chiromancy of Robert Flud,* one of several books that the unnamed narrator of "THE FALL OF THE HOUSE OF USHER" declares to be "in strict keeping with this character of phantasm."

Folio Club, the An imaginary literary society comprised of 11 DUNDERHEADS," to whom Poe attributed the writing of his collection "TALES OF THE FOLIO CLUB." Poe labeled his imaginary authors "a mere Junto of Dunderheadism. I think too the members are quite as ill-looking as they are stupid. I also believe it is their settled intention to abolish literature, subvert the Press, and overturn the Government of Nouns and Pronouns." Among the members of this imaginary literary society are Mr. Snap, the President, and nine other members: Mr. Convolvulus Gondola; De Rerum Natura, Esqr.; Mr. Solomon Seadrift; Mr. Horribile DICTU; Mr. Blackwood Blackwood; Mr. Rouge-et-Noir; Chronologos Chronology; and two unnamed Dunderheads, "a very little man in a black coat with very black eyes" and "a stout gentleman who admired Sir Walter Scott." The members would each read a story at one of the monthly meetings.

Foote, Arthur (1853–1937) American composer. In 1901 Foote wrote a four-part chorus for the first stanza of Poe's poem "THE BELLS." Foote also composed orchestral pieces inspired by other literary works; among these are *The Farewell of Hiawatha, The Wreck of the Hesperus,* and works by the Persian poet Omar Khayyam, as well as a symphonic prologue to *Francesca da Rimini.*

"For Annie" Poem by Poe that first appeared in the April 28, 1849, issue of the *FLAG OF OUR UNION* and in the *Home Journal* on the same day. Written for Annie RICHMOND after their close friendship ruptured, the tender and melodious poem describes Poe's gratitude in recovering from the severe illness that ensued when he attempted suicide by overdosing on laudanum in November 1848. It speaks of Poe's conquest at last of "the fever called 'Living'," and the cessation of "The moaning and groaning, / The sighing and sobbing" that had tortured him. A little more than halfway through the poem, the speaker has "A dream of the love / And the beauty of Annie" in which the Annie of the poem is tenderly maternal, comforting Poe with a gentle and protective embrace: "She tenderly kissed me, / She fondly caressed, / And then I fell gently / To sleep on her breast—Deeply to sleep / From the heaven of her breast." From his suffering state at the beginning of the poem, the speaker develops a heart "brighter / than all of the many / Stars of the heaven / For it sparkles with Annie." He recovers because of the loving care that Annie has provided to him.

Forrest, Hamilton (1901–1984) American composer who in 1928 created *The Masque of the Red Death, A Satire in Rhythmical Dissonance* for mixed chorus and orchestra.

Forsyth, Cecil (1870–1943) English composer, conductor, and author of music treatises. Forsyth wrote a part-song for unaccompanied men's voices, to Poe's poem "TO HELEN," as well as a setting of Keats's "Ode to a Nightingale," orchestral studies for Victor Hugo's *Les Misérables,* and the operas *Westward Ho!* and *Cinderella.*

Fortunato Character in the short story "THE CASK OF AMONTILLADO." A drunken fool whose name means "The Fortunate One," he is the victim of the story. The narrator, MONTRESOR, relates that Fortunato is in most regards "a man to be respected and even feared," but he has one weak point that the narrator exploits: "He prided himself on his connoisseurship in wine." Fortunato's pride allows Montresor to lure him into the catacombs and to kill him.

"The Fortune Hunter; or The Adventures of a Man About Town. A Novel of New York Society. By Mrs. Anna Cora Mowatt, Author of Fashion, Etc. New York. William Taylor"   Review by Poe that appeared in the August 2, 1845, issue of the *BROADWAY JOURNAL.* Poe admits in the review that the *Journal* received the novel too late to do more than to merely mention it, and he promises that "Hereafter we shall do it that full justice which is demanded by the celebrity and varied talent of its fair author." Poe reprinted chapter four of the novel with the review.

Foulds, John Herbert (1880–1939)   English composer and conductor who in 1924 created a dramatic monologue with a simplified pianoforte arrangement from an orchestral score for Poe's "THE TELL-TALE HEART." The composer also wrote music for theater productions, concert opera, chamber music, songs, and piano pieces.

"Four Beasts in One: The Homo-Cameleopard"   Short story. The "homo-cameleopard" created by Poe in this story is a combination of man, camel, lion, and panther that looks like a bizarre giraffe. The name "cameleopard" is taken from the Greek word for giraffe, *kamelopardalis,* modified by Poe to reflect his "four beasts in one."

The story is one of Poe's most successful comic efforts, although comedy seems to mask a serious statement about the relationship between despots and those they rule. In the midst of a city through which domesticated wild animals roam streaks an undignified ruler who seeks to associate with himself the characteristics of the camel, the lion, and the panther. He assumes the skins and the behaviors of the animals and creates chaos, destruction, and death, yet regains the love of the populace when he exhibits "superhuman agility" and offers a promise of victory "at the celebration of the next Olympiad." One can perpetrate any number of horrors upon a people, as long as physical efforts are shown to be successful.

PUBLISHING AND DRAMATIZATION HISTORY

The story was first published in the March 1836 issue of the *SOUTHERN LITERARY MESSENGER* under the title of "Epimanes," and it was included under this title again in *TALES OF THE GROTESQUE AND ARABESQUE* in 1839. When Poe revised the story for publication in the December 6, 1845, issue of the *BROADWAY JOURNAL,* he also changed the title.

The story begins with the epigraph *Chacun a ses vertus* [Each person has his virtues], taken from *Xerxes,* a play written in 1714 by Prosper Joylot de Crébillon.

No film has been made of "Four Beasts in One" to date.

CHARACTERS

ANTIOCHUS EPIPHANES, unnamed narrator.

PLOT SYNOPSIS

The narrator appears to be a historian of antiquity who tells the tale in the Syrian city of Antioch in the year 175 B.C. and invites the reader to enjoy a rare spectacle. The story tells of the triumphant return of a legendary ruler Antiochus Epiphanes, whose private life and reputation are made up of "impious, dastardly, cruel, silly, and whimsical achievements." Wild animals roam the streets "entirely without restraint," for leopards, tigers, and lions have been domesticated and "trained without difficulty to their present profession, and attend upon their respective owners in the capacity of *valets-de-chambre.*" Despite the "prodigious number of stately palaces . . . the numerous temples, sumptuous and magnificent" in Antioch, the city also contains "an infinity of mud huts, and abominable hovels." The quietly domesticated animals contrast strongly with the strange, bestial behavior of King Antiochus, who enters the city "ensconced in the hide of a beast and doing his best to play the part of a cameleopard," a four-part animal with the head of a man and a tail "held aloft by his two principal concubines." The spectacle so offends the domesticated wild animals that they mutiny and attack the citizens of Antioch, devouring some. The citizens then pursue the royal four-part beast to the Hippodrome, where he will either be presented a wreath for outrunning them or be torn to pieces in anger. The ending is ambiguous, as the narrators propose to leave town before either event takes place, although they believe it more likely that, despite the lives lost, the people will "invest his [the king's] brows . . . with the wreath of victory in the stadium of the foot races."

Fox, George (1854–?)   British composer and dramatic baritone who sang with the Italian Opera at Her Majesty's Theatre and the Royal English Opera Company. He wrote a cantata to Poe's poem "THE BELLS."

Francis, John Wakefield (1789–1861)   Physician who attended the Poes from 1844 to 1846. He warned Poe at various times to abstain from drinking for the sake of his health, and in 1847 he warned that Poe's heart was weak and he would not live long. Francis also appears in Poe's "THE LITERATI OF NEW YORK CITY," in which he is honored "in his capacity of physician and medical lecturer." Poe speaks highly of the physician's philanthropy, noting that "[h]is professional services and his purse are always at the command of the needy; few of our wealthiest men have ever contributed to the relief of distress so bountifully."

French critics and criticism Poe exercised great influence on the French poet and critic Charles BAUDELAIRE, who wrote several articles about him and translated Poe's work. Baudelaire's work, and Poe's work through him, attracted a group of French poets and prose writers in the last three decades of the 19th century whose works show the influence of the two earlier writers. Known both as Symbolists and in a narrower group as Decadents, for their interest in the morbid and perverse, as well as for their unconventional social behavior and sensational temperaments, they placed emphasis on pure art and creative self-expression. These rebellious artists and writers revolted against realism and chose, instead, to depict and explore the human psyche and to re-create—not merely record—human consciousness. The symbols pervading their work are highly personal, often esoteric, and the techniques used were attempts to free art from conventional restrictions. Form and function were forced to yield to a fluidity in both poetry and prose. The Symbolist leaders Stéphane MALLARMÉ, Arthur Rimbaud, and Paul Verlaine and their followers valued all of Poe's writings. Later French critics, such as Paul Claudel and Paul Valéry, who particularly admired "EUREKA," praised Poe's genius to a young André GIDE. Most English language readers saw "Eureka" only as pseudoscience, but Claudel called it "magnificent." Gide later credited Poe as "one of the inventors of *le monologue intérieur* [interior monologue]." The Symbolists adopted the musicality of Poe's verse as their own, as well as his synthesizing of the senses in which all objects take on symbolic meaning through a correspondence among visual, auditory, and sensory perceptions.

Fricassee Character in the short story "LIONIZING." He is a gourmet and a guest at the Prince of Wales's literary banquet. He has come from Rocher de Cancale, a fictional country Poe named after a well-known Paris restaurant of the time. Fricassee mentions real dishes, such as muriton of red tongue, cauliflowers and *velouté* sauce, and other foods for which recipes appear as recently as in the 1961 edition of *Larousse Gastronomique*, often referred to by culinary masters as the French national cookbook.

Frogpondians Poe's derogatory name for the New England and Boston literati. Boston itself was "the Frogpond." In many reviews of such luminaries as Henry Wadsworth LONGFELLOW, Poe spoke of the pretentious behavior by Boston literati who fancied themselves to be equals of the great British writers living on the other side of the Atlantic Ocean (the great pond). Instead, Poe characterized them as small talents living in the limited boundaries of a frog pond (Boston). His hostility was heightened by their abuse of his work, and he openly attacked the Frogpondians in "BOSTON AND THE BOSTONIANS": "The Frogpondians may as well spare us their abuse. We despise them and defy them (the transcendental vagabonds!) and they may all go to the devil together."

Froissart, Monsieur Character mentioned in the short story "THE SPECTACLES." Born in Paris, he is the father of Napoleon Bonaparte FROISSART.

Froissart, Napoleon Bonaparte Birth name of a character in the short story "THE SPECTACLES." The character proudly traces his descent "from the immortal author of the 'Chronicles'" but changes his surname to Simpson "in order to receive a large inheritance left by a distant male relative, Adolphus Simpson."

Fuller, Hiram (1814–1880) Editor of the New York *EVENING MIRROR*. He sided with Poe's literary enemies Charles Briggs and Dr. Thomas Dunn English when they published their attacks on Poe in the May 26, 1846 issue of the *Evening Mirror* and the June 23, 1846 issue of the *New York Morning Telegraph*.

Fuller, [Sarah] Margaret [Ossoli] (1810–1850) American social reformer, author, and editor who espoused transcendentalism and championed the cause of equal rights for women. She was the literary critic for the *NEW YORK TRIBUNE* from 1844 to 1846 and gained a strong reputation in this field. She reviewed *TALES BY EDGAR A. POE,* published in 1845 by Wiley & Putnam, in the *Tribune* and found them to be "a penetration into the causes of things which leads to original but credible results. Where the effects are fantastic, they are not unmeaningly so." Unlike Poe, who took every opportunity to attack his critics, and even though Poe attacked her association with the Transcendentalists (see TRANSCENDENTALISM), she abstained from revenge and her opinion of Poe's abilities remained fair and just. In her review of *THE RAVEN AND OTHER POEMS,* published in 1845 by Wiley & Putnam, Fuller wrote that Poe's lines "breathe a passionate sadness, relieved sometimes by touches very lovely and tender."

Poe presents a complimentary view of Fuller's literary ability in "THE LITERATI OF NEW YORK CITY" and speaks of her style as "one of the very best with which I am acquainted." He views Fuller as "a marked exception" to the "ill-founded" belief that "the book of an author is a thing apart from the author's self" and notes with approval that Fuller's "personal character and her printed book are merely one and the same thing."

Furneaux, Lieutenant An actual English sailor and explorer. Readers learn in the *NARRATIVE OF ARTHUR GOR-*

DON PYM that he accompanied Captain Cook on the *Resolution* and joined him "in the Adventure," as Poe wrote in referring to the extensive journeys made by Cook.

Fuseli, Henry (1741–1825) Swiss-English painter whose works emphasized melodrama, fantasy, and horror and exerted an important influence on the Romantic movement in England. Best known were his imaginative fantasy paintings, filled with lurid nocturnal effects, apparitions, and the trappings of nightmares. Poe's unnamed narrator in "THE FALL OF THE HOUSE OF USHER" views with fear the paintings by Roderick USHER, which evoke "an intensity of intolerable awe, no shadow of which felt I ever yet in the contemplation of the certainly glowing yet too concrete reveries of Fuseli."

G——, Lieutenant Character in the short story "THE GOLD-BUG." His name was most likely inspired by Captain Henry GRISWOLD, one of Poe's officers at Fort Moultrie. In the story, the army officer takes the scarabaeus from William LEGRAND shortly after Legrand finds it. Lieutenant G—— promptly returns it the following morning after studying it. Lieutenant G—— begs Legrand to allow him to take the beetle to the fort, and thrusts it into his waistcoat immediately after permission is given. As Legrand tells the unnamed narrator of the story, "you know how enthusiastic he is on all subjects connected with Natural History."

G——, Monsieur Character in Poe's short stories "THE PURLOINED LETTER," "THE MYSTERY OF MARIE ROGÊT," and "THE MURDERS IN THE RUE MORGUE." He is the prefect of Parisian police who seeks the assistance of C. Auguste DUPIN in solving crimes that baffle official law enforcement. Poe may have selected a name beginning with *G* because Henri-Joseph Gisquet was Prefect of the Paris police from 1831 to 1836, immediately preceding the publication in 1841 of the first of the stories, "The Murders in the Rue Morgue." The prefect grudgingly approaches Dupin "to consult us, or rather to ask the opinion of my friend, about some official business which had occasioned a great deal of trouble," and often reacts in an ungracious manner after Dupin solves the crime. In "The Murders in the Rue Morgue," he "could not altogether conceal his chagrin . . . and was fain to indulge in a sarcasm or two, about the propriety of every person minding his own business." In "The Mystery of Marie Rogêt," Dupin makes an agreement with the prefect and states to his unnamed assistant that he "knows this gentleman well. It will not do to trust him too far." When Monsieur G—— reappears in "The Purloined Letter," Dupin's assistant says they "gave him a hearty welcome, for there was nearly half as much of the entertaining as of the contemptible about him." Despite the irritating behavior of the prefect, Dupin remains mildly amused by the man's intellectual obtuseness, noting at the end of "The Purloined Letter": "I like him especially for one master stroke of cant, by which he has attained his reputation for ingenuity. I mean the way he has *'de nier ce qui est, et d'expliquer ce qui n'est pas'* [of denying what is, and explaining what isn't]."

Gaffy Nickname that Poe acquired as student at the University of Virginia. Poe would often read his early short story efforts to friends that gathered with him in the evening. On one particular occasion, he read a story to friends who teased him about its merits and said that the name of the hero, Gaffy, had been used too frequently throughout the work. Angered by their teasing, Poe threw the story into the fire, even though his friends protested immediately that it was one of his best stories to date and that they had simply been having fun with him. For a long time afterward, these same friends called Poe by their new nickname for him, Gaffy.

Gaillard, Petit Character in the short story "THE SYSTEM OF DOCTOR TARR AND PROFESSOR FETHER." His name in French means "little sprightly dance." He is one of the inmates of the mental asylum in the story and believes that he is a pinch of snuff. As one onlooker relates, Gaillard "was truly distressed because he could not take himself between his own finger and thumb."

Galt, William (1755–1825) A successful merchant and one of the richest men in Virginia, Galt was the uncle of John ALLAN. He was born in Scotland and emigrated to the United States to make his fortune. After settling in Richmond, Virginia, Galt built a prosperous mercantile and tobacco trade at home and overseas. Records show that he had a strong sense of family responsibility and provided for orphaned family members on both sides of the Atlantic Ocean. When he died in March 1825, he left his fortune of several hundred thousand dollars (the equivalent of a few million dollars in contemporary terms), slaves, securities, merchandise, and real estate to Allan.

Garcio, Alfonzo Character in the short story "THE MURDERS IN THE RUE MORGUE." He is a native of Spain and an undertaker who resides in the Rue Morgue. He swears that he heard the gruff voice of a Frenchman arguing with a shrill-voiced Englishman before the murders, although he claims that he could not distinguish what was said. Garcio does not understand the English language, only its intonations, but he swears that the murderer was speaking English.

Gaul, Harvey (1881–1967) American conductor, organist, music critic, and composer of religious and choir music. He wrote *Poe's Fordham Prayer,* a four-part chorus for men's voices, with piano music for rehearsal only, which he based on Poe's poem "HYMN." Gaul was under the mistaken impression that "Hymn" was written while Poe was living in Fordham, New York. In fact, the poem was written before 1834, and Poe did not move to Fordham until 1846. When asked about his title, Gaul said, "I really thought that Poe wrote the piece while living in Fordham and that is the only raison d'être for the title."

Gay-Lussac, Joseph-Louis (1778–1850) French chemist and physicist known for experiments with the physical properties of gases. In 1804, he made several ascents in hot air balloons to study magnetic forces and to observe the composition and temperature of the air at different altitudes. Poe refers to his experiments in the short story "THE UNPARALLELED ADVENTURE OF ONE HANS PFAALL" and notes that "the greatest height ever reached by man was that of 25,000 feet, attained in the aeronautic expedition of Messieurs Gay-Lussac and Biot."

"Genius and the Character of Burns. By Professor Wilson. Wiley and Putnam's Library of Choice Reading. No. XXI" Review by Poe that appeared in the September 6, 1845, issue of the *BROADWAY JOURNAL.* Poe begins the review by praising Wilson's "enthusiastic appreciation of the beautiful, conjoined with a temperament compelling him into action and expression" and by complimenting him for possessing "ideality, energy and audacity." Within a few lines, however, the review lambastes Wilson for "his own inability to comprehend. He is no analyst. He is ignorant of the machinery of his own thoughts and the thoughts of other men." Damning Wilson's criticism as "superficial," Poe relates that the reader learns nothing new about either the poet Robert Burns or his poems, because Wilson has never "*demonstrated* anything beyond his own utter incapacity for demonstration." In the end, Poe can only recommend the work to readers who would be happy with "mere rhapsody," for herein they will not find "a guide to the real Burns."

"George Balcombe. A Novel. New York. Harper and Brothers" Review by Poe that appeared in the January 1837 issue of the *SOUTHERN LITERARY MESSENGER.* The review is largely complimentary, and more than half is devoted to a detailed summary of the work and its characters. The novel was published and submitted for review without revealing an author, but Poe states teasingly at the end of the review that no other than Judge Beverley TUCKER, of William and Mary College, Virginia, could think in the manner of the main character. In his "AUTOGRAPHY" sketch of Tucker, Poe labels the work "one of the best novels ever published in America" and notes that "for some reason the book was never a popular favorite." Discussing in the review the dramatis personae, Poe approves of Tucker's delineation of women in the novel and notes, "Upon the whole, no American novelist has succeeded, we think, in female character, even nearly so well as the writer of *George Balcombe.*" Despite the extensive praise, Poe expresses a few objections to the work, especially with Tucker "mere English." He identifies faulty constructions at some length and suggests that the author rethink the manner in which "the occasional *philosophy* of Balcombe himself" is expressed. Such minor flaws have little impact on Poe's enthusiasm for the work: "Nothing is wanting to a complete whole, and nothing is out of place, or out of time."

George, Dr. Miles Student acquaintance of Poe at the University of Virginia who often visited Poe's rooms. In a letter written on May 18, 1880, to Edward Valentine, a cousin of Mrs. Frances ALLAN, George described his memories of Poe's temperament as "very excitable and restless, at times wayward, melancholic and morose, but again—in his better moods, frolicksome, full of fun, and a most attractive and agreeable companion." The memory of 1826 also includes a foreshadowing of the problem that would plague Poe: "To calm and quiet the excessive nervous excitability under which he labored, he would too often put himself under the influence of the 'Invisible Spirit of Wine.'"

"Georgia Scenes, Characters, Incidents, &c In the First Half Century of the Republic. By a Native Georgian. Augusta, Georgia" Review by Poe that appeared in the March 1836 issue of the *SOUTHERN LITERARY MESSENGER.* The local sketches written by Augustus Baldwin Longstreet originally were published in newspapers under the two pseudonymous bylines of Hall and Baldwin. The collection, sketches that contain "fanciful combinations of real incidents and characters," was submitted anonymously to Poe, who credited the author as "a clever fellow, imbued with a spirit of the truest humor, and endowed, moreover, with an exquisitely discriminative and penetrating understanding of *character* in general, and of Southern character in particular." As proof for his assertions, Poe provides summaries and quotations from many of the sketches to support the humor of the material and the pleasure of his own reaction: "Seldom—perhaps never in our lives—have we laughed as immoderately over any book as over the one now before us."

"Geraldine, Athenia of Damascus, and Miscellaneous Poems" *See* "THE POETRY OF RUFUS DAWES."

Gibson, Thomas Ware   Poe's cadet roommate at West Point. In an account published in the November 1867 issue of *Harper's Magazine,* 30 years after they shared quarters, Gibson recalled the young Poe. At barely 20 years of age, Poe "had the appearance of being much older. He had a worn, weary, discontented look, not easily forgotten by those who were intimate with him." Gibson recalled that Poe was not amused by any remarks at his expense, and he became "not a little annoyed by a story that some of the class got up, to the effect that he [Poe] had procured a cadet's appointment for his son, and the boy having died, the father had substituted himself in his place." He also mentions Poe's remarkable memory for reciting prose and verse, as well as his failure to study anything at the Academy, making it "evident from the first that he had no intention of going through with the course." Evidence of Poe's later problem with drink is also present, as Gibson observes Poe "was seldom without a bottle of Benny Haven's best brandy. I don't think he was ever intoxicated while at the Academy, but he had already acquired the more dangerous habit of constant drinking."

Gide, André (1869–1951)   French novelist and literary critic who became an ardent admirer of Poe through his correspondence with Paul Valery and Paul Claudel, who had come to Poe through their admiration of French writer and critic Charles BAUDELAIRE. Gide proclaimed Poe the master of the "interior monologue," the presentation of a character's thoughts in a manner more controlled than stream-of-consciousness and on a level closer to direct verbalization. In many ways, Gide conducted a study of Poe through his early critical examination of the works of Russian novelist Fyodor Dostoyevsky, whose settings and characters he viewed from a context of perversity and self-torment that he likened to those of Poe. As Gide found, the characters of Dostoyevsky's works, like those in Poe's works, are often "profoundly warped by humiliation" and "find satisfaction in the resultant degradation, loathsome though it be."

"The Gift: A Christmas and New Years Present for 1836. Edited by Miss Leslie. Philadelphia: E. L. Carey and A. Hart"   Review that appeared in the September 1835 issue of the *SOUTHERN LITERARY MESSENGER.* The *Gift* was a popular annual issued by the Philadelphia publishers Carey and Hart that contained both illustrations and stories, and several of Poe's tales first appeared in the publication, including "WILLIAM WILSON," "ELEONORA," "THE PIT AND THE PENDULUM," and "THE PURLOINED LETTER." "MS. FOUND IN A BOTTLE" was reprinted there. The review gives special attention to the engravings, noting that the "are not all of a high order of excellence" and praising others as being "exquisite."

Of the writers whose works appeared, Poe stated, "Never had Annual a brighter galaxy of illustrious literary names in its table of contents—and in no instance has any contributor fallen below his or her general reputation."

Gilbert, Henry F. (1868–1928)   American composer who in 1904 wrote music for pianoforte inspired by Poe's tale "THE ISLAND OF THE FAY." He also composed orchestral and piano pieces, as well as a ballet and choral works.

Gill, William F. (1843–1882)   Poe's first American biographer and author of *The Life of Edgar Allan Poe* (Chatto & Windus, 1878). Gill attempted to refute Rufus GRISWOLD's vicious distortions printed in "The LUDWIG ARTICLE." In the book *Edgar Allan Poe and His Biographer: Rufus W. Griswold,* Gill bitterly defended Poe against Griswold's falsifications, including the charge that Poe was an alcoholic. In a grotesque gesture of respect that Poe himself might have appreciated, Gill acquired the bones of Virginia CLEMM Poe in 1875 when the cemetery of the Fordham Dutch Reformed Church, where she was buried, was destroyed. Gill rescued Virginia's remains and placed them in a box under his bed, thus exciting considerable curiosity among those who had believed Virginia to be the model of Annabel Lee in Poe's poem of the same name. A few years later, the bones were taken to Baltimore to be buried next to Poe. Gill's work was impotent in its attempts, and Griswold's distortions of Poe's life continued to be accepted as truth until the early 20th century.

Gillespie, William M. (1816–1868)   Amateur writer and coeditor of the *New York World,* as well as a professor of civil engineering at Union College in Schenectady, New York. Poe included him among the profiles in "THE LITERATI OF NEW YORK CITY," and referred to him as "the author of a neat volume entitled 'Rome as Seen by a New Yorker'—a good title to a good book." The profile expresses approval of Gillespie's originality in endeavouring "to convey Rome only by those impressions which would naturally be made upon an American" and describes the author's style as "pure and sparkling, although occasionally flippant and *dillettantesque.*" Of the man, Poe wrote that he was "warmhearted, excitable, nervous" and "somewhat awkward," prone to walking the streets "in a state of profound abstraction."

Gironne, Nicolas Eymeric di (c. 1320–1399)   Inquisitor-general for Aragon during the Inquisition. He also is author of "one favourite volume . . . a small octavo edition of the *Directorium Inquisitorum"* in the library of

Roderick USHER. The book is an account of the procedures and tortures of the Inquisition.

Glanvill, Joseph (1636–1680)   Mystic theologian and author of *Saducismus Triumphatus,* a work on witchcraft, who was also famous for his treatises on the new science and religion. Poe takes the epigraph for "A DESCENT INTO THE MAELSTROM" from Glanvill's *Essays on Several Important Subjects.* He purports to also take the epigraph to "LIGEIA," regarding the power of the will to overcome death, from Glanvill. Despite careful scrutiny, scholars have not located the source of the quotation, which Poe also integrates into the text of the story at two points. Many believe Poe made up the quotation and falsified attribution.

Glass, Corporal   Character in *THE NARRATIVE OF ARTHUR GORDON PYM.* He is a former corporal in the British artillery who claims to be "supreme governor of the islands" with a constituency of 21 men and three women. Glass sells Captain GUY 500 sealskins and some ivory.

Glendinning   Character in the short story "WILLIAM WILSON." Described as "a young parvenu nobleman" with easily acquired riches, Glendinning is a fitting subject to be cheated at cards. After allowing Glendinning to win considerable sums of money in several games, Wilson draws him into a card game and aims to cheat him of all of his money. Within a short period of time, Glendinning loses so heavily to Wilson that the game has "effected his total ruin." The unpitying Wilson continues to play, nonetheless, until his double enters the room and exposes him.

Gliddon, Mr.   Character in the short story "SOME WORDS WITH A MUMMY." He is probably based on George Robins Gliddon, whose book *Ancient Egypt* was reviewed in the *New World* in April 1843, and to whom John Lloyd Stephens referred as British consul in Egypt in *Arabia Petrae.* In the story, Gliddon serves as translator and intermediary between the mummy and the learned men.

Gluck   Character in "THE UNPARALLELED ADVENTURE OF ONE HANS PFAALL." He is a printer who is called upon to verify the source of the newspapers that are stuck all over the hot-air balloon. He observes that they are from Holland and that they were "dirty papers—very dirty—and Gluck, the printer, would take his Bible oath to their having been printed in Rotterdam."

Gniessin, Michael (1883–1971)   Russian composer who was influential in the development of Hebrew music. He wrote *Cherv-Pobeditel,* an arrangement for tenor voice and orchestra to accompany Poe's poem "THE CONQUEROR WORM."

Godey, Louis Antoine (1804–1878)   Editor and publisher of *GODEY'S MAGAZINE AND LADY'S BOOK* from 1830 to 1877. He was the first magazine publisher to successfully reach the audience of American women, and he and his staff did so by catering to the pure and pretty sentimentality of the times. His fashionable periodical provided its vast female audience with articles that emphasized fashion, morality, and profuse sentiment. Poe's editorial relations with Godey were reasonably amicable, although he did refer to Godey's publication as "a milliner's magazine." Still, from May through October 1846, Poe published "THE LITERATI OF NEW YORK CITY" in *Godey's Lady's Book* with little interference despite their too-frank content, which often contained scathing denunciations of the subjects. He also expressed the opinion that "Godey keeps almost as many ladies in his pay as the Grand Turk." Poe writes of Godey's signature in "AUTOGRAPHY" that it "gives evidence of a fine taste, combined with an indefatigability which will ensure his permanent success in the world's affairs. No man has warmer friends or fewer enemies."

Godey's Magazine and Lady's Book   Usually referred to by its shortened title, *Godey's Lady's Book* was an eloquent periodical with a largely female readership. Despite his contempt for what he termed "a milliner's magazine," Poe contributed short stories and articles to the publication and enjoyed prompt and relatively good payment. "THE VISIONARY" appeared in the January 1834 issue; "A TALE OF THE RAGGED MOUNTAINS" in the April 1844 issue; "THE OBLONG BOX" in the September 1844 issue; "THOU ART THE MAN" in the November 1844 issue; a review of Nathaniel Hawthorne's work in the November 1847 issue; and "THE LITERATI OF NEW YORK CITY," a series of articles, appeared from May through October 1846. The November 1845 issue contained a review of Poe's *TALES OF THE GROTESQUE AND ARABESQUE,* originally published in 1839 that called Poe "one of the most accomplished authors in America" for his "skill in the 'building' of marvelous and grotesque stories which make the Arabian Nights seem tame and prosaic in comparison." The review continued, "We like a writer of this character and calibre. We are tired of being merely satisfied; and we like occasionally to be astonished."

Godwin, Bishop Francis (n.d.)   Author, under the pseudonym of Domingo Gonsales, of *The Man in the Moon; or a Discourse of a Voyager thither, by Domingo Gonsales the Speedy Messenger.* In a note at the end of "THE UNPARALLELED ADVENTURE OF ONE HANS PFAALL," Poe

Although Poe criticized Godey's Lady's Book *for its fashion pages like the one shown here, he published many short stories and articles in the magazine.* (Library of Congress)

PUBLISHING AND DRAMATIZATION HISTORY

The story was first published in two installments in the June 21 and 28, 1843, issues of the *Dollar Newspaper* in Philadelphia after winning a first prize of $100 in a contest sponsored by the paper. It was reprinted in newspapers across the country after winning the prize. In 1847, a pirated edition was published in England and the story was translated into French for several publications.

The story is preceded by a falsely attributed epigraph: "'What ho! what ho! this fellow is dancing mad! / He hath been bitten by the Tarantula.'—*All in the Wrong.*" These lines are not found in Arthur Murphy's comedy *All in the Wrong* (1761). Poe made up the lines to exploit the folk belief of southern Italy that dancing the tarantella, a folk dance, can cure a bite by the tarantula, thought to be the cause of tarantism, a nervous disorder characterized by spasms and twitching.

In August 1843 a stage production of the story appeared in Philadelphia. Although no film has been made of this story alone, *Manfish* (1956) contains a similar plot of murder and treasure hunting in the Caribbean.

CHARACTERS

Lieutenant G———, JUPITER, Mr. William LEGRAND, unnamed narrator.

This illustration accompanied the original publication of "The Gold-Bug" in the Philadelphia Dollar Newspaper. (Library of Congress)

claims "I have lately read a singular and somewhat ingenious little book" and proceeds to summarize its main argument. The author claims to have traveled to the moon through the assistance of swans (*ganzas*) that lifted him aloft while he sat astride a broomstick-like contraption, and he includes in the book an illustration of the event.

"The Gold-Bug" Short story. This tale was the most widely read, most popular of Poe's short stories during his lifetime, despite a warning from Nathaniel Parker WILLIS that using the word "bug" in the title might hurt sales in England, because the word is synonymous with "louse" in that country. This is one of the earliest serious stories to use the search for buried treasure as its theme and the first to introduce a message in cipher.

PLOT SYNOPSIS

This tale of treasure hunting and deciphering of secret messages features William Legrand, a cryptographer who lives alone on Sullivan's Island in the harbor of Charleston, South Carolina. Poe knew Sullivan's Island and the Charleston area well, because he was stationed there at Fort Moultrie from November 1827 through December 1848. As the story opens, the unnamed narrator has arrived to visit Legrand and his old African-American servant, Jupiter. Legrand has discovered a "scarabaeus," or dung beetle, "of a brilliant gold color" that dialect-speaking Jupiter insists "is a goole-bug, solid, ebery bit of him, inside and all."

The bug's unusual markings and lack of antennae suggest to Legrand that it is a clue to a greater treasure, and he decides to lead an expedition into the hills of the island. The characters soon uncover a treasure chest worth $1.5 million in "gold of antique date and of great variety," as well as precious stones and two complete skeletons apparently left behind by the legendary pirate Captain Kidd.

Afterward, Legrand explains his "methodical investigation of the affair" and reveals the shrewd methods that he used to crack the codes and to find the wealth. The key lies in a small, dirty scrap of parchment on which Legrand had drawn the bug. Really a treasure map, it contains the solution, lodged between the emblems of a skull and a goat, that Legrand needs in order to solve the cipher, which discloses the exact location of the treasure. Once the treasure hunters have reached the final location and begin to search, Legrand attaches a whipcord to the gold beetle and twirls it around to use it as a surveyor's plumb bob to pinpoint the spot. "The Gold-Bug" contains many of the same qualities and attitudes that appear in Poe's detective tales, for Legrand must use his ratiocinative abilities to solve the puzzle of the Gold-Bug. As is Auguste DUPIN, Legrand is misunderstood by those who lack his vision and think him mad, yet these men also exact their revenge, as does Legrand, who had "resolved to punish [him] quietly, in my own way, by a little bit of sober mystification."

Goldsmith, Oliver   *See* "THE VICAR OF WAKEFIELD."

Goncourt, Edmond Louis Antoine Hout de (1822–1896) and Jules Alfred Hout de Goncourt (1830–1870) French art critics, novelists, and early leaders in the Naturalism movement whose work was largely jointly created. After reading Charles BAUDELAIRE's translations of Poe's work, the Goncourt brothers were deeply impressed by Poe and proclaimed him a genius. They declared that Poe's originality and decadence, as well as the rich fantasy life depicted in his fiction, anticipated the fiction of the future, which would "present all the revolutions of the soul in the sufferings of the body."

Goodfellow, Charles   Character in the short story "THOU ART THE MAN." He is the alcoholic friend and the next door neighbor of Mr. Barnabas Shuttleworthy. Sometimes called "Charley Goodfellow" or "Old Charley Goodfellow," he possesses an "ingenuous face which is proverbially the very 'best letter of recommendation'." He fools the townspeople into charging another man with the murder that he commits and for which he nearly escapes punishment.

gothic   A type of literature characterized by gloomy medieval settings, supernatural effects, horror, and violence. The genre was named and introduced by Horace Walpole in *The Castle of Otranto* (1764), with the goal of leaving behind the familiar realism of Samuel Richardson and other 18th-century English novelists. Novelists in England created the standard in this genre: William Beckford, in *Vathek* (1786), Ann Radcliffe in *The Mysteries of Udolpho* (1794), Matthew Lewis in *The Monk* (1795), and William Godwin in *Caleb Williams* (1794) popularized such subject matter as haunted castles and abbeys, mysterious monks, dark family secrets, and ancient curses. In the United States, Charles Brockden Brown used the wilderness as a source of gothic elements in *Wieland* (1798). The gothic influence can be found in many of Poe's works, as well as in works written by Nathaniel HAWTHORNE.

Gottschalk, Louis F. (1869–1934)   American composer, conductor, and producer of light operas who wrote "The Cask of Amontillado," a song with words in the nature of a drinking song that uses verse to tell the story of Poe's tale of the same name. Gottschalk conducted *The Merry Widow* when it was first produced in 1907. He also produced the first film version of *The Wizard of Oz* (1914) and arranged scores for such movies as *The Curse of Eve* (1917), *The Three Musketeers* (1921), *Little Lord Fauntleroy* (1921), *Rosita* (1923), and *Romula* (1924).

Gove, Mary Neal (Mrs. Nichols) (1810–1884)   A phrenologist, Swedenborgian, and homeopathist, she attended Virginia CLEMM Poe during her terminal illness, often "bringing dainties and comforts from town." Gove also left one of the most living, contemporary accounts of Virginia's dying days and of the sad life that the melancholy little family lived in the Fordham cottage. Her account appeared in the February 1863 issue of *Six Penny Magazine*. Gove also published numerous articles under the pseudonym of Mary Orme and gave lectures on mesmerism. Grateful for her help, Poe published a complimentary profile of her in "THE LITERATI OF NEW YORK CITY."

Gowans, William New York City bookseller, described later by James Harrison, compiler of Poe's works, as a "wealthy and eccentric bibliopolist," who was a lodger in the boardinghouse run by Maria CLEMM, first at Sixth Avenue and Waverley Place and later on Carmine Street in New York City from February through September 1837. He had daily contact with Poe, Virginia, and Maria, and later wrote affectionately of them. In a personal account, Gowans remembered Poe as "one of the most courteous, gentlemanly, and intelligent companions I have ever met, and I must say I never saw him in the least affected with liquor, nor even descend to any known vice." To Gowans's view, Virginia was a young beauty whose "eye could match that of any hour, and her face defy the genius of a Canova to imitate." Through his work, Gowans had widespread literary contacts, and he shared them freely with Poe. He invited Poe to be his guest at the annual booksellers' dinner at the City Hotel on March 30, 1837, because numerous prominent literary figures and some well-known artists were expected to be present. In the same personal account, Gowans wrote, "The affair was a brilliant one and marked the first appearance of the young Southern critic and poet among the Knickerbockers," which included Washington IRVING, William Cullen BRYANT, James K. Paulding, Fitz-Green HALLECK, and Chanceller Kent.

Graham, George Rex (1813–1894) Philadelphia journal entrepreneur and founder of *GRAHAM'S MAGAZINE,* with interests in the *Saturday Evening Post* and *Atkinson's Casket.* He acquired *BURTON'S GENTLEMAN'S MAGAZINE* in December 1840 from William E. BURTON and merged its subscription list of 3,500 with the 1,500-member subscription list of his own publication, *Atkinson's Casket.* Graham was one of the few editorial authority figures in Poe's life with whom Poe did not openly feud. As Poe wrote, "With Graham who is really a very gentlemanly, although exceedingly weak man, I had no misunderstanding." After Poe's death, Graham wrote and published in his magazine two defenses of Poe and his art: "Defence of Poe" (March 1850) and "The Genius and Characteristics of the Late Edgar Allan Poe" (February 1854). Both pieces refuted the charges against Poe's character that appeared in the obituary written by Rufus GRISWOLD. Poe possessed, in Graham's estimation, a "management of the supernatural never attained or approached by any other writer." Poe's brief remark about Graham in "AUTOGRAPHY" says simply: "For both of these journals he has written much and well."

Graham's Magazine Begun in December 1840 after publisher George Rex GRAHAM combined *BURTON'S GENTLEMAN'S MAGAZINE* and *Atkinson's Casket, Graham's Magazine* hired Poe as book review editor in February 1841.

George Rex Graham, founder and owner of Graham's Magazine. (Edgar Allan Poe Society)

The new publication appealed in a popular manner to both men and women. It contained fashion, sketches and photographs, music, and short stories in addition to criticism and reviews. Poe remained the editor until April 1842, although he eventually became resentful of his own $800 annual salary at a "nambypamby" magazine in a year when Graham made a profit of $25,000. Despite his contempt, Poe was smart enough to exploit his association with the publication, which allowed him great freedom to express his literary opinions in frequently extensive articles. Looking back at Poe's reviews in *Graham's Magazine,* George Bernard Shaw became so impressed with the young critic that he labelled Poe as "the greatest journalistic critic of his time" and accused American critics of misunderstanding Poe's genius. In addition to literary criticism and reviews, Poe also published in the magazine such tales as "THE MURDERS IN THE RUE MORGUE," "A DESCENT INTO

THE MAELSTROM," "THE ISLAND OF THE FAY," "THE COLLOQUY OF MONOS AND UNA," and "NEVER BET THE DEVIL YOUR HEAD." Despite his prolific literary output, Poe found work at *Graham's* draining, as he said in a letter written in May 1841 to Frederick William Thomas: "I would be glad to get almost any appointment, even a $500.00 one, so that I have something independent of letters for a subsistence. To coin one's brain into silver, at the nod of a master, is, to my thinking, the hardest task in the world. . . ." Poe was succeeded by Rufus W. GRISWOLD, who remained for a year. *Graham's Magazine,* flourished until the competition from *Harper's New Monthly Magazine* forced circulation to drop in 1850. Publication ended in 1858.

"Grammar of the English Language, in a Series of Letters, Addressed to Every American Youth. By Hugh A. Pue. Philadelphia, Published by the Author" Review that appeared in the July 1841 issue of *GRAHAM'S MAGAZINE.* Early in the review, Poe points out the irony that the two-page preface of a grammar book should contain "some half dozen distinct instances of bad Grammar." After first questioning if Pue "means to include himself among the ignoramuses," Poe delineates the errors in the book. Following this analysis, he questions if he is, perhaps, "treating this gentleman discourteously. His book may be merely intended as a good joke." He quotes Pue's intention not only to inform students but also to entertain them, then discards the assumption that this "queer little book" is a joke and concludes that whether the book "will meet the views of 'Every American Youth'" will depend upon "whether 'Every American Youth' be or be not as great a nincompoop as Mr. Pue."

Grandjean, Auguste Character mentioned in "THE ANGEL OF THE ODD" and "LOSS OF BREATH." In the first story, Grandjean has supplied the narrator with a wig to cover the "serious loss of my hair, the whole of which had been singed off by the fire." In the second story, the narrator rummages in a dressing case and accidentally demolishes "a bottle of Grandjean's Oil of Archangels—which, as an agreeable perfume, I here take the liberty of recommending." In reality, Grandjean was a New York–based hair-compound maker in business around 1844.

Graves, Sergeant Samuel "Bully" One of several soldiers with whom Poe was stationed at Fort Moultrie, and a central figure in Poe's final estrangement from John ALLAN. To convince Graves to wait longer for money Poe owed him, Poe wrote to Graves in 1829 that he could not get the money from his guardian. To make the excuse more convincing, Poe added that "Mr. Allan is not very often sober." When Poe had not repaid the debt by the end of 1830, Graves went to Allan with the letter and its damaging assertion. Allan paid the debt immediately, then "banished Poe from his affections."

Greeley, Horace (1811–1872) Influential American journalist and political leader, as well as the editor of the *NEW YORK TRIBUNE* and the *New-Yorker,* the first penny newspaper, begun in 1834. A strong opponent of slavery, he is best remembered for the advice that he gave to a Congregational minister who had lost his voice and had to leave the ministry: "Go west, young man." Poe describes Greeley in "AUTOGRAPHY" as "one of the most able and honest of American editors. He has written much and invariably well." Greeley's endorsement of a note in the amount of $50 in 1845 enabled Poe to purchase the *BROADWAY JOURNAL,* but Poe never repaid the debt.

Greely Character mentioned in the novel *THE NARRATIVE OF ARTHUR GORDON PYM.* He is one of the mutinous sailors aboard the *Grampus* who is killed by Dirk PETERS after the loyal sailors learn that he and William ALLEN "had gone over to the mate, and were resolved to turn pirates."

Greely brothers Characters in *THE JOURNAL OF JULIUS RODMAN.* Frank, John, Meredith, Poindexter, and Robert Greely are brothers from Kentucky who participate in the exploring adventure. They are all bold and fine-looking men, as well as "experienced hunters and capital shots," but two stand apart. John, the eldest, "was the stoutest of the five and had the reputation of being the strongest man, as well as the best shot in Kentucky." Six feet tall and "of most extraordinary breadth across the shoulders, with large strong-knit limbs," he is "exceedingly good-tempered." Poindexter is as tall as John, "but very gaunt, and of a singularly fierce appearance, but, like his older brother, he was of peaceable demeanor." The five brothers agree to divide five ways a one-third share of the proceeds of their adventure with Julius RODMAN and Pierre JUNOT.

Green, Charles (1785–1870) Scientist mentioned in the short story "THE BALLOON-HOAX" on whose experiments the adventures in the story are based. Green invented the guide rope for use on the hot-air balloon. He was the son of a London fruit seller, but he made important contacts in Parliament that led to backing for 526 balloon ascents, the first from Green Park, London, in July 1821, for the coronation of George IV. He made history in 1836 when he and Thomas Monck MASON traveled 500 miles in a hot-air balloon in just 18 hours, leading Green to speculate about regularly scheduled flights and even a propeller-driven balloon to cross the Atlantic Ocean.

Grenouille, Prince de   Character in the short story "LIONIZING." His name means "frog" in French and he greets the nosologist narrator with the phrase, *"Mille tonnerres!"* (A thousand thunders!) at the uproar that ensues with Robert's appearance.

Gresset, Jean Baptiste (1709–1777)   French author whose works are found in the library of Roderick USHER. With the narrator, Usher pores over Gresset's anticlerical satire, *Ververt et Chartreuse,* in "THE FALL OF THE HOUSE OF USHER."

Grey, Edward S. T.   An alias sometimes used by Poe in his correspondence meant to elicit information from contemporaries in 1848 and 1849. In one instance, he sent a note in a disguised hand and signed as "Grey" to find out if Mrs. Sarah WHITMAN, who was avoiding him, was home.

Griffis, Elliot (1893–1976)   American composer and educator who wrote orchestral pieces, works for string quartets, a song cycle, and arrangements for more than 40 folk songs. He composed settings of Poe's poems "ELDORADO" and "TO HELEN" in 1937.

Grimm, M.   Character in "THE UNPARALLELED ADVENTURE OF ONE HANS PFAALL." He has invented an apparatus that improves "the condensation of the atmosphere air." Using "the very ingenious apparatus of M. Grimm," Pfaall is able to condense the air "in sufficient quantities for the purposes of respiration."

Griswold, Captain Henry (n.d.)   One of Poe's superior officers at Fort Moultrie. On May 6, 1829, John ALLAN wrote to Griswold and asked him "to aid this youth [Poe] in the promotion of his future prospects."

Griswold, Rufus Wilmot (1815–1857)   Baptist clergyman who replaced Poe as the editor of GRAHAM'S MAGAZINE. Poe and Griswold were literary and personal rivals for the favors of Frances OSGOOD, yet both recognized the power that each carried in the literary world, so they maintained a tentative friendship. Poe's fatal error was to appoint Griswold as his literary executor. The power and authority that such an appointment brought led the public to believe every scurrilous word of the infamous obituary of Poe that Griswold published on October 9, 1849, under the pseudonym "Ludwig," and which has come to be known as "THE LUDWIG ARTICLE." This libelous obituary was the beginning of a reign of character assassination by Griswold, who later expanded the obituary into the "Memoir of the Author" that he used to introduce the 1850 "authorized" edition of Poe's works. Given the commission to edit the works "in case of Poe's sudden confrontational nature of their relationship, which Poe

exacerbated during his lifetime, the choice of literary executor is an egregious error. While on the staff of the *Philadelphia Daily Standard,* Griswold compiled in 1842 an anthology that he titled THE POETS AND POETRY OF AMERICA. Poe's critical responses and his later characterization of Griswold in "AUTOGRAPHY" exhibit his ambivalence toward the man. Although Poe first called Griswold's anthology "the best collection of the American Poets that has yet been made" in a *Graham's Magazine* review in June 1842 (see "THE POETS AND POETRY OF AMERICA"), he later made an enemy of Griswold by deriding the anthology in various public lectures and in an extensive review of the third edition of the work, which appeared in the July 1843 issue of the PHILADELPHIA SATURDAY MUSEUM. Poe also mocked Griswold in several tales by making characters resemble him or by having characters read works known to be written by Griswold. The intoxicated narrator of "THE ANGEL OF THE ODD," for example, states that he is "made more stupid" by reading Griswold's "Curiosities." Yet, in analyzing Griswold's signature in "AUTOGRAPHY" in 1836, Poe had written generously that "his knowledge of American literature, in all its details, is not exceeded by that of any man among us."

Although Griswold, six years younger, could not have been certain that he would outlive Poe, he appears to have saved his most potent attacks to be published after Poe's death. Letters show that Griswold spread lies about Poe to Charles BRIGGS and others, but he began his most concentrated campaign to destroy the man's reputation after Poe was dead and could no longer retaliate. Despite efforts by John R. THOMPSON, who published "The Late Edgar A. Poe" in the November 1849 issue of the SOUTHERN LITERARY MESSENGER, and George R. GRAHAM, who published in his magazine "Defence of Poe" in March 1850 and "The Genius and Characteristics of the Late Edgar Allan Poe" in February 1854, Griswold's vitriolic characterization of Poe became the unofficial biographical record that extended well into the 20th century and kept Poe from achieving his full literary due. Griswold's lies included claims that Poe was expelled from the University of Virginia, that he deserted from the U.S. Army, and that he had been "sexually aggressive" toward John Allan's second wife. Griswold also made a pronounced effort to prove that Poe was morally negligent and a drug addict whose concerns were only for himself. In his introduction to the 1850 edition of Poe's works, Griswold misled readers by suggesting that Poe had based the portrayals on personal experience.

Griswold also proved to be pitiless and uncharitable toward Rosalie POE and Maria CLEMM, for he never gave either woman any proceeds from the sales of Poe's works. Instead, once he had secured from Poe the commission to edit the works "in case of Poe's sudden

Rufus Griswold in later life, when he published the defamatory "Ludwig" article. (Edgar Allan Poe Society)

death," he ignored a letter on August 27, 1849, from Maria Clemm, who appealed to him for money to buy bread when she nearly starved to death in Fordham while Poe was in Richmond. After Poe's death, when she was reduced to begging for a few dollars from various acquaintances and landed eventually in the Church Home in Baltimore, Griswold gave as payment several complete sets of Poe's works that she tried desperately to sell. Griswold did not, however, share the proceeds from sales.

Grogswigg Character mentioned in the short story "THE DEVIL IN THE BELFRY." He has traced the derivation of the name of the borough of Vondervotteimittiss, but his work is portrayed as a relatively useless exercise—Poe's private mockery of academics.

Guy, Captain Character in the novel *THE NARRATIVE OF ARTHUR GORDON PYM.* He is skipper and part owner of the *Jane Guy,* the vessel that picks up Pym and Dirk PETERS after the shipwreck of the *Grampus.* He is "a gentleman of great urbanity of manner" who has had extensive experience in sailing the South Seas, "to which he has devoted a great portion of his life." He has been assigned to cruise the South Seas in search of any cargo of interest, for which he will trade the beads, mirrors, saws, and other objects on the ship. The narrator finds him deficient in energy and lacking in the spirit of enterprise "which is here so absolutely requisite."

"Guy Fawkes; or, The Gunpowder Treason. An Historical Romance. By William Harrison Ainsworth. Author of 'The Tower of London,' 'Jack Sheppard,' Etc. Philadelphia, Lea & Blanchard" Review by Poe that appeared in the November 1841 issue of GRAHAM'S MAGAZINE. Poe declared the novel to be an "admixture of pedantry, bombast, and rigmarole." Condemning the style as "turgid pretension," Poe states that "the elaborately interwoven pedantry irritates, insults, and disgusts."

As was customary in Poe's reviews, this one contains more of Poe's ideas than details of the work. The novel, however, is a highly romanticized version of a historical incident, the Gunpowder Plot. Led by Robert Catesby and Guy Fawkes, a group of Roman Catholics plotted to blow up the House of Parliament while the king, lords, and commons were assembled. They were betrayed and arrested on November 4, 1605. Fawkes was executed.

The review accuses Ainsworth of padding the book by randomly inserting "second-hand bits of classical and miscellaneous erudition" that do not add to the aura of scholarship; on the contrary, "he may be as really ignorant as a bear." Poe declares the plot to be "monstrously improbable," and the author has "now accomplished exactly nothing. If ever, indeed, a novel were *less* than nothing, then that novel is 'Guy Fawkes'."

H

Haasz, Richard (n.d.) Composer of a 1913 symphonic poem for grand orchestra, and a piano transcription thereof, inspired by Poe's poem "THE RAVEN."

Hale, David Emerson (1814–1839) A cadet at the UNITED STATES MILITARY ACADEMY AT WEST POINT, to which Poe was appointed in March 1830 and left in February 1831. His mother was Sarah Josepha HALE, editor of *GODEY'S MAGAZINE AND LADY'S BOOK.* In a letter to his mother from West Point, he mentions that Poe "is thought a fellow of talent here."

Hale, Sarah Josepha (1788–1879) Editor of *GODEY'S MAGAZINE AND LADY'S BOOK,* as well as an important figure in the emancipation of women. She wrote novels and verse and is best known for composing "Mary Had a Little Lamb" (1830). In 1828, she became the editor of *The Ladies' Magazine,* then continued with and added to the success of the magazine when Louis GODEY bought it in 1837 and transformed it into *Godey's Lady's Book.* Her novel *North-wood, or, Life North and South,* published in 1827, was one of the first fictional denunciations of slavery. In "AUTOGRAPHY," Poe wrote that her large handwriting "is indicative of a masculine understanding. . . . Mrs. Hale is well known for her masculine style of thought."

Halleck, Fitz-Greene (1790–1867) American poet. Poe appealed to him for money when the *BROADWAY JOURNAL* was in danger of going under, and received a signed note of endorsement. A portrait of Halleck is included in "THE LITERATI OF NEW YORK CITY," and Poe reviewed Halleck's collection *Alnwick Castle* and other poetry in several essays. In particular, Poe found Halleck's poem "Fanny" "to uncultivated ears . . . endurable, but to the practiced versifier it is little less than torture," and remarked that "Alnwick Castle" is "sadly disfigured by efforts at the farcical," and "Wyoming" is "also disfigured with some of the merest burlesque." At the end of a review of Halleck's work that appeared in the September 1843 issue of *GRAHAM'S MAGAZINE,* Poe expresses regret that the author "has nearly abandoned the Muses, much to the regret of his friends, and to the neglect of his reputation." (*See* "ALNWICK CASTLE, WITH OTHER POEMS.")

Hammerhead, Marmaduke Satiric name for Poe that Dr. Thomas Dunn ENGLISH used in *Eighteen Forty-Four,* published in serial form in the New York *EVENING MIRROR* from 1844 through 1846. The character Marmaduke Hammerhead closely resembled Poe and was credited with writing "The Black Crow" and "The Humbug, and Other Tales." English's portrayal of Poe as a surly and arrogant writer who "never gets drunk more than five days a week" resulted in a violent literary war between the two.

Hannay, James (n.d.) Author of *The Poetical Works of Edgar Allan Poe,* published in London in 1863, and one of the first critics to attempt a critique of Poe's entire body of writing, as well as one of the first to misread him. With singleminded determination, he praised Poe as being "perfectly poetic in his own province. . . . His poetry was sheer poetry, and borrows nothing from without," Hannay observed, but he denies that the author had a sense of humor: "He has, for instance, no Humor—had little sympathy with the various forms of human life."

"Hans Phaall—A Tale" Original title of the short story and spelling of the character's name in the story now known as "THE UNPARALLELED ADVENTURE OF ONE HANS PHAALL." The spelling of the character's name varied in other printings and in Poe's letters.

Hansson, Ola (1860–1925) Swedish poet and novelist, and Poe's first psychological critic. Expressing an opinion of Poe that echoes Charles BAUDELAIRE, Hansson wrote in a 1889 essay that Poe is "one of the great maladies of mankind. His sickness is the sickness of beauty at its most sublime. Like most princes of culture, he is in one person the cloven trunk of madness and genius." Hansson further viewed Poe's studies of hypnosis, loss of consciousness, criminal psychology, and double personalities as similar to the concept of the unconscious, later to be studied by Sigmund Freud.

"The Happiest Day, the Happiest Hour" Poem in six quatrain stanzas first published in the September 15, 1827, issue of the *North American,* and as part of Poe's first collection in *TAMERLANE AND OTHER POEMS* in 1827. The poem appears to have been written while Poe was serving in the army. Poe sent it to his brother William Henry POE, who sent it to the magazine. Despite the relative youth of its 19-year-old author, this poem is a self-pitying lament for the lost visions of youth and the "highest hope of pride and power" that "have vanish'd long, alas!" The time of composition suggests that the poem also reflects Poe's feelings of despondence over losing the love of Elmira ROYSTER.

Hardy, Captain Character in the short story "THE OBLONG BOX." The captain of the packet-ship *Independence*, he helps a passenger secretly bring his dead wife's body aboard ship.

Harris, Alfred Character in Poe's novel *THE NARRATIVE OF ARTHUR GORDON PYM*. One of the sailors aboard the *Jane Guy* and a London native, he volunteers to remain behind on the island to clear the land and to complete the buildings for the captain and crew of the ship. He is later killed by the natives.

Harris, Cuthbert (1870–1932) English composer, organist, and educator who wrote orchestral and chamber music, as well as cantatas, anthems, organ music, and songs. In 1922 he composed "Silver Sleigh Bells," a trio for women's voices also arranged for mixed voices that was inspired by the first stanza of Poe's "THE BELLS."

Hart, Mr. Sculptor who frequented the same social and salon gatherings as Poe in New York City during the winter of 1845–46. He had been commissioned to sculpt in marble a statue of the politician Henry Clay.

"The Haunted Palace" Poem first published in the April 1839 issue of *Baltimore Museum* magazine, then incorporated by Poe into "THE FALL OF THE HOUSE OF USHER." In the story, the poem is said to have been written by Roderick USHER. An allegory, the poem focuses on a king who feels that sinister forces threaten him and his palace: "evil things in robes of sorrow, / assailed the monarch's high estate." The six eight-line stanzas describe "a hideous throng" that "rush out forever, / And laugh—but smile no more." Windows are "red-litten" through which may be seen "vast forms that move fantastically to a discordant melody; / While, like a rapid ghastly river, Through the pale door" rush the throng. The changing tone and content of the stanzas are similar to the development of the story, leading to the eventual collapse of the house and the accompanying destruction of the family. Like the story, the poem depicts the progress of madness. Rufus Wilmot GRISWOLD included the poem in his 1842 anthology *POETS AND POETRY OF AMERICA*. For the biographical sketch, Poe informed Griswold that "by 'The Haunted Palace' I meant to imply a mind haunted by phantoms—a disordered brain." In 1963, Roger CORMAN directed a film titled *The Haunted Palace*, which used only Poe's title for its story of a New Englander in 1875 who inherits an old mansion and is haunted by his violent ancestor. Corman's movie has all the elements of a Poe horror story, but the plot is not specific to one story.

Havens, Benny Owner of a tavern near the United States Military Academy at West Point that catered to the off-limits drinking of the cadets. "Old Benny Havens" would trade brandy for whatever the cadets might bring, including candles, clothes, blankets, equipment, and various petty luxury items. Poe frequently made the run to the Havens's Tavern during his cadet days.

Hawk, Thomas Character mentioned in the short story "THE LITERARY LIFE OF THINGUM BOB, ESQ." Thingum BOB uses this pseudonym to write savage reviews for a magazine named the *Lollipop*. The name is a variation on the term "tomahawk," a term applied by writers to Poe himself because of the vicious way in which he "chopped" up their work in his reviews.

Hawks, Dr. Francis Lister (1798–1866) Rector of St. Stephen's Episcopal Church in New York City and editor of the *New York Review*, a religious quarterly to which Poe contributed a review, "INCIDENTS OF TRAVEL IN EGYPT, ARABIA PETRAEA, AND THE HOLY LAND," in October 1837. Poe observes in "AUTOGRAPHY" that "his style, both as a writer and as a preacher, is characterized rather by perfect fluency than by any more lofty quality," and whose sermons Poe was "at some pains to proclaim boresome."

"The Hawks of Hawk-Hollow; a Tradition of Pennsylvania. By the Author of Calavar and the Infidel. Philadelphia: Carey, Lea & Blanchard" Review by Poe that appeared in the December 1835 issue of the *SOUTHERN LITERARY MESSENGER*. Poe praises Robert Montgomery BIRD for his earlier novels and declares this work to be unfavorably written in imitation of the style and content of works by Sir Walter SCOTT. After providing a lengthy synopsis of the complicated plot, Poe examines the numerous characters and finds them to be of inconsistent quality, ranging from one described as "one of the sweetest creations ever emanating from the fancy of poet, or of painter" to one who is "a mere excrescence." Poe asserts that, despite a few passages "of great eloquence and beauty," many passages are guilty of "sinking into the merest childishness and imbecility," In the final analysis, the review declares the novel to have "no pretensions to originality of manner, or of style . . . and very few to originality of matter."

Hawthorne, Julian (1846–1934) American author and son of the novelist Nathaniel HAWTHORNE. His fictional account—a short story six pages in length—of an encounter with Poe, titled "My Adventures with Edgar Allan Poe," appeared in *Lippincott's Magazine* in 1891. The imagined meeting was based solely on written accounts of Poe: Julian was only three years old when Poe died, and although Nathaniel Hawthorne had carried on a correspondence and traded fiction with Poe, the two men had never met. The story incorporates the popular physical description of the Byronic figure in black engaging in witty and intelligent discussion, but it merely repeats long-held beliefs without adding any new information about Poe.

Hawthorne, Nathaniel (1804–1864)   American novelist and short story writer. Hawthorne and Poe exchanged letters and read each other's fiction, but they never met. One of the first critics to acknowledge Hawthorne as a major American writer who demonstrated "more originality" than Washington IRVING in his handling of American life, Poe was most impressed by Hawthorne's command of the short story form. He also expressed admiration for Hawthorne's ability "to carry out the fulness of his intention" and for placing the reader inside a fictional world where "there are no external or extrinsic influences." In a brief review of Hawthorne's *Twice-Told Tales* that appeared in the April 1842 issue of GRAHAM'S MAGAZINE, Poe praised the work for a tone that "is singularly effective—wild, plaintive, thoughtful, and in full accordance with his themes." He also found that Hawthorne's "*originality* both of incident and of reflection is very remarkable." He did, however, object that "there is insufficient diversity in these themes themselves, or rather in their character."

Poe published a more detailed review of the tales in the May 1842 issue of *Graham's Magazine*. This review praises Hawthorne for skill that, in Poe's estimation, belongs "to the highest region of Art—an Art subservient to genius of a very lofty order." He commends Hawthorne for his distinctive traits of "invention, creation, imagination, originality" and states that "Mr. Hawthorne is original at *all* points." In "Literary Intelligence," which appeared in the February 6, 1845, issue of the New York EVENING MIRROR, Poe bemoaned the fact that *Twice-Told Tales* had gone out of print. In his "Editorial Miscellany" column in the BROADWAY JOURNAL of August 23, 1845, Poe referred to Hawthorne as "a prose poet, full of originality, beauty, and a refinement of style and conception." In "THE PHILOSOPHY OF COMPOSITION," published in 1846, Poe declared the traits that he most admired in Hawthorne's tales—his artistry in composition, structure, and atmospheric depth of setting—to be imperatives for all writers. Poe's judgment of Hawthorne's talents was to prove prophetic for both the writer and for American literature. When Poe praised Hawthorne's work and predicted its impact on the future of American literature, he had not yet published his major works *The Scarlet Letter* (1850), *The House of the Seven Gables* (1851), and *The Marble Faun* (1860). Also still ahead was Hawthorne's friendship with and influence on Herman Melville, 15 years his junior. *See also* "TALE-WRITING."

Hearne, Samuel   Character in THE JOURNAL OF JULIUS RODMAN. According to the "journal," Hearne conducted an important expedition in the northern portion of America from 1769 to 1772, "with the object of discovering copper mines." In doing so, he traversed from the Prince of Wales's Fort, in Hudson's Bay, as far as the shores of the Arctic Ocean.

Heath, James Ewell (1792–1862)   Editor of the SOUTHERN LITERARY MESSENGER for the first five or six months of its existence, who worked at first in an unpaid advisory capacity while he kept his lucrative position as second auditor of the State of Virginia. He had published a novel titled *Edge Hill* that, according to Poe, was "a well-written novel, which owing to the circumstances of its publication, did not meet with the reception it deserved." In "AUTOGRAPHY," Poe judged that Heath's "writings are rather polished and graceful, than forcible or original." Reviewing Poe's fiction in October 1839 issue of the *Messenger,* Heath praised Poe's artistic endowments as, "a taste classical and refined, an imagination affluent and splendid, . . . a singular capacity for minute and mathematical detail."

Helen (1)   Poe's name for Jane Stith STANARD, the mother of a school friend from the academy he attended in Richmond. Poe met her when he was 14 and immediately began to idolize her for her "gentle and gracious words of welcome . . . the sweet and gracious words that made the desolate world so beautiful to him." Poe thought her first name was too prosaic for such an extraordinary woman, and he preferred to think of her as the classical Helen of Troy, a fact that he revealed in later years. His "Helen" died in 1824 at the age of 31. Acquaintances and critics have generally accepted that "TO HELEN" (1), written in 1831, was inspired by her.

Helen (2)   Sarah Helen WHITMAN, a widow, was the great love of Poe's later life, and the woman to whom he addressed at least one impassioned letter: "Helen—my Helen—the Helen of a thousand dreams!" The widow and Poe, by then a widower, coincidentally shared the same birthdate. They became engaged in 1848, despite the dire warnings of friends and family about Poe's unstable nature and continued drinking, but the strains of the outside disapproval of a Poe as the choice of husband drove them apart. She became the inspiration for a second poem entitled "TO HELEN" (2), written in November 1848.

Hemberger, Theodor (1871–1946) German-American composer, conductor, and violinist. He composed a symphony, music for a string quartet, and arrangements for string orchestra. In 1910, he wrote a musical composition titled *Lenore,* op. 35, no. 1, to accompany the fifth stanza of Poe's poem "THE RAVEN."

Henderson Character mentioned in Poe's novel THE NARRATIVE OF ARTHUR GORDON PYM. He is the first mate of the *Penguin* and rescues Arthur Gordon PYM and Augustus Barnard when their boat, the *Ariel,* is run down. When the ship's captain grows angry and denies that he has a responsibility to save people who have put themselves in danger, Henderson stands up to him, stating that the captain is "a fit subject for the gallows" for his views, and takes control of the helm.

Hennepin, Louis (1640–1706) Flemish Recollect friar and explorer in North America, as well as the first European to explore the upper Mississippi River, mentioned in THE JOURNAL OF JULIUS RODMAN. After returning to France in 1683, Hennepin published *A Description of Louisiana,* an account of his travels, which was later exposed to be a plagiarism of an account by the French explorer Robert Cavelier, Sieur de LaSalle, who navigated the length of the Mississippi River and claimed the region of Louisiana for France. For this plagiarism, Hennepin was exiled from France. In his "journal," Julius RODMAN writes that the travels of Hennepin and his friends were "perhaps the earliest travels of any extent made in North America by white people . . . in 1698—but his researches were mostly in the south, we do not feel called upon to speak of them more fully."

Henry, Professor Caleb Sprague (1804–1884) Orator, essayist, political journalist, and educator at Bristol College who was also as Poe described him in "AUTOGRAPHY" one of the "originators of the *New York Review* with Dr. Hawks and Professor Anthon." In "Autography," Poe states further that Henry's inconsistent penmanship, "now neat and picturesque . . . and now excessively scratchy, *clerky,* and slovenly" reveals "a vacillating disposition with unsettled ideas of the beautiful. None of his epistles, in regard to their chirography, end as well as they begin. This trait denotes *fatigability.*" *See also* Charles ANTHON, Francis Lister HAWKS.

Henson, William Character in the short story "THE BALLOON-HOAX." He is based on an obscure businessman of the same name who organized the Aerial Steam Transportation Company in 1842. After the company failed, he moved to the United States and was never heard from again.

Hermann, Johann Character in the short story "MYSTIFICATION." He shows exceptional interest in Baron Ritzner VON JUNG's pontificating upon the history, nature, and etiquette of the duel. He is "an original in every respect—except, perhaps, in the singular particular that he was a very great fool." Highly successful in a great many duels, he also prides himself "upon his minute acquaintance with the etiquette of the *duello,* and the nicety of his sense of honor." In short, he is an "especial object" for the "whimsical nature" of the Baron, who was "ever upon the lookout for the grotesque."

"The Heroine: or Adventures of Cherubina. By Eaton Stannard Barrett, Esq. New Edition. Richmond: Published by P. D. Barnard" Review by Poe that appeared in the December 1835 issue of the SOUTHERN LITERARY MESSENGER. Poe enthusiastically recommends the novel, which is a vicious and funny satire on the Gothic romance genre. Not only is the book "charmingly written," but it also boasts a heroine who is "that most spiritual, that most ill-treated, that most accomplished of women—of that most consummate, most sublimated, most fantastic, most unappreciated, and most inappreciable of heriones," Cherubina Wilkinson. Poe asserts, "Everybody has read Cherubina. There is no one so superlatively unhappy as not to have done this thing." To those who have not, however, Poe commands that they purchase it "forthwith," because there are "few books written with more tact, spirit, naiveté, or grace." After a detailed summary of the plot, and with further praise for the "varied and brilliant talents of its author" and the "racy, dashing, and palpable" nature of the humor in the book, the review concludes that the novel "should be upon the shelves of every well-appointed library."

Herring, Elizabeth ("Eliza") Poe (1792–1822) Poe's aunt. In 1813, when four-year-old Edgar had been in the Allan household for two years, she wrote to Mrs. Allan to inquire after his well-being and to tell her that his older brother, William Henry Leonard POE, "often speaks of his little brother and expresses a great desire to see him." She also expressed the wish that "the Almighty Father of the Universe grant that he may never abuse the kindness he [Edgar] has received." This was the second letter that she had written to Mrs. Allen, who seems to have been afraid of losing her foster son if he had contact with his biological family. Poe donated several poems to the keepsake album of her daughter, Elizabeth Rebecca HERRING.

Herring, Elizabeth Rebecca (1815–1889) Poe's cousin. She came to Fordham cottage during Virginia CLEMM's last days in 1846. Poe wrote several acrostic poems for her, including "AN ACROSTIC."

Herring, Henry (1791–1868) The husband of Poe's aunt Elizabeth ("Eliza") Poe HERRING. He was a prosperous lumber dealer and his house provided a pleasant social background to which Poe gravitated when he first began living with Maria CLEMM and Virginia CLEMM in Baltimore. Poe was much in demand at the Herring social gatherings, reciting poetry and writing in his cousin's album, leading their contemporaries to believe as Hervey Allen wrote in *Israfel* that he became "extremely fond of this Miss Herring [Elizabeth Rebecca], if not in love." Henry Herring was also acquainted with several literary men and editors, and he arranged introductions for the young writer. With Judge Neilson POE, he took charge of Poe's remains and arranged the funeral in Baltimore on October 8, 1849.

Herschel, Sir John Frederick William (1792–1871) English astronomer and chemist and the author of *The Outline of Astronomy.* He led an expedition to the Cape of Good Hope in 1834 to study the stars of the Southern Hemisphere, and published the results in 1847. Poe quotes from Herschel's writings in "EUREKA" in regard to the conception of the solar system, as well as in reference to star clusters in "a state of progressive collapse." This negative convergence of stellar forces related to the central thesis of "Eureka," which deals with the tendency of the universe to return to primal nothingness.

Hewitt, John Hill (1801–1890) Baltimore journalist and editor of the *BALTIMORE SUNDAY VISITER.* In 1833, he entered the *Baltimore Sunday Visiter*'s literary contest for the short story and poetry. Under a pseudonym, Hewitt submitted a poem, "The Song of the Winds," that won first prize for poetry after Poe won first prize for his short story "MS. FOUND IN A BOTTLE." Poe won second prize in the poetry category for "THE COLISEUM," and angrily suggested that he would have won first prize in the poetry contest as well, had he not already won first prize in the short story competition. A judge later left a written record that unofficially agreed with this view. Poe was insulted and angered by the matter of the literary prize. When the two writers met on a Baltimore street, Poe accused Hewitt of conduct unbecoming a gentleman. In an account of the incident written to a friend, Hewitt explains that he retaliated by dealing Poe "a blow which staggered him, for I was physically his superior."

Hewitt, Mary Elizabeth (1818–1850) Amateur poet, member of the New York City literary crowd, and sister-in-law of John Hill HEWITT. Poe favorably reviewed her collection, "THE SONGS OF OUR LAND AND OTHER POEMS," in two different publications within the space of six months. In his portrait of her in "THE LITERATI OF NEW YORK CITY," Poe describes her poems as "numerous and often excellent" and says they "evince the author's poetic fervor, classicism of taste and keen appreciation of the beautiful, in the moral as well as in the physical world." The assessment also points out the flaws in her work: "[N]o one of them, perhaps, can be judiciously commended as a whole, but no one of them is without merit." He cites several passages from her poetry and adds that her verses are "rather particularly than generally commendable. They lack unity, totality, ultimate effect."

Hicks, Absalom Character mentioned in *THE NARRATIVE OF ARTHUR GORDON PYM.* One of the 13 surviving sailors aboard the *Grampus,* he is murdered by Dirk PETERS, who "seized him by the throat, and, by dint of sheer strength, strangled him instantaneously."

Higginson, Colonel Thomas Wentworth (1823–1911) American editor and critic. Although Poe and Higginson never met, Higginson heard Poe read at the Boston Lyceum on October 16, 1845, and was impressed that "every syllable was accentuated with such delicacy, and sustained with such sweetness as I never heard equaled by other lips." He was impressed with Poe's recitations of "AL AARAAF" and "THE RAVEN," yet disturbed by the speaker. As he wrote in a letter to an unidentified contemporary, "It was a face to rivet one's attention in any crowd; yet a face that no one would feel safe in loving." Higginson also reported that when Poe read "Al Aaraaf" and reached the words "Ligeia! Ligeia!" "his voice seemed attenuated to the finest golden thread; the audience became hushed, and, as it were, breathless; there seemed no life in the hall but his." Higginson is best remembered today for his correspondence with Emily Dickinson.

Hill, Edward Burlingame (1872–1956) American composer of orchestral works, songs, choral works, piano pieces, and symphonies. In 1920, he composed a symphonic poem inspired by Poe's short story "THE FALL OF THE HOUSE OF USHER."

Hill, George Handel (1809–1849) American poet and actor who specialized in unsophisticated roles. Poe charged that Hill, in his work "The Ruins of Athens and Other Poems," published in 1842, plagiarized a poem called "A Heath," written by Edward C. Pinckney "A long time ago—twenty-three or four years at least."

The original poem, Poe wrote, was "profoundly admired by the critical few, but had little circulation." To prove the accusation, Poe cited eight lines from "A Heath" and compared them to eight lines from Hill's poem.

Hirst, Henry Beck (1817–1874) Philadelphia poet and Poe's best friend during his years in Philadelphia, 1841–44. Hirst published a biographical essay on Poe in the February 25, 1843, and March 4, 1843, issues of the PHILADELPHIA SATURDAY MUSEUM. A heavy drinker of brandy, Hirst listened to Poe's discussions of plans for "THE RAVEN." Later in life, mentally weakened and addicted to alcohol, Hirst would mutter that he had been the author of the poem. In the July 12, 1845, issue of the BROADWAY JOURNAL, Poe reviewed Hirst's "THE COMING OF THE MAMMOTH," and decreed "nor has it one individual point of redeeming merit." In his 1846 portrait of Hirst in "THE LITERATI OF NEW YORK CITY," Poe accused Thomas Dunn ENGLISH of plagiarizing Hirst's work. Then, in a posthumously published review, Poe accused Hirst of plagiarizing his own work. To support this latter charge, Poe offered passages from his work and Hirst's and stated that "his poems, upon the whole, are little more than our conversations done into verse." In summing up the controversy with Hirst, Poe asserted, "I do *not* object to him stealing my verses; but I do object to his stealing them in bad grammar. My quarrel with him is *not*, in short, that he *did* this thing, but that he has went and *done did* it." In other words, as Poe states, had Hirst provided polished, grammatically correct plagiarisms, Poe would not have raised a challenge.

"Historical Sketch; of the Second War between the United States of America and Great Britain, Declared by Act of Congress, the 18th of June, 1812, and Concluded by Peace, the 15th of February, 1815. By Charles J. Ingersoll. In Three Volumes. Vol. I. Embracing the Events of 1812–13. Philadelphia. Lea & Blanchard" Review by Poe that appeared in the October 11, 1845, issue of the BROADWAY JOURNAL. After quoting two lengthy passages from the work, Poe criticizes what he finds to be the ambiguity of the material and awkwardness in stating several facts. Despite such "trifles," he praises the work because "it gives a plain, discerning and evidently faithful view of the events of the war, and will be received with favor by all who are competent to decide upon the worth of an historical treatise."

"The History of Texas: Or the Emigrants', Farmers', and Politicians' Guide to the Character, Climate, Soil, and Productions of That Country; Geographically Arranged from Personal Observation and Experience. By David B. Edward, Formerly Principal of the Acad- emy, Alexandria, Louisiana; Late Preceptor of Gonzales Seminary, Texas. Cincinnati: J. A. James & Co." Review by Poe that appeared in the August 1836 issue of the SOUTHERN LITERARY MESSENGER. Poe classifies the book as a "useful oddi[ty]. . . . Its style is somewhat *over-abundant.*" He praises the fortitude of the author, who spent six months in 1836 "in examining the improvements made throughout every locality" and determined that the work provides a "flattering little picture of Texan comfort and abundance." In particular, the review expresses faith in the veracity of the author's statements and regards the book "with a most favorable eye."

Hoffman, Charles Fenno (1806–1884) American poet, New York City literary figure, and editor of the KNICKERBOCKER MAGAZINE and the *New York World* during 1847–48. In a review called "THE POETS AND POETRY OF AMERICA," Poe questioned the extent of his inclusion in Rufus GRISWOLD's work, asking "How comes it that C. Fenno Hoffman is the greatest poet in America, and that his articles figure more than two to one over Bryant, and ten to one over Lowell, Longfellow, &c?" In "THE LITERATI OF NEW YORK CITY," Poe states that Hoffman will suffer "irreparable injury" because of Griswold's attention to his career: "Whatever may be the merits of Mr. Hoffman as a poet, it may easily be seen that these merits have been put in the worst possible light by the indiscriminate and lavish approbation bestowed on them by Dr. Griswold in his 'Poets and Poetry of America.'" Although Poe does not agree with Griswold's high opinion of Hoffman, he praises Hoffman for being a man "universally esteemed and admired" and says "it is impossible that he should have an enemy in the world."

Holberg, Ludvig (1684–1754) Danish writer and founder of Danish literature. His 1741 novel *The Subterranean Voyage of Nicholas Klimm* is among the works pored over by the unnamed narrator and Roderick USHER in "THE FALL OF THE HOUSE OF USHER." The choice of reading matter exhibits well Roderick Usher's state of mind. The "subterranean voyage" is both physical and psychological, and the title reflects the manner in which the house of Usher represents the human mind, with Roderick and Madeline as the conscious and unconscious aspects.

Holbrooke, Josef (1878–1938) English composer, conductor, and critic who was a prolific composer of accompaniments to Poe's works, including a symphony for string orchestra to "AL AARAAF"; a dramatic overture for orchestra to "THE CASK OF AMONTILLADO"; a ballad for tenor or baritone and orchestra or piano to accompany "ANNABEL LEE"; a dramatic poem for chorus and grand orchestra to "THE BELLS"; a dance symphony for piano and orchestra to "BON-BON"; accompaniment for harp and flute to "DREAMS"; a piano suite to "ELDORADO"; a ballad for horn and piano to "EULALIE"; a nocturne trio for piano, oboe, and violin to "FAIRY-LAND"; a dramatic choral symphony titled *Homage to E. A. Poe;* a nonetta and a symphonietta for flute, oboe, B-flat clarinet, and violins to "THE SLEEPER"; a sextet in F minor for pianoforte and wind instruments to "ISRAFEL"; a piano suite to "THE LAKE"; a quintet for two violins, viola, cello, and clarinet to "LIGEIA"; an orchestral score to "A DESCENT INTO THE MAELSTROM"; a fantasie sonata for the pianoforte to "THE MAN OF THE CROWD"; two ballets to "THE MASQUE OF THE RED DEATH"; a fantasie for orchestra to "THE PIT AND THE PENDULUM"; a poem for grand orchestra to "THE RAVEN"; a double concerto for clarinet and small orchestra or piano to "TAMERLANE"; a dramatic choral song for mixed voices for "TO ZANTE"; and a poem for orchestra to "ULALUME."

Holmes, Oliver Wendell (1809–1894) Professor of anatomy and physiology at Dartmouth College and amateur poet. In "AUTOGRAPHY," Poe relates that Holmes "has written many productions of merit, and has been pronounced by a very high authority, the best of the humorous poets of the day." In a September 1842 review of *The Poems of Alfred Tennyson* that appeared in GRAHAM'S MAGAZINE, Poe repeated his praise and added, "as a verisifier Holmes is equal to Tennyson, and with the same patient effort and care, he would in every way surpass him."

"Hop-Frog" Short story. This tale of terror relates the effective revenge taken by a court jester against his abusive king and the king's ministers.

The inspiration for this story may have come from a historical incident involving Charles VI of France and five of his nobles, who dressed in similar disguises and chained themselves together to amuse a wedding party in 1393. A curious noble accidentally set the chained party aflame when he brought a torch too close to the costumes while seeking their identities. Four of those men died, but the king and one other survived. The story was chronicled in history, but an account entitled "Barbarians of the Theater" also appeared in the February 1, 1845, issue of BROADWAY JOURNAL, edited by Poe.

PUBLISHING AND DRAMATIZATION HISTORY

The story first appeared in print on March 17, 1849, in the FLAG OF OUR UNION, a Boston newspaper.

The story was adapted in 1910 and filmed by the Gaumont Company in France with director Henry Desfontaines in a production titled *Hop-Frog.* The story was also the inspiration for a symphony also entitled *Hop Frog* written in 1926 by Eugene COOLS.

CHARACTERS

Hop-Frog, an unnamed king, the king's seven ministers (unnamed), TRIPPETTA.

PLOT SYNOPSIS

The plot relates the story of Hop-Frog and Trippetta, male and female respectively, who were taken from their homelands and who must endure abuse and humiliation by the king and his ministers. Named for his distorted legs and odd manner of walking, Hop-Frog is compelled to wear the motley outfit, cap, and bells of a court jester and to play the fool for the king and his court. In contrast to Hop-Frog's deformed appearance, Trippetta is an exquisitely proportioned and beautiful little woman who is usually admired and favored by all. At a meeting to plan the grand masquerade ball, the king forces Hop-Frog to drink wine, which he knows will affect the jester's brain in a bizarre manner. When Trippetta pleads with the king to stop, she is hit in the face with a goblet full of wine.

That action motivates Hop-Frog to plan a deadly revenge. In a move of apparent reconciliation, the jester suggests a novel masquerade for the king and his ministers. He suggests that they pretend to be orangutans, an idea made more appealing by the prospect of frightening all of the ladies present. The costume requires that the king and ministers dress in closely fitting shirts and pants and coat themselves with tar, then cover the tar with strands of flax. To make the scene realistic, Hop-Frog suggests that they be chained into a circle, with chains crossing the circle in the manner that animals from the wild have been paraded. The group agrees to the plan. On the night of the ball, the doors are all locked from the outside on the pretense of keeping the frightened guests captive to fully carry out the practical joke. The "orangutans" march into the ballroom and elicit the desired effect. The agitated crowd urges the disguised men to reveal themselves, and Hop-Frog grabs a torch and pretends to draw close to the costumed men to give the crowd a better look. The flames of the torch set the flax on fire and the locked doors prevent anyone from rushing out to obtain help. As the king and his ministers burn to death, Hop-Frog hoists himself up a chain to the skylight and disappears. Neither he nor Trippetta are ever seen again.

"Hop-Frog; Or, The Eight Chained Ourangoutangs" Original title for the short story "HOP-FROG."

Hopkins, Charles D. (n.d.) American actor and light comedian whom Elizabeth Arnold POE married in July 1802. The two were married until Hopkins's death on October 26, 1805, and the marriage produced no children.

Hopkins, Reverend John Henry, Jr. (1820–1891)
Clergyman and author whose summary of Poe's February 3, 1848, lecture on the universe appeared in the February 4, 1848, edition of the New York *Morning Express*. Hopkins also was an acquaintance who warned Marie Louise SHEW against continuing her relationship with Poe, threatening that Poe's atheistic ideas and the especially dangerous pantheism that he identified in "EUREKA" would contaminate her religious faith.

Horne, Richard Henry (or Hengist) (1803–1884)
British poet and playwright, Poe correspondent, and author of the epic poem "ORION," which Poe reviewed in the March 1844 issue of GRAHAM'S MAGAZINE. In the lengthy essay "THE RATIONALE OF VERSE," Poe praised Horne for his use of "the Heroic measure which every one knew consisted of feet of two syllables" and because he "upholds Chaucer in its frequent use; maintains his superiority, *on account* of his so frequently using it, over all English versifiers."

"Horse-Shoe Robinson: A Tale of the Tory Ascendancy. By the Author of 'Swallow Barn.' Philadelphia: Carey, Lea & Blanchard"   Review by Poe that appeared in the May 1835 issue of the SOUTHERN LITERARY MESSENGER. Poe declares that this historical novel by John Pendleton KENNEDY will place the author "at once in the very first rank of American novelists." After a brief summary of the plot, Poe declares that Kennedy has made "good choices in regard to the epoch, scene and subject" and "has done them all the fullest justice." He praises the work as "a book of no ordinary character" and commends the author for having "made another innovation. He has begun at the beginning. We all know this to be an unusual method of procedure." Poe is similarly impressed that Kennedy introduces the prominent characters at the outset of the novel, to allow the reader to "go with them at once, heart and hand, in the various and spirit-stirring adventures which befall them." The high praise accorded this novel is only slightly diminished by Poe's concern for punctuation: "[T]he two volumes before us are singularly deficient in this respect." He singles out the overuse of the dash as particularly disruptive to the narrative and offers an example from the work with his corrections. Overall, Poe recommends the work enthusiastically "to the lovers of the forcible, the adventurous, the stirring, and the picturesque" and predicts that the work "will be eagerly read by all classes of people."

"How to Write a Blackwood Article"   Short story. This tale, written in the form of a mock essay, is one of Poe's best comic writings, and it also provides insight into his writing methods. The tale, which is a companion piece to "A PREDICAMENT," contains Poe's only female narrator.

PUBLISHING AND DRAMATIZATION HISTORY

The story was first published under the title "THE PSYCHE ZENOBIA" in the November 1838 issue of the Baltimore *American Museum*. The same issue also printed "THE SCYTHE OF TIME" (later titled "A Predicament"), which appears to offer a sample of a model *Blackwood* article, which was characterized by repetitive horror writing and sensationalizing. The story appeared under the title "How to Write a Blackwood Article" in the July 12, 1845, of the BROADWAY JOURNAL.

An epigraph that is the common cry of a Turkish fig-peddler prefaces the story: "In the name of the Prophet—figs!!" The phrase provides a burlesque of the usually solemn language that appears in everyday common verbal interaction in Middle Eastern countries. In the same manner, Poe's story burlesques the manner of story that *Blackwood* presented with all seriousness.

CHARACTERS

William BLACKWOOD, Suky SNOBBS (1), Miss Tabitha TURNIP, Signora Psyche ZENOBIA.

PLOT SYNOPSIS

Poe appears to engage in self-parody as he mocks some of his own methods and the repetitive types of horror writing that were typical of *Blackwood* magazine. The narrator is Signora Psyche Zenobia, who appears again in "A Predicament." She is proud of her unusual name Psyche, "which is good Greek," and resents the alias of "Suky Snobbs," given to her by the gossip Miss Tabitha Turnip. Zenobia learns the "how" of writing a successful *Blackwood* article in an interview with William Blackwood himself, whose advice consists of representative passages from Schiller and Cervantes mixed in with Chinese and Chickasaw expressions and the encouragement to throw in some "nice Latin phrases" and Greek, whether she knows the language or not. He gives her guidance in writing stories of imminent horrible death, telling her, "[T]hen only think of the sensations"—a piece of advice that she follows to the letter in composing "A Predicament." This advice mirrors Poe's approach in such tales as "THE PIT AND THE PENDULUM" and "A DESCENT INTO THE MAELSTROM." Each of these stories creates a slow and steady progression of events that evoke increasingly intense sensations in the characters and readers as we are led toward what seems to be an inevitable death. The final action is less important to the story than are the sensations that lead to it.

Howard, Lieutenant J. (n.d.)   Officer who served with Poe at Fort Moultrie and assisted Poe in obtaining an early discharge from the army. Howard took an interest in helping Poe and promised to discharge him if Poe could reconcile with John ALLAN. In a letter dated April 20, 1829, Howard wrote that Poe had served under his command from June 1827 to January 1829, "during which time his conduct was unexceptionable. He once performed the duties of clerk and assistant in the Subsistent Department, both of which duties were promptly and faithfully done. His habits are good and entirely free from drinking."

Hoyle, Edmond (1672–1769) British author of *A Short Treatise on the Game of Whist*, published in 1742, which standardized the rules of the card game in a form followed until 1864. In a review of the Dickens novel *Barnaby Rudge*, Poe states that it is not his purpose "to ask them why, if the popularity of a book be the measure of its worth, we should not be at once in condition to admit the inferiority of 'Newton's Principia' to 'Hoyle's Games.'" The rules of Hoyle are also referred to by the narrator of "THE MURDERS IN THE RUE MORGUE," for whom they function as a touchstone with the logical and the comprehensible; in other words, limited and suspect.

Hoyt, Reverend Ralph (1806–1878) American clergyman poet and author, whose "A CHAUNT OF LIFE AND OTHER POEMS" Poe reviewed in the July 26, 1845, issue of the *BROADWAY JOURNAL*. In a profile of Hoyt in "THE LITERATI OF NEW YORK CITY," Poe praised Hoyt's writing, and expressed the hope that further essays and sketches would be forthcoming.

Hudson, Henry Norman (1814–1886) Shakespearean scholar and lecturer. Poe met him after Hudson lectured on a portion of *King Lear* at the Society Library in October 1845. In an assessment of Hudson that appeared in the December 13, 1845, issue of the *BROADWAY JOURNAL,* Poe stated: "He did not favorably impress us. His good points are a happy talent for fanciful, that is to say for unexpected (too often farfetched) *illustration,* and a certain cloudy acuteness in respect to motives of human action." Poe followed this with a methodical delineation of Hudson's negative aspects: "His bad points are legion." Among other complaints, Poe asserted that Hudson had "an elocution that would disgrace a pig, and an odd species of gesticulation of which a baboon would have excellent reason to be ashamed." Poe mentions Hudson in connection with other "FROGPONDIANS" in "BOSTON AND THE BOSTONIANS," and provides several negative comments of Hudson's abilities as a literary critic in "MARGINALIA."

Hughes, Judge Robert W. (n.d.) Richmond attorney, who wrote a column on economic topics for the *RICHMOND EXAMINER.* He told of Poe sitting hour upon hour at the office of the *Examiner* in August 1849, revising his poems and having them set up in the composing room

for reference. Hughes was among the few people to see Poe on the night of September 26, 1847, the author's last night in Richmond less than two weeks before his death.

Huhn, Bruno Siegfried (1871–1947) Composer, choral conductor, and voice coach whose compositions include song cycles and songs for vocal quartets, duets, women's chorus, men's choruses, anthems, cantatas, and piano pieces. In 1913 he composed music inspired by "ISRAFEL," and in 1914, a song setting of "ELDORADO."

"Human Magnetism; Its Claim to Dispassionate Inquiry. Being an Attempt to Show the Utility of Its Application for the Relief of Human Suffering. By W. Newnham, Esq., M.R.S.L., Author of the 'Reciprocal Influence of Body and Mind,' Etc. New York: Wiley & Putnam" Review by Poe that appeared in the April 5, 1845, issue of the *BROADWAY JOURNAL.* Poe calls the work one "of vast importance and high merit, but one of which (on account of its extent of thesis) it is almost impossible to speak otherwise than cursorily, or at random, within the limits of a weekly paper." Although Poe "disagree[s] with the author in some of the ideas of the curative effects of magnetism," he does not dispute "in any degree, the prodigious importance of the mesmeric influence in surgical cases." He suggests that readers "dip into some medical works of authority before forming an opinion on such topics."

Hunt, Freeman (1804–1858) Editor and proprietor of the well-known *Merchants' Magazine,* which Poe called "one of the most useful of our monthly journals, and decidedly the best 'property' of any work of its class." He favorably reviewed THE RAVEN AND OTHER POEMS and testified as a character witness in Poe's libel suit against Dr. Thomas Dunn ENGLISH. In his profile of Hunt that appeared in "THE LITERATI OF NEW YORK CITY," Poe praises Hunt's efforts to "without aid put the magazine [*Merchants' Magazine*] upon a satisfactory footing as regards its circulation" and success in making the publication the "absolute authority in mercantile matters." Poe is equally complimentary about Hunt's character, writing that he is a "true friend, and the enemy of no man."

Huxley, Aldous (1894–1963) English novelist and critic. In his 1930 work *Vulgarity in Literature,* he claimed that the French adoration of Poe was misplaced, and, instead, accused Poe of providing a primary example of vulgarity. According to Huxley, who seems to have disliked Poe almost as much as his expressed dislike of Percy Bysshe Shelley, "Baudelaire, Mallarmé, and Valery are wrong and Poe is not one of our major poets." He claimed Poe was "unhappily cursed with incorrigibly bad taste" and mocked what he termed the awkwardness of a "walloping dactylic metre" of "ULALUME." The attack on Poe actually places him in good company, because Huxley also expressed distaste for the leading English Romantic poets.

Huybrechts, Albert (1899–1938)   Belgian composer who wrote orchestral pieces, sonatas, and accompaniments for violin and piano. In 1928 he wrote *Trois poémes d'Edgar Poe,* a song for the piano, with words from "ELDORADO," "TO———"["I heed not that my earthly lot"], and "TO THE RIVER."

"Hymn"   Poem of 16 lines first published as a song sung by MORELLA in the first printing of the story "MORELLA," and later published separately as "A Catholic Hymn" in the August 16, 1845, issue of the *BROADWAY JOURNAL.* Addressed to the Holy Virgin, the poem, which consists of twelve lines of rhyming couplets, is a plea by the heroine to the Blessed Virgin, and it is unusual in its hopeful expression of a radiant future.

"Hyperion: A Romance. By the Author of 'Outremer.' Two Volumes. Samuel Colman, New York"   Review appearing in the October 1839 issue of *BURTON'S GENTLEMAN'S MAGAZINE.* Poe attacks the poem, written by Henry Wadsworth LONGFELLOW, as equivalent to placing "into a bag the lofty thought and manner" of one work with "the quirks and quibbles and true humour" of another, "not forgetting a few of the heartier drolleries of Rabelais," then shaking up and throwing out the results. He accuses the author of producing one of the works that "are the triumphs of Tom O'Bedlam, and the grief of all true criticism," because he has made "no scruple of scattering at random a profusion of rich thought in the pages of such farragos as 'Hyperion'." Poe does not analyze the poem methodically, but instead dismisses it "in brief," declaring it a work "without design, without shape, without beginning, middle, or end."

hypnosis   *See* MESMERISM.

"I Promessi Sposi, or the Betrothed Lovers; a Milanese Story of the Seventeenth Century: as Translated for the Metropolitan, from the Italian of Alessandro Manzoni, by G. W. Featherstonhaugh. Washington: Stereotyped and Published by Duff Green. 1834. 8vo. pp. 259" Review by Poe that appeared in the May 1835 issue of the SOUTHERN LITERARY MESSENGER. Poe's review begins with a lengthy consideration of the past "dynasties reigning over the regions of romance," each becoming less effective than those preceding, then focuses negative attention on Edward BULWER-LYTTON, who "learned the craft of plagiarism in the Spartan school, where detection was the only disgrace." Poe then discusses the novel, which he assesses to be "in every sense of the word, original." Impressed by Manzoni's use of the Italian past, Poe commends the author for a willingness to depict honestly the abuses of the "Romish Church" and to present realistically the scene of a young girl confined by her parents to a convent. He praises the original novel but also states that "the translation has many faults," which are the result of haste because "the translator, we fear was hungry; a misfortune with which we know how to sympathize." The translation style mixes Italian rhythms with English words, "a great fault," yet Poe states that "it gives a quaint raciness which is not unacceptable."

Ianthe Character in the poem "AL AARAAF." She is "a maiden angel" who encourages her lover ANGELO to be happy on the star AL AARAAF, a medium between heaven and hell, where no one is punished but no one achieves perfect happiness and tranquillity. In an effort to make him content with his new home, Ianthe tells Angelo that "A brighter dwelling-place is here for thee . . . grey Time unfurled / Never his fairy wing o'er fairier [*sic*] world!"

"Ideals and Other Poems. By Algernon Henry Perkins. Philadelphia" Review by Poe that appeared in the April 1842 issue of GRAHAM'S MAGAZINE. Poe wrote that the author of the poetry in this collection could claim, at best, "a tripping prettiness, in thought and expression . . . [but] the air of the whole is nevertheless commonplace." The review attacks the collection for imitating "with close precision" LONGFELLOW's "Ballads" and for drawing heavily upon the "hyper-ridiculous eli-sions in prose" of the English critic and essayist Thomas CARLYLE. Of merit, the review declares that the work "has nothing, except its mechanical execution, to distinguish it from the multitudinous ephemera with which our national poetical press is now groaning."

"Imitation" Poem that first appeared in the 1827 collection TAMERLANE AND OTHER POEMS. A 20-line meditation in rhymed couplets, the poem appears to reflect Poe's deteriorating relationship with John ALLAN. The speaker contemplates his youth as a beautiful dream that contrasts sharply with an uncertain and increasingly difficult present. The speaker appears despondent and views his past as forever lost: "For that bright hope at last / And that light time have past [*sic*], / And my worldly rest hath gone / With a sigh as it pass'd on."

"Imitation—Plagiarism" *See* "A CONTINUATION OF THE VOLUMINOUS HISTORY OF THE LITTLE LONGFELLOW WAR."

"The Imp of the Perverse" Short story. The tale has two primary interpretations among critics. The first is that the Imp of the Perverse represents the self-destructive tendencies of the narrator, and that this tendency is present in all people. The second is that the imp is the narrator's excuse for avoiding moral responsibility. Critics have identified passages in this story that reflect the narrator's unconscious desire to be caught, a desire also found in the narrators of "THE TELL-TALE HEART" and "THE BLACK CAT." Critical biographers of Poe have also identified connections between the tale and the many self-destructive choices Poe made throughout his life and in his interpersonal relationships, including his self-indulgence, his feuds with authority figures, his alcohol abuse, and his erratic treatment of both friends and colleagues.

PUBLISHING AND DRAMATIZATION HISTORY

The story was first published in the July 1845 issue of GRAHAM'S MAGAZINE. Unlike most stories written by Poe, this one is not prefaced by an epigraph. The story has not been dramatized to date.

CHARACTERS

The Imp of the Perverse; unnamed narrator.

PLOT SYNOPSIS

The tale begins as an essay in which the narrator comments objectively upon the perversity of human nature and the tendency to commit morally questionable acts, after which he states, "you will easily perceive that I am one of the many uncounted victims of the Imp of the Perverse." After relating the way in which he committed a murder by burning a poisoned candle in the "narrow and ill-ventilated" room of the victim, the narrator happily relates, "having inherited his estate, all went well with me for years." For a time, the narrator revels in the perfect nature of his crime, and states, "The idea of detection never once entered my brain," but he soon becomes plagued by "the spirit of the *Perverse*," which leads people to perform actions "merely because we feel we should *not*." Unable to offer any explanation, he determines that one might attribute "this perverseness to be a direct instigation of the arch-fiend, were it not occasionally known to operate in furtherance of good." The narrator's self-destructive impulses, embodied by the Imp, make him "fool enough to confess the murder of which I had been guilty," and he shouts out testimony of his crime—not from any desire to unburden his soul but only from the perverse desire to publicize his actions.

"Inaugural Address of the Reverend D. L. Carroll, D.D., President of Hampden Sidney College. Delivered on His Induction into That Office. Published by Request of the Board of Trustees. Richmond: T. W. White, 1835" Review by Poe that appeared in the December 1835 issue of the SOUTHERN LITERARY MESSENGER. Poe recounts the note that accompanied the manuscript, which stated that it was "prepared with great haste, amidst anxieties and efforts to regain health, and amidst all the inquietudes of journeying and absence from home." The review rejects the need for such apology and, instead, praises both the text and its message of "moral influence." Poe observes that "the conclusion of Mr. Carroll's Address is full of fervid eloquence, rendered doubly interesting by a vein of that truest of all philosophy, the philosophy of the Christian," to which he adds his approval.

"Incidents of Travel in Central America, Etc. By John L. Stephens. Two Volumes. New York, Harper and Brothers" Review by Poe that appeared in the August 1841 issue of GRAHAM'S MAGAZINE. After giving considerable attention to perceived deficiencies in Stephens's earlier work, *Incidents of Travel in Egypt, Arabia Petraea and the Holy Land,* in which Poe believes there exist "some errors of magnitude," he admits "we are not prepared to say that misunderstandings of this character will be found in the present." Poe can only speak of the merits of the book "from a general report and from the cursory perusal which has been afforded us by the politeness of a friend," for he had not yet received a copy of the book from the publisher. Undaunted by the lack of a text, Poe nonetheless asserts that the book is a "a magnificent one—perhaps the most interesting book of travel ever published." He declares that the "incidents', moreover, are numerous and highly amusing . . . and his hair-breadth escapes are particularly exciting."

"Incidents of Travel in Egypt, Arabia Petraea, and the Holy Land" *See* "REVIEW OF STEPHENS' ARABIA PETRAEA."

"The Indicator and Companion. By Leigh Hunt. Wiley & Putnam's Library of Choice Reading. No. XX. Part II" Review by Poe that appeared in the August 30, 1845, issue of the BROADWAY JOURNAL. Poe expresses disdain for Hunt's "easy writing which is not the easiest reading" and writes that "we find here too much of slipshodiness, both in thought and manner, and too little of determined purpose." Rather than to attribute the tone to that of "a bold genius uttering vigorous things carelessly and inconsiderately, with contempt or neglect of method or completeness," Poe labels Hunt's process as resulting from "a naturally immethodical and inaccurate intellect." The greater portion of the review is devoted to highlighting Hunt's inadequacies as a writer and a critic, as "a rambling essayist" who is more imitator than innovator and as a critic who "is merely saucy, or lackadaisical, or falsely enthusiastic, or at best pointedly conceited." In final summation, Poe declares, "as an author he is fit for very little, if really for anything at all."

"Infatuation" *See* "SATIRICAL POEMS."

"The Infidel; or The Fall of Mexico, a Romance, by the Author of Calavar. Philadelphia: Carey, Lee & Blanchard" Review by Poe that appeared in the June 1835 issue of the SOUTHERN LITERARY MESSENGER. Poe praised this second historical novel by Robert Montgomery BIRD as "a work of great power." After summarizing the plot, which takes place a few months "after the disastrous retreat of the Spaniards from Mexico," Poe extracts a lengthy scene that shows Bird's power in painting "to us the vastness of the barbarian multitude. His descriptions of myriads appeal to the sense with graphic effect." The review also contains praise for the author's "fertility of imagination [which] displays itself in the constant recurrence of dramatic situations, striking incidents and stirring adventures; so much so, that the interest of the reader . . . is often painfully excited." Poe does identify one minor fault in the writing, the author's habitual use of "the word working in describing the convulsions of the countenance, under the influence of strong passions: as, 'his working and agonized visage'—'his face worked convulsively,' &c." Overall, the review asserts "the enduring excellence of the work."

"In Youth I Have Known One with Whom the Earth"
Poem that was untitled when it appeared in Poe's first poetry collection TAMERLANE AND OTHER POEMS, published in July 1827. The poem was retitled "Stanzas" by George E. WOODBERRY and Edmund C. Stedman when they compiled a 10-volume edition of Poe's works in 1894–96. In a letter to James Russell LOWELL, Poe identified the poem as influenced by Lord BYRON's poem "The Island," which was "a powerful influence" on his thinking and artistic expression. John R. THOMPSON, one-time editor of the SOUTHERN LITERARY MESSENGER, suggested to friends that Poe's account to him of "a dream vision" seems to have provided an additional influence for the poem, in the form of an early experience in which "the soul separates itself from the body." Poe related that he dreamt of having been "taken out over Philadelphia by a woman of seraphic beauty who later turned into a vast black bird, typifying the cholera epidemic which was then raging there." The poem consists of four octaves addressed to "one with whom the Earth / In secret communing held—as he with it, / In day light, and in beauty from his birth: / Whose fervid, flick'ring torch of life was lit / From the sun and stars." A "wild light" infuses the world of the poem and other images of luminosity exist to exhibit "the intense / Reply of HERS [Nature's] to OUR intelligence!"

Inghelbrecht, Désiré-Emile (1880–1937) French composer and conductor who conducted first productions of several works by Claude DEBUSSY and became known as the chief interpreter of Debussy. Inghelbrecht composed two works based on Poe's short story "THE DEVIL IN THE BELFRY": a ballet with the same title as the story and a fox trot, extracted from the ballet, titled "The Little Black Man."

Ingram, John Henry (1842–1916) Poe's first English biographer. Ingram's *Edgar Allan Poe: His Life, Letters and Opinions* (1874) expanded to two volumes in 1880. By day, Ingram was a civil servant who worked in the post office, and by night he wrote lengthy correspondence to everyone he could locate who had ever had any contact with Poe. He traced many Poe letters and corresponded extensively with Sarah Helen WHITMAN and Annie RICHMOND, using all the information that he could to refute the many venomous lies that Rufus Wilmot GRISWOLD told and wrote about Poe's relationships with women. Ingram's enthusiastic defense of Poe aided in reversing the common 19th-century misperceptions regarding Poe's character. Ingram also worked hard to bring Poe's less-known writing to light.

To this end, he published nearly 50 articles and edited a four-volume edition of Poe's works.

"Irene" Original title of the poem "THE SLEEPER."

Irene Character in the poem "THE SLEEPER." She is one of many beautiful women mourned by Poe's narrators and speakers. Now dead and the subject of the speaker's grief, she lies in a vault "Against whose sounding door she hath thrown, / In childhood, many an idle stone—." The grieving lover fantasizes that the moon will address his love and call to her "Lady, awake! lady awake!" but he also realizes that "The lady sleeps: the *dead* all sleep." Still, he hopes that the dead woman will rest peacefully, praying that "No icy worms about her creep: / I pray to God that she may lie / Forever with as calm an eye."

Irving, Washington (1783–1859) Leading American author of Poe's era, and the first American author to achieve international renown. He is probably best known as the creator of the fictional characters Ichabod Crane and Rip Van Winkle. Despite Irving's fame, Poe felt that his work and reputation were "much overrated and a nice distinction might be drawn between his just and his surreptitious and adventitious reputation." In a review, "THE BIOGRAPHY AND POETICAL REMAINS OF MARGARET MILLER DAVIDSON," written in 1841, Poe commends Irving for conveying "a just idea of the exquisite loveliness of the picture here presented to view," but he also criticizes Irving for overestimating the artistry of the works and states that "his words, however, in their hyperbole, do wrong to his subject, and would be hyperbole still, if applied to the most exalted poets of all time." In contrast, in 1847 he praises Irving's "Tales of a Traveler" as "graceful and impressive narratives." Years earlier, in the first installment of "AUTOGRAPHY," appearing in the February 1836 issue of the SOUTHERN LITERARY MESSENGER, Poe stated that "Mr. Irving's hand writing is common-place. There is nothing indicative of the genius about it. . . . It is a very usual clerk's hand . . . an eye deficient in a due sense of the *picturesque*." While in 1841, in "A Chapter on Autography," which appeared in the November 1841 issue of GRAHAM'S MAGAZINE, Poe extended his criticism to state that Irving "has become so thoroughly satiated with fame as to grow slovenly in the performance of his literary tasks." Despite Poe's unenthusiastic view of Irving as a writer, critics consider him to have been an influence on Poe's life and work, especially in the nature of the tone, style, and sense of humor that appear in such Poe comic pieces as "THE DEVIL IN THE BELFRY." In letters written to Poe during the autumn of 1839, Irving made faintly favorable comments regarding "THE FALL OF THE HOUSE OF USHER," which Poe later used to promote TALES OF THE GROTESQUE AND ARABESQUE.

"The Island of the Fay"   Short story. One of four stories in which Poe expressed a rapturous appreciation of natural beauty; the others are "THE ELK," "THE DOMAIN OF ARNHEIM," and "LANDOR'S COTTAGE." In this work, people are not the center of attention; nature is. The story was written to accompany a steel engraving by John SARTAIN of a painting by the melodramatic English painter John Martin (1789–1854), who developed a type of enormous canvas crowded by tiny figures set in elaborate architectural and natural settings.

PUBLISHING AND DRAMATIZATION HISTORY

The story first appeared in the June 1841 issue of GRAHAM'S MAGAZINE. To the first publication of the story, Poe attached the following early poem "To Science," in which the scientific spirit and the spirit of poetry are opposed. He did not identify the poem as his and he changed the final two lines. The original lines appear in brackets, as follow:

> Has thou not dragged Diana from her car,
> And driven the Hamadryad from the wood
> To seek shelter in some happier star?
> Hast thou not torn the Naiad from her flood,
> The elfin from the grass?—the dainty *fay*, [The Elfin
> from the green grass, and from me]
> The witch, the sprite, the goblin—where are they?
> [The summer dream beneath the
> tamarind-tree?]

When the story was published a second time in the October 4, 1845, issue of the *BROADWAY JOURNAL*, Poe replaced the epigraph with *"Nullus enim locus sine genio est"* [No place is without its genius], from Servius's commentary on Virgil's *Aeneid*, book five. Critics suggest that Poe probably did not use the original source but, most likely, found the quotation prefacing chapter five of book seven of Victor Hugo's 1831 novel *Notre-Dame de Paris*.

In 1904, American composer Henry GILBERT wrote a piano piece inspired by the story.

CHARACTERS

The Fay, unnamed narrator.

PLOT SYNOPSIS

The tale offers a serene vision of nature and an appreciation of God's role in "nature's holy plan." The lonely, wandering narrator experiences a transcendental vision while experiencing "the dark valleys, and the gray rocks, and the waters that silently smile, and the forests that sigh in uneasy slumbers, and the proud watchful mountains that look down upon all." In contrast, the landscape changes when the narrator comes upon the race of the fay at the eastern end of the island, becoming haunted and bleak. He sees "the form of one of those very fays . . . as it made its way slowly into the darkness from out the light at the western end of the island. . . . [H]er shadow fell from her, and was swallowed up in the dark water, making its blackness more black." The vision of paradise dissolves as the fay disappears "into the region of the ebony flood . . . and I beheld her magical figure no more." As with all living things, the natural beauty of the fay is transitory and her life span short. The narrator views the fay as representing the cruel impermanence that exists in both the natural and the supernatural world, "and I beheld her magical figure no more."

"Israfel"   Poem in eight stanzas, varying in lengths of five, six, seven, and eight lines, and written while Poe was a cadet at the UNITED STATES MILITARY ACADEMY AT WEST POINT. The poem first appeared in April 1831 in *POEMS OF EDGAR A. POE*, printed by Elam Bliss. It also was published in a reworked and refined form in the August 1836 issue of the *SOUTHERN LITERARY MESSENGER*. In his note to the poem, Poe incorrectly states that in the Koran, Israfel is described as an angel "whose heart-strings are a lute, and who has the sweetest voice of all God's creatures." The real source is George Sale's "Preliminary Discourse," his 1764 introduction to the Koran, in which the quotation appears as follows: "the angel Israfil [*sic*], who has the most melodious voice of all God's creatures." Critics suggest that Poe was likely influenced by his readings of voyages to the Mediterranean and stories of "the mysterious interior of Arabia" as well as the "secondary Oriental literature" that dominated his reading at West Point. Poe uses Israfel to examine the plight of earth-bound poets whose mortality places burdens on them and interferes with their ability to sing joyously and melodiously. Critics have frequently identified Poe with Israfel, and one of the most comprehensive studies of Poe's life and work, a study published by critic Hervey Allen in 1934, makes the connection in the title, *Israfel: The Life and Times of Edgar Allan Poe*. Israfel is the symbol of the ideal poet who sings in heaven and captivates everyone with his sublime voice, which causes "the stars [to] be mute." In contrast, the earth-bound poet must reside in "a world of sweets and sours." The burdens of the earthly world make the poet dream of changing places with Israfel and to enter his poetic paradise. Chained to the earth, Israfel "would not sing so wildly well," but, given freedom from "mortal melodies," the poet would strike "a bolder note" upon his "lyre within the sky."

Jacinta Character in Poe's drama *POLITIAN*. She is a servant maid to LALAGE, ward of the Duke di BROGLIO. At outset of the play, she demands that the other servants call her "Madame Jacinta if you please" and proclaims herself "the riches waiting maid in Rome / The riches vintner's daughter owning these jewels!" She wears a variety of jewels, including pearls, rubies, emeralds and a topaz, as well as the distinctive cross of rubies that once belonged to Lalage and a ring that the count CASTIGLIONE gave to Lalage "as a token of his love / Last year." When UGO, another servant, leers at her and suggests that she has received the jewels from his master the count, she sets him right and tells him that Lalage gave her the jewels "as a free gift, and for a marriage present / All of her jewels!—every one of them!" When certain that Lalage has given her all the jewels available, Jacinta turns sullen and insulting to her mistress, then leaves her to serve Alessandra, "a change for the better." Believing that Lalage has been dishonored, Jacinta dresses up in the jewels she has been given and parades in front of the other servants while condemning her former mistress as having "nothing of the lady about her—not a tittle! One would have thought / She was a peasant girl, she was so humble." In contrast, she idolizes her new mistress for being "so loud, so ladylike, and so commanding!"

Jefferson, Thomas (1743–1826) American author, scientist, statesman, and philosopher; secretary of state; third president of the United States. He conceived the idea of a university that would "develop the reasoning faculties of our youth, enlarge their minds, cultivate their morals, and instill into them the precepts of virtue and order." These goals took physical form in the University of Virginia, conceived as nonsectarian, with no church on campus and no requirement to attend chapel—factors that may have influenced the young Poe to stray from his religious training when he entered this "most dissolute college in America" in February 1826, only a year after "Jefferson's experiment" opened. Although Jefferson and the trustees began the college with the democratic theory that the students should be self-governing and would take care of their own morals and manners "on their honor," they soon came to the conclusion that outside police were "essential to the comfort and reputation of both students and professors" because "scholastic anarchy and student escapades disturbed the peace of the College, Charlottesville, and the plantations about." Although gambling and drinking were still rampant when Poe first entered the university, a movement toward instilling rules was under way. Poe likely met and even dined with Jefferson, who often invited students to Monticello and remained active in academic life. When Jefferson died on July 4, 1826, Poe was still a student at the university. Poe appears to have remained untouched politically by his association with Jefferson, for he stated in an 1842 discussion with Thomas Holley CHIVERS that he admired George WASHINGTON and Chief Justice John MARSHALL, but not Jefferson.

Jennings Character in "SOME WORDS WITH A MUMMY." The doctor provides "a black dress coat, made in Jennings' best manner" to the naked, shivering mummy.

Jochaides, Simeon Cited as the author of a work in "THE THOUSAND-AND-SECOND TALE OF SCHERAZADE." Poe refers to a fictional title, Tellmenow Isitsoornot, "which (like the "Zohar" of Simeon Jochaides) is scarcely known at all, even in Europe." The work, attributed to Rabbi Simeon ben Jochai (first century A.D.), actually exists and it is a commentary on the Pentateuch, the first five books of the Old Testament. Washington IRVING mentions the work in a similar manner in his *History of New York by Dietrich Knickerbocker,* published in 1809.

John Reference in the short story "MELLONTA TAUTA." The futuristic narrator states of Poe's time that from "a hasty inspection of the fac-similes of newspapers, &c. &., I find that the great men in those days among Amriccans [*sic*], were one John, a smith, and one Zacchary, a tailor."

Johns, Reverend John (n.d.) Minister of Old Christ Church in Baltimore, and later bishop of Virginia, who was rumored to have conducted the first marriage ceremony uniting Poe with Virginia CLEMM soon after they obtained a license to marry on September 22, 1835. The Johns family has always stated that "no tradition of such a marriage was known to the Johns family," and the records of Christ Church in Baltimore contain no record of the first Poe-Clemm marriage.

Johnson, Dr. Samuel (1709–1784)   English essayist, critic, lexicographer, wit, and author, a leading figure of the English Enlightenment. In a review ("A NEW DICTIONARY OF THE ENGLISH LANGUAGE") of a work by Charles Richardson, Poe expresses his respect for Johnson as a pioneer lexicographer, and he suggests that Johnson would have achieved even greater success had he followed his original intention, as stated in a 1747 letter to Lord Chesterfield, which "communicated a *plan* of his undertaking." Johnson's original plan was to give first "the natural and primitive meaning of words; secondly, the consequential—and thirdly the metaphorical, arranging the quotations chronologically." Yet, as Poe points out, the book was published in 1755, "*without the plan,* and strange to say, in utter disregard of the principles avowed in the letter to the Earl of Chesterfield." In Poe's view, the principles "were well-conceived, and that if followed out, they would have rendered important service to English lexicography. . . . [T]he necessity for something of the kind which was felt then, is more strongly felt now." In references in "MARGINALIA," Poe corrected several misstatements by Johnson regarding literature. He also makes unflattering comparisons between Johnson's neoclassic style and that of Charles ANTHON in "Marginalia," characterizing Anthon's notes to the Classical Dictionary as being diffuse, "sometimes running into Johnsonism, of style."

Johnson, Hunter (1909–1987)   American composer whose works include chamber music, a piano concerto, and scores for flute and strings. At the age of 14 he composed a piece titled *Nevermore,* a piano accompaniment to Poe's "THE RAVEN."

Jones, Davy   Reference in "KING PEST." The term is a sailor's name for the evil spirit of the sea, and it seems to have grown out of a corruption of the word "duffy" or "duppy," a term used among the black population of the West Indies for a haunting spirit or ghost, and "Jonah," the Old Testament prophet who is thrown into the sea. In "King Pest," when the pseudointellectual King PEST pontificates upon "that earthly sovereign whose reign is over us all, whose dominions are unlimited, and whose name is 'Death,'" Hugh TARPAULIN retorts "Whose name is Davy Jones!" before pouring a skull-full of wine.

Jones, Robert   The narrator of the short story "LIONIZING." He is a large-nosed expert on nosology who states at the beginning of the story that "the first action of my life was the taking hold of my nose with both hands," which makes his mother call him a genius and his father weep for joy. He decides to develop the full power of his nose, after he "came to understand that, provided a man had a nose sufficiently conspicuous, he

might, by merely following it, arrive at a Lionship." Not content to depend upon mere theory, Jones becomes a serious student of nosology, which he calls "the science of Noses," although the true meaning is the classification of diseases, and also actively develops the physical qualities of his nose: "Every morning I gave my proboscis a couple of pulls and swallowed a half dozen of drams [of liquor]." This misappropriation of terms is further evidence of Poe's satire on pseudointellectuals and false erudition. Jones becomes a welcome guest in the houses of the rich and mighty, offering his profound theories among all of the other intellectual lions, and drawing praise from all who view his nose. He enjoys wide fame until he engages in a duel with the Elector of BLUDDENNUFF, whose nose he shoots off. Within an instant, Jones is proclaimed "Bete!" "Ass!" "Fool!" "Dolt!" "Ninny!" and "Noodle!" and condemned to obscurity, for, as Jones's father reminds him, "there is not competing with a lion who has no proboscis at all."

Jones, William Alfred (1817–1900)   American critic, who Poe apparently regarded with mixed feelings. In a review of the contents of the September 1845 issue of the *Democratic Review* that appeared in the September 20, 1845, issue of the BROADWAY JOURNAL, Poe expressed contempt for Jones's essay "American Humor," which he labeled "insufferable" and "a nuisance." In contrast, in his assessment of Jones that appeared in "ABOUT CRITICS AND CRITICISM: BY THE LATE EDGAR A. POE," a posthumously published review that appeared in the January 1850 issue of GRAHAM'S MAGAZINE, Poe declared him to be "our most analytic, if not altogether our best critic. . . . [H]is summary judgments of authors are, in general, discriminative and profound." In an assessment of Jones's analyses of Ralph Waldo Emerson and Thomas MACAULEY, Poe states that "they are at once pointed, lucid and just:—as summaries, leaving nothing to be desired."

"Joseph Rushbrook: or, The Poacher. By Captain Marryat, Author of 'Peter Simple,' 'Jacob Faithful,' Etc., Etc. Two Volumes. Philadelphia, Carey & Hart"   Review by Poe that appeared in the September 1841 issue of GRAHAM'S MAGAZINE. Poe states that Marryat "has always been a very *popular* writer in the most rigorous sense of the word. His books are essentially 'mediocre'. His ideas are the common property of the mob." Claiming that he has looked in vain "for the slightest indication of originality," Poe reviews *Joseph Rushbrook* in detail, pointing out character "plagiarisms" from Charles DICKENS's Oliver Twist and plot devices borrowed from other writers. Asserting that the later novels of Marryat "are evidently written to order," Poe declares that *Joseph Rushbrook* "deserves little more than an announcement" for "its English is excessively slovenly, . . . events are monstrously improbable, . . . it is a pitiable production."

Jourdain, Monsieur Character in Molière's *Le Bourgeois Gentilhomme* [The Would-Be Gentleman]. In act I, scene 2, he calls for his *robe de chambre* [bathrobe] in order to better appreciate chamber music. In "THE MURDERS IN THE RUE MORGUE," C. Auguste DUPIN compares the methods of the Paris police to that of Jourdain, "so ill adapted to the objects proposed."

"Journal—By Frances Anne Butler. Philadelphia: Carey, Lea & Blanchard. (Presented to the Editor of the Messenger, by Mr. C. Hall)" Review by Poe that appeared in the May 1835 issue of the *SOUTHERN LITERARY MESSENGER*. The first theatrical reminiscences of the English actress Fanny Kemble (1809–1893), who was only 26 years old at their publication, gathered high praise from Poe. She had married an American plantation owner in 1834, becoming Mrs. Frances Butler and retiring from the London stage. In 1848, she would divorce her husband and return to the theater, then publish yet another journal of reminiscences in 1863. Poe claimed to have read the first journal "with untiring interest," and he praised it highly for "the vivacity of its style, the frequent occurrence of beautiful descriptions, of just and forcible observations, and many sound views of the condition of society in this country." Despite his enthusiasm for the anecdotes regarding acting and travel, however, he felt that these "cannot redeem, her innumerable faults of language, her sturdy prejudices, her hasty opinions, and her ungenerous sarcasms." The review also finds that "the style and language is often coarse, we might say vulgar; and her more impassioned exclamations are often characterized by a vehemence which is very like profanity, an offence that would not be tolerated in a writer of the other sex." Poe concludes with the ambiguous judgment "that there is much to admire and much to condemn in this work."

The Journal of Julius Rodman, Being an Account of the First Passage across the Rocky Mountains of North America Ever Achieved by Civilized Man Unfinished serialized novel. The work is heavily reliant upon sources, many of which Poe mentions in the text of the story. Poe reviewed his main source, Washington IRVING's "ASTORIA," in the January 1837 issue of the *SOUTHERN LITERARY MESSENGER*, and also included material found in Alexander Mackenzie's *Voyages in 1789 and 1793*, published in 1801, and *History of the Expedition under the Command of Captains Lewis and Clark*, published in 1814.

The realism of the work deceived many readers, and many accepted it as being factual. In an ironic twist, Poe's heavily borrowed tale became part of a government report prepared for the United States Senate in 1840, when details of the geography and geology contained in the work were incorporated into the official report on the Oregon Territory.

PUBLISHING AND DRAMATIZATION HISTORY

The unfinished novel was published in six installments in *BURTON'S GENTLEMAN'S MAGAZINE*, beginning with the January 1840 issue and ending with the sixth installment in the June 1840 issue, after the proprietor, William BURTON, removed Poe as editor. In response to the dismissal, Poe refused to continue the novel serialization.

CHARACTERS

Frank, John, Meredith, Poindexter, and Robert—the GREELY BROTHERS; Samuel HEARNE; JULES THE CANADIAN; Pierre JUNOT; Jacques LAUZANNE; LITTLE SNAKE; MISQUASH; PERRINE; James RODMAN; Jane RODMAN; Julius RODMAN; Andrew THORNTON; TOBY; Alexander WORMLEY.

PLOT SYNOPSIS

The unfinished adventure is heavily padded with factual material taken from accounts of the explorations of John Jacob ASTOR, Captains Meriwether LEWIS and William CLARK, and Captain Benjamin BONNEVILLE, as well as with details regarding the weather and geography of the little explored regions. Set in 1792 and presented as a journal to aid in its acceptance as factual, this fictional work seeks to tell the story of the first crossing of the Rocky Mountains. Poe's hero is Julius Rodman, an English adventurer who braves the dangers of the wilderness with a party of companions. Rodman's initial impetus for the adventure is that it will serve as a health cure; he has lost his father and his two sisters to smallpox. He is a melancholy man who seeks "in the bosom of the wilderness, that peace which his peculiar disposition would not suffer him to enjoy among men." The group must confront dangerous illnesses, attacks by wild animals, stampeding antelopes, capsized boats, and ferocious Sioux Indians. Poe's abrupt dismissal from *Burton's Gentleman's Magazine* ended his interest in the story, and he made no further attempts to complete the work.

Joyce, James (1882–1941) Irish novelist and short story writer. Joyce mentions Poe more than a dozen times in *Dubliners, Finnegan's Wake*, and *Ulysses*, especially in his reference to the "life preserving coffins" in the latter work that provide the same mix of humor and horror as in Poe's "THE PREMATURE BURIAL." For both, the coffins are only temporary enclosures that contain the living—in Poe, the living dead, and in Joyce, the spiritually alive yet physically dead. In an address on the 19th-century Irish poet James Clarence

Mangan, delivered to the Literary and Historical Society of University College in Dublin on February 15, 1902, Joyce called Poe "the high priest of most modern schools" of literature.

Joyeuse, Madame   Character in the short story "THE SYSTEM OF DOCTOR TARR AND PROFESSOR FETHER." An old woman whose name means "joyful," she tells the visitors to the asylum about a woman who "found, upon mature deliberation, that, by some accident, she had been turned into a chicken-cock; but, as such, she behaved with propriety." While telling the story, she begins to flap her wings and to crow loudly and repeatedly, until she is reprimanded. The reader recognizes that the woman she has described is Madame Joyeuse herself.

"Judge Story's Discourse on Chief-Justice Marshall"   Brief review by Poe of two eulogies for "our great and lamented countryman, fell-townsman, neighbor, and friend," Chief Justice John Marshall, that appeared in the December 1835 issue of the SOUTHERN LITERARY MESSENGER. Poe stated that Story's Discourse, "pronounced . . . in Boston" had arrived at the same time as "BINNEY'S EULOGIUM," "pronounced at Philadelphia" and promised "a more extended notice of them and of their great subject" in a subsequent issue.

Jules, the Canadian   Character in the unfinished novella THE JOURNAL OF JULIUS RODMAN. He is one of Rodman's Canadian men who serve as interpreters, and he transacts business with them for Rodman when they first meet the Sioux Indians. When bears attack, he becomes "frightened out of his senses" and runs away, then leaps over the edge of a precipice. The rest of the party loses sight of him and presumes that he has been killed. The party later find him "cruelly bruised" but alive, for he had lodged in one of the ravines and made his way down to the river shore.

Juniper   Character mentioned in "HOW TO WRITE A BLACKWOOD ARTICLE." Signora ZENOBIA receives instruction in the art of article writing from Mr. William BLACKWOOD himself. He tells her that many believe that Samuel Taylor COLERIDGE wrote *Confessions of an English Opium-Eater*, but asserts the truth is that "it was composed by my pet baboon Juniper, over a rummer of Hollands [a brand of gin] and water, 'hot, without sugar.'" The baboon is appropriately named after the plant producing the berries that give gin its distinctive taste, the juniper.

Junot, M.   Character in the novella THE JOURNAL OF JULIUS RODMAN. After Julius RODMAN's sisters and father die, he sells the family plantation "at a complete sacrifice to M. Junot." The new owner gives his son Pierre JUNOT $300 and agrees that he join Rodman on the first river expedition.

Junot, Pierre   Character in the novella THE JOURNAL OF JULIUS RODMAN. He is the eldest son of the neighbor who purchases the family plantation from Julius RODMAN, "a man of strange manners and somewhat eccentric turn of mind, but still one of the best-hearted fellows in the world, and certainly as courageous a man as ever drew breath, although of no great bodily strength." Pierre is of Canadian descent and experienced in excursions for the Fur Company, for which he acted as a *voyageur*. He was a close acquaintance of James RODMAN and "a great favorite" with Jane RODMAN, Julius's younger sister who dies, but Julius believes that "they would have been married had it been God's will to have spared her." Pierre becomes vital to the success of the expedition, and Julius depends upon him to hire able men and to acquire appropriate supplies. Julius and he agree to share equally in the profits, with each taking one-third of the proceeds and the remaining third to be divided by remaining members of the expedition. Despite their amiable business relationship, Rodman relates that "there was not the tie of reciprocal thought between us—that strongest of all mortal bonds. His nature, although sensitive, was too volatile, to comprehend all the devotional fervor of my own."

Jupiter   Character in the short story "THE GOLD-BUG." He is the old black servant of William LEGRAND and Poe employs his dialect to provide comic relief in the story. Jupiter has been with the Legrand family through its changes in fortune and, even though the present Legrand cannot afford to keep servants, Jupiter "could not be induced, neither by threats nor by promises, to abandon what he considered his right of attendance upon the footsteps of his young 'Massa Will'." The narrator of the story suggests that Jupiter's steadfastness is less the result of devotion and more due to the commands of Legrand's relatives who consider their young nephew unbalanced and who are using Jupiter to engage in "supervision and guardianship of the wanderer." Although wary of Legrand's excursion, he is devoted to his master and helps in the digging that reveals Captain Kidd's treasure. The thickness of the dialect that Poe places in Jupiter's mouth has been viewed by critics as "the most embarrassing feature of Poe's prose," and his portrayal reflects Poe's upbringing as a son of the South, which viewed African Americans as "inferior, little more than childlike, and with the affection and intellect of the family dog."

Karnavicius, Jurgis (1884–1968) Lithuanian composer, known also by the Russian name of Jurij Karnovich, whose compositions include four string quartets; two chamber-music concerts (musical accompaniments); a cantata for tenor solo, choir, and orchestra; two operas; and a ballet, in addition to numerous musical compositions inspired by works by Poe. In 1916, Karnavicius wrote *Remembrances in the House of Usher* (known in Russian as *Vechera v Dome Usher* ["Evenings in the House of Usher"]), a chamber-music concert, op. 6, part I: String Quatuor (D minor, no. 2). That same year, Karnavicius completed *Ulalume,* a symphonic poem. In 1924, Karnavicius completed *Love* (known in Russian as *Lubov*), a song cycle for soprano, mezzo-soprano, piano, violin, and cello consisting of seven settings of poems by Poe: *To Helen,* a poem for piano, violin, and cello; *To Helen,* a romance for mezzo-soprano and piano; *To F——,* a romance for soprano, violin, and piano; *To Frances S. Osgood* [*To F——s S. O—d*], a romance for mezzo-soprano, cello, and piano; *To Mary Louise* [*To M. L. S.*], a duet for soprano and mezzo-soprano, with piano; *Intermezzo,* for piano, violin, and cello; *For Annie,* for soprano, mezzo-soprano, piano, violin, and cello. Poe's short story "THE OVAL PORTRAIT" inspired a symphonic poem of the same name in 1927. In describing the work, Karnavicius stated that "in the painter and his wife, as they are characterized by E. Poe, you will find all a composer might dream of for a symphonic construction: two themes and so brightly contrasting; one—full of motion and vigour, the other—tender and mild, as only women in Poe's tales may be."

Kate Character in the short story "THREE SUNDAYS IN A WEEK." She is the betrothed of the narrator, Bobby, also her cousin. "Barely fifteen" but "a firm friend," as well as "a good girl," she has promised to marry the narrator "whenever I could badger my grand-uncle [and Kate's father] Rumgudgeon into the necessary consent" required by her youth. Her father only consents to the marriage *"when three Sundays come together in a week!"* Despite her young age, Kate listens as Captain SMITHERTON and Captain PRATT tell of their journeys and, after hearing that one went round Cape Horn and the other doubled the Cape of Good Hope, proves the assembled group actually has experienced three Sundays in a week.

Katholim Reference in Poe's "A TALE OF JERUSALEM." When facing failure in obtaining the necessary offerings for their altar sacrifices, the Pharisee becomes upset and states that their failure will result in their being "turned out of office by the Katholim." Critics disagree whether Poe refers here to Katholikin, who were overseers of the Treasury, or if he had in mind an ironic reference to Roman Catholics, for which the modern Hebrew word translates as *Katholim.*

Keats, John (1795–1821) English Romantic poet. Although Poe did not review works by Keats, he did express his admiration for the poet in a review ("BALLADS AND OTHER POEMS") a work by Henry Wadsworth LONGFELLOW, writing: "Of the poets who have appeared most fully instinct with the principles now developed, we may mention Keats as the most remarkable. He is the sole British poet who has never erred in his themes. Beauty is always his aim." Throughout his writing career, Poe appears to have had an affinity for the moods and sound qualities of Keats's poetry. In 1832, he opened the short story "THE DUC DE L'OMELETTE" with the reference: "Keats felled by a criticism." This was Poe's commentary that Keats's death was the result of a hostile, critical review, a revelation of the extent to which the artist must suffer at the hands of critics. In truth, the hostile critical attack that Keats was wounded by and suffered in the pages of *BLACKWOOD'S MAGAZINE* occurred in 1818, but the poet did not die until 1821, of tuberculosis and not a broken heart.

Keith, Alexander (1791–1880) Biblical scholar mentioned in Poe's "REVIEW OF STEPHENS'S ARABIA PETRAEA," "SACRED PHILOSOPHY OF THE SEASONS," "INCIDENTS OF TRAVEL IN CENTRAL AMERICA," and in "MARGINALIA" for his work "upon the literal fulfilment of Biblical prophecies." In the review of *Arabia Petraea,* Poe criticizes Keith for "a palpable mistranslation" in a passage that refers to the prophet Isaiah and notes that is "a passage which Dr. Keith should have examined critically in the original before basing so long an argument upon it." Poe repeats nearly the same criticism in the review of *Incidents of Travel in Central America* in pointing out that "both he [Stephens] and Dr. Keith might have spared themselves much trouble by an examination of the Biblical text in the original before founding a question upon it." Despite his questioning of Keith's accuracy, Poe consulted his book *Evidence of the Truth of the Christian Religion Derived from the Literal Fulfilment of Prophecy* while writing *THE NARRATIVE OF ARTHUR GORDON PYM*.

Kelley, Edgar Stillman (1857–1924) American composer, conductor, author, and lecturer. His compositions, performed by major symphony orchestras and choral societies, include the *New England Symphony; Gulliver—His Voyage to Lilliput,* a symphony; *Alladin,* an orchestral suite; *Alice in Wonderland,* a symphonic suite; and music to *Prometheus Bound, Macbeth,* and *Ben Hur.* In 1891, Kelley completed the song "Eldorado", op. 8, no. 1, a setting of Poe's poem of the same name; in 1901, "Israfel", op. 8, no. 2, a song setting of Poe's poem of the same name, as well as an arrangement for women's chorus and orchestra; in 1904 "The Sleeper", for mixed chorus with piano accompaniment, inspired by the first stanza of Poe's poem of the same name; and in 1925, *The Pit and the Pendulum,* a symphonic poem inspired by Poe's short story.

Kempelen, Baron Wolfgang von (1734–1804) Hungarian nobleman, the inventor of the chess-playing robot or intelligent machine discussed in "MAELZEL'S CHESS-PLAYER." He is also the subject of Poe's "VON KEMPELEN AND HIS DISCOVERY." Despite the initial assertions of Poe and others that the chess-player is "the most wonderful of the inventions of mankind," Baron Kempelen "had no scruple in declaring it to be a 'very ordinary piece of mechanism—a *bagatelle* whose effects appeared so marvellous only from the boldness of the conception, and the fortunate choice of the methods adopted for promoting the illusion.'" The baron invented the automaton chess-player in 1769, and it was exhibited throughout the United States by Johann Nepomuk MAELZEL. The chess-player was built to appear as if a mechanical man were playing chess games with humans and beating them, but the contraption actually contained a human being who operated it. In 1836, Poe exposed the trick in the essay "Maezel's Chess-Player," making the name von Kempelen synonymous with "hoax."

Kennedy, John Pendleton (1795–1870) Baltimore lawyer and amateur writer. A friend and literary patron of Poe, he recognized Poe's genius as well as his psychological disparities. In 1833, he served on the committee that judged Poe's prize story for the *BALTIMORE SATURDAY VISITER*, "MS. FOUND IN A BOTTLE." In December 1834, Kennedy recommended Poe's short story collection to the publishing firm of Carey & Lea and, from

his own pocket, supplied Poe with a small advance and invited him to dinner. Poe's response, dated Sunday, March 15, 1835, and often quoted, exhibits the depth to which Poe's fortunes had fallen. Humiliated by his impoverished state and appearance, Poe refused Kennedy's invitation with the following note:

> Dr. Sir,—Your kind invitation to dinner today has wounded me to the quick. I cannot come—for reasons of the most humiliating nature in my personal appearance. You may conceive my deep mortification in making this disclosure to you—but it was necessary. If you will be my friend so far as to loan me $20, I will call on you tomorrow—otherwise it will be impossible, and I must submit to my fate.
>
> Sincerely yours,
> E. A. Poe
>
> Sunday 15th

Touched by Poe's plight, Kennedy also took the forlorn writer under his wing, supplying him with money and clothes, and inviting him to dinner while making certain that Maria CLEMM and Virginia CLEMM Poe were given generous amounts of food. He also introduced Poe to Thomas Willis WHITE, editor of the *SOUTHERN*

John Pendleton Kennedy, Poe's friend and literary patron.
(Edgar Allan Poe Society)

LITERARY MESSENGER, and recommended that White not only publish Poe's fiction but help him in "drudging upon whatever may make money." In a May 1835 review of Kennedy's novel HORSE-SHOE ROBINSON: A TALE OF THE TORY ASCENDENCY that appeared in the Messenger, Poe placed the author "at once in the very first rank of American novelists." In "AUTOGRAPHY," Poe noted Kennedy "[to have] the eye of a painter, more especially in regard to the picturesque—to have refined tastes generally—to be exquisitely alive to the proprieties of life—to possess energy, decision, and great talent—to have a penchant also for the bizarre."

Kerrison, Davenport (1833–1929) American composer whose compositions include Canada, a symphonic overture; a piano concerto in E minor; and a grand opera, with a libretto by the composer, titled The Last of the Aztecs. In 1908, Kerrison composed The Bells, a symphonic poem in four movements, based on Poe's poem of the same name.

King, the Unnamed royal character in the short story "HOP-FROG." He keeps the physically impaired dwarf Hop-Frog as his court fool and heaps abuse upon the weaker members of his court.

King, Oliver (1855–1923) English pianist, organist, and composer whose compositions include choral and orchestral works; a chorus and orchestral arrangement of the 137th Psalm; Night, a symphony; and various cantatas, services, and voluntaries. In 1887, King composed "Israfel," a song inspired by Poe's poem of the same name.

"King Pest the First. A Tale Containing an Allegory" Short story. The tale is considered by critics to be one of Poe's most puzzling stories in its disturbing combination of horror and humor. In reviewing John H. INGRAM's edition of Poe's works in 1875, Robert Louis Stevenson determined that this story, which describes wanton drunkenness during a plague, marked Poe as an unsympathetic individual: "He who could write 'King Pest' had ceased to be a human being."

PUBLISHING AND DRAMATIZATION HISTORY

The story was first published in the September 1835 issue of the SOUTHERN LITERARY MESSENGER and signed by Lyttleton BARRY, one of Poe's pseudonyms. He later included the story as one of the "grotesques" in the short story collection TALES OF THE GROTESQUE AND ARABESQUE, published in 1839, then revised it for republication in the BROADWAY JOURNAL in the October 18, 1845, issue.

An epigraph from Gorboduc: Ferrex and Porrex, a drama published in 1561 by Thomas Norton and Thomas Sackville, Lord Buckhurst, precedes the tale: "The gods do bear and well allow in kings / The things which they abhor in rascal routes." The play, the earliest English tragedy in blank verse, is named after the two sons of the mythical English king Gorboduc and relates the manner in which Porrex first drove his brother Ferrex from Britain, then killed him when Ferrex, returned with an army. Porrex was later put to death by their mother.

CHARACTERS

Her Serene Highness the Arch Duchess ANA-PEST, LEGS, King PEST, Queen PEST, His Grace Arch Duke PEST-IFEROUS, His Grace Duke PEST-ILENTIAL, Hugh TARPAULIN, Duke TEM-PEST.

PLOT SYNOPSIS

Set in one of the three periods in which the Black Death, or plague, struck England during the rule of Edward III, who reigned from 1327 to 1377, the tale mixes macabre horror with disgusting humor in recounting the adventures of a pair of seamen, Legs and Hugh Tarpaulin. After running out without paying their bar bill at the Jolly Tar alehouse while "intoxicated beyond moral sense," they wander into the area of London where the plaque ban remains in effect. The district resembles a metropolitan mortuary where "the whole mass of forbidden buildings was, at length, enveloped in terror as in a shroud . . . leaving the entire vast circuit of the prohibited district to gloom, silence, pestilence, and death." As they run through the streets, in which "the most fetid and poisonous smells everywhere prevailed," the two find the bodies of plague victims strewn everywhere, and "it was by no means seldom that the hand fell upon a skeleton or rested upon a more fleshy corpse." They reach what appears to be a welcoming doorway and "staggered into the midst of things with a volley of curses," only to find that the structure is the shop of an undertaker. They open a trapdoor that leads to a wine cellar and find the family court of King Pest with a company of relatives in various stages of decay. The narrator describes each of member of the Pest court, offering the reader the horrendous details of the emaciation of one, the dropsy of another, the delirium tremens of a third, and so on. "Before each of the party lay a portion of a skull, which was used as a drinking cup." Each character also represents a different type of "pest," from the intellectual who produces nothing original to the drunkard. King Pest accuses the two seamen of treason for violating his privacy and that of his family and sentences them to "'be tied neck and heels together and duly drowned as rebels in yon hogshead of October beer!'" When Tarpaulin is dunked into the barrel of beer, Legs goes to his rescue and knocks over the barrel, creating a "deluge of liquor" that drowns most of King Pest's court. Tarpaulin and Legs seize two of the women and rush away with them, heading for their ship, the *Free and Easy*.

Kircher, Athanasias (1601–1680) German Jesuit archeologist, mathematician, biologist, and physicist who studied subterranean forces. He connected the concept of the Maelstrom with Charybdis, a whirlpool near Sicily that appears in the 12th book of Homer's *Odyssey*. Bishop Pontoppidan wrote in his 1755 book *The Natural History of Norway* that Kircher believed the Maelstrom to be "a sea-vortex, attracting the flood under the shore of Norway, where, through another abyss, it is discharged into the gulph [*sic*] of Bothnia." Poe commented on Kircher's theories about whirlpools and sea vortexes in the short story "A DESCENT INTO THE MAELSTROM."

Kirkland, Caroline Matilda (1801–1864) New York author and editor of the *Union Magazines* who rejected Poe's "ULALUME" for publication in 1847. Poe's review of her in "THE LITERATI OF NEW YORK CITY" is positive, and he praises her "life-like" representations and her handling of western scenes and pioneer character. He finds her re-creation of life to be notable, and asserts that "she has represented 'scenes' that could have occurred only *as* and *where* she has described them." Declaring "unquestionably, she is one of our best writers, has a province of her own, and in that province has few equals," Poe writes that her work contains "a certain freshness of style, seemingly drawn, as her subjects in general, from the west."

Kirkland, William (1800–1846) American essayist and journalist. Poe included a profile of Kirkland in "THE LITERATI OF NEW YORK," singling out for praise his articles "The Tyranny of Public Opinion in the United States" and "The West, Paradise of the Poor." He writes that "whatever Mr. Kirkland does is done carefully," despite having a style that is "occasionally very caustic, but seldom without cause." Overall, the review declares Kirkland's style to be "vigorous, precise, and notwithstanding his foreign acquirements, free from idiomatic peculiarities." In his review "AMERICA AND THE AMERICAN PEOPLE," Poe chastises the translator William Turner for omitting either accidentally or "from some motives of publishing policy" to give Kirkland credit for assisting in the monumental task of translating the work into English: "We have been much surprised to find, in the Translator's Preface, no acknowledgment of his indebtedness to those who aided him in this difficult task—to Mr. Kirkland, for example, and to the accomplished

Mrs. ELLET—who, between them, prepared nearly, if not quite, one half the book."

Kissam, Mr. Character mentioned in "VON KEMPELEN AND HIS DISCOVERY" who claims to have made the discovery of how to turn lead into gold that has been widely attributed to Baron Von KEMPELEN. The unnamed narrator refuses to give credence to Kissam's assertion, stating, "It does not *look* true. Persons who are narrating facts, are seldom so particular as Mr. Kissam seems to be, about day and date and precise location." He suggests that "Mr. Kissam's (or is it Mr. Quizzam's?) pretensions to the discovery" are very hard to believe and have "an amazingly moon-hoax-y air."

Knickerbocker Magazine New York journal edited by Lewis Gaylord CLARK, a Poe foe who used his column "Editors' Table" to attack Poe's writing, printing one particularly virulent attack on *THE NARRATIVE OF ARTHUR GORDON PYM* in 1838. Clark's attacks combined with Poe's rebuttals to create a highly public feud in print that led in 1845 to physical violence when Poe attacked Clark on a New York street. The review of *The Narrative of Arthur Gordon Pym* that appeared in the August 1838 issue stated, "There are a great many tough stories in this book, told in a loose and slip-shod style. . . . The work is one of much interest with all its defects, not the least of which is, that it is too liberally stuffed with 'horrid circumstance of blood and battle.'" The November 1846 issue contained a satiric poem mocking Poe in "Epitaph on a Modern 'Critic'." "Here ARISTARCHUS lies, (nay, never smile,) / Cold as his muse, and stiffer than his style; / But whether BACCHUS or MINERVA claims / The crusty critic, all conjecture shames; / Nor shall the world know which the mortal sin, / Excessive genius or excessive gin." In a description of the publication, which appeared in his profile of Clark in "THE LITERATI OF NEW YORK CITY," Poe says the title, "for a merely local one, is unquestionably good." He also expresses admiration for the choice of contributors, who "have usually been men of eminence" and their contributions, which "have been excellent." Despite these admirable aspects, the work "has never succeeded in attaining *position* among intelligent or educated readers." Poe asserts that the blame for this lies in the manner in which the magazine was edited, "the work is deficient in that absolutely indispensable element, *individuality*. As the editor has no precise character, the magazine, as a matter of course, can have none. . . . [A]n apple, in fact, or a pumpkin, has more angles."

Kranich, Alvin (1865–1946) American composer and pianist whose compositions include the orchestral works *Rhapsodies, Americana,* and *Mary Magdalene;* a cantata *The Watchtower;* an opera *Doktor Eisenhart; Dante Sonata;* and overtures and piano concertos. In 1908, Kranich completed *The Raven,* a melodrama consisting of incidental music for piano, to be used in connection with the narration of Poe's poem of the same name. In 1925, Kranich wrote *The Raven* [*Der Rabe*], a symphonic poem whose score was completed in Weimar, Germany, and first performed in 1927 in Naumburg, Germany.

Kreutzenstern, Captain Russian navigator and oceanic explorer mentioned along with Captain LISIAUSKY in chapter 16 of *THE NARRATIVE OF ARTHUR GORDON PYM.* In 1803, he is sent by Czar Alexander I of Russia to circumnavigate the globe. As he and his crew attempt to go south, they meet with strong currents setting easterly, where they find an abundance of whales but no ice. The narrator states that had the expedition arrived earlier in the season—they arrived in March—they would have encountered ice, for the winds carry the floes great distances.

Kroeger, Ernest Richard (1862–1934) American composer, pianist, organist, and educator whose compositions include the orchestral suite *Lalla Rookh,* the symphonic poem *The Mississippi, Father of Waters;* the song "Bend Low O Dusky Night," and chamber music, choral music, and piano and choral works. In 1890, Kroegar completed "I Saw Thee on Thy Bridal Day," a song inspired by Poe's poem "SONG: TO———" and in 1906, Kroeger completed "Annabel Lee," op. 65, no. 7, a song inspired by Poe's poem of the same name.

Kroutaplenttey Character mentioned in the short story "THE DEVIL IN THE BELFRY." He has traced the origin of the name of the borough of Vondervotteimitiss. The name seems to translate to "plenty of Krauts," with "kraut" used as a slang term for "German" and obviously coming from sauerkraut, a well-known German cabbage dish.

Lackobreath, Mr.   *See* "LOSS OF BREATH."

Lacy, Frederick St. John (1862–1935)   Irish composer known for musical compositions and lecture-recitals. Lacy composed more than 100 works, most of them vocal. In 1887 he wrote a cantata setting of Poe's poem "ANNABEL LEE" for tenor solo, chorus, and orchestra.

Lafayette, Marie Joseph Paul Yves Roch Gilbert du Motier, Marquis de (1757–1834)   French general and hero of the American Revolution whom Poe characterizes as "the intimate friend" of Poe's paternal grandfather General David Poe, a quartermaster general in the Maryland line during the Revolutionary War. As Poe reported in an autobiographical memorandum to Rufus Wilmot GRISWOLD, when Lafayette visited Richmond in October 1824, he "called personally upon the Gen.'s widow, and tendered her his warmest acknowledgments for the services rendered him by her husband." Poe was made a lieutenant among a group of well-born young gentlemen attending Burke's Academy, run by William BURKE, who were organized into a military company called the Richmond Junior Volunteers. The company members were provided with uniforms consisting of fringed frontier hunting shirts and equipped with swords and guns. Reports suggest that Poe probably met Lafayette while on parade in Capitol Square as a member of the volunteer company of riflemen that served as Lafayette's honorary bodyguard during the French general's Richmond visit.

"Lafitte: The Pirate of the Gulf. By the Author of the South-West. New York: Harper and Brothers"   Review by Poe that appeared in the August 1836 issue of the *SOUTHERN LITERARY MESSENGER.* Poe asserts that the author of this historical novel, Professor Joseph H. Ingraham, seems to have based the novel "in a great degree" upon several historical accounts, but he does not use these as the basis upon which he will assess the current work: "We are not, however, to decide upon the merits of the story—which runs nearly thus—by any reference to historical truth." Instead, Poe provides a lengthy summary of the work, in which he finds deficiencies of the syntax, orthography, and typography. He chastises Ingraham for being "too minutely, and by far too frequently *descriptive.* We are surfeited with unnecessary detail."

Poe states "our principal objection is to the tendency of the tale" to glorify Lafitte while portraying the pirate hero as "a weak, a vacillating villain, a fratricide, a cowardly cut-throat. . . . Yet he is never mentioned but with evident respect." In the final analysis, Poe praises Ingraham's talent but expresses the desire that he "would either think it necessary to bestow a somewhat greater degree of labor and attention upon the composition of their novels, or otherwise, would *not* think it necessary to compose them at all."

Lafourcade, Mademoiselle Victorine   Character in "THE PREMATURE BURIAL." She is the subject of one of the case studies of premature interment created by Poe for this story. A beautiful, young girl of a wealthy and illustrious family, she was said to have fallen in love with Julien Bossuet, a young Parisian journalist, but pride made her reject him to marry, instead, Monsieur RENELLE, "a banker and diplomatist of some eminence." After several "wretched years" of marriage, during which her husband was rumored to have neglected and, "perhaps, more positively ill-treated her," she dies, or "at least her condition so closely resembled death as to deceive every one who saw her." When Bossuet hears of her death, he frantically seeks her grave with the goal "of disinterring the corpse, and possessing himself of its luxuriant tresses." As her coffin opens, Victorine slowly opens her eyes to reveal that she was buried alive, it is only through Bossuet's frantic efforts that she revives fully. After he nurses her back to health, she leaves with him for America, where the two remain for 20 years. When they later return, Victorine's husband recognizes her and asserts his claim, but "a judicial tribunal sustained her in her resistance."

"The Lake"   Poem first published in 1827 in the collection *TAMERLANE AND OTHER POEMS.* The poem also appeared under the title "The Lake—To———" in the 1829 collection *AL AARAAF, TAMERLANE, AND OTHER MINOR POEMS,* Poe's second collection of poetry and the first to be commercially published. The poem is both a celebration of solitude and a meditation on the self inspired by the lake. The narrator states "So lovely was the loneliness / Of a wild lake," an isolated body of water surrounded by tall pines in which he experiences exquisite pleasure for "that terror was not fright— /

But a tremulous delight." The speaker finds that "Death was in that poisonous wave," yet he is not frightened because the terror of the lonely lake is actually a path to the hidden imagination, "For him who thence could solace bring / To his dark imagining." The inspiration of his surroundings would stimulate the speaker "Whose wild'ring could even make / An Eden of that dim lake."

Lalage Character in Poe's drama *POLITIAN*. She is the last surviving member of an illustrious family and the ward of the Duc di BROGLIO. Count CASTIGLIONE, the duke's son, has seduced Lalage and abandoned her to marry another woman. Although the duke forgives his son for the indiscretion, he "is most wroth with her / And treats her with such marked severity / As humbles her to the dust." She must now watch while Castiglione marries his cousin Alessandra, once "the bosom friend of the fair lady Lalage / Ere this mischance." Late in the play, she learns that she is loved by POLITIAN, an English nobleman who saw her sometime before and fell in love with her. When he learns of what Castiglione has done to her, he vows revenge.

Lalande, Madame Eugenie Character in the short story "THE SPECTACLES." She is an 82-year-old woman with whom the nearsighted Napoleon Buonoparte FROISSART falls in love, fooled by his bad eyesight into thinking that she is a young woman of 27. She is immensely wealthy, having been widowed twice without any children, and "by the aid of pearl-powder, or rouge, of false hair, false teeth, and false *tournure,* as well as of the most skilful modistes of Paris, she contrived to hold a respectable footing among the beauties *peu passées* of the French metropolis." She is actually the great-great-grandmother of Froissart and joins his friends in deceiving him into proposing and carrying out a marriage to her as a means of reproof for his refusal to wear spectacles.

Lalande, Madame Stephanie Character in the short story "THE SPECTACLES" and a relative of Madame Eugenie LALANDE's second husband. She is the true object of Napoleon Buonaparte FROISSART's passion and becomes his wife after he is humiliated when his poor eyesight has led him to propose marriage to his own great-great-grandmother.

Landor, Mr. Character in the short story "LANDOR'S COTTAGE." The narrator describes him as "civil, even cordial in his manner," and he offers no further description because the intention of the tale is to describe the cottage. The name is taken from the pseudonym William LANDOR, used by American novelist Horace Binney Wallace.

Landor, William Occasional pseudonym of Horace Binney Wallace, an American novelist who also published occasionally in periodicals. Poe wrote in "AUTOGRAPHY" that he has "acquired much reputation as the author of 'Stanley,'" a work that was warmly commended by the press throughout the country. Nothing that Landor has also "written many excellent papers for the Magazines," Poe assesses his style as that of "an elaborately careful, stiff, and pedantic writer, with much affectation and great talent."

"Landor's Cottage. A Pendant to 'The Domain of Arnheim'" Short story. This charming piece, more of a descriptive narrative, is the last story of Poe's printed in his lifetime. Friends of Poe such as Mary GOVE have written that the cottage Poe describes is actually an idealized version of his Fordham cottage, his "little cottage at the top of a hill."

The "Annie" of the story has been identified as Poe's friend Mrs. Annie RICHMOND, who is similar in appearance and for whom Poe wrote the poem "FOR ANNIE."

PUBLISHING AND DRAMATIZATION HISTORY

The story was first published in the June 9, 1849, issue of the *FLAG OF OUR UNION*. It contains no epigraph.

CHARACTERS

ANNIE (2), MR. LANDOR, unnamed narrator.

PLOT SYNOPSIS

The speaker states that the only purpose of the work is to "give, in detail, a picture of Mr. Landor's residence—*as I found it.*" To this end, the unnamed narrator takes a walk throughout one or two river counties of New York State with no particular direction or goal. He wanders into a gorge, where he is overwhelmed by the luxuriant beauty of the natural world, then moves on to listen to the murmur of water and to watch the fog dissipate and the sun making its way over the hills. As he marvels at the harmony among the disparate entities of nature—the rocks, trees, lake, and other natural elements that created one cohesive picture—he concludes that "Everywhere was variety in uniformity." In the distance, he sees a peninsula on which has been built a cottage that strikes him "with the keenest sense of combined novelty and propriety—in a word, of *poetry.*" The narrator is mesmerized by the house and describes it in detail, stating that "nothing could be more simple—more utterly unpretending than this cottage." The chief attraction lies in its artistic placement among the natural beauty surrounding, as if "some eminent landscape-painter had built it with his brush." When he approaches the cottage, he is greeted by a slender woman of medium height and approximately 28 years old, whose "spiritual gray" eyes captivate him. From inside the cottage, he hears someone call "Annie, darling!" as she issues to him "her most courteous of invitations" to enter the cottage. There he meets Mr. Landor himself, whose "keenest sense of combined novelty and propriety" has given perfect artistic balance to the neat and graceful cottage and the sublime natural scenery.

"The Landscape Garden" Sketch first published in the October 1842 issue of *Snowden's Ladies' Companion.* The sketch later became the first 15 paragraphs of an expanded version of the tale that was retitled "THE DOMAIN OF ARNHEIM."

Laplace, Mam'selle Character in the short story "THE SYSTEM OF DOCTOR TARR AND PROFESSOR FETHER." One of the asylum inmates who attend the mad banquet, she is an old lady who reprimands Monsieur DE KOCK for kicking up his heels like a donkey and spoiling her brocade dress. She is appeased when Mr. De Kock apologizes, kisses her hand "with much ceremony," and drinks a glass of wine with her.

Latrobe, John Hazelhurst Boneval (1803–1891) One of three judges, with John Pendleton KENNEDY and Dr. James MILLER, he judged Poe's prizewinning story "MS. FOUND IN A BOTTLE" for a competition sponsored in 1833 by the *BALTIMORE SUNDAY VISITER.* In later accounts he described Poe as having the air of a gentleman: "Gentleman was written all over him." Latrobe wrote that Poe "was dressed in black, and his frock-coat was buttoned to the throat, where it met the black stock, then almost universally worn. Not a particle of white was visible." He noted that the clothes were well-worn and mended and that "on most men his clothes would have looked shabby and seedy," but that Poe's sense of dignity made the terms inapplicable to him.

Lauzanne, Jacques Character in *THE JOURNAL OF JULIUS RODMAN.* He is a Canadian who accompanies Rodman on his journey and dies of a snakebite.

Lawson, James (1799–1880) New York author whom Poe profiles in "THE LITERATI OF NEW YORK CITY." He is the author of *Giordano* (1832), a tragedy which, Poe informs readers, was "condemned (to use a gentle word) some years ago at the Park Theatre; and never was condemnation more religiously deserved." Poe professes to know very little about other writings by Lawson, aside from another work titled *Tales and Sketches by a Cosmopolite,* which contains "The Dapper Gentleman's Story," "in manner, as in title, an imitation of one of Irving's 'Tales of a Traveller'." Of the man, Poe states that he is a fluent conversationalist who "tells a good story" and is socially adept. In particular, Poe

asserts that Lawson, "with no taste whatever, is quite enthusiastic on all topics appertaining to Taste."

Le Blanc, Monsieur Character in the short story "THE MYSTERY OF MARIE ROGÊT." He is the proprietor of a *parfumerie,* a perfume shop in the Palais Royal. Marie ROGÊT had worked there three-and-a-half years earlier, at which time she disappeared for a week, then was reemployed by Le Blanc until her final disappearance prior to her murder.

Le Bon, Adolphe Character in the short story "THE MURDERS IN THE RUE MORGUE." He is a clerk in the banking firm Mignaud et Fils who accompanies Madame L'ESPANAYE to her residence, carrying with him 4,000 francs divided into two bags. He claims that, when he reached her residence, Madame L'Espanaye took one bag of money from him and Mademoiselle L'ESPANAYE took the other, after which he simply bowed and left the two women. His name, Le Bon, means "the good" in French, and he ironically is the first person whom the police accuse of the murders. After C. Auguste DUPIN enters the case, Le Bon is exonerated.

Le Brun, Pere Reference in "THE DUC DE L'OMELETTE" to Charles Le Brun (1619–1690), a virtual dictator of the arts in France under Louis XIV. He laid down a strict system of rules for artistic expression for the French Academy and even wrote a treatise on the appropriate means of expressing the passions. When faced with one final card game with the devil for his soul, the desperate Duc de l'Omelette wracks his brain to remember anything that might help him and recalled "had he not skimmed over Pere Le Brun?"

Ledyard, John Mentioned in *THE JOURNAL OF JULIUS RODMAN* as a former associate of Captain James COOK. In the story, he is credited as one of the earliest explorers of the northern portion of the United States, and "Mr. Jefferson, in speaking of Ledyard's undertaking, erroneously calls it 'the *first* attempt to explore the western part of our northern continent.'"

"Legends of a Log Cabin. By a Western Man. New York: George Dearborn, Publisher" Review by Poe that appeared in the December 1835 issue of the *SOUTHERN LITERARY MESSENGER.* Poe claims to "have been much interested in this book in spite of some very glaring faults and absurdities with which it is besprinkled." This book of seven tales is based on an old plot device: A heterogeneous group of people accidentally come together, then amuse each other by telling stories to pass the time. Although Poe finds several of the tales —most notably "The Hunter's Vow"—well executed, others are assessed to be "uninteresting," "neither so verisimilar, nor so well told," "a failure," or "not very good." Despite such faultfinding, Poe recommends the work to readers and states that "It is excellently gotten up."

Legrand, William　Character in the short story "THE GOLD-BUG." He finds a real gold bug and an old piece of parchment containing a mysterious cipher on the isolated island where he resides. Despite the skepticism of his servant JUPITER and the unnamed narrator, Legrand discovers a coded message that leads him to the burial place of Captain Kidd's treasure, as well as precious stones and two complete skeletons apparently left behind by Captain Kidd. Afterward, Legrand explains his "methodical investigation of the affair" and reveals the shrewd methods and the ratiocinative abilities that he used to crack the codes and to find the wealth. Once the treasure hunters have reached the final location, Legrand uses the gold beetle as a surveyor's plumb bob to pinpoint the spot, thus providing an explanation of his attaching the bug to a bit of whipcord and twirling it as the treasure hunters search.

Legs　Character in the short story "KING PEST." With his drinking companion and fellow member of the crew of the ship *Free and Easy,* Hugh TARPAULIN, Legs meets King Pest and the Pest family court during the London plague. Six-and-a-half-feet tall, he walks with "an habitual stoop in the shoulders [that] seemed to have been the necessary consequence of an altitude so enormous." He is also extremely thin, and his fellow crewmen assert that he might "have answered, when drunk, for a pennant at the mast-head, or, when sober, have served for a jib-boom." He has high cheekbones, a large hawk-nose, retreating chin, fallen underjaw, and huge protruding white eyes, all joined to convey an attitude of "dogged indifference to matters and things in general." At the end of the story, after saving his shipmate from drowning in a "hogshead full of October ale," Legs seizes "by the waist the fat lady in the shroud, rushed out with her into the street, and made a beeline for the 'Free and Easy'."

Leicester, Earl of　*See POLITIAN.*

"Lenore"　Poem that first appeared under the title "A Paean" in Poe's first commercially printed poetry collection, *Poems,* published by Elam Bliss in 1831. Originally consisting of 11 simple quatrains with only one speaker, the bereaved husband, the poem did not originally contain the name LENORE (1). The poem went through eight revisions in Poe's lifetime, with the first major revision retitled "Lenore" appearing in the February 1843 issue of the *Pioneer,* a periodical published by the poet James Russell LOWELL. In this version, Poe achieves a dramatic contrast by dividing the poem into a tale between two speakers, in which he

shortens the lines and creates stanzas that are from 13 to 16 lines long. In the final version, published in the August 16, 1845, issue of the *BROADWAY JOURNAL,* the poem is compressed into three stanzas that contain longer lines with interstanzaic rhyme. In the poem, Guy DE VERE, Lenore's grieving lover, fails to weep when he looks at her beautiful form lying on the funeral bier; yet the conflicting views that he expresses about her death as he rants throughout the poem show his deep devotion to her. De Vere accuses Lenore's family and friends of treating her in a cold and unfeeling manner while she was alive, and he states that in his love for her "No dirge will I upraise." Instead of mourning, he will sing a song of triumph as "her sweet soul" leaves the earth that caused her so many tears. The lamentation for a young woman whose death is welcomed, and perhaps caused, by a "slanderous tongue / That did to death the innocence that died, and died so young. Defeating her persecutors" is similar to the death in "ANNABEL LEE," a poem which also contains a callous family.

Lenore (1)　Dead young woman in Poe's poem "LENORE" who has been sent to her death by a wicked and unfeeling family. Her bereaved husband Guy DE VERE mourns her and claims her family "loved her for her wealth, and ye hated her for her pride; / And when she fell in feeble health, ye blessed her—that she died."

Lenore (2)　Dead young woman in Poe's poem "THE RAVEN" for whom the speaker mourns in his "sorrow for the lost Lenore" as he glorifies her "whom the angels name Lenore." As the torment of the speaker in the poem increases, he asks for "respite and nepenthe from thy memories of Lenore" and asks to "forget this lost Lenore." Her status as "a sainted maiden" and "a rare and radiant maiden" remains intact throughout the poem, and near the end of the poem the speaker states twice that she is the maiden "whom the angels name Lenore."

Some critics have taken Lenore to represent the loss of the love of Poe's young life—Sarah Elmira ROYSTER—to marriage, not death. Others have interpreted the name as a symbol of the creative impulse that is rare, precious, and too easily lost.

Leoni, Franco (1865–1947)　Italian composer. Leoni's compositions include 10 operas, three oratorios, chamber music, and various songs. In 1908, he composed a vocal scena for baritone or contralto with orchestra, to Poe's poem "THE BELLS."

Le Poer　The ancestral name that Poe's friend Mrs. Sarah Helen Power WHITMAN claimed to have identified for Poe after observing the similarity between her family name, Power, and that of Poe. She claimed that she and Poe shared a magnificent common ancestry, and stated that Poe was modified from an old Norman family surname, Le Poer—a name that Walt Whitman called "conspicuous in Irish annals."

Le Rennét, Henri Alias that Poe used in 1827 when he left John ALLAN's house after a quarrel resulting from Allan's refusal to cover the debts that Poe had accumulated while attending the University of Virginia. In order to avoid arrest on a debtor's warrant and to cover his departure, Poe assumed the name of Le Rennét when he left Richmond for Boston.

Leslie, Henry (1822–1896) English conductor, composer, and cellist whose compositions include operas, oratorios, symphonies, part-songs, and church, chamber, and piano music. In 1891, Leslie composed "Annabelle Lee: The Beautiful Classic Ballad," a song for the concert hall and the parlor, inspired by Poe's poem "ANNABEL LEE."

L'Espanaye, Madame Character in the short story "THE MURDERS IN THE RUE MORGUE." She is one of the murder victims; her body is found in a small paved yard in the rear of the building in which she lived, "with her throat so entirely cut that, upon an attempt to raise her, the head fell off." The body is also extensively mutilated, "so much so as scarcely to retain any semblance of humanity." C. Auguste DUPIN also mentions her case in "THE MYSTERY OF MARIE ROGÊT."

L'Espanaye, Mademoiselle Camille Character in the short story "THE MURDERS IN THE RUE MORGUE." She is one of the murder victims. Her body is stuffed into the fireplace chimney, "head downward," and the police have to drag the still-warm body out, "it having been thus forced up the narrow aperture for a considerable distance." The police observe that the body is covered with numerous scrapes and bruises, as well as many severe scratches on the face and, "upon the throat, dark bruises, and deep indentations of finger nails, as if the deceased had been throttled to death."

"Letter to B———" The preface to Poe's third collection *POEMS*, published by Elam Bliss in 1831, as "Letter to Mr.——— ———," and addressed "Dear B———." The preface later appeared under the title "Letter to B———" in the July 1836 issue of the *SOUTHERN LITERARY MESSENGER*. This rambling epistolary essay marks Poe's early effort to establish himself as critic and theorist of American literature. He discusses the works of Shakespeare and Milton. He also discusses the lessons that he has learned by paring and revising his earlier poems to those included in the current edition with "the trash taken away from them in which they were embedded." Critics find the

epistle significant primarily because it contains for the first time Poe's theory of poetic criticism, as well as the germ of the famous later lecture on "THE POETIC PRINCIPLE." Poe speaks of the difficulty of being taken seriously experienced by American writers and expresses the strong influence of Samuel Taylor COLERIDGE's ideas in defining his distinctions between a poem and other works. As he would later insist in "The Poetic Principle," poetic pleasure arises by virtue of the musical qualities inherent in the poem itself: "Music, when combined with a pleasurable idea, is poetry; music, without the idea, is simply music; the idea, without the music, is prose from its very definitiveness."

"Letters, Conversations, and Recollections of S. T. Coleridge. New York: Harper and Brothers" Review by Poe that appeared in the June 1836 issue of the *SOUTHERN LITERARY MESSENGER*. Poe asserts that the letters and conversations recounted in the volume reviewed exhibited Coleridge's "heart, as in his own works we have beheld the mind, of the man," and he praises "Coleridge—the man to whose gigantic mind the proudest intellects of Europe found it impossible not to succumb." He expresses a strong feeling of "indignation and disgust" that the "Narcissi of critical literature have had the infinite presumption to breathe against the majesty of Coleridge." Declaring that "no man was more richly-gifted with all the elements of mental renown, so none was more fully worthy of the love and veneration of every truly good man," Poe chastises American publishers for not bringing out an edition of Coleridge's *Biographia Literaria*. To do so, he asserts, would afford "a clearer view into his mental constitution than any other of his works."

"Letters Descriptive of the Virginia Springs—The Roads Leading Thereto and the Doings Thereat. Collected, Corrected, Annotated, and Edited by Peregrine Prolix. With a Map of Virginia. Philadelphia: Published by H. S. Tanner" Review by Poe that appeared in the August 1836 issue of the *SOUTHERN LITERARY MESSENGER*. Poe heartily recommends the book, written under a pseudonym by Philip H. Nichelin, to "every person about to pay a visit to our Springs . . . and every person not about to pay them a visit . . . [so] that he may have the pleasure of changing his mind." The review states that the volume is "increased in value by the addition of a Tanner's Map of Virginia" on which are marked in different colors several routes to the Springs. Poe ends with an endorsement for Red Sulphur Springs, an establishment run by "our old and highly esteemed friend, Mr. Burke," who has made the business "every thing the tourist or the valetudinarian could desire."

"Letters of Eliza Wilkinson, During the Invasion and Possession of Charleston, S.C. by the British, in the Revolutionary War. Arranged by Caroline Gilman" Review of the 12 letters that comprise the book that Poe published in "MARGINALIA." Although he acknowledged the truth of the assertion in the preface that "few records exist of American women either before or during the war of the Revolution, and that those perpetuated by History want the charm of personal narrative," he judged these letters "silly" and stated that he could not "conceive why Miss Gilman thought the public wished to read them." Poe claims to have looked "in vain" for any useful information in the book.

"Letters to Young Ladies. By Mrs. L. H. Sigourney. Second Edition. Hartford: Published by Wm. Watson" Review by Poe that appeared in the July 1836 issue of the SOUTHERN LITERARY MESSENGER. Poe praised the collection "as a code of morals and *manner* for the gentler sex" and stated "we have seen nothing whatever which we would more confidently place in the hands of any young female friend." The 12 letters are on the following subjects: "Improvement of Time," "Domestic Employment," "Health and Dress," "Manners and Accomplishments," "Books," "Friendship," "Cheerfulness," "Conversation," "Benevolence," "Self-Government," "Utility," and "Motives in Perseverance." Poe contends that "it would be difficult to find fault with the construction of more than a very few passages in the Letters" and admits that the general quality of the collection would make any fault-finding "a matter of hyper-criticism."

Levey, William Charles (1837–1894) Irish dramatic composer and conductor whose works include many operas produced in London, as well as cantatas, songs, and piano pieces. In 1866, he wrote "Many a Year Ago," a song whose text was taken from Poe's "ANNABEL LEE."

Lewis, Captain Meriwether (1774–1809) American explorer. In 1803 he was appointed by President Thomas Jefferson as commander of an expedition to explore the newly acquired Louisiana Territory and chose William CLARK as joint commander of what became known as Lewis and Clark Expedition (1803–06). Poe included references to Lewis's explorations in THE JOURNAL OF JULIUS RODMAN and his review of Washington IRVING's "ASTORIA; OR, ANECDOTES OF AN ENTERPRISE BEYOND THE ROCKY MOUNTAINS."

Lewis, Sarah Anna "Stella" (1824–1880) Amateur poet who knew Poe at the Fordham cottage after Virginia CLEMM Poe's death. Lewis and her husband paid Poe $100 to assure that he would write a complimentary review of her collection *The Child of the Sea and Other Poems*. The review appeared in the September 1848 issue of the SOUTHERN LITERARY MESSENGER. Born Sarah Anna Robinson, Lewis spent much of her early life in Cuba, where her father, a distinguished Cuban of English and Spanish heritage, owned a thriving business. In an unpublished manuscript that Rufus GRISWOLD later included in his first edition of Poe's works, Poe praised her for being "a thorough linguist in the ancient and modern languages" and for her translations as well as for her poetry. In the essay entitled "Estelle Anna Lewis," Poe declared that she was "the best educated, if not the most accomplished of American authoresses." Despite such praise, Marie Louise SHEW revealed Poe's true feelings toward Stella, noting that he "hated the fat, gaudily dressed woman" who spent considerable time in Maria CLEMM's kitchen and that he "rushed out to escape her." He confessed to Shew that "She [Lewis] is really commonplace, but her husband was kind to me."

Lewis, Sylvanus D. (n.d.) Brooklyn attorney who sent money to Poe after the death of Virginia CLEMM Poe when he saw the statement of the poet's property while engaged in one of the city courts. He was the husband of Sarah Anna LEWIS.

Liebling, George (1865–1948) German composer and pianist who later settled in Hollywood, California. His works included operas, violin and piano concertos, sonatas, piano pieces, and over 150 songs. In 1934, he published a musical setting of Poe's poem "ANNABEL LEE."

"Life and Literary Remains of L. E. L. By Laman Blanchard. Two Volumes. Lea and Blanchard" Review by Poe that appeared in the August 1841 issue of GRAHAM'S MAGAZINE. In his review of this posthumous biography of the poet Letitia Elizabeth Landon, Poe praises her "genius" and states that "few equalled her . . . in the *passionate purity* of her verse." Although he regarded her as one of the "loftiest of the female poets of the present generation," he also admits that "her great faults were a want of method, and a careless, rapid habit of composition." As a result, she "consequently was often trite, and always careless." Still, in the final analysis, he notes, "we may say that she has left no living female poet to compete with her in fame."

"The Life and Surprising Adventures of Robinson Crusoe, of York, Mariner: With a Biographical Account of Defoe. Illustrated with Fifty Characteristic Cuts, from Drawings by William Harvey, Esq. and Engraved by Adams. New York: Published by Harper and Brothers" Review by Poe that appeared in the January 1836 issue of the SOUTHERN LITERARY MESSENGER. Poe begins the review by rhapsodizing over the widespread popularity of the work, and by recalling "those enchanted days of our own boyhood when we first learned to grow serious over Robinson Crusoe!—when we first found the spirit of wild adventure enkindling within us." While he acknowledges the power of the adventures to entertain, Poe asks readers to also view the work "in the light of a literary performance." In addition to praising Defoe's skills in writing this work, Poe reminds readers that Defoe wrote "no less than two hundred and eight works" that receive considerably less attention. To correct this lack, he identifies and describes briefly 17 of those works, and also notes that Defoe edited a magazine of largely political material for nine years.

"Life in Death"   First title for the short story "THE OVAL PORTRAIT."

"A Life of George Washington, in Latin Prose: By Francis Glass, A.M. of Ohio. Edited by J. N. Reynolds. New York: Published by Harper and Brothers"   Review by Poe that appeared in the December 1835 issue of the SOUTHERN LITERARY MESSENGER. Poe confesses that he thought the early announcement of a life of George Washington written in Latin was a hoax and that "the thing was improbable, we thought." Once having read the work, Poe enthusiastically commends it and states that "we really can call to mind, at this moment, no modern Latin composition whatever much superior to the Washington Vita of Mr. Glass." Poe praises both the ingenuity and the grammatical skill of Francis Glass, but he claims that "a large proportion of the work—disguise the face as we may, is necessarily not Latin at all" because it treats "of events and incidents occurring in a manner utterly unknown to the Romans, and at a period many centuries after their ceasing to exist as a nation." Despite Poe's enthusiasm for the work, he observes that it has little value in teaching students classical Latin, for "our object, then, at present, is simply to imbue the mind of the student with the idiom, the manner, the thought, and above all, with the words of antiquity."

"Life of Petrarch. By Thomas Campbell, Esq., Author of 'The Pleasures of Hope,' Etc., Complete in One Volume. Philadelphia, Carey and Hart"   Review by Poe that appeared in the September 1841 issue of GRAHAM'S MAGAZINE. Poe began the review by alerting readers to his lack of enthusiasm for Petrarch and his work: "[W]e are not among those who regard the genius of Petrarch as a subject for enthusiastic admiration." Despite this lack of enthusiasm for the subject or his poetry, Poe praises the importance of Petrarch as a historical figure and devotes nearly one-fourth of the review to identifying areas in which he excelled. Of the craftsmanship of the biography, he holds a low opinion, noting that Campbell is usually "scrupulously correct" but observing that the author is guilty in this instance of a "slovenliness of style" and "the want of comprehensive analysis of the poet's character, and of the age in which he lived." In short, Poe contends that "the biographer has swallowed the philosopher."

"A Life of Washington. By James K. Paulding. New York: Harper and Brothers"   Review by Poe that appeared in the May 1836 issue of the SOUTHERN LITERARY MESSENGER. Poe praised Paulding's thorough examination of Washington's life, including "the private affections, aspirations, and charities of that hero" and predicted that the work would "not fail to take a deeper hold upon the public mind, and upon the public affections, than any work upon the same subject." He also expressed approval of Paulding's style, and stated that "there is no better literary *manner* than the manner of Mr. Paulding." Poe praised the character of the work under review for avoiding the mistakes of those who substitute for "style the fine airs at second hand of the silliest romancers" and recommended that copies of the book should immediately be introduced "into every respectable academy in the land."

"Life on the Lakes: Being Tales and Sketches Collected During a Trip to the Pictured Rocks of Lake Superior. By the Author of 'Legends of a Log Cabin'. New York: Published by George Dearborn"   Review by Poe that appeared in the July 1836 issue of the SOUTHERN LITERARY MESSENGER. Poe found the title to be "in shockingly bad taste" after the plethora of recent burlesques, "all partaking of caricature." He also finds fault with the narrative, which contains "a rawness, a certain air of foppery and ill-sustained pretension . . . which will cause nine-tenths of the well educated men who take up the book, to throw it aside in disgust, after perusing the initial chapter." Despite these defects, Poe states that the work can be found "a very amusing performance" once these difficulties are overlooked. He ends the review by quoting from a "piquant Indian Story, narrated by an Indian."

"Ligeia"   Short story. The tale is one of Poe's most critically acclaimed stories, as well as the tale that he identified as his personal favorite. Critics have considered this story one of his most complex, and it has aroused considerable critical controversy and disagreement as to the meaning of the plot and the characters' actions. Many critics echo the words of the British critic and playwright George Bernard Shaw: "The story of the Lady Ligeia is not merely one of the wonders of literature: it is unparalleled and unapproached. There is really nothing to be said about it: we others simply take off our hats and let Mr. Poe go first."

PUBLISHING AND DRAMATIZATION HISTORY

The story was first published in the September 1838 issue of the *Baltimore American Museum*. Although the story would remain essentially the same in later publications, the first printing of the tale did not include the poem "THE CONQUEROR WORM," which was incorporated into the text when the story was published in the February 15, 1845, issue of the *New York World* and reprinted in the September 27, 1845, issue of the *BROADWAY JOURNAL*. Poe made the poem the dying words of the doomed LIGEIA to correct the impression that Ligeia's return suggested too strongly that she had successfully escaped death. Although originally published separate from the tale, the poem is represented as the creation of Ligeia, and it functions to reveal her anxiety about the decay of the body and her desire to escape death. The death envisioned in the poem is violent, "And the seraph sob at vermin fangs / In human gore imbued."

Aside from the disagreement as to what actually happens in the tale, scholars question the source of the epigraph that precedes the story:

> *And the will therein lieth, which dieth not. Who knoweth the mysteries of the will, with its vigor? For God is but a great will pervading all things by nature of its intentness. Man doth not yield himself to the angels, nor unto death utterly, save only through the weakness of his feeble will.*

Although Poe attributes this passage to Joseph GLANVILL, scholars have not located the source and suspect that Poe merely created a convenient quotation, which he also integrates into the text of the story at two points, and falsified its attribution. The choice of Glanvill is appropriate, nonetheless, because mixed among his treatises on the "new science" and religion are writings that show his belief in spiritual manifestations and the eternal nature of the soul.

The tale was made into a film titled *The Tomb of Ligeia* (also distributed in the United States and abroad as, variously, *The House at the End of the World*, *Ligeia*, and *Last Tomb of Ligeia*), produced and directed in 1964 by Roger CORMAN and starring Vincent PRICE. The movie was the last of Corman's eight screen adaptations of works written by Poe, and it has been acclaimed by critics as his best, and closer in spirit to the original than most adaptations of Poe's work.

CHARACTERS

Ligeia, Lady Rowena TREVANION of Tremaine, unnamed narrator.

PLOT SYNOPSIS

The story combines three of Poe's most common themes: the death of a mysterious and beautiful woman, a bereaved narrator of doubtful stability, and a gruesome resurrection. In an indefinite setting, the story opens with the narrator's statement "I cannot, for my soul, remember how, when or even precisely where, I first became acquainted with the lady Ligeia." After wracking his brain, he feebly recalls: "Yet I believe that I met her first and most frequently in some large, old, decaying city near the Rhine." He states with wonder, "a recollection flashes upon me that I have *never known* the paternal name of her who was my friend and my betrothed, and who became the partner of my studies, and finally the wife of my bosom." Seemingly unconcerned by this lack of knowledge, the narrator muses only briefly whether Ligeia kept this information from him, he was simply so devoted that he did not care, or he has forgotten what he once knew. His later admission of his opium addiction—"for I was habitually fettered in the shackles of the drug"—and the description of her beauty as "the radiance of an opium dream" suggest that blurred memory rather than mystery may be at fault. Nonetheless, he does remember "the person of Ligeia" and can describe her beauty in detail, from her strange, large eyes to the proportions and contours of her skull. For all of her seeming outward calm, "the ever-placid Ligeia, was the most violently a prey to the tumultuous vultures of stern passion," of which the narrator is made aware through "the wild words which she habitually uttered." The physical beauty of Ligeia is far less enticing to the narrator than her great learning, and he soon yields "with a child-like confidence, to her guidance through the chaotic world of metaphysical investigation at which I was most busily occupied during the early years of our marriage."

Ligeia's philosophy seems to be a variation of that expressed in the epigraph to the story, falsely attributed to the mystic theologian Joseph Glanvill, that views the human will as stronger than death or decay. Ligeia succumbs to a fatal illness, but not before the narrator must watch "the fierceness of the resistance with which she wrestled with the Shadow. . . . [N]ot until the last instance, amid the most convulsive writhings of her fierce spirit, was shaken the external placidity of her demeanor." Ligeia asks the narrator to recite "The Conqueror Worm," a poem she has composed, which he does "at the high noon of the night in which she departed."

After Ligeia dies, the narrator abandons his home in "the dim and decaying city by the Rhine" and purchases an ancient abbey "in one of the wildest and least frequented portions of fair England." At the same time, he degenerates into "a bounden slave in the trammels of opium." Within a short time, the narrator marries once again, this time to "the fair-haired and blue-eyed Lady Rowena Trevanion, of Tremaine," whose appearance contrasts sharply with that of the darkly beautiful Ligeia. The two contrast in appearance, but even more of a contrast is the extent to which the narrator knows Rowena's family, as he questions, "Where were the souls of the haughty family of the bride, when, through thirst of gold, they permitted to pass the threshold of an apartment so bedecked, a maiden and a daughter so beloved?" The room to which he alludes is the bridal chamber, which contains "wild and grotesque specimens," "melancholy vaulting," and a bridal couch "low, and sculptured of solid ebony, with a pall-like canopy above." Adding to the sepulchral air, "in each of the angles of the chamber stood on end a gigantic sarcophagus of black granite, from the tombs of the kings over against Luxor."

Within days, the narrator loathes his bride "with a hatred belonging more to demon than to man" and takes pleasure that she "dreaded the fierce moodiness of my temper." At the beginning of the second month of the marriage, Rowena becomes seriously ill and hallucinates. After seeming to recover, she suffers a relapse and becomes even more violently ill than before. When he rushes to obtain a goblet of wine prescribed by Rowena's doctor, the narrator thinks that he sees "a faint, indefinite shadow of angelic aspect" and believes that he sees "three of four large droplets of a ruby colored fluid" fall into the goblet, emanating as if "from some invisible spring in the atmosphere of the room." He cannot, however, be sure because he is "wild with the excitement of an immoderate dose of opium, and heeded these things but little."

Rowena dies three days later. On the fourth day, as the narrator watches by the body, he hears a sigh and watches as the cheeks and forehead of the dead woman seem to fill with color. He momentarily believes that he has been too quick in declaring Rowena dead, but the color soon fades and the body remains still. As he has visions of Ligeia, the narrator sees the corpse move and rise, until "the thing that was enshrouded advanced boldly and palpably into the middle of the apartment." As the wrappings fall from the body, the narrator joyously sees streaming downward "huge masses of long and dishevelled hair; *it was blacker than the raven wings of midnight!*" When the corpse opens her eyes, the narrator shrieks aloud, "these are the full, and the black, and the wild eyes—of my lost love—of the lady—of the LADY LIGEIA." The story ends here, leaving critics and other readers to question what has really happened in the story. Is this simply a tale of the opium-induced hallucinations of the narrator in which either or both Ligeia and Rowena are figments of the narrator's imagination? Is the story meant to provide a validation of Ligeia's theory of willpower, in which the narrator uses his willpower to summon her back to life? Is Ligeia a vampire-like creature who has fed on the soul of Rowena and inhabited her body to be reanimated? Numerous critics have advanced theories to support

each of the preceding, but no consensus regarding the meaning of the tale has been reached.

Ligeia   Character in Poe's short story "LIGEIA." She is a mysterious and beautiful woman, "tall, somewhat slender, and, in her latter days, even emaciated," whom the unnamed narrator of the tale first met "in some large, old, decaying city near the Rhine." Her features "were not of a classic regularity," but she has "skin rivalling the purest ivory, . . . the raven-black, the glossy, the luxuriant and naturally-curling tresses, . . . the delicate outlines of the nose . . . the sweet mouth." Of even more note to the narrator are Ligeia's eyes, "the hue of the orbs was the most brilliant of black, and, far above them, hung jetty lashes of great length." The "ever-placid Ligeia" is also "deeply proficient" in the classical tongues and learned in metaphysical philosophy. Ligeia dies, but she is later rejuvenated through the death of the narrator's second wife.

Lincoln, Robert Todd (1843–1926)   American lawyer and son of President Abraham Lincoln. He served as a captain in the Union army in the last year of the Civil War, and was United States secretary of war from 1881 to 1885. While secretary of war, he confirmed for Professor George E. Woodberry, author of the 1885 *Life of Edgar Allan Poe, Personal and Literary, with His Chief Correspondence with Men of Letters,* the vital fact that 1827 was the year of Poe's enlistment at Boston in the United States Army under the assumed name of Edgar A. Perry.

"The Linwoods; or, "Sixty Years Since" in America. By the Author of "Hope Leslie," "Redwood," &c. New York: Published by Harper and Brothers"   Review by Poe that appeared in the December 1835 issue of the SOUTHERN LITERARY MESSENGER. Opening his review with substantial praise for the skills of Catherine Sedgwick, the author of the novel, Poe identifies her as "one among the few American writers who have risen by merely their own intrinsic talents, and without the a priori aid of foreign opinion and puffery." Declaring of Sedgwick, "of American female writers we must consider her the first," Poe waxes poetic about the nature of all women writers, stating that "woman is, after all, the only true painter of that gentle and beautiful mystery, the heart of woman. She is the only proper Scheherazade for the fairy tales of love." Despite his praise of the author and description of the novel as being "full of deep natural interest, rivetting attention without undue or artificial means for attaining that end," however, Poe finds fault with it. Aside from having "no pretensions to a connected plot of any kind," the novel also contains characters that contain slight discrepancies in portrayal, and "very few trifling inadvertences into which she [the author] has been betrayed." Among the flaws are one character's deficiency in spelling, "some slight liberties taken with the King's English" in the creation of verbs, and the use of "the vulgarities of such a phrase as 'I put in my oar'—meaning 'I joined in the conversation.'" Although he claims to be "heartily ashamed of finding fault with such trifles," Poe also objects to misspellings and suggests that the author "should look over her proof-sheets, or, be responsible for the blunders of her printer."

In closing, Poe recommends the work "to all persons of taste" and warns "let none others touch it."

"Lionizing. A Tale"   Short story. The tale is considered one of Poe's best comic efforts. It was one of the six tales that Poe submitted to a literary competition sponsored by the the *Baltimore Saturday Visiter* that he won with "MS. FOUND IN A BOTTLE." In reference to "Lionizing" and other tales, John Pendleton KENNEDY wrote to Poe in 1835, "Several of your *bizarreries* have been mistaken for satire—and admired, too, in that character. They deserved it, but *you* did not, for you did not intend them so." In a reply to Kennedy, dated February 11, 1836, Poe wrote that the story is a satire "properly speaking—at least so meant— . . . of the rage for Lions and the facility of becoming one." A lion is a person or celebrity who is socially sought after, without established criteria as to the value of the reason for that celebrity status.

The story is a parody of experiences recounted by Nathaniel Parker WILLIS in a series of articles that were later collected and published in 1835 in *Pencillings by the Way*. Among the adventures that Willis claimed to have enjoyed during his 1831 tour of Europe are a duel, friendships with English royalty, and meetings with members of the British literati.

PUBLISHING AND DRAMATIZATION HISTORY

The story was first published in the May 1835 issue of the *Southern Literary Messenger*, then revised for inclusion in *TALES BY EDGAR A. POE*, published in 1845 by Wiley & Putnam.

The following epigraph precedes the story: "'—all people went/Upon their ten toes in wild wonderment.'—Bishop Hall's Satires." This is an altered version of the following quotation that appeared in *Satires*, published by Bishop Joseph Hall in 1597: "Genus and Species long since barefoote went/Upon their ten-toes in wilde wonderment."

No film has been made of "Lionizing" to date.

CHARACTERS

Miss Big BAS-BLEU, Miss Little BAS-BLEU, Mrs. BAS-BLEU, Duchess of BLESS-MY-SOUL, Elector of BLUDDENNUFF, BUBASTIS, Count CAPRICORNUTTI, Aestheticus ETHIX, EUSEBIUS of Caesarea, Ferdinand Fitz Fossillus FELTSPAR, FRICASSEE, Prince de GRENOUILLE, Robert JONES.

PLOT SYNOPSIS

The tale satirizes the social milieu that makes sought-after celebrities out of sometimes foolish and unworthy individuals. The cult of celebrity is best exposed through Poe's burlesque account of a literary banquet in the city of Fum-Fudge attended by the self-proclaimed "nosologist" Robert Jones, whose monograph on the topic has earned him instant fame. The true meaning of the term *nosology* is the classification of diseases, a term known to Poe, who uses the misappropriation of meaning to further satirize pseudointellectualism. Jones encounters a gallery of oddly named, eccentric men and women to whom he proudly shows his source of celebrity, his proboscis, then sends the royal family "the ninety-ninth edition of the 'Nosology,'" with a portrait of his nose. In gratitude, he is invited to dine with the Prince of Wales. Poe further satirizes the egotistic business of becoming a literary lion as Jones lists the names of the guests also at the Prince of Wales's banquet and the reasons for their celebrity. Speaking of himself, Jones provides the ultimate example of lionizing: "There was myself. I spoke of myself;—of myself, of myself, of myself;—of Nosology, of my pamphlet, and of myself. I turned up my nose, and I spoke of myself." After Jones is insulted by the Elector of Bluddennuff, the two engage in a duel in which Jones shoots off the Elector's nose. This turns public opinion against the formerly famed nosologist, who returns home to his father to inquire, "what is the chief end of my existence?" His father informs him that "in Fum-Fudge the greatness of a lion is in proportion to the size of his proboscis—but, good heavens! there is no competing with a lion who has no proboscis at all."

"Lion-Izing. A Tale"   The short story "LIONIZING. A TALE" was originally published under this title.

Lisiausky, Captain   Russian navigator and oceanic explorer mentioned along with Captain KREUTZENSTERN in chapter 16 of *THE NARRATIVE OF ARTHUR GORDON PYM*. In 1803, he is sent by Czar Alexander I of Russia to circumnavigate the globe. As he and his crew attempt to go south, they meet with strong currents setting easterly, where they find an abundance of whales but no ice. The narrator states that had the expedition arrived earlier in the season—it arrived in March—it would have encountered ice, for the winds carry the floes great distances. The narrator contrasts the success of Lisiausky with the failures of Captain Cook and other ship's captains to penetrate Antarctica and their mistaken assessment of the ice floes—due to the time of year of their arrivals—as being land mass. The success, thus, depended on the season of navigation.

"literal Fulfilment of the Biblical Prophecies"   *See* KEITH, Alexander.

"The Literary Life of Thingum Bob, Esq. Late Editor of the 'Goosetherumfoodle.' by Himself"   Short story. The tale is one of Poe's most highly autobiographical and ironical sketches. He returns to the scenes of his youth in Richmond in this thinly disguised satire of his conversations with John ALLAN about a literary future, and in incidents that reflect his life in Richmond and around the warehouse of Ellis & Allan, the mercantile company co-owned by Allan. Poe may have taken special pleasure in publishing the story first in a Richmond publication.

PUBLISHING AND DRAMATIZATION HISTORY

The short story originally appeared, unsigned, in the December 1844 issue of the SOUTHERN LITERARY MESSENGER, which was published in Richmond, Virginia, the locale it satirized. Poe revised the story for republication the following year, and it appeared under his name in the July 26, 1845, issue of the BROADWAY JOURNAL. The revised version contained more specific sarcasm directed at Poe's literary enemy Lewis Gaylord CLARK. Poe might have left the story unsigned had not James Russell LOWELL identified him as the author in an article published in the February 1845 issue of GRAHAM'S MAGAZINE, "Our Contributors, No. XVII: Edgar Allan Poe."

CHARACTERS

Thingum BOB, Thomas BOB, Mr. CRAB, Mr. FATQUACK, Mrs. FIBALITTLE, Thomas HAWK, Mr. MUMBLETHUMB, Mr. SLYASS, Mrs. SQUIBALITTLE, UGOLINO.

PLOT SYNOPSIS

The tale satirizes the publishing profession, and especially the pettiness of the editors of literary magazines who did not always deal fairly with such writers as Poe but who often rewarded the lesser quality work of hacks and "quill drivers." From the opening sentence, the reader is aware that the story is told tongue in cheek, as Thingum Bob, the narrator, observes, "I understand that Shakespeare and Mr. Emmons are deceased—it is not impossible that I may even die." The story is framed as the autobiography of Thingum Bob, who has "resolved at once to become a great man" by his pen and who never misses the opportunity to extol his literary virtues or brag of his successes. He achieves literary fame with the publication of his two-line ode, "The Oil-of-Bob," and is offered the position of Thomas H.

Hawk, or "Tomahawk," by Mr. Crab, publisher of the *Lollipop,* which permits him to hack up literary adversaries through savage reviewing, or "tomahawking." Thingum Bob finally succeeds in the magazine world by launching a huge magazine of his own, "one magnificent Magazine known everywhere as the *Rowdy-Dow, Lollipop, Hum-Drum,* and *Goosetherumfoodle,"* a feat attempted by Poe but never achieved. In a speech on literary fame in the final paragraphs of the story, Poe speaks through Thingum Bob to candidly reveal his own experiences in the periodical world and to express frustrations that he often felt in their dealings with contributors: "Look at *me!*—how I labored—how I toiled—how I wrote! Ye Gods, did I *not* write? I knew not the word 'ease.' By day I adhered to my desk, and at night, a pale student, I consumed the midnight oil. You should have seen me—you should."

"Literary Remains of the Late William Hazlitt, with a Notice of his Life by his Son, and Thoughts on his Genius and Writings, By E. L. Bulwer, M.P. and Mr. Sergeant Talfourd, M.P. New York: Saunders and Otley"   Review by Poe that appeared in the September 1836 issue of the SOUTHERN LITERARY MESSENGER. Poe presents an extensive summary of the content of the essays collected in the work and states that "there is a piquancy in the personal character and literary reputation of Hazlitt, which will cause this book to be sought with avidity by all who read." He begins with a sketch of Hazlitt's life, using information drawn from the work, then identifies the content of essays and connects them with events. Poe also compares the differences between Bulwer's and Talfourd's thoughts on Hazlitt's life and works, identifying the efforts of the former as appearing "to be a compulsory thing" and the latter as appearing "to write with a vivid interest in the man, and a thorough knowledge of his books." Poe concludes the review by quoting the following words of Bulwer, that "a complete collection of his works is all the monument he demands."

"Literary Small Talk"   Article by Poe that appeared in the January/February 1839 issue of the AMERICAN MUSEUM OF SCIENCE, LITERATURE, AND THE ARTS. Poe begins his essay by refusing "to feel any goadings of conscience for undue severity" and, instead, "my remorse lies somewhat in the other way." He then offers a critique of Edward BULWER-LYTTON's approach to writing, asserting that it "wants the true vigour of intellect which would prompt him to seek, and enable him to seize the truth upon the surface of things." Poe faults Lytton for "perpetually refining to no purpose upon themes which have nothing to gain, and everything to lose in the process." Lytton's novel *The Last Days of Pompeii* is singled out for being "ridiculously full" of the author's "love of the 'far-fetched.'" Poe also scrutinizes

Edward Gibbon's *Decline and Fall of the Roman Empire* and expresses impatience with Gibbon's "*indirectness* of observation, then, which forms the soul of the style of Gibbon, of which the apparently pompous phraseology is the body." In further "small talk," Poe also finds fault with work by the Abbé de la Breterie, and his use of a "laughable Gibbonism," i.e., pompous phrasing, and Voltaire, whom Poe states "betrays, on many occasions, an almost incredible ignorance of antiquity and its affairs."

"The Literati of New York City"   Series of literary and biographical profiles that appeared in the May through October 1846 issues of *GODEY'S MAGAZINE AND LADY'S BOOK*. The series was so popular that the magazine reprinted the first six in the June 1846 issue when the additional numbers were printed. The 38 writers discussed included well-known literary lights, both male and female, who had distinguished themselves in poetry, criticism, and journalism. Although Poe insisted that he had selected the names at random, the first six that appeared in the May 1846 issue seemed better known to Poe than to the general public: Charles F. BRIGGS, George BUSH, George Hooker COLTON, John Wakefield FRANCIS, William M. GILLESPIE, and Nathaniel Parker WILLIS. Most of the later literati profiled are poets, and most are discussed with gentle praise instead of the excoriation that would be more typical of the fierce literary critic: William KIRKLAND, Anna Cora MOWATT, George B. CHEEVER, Charles ANTHON, Ralph HOYT, Gulian VERPLANCK, Freeman HUNT, Piero MARONCELLI, Laughton OSBORN, Fitz-Green HALLECK, Ann S. STEPHENS, Evert A. DUYCKINCK, Mary GOVE, James ALDRICH, Thomas Dunn ENGLISH, Henry CARY, Christopher Pearse CRANCH, Sarah Margaret FULLER, James LAWSON, Caroline M. KIRKLAND, Prosper M. WETMORE, Emma C. EMBURY, Epes SARGENT, Frances S. OSGOOD, Lydia M. CHILD, Elizabeth BOGART, Catherine M. SEDGWICK, Lewis Gaylord CLARK, Anne C. LYNCH, Charles Fenno HOFFMAN, Mary E. HEWITT, and Richard Adams LOCKE. Poe's eagerly read column commented upon the state of American letters through his often intensely personal examination of literary friends and enemies, as well as of writers who had appeared in his earlier critical reviews. The profiles, in which Poe often commented upon the connection between the author's work and his or her personality, ranged from the complimentary to the brutally scathing in describing both the author's work and personal appearance, largely because the nature of each profile developed from the nature of Poe's relationship with his subject. In announcing the planned series, Louis GODEY stated with confidence, "We are much mistaken if these papers of Mr. Poe do not raise some commotion in the literary emporium." Poe not only discussed the literary character of his subjects, but he also frequently evaluated their physical appearance, mental properties, habits of fashion and dress, education, financial status, and general standing in the community. The first series was so popular that *Godey's Lady's Book* reprinted Poe's first installment in the June 1846 issue with the second series, and further offered to buy back from subscribers any and all copies of the May issue for resale. After the first series of profiles appeared, several New York newspapers censured Poe for his intrusions into private lives. *Godey's* also responded in its "Editor's Book Table" forum in the June 1846 issue to reader complaints regarding the first series of profiles by denying any responsibility for the content:

> We have several letters from New York, anonymous, and from personal friends, requesting us to be careful what we allow Mr. Poe to say of the New York authors, many of whom are our personal friends. We reply to one and all that we have nothing to do but publish Mr. Poe's opinion, not our own. Whether we agree with Mr. Poe or not is another matter. We are not to be intimidated by a threat of the loss of friends or turned from our purpose by honeyed words. . . .

In the September 1846 "Editor's Book Table," Godey once again addressed complaints and denied any involvement:

> We hear of some complaints having been made by those writers who have already been noticed by Mr. Poe. Some of the ladies have suggested that the publisher has something to do with them. This we positively deny, and we as positively assert, that they are published as written by Mr. Poe, without any alteration or suggestion from us.

Poe eventually concluded the series because "people insisted on considering them elaborate criticisms when I had no other design than critical gossip." Even when the critical judgments do creep in, they are usually taken from Poe's earlier reviews and do not include new opinions. The truth about the sketches is that they were not meant as literary criticism. Rather, they were hastily completed journalistic pieces meant for public consumption and authorial profit. At the same time, Poe treated his subjects with a great deal of candor and used his personal knowledge of them to create sketches that often read like a betrayal of conversational confidences. In his critical text *Hawthorne*, published in 1879, the American author Henry James examined the literati sketches and proclaimed them to be "the most complete and exquisite specimen of *provincialism* ever prepared for the edification of man. Poe's judgments were pretentious, spiteful, vulgar, but they contained a great deal of sense and discrimination as well."

Little, Arthur Reginald (born c. 1902)   American composer who wrote a piano accompaniment to Poe's poem "ULALUME" and a song setting of the first and second stanzas of Poe's poem "TO HELEN (1)."

Little Snake   Character in THE JOURNAL OF JULIUS RODMAN. He is a Native American chief who befriends the members of Rodman's expedition and temporarily provides them with safe passage and supplies.

"Lives of the Cardinal de Richelieu, Count Oxenstiern, Count Olivarez, and Cardinal Mazarin. By G. P. R. James. Republished by Carey, Lea & Blanchard"   Review by Poe that appeared in the October 1836 issue of the SOUTHERN LITERARY MESSENGER. The major part of the review discusses the author as novelist, and the biographies are not discussed until the final paragraph of the review. Poe states that G. P. R. James's novels "have been of questionable character—neither veritable history, nor endurable romance—neither 'fish, flesh, nor gude [sic] red herring.'" Labeling James "an indifferent imitator" of Scott, Poe observes that those who laud the author do so "from mere motives of duty, not of inclination—duty erroneously conceived." Although he agrees that James's "sentiments are found to be pure—his morals unquestionable, and pointedly shown forth—his language indisputably correct," Poe views these as duties that all authors owe their readers, not as signs of exceptional talent. "To genius of any kind, it seems to us, that he has little pretension." Only the concluding paragraph of the review comments on the biographies, which it praises faintly: "Of the volumes now before us we are enabled to speak more favorably—yet not in a tone of high commendation. What is done, however, is done with more than the author's usual ability."

"Lives of the Necromancers: Or An Account of the Most Eminent Persons in Successive Ages, Who Have Claimed for Themselves, or to Whom Have Been Imputed by Others, the Exercise of Magical Power. By William Godwin, Author of 'Caleb Williams,' &c. New York: Published by Harper & Brothers"   Review by Poe that appeared in the December 1835 issue of the SOUTHERN LITERARY MESSENGER. Poe praises Godwin's "air of mature thought" and his "fuller appreciation of the value of words," remarking that "none is more nicely discriminative between closely-approximating meanings." The review of the Harper reprint of William Godwin's collection of biographical portraits of alchemists, sorcerers, and necromancers labels it "an invaluable work, evincing much labor and research, and full of absorbing interest." Poe states that rather than to deal with the sensational aspects of magic, the design of the work "is to display in their widest extent, the great range and wild extravagancy of the imagination of man." The only negative commentary in the review is Poe's reference to "the author's unwelcome announcement in the Preface, that for the present he winds up his literary labors with the production of this book."

Locke, Jane Ermina (1805–1859)   Amateur poet, sister-in-law of Frances Sargent OSGOOD. Her relationship with Poe began in December 1846 when she sent him her poem "An Invocation to Suffering Genius," her sympathetic view of Poe's situation. She arranged for Poe to lecture in Lowell, Massachusetts, on July 10, 1848, on the topic of "The Poets and Poetry of America." Although Locke was a married woman in her 40s, with five children, she led Poe to believe that she was a widow. When he learned the truth and began to court her young neighbor Annie RICHMOND, Locke retaliated by writing vindictive letters to Richmond that lied about Poe's activities and exaggerated his personal failings. Although Annie Richmond knew Poe well enough to discount the truth of Locke's acrimonious correspondence, the fear of public embarrassment made her end the relationship.

Locke, Lieutenant Joseph Lorenzo (1808–1864)   Military tactics instructor at the UNITED STATES MILITARY ACADEMY AT WEST POINT while Poe was a cadet. Poe regarded him as a ridiculous martinet and mocked his vanity in a comic poem titled "Lines on Joe Lock," noting that "John Locke is a notable name / Joe Locke is a greater." This was one of a series of comic poems that Poe shared with his fellow cadets about instructors at the U.S. Military Academy.

Locke, Richard Adams (1800–1871)   New York City journalist whom Poe profiled in one his most lengthy entries in the series "THE LITERATI OF NEW YORK CITY." The profile begins with a thorough discussion of Locke's relationship with the NEW YORK SUN, then provides a detailed dossier of Locke's writings. Of particular interest to Poe is "Moon-Hoax," which appeared in the August 1835 issue of the Sun under the title "Great Astronomical Discoveries, Lately Made by Sir John Herschel," because Poe believed that his balloon-hoax story, "THE UNPARALLELED ADVENTURE OF ONE HANS PFAALL," had inspired Locke's charade. Poe writes, "It was three weeks after the issue of 'The Messenger' containing 'Hans Pfaall,' that the first of the 'Moon-hoax' editorials made its appearance in 'The Sun,' and no sooner had I seen the paper than I understood the jest, which not for a moment could I doubt had been suggested by my own jeu d'esprit." After a detailed comparison of the two works, Poe spends only one page addressing Locke's skills as a writer, calling his prose style "noticeable for its concision, luminousness, completeness—each quality in its proper place." He further asserts that everything Locke writes is "a model in its peculiar way, serving just the purposes intended and nothing to spare."

Loeffler, Charles Martin (1861–1935) Alsatian-born American impressionist composer whose compositions include symphonic poems, songs for chorus and orchestra, and solo pieces. In 1906, he composed *To Helen,* op. 15, no. 3, one segment of a composition titled *Four Poems Set to Music for Voice and Piano.*

"Loiterings of Travel" *See* "DASHES AT LIFE WITH A FREE PENCIL."

"L'Omelette, Duc de" *See* "THE DUC DE L'OMELETTE."

Long, George (1800–?) Professor of ancient languages at the University of Virginia during Poe's residency who later taught at the University of London. He was an eminent Greek and Latin scholar who translated and edited works by Herodotus, Epictetus, Plutarch, Cicero, Caesar, and Marcus Aurelius. He also wrote numerous books on classical languages, Egyptology, geography, history, politics, and education.

Long, Stephen H. (n.d.) American explorer mentioned in *THE JOURNAL OF JULIUS RODMAN*. In 1823, he proceeded to the source of the St. Peter's River, to Lake Winnipeg, to the Lake of the Woods, and to other sites and left accounts that Julius RODMAN uses to guide his expedition.

Longfellow, Henry Wadsworth (1807–1882) American poet whom Poe often accused of plagiarism. Longfellow refused to respond to Poe's charges of plagiarism and, after Poe's death praised him and attributed the charges to "a sensitive nature chafed by some indefinite sense of wrong." In the "Author's Introduction" to "THE LITERATI OF NEW YORK CITY" series, Poe writes: "Mr. Longfellow, who although little quacky per se, has, through his social and literary position as a man of property and a professor at Harvard, a whole legion of active quacks at his control—of him what is the apparent popular opinion? . . . [H]e is regarded with one voice as a poet of far more than usual ability, a skilful artist and a well-read man, but as less remarkable in either capacity than as a determined imitator and a dexterous adapter of the ideas of other people." Poe reiterates his charge in "AUTOGRAPHY," noting that "[Longfellow's] good qualities are all of the highest order, while his sins are chiefly those of affectation and imitation—an imitation sometimes verging upon downright theft."

The poet Henry Wadsworth Longfellow, whom Poe accused of plagiarism. (Library of Congress)

Longfellow Wars, the *See* "A CONTINUATION OF THE VOLUMINOUS HISTORY OF THE LITTLE LONGFELLOW WAR— MR. POE'S FURTHER REPLY TO THE LETTER OF OUTIS."

"Loss of Breath: A Tale à la Blackwood" Short story. This tale is not ranked by critics as among Poe's best. It has received little critical attention aside from a lengthy psychological interpretation undertaken by the psychologist Marie Bonaparte, who has characterized it as an unconscious parable about Poe's fears of impotence and castration. She interprets the "loss of breath" as an expression of psychological castration.

PUBLISHING AND DRAMATIZATION HISTORY

The story first appeared under the title "A Decided Loss" in the November 1832 issue of the *Philadelphia Saturday Courier.* Poe used the pseudonym Lyttleton BARRY and changed the title to "Loss of Breath: A Tale à la Blackwood" when the story was printed in the September 1835 issue of the SOUTHERN LITERARY MESSENGER.

The story is preceded by the epigraph "O breathe not, &c. —Moore's Melodies." The quotation is taken from the title of "Oh! Breathe Not His Name," a song in the collection *Irish Melodies,* written by Thomas Moore.

No film has been made of "Loss of Breath" to date.

CHARACTERS

Mr. Lackobreath, Mr. WINDENOUGH.

PLOT SYNOPSIS

The newly married Mr. Lackobreath wakes up one morning and begins to shout viciously at his new wife, who appears to have been unfaithful. In the middle of his shouting he begins to lose his breath, a condition he attempts to hide from his wife until he is sure of the extent of his loss. As he begins a search for his breath, Mr. Lackobreath discovers "a set of false teeth, two pair of hips, an eye, and a number of *billets-doux* [love letters] from Mr. Windenough to my wife," proof that his wife has been carrying on a romantic extramarital relationship. Throughout the remainder of the story, the narrator attempts to catch his breath in a series of darkly absurd adventures. On one occasion, a surgeon pronounces the narrator dead, and on another he is partially eviscerated despite his "most furious contortions." As he escapes from the autopsy by leaping from a window into the passing cart of a hangman, he finds that the cart is on its way to the gallows, where he is promptly hanged. "Interred in a public vault," he inspects the "numerous coffins" and pries them open in "speculation about the mortality within." One coffin brings a surprise, because it contains the corpse of Mr. Windenough, who has also been interred mistakenly. After Lackobreath tugs at Mr. Windenough's nose to drag the corpse into a sitting position, the man revives so energetically that Lackobreath decides "the breath so fortunately caught by the gentleman (whom I soon recognized as my neighbor Windenough) was, in fact, the identical expiration mislaid by myself in the conversation with my wife." Still unable to speak, Lackobreath now attempts to recapture his lost breath from Windenough, whom he believes to have been his wife's lover. The story ends with the two men being rescued from the burial vault after they use "the united strength of our resuscitated voices" to attract attention. The story ends with no further reference to Lackobreath's wife nor indication of his future. Instead, Poe waxes philosophical and recalls the belief "among the ancient Hebrew . . . that the gates of Heaven would be inevitably opened to that sinner, or saint, who, with good lungs and implicit confidence, should vociferate the word '*Amen!*'"

"The Lost Pleiad; And Other Poems, By T. H. Chivers, M.D. New York: Edward O. Jenkins"   Review by Poe that appeared in the August 2, 1845, issue of the *BROADWAY JOURNAL*. Poe praises the collection written by Thomas Holley CHIVERS as "evidently the honest and fervent utterance of an exquisitely sensitive heart which has suffered much and long." Although the

poems are about death, the review makes clear that the collection "is no mere Byronic affectation of melancholy." Instead, "the poet seems to have dwelt among the shadows of tombs, until his very soul has become a shadow." Poe ends the review by stating that he has no hesitation in declaring the poetry in this volume "as possessing merit of a very lofty—if not of the very loftiest order."

The Loves of Edgar Allan Poe   Biographical film about Poe's life. The movie focuses on the life of the adult Poe, his alcoholism, and the women who influenced him, with particular attention to the sufferings of the fragile Virginia CLEMM. Sixty-seven minutes in length, this B-movie effort was produced by Bryan Foy at Twentieth Century–Fox, directed by Harry Lachman, and released in 1942. Samuel Hoffenstein and Tom Reed wrote the screenplay, and Emil Newman composed the score. The film starred John Sheppard, Linda Darnell, Virginia Gilmore, Jane Darwell, Frank Conroy, and Henry Morgan.

Lowell, James Russell (1819–1891)   American poet and essayist who also founded and edited the Boston monthly the *Pioneer*. In his June 1842 review of Rufus Wilmot GRISWOLD's "THE POETS AND POETRY OF AMERICA," which appeared in GRAHAM'S MAGAZINE, Poe expressed dismay that the editor had given little notice to Lowell: "We would have been better pleased to have seen a more liberal notice of his poems." That same year, Poe wrote in "AUTOGRAPHY" that Lowell surpassed "any of our writers" in "the vigor of his *imagination*—a faculty to be first considered in all criticism upon poetry," but he also wrote that Lowell's "ear for rhythm . . . is imperfect." Two years later, in a March 1844 review, "POEMS BY JAMES RUSSELL LOWELL," also in *Graham's Magazine*, Poe praised Lowell as having "as high poetical genius as any man in America." Although the two only met once, in May 1845, in January of that year Lowell aided Poe in obtaining an editorial appointment to the *BROADWAY JOURNAL*, then published a laudatory biographical essay of Poe in the February 1845 issue of *Graham's Magazine* that further enhanced Poe's stature.

Soon after their only meeting, Poe's admiration turned to scorn as he tried to minimize any assistance rendered by Lowell and accused him of plagiarizing from Wordsworth. Feeling betrayed, Lowell retaliated. He included Poe in his 1848 satiric poem *A Fable for Critics*, commenting in general on Poe's often overly elaborate prose, exaggerations in his criticism, and unjust accusations against Henry Wadsworth LONGFELLOW. Following are the relevant lines from that poem:

There comes Poe, with his raven, like Barnaby Rudge,
Three-fifths of him genius and two-fifths sheer fudge;
Who talks like a book of iambs and pentameters

The poet James Russell Lowell in 1844. (National Archives—Stills Division)

> In a way to make people of common sense damn
>   meters;
> Who has written some things quite the best of their
>   kind,
> But the heart somehow seems all squeezed out by the
>   mind;
> Who—But hey-day! What's this? Messieurs Matthews
>   and Poe,
> You mustn't fling mud-balls at Longfellow so!

Poe took offense at the satire and responded in a review of *A Fable for Critics* that appeared in the March 1849 issue of the SOUTHERN LITERARY MESSENGER. The review methodically attacked Lowell's views on a range of topics, including slavery, and declares the work to be "'loose'—ill-conceived and feebly executed, as well in detail as in general . . . we confess some surprise at his putting forth so unpolished a performance."

Luchesi Character mentioned in the short story "THE CASK OF AMONTILLADO." He is a wine expert whose name MONTRESOR invokes to lure FORTUNATO into Montresor's wine cellar. Fortunato disdainfully states that "Luchesi cannot tell Amontillado from Sherry" and "cannot distinguish Sherry from Amontillado." When Fortunato appears to falter in his steps on the way to the wine cellar, Montresor again invokes Luchesi's name, to which Fortunato immediately responds, "He is an ignoramus."

the "Ludwig" article Damaging obituary of Poe written by Rufus Wilmot GRISWOLD and signed with the pseudonym "Ludwig." Printed in the October 9, 1849, issue of the New York *Daily Tribune,* the piece destroyed Poe's reputation and remained the "official" view of the poet's life for nearly half a century. As soon as Poe was dead, Griswold began the process of exacting posthumous revenge against him, stating of his death that "few will be grieved by it" and depicting him as a mentally unstable misanthrope who "had few or no friends." Still bitter from Poe's attacks on his work, Griswold condemned Poe as "little better than a carping grammarian" who also had "little or nothing of the true point of honor." Despite efforts by John R. THOMPSON, who published "The Late Edgar A. Poe" in the November 1849 issue of the SOUTHERN LITERARY MESSENGER, and George R. GRAHAM, who published in his magazine "Defence of Poe" in March 1850 and "The Genius and Characteristics of the Late Edgar Allan Poe" in February 1854, Griswold's vitriolic characterization of Poe became the unofficial biographical record that extended well into the 20th century and kept Poe from achieving his full literary due. Griswold's lies included claims that Poe was expelled from the University of Virginia, that he deserted from the U.S. Army, and that he had been "sexually aggressive" toward John ALLAN's second wife. Griswold also made a pronounced effort to prove that Poe was a morally negligent drug addict whose concerns were only for himself. In his introduction to the 1850 edition of Poe's works, Griswold misled readers by suggesting that Poe had based the portrayals in his bizarre stories on personal experience.

Lummis, Colonel William (n.d.) Mrs. Elizabeth ELLET's brother. He confronted Poe to obtain intensely personal letters that his sister had sent to the author and refused to believe that Poe had returned the letters the day before. Poe was insulted by Lummis's insistence that the letters were still in his possession, and he challenged Lummis to a duel. Poe went to the home of Thomas Dunn ENGLISH and demanded the loan of a pistol. English refused, and the ensuing argument led to a fistfight between the two men that put Poe into a state of collapse that required him to spend several days in bed.

Lynch, Anne Charlotte (1815–1891) Literary salon hostess who knew Poe in New York in 1845. Although Poe included her among "the most *skilful merely*" in his review of Rufus Wilmot GRISWOLD's "THE FEMALE POETS OF AMERICA," Poe's profile of her in "THE LITERATI OF NEW YORK CITY" praises her poems "Bones in the Desert," "Farewell to Ole Bull," "The Ideal," and "The Ideal Found" for their "modulation and vigor of rhythm, in dignity and elevation of sentiment, in metaphorical appositeness and accuracy, and in energy of expression." Lynch removed Poe from her guest list after she heard of Poe's contemptuous treatment of Elizabeth Fries ELLET and the fight over Ellet's letters. *See also* LUMMIS, COLONEL WILLIAM.

Lytton, Edward George Frank Bulwer   *See* BULWER-LYTTON, EDWARD GEORGE EARLE.

Macaulay, Thomas Babington, 1st Baron Macauley (1800–1859) English historian, essayist, and statesman whose best-known work is the five-volume *History of England*. Poe's early reviews do not exhibit his later admiration for the "critical learning" that lay behind Macaulay's analytic and stylistic powers as a critic. In "CRITICAL AND MISCELLANEOUS ESSAYS," which appeared in the June 1841 issue of GRAHAM'S MAGAZINE, Poe declares that Macauley's "deservedly great" reputation was "yet in a remarkable measure undeserved," and that those who viewed him as "a comprehensive and profound thinker, little prone to error, err essentially themselves." Poe's review "ABOUT CRITICS AND CRITICISM," written in 1849 and published posthumously in 1850, shows that his respect for Macaulay had grown over a decade. He offers Macaulay as an example of one critic who is able "to accomplish the extremes of unquestionable excellences—the extreme of clearness, of vigor (depending upon clearness), of grace, and very especially of thoroughness."

MacDowell, Edward (1861–1908) American composer whose works include piano sonatas, concertos, suites, virtuoso studies, choruses for male voices, part-songs, and such orchestral pieces as *Hamlet and Ophelia*, *Launcelot and Elaine*, and *Lamia*. The Library of Congress contains an unfinished original manuscript of a four-part chorus for male voices inspired by Poe's "ELDORADO."

Mackenzie, John Hamilton (n.d.) Boyhood friend of Poe whose parents, William and Jane Scott MACKENZIE, adopted Poe's sister, Rosalie. Mackenzie became the guardian of Rosalie POE after his father's death and shared his memories with later biographers such as Susan Archer Weiss Talley, who included them in her 1907 *Home Life of Poe*. He offers an unflattering view of John ALLAN, a view consistent with Poe's. Mackenzie speaks of Allan as "a good man in his way," and states that "often when angry with Edgar he would threaten to turn him adrift, and that he never allowed him to lose sight of his dependence on his charity." Mackenzie accompanied Poe into Richmond on September 26, 1849, and, with other friends, they spent the evening together before Poe boarded the boat for Baltimore—Poe's final trip—the next morning.

Mackenzie, Lieutenant Alexander Slidell (1803–1848) American naval officer and author. He was the commanding officer of the Brig-of-War *Somers* during the mutiny of December 1841. Poe's review "THE AMERICAN IN ENGLAND" in the February 1836 issue of the SOUTHERN LITERARY MESSENGER discusses a book of this title by Mackenzie. Poe referred to this and a second work, *A Year in Spain*, in his "AUTOGRAPHY" entry for Mackenzie, stating that "Both these books abound in racy description, but are chiefly remarkable for their gross deficiencies in grammatical construction." His assessment of the author is even less complimentary, for he attributes Mackenzie's success to influence rather than to talent. Poe states that "his reputation at one period was extravagantly high—a circumstance owing, in some measure, to the *esprit de corps* of the navy, of which he is a member, and to his private influence, through his family, with the Review-cliques."

Mackenzie, William and Jane Scott (n.d.) Wealthy Richmond couple who adopted Poe's sister, Rosalie, although they already had two children, John and Mary. They would have eight more children of their own. As a child, Poe was a frequent visitor to their home, Duncan Lodge, which was near the home of his adoptive family, the Allans. Poe spent the night of September 26, 1849, his final night in Richmond, at Duncan Lodge before setting sail for Baltimore, where he died.

"Madrid in 1835. Sketches of the Metropolis of Spain and Its Inhabitants, and of Society and Manners in the Peninsula. By a Resident Officer. Two Volumes in One. New York: Saunders & Otley" Review that appeared in the October 1836 issue of the SOUTHERN LITERARY MESSENGER. Poe reviewed both volumes and found the second volume "upon the whole more entertaining" than the first. His chief objection to the first volume is that several passages are "somewhat overcoloured," but he concedes that "the most striking features of the life and still-life of the Metropolis are selected with judgment, and given with effect." The inclusion in the second volume of "some memorabilia of the year 1835—the Cholera and the Massacre of July" enhances its appeal for Poe, who also compliments the way in which the author deals knowledgeably "with the Ministry, the

Monasteries, the Clergy and their influence, with Prisons, Beggars, Hospitals and Convents."

"Maelzel's Chess-Player" Essay by Poe that appeared in the April 1836 issue of the SOUTHERN LITERARY MESSENGER. The title refers to a device that purportedly used an automaton dressed in Turkish clothing to play chess against human opponents. A traveling confidence man named Johann Nepomuk Maelzel perpetrated the hoax. Before focusing on the device in the title, Poe reviews other "automata," or mechanical wind-up toys, including a coach invented by M. Camus for the amusement of the child Louis XIV, the Magician of M. Maillardet, and the duck of Vaucanson, "so perfect an imitation of the living animal that all spectators were deceived." Among these wonders, Poe also includes the "calculating machine of Mr. Babbage," the precursor to modern computers, "which cannot only compute astronomical and navigation tables to any given extent, but render the exactitude of its operations mathematically certain through its power of correcting its possible errors." Before exposing the hoax of the chess-player, Poe first identifies Baron Wolfgang von KEMPELEN as the inventor of the automaton chess-player in 1769, and informs readers that it was exhibited throughout the United States by Johann Nepomuk Maelzel. The chess-player was built to appear as if a mechanical man were playing chess games with humans and beating them, but the contraption actually contained a human being inside who operated it. In the process of his exposé, Poe analyzes the steps that are followed in a game of chess and concludes that the nature of the game requires human intervention, "the only question then is the *manner* in which human agency is brought to bear." Poe then delineates the steps that Maelzel follows in introducing the chess-player to the audience and recounts the mechanical sounds that are heard when the Maelzel activates an automaton seated at a chessboard. Poe exposes the hoax by observing that the chess-player played each game with his left arm only, and he lists 17 sequential points to support his deductive methodology.

Maginn, William (1793–1842) Author of a Gothic tale, "The Man in the Bell," that appeared in the November 1821 issue of BLACKWOOD'S MAGAZINE. The story is about a young man who falls asleep under the clapper of a huge church bell and awakens when the bell tolls for a funeral. The sound drives him mad, and, as he is sinking into madness, he records on a writing tablet his sensations of auditory torture. In mentioning this plot device in "HOW TO WRITE A BLACKWOOD ARTICLE," Poe, in the guise of William BLACKWOOD, advises readers satirically through his main character, "Should you ever be drowned or hung, be sure and make a note

of your sensations—they will be worth to you ten guineas a sheet. If you wish to write forcibly, Miss Zenobia, pay minute attention to the sensations."

Magruder, Allan B. (n.d.) Virginia native and fellow cadet with Poe at the UNITED STATES MILITARY ACADEMY AT WEST POINT. In interviews with Professor George E. WOODBERRY, whose *The Life of Edgar Allan Poe* in 1885 reversed some of the damage to Poe's reputation, Magruder recalled that Poe associated almost exclusively with Virginians at West Point, and that "he was a great devourer of books, but his great fault was his neglect and apparent contempt for military duties."

"Mahmoud. New York. Published by Harper and Brothers" Review by Poe that appeared in the March 1836 issue of the SOUTHERN LITERARY MESSENGER. Poe questions the origin of this anonymous collection of Turkish sketches, which claims in an accompanying advertisement that "with the exception of a few of the inferior characters, and the trifling accessories necessary to blend the materials, and impart a unity to the rather complex web of the narrative, the whole may be relied upon as perfectly true." The reviewer expresses limited interest in the work and asserts that it compares unfavorably to Thomas Hope's novel *Anastasius* (1819), "that most excellent and vivid (although somewhat immoral) series of Turkish paintings."

Maillard, Monsieur Character in the short story "THE SYSTEM OF DOCTOR TARR AND PROFESSOR FETHER." He is the former superintendent of the Maison de Sante, or madhouse, who becomes insane. After he is imprisoned, he incites his fellow inmates to rebellion and aids them in imprisoning the guards, whom they cover with tar and feathers.

Maiter-di-dauns, Mounseer (the Count A. Goose; Look-aisy) Character in the short story "WHY THE LITTLE FRENCHMAN WEARS HIS HAND IN A SLING." As the narrator of the story Sir Pathrick O'GRANDISON, Barronnitt says in his thick Irish brogue, Maiter-di-dauns is "the little ould furrener Frinchman as lived over the way" from the narrator. The two compete for the attentions of a lady, one sitting on each side of her, and each putting an arm around her back to clasp what they believe is her arm on the other side. As they compete with witty remarks, they alternately squeeze what they believe to be her arm and receive a squeeze in return. After she leaves them, they realize that they have been squeezing each other's arms, and O'Grandison then gives Maiter-di-dauns's arm "a nate little broth of a squaze, as made it all up into a raspberry jam." The result is an injury to the Frenchman, who must wear his left hand in a sling.

Mallarmé, Stéphane [Etienne] (1842–1898) French poet and member of the French Symbolist movement. He was the force that encouraged the FRENCH CRITICS to embrace Poe's work. Poe's work influenced Mallarmé to make poetry a conscious enterprise that was based not on chance but instead upon a careful process of composition in which the poet calculates the importance of every word. In 1876, he wrote the memorial sonnet, "Le Tombeau d'Edgar Poe," which portrayed Poe as a transcendent artist whose understanding of beauty has made him an angelic figure existing far above the mediocrity of mortal existence. Mallarmé's view of Poe as an artist echoes that of Charles BAUDELAIRE, who saw Poe as a tortured genius, the product of suffering and sacrifice confronting the world's ignorance and vulgarity.

Mallinson, Albert (1870–1948) English composer who wrote more than 200 songs. In 1901, he composed a setting of Poe's poem "ELDORADO."

Mann, Captain Character in "THE MAN THAT WAS USED UP." The story of his duel becomes the focus of Mrs. O'TRUMP's story that interrupts the narrator's attempt to obtain information about Brevet Brigadier General SMITH. Mrs. O'Trump babbles on "all about a certain Captain Mann who was either shot or hung, or should have been both shot and hung." When the narrator asks another character for information, he is, once again, confronted with an offer of information about Captain Mann, to which he replies, "'Captain Mann be d——d!'"

"The Man of the Crowd" Short story. This tale is one of conscience, featuring a stranger who seems doomed to wander forever in order to make up for some unnamed crime. It contains London scenes that Poe probably recollected from his time spent there as a young boy with John ALLAN and his family. The story is unusual among Poe's work because none of the characters is given a name, nor does Poe reveal the crime committed by the nameless narrator that is responsible for his aimless wanderings. Critics have also viewed the story as exceedingly modern in its themes of the isolation of the artist and the alienation of the individual in an urban environment.

PUBLISHING AND DRAMATIZATION HISTORY

The story first appeared simultaneously in the December 1840 issues of *Atkinson's Casket* and of *BURTON'S GENTLEMAN'S MAGAZINE*, the latter periodical's last issue.

The story is preceded by the following epigraph: "*Ce grand malheur, de ne pouvoir etre seul* [That great misfortune, not to be able to be alone]. —*La Bruyère*. The quotation is taken from *Les Caractères de l'homme* [The Characters of Man], by Jean de La Bruyère

(1645–1696), and Poe also uses the quotation in "METZENGERSTEIN."

The story has not been adapted for stage or screen.

CHARACTERS

Unnamed narrator and characters.

PLOT SYNOPSIS

The story opens with mysterious references to dark secrets "which do not permit themselves to be told" and "the hideousness of mysteries which will not *suffer themselves* to be revealed." The nameless narrator, convalescing after a long illness, sits in a coffeehouse observing a busy street scene. The "tumultuous sea of human heads" fascinates him and expresses the irony that people in a city feel "solitude on account of the very denseness of the company around." Taking careful note of how passersby are dressed, as well as their "air, gait, visage, and expression of countenance," he deduces their occupations and social class based on their physical characteristics. The story begins in early evening on one day and proceeds until early evening the next, while the narrator keeps time for the reader, indicating as deep night falls, when 11 in the evening strikes, the coming of daybreak, and the coming of "the shades of the second evening."

With the deepening of the evening, which signals the "retiring in the gradual withdrawal of the more orderly portion of the people, and its harsher ones coming out into bolder relief," the narrator's attention becomes focused on "a decrepit old man, some sixty-five or seventy years of age" who is dressed in filthy, ragged clothes through which peek a diamond and a dagger. The narrator can hardly contain his excitement as he hurries out of the coffeehouse to follow the man throughout the night. The old stranger races through the London streets, then aimlessly forces his way through a large street bazaar and later enters shop after shop—looking at everything but buying nothing. As time passes, the old man heads to a less desirable part of the city, "where every thing wore the worst impress of the most deplorable poverty, and of the most desperate crime." The dammed-up gutters of the streets contain "horrible filth," and the people are "the most abandoned of London." They stop in front of "one of the huge suburban temples of Intemperance— one of the palaces of the fiend, Gin," but the manager is closing up, so the stranger turns and begins to walk back to "the heart of the mighty London." All day, the stranger and the nameless narrator walk through the busy streets of London, until the narrator becomes too tired to continue. He steps in front of the old man and "gazed at him steadfastly in the face," but even then the man fails to notice him. As the narrator then ceases his endless walking, he concludes that the old man "is the type and the genius of deep crime. He refuses to be alone. *He is the man of the crowd.* It will be in vain to follow; for I shall learn no more of him, nor of his deeds."

The reader is never told why the narrator is haunted by the old man, but the story implies that the two are each sides of the same person and that the old man, thus, represents a secret side of the narrator. A similar situation appears in "WILLIAM WILSON," but that story contains a confrontation that never occurs in the current story despite the best efforts of the narrator. As a result, this is more a story of noncommunication and of unresolvable loneliness, for after overtaking the man of the crowd, the narrator gazes at him steadfastly in the face. "He noticed me not, but resumed his solemn walk, while I ceasing to follow, remained absorbed in contemplation."

"The Man That Was Used Up. A Tale of the Late Bugaboo and Kickapoo Campaign"   Short story. This tale has been identified by Poe's contemporary Nathaniel Parker WILLIS as one of Poe's personal favorites among his satires. Critics associate "the man that was used up" in the story with General Winfield SCOTT, a Virginian as well as a close relative of John ALLAN's second wife, Louisa Gabriella PATTERSON. A professional military officer, Scott won early fame fighting in the War of 1812 and was a leader in military campaigns against the Seminole and Creek tribes, in which he was wounded. He was an unsuccessful candidate for president in 1852. Critics suggest that Scott the well-known public figure is reflected in the self-promotion of the central character as well as in the way that he greets the narrator: "Man alive, how *do* you do? why, how *are ye? very* glad to see ye, indeed!" In addition, similar to the general in the story, Scott was also a "brevet," an officer who is raised by government action to a nominal rank without a corresponding increase in pay.

PUBLISHING AND DRAMATIZATION HISTORY

The story was first published in the August 1839 issue of *BURTON'S GENTLEMAN'S MAGAZINE,* then revised for publication in 1840 in *TALES OF THE GROTESQUE AND ARABESQUE.*

The story is preceded by the following epigraph, taken from *Le Cid* (III, iii, 7–8) by Pierre Corneille (1606–1684):

> *"Pleurez, pleurez, mes yeux, et fondez-vous en eau!*
> *La moitiè de ma vie a mis l'autre au tombeau."*

["Weep, weep, my eyes, and float yourself in tears! / The better half of my life has laid the other to rest."]

No film has been made of the tale to date.

CHARACTERS

Miss BAS-BLEU, Miss Arabella COGNOSCENTI, Miss Miranda COGNOSCENTI, Reverend Doctor DRUMMUMMUPP, Captain MANN, Mrs. Kathleen O'TRUMP, Miss PIROUETTE, POMPEY, Mr. Theodore SINIVATE, Brevet Brigadier General A. B. C. SMITH, Miss Tabitha T., Mr. TATTLE, Mr. THOMPSON.

PLOT SYNOPSIS

Upon first meeting Brevet Brigadier General John A. B. C. Smith, the narrator believes him to be "one of the most remarkable men of the age," a magnificent physical specimen six feet tall with "richly flowing" black hair, eyes that are "large and lustrous," a powerful set of shoulders "which would have called up a blush of conscious inferiority into the countenance of the marble Apollo," "a mouth utterly unequalled," and other physical attributes that speak of "the supreme excellence of his bodily endowments." The general's speeches are as grand as his appearance, containing as they do boasts of his triumphs over his inferiors and magnificent statements about the progress of the age. Despite being initially impressed, the narrator seeks to learn more about this military hero and finds that everyone he asks simply hints about this being "a wonderful age for invention . . . a wonderfully inventive age . . . the age of invention." Convinced that Smith is hiding some secret, the narrator decides to make an unexpected visit to the general's home. He is ushered into the general's bedroom where he finds "a large and exceedingly odd looking bundle of something which lay close by [his] feet on the floor," which he nudges with his foot. The bundle begins to talk, and as its one arm draws a stocking on its single leg, the narrator realizes that this is all remaining of the general after his many losses in battle. As the fascinated narrator watches, the general's valet Pompey literally assembles the general, piece by piece. A second leg and arm are screwed on, shoulders and a chest are added, as are a wig, a glass eye, and false teeth, until finally the handsome general emerges once more. Without self-consciousness, the general assures the amazed narrator that, should the need ever arise, he can recommend any number of skilled men to perform similar services for him.

After the reconstruction is complete, the narrator leaves the general "with a perfect understanding of the true state of affairs—with a full comprehension of the mystery which had troubled me so long. It was evident. It was a clear case. Brevet Brigadier General John A. B. C. Smith was the man—was *the man that was used up."* This creation of apparent substance from literally nothing suggests the story is an allegory that signals a contempt on the author's part for the masses who can so easily be fooled.

"Marginalia" A series of "learned and gossipy paragraphs" on various subjects that appeared in different publications over a period of five years, from November 1844 through September 1849. The passages reflect Poe's "chit-chat habit" and contain many instances of repetition, such as recurrences of the same topic or discussions of the same literary men and women, extended over the five-year period. At times, the passages are fragments of literary reviews or profiles that appeared in lengthier form in earlier publications. Some of the marginalia are self-contained literary reviews, complete with reprints of stanzas of poetry; others are sarcastic, despondent, or cynical observations, and still others seem to be pseudointellectual nonsense. All, however, are intentional, for Poe indicated in his preface to the first installment of "Marginalia," published in the November 1844 issue of the *Democratic Review,* that their underlying feature would be a prevalent spirit of nonsense: "It may be as well to observe, however, that just as the goodness of your true pun is in direct ratio of its intolerability, so is nonsense the essential sense of the Marginal Note." The second installment appeared in the December 1844 issue of the *Democratic Review,* followed by a third installment that appeared in the August 1845 issue of GODEY'S MAGAZINE AND LADY'S BOOK under the title "Marginal Notes—No. 1: A Sequel to the 'Marginalia' of the 'Democratic Review'." A fourth installment was printed in the September 1845 issue of *Godey's Lady's Book* under the title of "Marginal Notes—No. 2: More 'Marginalia'." Additional installments of "Marginalia" appeared in the March, April, November, and December 1846 issues of GRAHAM'S MAGAZINE; the April and July 1846 issues of the *Democratic Review;* the January, February, and March 1848 issues of *Graham's Magazine;* and the April, May, June, July, and September 1849 issues of the SOUTHERN LITERARY MESSENGER. Poe's tone throughout is one of amused cynicism.

Maroncelli, Piero (1795–1846) Exiled Italian poet living in America whose profile Poe included in "THE LITERATI OF NEW YORK CITY." Poe reviews the essays and poems Maroncelli published in the United States, finding the "Essay on the Classic and Romantic Schools" to be "strongly tinctured with transcendentalism," yet admitting that "there is at least some scholarship and some originality in this essay." Although Poe observes that the author "speaks hurriedly and gesticulates to excess," he also commends Maroncelli for "he is quite enthusiastic in his endeavours to circulate in America the literature of Italy."

Marshall, John (1755–1835) American statesman, jurist, and the fourth chief justice of the Supreme Court. He was principally responsible for developing the power of the United States Supreme Court and for formulating constitutional law in the nation. Poe included his signature in "AUTOGRAPHY," in which he states that Marshall's writing "in its utter simplicity, is strikingly indicative of the man." Poe also reviews two eulogies that appeared after Marshall's death, "BINNEY'S EULOGIUM" and "JUDGE STORY'S DISCOURSE ON CHIEF-JUSTICE MARSHALL."

Marston, George (1840–1901) American composer of church music, including music for church services, sacred cantatas, part-songs for male voices and choruses for female voices, as well as piano music, trios, and quartets. In 1876 he published the song "To One in Paradise," a setting of Poe's poem of the same name.

Marx, Issacher Pseudonym of a character M. VALDEMAR in the short story "THE FACTS IN THE CASE OF M. VALDEMAR." Under this pen name, Valdemar supposedly has written Polish versions of *Wallenstein,* which actually was written by Johann Christoph Friedrich von Schiller, and *Gargantua,* written by François Rabelais. The name is actually an example of Poe's sly humor, for the name appears in the Bible, in Genesis 49.14: "Issachar is a strong ass crouching down between two burdens."

Mary *See* DEVEREAUX, Mary.

Mason, Monck Character in the short story "THE BALLOON-HOAX." He is one of the balloon *Victoria*'s pilots and the supposed inventor of the "steering balloon." Poe based the character on Thomas Monck Mason and borrowed heavily from Mason's book *Account of the Late Aeronautical Expedition from London to Weilburg, accomplished by Robert Hollond, Esq., Monck Mason, Esq., and Charles Green Aeronaut,* published in 1836.

"The Masque of the Red Death" Short story. Critics generally regard this tale as an undisputed masterpiece and one of the most unusual of Poe's short fiction efforts. One of Poe's few stories to use a third-person narrator, the story contains opulent, highly descriptive language that imparts a dreamlike rhythm to the narrative.

Originally titling it "The Mask of the Red Death: A Fantasy," to place focus on the mysterious figure who appears at the end of the story, Poe later changed the title to focus attention on the masque, a private ball that flourished in Renaissance Italy.

PUBLISHING AND DRAMATIZATION HISTORY

The story first appeared in the May 1842 issue of GRAHAM'S MAGAZINE under the title "The Mask of the Red Death." Poe changed the title to "The Masque of the Red Death" when he published a revised version of the story in the July 19, 1845, issue of the BROADWAY JOURNAL.

The story is not preceded by an epigraph, making it unusual in that respect among tales by Poe.

Several film versions of the story have appeared. The story inspired *A Spectre Haunts Europe*, a Russian film directed by Vladimir R. Gardin in 1921. Roger CORMAN has made two versions of the film. Corman's *The Masque of the Red Death* (1964), an ultrastylish adaptation starring Vincent PRICE as the dissipated Prince PROSPERO and featuring Hazel Court, Jane Asher, Patrick Magee, and Nigel Green, concentrated on the literary and symbolic aspects of the story in what has generally been viewed as Corman's best film. Corman also worked in elements of Poe's short story "HOP-FROG" as a subplot. In his 1989 remake, titled *Masque of the Red Death*, starring Adrian Paul, Clare Hoak, Jeff Osterhage, Patric Macnee, and Tracey Reiner, Corman makes Prince Prospero more troubled and thoughtful, but the more literate and more verbose Red Death slows the pace of the production and detracts from the suspense.

The story has inspired symphonic works by the French composer Andre CAPLET and the English composer Joseph HOLBROOKE.

CHARACTERS

Prince PROSPERO, RED DEATH, unnamed guests.

PLOT SYNOPSIS

The story appears similar to Boccaccio's *Decameron*, written in 1353, in its premise of gathering a group of aristocrats in a secluded abbey in the attempt to escape a devastating plague, as well as in the author's revelation that this attempt is futile. The wealthy and powerful Prince Prospero seeks safety from the raging plague of the "Red Death" with his "thousand hale and light-hearted friends." Because all within the walls of the abbey remain safe and secure, no one seems concerned about the fate of those left to confront the pestilence outside the walls of the abbey in his "half-depopulated" dominions where the plague rages: "Without was the 'Red Death.' The external world could take care of itself. In the meantime it was folly to grieve or to think." Poe names his protagonist after Prospero, William SHAKESPEARE's exiled Duke of Milan in *The Tempest*, who creates his own private world and uses magic to control the destinies of other characters in the play. In contrast, Poe's Prospero makes the same attempt but learns that his attempts are only illusion. He decorates the abbey to please the senses of his guests, providing them with seven elaborately decorated rooms, each a different color—blue, purple, green, orange, white, violet, and black—and has provided his retinue with "a voluptuous scene" even as the plague rages outside the abbey walls: "There were buf-foons, there were improvisatori, there were ballet-dancers, there were musicians, there was Beauty, there was wine. All these and security were within." Critics suggest that the abbey's seven pleasure chambers correspond to the seven ages of man, as well as to the seven deadly sins, the worst of which is pride. Connected by a corridor running from east to west to track the movement of the sun, the chambers end with the westernmost, decorated entirely in black with a giant ebony clock that chimes and makes the giddiest grow pale.

At the height of the plague, Prince Prospero entertains his guests with a lavish masque, a masquerade ball during which "the license of the night was nearly unlimited." The appearance of an uninvited guest wearing a mask and costume that resembles "the countenance of a stiffened corpse" infuriates the prince, who pursues it to the black chamber, then threatens the "tall and gaunt" figure with a dagger. As the figure turns to confront him, Prince Prospero falls dead. The revellers attack the figure, then gasp "in unutterable horror at finding the grave-cerements and corpse-like mask which they handled with so violent a rudeness. . . . [O]ne by one dropped the revellers in the blood-bedewed halls of their revel, and died each in the despairing posture of his fall." As the story ends, death triumphs once more, as "the Red Death held illimitable dominion over all."

Masetti, Enzo (1893–1968) Italian composer and music critic whose works include music for mixed chorus, orchestral pieces, and vocal, theatrical, and cinematographic music. In 1925, he published *Bubboli*, music to accompany the first stanza of Poe's poem "THE BELLS."

"Master Humphrey's Clock. By Charles Dickens. (Boz.) With Ninety-One Illustrations by George Cattermole and Hablot Browne. Philadelphia, Lea & Blanchard"
"The Old Curiosity Shop, and Other Tales. By Charles Dickens. With Numerous Illustrations by Cattermole and Browne. Philadelphia, Lea & Blanchard" Review by Poe that appeared in the May 1841 issue of GRAHAM'S MAGAZINE. Poe opens the review with his criticism of the publisher's confusing combination of the novel with the stories in one volume, stating that it creates "a certain confusion and hesitation observable in the whole structure of the book itself." In particular, Poe objects to the practice of "intimating the *entireness* of the volume now before us, that '*The Old Curiosity Shop, and Other Tales,*' has been made not only the primary and main title, but the name of the whole publication as indicated by the back." In truth the volume was only one of a series—"only part of a whole." Before his examination of *Master Humphrey's Clock*, Poe addresses rumors that Dickens

had become mentally unstable during the writing of the story collection, noting "we do not think it altogether impossible." He qualifies this position: "[W]e mean to say that the mind of the author, at the time, might possibly have been struggling with some of those manifold and multiform *aberrations* by which the nobler order of genius is so frequently beset, but which are still very far removed from disease." Poe sees these presumed "aberrations" in the "hesitancy and indefinitiveness of purpose" of the work and finds the design of the work to be "simply the common-place one of putting various tales into the mouths of a social party." Dickens's execution of the plan does not earn praise from Poe, who suggests that "because the work was done in a hurry, Mr. Dickens did not precisely know how his own plans when he penned the five or six first chapters of 'Clock.'" He asserts, "we feel displeased to find Master Humphrey commencing the tale [*The Old Curiosity Shop*] in the first person. . . . All is confusion." Poe provides an extensive analysis of the plot of *The Old Curiosity Shop,* finding Dickens's approach to contrast greatly with that of *Master Humphrey's Clock* and expressing approval of its "excellences" in several instances, writing, "In truth, the great feature of the 'Curiosity Shop' is its chaste, vigorous, and glorious imagination. This is the one charm, all potent, which alone would suffice to compensate for a world more of error than Mr. Dickens ever committed." After extolling the virtues of Dickens's characterization and establishment of setting, Poe concludes, "we think the 'Curiosity Shop' very much the best of the works of Mr. Dickens. It is scarcely possible to speak of it too well."

Mathews, Cornelius (1817–1899)   New York author, literary friend of Evert A. DUYCKINCK, and editor of the monthly magazine *Arcturus.* Poe lists his best works in "AUTOGRAPHY," although he labels Mathews's *Puffer Hopkins* "a clever satirical tale somewhat given to excess in caricature." In a negative review of Mathews's epic "WAKONDAH, THE MASTER OF LIFE. A POEM", Poe claimed that "we had been sincerely anxious to think well of his abilities." In contrast, Poe's review of Mathews's "BIG ABLE AND THE LITTLE MANHATTAN" is positive. Mathews reacted to Poe's mention in "Autography" of his *The Motley Book* by stating, "It is not fair to review my book without reading it," to which Poe replied, "Mr. Mathews will not imagine that I mean to blame *him.* The book alone is in fault, after all."

"Maury's Navigation"   Review appearing in the June 1836 issue of the SOUTHERN LITERARY MESSENGER. Written by United States Navy Lieutenant Matthew Maury, the manual earns Poe's praise: [T]his volume . . . strongly commends itself to notice." After identifying the many errors that most navy and general military personnel make in writing, which include a lack of "clearness of arrangement" of facts and formulae and the tendency to encumber the work with too many unimportant rules and principles, Poe commends Maury for avoiding these errors: "With great propriety he has rejected many statements and rules which in the progress of nautical science have fallen into disuse." Declaring that the manual's "style is concise without being obscure," Poe asserts that Maury has worked hard to credit a work of such merit and that doing so "required the exercise of a discriminating judgment, guided by a thorough acquaintance with all the points in nautical science."

Mayo, Colonel John (n.d.)   Friend of John ALLAN and uncle through marriage of Allan's second wife, Louisa Gabriella PATTERSON. After Frances ALLAN died, Mayo offered Allan the hospitality of his Belleville Plantation, situated near Richmond, Virginia, where Allan first met his second wife.

McBride, Admiral James (n.d.)   Member of the British navy whose daughter Jane MCBRIDE married Poe's paternal grandfather, David POE. In the account of his early life provided to Rufus Wilmot GRISWOLD, Poe states that Admiral McBride was "noted in British naval history, and claim[ed] kindred with many of the most illustrious house of Great Britain." Griswold repeated this information in the THE "LUDWIG" ARTICLE, the October 9, 1849, obituary that he wrote after Poe's death.

McBride, Jane (n.d.)   The daughter of Admiral James MCBRIDE, a noted British naval officer, she was the wife of John POE, and the mother of David POE, Poe's paternal grandfather.

McHenry, James (1785–1845)   American poet and historical novelist. In a review, "THE ANTEDILUVIANS, OR THE WORLD DESTROYED," Poe skewered McHenry's pretentious epic and attacked what he saw as McHenry's arrogance in presuming to associate his work with that of John MILTON. He compared McHenry to "a tom-tit twittering on an eagle's back" and advised him to give up poetry. Poe expressed the opinion that McHenry need never fear being accused of being a poet, for "no sane jury would ever convict him; and if, as most likely, he would plead guilty at once, it would be as quickly disallowed, on that rule of law which forbids the judges to decide against the plain evidence of their senses."

Mcintosh, Maria Jane (1803–1878)   Casual acquaintance of Poe in New York City and writer of children's stories under her pen name "Aunt Kitty." She was present at a party in Fordham at which Poe raved about his attraction to Mrs. Sarah Helen WHITMAN, whom he had never met but with whom he claimed to be very much in love. Visiting Whitman a few months later, Mcintosh spoke of the infatuated poet and was asked to deliver an unsigned poem to him. She later acted as the conduit through which Poe met Mrs. Whitman.

McMichael, Morton (1807–1879)   American poet and journalist. He published in the January 1840 issue of GODEY'S MAGAZINE AND LADY'S BOOK a highly favorable review of Poe's TALES OF THE GROTESQUE AND ARABESQUE. In the review, McMichael made specific mention of Poe's expert sense of "the comically absurd," and he stated that the collection contained "some of the most vivid scenes of the wild and wonderful which can be found in English literature." In his sketch in "AUTOGRAPHY," Poe praised McMichael highly, noting that his poetry contains "some remarkably vigorous things. We have seldom seen a finer composition than a certain celebrated 'Monody.'"

Mela, Pomponius (c. 1st century A.D.)   Roman geographer whose Geography, published in 1471, contains stories of satyrs and goatmen in Africa. In "THE FALL OF THE HOUSE OF USHER," Roderick USHER "would sit dreaming for hours" over passages of Mela's work. Usher's preoccupation with such works emphasizes his estrangement from ordinary human experience and his obsession with the supernatural.

Melamet, David (1861–1932)   German composer and conductor whose musical compositions include cantatas and other vocal and instrumental works. He wrote a setting of Poe's poem "ANNABEL LEE" for chorus and solo voice.

"Mellonta Tauta"   Short story. This tale, which Poe dates as having been written on April Fool's Day in the year 2848, contains some of Poe's most important inferences about the future. It also provides an interesting satire on Poe's era, especially its social theories, fashions, and architecture. Poe quoted from this story in the introduction to "EUREKA: AN ESSAY ON THE MATERIAL AND SPIRITUAL UNIVERSE," and the tale elaborates many of the points discussed in the prose poem. Critics have identified views in the story that are similar to those in such Poe stories as "THE UNPARALLELED ADVENTURE OF ONE HANS PFAALL," "SOME WORDS WITH A MUMMY," "THE ANGEL OF THE ODD," and "THE BALLOON-HOAX."

PUBLISHING AND DRAMATIZATION HISTORY

The story was first published in the February 1849 issue of GODEY'S MAGAZINE AND LADY'S BOOK, although Poe wrote the story early in 1848. Poe submitted the story soon after he completed writing it, but Godey's Lady's Book waited to publish it, so he made minor changes in the tale, retitled it "A Remarkable Letter," and attached it to his prose poem "Eureka."

The story does not open with an epigraph. The title is taken from Sophocles's tragic drama Antigone, but Poe must also have found it in Edward BULWER-LYTTON's 1837 novel Ernest Maltravers, in which the author states that in Greek Mellonta Tauta means "These things are in the future."

No film has been made to date.

CHARACTERS

Mr. MILL, PUNDIT, PUNDITA.

PLOT SYNOPSIS

The story is framed as "a long gossiping letter" from the intrepid Pundita to the editor of Godey's Lady's Book in which she promises to punish the editor for all "impertinences by being as tedious, as discursive, as incoherent, and as unsatisfactory as possible." The writer of the letter quotes liberally from Pundit, whose relationship to Pundita is not specified but whose name is derived from the Hindu word for a Brahmin who is thoroughly versed in Sanskrit, philosophy, law, and religion, making him the authority to whose great wisdom Pundita defers throughout. The letter, dated April Fool's Day, April 1, 2848, relates details of a voyage on the hot-air balloon Skylark. The philosophy expounded by Pundita is that of Poe, who held a pessimistic view of politics and claimed to have an aversion to democracy, calling it "a very admirable form of government—for dogs." The guarantees of equality for all men that appear in the Declaration of Independence, democratic institutions, and rule by the mob all come under severe criticism during the course of the voyage, while Pundit and Pundita exchange intellectual and pseudoscientific nonsense. In the process, the two examine theories from the research of "the Hindoo Aries Tottle" and his disciples "one Neuclid and one Cant." They also confuse the philosopher Sir Francis Bacon with the poet James Hogg, noting that "'Baconian,' as you must know, was an adjective invented as equivalent to Hog-ian and more euphonious and dignified." The English logician and economist John Stuart MILL, "one Miller," is also dismissed among "these ancients so much because their logic is, by their own showing, utterly baseless, worthless and fantastic altogether, as because of their pompous and imbecile proscription of all *other* roads to Truth, of all *other* means for its attainment."

"A Memoir of the Reverend John H. Rice, D.D. First Professor of Christian Theology in Union Theological

Seminary, Virginia. By William Maxwell. Philadelphia: Published by J. Whetham" Review by Poe that appeared in the December 1835 issue of the SOUTHERN LITERARY MESSENGER. Poe states that the memoir, which consists largely of Rice's letters, "will be received and read with pleasure generally." After identifying the three types of letters included—narrative accounts of the man in different periods of his life, pastoral letters to different members of the church, and ordinary letters of friendship—Poe states that all "give evidence of an elevated, a healthy, cheerful, powerful, and well-regulated mind." The review also praises Maxwell for allowing the letters to tell Rice's story in his own words, and it ends with the reprint of one letter as an example.

"Memoirs and Letters of Madame Malibran. By the Countess de Merlin. With Notices of the Progress of the Musical Drama in England. In Two Volumes. Carey and Hart, Philadelphia" Review by Poe that appeared in the May 1840 issue of BURTON'S GENTLEMAN'S MAGAZINE. Poe begins the review by praising highly the life and career of Madame Malibran, who died tragically at the age of 25. Poe chastises the author for not identifying a definite cause for the subject's demise, for speaking only in vague terms, with "an indistinctness. . . . She seems never to approach the truth." On the other hand, the review praises the ability of the memoirs to "convey a vivid picture of their subject." The memoir appears in two volumes, the first dealing with the subject's life and career and the second providing a minute account of the death and funeral. The work also includes critical notices of her performances, both of which Poe finds "highly entertaining," especially "the merely private anecdotes."

"Memoirs of an American Lady. With Sketches of Manners and Scenery in America, as They Existed Previous to the Revolution. By the Author of 'Letters from the Mountains.' New York: Published by George Dearborn" Brief review by Poe that appeared in the July 1836 issue of the SOUTHERN LITERARY MESSENGER. Written by Anne Grand, the book is "a memorial of the epoch immediately preceding our Revolution," and, as such, it contains a means of comparing society with the present. Poe wrote that the book had long been out of print, but that it had remained a favorite of many readers, "and we are glad to see it republished." Although the review states that the work will be read with pleasure everywhere, "as an authentic and well written record of a most exemplary life," Poe also writes that it will be of specific interest "[i]n Albany and New York [where] it will possess a local interest of no common character," and that remarks on slavery "will apply with singular accuracy to the present state of things in Virginia."

"Memoirs of Lucian Bonaparte (Prince of Canino), Written by Himself. Translated from the Original Manuscript, Under the Immediate Superintendence of the Author. Part the First, (From the Year 1792, to the Year 8 of the Republic.)" Review by Poe that appeared in the October 1836 issue of the SOUTHERN LITERARY MESSENGER. Poe asserts that the work is "of deep interest" and states that it "must be read, by every person who pretends to read at all." Nonetheless, he finds fault with the author's inclusion of "personal and private anecdotes which have a very shadowy bearing, if any, upon the political movements of the times" and observes that the book possesses "many of those peculiarities of manner, which in so many a measure distinguished, and we must say disfigured, the author's poem. . . . the same affectations, the same Tacitus-ism, and the same indiscriminate elevation of tone."

"Memorials of Mrs. Hemans, with Illustrations of Her Literary Character from Her Private Correspondence. By Henry F. Chorley. New York: Saunders and Otley" Review by Poe that appeared in the October 1836 issue of the SOUTHERN LITERARY MESSENGER. This lengthy review devotes almost as much space to a discussion of Chorley's skill in portraying clearly the work of English poet Felicia Dorothea Hemans and her life as it does to examining her work. Clearly appreciative of Hemans's skills, Poe states that there exist "few persons now living upon whose appreciation of a poetical character we would look with a higher respect." He also praises Chorley's selection of details and "truly exquisite narration," which has resulted in "something far more impressive than we can imagine any legitimate biography." The review also includes brief analyses of select writings by Hemans, comparing her favorably with other renowned writers of her time. In closing the review, Poe observes that "the reader will not fail to be struck with the evidence they contain of a more than ordinary joyousness of temperament in Mrs. Hemans" and praises the memorialist for writing a work in which "no shadow of vanity or affectation could be discerned in either the Memorialist or his subject."

Mentoni, Marchesa Aphrodite di Character in Poe's short story "THE ASSIGNATION." The beautiful wife of the seemingly passionless Marquese di MENTONI, she accidentally drops her baby into a Venetian canal, from which it is rescued by a former lover as her husband looks on and plays the guitar. After being reunited with her baby, she agrees a short while later to a suicide pact with her former lover.

Mentoni, Marchese di Character in Poe's short story "THE ASSIGNATION." The "old and intriguing Mentoni," described as "a Satyr-like figure," stands strumming a guitar and "seemed ennuyé to the very death" as he gives directions for the recovery of the child who has fallen into a Venetian canal. He conveys an atmosphere of cruel indifference toward the plight of his wife and the fate of his child.

"Mephistopheles in England, or the Confessions of a Prime Minister, 2 vols. Philadelphia: Carey, Lea & Blanchard" Review by Poe that appeared in the September 1835 issue of the SOUTHERN LITERARY REVIEW. The political satire, discovered later to have been written by R. F. Williams, is condemned by Poe, who states that it "abounds with the coarsest and most malignant satire, at the same time evincing less of the power than of the will for causticity—and being frequently most feeble when it attempts to be the most severe." Although Poe praises the work for containing imagination "of the most etherial [sic] kind . . . and bears on every sentence the impress of genius," he also finds that it seems "to have no just object or end." Because of this lack, the reviewer states that "the work must, therefore, as a whole be condemned."

"Mercedes of Castile, A Romance, By James Fenimore Cooper. Two Volumes, Lea & Blanchard, 1840" Review by Poe that appeared in the January 1841 issue of GRAHAM'S MAGAZINE. Poe opens his review by attacking the work as "the worst novel ever penned by Mr. Cooper" and states further, "as a history this work is invaluable; as a novel, it is well nigh worthless." To prove that assertion, Poe provides readers with "a hasty sketch of the plot" as he attacks Cooper's lack of skill in characterization: "We did not look for character in it, for that is not Cooper's forte; nor did we expect that his heroine would be aught better than the inanimate thing she is." What does disappoint Poe is that Cooper fails to include "another of those magnificent sea-pictures for which, in all their sternness and sublimity, he is so justly celebrated." Lacking this, the novel holds little attraction for Poe, who states that the interest of the reader "does not begin until we are about to close the book."

Mesmer, Franz Friedrich Anton (1734–1815) Austrian physician known for using MESMERISM, a method for putting a subject into trance-like state today called "hypnotism," as a treatment for patients. He viewed the "magnetic principle" his alternate term for mesmerism as free of any spiritual associations and as only physical in existence. In 1772, Mesmer claimed to have discovered the existence of a power, similar to magnetism, that had an extensive influence over human behavior. Calling this power "animal magnetism," he experimented with it and claimed that it resulted in medical benefits to patients. Results of an investigation into the theory by a committee of physicians and scientists appointed by the French government, however, did not

support his findings. Their unfavorable report turned opinion against Mesmer, and he died in obscurity. Poe showed an interest in mesmerism, despite its status as a pseudoscience, and mentioned it in several works.

"Mesmeric Revelation" Short story. The framing of the story as the report of a scientific investigation using MESMERISM was so convincing that it was reprinted as an authentic scientific report in the September 1845 issue of the *American Phrenological Journal.* Poe was upset that the journal editors had taken his writing as fact and that they failed to realize, as Poe stated, "The story is pure fiction from beginning to end." Critics suggest that "THE FACTS IN THE CASE OF M. VALDEMAR" is a sequel to the present story.

PUBLISHING AND DRAMATIZATION HISTORY

The story was first published in the August 1844 issue of the *Columbian Magazine* and reprinted without modification in the August 31, 1844, issue of the PHILADEL-PHIA SATURDAY MUSEUM.

The story is not preceded by an epigraph.

No film has been made of "Mesmeric Revelation."

CHARACTERS

Unnamed physician, Mr. VANKIRK.

PLOT SYNOPSIS

The tale develops the theme of using mesmerism to place a person into a hypnotic trance in order to explore survival after death. As the story opens, the unnamed physician, P., has been summoned to the bedside of an invalid patient "suffering with acute pain in the region of the heart, and breathed with great difficulty, having all the ordinary symptoms of asthma." The patient, Mr. Vankirk, whose name means "of a church," tells P. that "the mesmeric exaltation enables me to perceive a train of ratiocination which, in my abnormal existence, convinces, but which, in full accordance with the mesmeric phenomena, does not extend, except through its *effect,* into my normal condition." He asks P. to place him into a "mesmeric sleep," during which P. interviews him on a variety of metaphysical topics, including the nature of God, the materiality of deity, and postmortem survival. The interview terminates suddenly when Vankirk dies. P. attempts to bring Vankirk back to life, but Vankirk refuses the effort because while on the "other side" during the trance he has experienced a mesmeric revelation induced by "keenly refined perception." This convinces Vankirk to choose to remain in this ideal state of being, and he smiles blissfully as he dies, leaving P. frustrated and alarmed without answers regarding the soul's immortality or any control over his subject's condition.

mesmerism Method, now called "hypnotism," for putting a subject into trance-like state, used by the Austrian physician Franz Friedrich Anton MESMER to treat patients in the late 18th century. Although mesmerism was considered a pseudoscience even in Poe's time, his interest in mesmeric or hypnotic phenomena can be seen in his mention of Mesmer in several short stories, such as "MESMERIC REVELATION," "A TALE OF THE RAGGED MOUNTAINS," "SOME WORDS WITH A MUMMY," and "THE FACTS IN THE CASE OF M. VALDEMAR." Poe became familiar with the concept when he attended a series of lectures given in 1838 by the French magnetist Charles Poyen; he also attended a series of similar lectures given by Andrew Jackson Davis in 1845 in New York.

"Mesmerism/ 'In Articulo Mortis' / An Astounding and Horrifying Narration / Shewing the Extraordinary Power of Mesmerism / In Arresting the / Progress of Death / By Edgar A. Poe, Esq. / of New York / London / Short & Co., 8, King Street, Bloomsbury. / 1846. / Three pence" The second English reprint of Poe's story "THE FACTS IN THE CASE OF M. VALDEMAR" that appeared in booklet form in London, 1846, under the title of "Mesmerism 'In Articulo Mortis'." The following advertisement appeared on the cover of the booklet:

> The following astonishing narrative first appeared in the American Magazine, a work of some standing in the United States, where the case has excited the most intense interest.
>
> The effects of the mesmeric influence, in this case, were so astounding, so contrary to all past experience, that no one could have possibly anticipated the final result. The narrative though only a plain recital of facts, is of so extraordinary a nature as almost to surpass belief. It is only necessary to add, that credence is given to it in America, where the occurrence took place.

"Metzengerstein: A Tale In Imitation of the German" Short story. This tale was Poe's first to appear in print.

Because this story is the earliest of the horror tales, critics have questioned if the tale is a spoof or a hoax of the very popular hair-raising German gothic thrillers that were prevalent in the magazines of the period, or if it is a "serious imitation of the German" as the subtitle proclaims. Whichever it is, "Metzengerstein" confirms Poe's early and longstanding attraction to the elements of gothic fiction, which he later tempered with extensive psychological insight.

PUBLISHING AND DRAMATIZATION HISTORY

The story first appeared in the January 14, 1832, issue of the Philadelphia *Saturday Courier.*

The following epigraph, taken from a hexameter by Martin Luther and directed to the papacy, precedes the story: *Pestis eram vivus—moriens tua mors ero.* ["Living I have been your plague, dying I shall be your death."]

The tale was filmed as one segment of the French-Italian film titled *Tales of Mystery and Imagination,* directed in 1968 by Roger Vadim and starring Jane Fonda and Peter Fonda. Although the segment is entitled "Metzengerstein," the plot bears little resemblance to Poe's story.

CHARACTERS

Count Wilhelm BERLIFITZING, Baron Frederick METZENGERSTEIN, Lady Mary METZENGERSTEIN.

PLOT SYNOPSIS

The story contains many of the standard devices found in such 18th-century gothic thrillers as Horace Walpole's *The Castle of Otranto,* published in 1764, as well as the warning at the outset that "horror and fatality" have existed throughout the "all ages." Following the conventions of the genre, the story includes dark and brooding castles, hints at secret obsessions and sins, foreboding prophecies, family rivalry, a nightmare-like atmosphere, and horrible conflagrations. Poe's contribution to this standard fare is the introduction of an unusual phenomenon, the psychic transmigration of a soul from a human to a horse. The young Baron Frederick Metzengerstein inherits his family's vast possessions at the age of 18 and immediately "the behavior of the heir out-Heroded Herod. . . . Shameful debaucheries—flagrant treacheries—unheard-of atrocities—gave his trembling vassals quickly to understand that no servile submission on their part—no punctilios of conscience on his own—were thenceforward to prove any security against the remorseless fangs of a petty Caligula." On the fourth day of Metzengerstein's celebration of his inheritance, the stables of his family's rival Berlifitzing burn, taking with them the life of the "infirm and doting old man." During the fire, the young baron sits in his private apartment and stares at a tapestry that pictures an epic battle between the two families, and his eyes are drawn to "an enormous and unnaturally colored horse" that belonged to an ancestor of his rival. Metzengerstein looks away, and when his gaze returns to the tapestry he sees that the head of the gigantic horse appears to have moved, and the eyes "now wore an energetic and human expression." He staggers out of his room and learns that his rival burned to death trying to save his horses. His grooms have with them "a gigantic and fiery-colored horse," which bears the initials *W. V. B.* on its forehead but which no one at the Berlifitzing stables will claim, so the grooms assume that it belongs to the young baron. The Baron soon develops "a perverse attachment to his lately acquired charger. . . . an attachment which seemed to attain new strength from every fresh example of the animal's ferocious and demonlike propensities." From this point, the baron begins to isolate himself from all social events, and lives "utterly companionless" aside from his unusual attachment to the strange stallion with its "human-looking eye." One night, while the young baron is out riding, a raging fire spreads throughout the Palace Metzengerstein. When he returns to the castle, the strange horse which he is riding plunges into the castle, "far up the tottering staircases of the palace," and into the flames. As the white smoke rises above the flaming Castle Metzengerstein, the onlookers see a cloud of smoke "settled heavily over the battlements in the distinct colossal figure of— *a horse.*" The reader is left to believe that the Count Berlifitzing has returned to wreak his revenge on the sole remaining bearer of the name Metzengerstein.

Metzengerstein, Baron Frederick   Character in the short story "METZENGERSTEIN." His parents die when he is young and he inherits vast properties at the age of 18. After four days of debauchery and celebration, he sets fire to the stable of the longtime family rival, Count BERLIFITZING. His strange attachment to a horse that appears on the night of the fire leads to his isolation and, eventually, to his death.

Metzengerstein, Lady Mary   Character in the short story "METZENGERSTEIN." She is Baron Frederick MET-ZENGERSTEIN's mother, who dies shortly after her husband's death, leaving the baron an orphan at the age of 18.

Miaskovsky, Nikolai (1881–1950)   Prolific Russian composer who wrote at least 27 symphonies, as well as numerous string quartets, piano sonatas, songs, and various other works. His symphonic poem *Silentium* (1910) was inspired by Poe's poem "SILENCE—A SONNET."

Middleton, Henry (n.d.)   American consul in St. Petersburg, Russia. In Poe's account of his life furnished by him to Rufus Wilmot GRISWOLD to accompany publication of the complete works, Poe claimed to have run away from home in 1827 to join the Greeks in their fight for liberty; however, he claims, he was sidetracked and landed in St. Petersburg, Russia, where he "Got into many difficulties, but was extricated by the kindness of Mr. H. Middleton, the American consul at St. P."

Mignaud, Jules   Character in the short story "THE MURDERS IN THE RUE MORGUE." A banker with the firm of Mignaud et Fils, he confirms Madame L'ESPANAYE's banking habits. He tells investigators that she opened an account with his firm eight years previously, made frequent small deposits, and withdrew the sum of 4,000 francs in gold three days prior to her death, receiving the money from a clerk dispatched by the bank.

Mill, John Stuart (1806–1873)   British political writer and utilitarian thinker. He was considered a radical because he supported such measures as the public ownership of natural resources, equality for women, compulsory education, and birth control. His stand on women's suffrage, expressed in *The Subjection of Women* (1869), contributed to the formation of the suffrage movement. Poe's narrator PUNDITA in "MELLONTA TAUTA" dismisses Mill as "one Miller" representing the ancients whose "logic is, by their own showing, utterly baseless, worthless and fantastic altogether, as because of their pompous and imbecile proscription of all *other* roads to Truth, of all *other* means for its attainment."

Millard, Harrison (1830–1895)   American composer and singer whose compositions include more than 350 songs, many adaptations from French, Italian, and German; church music, and opera. In 1889, he published *Annabelle Leigh: A Parody Ballad of the Sea,* inspired by Poe's poem "ANNABEL LEE."

"Mille, Mille, Mille"   The title of a Latin hymn meaning "A thousand, a thousand, a thousand" that is sung to praise the valor of ANTIOCHUS EPIPHANES, the king of Syria in "FOUR BEASTS IN ONE; THE HOMO-CAMELEOPARD." He and his army march triumphantly into Antioch after battling and beating the Hebrew army, having "knocked over a thousand so fine," his troops "singing it as they go."

Miller, James Henry (1788–1853)   One of three judges, with John Pendleton KENNEDY of John Hazelhurst Boneval LATROBE, who judged Poe's prizewinning story "MS. FOUND IN A BOTTLE" for a competition sponsored in 1833 by the *BALTIMORE SUNDAY VISITER*. The committee awarded Poe the $50 prize for his story.

Miller, Joseph   Persona created by Poe as "our friend and particular acquaintance, Joseph Miller, Esq., (who, by the way, signs his name, we think, Joseph A. Miller, or Joseph B. Miller, or at least Joseph C. Miller)" who has "a passion for autographs." Poe introduces him in the prefatory pages of "AUTOGRAPHY," published in the February 1836 issue of the *SOUTHERN LITERARY MESSENGER,* as a character who changes his middle initial with each self-mention, running consecutively through the alphabet but omitting use of the letters *J* and *U*. At the end of the introduction, the autographer and collector of signatures gives Poe 24 letters from various contemporary prominent individuals—each sent to Joseph Miller using a different middle initial, minus *J* and *U*—and offers them for publication. "The package handed us by Mr. M. we inspected with a great deal of pleasure . . . . We print them *verbatim,* and with facsimiles of the signatures, in compliance with our friend's suggestion."

Milton, John (1608–1674) Poet often cited as the greatest English poet after Shakespeare. His work influenced the course of English poetry for three centuries after his death, and both his poetry and prose are marked by cosmic themes and lofty religious idealism. Poe read Milton early in life and his work often shows Milton's influence. The "Nicean barks" of "TO HELEN (1)" and the epigraph to the volume *TAMERLANE AND OTHER POEMS* suggest the grandeur of Milton's theme, diction, and style. In "THE POETIC PRINCIPLE," Poe mentions Milton's *Paradise Lost,* and he comments favorably on Rufus Wilmot GRISWOLD's edition of *The Prose Works of John Milton* in the September 27, 1845, issue of the *BROADWAY JOURNAL.* In "PINAKIDIA," Poe comments that "the noble simile of Milton, of Satan with the rising sun in the first book of 'Paradise Lost,' has nearly occasioned the suppression of that epic: it was supposed to contain a treasonable allusion." Also in "Pinakidia," Poe cites numerous instances in which later poets use lines suggested by Milton's works. Critics have suggested that Poe's name for LIGEIA may have been taken from line 880 in Milton's masque *Comus:* "And fair Ligea's golden comb."

Minor, Benjamin Blake (1818–1905) Editor of the *SOUTHERN LITERARY MESSENGER* in the 1840s. Poe made a special arrangement with him to print a revised version of "THE RAVEN" in March 1845.

Minor, Lucian Temperance advocate and frequent contributor to the *SOUTHERN LITERARY MESSENGER.* Thomas Willis WHITE, editor of the *Messenger,* wrote to Minor in 1841 that he had retained Poe as a copyreader, not editor, at the *Messenger,* because "he is unfortunately rather dissipated,—and therefore I can place very little reliance upon him." In the December 1835 issue of the *Messenger,* Poe reviewed Minor's "AN ADDRESS ON EDUCATION, AS CONNECTED WITH THE PERMANENCE OF OUR REPUBLICAN INSTITUTIONS," a speech delivered to the Institute of Education of Hampden Sidney College at its anniversary meeting on September 24, 1835.

Misquash Character in *THE JOURNAL OF JULIUS RODMAN.* A member of the Minnetaree tribe and the son of Chief WAUKERASSAH, he joins Julius RODMAN as interpreter for the expedition for part of the journey. He is especially valuable to the party when they confront the Assiniboins tribe, members of which seem to be hostile when they are merely exhibiting curiosity about the white travelers.

Moissart, Mademoiselle Character in Poe's short story "THE SPECTACLES." Known as Madame Eugenie LALANDE, she tricks the hero of the story, Napoleon Bonaparte FROISSART, her great-great-grandson, into thinking that he has married her to teach him a lesson.

Moneypenny, Dr. Character in Poe's short story "HOW TO WRITE A BLACKWOOD ARTICLE." He is an acronymist, and "such a queer little man that I am never sure when he is telling the truth." He is also "[a] vulgar man . . . but he's deep," and is a member of the Society for the Diffusion of Useful Knowledge. His pretentious comments allow Poe to satirize the pseudointellectuals whose articles found a home in *BLACKWOOD'S MAGAZINE.*

Monk Character in Poe's unpublished drama *POLITIAN.* Lady LALAGE's religious adviser, he urges her to "Give up thy soul to penitence, and pray!" When she asks for a crucifix he offers his own, then shrinks back in horror as she holds a dagger high and calls it her crucifix. He begs her to "tempt not the wrath divine!"

Monos Character in Poe's short story "THE COLLOQUY OF MONOS AND UNA." Monos describes in painful detail his dying and death, the funeral preparations, the grieving by those left behind, and the bodily sensations remaining after death. He also describes the sensations of dying, including the hyperexcitation of his senses and his eerie awareness, exhibiting more of life than he experienced while fully living. He disparages passion as "the affliction of an impure nature" that marks one who is not sufficiently devoted to transcending the earthly state to become worthy of inhabiting the paradise where pure spirits dwell. As the tale ends, Monos expresses the peace that he felt when, at last, all form and sentience had left him and "for all this nothingness, yet for all this immortality, the grave was still a home, and the corrosive hours, co-mates."

Montagu, Lady Mary Wortley (1689–1762) English intellectual known for her lively correspondence and gatherings of intellectuals. In a discussion of gossip in "MARGINALIA," Poe speaks of "Mary Wortley Montague [*sic*], who made it a profession and a purpose."

Montani, Alberto Character in Poe's short story "THE MURDERS IN THE RUE MORGUE." He is the first person to ascend the stairs that lead to the apartment of the murdered women. An Italian confectioner, he claims to have heard a gruff voice speaking in French and a second shrill voice that is "the voice of a Russian," although he admits that he has "never conversed with a native of Russia."

Montani, Nicola (1880–1949) American composer and conductor who wrote hymns, anthems, motets, sonatas, and songs. In 1917 he published *The Bells,* a contata for women's voices with soprano and alto solos and pianoforte or orchestral accompaniment. The piece was inspired by Poe's poem of the same name.

Montresor   Character in Poe's short story "THE CASK OF AMONTILLADO." He narrates the account of an ancient enmity that exists between his family and that of FORTUNATO, against whom he extracts his revenge during "the supreme madness of carnival season." He cunningly tricks his enemy into insisting that they sample the barrel of amontillado (a type of sherry) that he claims to have purchased, first luring Fortunato into the catacombs containing his wine cellar, then encasing him behind a wall and sealing it off.

Moog, Wilson Townsend (1881–1954)   American composer, organist, and teacher whose compositions include organ and piano music and songs. In 1909, for the Poe Centenary Exercises at the Edgar Allan Poe School near Westminster Churchyard in Baltimore, Poe's burial place, he composed a choral setting for children's voices of the first stanza of Poe's poem "THE BELLS."

Moran, Dr. John J.   The 27-year-old resident physician at Baltimore's Washington College Hospital who provided Poe with medical attention in the author's final two days of life. In a letter to Maria CLEMM on November 15, 1849, five weeks after Poe's death, Moran wrote the following:

> When brought to the hospital he [Poe] was unconscious of his condition—who brought him or with whom he had been associating. He remained in this condition from 5 in the afternoon—the hour of his admission—until 3 next morning. This was on 3rd Oct.
>
> To this state succeeded tremor of the limbs, and at first a busy, but not violent or active delirium—constant talking—and vacant converse with spectral and imaginary objects on the walls. His face was pale and his whole person drenched in perspiration. We were unable to induce tranquility before the second day after his admission.

The doctor also reported that Poe shouted for the explorer Jeremiah REYNOLDS, "which he did through the night up to three on Sunday morning. . . . At this time a very decided change began to affect him. Having become enfeebled from exertion he became quiet and seemed to rest for a short time, then gently moving his head he said, *'Lord help my poor soul'* and expired." Although Moran judged the cause of Poe's death to be drunkenness and a severe case of delirium tremens, the exact medical cause of Poe's death remains uncertain.

Moran, Mrs. Mary   Wife of Dr. John J. MORAN, the physician who attended Poe in his final illness. She visited Poe's bedside and read to him from the Bible in an effort to comfort him as he was dying. She hoped that "the words of the Great Physician" (Jesus) would ease his suffering, so she read from the 14th chapter of the Gospel of St. John. Moran also attended to his physical needs by giving him water, wiping the perspiration from his forehead, smoothing the sheets, and making his shroud.

More, Sir Thomas (1478–1535)   English statesman, writer, and martyr whose stand against King Henry VIII led to his death. He was the author of *Utopia.* Legend has that he stood laughing before kneeling at the block to be beheaded. Poe refers to More in his short story "THE ASSIGNATION" through the speech of the mysterious, Byronic stranger to the unnamed narrator: "To die laughing must be the most glorious of all glorious deaths! Sir Thomas More—a very fine man was Sir Thomas More—Sir Thomas More died laughing, you remember."

Moreau, Pierre   Character in Poe's short story "THE MURDERS IN THE RUE MORGUE." He is a Parisian tobacconist who testifies that Madame L'ESPANAYE has been one of his customers, buying "small quantities of tobacco and snuff" for nearly four years. He also provides the police with some history of the residents of the victims' house, the personality and habits of the old woman and her daughter, and the existence of any visitors.

Morrell, Captain Benjamin   Character referred to in Poe's novel *THE NARRATIVE OF ARTHUR GORDON PYM.* The captain of the American schooner *Wasp,* he has sailed through the same waters as Arthur Gordon PYM on January 11, 1823, "with a view of penetrating as far south as possible" to the Antarctic Circle. Morrell is unable to complete the journey and, "nearly destitute of fuel and water, and without proper instruments," he must turn back without completing his journey. Captain GUY reads his account in the ship's log and resolves to push the crew of the *Jane* "boldly to the southward."

"Morella"   Short story. The tale is one of metempsychosis, the passage of the soul from one body to another, with which Poe also dealt in "METZENGERSTEIN," "LIGEIA," "A TALE OF THE RAGGED MOUNTAINS," and "THE BLACK CAT." Critics suggest that "Morella" is the best of the tales dealing with the topic.

PUBLISHING AND DRAMATIZATION HISTORY

The story was first published in the April 1835 issue of the *SOUTHERN LITERARY MESSENGER* and reprinted in the

November 1839 issue of BURTON'S GENTLEMAN'S MAGAZINE. The first publication of the story contained "HYMN," a poem of 16 lines first published as a song sung by MORELLA (1) in the first printing of the story and later published separately as "A Catholic Hymn" in the August 16, 1845, issue of the BROADWAY JOURNAL. The poem, which consists of 12 lines of rhyming couplets, is a plea by the heroine to the Blessed Virgin, and it is unusual in its hopeful expression of a radiant future.

An epigraph taken from Plato's *Symposium* and adapted by Henry Nelson Coleridge, who placed it in his 1831 *Introduction to the Study of the Greek Classic Poets,* where Poe found it, precedes the story: "Itself—alone by itself—eternally one and single." The theme of one entity eternal reverberates throughout the story, which relates the domination of one malign spirit over those bodies it inhabits.

The story was one of three stories by Poe, with "THE FACTS IN THE CASE OF M. VALDEMAR" and "The Black Cat," that were filmed by the director Roger CORMAN as *Tales of Terror* (1962), starring Vincent PRICE, Peter Lorre, Basil Rathbone, and Debra Paget.

CHARACTERS

MORELLA (1), MORELLA (2), unnamed narrator.

PLOT SYNOPSIS

The tale relates the theme of the psychic survival of a malign spirit that transfers from the dying mother to the daughter at the moment of birth. The unnamed narrator marries Morella (1) with a soul that "burned with fires it had never before known; but the fires were not of Eros, and bitter and tormenting to my spirit was the gradual conviction that I could in no manner define their unusual meaning, or regulate their vague intensity." His new wife's "erudition is profound. . . . [H]er talents were of no common order—her powers of mind were gigantic," and the narrator enters into study with her, including her studies "over forbidden pages." As the two delve more deeply into mystical writings, the narrator states, "I found a forbidden spirit kindling within me." He becomes weary, "when the mystery of my wife's manner oppressed me as a spell." He soon can no longer bear her touch, and Morella (1) appears to sense the narrator's "consuming desire for the moment of [her] decease." As she is dying in childbirth, she warns the narrator, "thy days shall be days of sorrow—that sorrow which is the most lasting of impressions." She vows to return and predicts "her whom in life thou didst abhor, in death thou shalt adore." As Morella (1) dies, their daughter is born and becomes the reincarnation of her mother. The narrator refuses to name his child, who "was the perfect resemblance of her who had departed," and he grows to love her "with a love more fervent than I had

believed it possible to feel for any denizen of earth." When the child is an adult, she is so much like her mother that the narrator becomes frightened "at its too perfect *identity*—that her eyes were like Morella's." He determines that he will have her baptized as "a present deliverance from the terrors of my destiny." During the ceremony, when he must provide the young woman a name, some "fiend spoke from the recesses of my soul," and he whispers Morella's name to the priest. The reaction is immediate, and his daughter "turned her glassy eyes from the earth to heaven, and, falling prostrate on the black slabs of our ancestral vault responded—'I am here!'" The narrator watches his daughter convulse and die. When he inters Morella (2) in the family tomb, he laughs "a long and bitter laugh" as he finds no traces of his dead wife. She appears to have wreaked her revenge for his hatred toward her during her first physical life, as Morella (1).

Morella (1)   Character in Poe's short story "MORELLA." An erudite woman who shuns society and attaches herself to her husband alone, she has "a Pressburg education"; Pressburg, in Hungary, was in 1835 not only the site where kings were crowned and the home of a great university, but was also considered the center for "the Black Arts," so called by Poe, whose meaning appears to be the use of magic for evil purposes. Mystical writings are Morella's "favorite and constant study." Soon hated by her husband, she dies in childbirth; but on her deathbed she warns that he will love her in death as much as he has hated her in life. She seems to return to life through her daughter.

Morella (2)   Born at the moment that her mother dies, she lives her life nameless until she reaches adulthood and resembles her late mother MORELLA (1) so completely that her father decides that she must be baptized to protect them both from the evil that her mother's studies had generated. When she and her father stand with the priest at the baptismal font and her father must select a name, he utters her mother's name, "Morella." Within moments, Morella the daughter convulses and falls dead to the ground after responding "I am here!"

Morgan, Appleton (n.d.)   President of the New York Shakespeare Society, he led an effort in 1897 to get passed a bill in the New York legislature that would establish Poe Park and remove to it the Fordham cottage where Virginia CLEMM Poe died. Writing in *Munsey's Magazine* in July 1897, Morgan reported that his interviews with people, "or whose fathers or mothers have so testified to them, have assured me that Poe never drank liquor simply because his stomach was so delicate that a single glass of wine was poison to him, and that he could not, even by a physical effort, swallow, much less retain, a drop of ardent spirits." Opposition to the bill was based on Poe's unfavorable reputation, which persisted from the publication of THE "LUDWIG" ARTICLE. Through persistence, the bill eventually passed and the Park is now under the aegis of the federal government.

"Morning on the Wissahiccon"   Travel sketch by Poe; better known under the title "THE ELK."

Morphine, Dr.   Original name of Dr. OLLAPOD, a character in the short story "A PREDICAMENT."

Morris, George Pope (1802–1864)   Editor and co-owner, with Nathaniel Parker WILLIS, of the New York *EVENING MIRROR*. The two men sold the *Evening Mirror* and founded the *Home Journal,* one of the outstanding and most successful ventures of the time, which left a lasting mark on American magazines. Poe wrote in "AUTOGRAPHY" with admiration of Morris's songs, "which have taken fast hold upon the popular taste, and which are deservedly celebrated." Poe further remarked that "he has caught the true *tone* for these things, and hence his popularity—a popularity which his enemies would fain make us believe is altogether attributable to his editorial influence."

"Mosses from an Old Manse"   Short story collection by Nathaniel HAWTHORNE, reviewed by Poe as part of a lengthy review of works by Hawthorne, in an article titled "TALE-WRITING—NATHANIEL HAWTHORNE" in the November 1847 issue of *GODEY'S MAGAZINE AND LADY'S BOOK.*

Mott, Valentine (1785–1865)   Physician at the New York University School of Medicine who examined Poe in 1847, in the months after Virginia CLEMM's death. He was told of Poe's symptoms by Marie Louise SHEW, a medically trained doctor's daughter who had served as Virginia's nurse. Shew noticed and reported to Mott that Poe's "pulse beat only ten regular beats, after which it suspended or intermitted." He agreed with her conjecture that Poe might have a lesion on one side of the brain and recommended that Poe refrain from all stimulants and tonics—even sedatives—the use of which would intensify hallucinations and lead to greater mental instability. Despite his confirmation of Shew's suspicions, Mott did not medically confirm the brain lesions, nor did he provide treatment.

Mowatt, Anna Cora (1819–1870)   Playwright, socialite, and author of the comedy *Fashion,* which Poe reviewed in his portrait of her in "THE LITERATI OF NEW YORK CITY," appearing in the June 1846 issue of *GODEY'S MAGAZINE AND LADY'S BOOK.* Poe opens the review by declaring Mowatt to be "in some respects a remarkable

Anna Cora Mowatt, stage actress, novelist and dramatist, whom Poe called "in some respects a remarkable woman." (Edgar Allan Poe Society)

woman, and [a person who] has undoubtedly wrought a deeper impression upon *the public* than any one of her sex in America." Despite his opening praise, Poe finds her tales to be "conventional" and the subjects often "hackneyed." He likes her poetry no better, and he says "in very few of them do I observe even noticeable passages." Her problem, as he assesses it, is that "she evinces more feeling than ideality." Her writing of drama has different results, and Poe notes that "her first decided success was with her comedy [*Fashion*], although the play is in imitation of Congreve." Poe praises the manner in which Mowatt manages such imitation and observes that it "owes what it had of success to its being the work of a lovely woman who had already excited interest, and to the very commonplaceness or spirit of conventionality which rendered it readily comprehensible and appreciable by the public proper." In contrast to his lukewarm appreciation of her writing, Poe enthusiastically praises Mowatt's appearance on stage, attributing her success to her "rich and voluminous" voice, "the perfection of grace" of her step, the "well-controlled impulsiveness" of her movements—"the great charm of her manner is its nat-

Moyamensing Prison, where Poe spent one night in September 1849. (Library of Congress)

uralness." In other reviews of Mowatt's work, including "THE NEW COMEDY," "THE DRAMA," "PROSPECTS OF THE DRAMA," and "THE FORTUNE HUNTER," Poe is inconsistent in his praise.

Moyamensing Prison Philadelphia jail where Poe was detained for public drunkenness in July 1849 after he became hallucinatory and attempted suicide. While in the prison, he claimed to have seen the vision of a white female form that warned him against suicide. When he appeared before Philadelphia Mayor Gilpin the following morning, the mayor recognized him as "Poe, the poet" and dismissed him without charging a fine. Poe's biographers note the first onset of the author's delirium tremens during this incarceration.

"Mr. Griswold and the Poets" Review by Poe that appeared in the November 1842 issue of *Boston Miscellany*. Rufus Wilmot GRISWOLD contacted Poe in July 1842 and offered him a fee to review his (Griswold's) anthology *THE FEMALE POETS OF AMERICA* and include remarks about an earlier anthology, *THE POETS AND POETRY OF AMERICA*. Griswold believed that "the name of Poe—gratuitously furnished—might be of some consequence." Because he paid for the review, Griswold expected high praise for his work; but Poe retained his sense of integrity by assessing the work fairly and expressing reservations. Displeased with the result, Griswold debated whether he should withhold the review, but decided to publish it to avoid a confrontation, "lest Poe should think I had prevented its publication." Poe's review disagreed with Griswold's critical assumptions and taste in New England poets, and Griswold's anthology of female poets won Poe's praise for being "a man not more of taste than—shall we say it?—courage." Of *The Poets and Poetry of America*, Poe wrote that "the work before us is indeed so vast an improvement upon those of a similar character which have preceded it, that we do its author some wrong in classing all together." In the same vein, Poe identifies the structure of the work and content, and expresses his approval "of the general plan and execution of the work." That said, he asserts, "We disagree then, with Mr. Griswold in *many* of his critical estimates. . . . He has omitted from the body of his book, some one or two whom we should have been tempted to introduce. . . . [H]e has scarcely made us amends by introducing some one or two dozen whom we should have treated with contempt." In the final summation, however, Poe pronounces *The Poets and Poetry of America* to be "*the most important addition which our literature has for many years received. It fills a void which should have been long ago supplied.*"

"MS. Found In a Bottle"   Short story. The author Joseph Conrad considered this tale "about as fine as anything of that kind can be—so authentic in detail that it might have been told by a sailor of sombre and poetical genius in the invention of the phantastic." In 1833, this story won the top prize of $50 and publication as the best prose tale entered in a contest sponsored by the BALTIMORE SUNDAY VISITER. The judges declared that Poe's tale was "eminently distinguished by a wild, vigorous and poetical imagination, a rich style, a fertile invention, and varied and curious learning."

The story is similar in setting, characterization, and situation to two later sea tales by Poe, "THE NARRATIVE OF ARTHUR GORDON PYM" and "A DESCENT INTO THE MAELSTROM."

PUBLISHING AND DRAMATIZATION HISTORY

The story was first published in the October 19, 1833, issue of the *Baltimore Sunday Visiter.*

The epigraph that precedes the story is taken from Philippe Quinault's *Ays,* I, vi., 15–16:

> *Qui n'a plus qu'un moment a vivre*
> *N'a plus rien a dissimuler.*
> [He who has but a moment to live / has no longer anything to dissemble.]

No film has been made of the story to date.

CHARACTERS

Old Swede, unnamed captain, unnamed narrator.

PLOT SYNOPSIS

Told in the first person, the tale is framed as an account in a journal found in a bottle that has been floating in the ocean. The story tells of a shipwreck and of the strange voyage that the narrator makes aboard the ship that rescues him, "a gigantic ship, of perhaps four thousand tons. . . . Her hull was of a deep dingy black, unrelieved by any of the customary carvings of a ship." The ship has a spectral crew of ancient mariners: "their shriveled skins rattled in the wind; their voices were low, tremulous, and broken; their eyes glistened with the rheum of years; and their gray hairs streamed terribly in the tempest." The ship appears to be caught in a current that is pulling it toward the South Pole, a phenomenon that leads the narrator to write of the bizarre experience in a journal as the ship moves ever closer to the abyss. Not merely moving passively, the ship is propelled toward the immense whirlpool by nature, in the form of the simoom, tempest, hurricane, and tornado. The journal gives accounts of the mysterious crew, as well as of the overwhelmingly destructive power of nature. The narrator also writes in his journal about the opportunity for knowledge in such a self-destructive moment, noting, "Yet a curiosity to penetrate the mysteries of these awful regions, predominates even over my despair, and will reconcile me to the most hideous aspect of death. It is evident that we are hurrying onward to some exciting knowledge—some never-to-be-imparted secret, whose attainment is destruction."

When the end is imminent, the narrator sees the ice open suddenly and the ship begin to whirl in immense concentric circles. He writes his final words, recording that "the ship is quivering, Oh God! and—going down." As the ship disappears into "the borders of a gigantic amphitheatre," the narrator places the manuscript in a bottle, then eagerly goes down with the *Discovery,* submitting to the force of the whirlpool, as do Arthur Gordon PYM and the unnamed narrator of "A DESCENT INTO THE MAELSTROM."

Mumblethumb, Mr.   Character mentioned in the short story "THE LITERARY LIFE OF THINGUM BOB, ESQ." Notice appears in the "Toad," a fictional gossip column, that the *Lollipop,* a literary magazine, paid Mumblethumb 50¢ for the literary contribution "Monody in a Mud-Puddle."

"The Murders In the Rue Morgue"   Short story. This tale introduced the world to the detective story, a genre (distinct from the mystery story) that emphasizes the "detector" as well as the crime and places the emphasis upon analysis instead of trial-and-error. The original title was "Murders in the Rue Trianon," but Poe changed the title to connect more directly with death. "Rue Morgue" suggests a street that contains a building that houses dead bodies.

The story also introduced C. Auguste DUPIN as the model for the detective—professional or amateur, a member of the official police force or a private investi-

Illustration for "Murders in the Rue Morgue" in Collected Works of Edgar Allan Poe *(1902).*

gator—who uses his intellectual powers—the power of ratiocination—to solve crime. Dupin's remarkable powers of deduction and idiosyncrasies, as well as the dual national association of a French detective created by an American writer, led to a range of successors both in the United States and abroad, the most famous of whom was Sir Arthur Conan DOYLE's Sherlock Holmes. Critics have also suggested that Agatha Christie had Poe's Dupin in mind in creating her Belgian detective Hercule Poirot, who insists that his powers of detection reside in his use of "the little gray cells" and whose idiosyncrasies are abundant.

PUBLISHING AND DRAMATIZATION HISTORY

The story was first published in April 1841 issue of GRAHAM'S MAGAZINE.

Poe precedes the story with an epigraph taken from chapter five of *Urn-Burial* by Sir Thomas BROWNE: "What song the Syrens sang, or what name Achilles assumed when he hid himself among women, although puzzling questions, are not beyond all conjecture."

The tale has inspired a number of films, some of which use only portions of the story. The first full-length version to use the story title appeared in 1932, directed by Robert Florey and starring Bela Lugosi, Sidney Fox, Leon Ames, Brandon Hurst, and Arlene Francis. This expressionist effort, which used shadowed lighting and a variety of other film techniques to soften the evidence of reality, cast Lugosi as the fiendish Dr. Mirakle who eyes Fox as a potential bride for his pet ape. In 1954, another film version was released: *Phantom of the Rue Morgue,* directed by Roy Del Ruth and starring Karl Malden, Claude Dauphin, Patricia Medina, Steve Forrest, and Merv Griffin. The plot here is closer to Poe's original, but the ape is replaced by a mad killer on the loose in Paris. In 1971, director Gordon Hessler reworked the story into a sensationalistic version, *Murders in the Rue Morgue,* placing the action in a Grand Guignol–style theater. This film starred Jason Robards, Herbert Lom, Christine Kaufmann, Lilli Palmer, and Adolfo Celi. The most recent reworking of the story appeared in 1986, in *The Murders in the Rue Morgue,* directed by Jeannot Szwarc and starring George C. Scott, Rebecca de Mornay, Ian MacShane, Neil Dickson, and Val Kilmer. Although made for television, this film adaptation is largely true to Poe's story, enhanced by atmospheric locations and high production values.

CHARACTERS

William BIRD, CHANTILLY, Pauline DUBOURG, Paul DUMAS, C. Auguste Dupin, Henri DUVAL, Alexandre ETIENNE, Alfonzo GARCIO, Monsieur JOURDAIN, Adolphe LE BON, Madame L'ESPANAYE, Mademoiselle Camille L'ESPANAYE, Jules MIGNAUD, Alberto MONTANI, Pierre MOREAU, Isidor MUSET, ODENHEIMER, unnamed narrator.

PLOT SYNOPSIS

The story opens with a prelude in which the unnamed narrator considers the logical moves of the mind and compares chess moves with the possible moves that that analytical mind might take: "It will be found, in fact, that the ingenious are always fanciful, and the *truly* imaginative never otherwise than analytic." The narrator assists Dupin in solving the horrifying murders of two women, a mother and daughter, in Paris. The narrator and Dupin first meet in an obscure library, "where the accident of our both being in search of the same very rare and very remarkable volume brought us into closer communion." The two become roommates in "a time-eaten and grotesque mansion, long deserted through superstitions into which we did not inquire, and tottering to its fall." The two have sequestered themselves from the world, admitting no visitors and waiting until dark to set out to walk the streets, "arm in arm, continuing the topics of the day, or roaming far and wide until a late hour."

Dupin becomes intrigued with the newspaper account of a double murder, in which the mother's body is badly mutilated "with her throat so entirely cut that, upon an attempt to raise her, the head fell off." The daughter's body is found stuffed up the chimney, feet first, with many scratches and bruises on the face and throat. The numerous witnesses contradict each other in their accounts. Each professes to be certain that the voice he or she heard spoke a foreign language, but no witness agrees with any other on the language spoken by the murderer.

Dupin asks the police for permission to investigate the premises. The lack of agreement about the language spoken leads him to conclude that no human speaker uttered those sounds. Once in the apartment, he observes clues that the police have overlooked: one of the nails that supposedly secured a locked window from the inside is broken, for example, although only an agile beast or a creature of superhuman strength could have climbed into the apartment by means of a lightning rod and window shutters.

Based on this information, Dupin shifts "the question from the mode of egress to that of ingress" as he avoids the error of the police, who assume a human perpetrator and a human motive. After he finds a hair that is "most unusual—this is no *human hair*," Dupin explores the possibility that a nonhuman killer is at fault and places an advertisement in the newspaper. When a sailor answers the ad, the detectives learn that an "OurangOoutang" brought from Borneo is responsible for the murders.

After Dupin solves the crime, the prefect of police "was fain to indulge in a sarcasm or two, about the propriety of every person minding his own business." Unfazed by the annoyance of the prefect, Dupin pronounces him "too cunning to be profound."

Muset, Isidor　Character in the short story "THE MURDERS IN THE RUE MORGUE." A police officer who is called to the house where the murders are in progress, he gives testimony that he heard "screams of some person (or persons) in great agony" and reports hearing "two voices in loud and angry contention," but he is unable to identify the gender of the speakers or repeat what was said.

The Mysteries of Paris　Criminal romance novel by Eugène Sue published in 1842 and reviewed by Poe in the "MARGINALIA" entry that appeared in the November 1846 issue of *GRAHAM'S MAGAZINE*. Poe called the novel in translation "a work of unquestionable power—a museum of novel and ingenious incident—a paradox of childish folly and consummate skill." However, Poe was less favorable in his assessment of the translation

from French into English: "The translation (by C. H. Town) is very imperfect, and, by a too literal rendering of idioms, contrives to destroy the whole *tone* of the original." He contends that the translation "abounds in misapprehensions of the author's meaning" and provides examples of the errors that he has identified throughout. Poe uses the "Marginalia" entry to eliminate any misapprehensions that readers may have about the relationship of the novel to his short story "MURDERS IN THE RUE MORGUE." He is "not a little surprised" to find in the novel a story related by one of the characters in which "one of its points has been suggested to M. Sue by a tale of my own." The story tells of an ape that is "remarkable for its size, strength, ferocity, and propensity to imitation." The ape's master wants to use it to commit a murder, so he teaches the ape "to imitate the functions of a barber, and incites it to cut the throat of a child." Poe expresses concern that "some of my friends would accuse me of plagiarising from it my 'Murders in the Rue Morgue.'" His fears are soon allayed as he recalls for readers that his story first appeared in the April 1841 issue of *Graham's Magazine*, and that it was printed in the *Paris Charivari* in 1842 without any identification of him as its author. He generously refuses to accuse Sue of appropriating his idea and, instead, observes, "The similarity *may* have been entirely accidental."

"The Mystery of Marie Rogêt. A Sequel to 'The Murders In the Rue Morgue'"　Short story. Poe transferred to Paris the tantalizing events that make up this story of a real murder that occurred in New York, making this the first detective story to attempt to solve an actual crime. The murder of Mary Cecilia ROGERS, a beautiful girl who worked in John Anderson's New York City cigar store, dominated the newspapers in August 1841. Using news reports and visits to the location where the body had been found, Poe finished one version of the story by June 1842 with an ending that suggested that the culprit was a secret lover. In a letter written to George Roberts on June 4, 1842, Poe wrote:

> I believe not only that I have demonstrated the fallacy of the general idea—that the girl was the victim of a gang of ruffians—but have indicated the assassin in a manner which will give renewed impetus to investigation. My main object, nevertheless, as you will readily understand, is an analysis of the true principles which should direct inquiry in similar cases.

Five months later, an article published in the November 26, 1842, issue of the New York *Tribune* forced Poe to revise the story. The newspaper reported that Mrs. Frederica Loss, "the woman who kept the refreshment house nearest the scene of her [Marie Rogers's] death," revealed on her deathbed that Marie Rogers had died in her house after a physician "undertook to procure for the unfortunate girl a premature delivery [abortion]." Mrs. Loss's son had then taken the body and placed it in the Hudson River.

Although subtitled "A Sequel to 'The Murders in the Rue Morgue,'" the only elements that the two tales have in common are the Paris setting, the involvement of C. Auguste DUPIN, and the heavy emphasis on newspaper accounts. Unlike his analysis of evidence in "Murders in the Rue Morgue," Dupin in this story spends his time disputing the newspaper accounts and suggests ways in which the crime could be solved, but Poe does not commit himself to a solution.

PUBLISHING AND DRAMATIZATION HISTORY

The story was first published in serialized form in the November and December 1842 and February 1843 issues of *Snowden's Ladies' Companion.*

The epigraph that precedes the story is a translation from "Moralische Anisichten" that appears in *Novalis Schriften* by the German writer Friedrich von Hardenburg, although Poe may have found it in Sarah Austin's *Fragments from German Prose Writers,* which he reviewed in *Graham's Magazine* in December 1841: "There are ideal series of events which run parallel with the real ones. They rarely coincide. Men and circumstances generally modify the ideal train of events, so that it seems imperfect, and its consequences are equally imperfect. Thus with the Reformation; instead of Protestantism came Lutheranism."

The film *The Mystery of Marie Rogêt,* released in 1942, was directed by Phil Rosen and starred Maria Montez, Maria Ouspenskaya, John Litel, Patric Knowles, and Charles Middleton. The plot is modified to feature a detective who must search for a music-hall actress who has disappeared.

CHARACTERS

Monsieur BEAUVAIS, Madame DELUC, C. Auguste Dupin, Monsieur LE BLANC, Estelle ROGÊT, Marie ROGÊT, Jacques ST. EUSTACHE, VALENCE, unnamed narrator.

PLOT SYNOPSIS

The lengthy short story is based upon the actual and unsolved murder of Miss Mary Cecilia Rogers, and includes a reappearance Poe's detective C. Auguste Dupin. Poe also transferred the American murder to Paris and made changes in the story and characters to suit the French setting. The last name "Rogers" became "Rogêt" (both names are pronounced the same way in French), the mutilated body of the victim is found in the Seine rather than in the Hudson River, the victim works at a perfumery instead of a tobacco

shop, and the Parisian police conduct the investigation, which they invite Dupin to join. One major similarity between the actual case and Poe's story is the role of the media: the fictional Parisian media sensationalizes the case as did the New York City newspapers, with both adding their own inventive details and solutions. As Dupin observes, "We should bear in mind that, in general, it is the object of our newspapers rather to create a sensation—to make a point—than to further the cause of truth." Dupin is equally dismissive of the courts and of formal hearings: "I would here observe that very much of what is rejected as evidence by a court, is the best evidence to the intellect." To make sense of the facts, Dupin attempts to enter the murderer's mind and to determine the pattern of this "ordinary, although an atrocious, instance of crime" using diverse newspaper accounts and the reports provided by his sidekick, the unnamed narrator. Using his skills of ratiocination, Dupin determines that the cloth belt reported to have been fastened around her waist was used to drag the body to the river. He similarly refutes the suggestions of several newspapers that she was attacked and murdered by a gang, and suggests, instead, that a single man killed her, then dumped the body from a boat into the river and set the boat adrift. Unlike his brilliant revelation of the murderer in "MURDERS IN THE RUE MORGUE," Dupin's manner is more subdued in this story. The detective suggests that the police will find the killer if they find the boat used: "This boat shall guide us, with a rapidity which will surprise even ourselves, to him who employed it in the midnight of the fatal Sabbath. Corroboration will rise upon corroboration, and the murderer will be traced." Dupin plays a less significant role in this story and exhibits less analytic brilliance than he does in "The Murders in the Rue Morgue" and "THE PURLOINED LETTER."

"Mystification"   Short story. This brief, humorous tale includes dueling, secret writing, and the concept of the double, or Doppelganger.

PUBLISHING AND DRAMATIZATION HISTORY

The tale was first published in the June 1837 issue of the New York *American Monthly Magazine* under the title "Von Jung, the Mystific." It was published in 1840 under the same title in TALES OF THE GROTESQUE AND ARABESQUE. Poe changed the title to "Mystification" when he published a revised version in the December 27, 1845, issue of the BROADWAY JOURNAL.

The epigraph that precedes the story is taken from Ben Jonson's play *Every Man in His Humour* (1616), and Poe attributes it to a name adapted from Jonson's "Edward Knowell": *"Slid, if these be your 'passados' and 'montantes,' I'll have none o' them."—Ned Knowles.*

CHARACTERS

Johann HERMANN, unnamed narrator, Baron Ritzner VON JUNG.

PLOT SYNOPSIS

The story relates the efforts of the Baron Ritzner Von Jung to teach a pompous and sneering duelist a lesson by using his pseudolearning against him. The clever intellectual Von Jung visits the unnamed narrator of the story at the university and becomes embroiled in a heated discussion of the gentlemanly benefits of dueling—an amazing feat, because the baron holds only contempt for the activity. Despite his aversion, the baron speaks on the subject "with an ardor, an eloquence, an impressiveness, and an affectionateness of manner, which elicited the warmest enthusiasm from his listeners." So effective is his discussion that he excites the animosity of one of the "gentleman duelists," Johann Hermann, who belittles Von Jung's command of the topic and insults him: "'I would say, sir, that your opinions are not the opinions to be expected from a gentleman.'" Hermann is jealous of the attention that the baron commands, for he considers himself to be the leading authority at the university on dueling. He prides himself on knowing the intricate details of the etiquette of the activity, "and the nicety of his sense of honor that he most especially prided him-

self." The baron decides to make a fool of Hermann and misleads him into thinking that a duel is imminent. In mock anger, the baron hurls a decanter of wine into the mirror facing Hermann, so that it smashes the duelist's reflection. Uncertain if the action constitutes an insult. Hermann retreats to his room to consult his books on dueling etiquette. When the two exchange letters, the baron directs Hermann to consult "the opinions of the Sieur Hedelin, as set forth in the ninth paragraph of the chapter of *'Injuriae per applicationem, per constructionem, et per se,'* in his *'Duelli Lex scripta, et non, aliterque.'*" The passage satisfies him that "the explanation offered was of the fullest, the most honorable, and the most equivocally satisfactory nature," yet this is a second humiliation that the baron has perpetrated on him, because the book is nonsense. Hermann's stupid and pompous nature makes him unable to admit that he does not understand what he reads, for the Duelli Lex Scripta is "framed so as to present to the ear all the outward signs of intelligibility, and even of profundity, while in fact not a shadow of meaning existed." To Hermann's greater embarrassment, when the second and third words of the sentences are alternately omitted as the treatise is read aloud, the text becomes "a most horribly absurd account of a duel between two baboons." Hermann would rather die a thousand deaths than admit his ignorance. Thus, a duel of wits is fought, and Hermann loses.

The Narrative of Arthur Gordon Pym Poe's only novel. The novel contains bloodcurdling murders, mutiny, shipwreck, strange characters and cannibal feasting, all in an effort to attract a popular audience. The work shows the influence of Poe's reading at the time, including Captain Benjamin MORRELL's *Narrative of Four Voyages to the South Seas,* Jeremiah N. REYNOLDS's "ADDRESS ON THE SUBJECT OF A SURVEYING AND EXPLORING EXPEDITION TO THE PACIFIC OCEAN AND SOUTH SEAS," the Harper Family Library *Description of Pitcairn's Island and Its Inhabitants with an Authentic Account of the Mutiny of the Ship Bounty,* Washington IRVING's "ASTORIA," and John Lloyd STEPHENS's *Travels in Arabia Petraea* (*see* "REVIEW OF ARABIA PETRAEA"). Silverman states critics have observed that "the main and central part of the story is largely a compilation of mutinies, murders, and the sufferings of shipwrecked mariners taken sometimes almost *verbatim* from the literary sources mentioned."

Critical reception of the book was unfavorable. Writing in *BURTON'S GENTLEMAN'S MAGAZINE,* the editor William E. BURTON was sarcastic in assessing the travel tale. He expressed indignation with the work, stating that "a more impudent attempt at humbugging the public has never been exercised." In a letter written on June 1, 1840, responding to Burton's assertion that Poe owed him $100, Poe alluded to the review:

> You once wrote in your magazine a sharp critique upon a book of mine—a very silly book—Pym. Had I written a similar criticism upon a book of yours, you feel that you would have been my enemy for life, and you therefore imagine a latent hostility towards yourself. . . . Your criticism was essentially correct, and therefore, although severe, it did not occasion in me one solitary emotion either of anger or dislike.

Poe was not as amiable toward criticism published by Lewis Gaylord CLARK, editor of the *KNICKERBOCKER MAGAZINE,* who used his column "Editors' Table" to print a particularly virulent attack on *The Narrative of Arthur Gordon Pym.* He chastised Poe for the "loose and slipshod style, seldom chequered by any of the more common graces of composition." Moreover, Clark asserted that the novel "is too liberally stuffed with 'horrid circumstance of blood and battle.'"

The realistic nature of the title and the narrative fooled many readers into believing that the work actually is a first-person account of adventures at sea. Even the publisher George Putnam believed the book to be a true account, and he noted, in a later reminiscence that appeared in the October 1869 issue of *Putnam's Magazine,* that "whole columns of these new 'discoveries,' including the hieroglyphics (!) found on the rocks, were copied by many of the English country papers as sober historical truth."

PUBLISHING AND DRAMATIZATION HISTORY

Poe began to write the novel after the publisher Harper & Brothers rejected the short story collection *TALES OF THE FOLIO CLUB* in 1836. In a letter dated March 3, 1836, that accompanied news of the rejection, the New York City author James K. Paulding suggested, "I think it would be worth your while, if other engagements permit, to undertake a Tale in a couple of volumes, for that is the magical number." Poe took the suggestion and wrote *The Narrative of Arthur Gordon Pym,* which appeared as a serial in the *SOUTHERN LITERARY MESSENGER* in 1836 and 1837.

After the successful serialization of the novel, Harper & Brothers published the novel in book form in July 1838. The publisher described the novel as follows:

> *The Narrative of Arthur Gordon Pym;* Comprising the Details of a Mutiny and Atrocious Butchery on Board the American Brig *Grampus,* on Her Way to the South Seas, in the Month of June, 1827. With an Account of the Recapture of the Vessel by the Survivors; Their Shipwreck and Subsequent Horrible Sufferings from Famine; Their Deliverance by Means of the British Schooner *Jane Guy;* the Brief Cruise of this Latter Vessel in the Antarctic Ocean; Her Capture, and the Massacre of Her Crew Among a Group of Islands in the Eighty-Fourth Parallel of Southern Latitude; Together with the Incredible Adventures and Discoveries Still Farther South to Which That Distressing Calamity Gave Rise. 12 mo., pp. 198. New York: Harper and Brothers, 1838.

Poe did not place his name on the title page of the novel. Instead he provided a preface signed by "A. G. Pym." According to "Pym,"

THE NARRATIVE

OF

ARTHUR GORDON PYM.

OF NANTUCKET.

COMPRISING THE DETAILS OF A MUTINY AND ATROCIOUS BUTCHERY
ON BOARD THE AMERICAN BRIG GRAMPUS, ON HER WAY TO
THE SOUTH SEAS, IN THE MONTH OF JUNE, 1827.

WITH AN ACCOUNT OF THE RECAPTURE OF THE VESSEL BY THE
SURVIVERS; THEIR SHIPWRECK AND SUBSEQUENT HORRIBLE
SUFFERINGS FROM FAMINE; THEIR DELIVERANCE BY
MEANS OF THE BRITISH SCHOONER JANE GUY; THE
BRIEF CRUISE OF THIS LATTER VESSEL IN THE
ANTARCTIC OCEAN; HER CAPTURE, AND THE
MASSACRE OF HER CREW AMONG A
GROUP OF ISLANDS IN THE

EIGHTY-FOURTH PARALLEL OF SOUTHERN LATITUDE;

TOGETHER WITH THE INCREDIBLE ADVENTURES AND
DISCOVERIES

STILL FARTHER SOUTH

TO WHICH THAT DISTRESSING CALAMITY GAVE RISE.

NEW-YORK:

HARPER & BROTHERS, 82 CLIFF-ST.

1838.

THE NARRATIVE

OF

ARTHUR GORDON PYM

OF NANTUCKET, NORTH AMERICA:

COMPRISING THE DETAILS OF A MUTINY, FAMINE,
AND SHIPWRECK,
DURING A VOYAGE TO THE SOUTH SEAS;

RESULTING IN VARIOUS

EXTRAORDINARY ADVENTURES

AND

DISCOVERIES

IN THE

EIGHTY-FOURTH PARALLEL OF SOUTHERN LATITUDE.

LONDON:

WILEY AND PUTNAM, 67, PATERNOSTER ROW;
WHITTAKER AND CO.; AND CHARLES TILT.

[ENTERED AT STATIONERS' HALL.]

1838.

Title pages for the American and the English editions of The Narrative of Arthur Gordon Pym. (Robert Gregor)

accident threw me into the society of several gentle-men in Richmond, Va., who felt deep interest in all matters relating to the regions I had visited, and who were constantly urging it upon me, as a duty, to give my narrative to the public. . . . Among those gentlemen in Virginia who expressed the greatest interest in my statement, more particularly in regard to that portion of it which related to the Antarctic Ocean, was Mr. Poe.

The preface also states that Poe merely wrote a narra-tive of the opening of the earlier portion of Pym's adventures, from facts Pym provided, and published the accounts "in The Southern Literary Messenger *under the garb of fiction* . . . and, in order that it might certainly be regarded as fiction, the name of Mr. Poe was affixed to the articles in the table of contents of the magazine." To complete the effort at convincing read-

ers that the account is real, "Pym" asserts that those noting the differences in writing style between Poe's early pages and his own will see clearly "where his por-tion ends and my own commences; the difference in point of style will be readily perceived."

The novel has not been filmed to date.

CHARACTERS

William ALLEN, Augustus BARNARD, Captain BARNARD, BENNET, Captain E. T. V. BLOCK, Jim BONNER, Captain John BRISCOE, Jim CARSON, Captain COLQUHON, EDMUNDS, the Messieurs ENDERBY, Lieutenant FURNEAUX, Corporal GLASS, GREELY, Captain GUY, Alfred HARRIS, HENDERSON, Absalom HICKS, Captain KREUTZENSTERN, Captain LISIAUSKY, Captain Benjamin MORRELL, Nu-Nu, Captain Manuel de Oyarvido, Captain PATTEN, Mr. PAT-

TERSON, Dr. James G. PERCIVAL, Captain Perkins, Dirk PETERS, Mr. PETERSON, Hartman ROGERS, Mr. E. RONALD, Mr. ROSS, Robert and Emmet Ross, SEYMOUR, Mr. Theodore SINIVATE, TIGER, Peter VREDENBURGH, WAMPOOS, Captain James WEDDELL.

PLOT SYNOPSIS

The tale relates five voyages undertaken by Arthur Gordon Pym, who introduces himself to readers in a manner that resembles the realistic beginnings of such novels as Daniel Defoe's *The Fortunes and Misfortunes of the Famous Moll Flanders,* Laurence Sterne's *The Life and Opinions of Tristram Shandy,* and Jonathan Swift's *Gulliver's Travels,* whose authors all sought to convey a sense of verisimilitude by setting their characters into a specific social class and providing biographical details: "My name is Arthur Gordon Pym. My father was a respectable trader in sea-stores at Nantucket, where I was born. My maternal grandfather was an attorney in good practice. . . . He was more attached to myself, I believe, than to any other person in the world, and I expected to inherit the most of his property at his death."

Pym's journey begins in Nantucket when he and a friend named Augustus Barnard drink too much liquor and impulsively sail away in Pym's sloop. The pair soon must be rescued when a whaler crushes the boat. In their second voyage, Pym is a stowaway aboard the *Grampus,* of which Barnard's father is the captain. The crew soon mutinies and, after tremendous fighting, only four remain: Pym, Augustus Barnard, Dirk Peters, and a crew member named Parker. They must resort to cannibalism to survive. Parker is sacrificed, and Augustus soon dies of a gangrenous infection in his leg. Pym and Peters survive to enjoy a few more adventures before falling into a cataract, or waterfall, at the South Pole and leaving the tale unfinished, a condition that Poe attempts to explain with a "Note" at the end of the novel. According to the note, "the circumstances connected with the late sudden and distressing death of Mr. Pym are already known to the public through the medium of the daily press," and the last three or four chapters "have been irrecoverably lost through the accident by which he perished himself." This conflicts with "Pym's" statements in the preface that suggest he survived the experience and returned to the United States "after the extraordinary series of adventure in the South Seas and elsewhere."

"National Melodies of America. By George P. Morris, Esq." Review by Poe that appeared in the December 1839 issue of *BURTON'S GENTLEMAN'S MAGAZINE* under the title "George P. Morris." The article was revised and given this title for its publication in April 1840 in the *SOUTHERN LITERARY MESSENGER.* The review devotes a considerable number of words to explaining Poe's theory of songwriting: "There are few cases in which mere popularity should be considered a proper test of merit; but the case of song-writing is, I think, one of the few." Poe defines songwriting in terms of poetry: "I mean, of course, the composition of brief poems with an eye to their adaptation for music in the vulgar sense." He designates Morris, "very decidedly, our best writer of songs—and, in saying this, I mean to assign him a high rank as *poet.*" He calls several of Morris's works, including "Woodman, Spare that Tree" and "By the Lake Droops the Willow," compositions "of which any poet, living or dead, might justly be proud. By these, if by nothing else, Morris is *immortal.*" The review closes with one of Morris's poems.

Neal, John Clay (1793–1896) American poet, critic, and novelist who wrote under the pen name of Jehu O'Cataract. He first became familiar with Poe through the intervention of Poe's cousin George Poe, who had known Neal when he lived and worked in Baltimore as an editor. By 1829, when Poe was showing *AL AARAAF, TAMERLANE, AND MINOR POEMS* to editors in the hope that it might be published, Neal had already left Baltimore and settled in Portland, Maine, where he started a paper that evolved into the *Yankee and Boston Literary Gazette.* George Poe wrote to his old friend and told him that he had directed Poe to send some poetry to Neal for his expert commentary, and he expressed complete confidence that Neal would honor their old friendship. The editor did more, and the young Poe was pleasantly surprised by the following notice in Neal's literary column in the September 1829 issue of the *Yankee and Boston Literary Gazette:* "If E. A. P. of Baltimore—whose lines about 'Heaven', though he professes to regard them as altogether superior to anything in the whole range of American poetry, save two or three trifles referred to, are, though nonsense, rather exquisite nonsense—would but do himself justice might [*sic*] make a beautiful and perhaps a magnificent poem. There is a good deal here to justify such a hope." Poe recalled this review as "[t]he very first words of Encouragement I ever remember to have heard." Neal also allowed Poe to print a letter covering four pages in the December 1829 issue of *Yankee,* which contained lengthy excerpts from the forthcoming work. The printed praise of a distinguished critic also opened doors to publishers for Poe, whose work was accepted in November 1829 by the Baltimore publisher Hatch & Dunning. Poe appeared to believe that, having once come to his aid, Neal should continue to do so, as he suggests in a letter date June 4, 1840, written to ask for assistance in launching a new magazine in Philadelphia:

MY DEAR SIR: As you gave me the first jog in my literary career, you are in measure bound to protect me and keep me rolling. I therefore now ask you to aid me with your influence in whatever manner your experience shall suggest.

It strikes me that I never write you except to ask a favor. But my friend Thomas will assure you that I bear you always in mind, holding you in the highest respect and esteem.

Most truly yours,
EDGAR A. POE

In an "AUTOGRAPHY" entry, Poe described Neal's signature as "exceedingly illegible, and very careless. . . . One might support Mr. Neal's mind (from his penmanship) to be bold, excessively active, energetic, and irregular."

Neptune Huge dog in THE JOURNAL OF JULIUS RODMAN. He belongs to Andrew THORNTON and seems to listen "with profound attention to every word that was said." He has been trained to react to various points in the anecdotes. When Thornton would say, "'Nep can swear to the truth of that—can't you, Nep?'" the dog "would roll his eyes up immediately, loll out his monstrous tongue, and wag his great head up and down, as much as to say—'Oh, it's every bit as true as the Bible.'"

Nesace Character in Poe's poem "AL AARAAF." She symbolizes ideal beauty and lives in perfect happiness on the star Al Aaraaf. As God's favorite, with a superior intelligence and the ruling presence on the star, she alone in the universe can hear God's voice directly. In part one, she begs him to restore the lower beings on Al Aaraaf to their former high spiritual plane. In part two, she calls together all of her subjects and instructs those assembled to devote their time to the contemplation of beauty and purify their natures so that their corporeal state will be transformed into pure idea.

"Never Bet the Devil Your Head: A Tale With a Moral" Short story. This satire was Poe's literary response to the charge by critics writing in the Transcendentalist magazine the *Dial* that his fiction lacked moral content. He takes the inclusion of a moral in the story to a ridiculous extreme by making every incident he relates a cause for the expression of yet another moral principle. (*See* TRANSCENDENTALISM.)

PUBLISHING AND DRAMATIZATION HISTORY

The story was first published in the September 1841 issue of GRAHAM'S MAGAZINE under the title "Never Bet Your Head: A Moral Tale." Poe revised the title to the present one when the story was revised for publication in the August 16, 1845, issue of the BROADWAY JOURNAL.

Despite assertions of his contemporaries that Poe's satire is aimed at literary pedanticism, transcendentalism, and the *Dial*, Poe denied having any specific targets. Instead, he wrote, "The tale in question is a mere Extravaganza levelled at no one in particular, but hitting right and left at things in general."

The tale opens with a quotation from *Cuentos en verso castellano*, written in 1828 by Tomas Hermenegildo de las Torres: "'As long as the habits of an author are pure and chaste, it matters very little if his works are less austere.'"

The story has been dramatized as "Toby Dammit" as one sequence in the 1968 film *Tales of Mystery and Imagination*, directed by Federico Fellini.

CHARACTERS

Mrs. Dammit, Toby DAMMIT, unnamed narrator.

PLOT SUMMARY

Poe opens the tale with his narrator's rebuttal to "certain ignoramuses" who have charged him with having never written a moral tale, "or, in more precise words, a tale with a moral," and promises that the current effort will precisely fill that void. By the time readers complete reading the tale, they realize that Poe has used his comic sketch to skewer TRANSCENDENTALISM. The tale is that of Toby Dammit, "a sad dog, it is true," who is overrun by vices for which he is not to blame: "They grew out of a personal defect in his mother." Toby's villainous behavior at the age of five months leads his mother to flog him, but her left-handedness detracts strongly from the benefits that might otherwise result from a flogging. As the narrator explains, "The world revolves from right to left. It will not do to whip a baby from left to right. If each blow in the proper direction [from right to left] drives an evil propensity out, it follows that every thump in an opposite one knocks its quota of wickedness in." Thus, Toby is doomed to a life of unalterable wickedness, and as an adult his chief wickedness is gambling. At the slightest provocation, "he could scarcely utter a sentence without interlarding it with a proposition to gamble." At first, Dammit wagers a dollar or states "I'll bet you what you please," until he reaches a point at which "he abandoned all other forms of wager, and gave himself up to *'I'll bet the Devil my head'*."

As the narrator walks across a bridge with Dammit, they find their path blocked by a turnstile. The narrator walks through the stile. Dammit, however, insists on leaping over it and bets the narrator that he can do so, uttering the phrase, "I'll bet the Devil my head." As Dammit utters this fateful phrase, the two hear the sound of "Ahem" and turn to see a very old, lame man wearing a full suit of black. The stranger assures Dammit that he will probably be able to clear the turnstile, but that they must have a trial to prove Dammit's ability. Dammit seems to be at a loss for words. The narrator muses that this is a remarkable situation, and wonders if it is the result of his last lecture, due to which "he [Dammit] is cured of the transcendentals." Within moments, the narrator watches as Dammit takes a leap, runs forward, and springs up from the floor of the bridge, then lands on the same side of the turnstile that he started. The old stranger reaches to the floor and quickly grabs something that he wraps in his coat before he rapidly limps away. The narrator discovers that Dammit struck a sharp iron bar five feet above the turnstile and was beheaded, but the head is nowhere to be found. The narrator assumes the costs for Dammit's funeral, then "sent in my very moderate bill to the transcendentalists [but] The scoundrels refused to pay it, so I had Mr. Dammit dug up at once and sold him for dog meat."

"The New Comedy. By Mrs. Mowatt" Review by Poe that appeared in the March 29, 1845, issue of the *BROADWAY JOURNAL.* Poe begins the review with a detailed plot summary of the play *Fashion,* then attacks the author's lack of originality in using hackneyed characters and situations, writing that "not even the author of a plot such as this, would be disposed to claim for it anything on the score of originality or invention." Claiming that "our fault-finding is on the score of deficiency in verisimilitude—in natural art—that is to say, in art based in the natural laws of man's heart and understanding," Poe identifies the numerous absurdities that occur on stage, "the crossings and recrossings of the dramatis personae" and the unnatural dialogue spoken by the unreal characters that result in "a total deficiency in verisimilitude." The review finds that "the colloquy in Mrs. Mowatt's comedy is spirited, generally terse, and well seasoned at points" and compliments her thorough knowledge of "ordinary stage effects," as it makes clear that the condemnation is not for "Mrs. Mowatt's comedy in particular, but the modern drama in general."

"A New and Compendious Latin Grammar; With Appropriate Exercises, Analytical and Synthetical. For the Use of Primary Schools, Academies, and Colleges. By Baynard R. Hall, A. M., Principal of the Bedford Classical and Mathematical Academy, and Formerly Professor of the Ancient Languages of the College of Indiana. Philadelphia: Harrison Hall" Review by Poe that appeared in the October 1836 issue of the *SOUTHERN LITERARY MESSENGER.* This brief notice appears after "the excellences of this grammar have been so well proved, and the work itself so heartily recommended by some of the first scholars in our country," and the reviewer feels "called upon to say but little in its behalf." Listing methodically the advantages of this grammar, Poe expresses only praise for the work and concludes by writing "were we a teacher, we would prefer its use to that of any other Latin Grammar whatever."

"A New and Comprehensive Gazeteer of Virginia, and the District of Columbia: Containing a Copious Collection of Geographical, Statistical, Political, Commercial Religious, Moral and Miscellaneous Information, Collected and Compiled From the Most Respectable, and Chiefly From Original Sources; by Joseph Martin. To Which Is Added a History of Virginia, From Its First Settlement to the Year 1754: With an Abstract of the Principal Events From That Period to the Independence of Virginia, Written Expressly for the Work, by a Citizen of Virginia. Charlottesville: Published by Joseph Martin. 1835" Review by Poe that appeared in the February 1836 issue of the *SOUTHERN LITERARY MESSENGER.* Poe strongly praises the efforts of the author who "disavows all pretension to literary attainment, and claims only the merit of enterprise and perseverance in the execution of his design." In addition to providing an overview of the information contained within the book, Poe takes the opportunity to chastise the "public indifference" of Virginians and "too little of that public spirit which has animated other communities" that made Martin's task "in amassing a large amount of valuable information" harder. The review states that the study is invaluable to "the man of business and to the traveller, and indeed to the general reader," and suggests that "public liberality" be used to sustain the author in producing future editions of the work.

"A New Dictionary of the English Language: By Charles Richardson. London: William Pickering—New York: William Jackson" Review by Poe that appeared in the August 1836 issue of the *SOUTHERN LITERARY MESSENGER.* The review traces briefly the development of the dictionary, beginning with Dr. Samuel JOHNSON's first effort in 1747, and examines the implications that Johnson's approach holds for the effort under present discussion. Poe suggests that Johnson would have achieved even greater success had he followed his original intention, stated in a 1747 letter to Lord Chesterfield, which "communicated a *plan* of his undertaking" to give first "the natural and primitive meaning of words; secondly, the consequential—and thirdly the metaphorical, arranging the quotations chronologically." Johnson's dictionary was published in 1755, "*without the plan,* and strange to say, in utter disregard of the principles avowed in the letter to the Earl of Chesterfield." In Poe's view, however, the principles "were well-conceived, and that it followed out, they would have rendered important service to English lexicography," and Poe declares that "the necessity for something of the kind which was felt then, is more strongly felt now." The review concludes by "heartily recommending" the new dictionary, noting the improvement Richardson has made in using the principles of Johnson and adding the system of Horne Tooke, "the greatest of philosophical grammarians."

Newman, Cardinal John Henry (1801–1890) Church of England clergyman and leader of the Oxford Movement, a revival of certain sacraments, rituals, and doctrines in the Anglican Church had been abandoned after the Reformation. He converted to Roman Catholicism in 1845. During a tour of the Mediterranean region in 1833, he wrote the famous hymn "Lead, Kindly Light," which contains the following couplet that imitates, either consciously or unconsciously, lines in Poe's "TAMERLANE," published in 1829: "Pride ruled my will / remember not past days." Poe's original lines in stanza nine are: "The soul, which knows such power, will still / Find Pride the ruler of its will—" Critics have observed that "Lead, Kindly Light" also "gives the fundamental note of 'Tamerlane'."

"A New Theoretical and Practical Treatise on Navigation" *See* "MAURY'S NAVIGATION."

New York Mail and Express Newspaper that revealed the pathetic circumstances of Poe and his wife, Virginia, after Mrs. Mary Elizabeth HEWITT took up a "subscription" for the couple among editors. Poe was embarrassed when the paper printed the following paragraph:

> We regret to learn that Edgar A. Poe and his wife are both dangerously ill with the consumption, and that the hand of misfortune lies heavy upon their temporal affairs. We are sorry to mention the fact that they are so far reduced as to be barely able to obtain the necessaries of life. This is indeed a hard lot, and we hope the friends and admirers of Mr. Poe will come promptly to his assistance in his bitterest hour of need.

New York Mirror *See* EVENING MIRROR.

New York Sun Daily newspaper published in New York City and the first "penny paper" in that city. The paper inaugurated a peculiarly American and sensational method of treating news, which was a feature of the new, native journalism. The paper was founded in 1833 with the aim of "supplying the public with the news of the day at so cheap a rate as to lie within the means of all." As Poe wrote in his profile of the *Sun*'s first editor, Richard LOCKE, "The consequences of the scheme, in their influence on the whole newspaper business of the country, and through this business on the interests of the country at large, are probably beyond all calculation." The *Sun* played a part in Poe's life early in its

founding. Three weeks after Poe's short story "THE UNPARALLELED ADVENTURE OF ONE HANS PFAALL" was published in the *SOUTHERN LITERARY MESSENGER,* the *Sun* ran a story entitled "Discoveries in the Moon," supposedly reprinted from the Edinburgh *Courant and Journal of Science.* Poe wrote to John Pendleton KENNEDY asking if he saw the similarity to Poe's tale and noting that "the general features of the two compositions are nearly identical." Poe selected the *Sun* to publish "THE BALLOON-HOAX," where it appeared on April 13, 1844, as a factual article. Proclaiming that it was the "sole paper which had the news," the paper created a rush for update editions that purported to follow the progress of the hot-air balloon *Victoria.*

New York Tribune New York City newspaper. Poe was informally connected to the paper through his association with Horace GREELEY, the editor and a columnist at the paper, who signed financial notes for Poe with expectation of repayment, and Margaret Fuller, the literary critic and an assistant editor of the paper from 1842 to 1845. The *Tribune* also published the damaging obituary of Poe written by Rufus Wilmot GRISWOLD and signed with his pseudonym "Ludwig." Printed in the October 9, 1849, issue, the piece destroyed Poe's reputation and remained the "official" view of the poet's life for nearly half a century.

Nicholls, Frederick (1871–1843) British composer of songs and piano pieces. In 1938, he published "Eldorado," a song inspired by Poe's poem "ELDORADO."

Nicolino Character in Poe's short story "THE OBLONG BOX." He is spoken of as "Nicolino, the Italian Jew" with whom the narrator's friend Cornelius WYATT has been bargaining about "something he wishes not to be put in the hold—something to be kept under his own eye." He is said to possess a copy of Leonardo da Vinci's painting *The Last Supper,* "done by Rubini the younger at Florence," and the narrator suspects that the painting is contained in the mysterious oblong box.

"Night and Morning: A Novel. By the Author of 'Pelham,' 'Rienzi,' 'Eugene Aram,' etc. Two Volumes. Republished by Harper & Brothers, New York" Review by Poe that appeared in the April 1841 issue of *GRAHAM'S MAGAZINE.* Poe begins this review of the novel by Edward BULWER-LYTTON with a summary of "the groundwork of the plot," then examines the meaning of plot and how it relates to the specific work. Poe asserts, "so careful has been our author in this working-up . . . that it is difficult to detect a blemish in any portion." Still, he does identify "a few defects," and discussion of these occupies more than a half of the review. Methodically working through the novel, Poe identifies errors in plot, characterization, and language: "His mere English is grossly defective—turgid, involved, and ungrammatical. There is scarcely a page of 'Night and Morning' upon which a schoolboy could not detect at least half a dozen instances of faulty construction." The review singles out "the predominant and most important failing" as Lytton's "absolute mania of metaphor—metaphor always running into allegory. . . . He is king-coxcomb of figures of speech. His rage for personification is really ludicrous." Poe concludes that he cannot agree with "that critical opinion which considers it the best novel of the author. It is only not his worst."

Nimrod   Figure mentioned in Poe's short story "BON-BON." In bargaining for the soul of Monsieur BON-BON, the devil says he has made "innumerable purchases of the kind" in his day, "and the parties never experienced any inconvenience. There were Cain and Nimrod, and Nero, and Caligula . . . and a thousand others." Nimrod is mentioned in Genesis as "A mighty hunter before the Lord" and the founder of Babylon.

Niobe   In Greek mythology, a descendant of the house of Thebes, wife to King Amphion, and the mother of six sons and six daughters. She commanded the people of Thebes to worship her instead of the goddess Leto. When the gods heard her commands, they punished her by directing Leto's children Apollo and Artemis to fire their arrows with deadly aim and to kill Niobe's children. The grief-stricken Niobe was turned to stone that remains ever wet with her tears. In Poe's short story "THE ASSIGNATION," the Marchesa Aphrodite di MENTONI wears only "a snowy-white and gauze-like drapery" as she watches the search for her child, who has fallen into the canal. So still is she that "no motion in the statue-like form itself, stirred even the folds of that raiment of very vapor which hung around it as the heavy marble hangs around the Niobe."

"Noble Deeds of Woman. 2 vols. Philadelphia: Carey, Lea, & Blanchard"   Review by Poe that appeared in the February 1836 issue of the SOUTHERN LITERARY MES-SENGER. Poe wrote that he presumed from the date and place found in the preface that the work originally was published in London, but he could not find the names of the author or original publisher. He thus assumed that the work was "merely a reprint. . . . But, be the 'Noble Deeds of Woman' English or American, we recommend them heartily to public attention." Poe identifies the chapter topics listed in the table of contents, but does not elaborate, and describes the structure of the work, which consists of numerous anecdotes related to household activities traditional for a woman

of the time, grouped under the chapter headings. The review ends with the reprint of two paragraphs from the work as illustration of its merit.

"Norman Leslie: A Tale of the Present Times. New York: Published by Harper & Brothers"   Review by Poe that appeared in the December 1835 issue of the SOUTHERN LITERARY MESSENGER. In the opening lines of the review, Poe mocks the fanfare that had preceded this novel, which was repeatedly described in the NEW YORK MIRROR as "'in press,' 'in progress,' 'forthcoming,' and written by or 'attributed to' Mr. Blank, and 'said to be from the pen' of Mr. Asterisk." Rather than continue the charade of the author's anonymity, Poe immediately identifies him as Theodore S. Fay, an editor at the *Mirror*, whose preface to the work claims that the material in the novel is founded on fact. Poe mockingly quotes phrases from the preface, and writes that "we, at least, are neither solemn nor sapient, and therefore, do not feel ourselves bound to show him a shadow of mercy." The review then provides a lengthy and detailed summary of the convoluted plot of the work that Poe declares to be "the most inestimable piece of balderdash with which the common sense of the good people of America was ever so openly or so villainously insulted." After pointing out specific flaws in the novel, complete with page numbers and representative phrases, Poe concludes that the novel is filled with absurdities and that not even a schoolboy "would fail to detect at least two or three gross errors in Grammar, and some two or three egregious sins against common-sense."

"Notices of the War of 1812. By John Armstrong. New York: George Dearborn"   Review by Poe that appeared in the June 1836 issue of the SOUTHERN LITER-ARY MESSENGER. The review praises the "Notices," written by the former United States Secretary of War, as "a valuable addition to our history, and to our historical literature, with especial attention to the Appendix, which will prove of great service to the future historian." Despite his approval of the range of topics covered by the "Notices," Poe indicates that he is "grieved, however, to see a piquancy and freedom of expression, in regard to the unhappy sources of animosity between America and the parent land, which can neither to-day nor hereafter answer any possible good end, and may prove an individual grain in a future mountain of mischief."

"Nuts to Crack: or Quips, Quirks, Anecdote and Facete of Oxford and Cambridge Scholars. By the Author of Facetiae Cantabrigienses, Etc., Etc., Etc. Philadelphia: E. L. Carey & A. Hart"   Review by Poe that appeared in the December 1835 issue of the SOUTHERN LITERARY

MESSENGER. The collection of quizzes, oddities, and eccentricities was not intended for an American audience, but Poe declared, "never was there a better thing for whiling away a few loose or unappropriate half hours." Although his comments on the collection generally are favorable, Poe points out inaccuracies in the attributions and a few blunders that are to him shocking "in a volume professing to be *Anecdote and Facete* (oh!—too bad) of Oxford and Cambridge *scholars.*" Poe ends the review by sharing a selection from the work with readers.

"The Oblong Box" Short story. This tale uses Poe's experience while stationed in Charleston, South Carolina, to provide a portion of the setting, especially in regard to life along the docks and the departure of the sailing packets from the Charleston Harbor.

PUBLISHING AND DRAMATIZATION HISTORY

The story was first published in the September 1844 issue of GODEY'S MAGAZINE AND LADY'S BOOK.

The 1969 British-American film *The Oblong Box*, directed by Gordon Hessler and starring Vincent PRICE and Christopher Lee, has only the title in common with Poe's story. The plot deals with a witch doctor who uses a special potion to make individuals appear dead.

CHARACTERS

Mrs. Adelaide CURTIS, Captain HARDY, NICOLINO, unnamed narrator, Cornelius WYATT, Marian WYATT.

PLOT SYNOPSIS

The story opens as the unnamed narrator begins a sea journey from Charleston to New York City aboard the packet ship *Independence*. He learns that his college acquaintance, the artist Cornelius Wyatt, is aboard the ship with his sisters and his wife, renowned for her beauty. As the narrator renews their acquaintance, he learns that Wyatt has also brought aboard the ship an oblong box, six feet long and two-and-half feet wide, that he keeps in his stateroom; the narrator believes that it contains a valuable copy of Leonardo da Vinci's painting *The Last Supper*. The narrator is surprised to find that the artist's wife is physically unattractive, despite what he had heard earlier, yet Wyatt claims to have married "for love, and for love only; and his bride was far more than worthy of his love." Each night, she sneaks out of the conjugal stateroom and stays in the extra stateroom until sunrise, when she then returns to Wyatt's room. While she is gone, the narrator hears in Wyatt's stateroom sounds of the box being pried open and what seems to be sobbing. When the *Independence* is hit by a hurricane and is about to sink, the captain and passengers manage to reach a lifeboat, but Wyatt refuses to leave without the box. The captain refuses to take the box aboard, so Wyatt uses a rope to lash himself securely to the box and sinks with it into the stormy waters. Months after they are rescued, the narrator meets Captain Hardy while in New York City and learns that the box actually had contained the body of Wyatt's late wife. Because the passengers and crew would not have sailed on a ship that contained a dead body, his wife's maid had pretended to be her mistress by day and retreated to her own stateroom each night.

O'Bumper, Bibulus Character in Poe's short story "LIONIZING. A TALE." A guest at the literary dinner given by the Prince of Wales, he is an expert on wines and seems conversant on all of the famous wine regions.

Odenheimer Character in Poe's short story "THE MURDERS IN THE RUE MORGUE." He is a restaurateur who volunteers his testimony regarding what he heard on the night that Madame and Mademoiselle L'ESPANAYE were murdered. A native of Amsterdam, he does not speak French, so he must be questioned through an interpreter. In his testimony, Odenheimer states that he was passing the house where the murders occurred and heard the shrill voice of a man—"of a Frenchman"—but he could not distinguish the words. He claims, however, that "the gruff voice said repeatedly '*sacré*,' '*diable*' and once '*mon Dieu*'."

O'Grandison, Sir Pathrick Character and narrator of Poe's short story "WHY THE LITTLE FRENCHMAN WEARS HIS HAND IN A SLING." He vies with Mounseer MAITER-DI-DAUNS, the Count A. Goose, Look-aisy, for the attentions of the "widdy . . . the purty Mistress TRACLE." Possessed of a thick Irish brogue, O'Grandison trades witty insults with "the little ould furrener Frinchman as lived over the way" as they alternately squeeze what they believe to be her arm and receive a squeeze in return. After she leaves them, they realize that they have been squeezing each other's arm, and O'Grandison then gives Maiter-di-dauns's arm "a nate little broth of a squaze," injuring it so the Frenchman must wear his left hand in a sling.

Oinos Character in Poe's short story "THE POWER OF WORDS." He is "a spirit new-fledged with immortality" who recently arrived from earth. He turns to AGATHOS and asks to be instructed in "the modes or the methods of what, during mortality, we were accustomed to call Creation." Agathos teaches him "the *physical power of words*." Oinos also appears in "SHADOW—A PARABLE."

"Old Curiosity Shop" *See* "MASTER HUMPHREY'S CLOCK."

Oldeb, Mr. Character in "THE TALE OF THE RAGGED MOUNTAINS." He is a British army officer who is shot with a poisoned arrow and dies during an insurrection of Cheyte Sing in the Indian city of Benares in 1780. Fifty years later, Augustus BEDLO, who looks exactly like a miniature portrait of Oldeb, tells a physician who knew Oldeb that he has had visions from the insurrection. A week later, Bedloe dies and the newspaper obituary leaves off the final "e" of his name, making it the exact opposite spelling of Oldeb.

"The Old World and the New; Or, a Journal of Reflections and Observations Made on a Tour in Europe. By the Reverend Orville Dewey. New York: Harper & Brothers" Review by Poe that appeared in the August 1836 issue of the SOUTHERN LITERARY MESSENGER. The review begins by contradicting the author's contention that the book is not an itinerary, for its methodical procedure "in which unconnected remarks follow one upon another—object upon object—day upon day—and all with a scrupulous accuracy in regard to dates" disproves the author's assertion. The reviewer declares "we cannot understand Mr. Dewey in declaring his book not to be what it most certainly is, if it is any thing at all." Despite his approval of the book as an itinerary, Poe does not recommend the book "*as a whole*," because it contains "very little, we think, of either novelty or morality," although he heartily approves of "its amusing *naiveté* of manner—a feature that will arrest the attention of every reader."

Ollapod, Dr. Character mentioned in "A PREDICAMENT." The ticking of a huge clock puts the narrator "in mind of the grateful sermonic harangues of Dr. Ollapod." The name appears to derive from a character in the farce *The Poor Gentleman*, written by George Colman (1762–1836). In the play, he looks for wit in the conversations of others and tries himself to speak in a witty manner.

Oquawka Spectator Weekly newspaper published in Oquawka, Illinois. James B. Patterson, the founder of the paper, was originally from Winchester, Virginia. When he died, he passed the paper on to his son Edward PATTERSON, who admired Poe and offered to back the STYLUS if a western edition could emanate from St. Louis, Missouri.

"Oration on the Life and Character of the Rev. Joseph Caldwell, D.D. Late President of the University of North Carolina, by Walter Andersen, A. M." Review by Poe appearing in the December 1835 issue of the SOUTHERN LITERARY MESSENGER. Admittedly a "hasty and imperfect notice" of the pamphlet containing the oration, the review, nonetheless, praises the exemplary life of Caldwell and the capability of Andersen in rendering that life, as well as the "especial beauty, we think, in the way in which he treats of his religious principles." The review contains two extracts from the pamphlet as proof of Andersen's "fine powers as a biographical writer" and expresses "the very great pleasure its perusal afforded us."

"Orion: An Epic Poem in Three Books. By R. H. Horne. Fourth Edition. Published by J. Miller: London" Review by Poe that appeared in the March 1844 issue of GRAHAM'S MAGAZINE. The lengthy review begins with high praise for the author and the reviewer's admission of having been "among the most earnest admirers of his high genius;—for a man of high, of the highest genius, he unquestionably is." This is followed by a vehement condemnation of the "cant" of the time, "of the mere opinions of the donkeys who bray thus—of their mere dogmas and doctrines, literary, aesthetical, or what not" but who understand very little about the creative process. Poe then uses the review as a forum for discussing his own ideas about poetry, and he creates a detailed summary of the epic poem to provide examples for his theory. After conducting "a careful methodical analysis," the review concludes that "we have left unsaid a hundred things" and declares the poem "to be one of the noblest, if not the very noblest poetical work of the age."

O'Rourke, Thomas Character mentioned in Poe's note following "THE UNPARALLELED ADVENTURE OF ONE HANS PFAALL." He is the gamekeeper of an Irish peer in *The Flight of Thomas O'Rourke*, a novel with an unnamed author that has been translated from German. His "flight" takes place on the back of an eagle.

Osborn, Laughton (1809–1878) Amateur American novelist with whom Poe became acquainted in New York City and whom he profiles in "THE LITERATI OF NEW YORK CITY." Poe identifies a large number of works written by Osborn, who "has made a great many 'sensations' anonymously or with a *nom de plume*"; but Poe admits that he is not sure if Osborn has published anything with his own name. Poe methodically points out the weaknesses of Osborn's works. *The Battle of Niagara*, he finds, contains "an excessive *force* but little of refined art"; *The Confessions of a Poet* is "not precisely the work to be placed in the hands of a lady"; *The Visions of*

Rubeta is "very censurably indecent—*filthy* is, perhaps, the more appropriate word." He asserts that Osborn "has no doubt been misapprehended, and therefore wronged by the world; but he should not fail to remember that the source of the wrong lay in his own idiosyncrasy."

Osgood, Frances "Fanny" Sargent (1811–1850) Poet and friend whose relationship with Poe Virginia CLEMM encouraged. Fanny Osgood met Poe in March 1845 after she and her husband, Samuel Osgood, had separated, but Samuel would later paint Poe's portrait. Fanny Osgood appears to have been the woman to whom Poe was most seriously attracted while married to Virginia Clemm, although all reports point to a passionate platonic friendship. Osgood wrote that she had to flee at various times to Albany, Boston, and Providence to avoid Poe's attentions. Osgood recorded in journal entries that Poe followed her each time and begged her to love him, requests that she refused to answer until Virginia Clemm added her pleas, stating that Osgood would save Poe from "infamy" if she were to show an interest in him. The two exchanged poetry, and Poe praised her work in a review of "A WREATH OF WILD FLOWERS FROM NEW ENGLAND" and in "THE LITERATI OF NEW YORK CITY." In his profile of Osgood, which appeared in the September 1846 issue of *GODEY'S MAGAZINE AND LADY'S BOOK,* Poe wrote that she had "been rapidly attaining distinction—and this, evidently, with no effort at attaining it." He chastised mildly Osgood's disregard for fame and wrote that "Mrs. Osgood has taken no care whatever of her literary fame." Their relationship came to an end in June 1846. While Poe was away, Mrs. Elizabeth Fries ELLET, a married mother of four and a would-be poet who had been writing Poe passionate letters, which he ignored, visited Maria CLEMM and found one of Osgood's letters lying open on the table. Ellet later visited Osgood and told her about the letter, suggesting that she would become the object of gossip. A fearful Osgood requested that Poe return all of her letters, which he did, and the friendship between them cooled. Seven months after Poe's death, and only shortly before her own, Osgood defended Poe's character in a letter to Rufus Wilmot GRISWOLD.

Only she would know to what extent Griswold's feelings for her influenced his vindictiveness, for his rivalry with Poe for Osgood's attention was known in their literary circle. Even as Osgood carried on her friendship with Poe, she sent Griswold a valentine in which her name was interwoven with that of Griswold. She often visited the ailing Virginia Clemm at the Fordham cottage, where she would also enjoy time with Poe, to whom she referred as the "Raven" when writing to friends. During that same winter of 1846, she also regularly attended the literary salon run by Elizabeth Oakes SMITH, where she was often joined by Griswold.

Frances Sargent Osgood, a poet and a confidante of Poe. (Edgar Allan Poe Society)

O'Trump, Mrs. Kathleen Character in the short story "THE MAN THAT WAS USED UP." She is a "lovely widow" who hosts a party attended by the narrator. She is encouraged by "some feminine interloper" to go on to tell a story totally irrelevant to the narrator's purposes: "Yes! Mrs. O'Trump, she went on, and I—I went off."

"Our Amateur Poets, No. I.—Flaccus" Review by Poe that appeared in the March 1843 issue of *GRAHAM'S MAGAZINE.* Poe identifies the poet as "merely a Mr.——— Ward, of Gotham, once a contributor to the New York 'American,' and to the New York 'Knickerbocker' Magazine." The review states that the first poet is not "altogether destitute of merit," yet Poe finds some of the entries to be affected and dull: "there is nothing very original in all this; the general idea is, perhaps, the most absolutely trite in poetical literature." In a review of the poems in the collection, Poe focuses special attention on the "Great Descender" and writes, "We are at a loss to know by what right, human or divine, twaddle of this character is intruded into a collection of what professes to be *Poetry.*" As Poe methodically examines each of the poems, he grudgingly doles out limited praise with more frequent negative criticism of the poet's technique. "To An Infant in Heaven" is "feeble as a whole" and terminates "lamely," while Ward's imagery "is, indeed, at rare intervals, good, it must be granted, on the other hand, that, in general, it is atrociously inappropriate, or low"; "of the ineffable *bad taste* we have instances without number." The review ends with Poe's question, "*Who calls Mr. Ward a poet? He is a second-rate, or a third-rate, or perhaps a ninety-ninth-rate poetaster.*"

"Our Amateur Poets, No. III. William Ellery Channing"   Review by Poe that appeared in the August 1843 issue of GRAHAM'S MAGAZINE. Channing's poetry is mentioned in a satiric context in the short story "HOW TO WRITE A BLACKWOOD ARTICLE."

The review disparages both the poet and his work. Poe begins by making clear to readers that Channing "is a, and by no means the, William Ellery Channing. He is only the son of the great essayist deceased. . . . It may be said in his favor that nobody ever heard of him. Like an honest woman, he has always succeeded in keeping himself from being made the subject of gossip." The review abounds with numerous other such clever insults. Poe writes that Channing's poems "are full of all kinds of mistakes, of which the most important is that of their having been printed at all." He asserts that the poems "are not precisely English—nor will we insult a great nation by calling them Kickapoo; perhaps they are Channingese." Comparing Channing unfavorably to Tennyson and Carlyle, Poe writes that the poet has been "inoculated with *virus* from Tennyson" and examines lines that exhibit his pretensions and the defects of his writing. At the close of the review, Poe suggests that Channing will ride to fame on his father's reputation and that people will buy his books not because of his skill, but because they believe it to be "the posthumous work of that truly illustrious author, the *sole* William Ellery Channing of whom anybody in the world ever heard."

"Our Contributors, No. VIII.—Fitz-Greene Halleck"   Review by Poe that appeared in the September 1843 issue of GRAHAM'S MAGAZINE. Poe opens the review by observing that despite being firmly established in the literary world, Fitz-Green HALLECK is unique among poets "of eminence" for having written so little. The review briefly sketches the poet's personal life and literary development, then quotes extensively what William Cullen BRYANT has said about his work. Focusing on Halleck's skills in versification, Poe asserts that the poet's rhythms are often defective, so that scanning his poems "is impossible." The review examines several of Halleck's best-known poems, including "Fanny," "Alnwick Castle," and "Wyoming," and finds each "disfigured with some of the merest burlesque." Although numerous lyrically rhythmic lines appear in these poems, they all have "rhythmical defects," as well as lines that "form an imperfect rhyme." The review concludes with Poe's assertion that the poet is "in the maturity of his powers" and the regret that Halleck "has nearly abandoned the Muses."

"Outis Paper"   *See* "A CONTINUATION OF THE VOLUMINOUS HISTORY OF THE LITTLE LONGFELLOW WAR—MR. POE'S FURTHER REPLY TO THE LETTER OF OUTIS."

"The Oval Portrait"   Short story. The tale appears to adapt ideas contained in *The Picture of Dorian Gray,* an 1891 novel written by Oscar Wilde, who had praised Poe's rhythmical expression in poetry in 1886.

PUBLISHING AND DRAMATIZATION HISTORY

The story was first published under the title "Life in Death" in the April 1842 issue of GRAHAM'S MAGAZINE. Poe retitled the story when he shortened and revised it for republication in the April 26, 1845, issue of the BROADWAY JOURNAL.

The original version of the story contained extensive passages in which the narrator prepared and smoked opium, as well as passages containing his reasoning for using the drug in the isolated mountain chateau to alleviate his feverish symptoms. Poe deleted those passages in revisions because he believed the emphasis upon the hallucinatory effects of the drug created a dreamlike effect in the story that dulled the horror.

No film has been made of the story, although elements of it appear in the French film *The Fall of the House of Usher* (1925), directed by Jean Epstein.

CHARACTERS

PEDRO, unnamed narrator.

PLOT SYNOPSIS

The story opens as the narrator enters a recently abandoned chateau that appears to be less of a home than a monument to art. The walls are hung with tapestry and armorial trophies, "together with an unusually great number of very spirited modern paintings in frames of rich golden arabesque." Of particular interest is an oval portrait of a beautiful young woman, actually "a young girl just ripening into womanhood," a painting that appears to pulse with life.

Obsessed by the image, the narrator eagerly seeks the volume that contains discussions of the paintings of the chateau and their histories. From Pedro, a manservant who lives there, he learns that the young woman is the wife of the man who painted the portrait and that the artist has endowed this painting with his young wife's life. The painting drew so much from its living model that she died as the portrait was completed and the artist placed the final color in her cheeks. In essence, the artist transferred the very life from his wife to the painting: so absorbed had he been in completing the painting that he ignored his wife and allowed her to wither away.

Oyarvido, Captain Manuel de   Character in *THE NARRATIVE OF ARTHUR GORDON PYM*. The commander of a ship named *Aurora*, owned by the Royal Phillippine [*sic*] Company, he is said to have discovered as early as 1790 the islands to which the *Guy* sails.

Pabodie, William J., Esq. (1815–1870) Author and intimate friend of Sarah Helen WHITMAN. He published two articles in the June 2 and June 11, 1852, issues of the NEW YORK TRIBUNE that defended Poe's reputation against the scurrilous allegations made by Rufus Wilmot GRISWOLD in THE "LUDWIG" ARTICLE. When in Providence, Rhode Island, in December 1848 to draw up a marriage contract with Whitman, Poe stayed at Pabodie's house, although Pabodie had once been Whitman's suitor and was said to still be very much in love with her. Pabodie also served as a witness when Poe signed a consent to the release of the property of Whitman on December 22, 1848.

"A Paean" *See* "LENORE."

Paixhan, General Henri J. (1783–1854) Designer of a gun for throwing explosive shells. His invention is mentioned by the narrator in Poe's short story "NEVER BET THE DEVIL YOUR HEAD," who says, "if I had shot Mr. D. through and through with a Paixhan bomb . . . he could hardly have been more discomfited than when I addressed him with these simple words."

"Palestine" Essay by Poe that appeared in the February 1836 issue of the SOUTHERN LITERARY MESSENGER. The writing provides a brief overview of the geography and the history of the area that Poe refers to as "The Holy Land." The essay identifies the tribes that have inhabited the region in various periods and explains the origins of divisions between the people of the region. The writer focuses particular attention on the Dead Sea, explaining the origin of the name and the relationship of the contemporary region to biblical descriptions. In addition to describing the topography, the essay also identifies the conquerors of the region.

Paradox, Sir Positive Character in Poe's short story "LIONIZING." He is a guest at the dinner given by the Prince of Wales, where he observes that "all fools were philosophers, and that all philosophers were fools."

"Paris and the Parisians in 1835. By Frances Trollope, Author of 'Domestic Manners of the Americans,' 'The Refugee in America,' &c. New York: Published by Harper & Brothers" Review by Poe that appeared in the May 1836 issue of the SOUTHERN LITERARY MESSENGER. Poe methodically describes the work, and he gives particular attention to the "eleven most admirable copperplate engravings" that provide "the most effectual method of imparting to our readers . . . a just conception of the work itself." Although Poe admires the writing, he gives little weight to the author's views: "[H]er mere political opinions are, we suppose, of very little consequence to any person other than Mrs. Trollope; and being especially sure that they are of no consequence to ourselves we shall have nothing further to do with them." Instead, he describes in detail each of the 11 engravings that appear in the volume, and, in conclusion, recommends the book "to all lovers of fine writing, and vivacious humor. It is impossible not to be highly amused with the book— and there is by no means any necessity for giving a second thought to the *political* philosophies of Madame Trollope."

Parish, F. Wilson (1869–1933) English choral conductor, composer, and organist. In 1918, he published "Eldorado," a part-song for choir of female voices with piano accompaniment, inspired by Poe's poem of the same name.

Parker, Richard Character in THE NARRATIVE OF ARTHUR GORDON PYM. He is one of the mate's party after the mutiny and later the only one left alive of the group that opposes PYM's group. Pym knocks him down with a pump handle at the beginning of the mutiny and, when he comes to, Parker begs for mercy. At first, Pym has him bound, but later releases Parker so that he can help work the pumps of the ship. When the only four survivors are cast out into the open sea, Parker turns to Pym and the others "with an expression of countenance which made [Pym] shudder" and proposes "that one of us should die to preserve the existence of the others." The irony is that Parker becomes the first victim of the cannibalism that he suggested.

Parmly Reference made in "THE MAN THAT WAS USED UP." While putting himself together and inserting his false teeth, Brevet Brigadier General John A. B. C. SMITH advises the narrator "for a *good* set of these you had better go to Parmly's at once; high prices, but excellent work." "Parmly" was the name of family of dentists in Philadelphia of Poe's time.

Parry, Sir William Edward (1790–1855) British explorer in the Arctic who made unsuccessful attempts to find the Northwest Passage and to reach the North Pole. Poe refers to him in THE JOURNAL OF JULIUS RODMAN, in writing of foods to take on the journey, "with which our readers have no doubt been familiarised in the journals of Parry, Ross, Back, and other northern voyagers."

"The Partisan: A Tale of the Revolution. By the Author of "The Yemassee," "Guy Rivers," &c. New York: Published by Harper & Brothers" Review of William Gilmore Simms's novel that appeared in the January 1836 issue of the SOUTHERN LITERARY MESSENGER. Poe begins the review by mocking the author's dedication "To Richard Yeadon, Jr. Esq. *Of South Carolina,*" which also contains a brief letter thanking Yeadon for "pleasant rambles in the field of literature." Poe's objection is that "it affects excessive terseness, excessive appropriateness, and excessive gentility," leading to the conclusion that the written dedication is Simms's substitute for "certain oral communication" of most individuals to their friends. Poe has little good to say of the novel itself, and notes that "there is very little plot or connexion in the book before us; and Mr. Simms has evidently aimed at neither." After relating the author's assurance that the historical facts in the novel are scrupulously accurate, Poe suggests that Simms's fact-driven design would have been "better carried into effect by a work of a character *purely* historical," because "the interweaving of fact with fiction is at all times hazardous." To exhibit the point, Poe summarizes the novel in detail and praises the representations of historical characters, but finds that the fictitious characters will not bear examination, and singles out for criticism one character who "deserves a separate paragraph of animadversion." Quoting extensively from the novel to support his position, Poe declares "Mr. Porgy" to be "an insufferable bore" who never opens his mouth "without making us feel miserable all over." Poe also finds offensive the novelist's "villainously bad taste" in providing minute details of two murders committed by "a maniac"; one of the murders described is "in a manner too shockingly horrible to mention" in the review. He also objects to Simms's detailed description of a flogging, with the attendant "screeches of the wretch" and his mother's cries of anguish, and the torture death of a terrapin by Mr. Porgy, "more particularly in the writhings and spasms of the head, which he assures us with a smile *'will gasp and jerk long after we have done eating the body.'*" Poe praises Simms for well-drawn concluding scenes and "exquisite" descriptions of swamp scenery, crediting the author for having "the eye of a painter." His final words, however, make his view of Simms's skills clear: "Perhaps, in sober truth, he would succeed better in sketching a landscape than he has done in writing a novel."

"Passaic, A Group of Poems Touching That River: With Other Musings, by Flaccus" *See* "OUR AMATEUR POETS, NO. I.—FLACCUS."

Patten, Captain Person referred to in THE NARRATIVE OF ARTHUR GORDON PYM. Pym records that Patten, captain of the ship *Industry* out of Philadelphia, reached the island of Tristan d'Acunha in August 1790 and stayed until April 1791. According to his journal, Patten gathered 5,600 sealskins and said "he would have had no difficulty in loading a large ship with oil in three weeks." At the time of his arrival, Patten "found no quadrupeds, with the exception of a few wild goats," leaving Pym to surmise that the abundance of valuable domestic animals currently on the island must have been brought by later navigators.

Patterson, Edward Howard Norton (1828–?) The son of a newspaper man born originally in Winchester, Virginia, Patterson inherited "a tidy sum of money" and a weekly newspaper, the *Oquawka Spectator,* from his father. He had read and admired Poe's work in GRAHAM'S MAGAZINE, GODEY'S MAGAZINE AND LADY'S BOOK, and other publications. After reading announcements of Poe's plans for the STYLUS, Patterson contacted Poe and offered to back the venture. In a letter to Poe dated May 7, 1849, Patterson wrote, "Of this magazine you are to have the entire editorial control." Poe replied with a request of an advance for $50, money that went toward a trip to Richmond, not toward any effort to bring out the *Stylus.*

Patterson, Captain John (n.d.) Officer in the British army who married Catherine Livingston of Livingston Manor, New York. He became the first United States collector of the port of Philadelphia after the American Revolutionary War. He was the grandfather of Miss Louisa Gabriella PATTERSON, the second wife of John ALLAN.

Patterson, John William (n.d.) Son of Captain John PATTERSON and a lawyer in the state of New York. He was the father of Miss Louisa Gabriella PATTERSON, the second wife of John ALLAN.

Patterson, Miss Louisa Gabriella *See* ALLAN, Louisa Gabriella Patterson.

Patterson, Mr. Character in Poe's novel THE NARRATIVE OF ARTHUR GORDON PYM. He is the chief mate aboard the *Jane Guy,* and he takes the boats out to search for seal.

Patterson, Mrs. Louisa (n.d.) Mother of Louisa Gabriella Patterson ALLAN. She was the daughter of John DE HART, a member from New Jersey of the Continental Congress of 1774–76. Her father was also a man of considerable financial means and influence, as well as the attorney general of his state and a well-known attorney.

"Paul Ulric: Or the Adventures of an Enthusiast. New York: Published by Harper & Brothers" Review by Poe, published in the February 1836 issue of the SOUTHERN LITERARY MESSENGER. Poe states that the novel in two volumes written by Morris Mattson, Esq., of Philadelphia, "is too purely imbecile to merit an extended critique," but he does promise readers that he will "have no hesitation, and spare no pains, in exposing fully before the public eye its four hundred and forty-three pages of utter folly, bombast, and inanity." After quoting the first-person narrator's assertion that his life has been "one of continual excitement, and in my wild career I have tasted of joy as well as of sorrow," Poe comments within brackets: "Oh remarkable Mr. Ulric!" In response to the narrator's declaration "I am growing metaphysical," Poe writes, "We had thought he was only growing absurd." Poe lampoons Mattson's florid writing as well as his convoluted and confusing plot. He also mocks the hero's numerous love affairs and adventures and relates lengthy passages containing absurd situations, such as Ulric's imprisonment "in a cavern of banditti, somewhere in the neighborhood of Philadelphia!!" Poe finds that other fantastic adventures are drawn almost whole from the works of earlier writers.

In the conclusion of the review, Poe declares that "the book is despicable in every respect" and charges Mattson with producing a work that contributes to the "daily discredit to our national literature." He is particularly incensed that such a work found a publisher: "We have no right to complain of being laughed at abroad when so villainous a compound, as the thing we now hold in our hand, of incongruous folly, plagiarism, immorality, inanity, and bombast, can command at any moment both a puff and a publisher."

Payne, Daniel The fiancé of Mary ROGERS, he committed suicide six weeks after her body was discovered floating in the Hudson River. He was found unconscious on a bench near the point that Rogers's body was found. An empty laudanum bottle, marked "Laudanum, Souillard & Delluc," was found near his body, together with a note stating, "To the World, Here I am on the spot. God forgive me for my misfortune, or for my misspent time." Witnesses reported that earlier in the day he had been seen wandering aimlessly around the area, apparently drunk.

Pedro Character in "THE OVAL PORTRAIT." He is a manservant whom the narrator bade "to close the heavy shutters of the room—since it was already night,—to light the tongues of the tall candelabrum which stood by the head of my bed, and to throw open far and wide the fringed curtains of black velvet which enveloped the bed itself."

The Penn Magazine In 1840, Poe presented a prospectus for a monthly literary journal that would be edited and published in Philadelphia. Poe informed potential subscribers that the new magazine would "endeavor to support the general interests of the republic of letters, without reference to particular regions—regarding the world at large as the true audience of the author." Poe also promised to produce a magazine of the highest quality, one that would exclude "any tincture of the buffoonery, scurrility, or profanity, which are the blemish of some of the most vigorous of the European prints." The magazine never appeared, the result of Poe's involvement as editor of BURTON'S GENTLEMAN'S MAGAZINE and various personal crises.

Pennifeather, Mr. Character in Poe's short story "THOU ART THE MAN." He is "a young man of very dissipated habits, and otherwise of rather bad character." The nephew of Barnabas SHUTTLEWORTHY, "one of the wealthiest and most respectable citizens of the borough," he is "so intimately cognizant of all the circumstances connected with his wealthy uncle's disappearance, as to feel authorized to assert, distinctly and unequivocally, that his uncle *was* a murdered man." Pennifeather is falsely accused of and tried for the murder of his uncle, but the true murderer is revealed right before Pennifeather is doomed to die. Once he is released from jail, he inherits his uncle's fortune.

Percival, Dr. James G. (n.d.) Physician and author whose views are mentioned in Poe's short story "THE FALL OF THE HOUSE OF USHER." In his mention that Roderick USHER's "opinion, in its general form, was that of the sentience of all vegetable things," Poe draws upon the research of Percival, who published an article on the perceptive powers of vegetables in *Memoir of the Literary and Philosophical Society of Manchester* (1785), volume two, number 14.

Perier, Casimir (1777–1832) French statesman referred to in Poe's short story "THREE SUNDAYS IN A WEEK." His "pert little query '*A quoi un poète est-il bon?*'" [what is a poet good for?] provides the inspiration for the "profound contempt" that RUMGUDGEON, a character in the story, holds for the fine arts, and especially for belles-lettres—and it is a phrase he was fond of using.

Perrine Character in Poe's unfinished novel *THE JOURNAL OF JULIUS RODMAN*. He is an agent of the Hudson Bay fur company who accompanies the Rodman expedition for 10 miles with three members of the Ricaree tribe. He leaves the expedition to return to the village where, as the voyagers learn afterward, "he met with a violent death from the hands of a squaw, to whom he offered some insult."

Perry, Edgar A. Alias that Poe used when he enlisted in the United States Army on May 26, 1827. Although only 18 years old, he gave his age as 22. He also stated that he was born in Boston and had worked as a clerk. The new recruit was assigned to Battery H of the First Artillery, then stationed in Boston Harbor at Fort Independence, where he lived in the barracks from May through October 1827. As "Perry," Poe's performance was exemplary, and on January 1, 1829, he was appointed regimental sergeant major, through whose hands the entire correspondence of a command passed. After appealing to John ALLAN for help in leaving the service, "Edgar A. Perry" was discharged from the army on April 15, 1829.

Pest, Queen Character in Poe's short story "KING PEST." The cadaverous "Serene Consort" of King Pest, she is "evidently in the last stage of a dropsy," a large woman with a face that is "exceedingly round, red, and full" and a body that resembles an ale barrel. Her mouth is her distinguishing feature: "Commencing at the right ear, it swept with a terrific chasm to the left—the short pendants which she wore in either auricle continually bobbing into the aperture." This noble lady lifts the seaman Hugh TARPAULIN high into the air, then drops him into a huge open barrel of ale.

Pest-Iferous, Arch Duke Character in Poe's short story "KING PEST." He is one of six rotting relatives of King PEST, the "exalted personages . . . all of our family," who wears "the insignia of the blood royal" under the title of archduke.

Pest-Ilential, The Duke Character in Poe's short story "KING PEST." He is a one of six rotting relatives of King PEST, the "exalted personages . . . all of our family," who wears "the insignia of the blood royal" under the title of duke.

Pest the First, King Character in Poe's short story "KING PEST." The king of plague and death, he is tall, gaunt, and emaciated, with a face "as yellow as saffron" and "a forehead so unusually and hideously lofty, as to have the appearance of a bonnet or crown of flesh superadded upon the natural head." His mouth is "puckered and dimpled into an expression of ghastly affability, and his eyes, as indeed the eyes of all at the table, were glazed over with the fumes of intoxication." He is dressed completely in richly embroidered black silk velvet, and "his head was stuck full of sable hearse-plumes, which he nodded to and fro with a jaunty and knowing air; and, in his right hand, he held a huge human thigh-bone."

"Peter Pendulum" *See* "THE BUSINESS MAN."

Peters, Dirk Character in Poe's novel *THE NARRATIVE OF ARTHUR GORDON PYM*. The son of an Indian woman of the tribe of Upsarokas and a fur-trader father, he "was one of the most ferocious-looking men" Arthur Gordon PYM has ever seen. He is short, "But his limbs were of Herculean mold." He has thick and powerful hands and arms, and a head that is "deformed, being of immense size, with an indentation on the crown . . . and entirely bald." To hide his baldness, Peters usually wears a wig "formed of any hair-like material . . . the skin of a Spanish dog or American grizzly bear." His protruding teeth, "never even partially covered, in any instance, by the lips," give his face a look of laughter "but a second look would induce a shuddering acknowledgment . . . the merriment must be that of a demon." Ferocious as he seems, Peters saves the life of Augustus BARNARD, Richard PARKER, and Pym after the mutiny.

Petersilea, Franz (?–1878) German musician. In 1849, he wrote *The Bells,* a musical score that may well be the first musical setting of any Poe text, a piece inspired by Poe's poem of the same name.

"Peter Snook" Essay by Poe that appeared in the October 1836 issue of the *SOUTHERN LITERARY MESSENGER*. Poe took issue with an article in which Evert DUYCKINCK undervalued the power of "Magazine Literature" in the United States. Poe argued that magazine writing in America was far inferior to that of the French and the English because American magazine writing paid poorly and failed to attain the artistic fulfillment of "the true magazine spirit." Poe noted that "we are lamentably deficient not only in invention proper, but in that which is, more strictly, *Art.*" Poe offered as one example the differences between the critical reviews written by Americans compared with those published by the English and the French: "What American, for instance, in penning his a criticism, ever supposes himself called upon to present his readers with more than the exact stipulation of his title—to present them with a criticism and *something beyond?* Who thinks of making his critique a work of art in itself—independently of its critical opinions?" Even more than in regard to articles, Poe finds that Americans "evince the most remarkable deficiency in skill" in "tale-writing." To provide an example of the artistic superiority of British and

French fiction over American fiction, he discusses in detail the "longest and best" of James Forbes Dalton's stories, "Peter Snook." After the lengthy summary and analysis, Poe ranks the tale "among the few tales which (each in its own way) are absolutely faultless."

Peterson, Charles Jacobs (1819–1887)   Assistant editor with Poe at GRAHAM'S MAGAZINE in mid-1841 and one of a family of magazine printers. His relationship with Poe began to deteriorate in the spring of 1842, when Poe's conduct suffered as his wife's health worsened and his personal difficulties increased. After months of growing tension, Poe and Peterson quarreled openly and Graham discharged Poe, having told the engraver John SARTAIN, "Either Peterson or Poe would have to go—the two could not get along together."

Peterson, Mr.   Character in Poe's novel THE NARRATIVE OF ARTHUR GORDON PYM. He is the grandfather of Arthur Gordon PYM, and he objects when Pym seeks to indulge his desire for travel and to sail with Captain BARNARD aboard the *Grampus*. Pym states, "my grandfather, from whom I expected much, vowed to cut me off with a shilling if I should ever broach the subject to him again." Pym decides to run off to sea and, while disguised with a dirty and thick seaman's cloak, runs into his grandfather on the day of embarkment. When Peterson recognizes his grandson, Pym assumes a seaman's dialect and berates the old man for being "sum'-mat mistaken."

Pfaall, Hans   Character in Poe's short story "THE UNPARALLELED ADVENTURE OF ONE HANS PFAALL." He is "an humble artizan [*sic*], by name Hans Pfaall, and by occupation a mender of bellows" who had disappeared from Rotterdam via hot-air balloon five years before the story occurs. He had disappeared with three others "in a manner which must have been considered unaccountable," but sends a letter to the president and vice president of the States' College of Astronomers that provides a journal of his adventures. The letter is supposedly delivered by "an inhabitant of the moon," where Pfaall claims in the epistle to live.

Pfaall, Grettel   Character in Poe's short story "THE UNPARALLELED ADVENTURE OF ONE HANS PFAALL." She is the wife of the balloonist Hans PFAALL and she utters "an exclamation of joyful surprise" when she sees the "enormous drab beaver hat" suspended from an unusual flying vehicle. Grettel "declared it to be the identical hat of her good man himself."

Philadelphia Dollar Newspaper   Newspaper with offices in the same building as GRAHAM'S MAGAZINE, located at Third and Chestnut Streets in Philadelphia. Poe published "THE GOLD-BUG" in the newspaper in the June 21

and 28, 1843, issues after winning a prize of $100. "THE SPECTACLES" appeared in the March 27, 1844, issue; "THE PREMATURE BURIAL," one of Poe's most genuinely morbid stories, appeared in the July 31, 1844, issue of the paper.

Philadelphia Saturday Museum   Periodical, published in Philadelphia, with which Poe had a strong connection in 1843. Poe used the columns of the publication to advertise himself as a literary figure and to announce the pending publication of his new magazine. Poe's friend and fellow writer and editor Henry Beck HIRST wrote a brief biography of Poe that appeared in the February 1843 issue of the publication, which other papers noticed and quoted from. In response to the interest shown by other papers, the *Museum* announced, "we have been so fortunate as to secure his services as associate editor of the *Saturday Museum*, where we intend [his fame] shall be placed beyond the reach of conjecture." The editors also informed readers, "so great was the interest excited by the biography and poems of Mr. Poe published in the *Museum* of last week, that to supply those who were disappointed in obtaining copies we shall be at the expense of an extra edition, which shall be printed with corrections and additions." In a letter written to James Russell LOWELL in March 1843, Poe remarked that the announcement of his accepting the position of assistant editor had been made "prematurely," which exhibits that he was only using the obscure paper to advertise himself and to develop a following for his potential publication of the STYLUS.

"The Philosophy of Composition"   Essay by Poe, published in the April 1846 issue of GRAHAM'S MAGAZINE. In the essay, Poe purports to demonstrate how he wrote "THE RAVEN" and how it should be read, as well. He claimed that many people would stop him and ask, "'Why, Mr. Poe, how did you write 'The Raven'?" This was his answer. Whatever its reason for creation, the work is a vital text in understanding Poe criticism. It contains a thorough analysis of his creative process, which has led to significant debate regarding the accuracy of Poe's description of his compositional process. Poe suggests that the essay will reveal the method that any author might follow in producing successful literature, beginning with "the consideration of an effect . . . after looking about me (or rather within) for such combinations of event, or tone, as shall best aid me in the construction of the effect." The author writes that he has often thought "how interesting a magazine article might be written by any author who would—that is to say who could—detail, step by step, the processes by which any one of his compositions attained its ultimate point of completion." Poe suggests that "autorial vanity" may be the reason that writers have omitted such

Poe lived and worked briefly in Philadelphia, shown here in the 1840s. (National Archives—Stills Division)

analysis, because "most writers—poets in especial—prefer having it understood that they compose by a species of fine frenzy—an ecstatic intuition." The opposite is actually true, notes Poe, and most writers "would positively shudder at letting the public take a peep behind the scenes . . . at the fully matured fancies discarded in despair as unmanageable—at the cautious selections and rejections—at the painful erasures and interpolations." After pointing out that most authors are "in no condition to retrace the steps by which his conclusions have been attained," Pope proposes to analyze for readers the composition process that he followed in writing "The Raven." He identifies issues that determine the success or failure of a poem, with emphasis upon length, the effect to be conveyed, and the province, beauty in this case. Poe asserts, "there is a distinct limit, as regards length, to all works of literary art—the limit of one sitting." Although he allows that a novel may require more time, the limit should never be exceeded in a poem. The choice of effect is a second consideration, and Poe argues that the poet should determine in advance the effect that he wishes to create. For Poe, the province of the poem should be Beauty, "because it is an obvious rule of Art that effects should be made to spring form direct causes." He then applies his observations to "The Raven" to provide examples of his theory. It is this very detailed and carefully delineated discussion that created debate as to how honest Poe was in assessing his writing of "The Raven." Critics who doubted the premise expressed doubt that the creative process could be so straightforward and logical.

"The Philosophy of Furniture" Essay by Poe, first published in the May 1840 issue of BURTON'S GENTLEMAN'S MAGAZINE. Poe retitled the essay "House of Furniture" when he published it in the May 3, 1845, issue of the BROADWAY JOURNAL. The work contains Poe's analysis of the differences in national temperaments as they are revealed in the "internal decoration, if not in the external architecture of their residences." The focus of Poe's criticism of taste appears directed mainly to Americans, who "alone are preposterous" for their substitution of "an aristocracy of dollars, the *display of wealth*," for good taste. He laments what he sees as "an evil growing out of our republican institutions, that here a man of large purse has usually a very little soul which he keeps in it." In general, Poe finds most nations, although their faults are less egregious, have little in the way of good taste in regard to interior decoration. "The Italians have but little sentiment beyond marbles and colours," the French "are too much a race of gadabouts to maintain those household proprieties. . . . [T]he Chinese and most of the eastern races have a warm but inappropriate fancy. . . . [T]he Scotch are poor decorists. . . . [T]he Russians do not furnish." Of all nations, "the English are supreme" and "the Yankees alone are preposterous." Poe attacks what he perceives to be the American manner of confounding cost with quality, decrying the fact that "the cost of an article of furniture has at length come to be, with us, nearly the sole test of its merit in a decorative point of view." He describes "the interior of what is termed in the United States—that is, to say, in Appallachia [*sic*]— a well-furnished apartment. Its most usual defect is a want of keeping." This want of keeping is seen in the "inartistic arrangement" of pieces of furniture or in the "undue precision" of the pieces of which "straight lines are too prevalent." Convinced that "the soul of the apartment is the carpet," Poe asserts that "a good judge of carpet *must be* a genius" and he decries the reality that carpets are often chosen by men "who could not be entrusted with the management of their own *moustaches*." The essay ends with Poe's detailed description of the model apartment, "a small and not ostentatious chamber with whose decorations no fault can be found."

"Philothea: A Romance. By Mrs. Child, Author of the Mother's Book, &c. Boston: Otis, Broaders & Co. New York: George Dearborn" Review by Poe that appeared in the September 1836 issue of the SOUTHERN LITERARY MESSENGER. The review sets a positive tone at the outset by noting that the difference of this novel from works previously published by Child "places the fair writer in a new and most favorable light." Poe provides readers with a lengthy summary of the plot, which is set in ancient Athens and abounds with classical names and references. The review warns that, however well written and worthy in topic, the novel will likely not become popular, because "we have little of purely human sympathy in the distantly antique; and this little is greatly weakened by the constant necessity of effort in conceiving *appropriateness* in manners, costume,

habits, and modes of thought, so widely at variance with those around us." The plot should be regarded as a "mere vehicle" for examining the aforementioned manners, costume, habits, and modes of thought, rather than for itself. The real value of the book is that it "might be introduced advantageously into our female academies. Its purity of thought and lofty morality are unexceptionable. It would prove an effectual aid in the study of Greek antiquity. . . . [I]ts purity of language should especially recommend it to the attention of teachers."

"Phrenology, and the Moral Influence of Phrenology: Arranged for General Study, and the Purposes of Education, from the First Published Works of Gall and Spurzheim, to the Latest Discoveries of the Present Period. By Mrs. L. Miles. Philadelphia: Carey, Lea & Blanchard" Review by Poe that appeared in the March 1836 issue of the SOUTHERN LITERARY MESSENGER. Poe opens the review by stating that "Phrenology [the study of shape and size of the skull to determine mental ability and personality] is no longer to be laughed at. . . . It has assumed the majesty of a science . . . involving consequences of the highest practical magnitude." He defends its use as providing individuals with "a perfectly accurate estimate of their own moral capabilities," before praising the "neat and convenient" work that places the study into perspective. Poe praises the work as being "lucid, compact and portable" and lists for the reader the classifications contained within, although he does note that the clarity of the arrangement has resulted in the sacrifice of "points of vital importance to the science."

"The Pic Nic Papers. By Various Hands. Edited by Charles Dickens, Esq., Author of 'The Pickwick Papers,' etc. Two Volumes. Lea & Blanchard, Philadelphia" Review by Poe that appeared in the November 1841 issue of GRAHAM'S MAGAZINE. The "papers" consist of a collection of articles from Dickens, Leitch RITCHIE, Allan Cunningham, Thomas MOORE, William H. AINSWORTH, G. P. R. James, Agnes Strickland, and others. Poe observes that "it might be supposed, of course, that the collection would be one of high interest; but we are forced to say that it is *not*." Instead, the review explains that when authors "are called upon to furnish *gratuitous* papers. . . . [T]hey content themselves with bestowing whatever Ms. they may have on hand, of least value." In essence, such "refuse labour of a man of genius is usually inferior" to his usual work because "the man of genius must write in obedience to his impulses." Thus, Poe views the collection under review in the same light and states that he has never encountered in any respectable-looking book "more consummate nonsense than the greater portion of the collection." The review also protest the prominent use of Dickens's name and the use of a title that so nearly reminds readers of Dickens's *Pickwick Papers,* suggesting that the current volume was written by him. In conclusion, Poe asks, "Now what is this but the worst species of *forgery?*"

Pike, Major Zebulon Montgomery (1779–1813) American explorer, army officer, and the man for whom Pike's Peak in Colorado is named. In his unfinished novel THE JOURNAL OF JULIUS RODMAN, Poe describes Pike's 1805 expedition to discover the source of the Mississippi River. Pike later explored the Louisiana Territory, where he was captured by the Spanish and charged with spying. After his release, he served as a brigadier general in the War of 1812, in which he was killed by an explosion.

"Pinakidia" An article by Poe, comprised of a collection of brief observations and random statements on miscellaneous subjects, that appeared in the 1836 issue of the SOUTHERN LITERARY MESSENGER. In his preface to the 173 statements, Poe defines the title as "tablets" culled from his notebooks that shed an interesting sidelight on his secondary sources. Simply an unconnected collection, similar material might be found in numerous periodicals of his time under such headings as "Random Thoughts," "Odds and Ends," "Stray Leaves," "Scraps," and "Brevities," most having "pretensions to originality." In contrast, Poe admits that his collection "is not original, and will be readily recognized as such by the classical and general reader." He has not cataloged his work: "[N]o arrangement has been considered necessary; and, indeed, so heterogeneous a farrago it would have been an endless task to methodize." Thus, the reader of "Pinakidia" learns "during the whole period of the middle ages, the Germans lived in utter ignorance of the art of writing," "of the ten tragedies attributed to Seneca (the only Roman tragedies extant), nine are on Greek subjects"; and "the translators of the Old Testament have used the word Eternity but once."

Pinxit Character in Poe's short story "LOSS OF BREATH." He attends the public hanging of the narrator and "availed himself of the opportunity to retouch, from a sketch taken upon the spot, his admirable painting of the Marsyas flayed alive." He has been identified with the painter Raphael (1483–1520), who created the painting mentioned.

Pirouette, Mrs. Character in Poe's short story "THE MAN THAT WAS USED UP." She is one of the women whom the narrator encounters at the party given by Mrs. Kathleen O'TRUMP, all of whom are eager to discuss Brevet Brigadier General A. B. C. SMITH. The "bewitching little angel, the graceful Mrs. Pirouette" dances

with the narrator, alternately speaking of "the dreadful business" of Smith and admonishing her dance partner "*do* turn out your toes" until she is "quite out of breath."

"The Pit and the Pendulum" Short story. This most widely read of Poe's tales deals with the Spanish Inquisition, which was independent of the medieval Inquisition and controlled entirely by the Spanish kings. The Spanish Inquisition was launched in 1478 to discover and punish converted Jews (*Marranos*), and later converted Muslims (*Moriscos*), who were not viewed as "true believers" because they had not been born into the Roman Catholic faith. By 1483, 2,000 people are reputed to have been burned at the stake in Spain. The Spanish Inquisition differed from the Inquisition in southern France, Italy, and Germany in severity and cruelty. The Spanish Inquisition investigated crimes against morality as well as heresy, and the use of torture was common. Punishments ranged from reprimands and warnings to burning at the stake.

The introduction of General Lasalle as the savior of the narrator appears to have been taken from Thomas Dick's account in the *Philosophy of Religion* (1825), which recounts the arrival in Toledo of the French in 1808 during the Peninsular War. Dick wrote, "General Lasalle visited the palace of the Inquisition. The great number of instruments of torture, especially the instruments to stretch the limbs, and the drop-baths, which cause a lingering death, excited horror, even in the minds of soldiers hardened in the fields of battle."

PUBLISHING AND DRAMATIZATION HISTORY

The story first appeared in the annual *The Gift: A Christmas and New Year's Present* for 1843, published by Carey & Hart. The story was republished with only slight revision in the May 17, 1845, issue of the BROADWAY JOURNAL.

Poe identifies the epigraph that precedes the story as a "quatrain composed for the gates of a market to be erected upon the site of the Jacobin Club House at Paris":

Impia tortorum longos hic turba furores
Sanguinis innocui, non satiata, aluit.
Sospite nunc patria, fracto nunc funeris antro,
Mor ubi dira fuit vita salusque patent.

[Here the wicked mob, unappeased,
Long cherished a hatred of innocent blood.
Now that the fatherland has been saved, and the cave
of death demolished;
Where grim death has been, life and health appear.]

Charles BAUDELAIRE wrote that the Marché St. Honoré, which was built on the site of the Old Jacobin Club, had no gates and, of course, no inscription. The Jacobins were a political group led by Maximilien Robespierre (1748–1794) during the French Revolution responsible for the 1793 Reign of Terror.

Films made of the story include such early versions as the 1910 *Le Puits et le pendule,* directed by Henri Desfontaines, and a 1913 English-language version directed by the film pioneer Alice Guy Blanche. In 1961, Roger CORMAN directed *The Pit and the Pendulum,* a commercial success that started the cycle of Poe films in the 1960s and starred Vincent PRICE, John Kerr, and Barbara Steele. The story borrowed only the setting and the devices of torture in this version that is set right after the Spanish Inquisition in which the character played by Price believes himself to be his late father, the most vicious torturer of the inquisition. The plot acquires a new framework of a brother arriving at a Spanish castle to investigate what he has been told is the mysterious death of his sister, while the sister, still alive but devious, and her lover plot to drive the brother mad for his money. The film ends with a shot of Steele being accidentally enclosed in the Iron Maiden by Price, to be locked in it forever.

The 1991 film version *The Pit and the Pendulum,* directed by Stuart Gordon and starring Lance Henriksen, Rona De Ricci, Frances Bay, Jeffrey Combs, and Oliver Reed, offers a twisted love story set in Spain in 1492 and uses a setting inspired by the atmosphere and torture devices of Poe's story but nothing of Poe's plot. Torquemada, Spain's Grand Inquisitor, has lust-filled desires for a baker's wife accused of witchcraft and, because he cannot give in to those desires, she and her husband must suffer the consequences.

CHARACTERS

General Lasalle, unnamed narrator, unnamed black-robed judges.

PLOT SYNOPSIS

The story relates the experiences of the nameless narrator, who is dragged before a court of the Spanish Inquisition in Toledo after long suffering, then sentenced to death by his similarly nameless accusers and judges for a crime that is never revealed. His punishment involves a range of ingeniously devised and increasingly horrible tortures. Placed in a rat-infested cell without light, he explores his surroundings through touch, attempting to determine the size and shape of his cell as he gropes his way around. Unable to see, he trips after catching his foot in the hem of his robe and falls to the ground, where he discovers "a somewhat startling circumstance," that he has nearly fallen into a deep pit. His chin rests on the ground, but his lips and the upper portion of his head, "although seemingly at a less elevation than the chin, touched

nothing. At the same time, my forehead seemed bathed in a clammy vapor, and the peculiar smell of decayed fungus arose to my nostrils." To test the depth, the narrator dislodges a small chunk of stone from the rim of the pit and throws it in. The stone takes several seconds to hit the water, signaling a great depth. When the narrator hears a door overhead open and close rapidly, as if someone is checking on him, he realizes that "To the victims of [the Inquisition's] tyranny, there was the choice of death with its direct physical agonies, or death with its most hideous moral horrors. I had been reserved for the latter." The realization discomfits him, and he crawls back to the wall to avoid the abyss, "*the pit* typical of hell, and regarded by rumor as the Ultima Thule of all their punishments." Exhausted, the narrator falls asleep and later awakens to find a loaf of bread and a pitcher of water, which he drains "at a draught." He then falls asleep again because the water has been drugged. When he awakens once more, the room is visible because of "a wild sulphurous lustre," perhaps meant to suggest hellfire, that allows him to see the extent and appearance of his prison. The metal walls surrounding him contain "all the hideous and repulsive devices to which the charnel superstition of the monks has given rise. The figures of fiends in aspects of menace, with skeleton forms, and other more really fearful images, overspread and disfigured the walls."

Now lying on his back and securely bound to a wooden frame by one long strap that covers most of his body and leaves only his head and left arm free to reach a nearby plate of meat, the narrator looks up and sees, 30 or 40 feet overhead, a painted picture of Time holding not the traditional scythe but instead a huge pendulum. As the narrator stares at the pendulum, it begins to move. He quickly turns his attention to the floor, where "several enormous rats" have left the abyss and are headed toward him. After he spends an hour or more scaring away the rats, he looks up at the pendulum, only to find that it has now increased in sweep and velocity and that is has perceptibly descended. Agonized, the narrator watches and counts the sweeps as the pendulum continues its downward descent. When it is near enough for him to smell "the odor of the sharp steel," he swoons, then recovers and reaches for the remaining food, for "even amid the agonies of that period the human nature craved food."

Consuming the food reawakens the narrator's hope and his ability to think. In minute detail, he considers the actions of the pendulum as it approaches. He imagines where it will make contact, what it will sever, and the sensations he will experience. He also recalls that a cut at any point on the one strap that binds him would set him free. He reaches for the meat in the dish and rubs it all over the strap wherever he can reach, hoping to attract the rats to gnaw at it. The plan works only moments after the pendulum has begun to cut through his robe and the linen beneath. As pendulum swings to one side, the narrator slides off the frame and watches with amazement as the movement of the pendulum stops and it is drawn upward through the ceiling. He is horrified to realize that his every movement is being watched, but his attention is soon occupied by the glowing heat he sees around the perimeter of the cell, and realizes that the metal walls are being heated by the flames of a furnace. For a moment he contemplates the coolness of the pit, but he draws back from the edge. The shape of the room is also changing, from its once square form to a shape with two acute angles and two obtuse, "that of a lozenge." The heated walls press more closely onto the narrator, forcing him closer to the pit in the center of the room and leading him to cry out for "Death . . . any death but that of the pit!" He is pressed closer, until "for my seared and writhing body there was no longer an inch of foothold on the firm floor of the prison." As he totters on the brink, he hears "a discordant hum of human voices . . . a loud blast as of many trumpets . . . a harsh grating as of a thousand thunders." An outstretched hand catches him just before he falls into the abyss. General Lasalle has arrived with the French army, and "the Inquisition was in the hands of its enemies."

Placide, Mr. C. (n.d.)   Actor-manager of the Charleston Players (also called the Richmond Players, depending upon their city of performance), of which Elizabeth POE was a member. On November 25, 1811, he placed an advertisement in the *Richmond Enquirer,* an appeal for Mrs. Poe "to the kind-hearted of the city" for financial assistance. Four days later, he placed an advertisement of a second benefit "in consequence of the serious and long continued indisposition of Mrs. Poe, and in compliance with the advice and solicitation of many of the most respectable families." His company was based in Charleston, South Carolina, and Placide later retired to that city after turning over the business to his son.

"Plato Contra Atheos.—Plato against the Atheists; or the Tenth Book of the Dialogue on Laws, Accompanied with Critical Notes, and Followed by Extended Dissertations on Some of the Main Points of the Platonic Philosophy and Theology Especially as Compared with the Holy Scriptures, by Tayler Lewis, LL.D., Professor of the Greek Language and Literature, in the University in the City of New York.—New York, Harper & Brothers"   Review by Poe that appeared in the June 21, 1845, issue of the *BROADWAY JOURNAL.* The review opens with the assumption that "the Laws of Plato were probably the work of his old age—of his extreme senility," an assertion that disputes the opinion of the annotator, Dr. Lewis, that this work represents Plato's mature and most settled opin-

ions. Poe then provides a synopsis of the work, which deals with laws enacted against violators of religion, and offers editorial commentary on Plato's views throughout. Although Poe acknowledges "the purity and nobility of the Platonian soul," he suggests that Platonic thought is archaic: "But if the question be put to-day, what is the value of the Platonian philosophy, the proper answer is, 'exactly nothing at all.' We do not believe that any good purpose is answered by popularizing his dreams; on the contrary we do believe that they have a strong tendency of ill—intellectually of course." Of Lewis's work, Poe is similarly critical and expresses a regret that the book contains only the Greek text without a translation, which seems to belie the stated object of the annotator, which "seems to have been the placing of the doctrines of Plato more immediately within the *reach of the public.*"

"The Pleasant Peregrination Through the Prettiest Parts of Pennsylvania. Performed by Peregrine Prolix. Philadelphia: Grigg and Elliot"   Review appearing in the June 1836 issue of the *SOUTHERN LITERARY MESSENGER.* The work is written under a pseudonym by Philip H. Nichelin, the author of "LETTERS DESCRIPTIVE OF THE VIRGINIA SPRINGS—THE ROADS LEADING THERETO AND THE DOINGS THEREAT," reviewed by Poe for the June 1836 issue of the *Messenger.* Although Poe begins the current review with the statement, "We know nothing farther about Peregrine Prolix than that he is the very clever author of a book entitled 'Letters descriptive of the Virginia Springs,' and that he is a gentleman on the wrong side of forty," he had already identified Nichelin as Prolix in the earlier review. Poe provides readers with synopses of the ten letters detailing the ramblings of Prolix from Philadelphia to points west, then home again, and he assures them that "his book is a very excellent thing."

Pluto   A cat, the narrator's favorite pet in Poe's short story "THE BLACK CAT." He is "a remarkably large and beautiful animal, entirely black, and sagacious to an astonishing degree." Pluto follows the narrator everywhere, and when the narrator begins to maltreat the other animals in his menagerie he spares the cat for a long while until "at length even Pluto, who was now becoming old, and consequently somewhat peevish—even Pluto began to experience the effects of my ill temper." The cat experiences cruel torture and mutilation by the narrator, who eventually "slipped a noose around its neck and hung it to a limb of a tree."

Poe, David, Jr. (1784–1811?)   Father of Edgar Allan Poe. A Baltimore native, he was approximately 22 years old and studying law when he first saw Elizabeth Arnold, who would later become his wife and the mother of Edgar. Despite his father's wishes that he become a lawyer, the young David Poe joined the Thespian Club in Baltimore. He was later sent to his uncle's house in Augusta, Georgia, which he left for Charleston, South Carolina, then a theatrical center, and the opportunity to go on stage. The December 1, 1803, issue of the *Charleston City Gazette* reports his first stage appearance there as "An Officer" in a pantomime titled *La Pérouse*. Three years later he joined the troupe in which the newly widowed Elizabeth Arnold Hopkins acted, and the two married six months later. Their marriage further widened the breech between Poe and his father, David POE, Sr., but the birth of their first child, William Henry Leonard, in 1807, brought a reconciliation. Sensitive about his limited stage talents, hot-tempered, and hard-drinking, David Poe was prone to outbursts and possessed of only meager earning capability. The births of Edgar in January 1809 and Rosalie in December 1810 strained both the Poes' finances and David Poe's patience as a father and a husband. He left his family in July 1811, and is believed to have died in Norfolk, Virginia, on or about December 11, 1811. Speculation about his disappearance ranges from the suggestion that he was ill and wanted to spare his family the agony to the more realistic possibility that he, a man in his mid-20s, had simply become tired of living with so many responsibilities and so few prospects. The circumstances and facts surrounding the death of David Poe, Jr., remain obscure, and they are further muddied by Edgar Allan Poe's letter to William Poe in Richmond on August 20, 1835, in which he notes that "my father David died when I was in the second year of my age. . . . [M]y mother died a few weeks before him." Whether Poe's statement is true, or a falsehood meant to protect the reputation of his mother and sister, remains in doubt.

Poe, David, Sr. (1742–1816)   Poe's paternal grandfather and a distinguished veteran of the American Revolution. He had held the rank of major during the war, although he used the courtesy title of "General" because of the large sum of money that he had invested in the war effort. He also became a close friend of French war hero the Marquis de LAFAYETTE, who honored the Poe family by visiting the General's widow and the grandfather's grave during his visit to Richmond in 1824. The General served as the deputy quartermaster general of Baltimore during the American Revolutionary War, but his grandson would later inflate that role and refer to him as having served as the quartermaster general of the United States Army. The General was highly upset when his favorite son and namesake, David POE, abandoned a law career to join an acting troupe and later marry an actress. The two reconciled after the birth of William Henry Leonard POE.

Poe, Edgar Allan (1809–1849)   American writer and critic who is credited with refining the short story form and inventing the modern DETECTIVE STORY. He was born on January 19, 1809, in a boardinghouse on Carver Street near the Boston Common while his actor parents, Elizabeth Arnold Hopkins POE and David POE, Jr., were on tour. After his father deserted the family and his impoverished mother died of tuberculosis in 1811 in Richmond, Virginia, young Edgar was taken into the home of John ALLAN, a wealthy Richmond merchant whose marriage had been childless. The Allans never formally adopted the child, but they provided him with a private school education when they traveled to England in 1815, and his education continued in private schools when they returned to the United States in 1820. In 1826, Poe entered the newly established University of Virginia, but John Allan made him leave one year later after young Poe racked up huge debts by drinking and gambling instead of attending classes. Poe was forced to return to Richmond as a clerk in Allan's mercantile firm, but he hated the work and ran off to Boston, where he enlisted in the army under the name of Edgar A. PERRY. He served two years, after which he pleaded with Allan to help him to leave the army. Allan agreed, provided that Poe obtain an appointment to the UNITED STATES MILITARY ACADEMY AT WEST POINT, to which he acquiesced. Frances ALLAN died in the last weeks of Poe's enlistment, but she had pleaded his case with her husband, who was willing to give him another chance. Poe quarreled with John Allan before entering West Point, and that argument, coupled with Allan's remarriage in October 1830 to Louisa Gabriella PATTERSON, created a final, irrevocable break. Already at the military academy but with little hope of financial support from Allan, Poe worked to be expelled, and succeeded. After he left, he began his publishing efforts in earnest. His first book, *TAMERLANE AND OTHER POEMS*, had appeared anonymously in 1827, and the second volume of verse—his first to be commercially published—*AL AARAAF, TAMERLANE, AND MINOR POEMS*, appeared in 1829. Poe's third book, *POEMS*, appeared in 1831, after which he moved to Baltimore to live with his paternal aunt Maria Poe CLEMM and her young daughter, Virginia. With this move Poe began a productive period of writing and publishing short stories while he also worked as an editor and established an important connection with the *SOUTHERN LITERARY MESSENGER*, where he served as editor from 1835 through 1837. In 1836, Poe married his 13-year-old cousin Virginia with Maria Clemm's blessing, but the marriage provoked the disapproval of acquaintances and members of his extended family, especially Neilson POE. During their 10 years of marriage, Poe moved the family, including Maria Clemm, to Philadelphia and then to New York City, where he worked as an editor on such periodicals as *BURTON'S GENTLEMAN'S MAGAZINE, GRA-*

This photograph of Poe was taken in 1848, when he was courting Sarah Helen Whitman. (Edgar Allan Poe Society)

HAM'S MAGAZINE, ALEXANDER'S WEEKLY MESSENGER, and GODEY'S MAGAZINE AND LADY'S BOOK, among others. He also published extensive criticism and numerous poems and short stories in these and other publications. He published his only novel, THE NARRATIVE OF ARTHUR GORDON PYM, in 1838; TALES OF THE GROTESQUE AND ARABESQUE, containing 25 stories, was published in 1840; THE RAVEN AND OTHER POEMS appeared in 1845, as did TALES BY EDGAR A. POE.

Within nine months of arriving in New York City in April 1844, Poe published "THE RAVEN," and his success was instantaneous. Thus began a round of literary gatherings, invitations to lecture, and acquaintances with other writers who were later profiled in "THE LITERATI OF NEW YORK CITY." Virginia died in 1847 of tuberculosis. Poe also became very ill and was nursed by Maria Clemm and Marie Louise SHEW, the medically trained daughter of a physician. Shew consulted the physician Valentine MOTT, who told her that Poe had had a brain lesion when young, and this was responsible for the erratic behavior throughout his life. In the

remaining two years of his life, Poe continued to publish and lecture. He died in Washington Hospital in Baltimore, on October 7, 1849, and was buried in Westminster Churchyard the following day. His reputation suffered severe damage when Rufus Wilmot GRISWOLD, using the pseudonym Ludwig, published an obituary of Poe in the October 9, 1849, issue of the New York *Daily Tribune.* The piece, which has come to be known as THE "LUDWIG" ARTICLE, destroyed Poe's reputation and remained the "official" view of the poet's life for nearly a half century. As soon as Poe was dead, Griswold began the process of exacting posthumous revenge against Poe, stating of his death that "few will be grieved by it" and depicting him as a mentally unstable misanthrope who "had few or no friends."

Poe, Elizabeth (Eliza) Arnold Hopkins (1787–1811)
Actress and the mother of Edgar Allan Poe. She was the daughter of two actors, Henry Arnold and Elizabeth Smith, both of whom appeared at the Covent Garden Theatre in London. They were married in June 1784 and Eliza was born in London in the spring of 1787. Six years after her father died, Eliza and her widowed mother left London for the United States in November 1795, and they arrived in Boston on January 3, 1796, as a shipping notice dated January 5, 1796, shows. Nine-year-old Eliza made her stage debut a month later, as a character named Biddy Bellair in David Garrick's farce *Miss in Her Teens.* A review in the *Portland Herald* praised her performance, saying "her powers as an Actress will do credit to any of her sex of maturer age." In 1802, at only 15, she married a fellow actor, Charles HOPKINS. She was widowed three years later. Six months after Hopkins's death she married David POE, Jr., in Richmond in April 1806. Their first child, William Henry Leonard, was born in January 1807, followed by their second child, Edgar, on January 19, 1809, both born in Boston. Their daughter Rosalie was born in Richmond in December 1810. Throughout her childbearing years, Eliza continued to act because she was desperate for money. Her husband's mediocre performances and harsh reviews had not made him popular on stage. After David Poe, Jr., deserted his wife and children in July 1811, Eliza took one more role before becoming too ill to continue. She appeared on stage for the last time on October 11, 1811, and lay ill with tuberculosis for two months before dying at the age of 24 on December 8, 1811. Only one portrait of Eliza Poe exists, an oval miniature that shows the 15-year-old young woman with her large doe-like eyes, cupid's-bow mouth, dangling curls, and childlike face. She is portrayed seated, wearing dangling earrings, a low-cut dress with a high sash under the bodice, and a bonnet covered with ribbons.

Poe's mother, Elizabeth Arnold Poe. (Edgar Allan Poe Society)

Poe, John (n.d.) Poe's great-grandfather. The son of a Protestant tenant farmer in Dring, County Cavan, Ireland, he married the sister of an admiral and emigrated to the United States in 1750, settling in Lancaster County, Pennsylvania.

Poe, Neilson (1809–1884) Poe's second cousin and a lawyer, as well as a journalist, publisher and editor. Poe never forgave him for trying to persuade Maria CLEMM to make Virginia wait a few years before marrying, believing that Neilson was planning to take her from him. Three years after the marriage, when Neilson failed to respond to a request that he publish a glowing account of Poe's achievements as editor and author, Poe wrote an angry letter to Dr. Joseph SNODGRASS, stating, "I believe him [Neilson Poe] to be the bitterest enemy I have in the world. He is the more despicable in this, since he makes loud professions of friendship."

Poe, Rosalie (1810–1874) Poe's younger sister, who was adopted by William and Jane Scott MACKENZIE. She has been described by observers as having been "backward," a dull, pathetic figure whose mental development never surpassed the age of 12. Whenever Poe visited her at the Mackenzies' home, Duncan Lodge,

she would dote over him to an extent that embarrassed him. Possessed of a tiresome and monotonous personality, Rosalie managed to earn a living as a young woman by teaching writing for nine years in a school run by Miss Jane Mackenzie, one of the Mackenzies' biological children. When the Mackenzies died, their son John became her guardian. In 1870, Rosalie entered a home for indigents, where she died four years later.

Poe, Virginia *See* Virginia CLEMM.

Poe, William Henry Leonard (1807–1831) Edgar Allan Poe's elder brother, known as Henry. He was sent to Baltimore to live with his paternal grandparents from the time he was two years old to adulthood. Henry journeyed to the Near East, the West Indies, Montevideo, the Mediterranean, and Russia during the late 1820s as a crewman aboard the American frigate *Macedonian*. His brother would later claim some of Henry's adventures for his own, hinting darkly of adventures in Russia and other distant places. When Henry returned to Baltimore in 1827, he and his widowed grandmother Elizabeth Poe moved in with Maria CLEMM, his grandmother's daughter and his aunt. He also wrote and published in October 27, 1827, issue of the *Baltimore North American* a short story titled "The Pirate," the subject of which is his brother's tragic love affair with Elmira ROYSTER and his eventual adventures as he sought to escape the pain. The story of the star-crossed lovers was the type of material that would appeal to the sentimental tastes of the period and especially to the romantic notions of youth. Henry also published under his own name in the *Baltimore North American* several poems that had appeared in Edgar's privately published *TAMERLANE AND OTHER POEMS*. In a letter dated August 10, 1829, Edgar wrote to John ALLAN that he had succeeded finding his grandmother and relatives in Baltimore, and his description of the pathetic household indicates Henry's condition at the time: "My Grandmother is extremely poor and ill. My Aunt Maria if possible is still worse and Henry entirely given over to drink and unable to help himself, much less me." Henry suffered from tuberculosis and he continued to drink heavily. On August 1, 1831, he died at the age of 24.

Poems By Edgar A. Poe The third collection of Poe's poems to be published and his second commercial publication. While attending the UNITED STATES MILITARY ACADEMY AT WEST POINT, Poe collected poems that he had published in Baltimore, as well as new poems written while living with Maria CLEMM, in Richmond, Virginia, and at West Point, into a book that would become his third published collection. While at West Point, he submitted the poems to Colonel Thayer,

Duncan Lodge, Rosalie Poe's home after the Mackenzies adopted her. (Edgar Allan Poe Library, Richmond)

superintendent of the Academy, and asked him to give the cadets permission to subscribe to the publication of the poems at 75¢ each, to be deducted from their pay. With this permission, Poe had guaranteed sales of several hundred copies, and he wrote to Elam Bliss, the New York City publisher, telling him of the guaranteed advance sales. The cadets were unaware of what the collection would contain, but they expected Poe would include humorous verse satirizing officers and the academy faculty. The collection was preceded by the following: "To the U.S. Corps of Cadets This Volume Is Respectfully Dedicated." Those cadets who read the work felt that Poe had deceived them. Much of the work was incomprehensible to them, and they expressed derision for it. The collection contained 11 poems: "ISRAFEL," "TO HELEN," "THE SLEEPER," "LENORE," "THE VALLEY OF UNREST," "ROMANCE," "FAIRY LAND," "A PAEAN," "THE DOMED CITY," "AL AARAAF," and "TAMER-LANE." The slender booklet of poems, bound in green cardboard, received little attention aside from a review appearing in the May 7, 1831, issue of the *NEW YORK MIRROR* that said, "The poetry of this little volume has a plausible air of imagination, inconsistent with the gen-

eral indefiniteness of the ideas. Everything in the language betokens poetic inspiration, but it rather resembles the leaves of the sybil when scattered by the winds."

"Poems. By Frances S. Osgood. New York: Clark & Austin"   Review by Poe that appeared in the December 13, 1845, issue of the *BROADWAY JOURNAL*. Poe praises the poet for having experimented in a wide range of poetic forms and states "there is not one in which she has not very creditably succeeded." This is the first collection of her poems, and the reviewer feels that in selecting some and omitting others she "is in danger of losing the credit to which she is so fairly entitled on the score of versatility." The review examines in detail five of the poems—"The Spirit of Poetry," "She Loves Him Yet," "Aspirations," "Lenore," and "A Song"—and includes the full text of each. Although Poe finds minor flaws in the poems, such as the need in one instance to substitute "you" for "thee" throughout—"the modern and colloquial for the ancient and so-called poetical pronoun"—the review conveys "a high opinion of the power of the poetess."

"Poems—By Miss H. F. Gould. Third Edition. Boston: Hilliard, Gray & Co. 1835" Review by Poe that appeared in the January 1836 issue of the SOUTHERN LITERARY MESSENGER. The reviewer praises Hannah F. Gould for her disposition "to seek beauty where it is not usually sought—in the homelinesses . . . and in the most familiar realities of existence." He also praises her "*abandon* of manner" as well as "a phraseology sparkling with antithesis, yet, strange to say, perfectly simple and unaffected." Poe focuses particular attention upon Gould's poem "The Dying Storm," which is "full, forcible, and free from artificiality."

"Poems by James Russell Lowell. Published by John Owen: Cambridge" Review by Poe that appeared in the March 1844 issue of GRAHAM'S MAGAZINE. The review opened by praising Lowell's new collection and by declaring that this new volume would place him "*at the very head* of the poets of America." Poe examines in detail the poet's "Legend of Brittany" and finds it "truly magnificent," filled with "the loftier merits," but he also observes that it suffers from "the error of didacticism. After every few words of narration, comes a page of morality." Further, the review observes minor errors in versification and "the harsh consonants are excessive." With apologies for the brevity of the review, Poe ends by repeating that Lowell "has given evidence of a least as high poetical genius as any man in America—if not a loftier genius than any."

"Poems, by William Cullen Bryant. Boston: Russell, Odiorne & Metcalfe. 1834" Review by Poe that appeared in the January 1835 issue of the SOUTHERN LITERARY MESSENGER. Poe praised the "new and beautiful edition" of poems and stated that "the pure white paper and excellent typography of the volume before us, will give a richer lustre to the gems of Mr. Bryant's genius." Behind the praise lies the suggestion that William Cullen BRYANT's best work is not contained within the attractive package, for Poe also makes the point that "the majority of mortals are governed by *appearances;* and even a dull tale will appear respectable in the pages of a hot pressed and gilt bound London annual." Placing the blame on the American public, which has largely ignored "native literature," Poe observes that Bryant's earlier "great intellectual power" is not evident in the current volume, which reflects the poet's "bitter regrets at the frowns of an unpoetical public."

"Poems; Translated and Original. By Mrs. E. F. Ellet, Philadelphia: Key & Biddle. 1835" Review by Poe that appeared in the January 1836 issue of the SOUTHERN LITERARY MESSENGER. The review notes that 39 of the 57 poems in the collection are original and the rest are

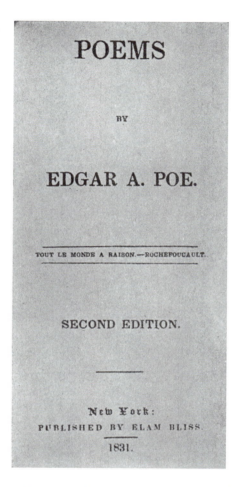

Title page of Poems *by Edgar A. Poe, published in 1831.* (Robert Gregor)

translations from the French, Spanish, Italian and German, and "these translations are very creditable to her [Elizabeth Fries ELLET]." Poe asserts that in instances where he has tested the accuracy of the translation by referring to the originals, "we have always found reason to be satisfied with her performances." In examining Ellet's original compositions, the reviewer observes that "Mrs. Ellet is a poetess of no ordinary rank," and he prints from the volume "a little poem rich in vigorous expression, and full of solemn thought. Its chief merits, however, are condensation and energy."

"Poe's Reply to His Critics" Essay published in a supplement to the July 1836 issue of the SOUTHERN LITERARY MESSENGER. The essay consists of a selection from the notices that the *Messenger* has received and quotes liberally from the letters of criticism. Poe assures readers that care has been taken in selecting among notices so that "no suspicion of unfairness in this selection should be entertained." The notices are quoted in their entirety, before Poe then responds to particular points.

"Poetical Remains of the Late Lucretia Maria Davidson. Collected and Arranged By Her Mother, With a Biography By Miss Sedgwick. Lea & Blanchard, Philadelphia" Review by Poe that appeared in the December 1841 issue of GRAHAM'S MAGAZINE. Poe praises the biographical portion of the work, and states "that nothing could be more intensely pathetic." He is more skeptical when approaching the poetry and states that he was forced "to dissent from that extravagant eulogium which had its origin, beyond doubt, in a confounding of the interest felt in the poetess and her sad fortunes with a legitimate admiration of her works." The review asks that the works be judged on their present merit, not on what the author might have written had she lived, and asserts that no further development may have occurred for "the mind is early matured only to be early in its decadence." Although the review acknowledges "warmth of admiration for the personal character" of the poet, Poe asks that critics focus on the "appreciation of their poetic ability." He notes that the distinction is "too obvious for comment; and its observation would have spared us much twaddle on the part of the commentators upon 'Amir Khan'," one of the poems in the collection.

"The Poetical Writings of Mrs. Elizabeth Oakes Smith. First Complete Edition. New York; J. S. Redfield" Review by Poe that appeared in the August 23, 1845, issue of the BROADWAY JOURNAL. The review observes that Smith owes her reputation as a poet to the publication of "The Sinless Child," "her longest and perhaps her most meritorious composition." Poe does not accept the merits of the poem in total, finding the conception to be "original, but somewhat forced" and the execution effective in parts, but he observes that "the conduct, upon the whole, is feeble, and the denouement is obscure, and inconsequential." The review suggests that critics should confine themselves to passages extracted from the poem, for many of such passages "possess merits of a lofty order." Poe then examines sections from the work to illustrate this point. He also compares a portion of Smith's poem "The Water" with lines from Henry Wadsworth LONGFELLOW, and concludes with the question, "If this is *not* a plagiarism, and a very bold one, on the part of Professor Longfellow, will anybody be kind enough to tell us what it *is?*"

"The Poetic Principle" Essay by Poe that appeared in the December 1848 issue of the SOUTHERN LITERARY MESSENGER. The essay closely resembles, and is based on, Poe's lecture on the same topic, first delivered on December 20, 1848, in Providence, Rhode Island. Poe uses excerpts from 11 poems by such writers as William Cullen BRYANT, George Gordon Lord BYRON, Thomas HOOD, Henry Wadsworth LONGFELLOW, Percy Bysshe SHELLEY, and Alfred Lord TENNYSON to provide examples to support his ideas. This essay combines with "THE RATIONALE OF VERSE" to form the foundation of Poe's critical theory. Poe suggests that true poetry results from a combination of "the simple elements which induce in the Poet himself the true poetical effect." Despite his own sometime lengthy poems, Poe states that "A long poem does not exist." Instead, the epic and other long poems are simply composed of "a series of minor poems." Some critics have seen this as Poe's own explanation for the unpopularity of "AL AARAAF" and his failure to finish other long works. In the essay, he also rejects didacticism and takes a stand against using poetry to convey moral principles or to teach. He argues that the sole reason for a poem's existence should be its aesthetic essence, and the poet should aim to create "this poem which is a poem and nothing more—this poem written solely for the poem's sake." He writes that the poet should be a creator and perfector of beauty, not the manufacturer of a tool that has a purpose to teach or preach. Poe suggests that poets may find truth in the simple elements that surround them, such as "the volutes of the flower . . . the clustering of low shrubberies . . . the waving of the grainfields . . . the blue distance of the mountains . . . the grouping of the clouds . . . the twinkling of half-hidden brooks . . . the gleaming of silver rivers . . . the repose of sequestered lakes . . . the star-mirroring depths of lonely wells." The poet may also perceive truth in "all noble thoughts—in all unworldly motives," as well as in a woman's beauty and love.

"The Poetry of Life. By Sarah Stickney, Author of 'Pictures of Private Life.' Philadelphia: Republished by Carey, Lea, & Blanchard" Review by Poe that appeared in the January 1836 issue of the SOUTHERN LITERARY MESSENGER. The review opens with a list of the categories into which Stickney has sorted the poems in this anthology, and Poe's comment that the title of the work should be more specific to indicate the rather limited design of the work. Examining Stickney's intention to "treat of poetic feeling, rather than poetry," Poe writes, "she is, we think, insufficiently alive to the *delicacies* of the beautiful—unable to fully appreciate the *energies* of the sublime." To support that assertion, Poe reprints without comment Stickney's attempt to bring a passage from BYRON's *Childe Harold* "down to the level of ordinary composition." In contrast, however, he cannot remain uncritical in her handling of lines from Percy Bysshe Shelley's "Ode to Naples," "of whose exquisite beauty she has evidently not the slightest comprehension." He ends the review with a recommendation that "Miss Stickney should immediately burn her copy of Shelley—it is to her capacities a sealed book."

"The Poetry of Rufus Dawes—A Retrospective Criticism" Review by Poe that appeared in the October 1842 issue of GRAHAM'S MAGAZINE. Poe opens his review of Dawes's work by quoting the opinion of Rufus Wilmot GRISWOLD that "the standing of Mr. Dawes is as yet unsettled; there being a wide difference of opinion respecting his writings." The review then examines the factors that have resulted in what Griswold called "Dawes's "high poetical reputation" and determines that this view "might be received as evidence of his actual merit . . . were it not too scandalously at variance with a species of criticism which *will not* be resisted." To test the validity of Griswold's assertion, Poe has made "inquiry into the true character of the volume to which we have before alluded, and . . . this inquiry has but resulted in the confirmation of our previous opinion; and we now hesitate not to say, that no man in America has been more shamefully over-estimated than the one who forms the subject of this article." To support this assertion, Poe analyzes in detail Dawes's poem "Geraldine." Calling it "a most servile imitation of the 'Don Juan' of Lord Byron" and "a mere mass of irrelevancy," Poe quotes stanzas from the poem, pointing out that "this *is* a droll piece of business" in which the poet's works "may be regarded as a theatrical world of mere verbiage, somewhat bedizened with a tinselly meaning well adapted to the eyes of the rabble." Poe addresses those who insist on lauding Dawes's poems that "his poems have not been condemned, only because they have never been read."

"The Poets and Poetry of America, with an Historical Introduction. By Rufus Wilmot Griswold. One Vol. Carey & Hart: Philadelphia" Review by Poe that appeared in the June 1842 issue of GRAHAM'S MAGAZINE. Poe wrote that the one-volume anthology "is the best collection of the American Poets that has yet been made, whether we consider its completeness, its size, or its literary worth." The review provides details about the work, noting that the selections begin with the poems of Philip Freneau and include the works of approximately 88 authors, each selection "prefixed [with] a short but clear biography." Halfway through the review, Poe writes that while his "*general* opinion of the book" is that it is superior to any other, "we do not, however, always coincide with the judgment of the editor." Poe especially disagrees with Griswold's choice of poets and feels that he "has scarcely done justice to some of our younger poets," in particular James Russell LOWELL, "to whom others than ourselves have assigned a genius of the highest rank." The reviewer also feels that the editor "has unduly favored writers of New England." Aside from these two negative observations, Poe finds the book, "as a whole, is one of high merit," and "a good work."

Politian Character in Poe's unfinished drama POLITIAN. Actually the Earl of Leicester, he has come to Rome from England to avenge the lost honor of LALAGE, who has been seduced and abandoned by CASTIGLIONE, the son of her guardian the Duc di BROGLIO.

Politian Unfinished drama. Written in blank verse, the play is based on the BEAUCHAMP-SHARP MURDER CASE, a celebrated crime of passion, also known as "The Kentucky Tragedy," that occurred in 1825. Poe set his drama in 16th-century Rome. His hero is named after a 15th-century poet, humanist, scholar, and teacher of the Italian Renaissance whose many works include Latin poems, *Miscellanea,* and *Orfeo,* a lyrical drama with musical accompaniment. After reading the play, John Pendleton KENNEDY suggested to Poe that he return to writing poetry and tales.

PUBLISHING AND DRAMATIZATION HISTORY

Excerpts from the play appeared in the December 1835 and January 1836 issues of the SOUTHERN LITERARY MESSENGER, in celebration of Poe's appointment as editor. Poe also included the play in THE RAVEN AND OTHER POEMS, published in 1845.

No film has been made of the drama.

A youthful Rufus Griswold, whose Poets and Poetry of America *Poe reviewed.* (Library of Congress)

CHARACTERS

ALESSANDRA, BALDAZZAR, Duc di BROGLIO, CASTIGLIONE, JACINTA, LALAGE, POLITIAN, UGO.

PLOT SYNOPSIS

The drama opens as servants in the di Broglio family discuss the debauchery of Castiglione and the recent "base seduction and abandonment" of his father's orphaned ward Lalage, to which they attribute "his low debaucheries—his gambling habits / And all his numerous vices." Castiglione becomes engaged to his cousin Alessandra, leading Lalage to cry and despair for her life. She gives all of her jewels to her maid Jacinta, as if she were dying. Instead, she finds strength in the appearance of Politian, the Earl of Leicester, whom she seems to know from a past visit to England. Lalage catches Politian's attention by singing a traditional ballad in English, and his reaction hints that his recent melancholy has been, in part, due to a loss of love. When the two meet, he speaks to her of love, but Lalage reproaches him and challenges him to avenge her honor by dueling with Castiglione. Despite his resolve, Politian is unable to carry out her request, and they meet amid the ruins of the Coliseum, at which point Poe introduces his poem "THE COLISEUM." As the play comes to an abrupt halt, Politian seems determined to try to carry, once again, the attempt to duel as he leaves Lalage.

Pompey (1)   Character in Poe's short story "THE MAN THAT WAS USED UP." He is "an old negro valet" who attends to the needs of Brevet Brigadier General John A. B. C. SMITH, screwing on arms and a leg, inserting Smith's teeth, and attaching and adjusting his wig. "The manipulations of Pompey" make "a very striking difference" in the appearance of Smith, turning him from "a large and exceedingly odd looking bundle of something" to the stalwart-looking general.

Pompey (2)   Character in Poe's short story "A PREDICAMENT." Signora Psyche ZENOBIA refers to him as "my negro!—sweet Pompey!" He is approximately three feet tall, and about 70 or 80 years old, corpulent and with bow legs. "Nature had endowed him with no neck, and had placed his ankles (as usual with that race) in the middle of the upper portion of the feet." He wears a "nearly-new drab overcoat" that was owned formerly by "the tall, stately, and illustrious Dr. Moneypenny." Although he serves the signora faithfully, she tears out "a vast quantity of the black, and crisp, and curling material [his hair]" after he accidentally trips her, but they make up. Later, he holds her upon his shoulders as she looks through the keyhole of a giant clock, but deserts the signora in terror when the clock's minute hand beheads her.

Ponnonner, Doctor   Character in Poe's short story "SOME WORDS WITH A MUMMY." He invites the narrator of the story and others to join him in unraveling a mummy at the City Museum. He prepares his instruments for dissection, but decides to postpone the internal examination until the next day while the assembled group experiments by applying electricity to the mummy. When the mummy reacts, its leg "bestowed a kick upon Doctor Ponnonner, which had the effect of discharging that gentleman, like an arrow from a catapult, through a window to the street below." Unhurt by the experience, Ponnonner returns and applies the electricity with a vengeance, animating the mummy, who chastises him for being "a poor fat little fool who *knows* no better."

Pontet, Henry (1840–1902)   Irish composer who also wrote under the pseudonym M. Piccolomini. He composed "A Dream Within a Dream," a song setting of Poe's poem of the same name.

"Posthumous Memoirs of His Own Time. By Sir N. W. Wraxall, Baronet. Author of 'Memoirs of My Own Time.' Philadelphia: Republished by Carey, Lea & Blanchard"   Review by Poe that appeared in the October 1836 issue of the SOUTHERN LITERARY MESSENGER. The reviewer praised the work, stating that "the Baronet's pages will excite no ordinary attention, and will be read with unusual profit and pleasure." Poe provides a detailed account of the work and includes a description of the information contained within as well as an account of the objections to various portrayals voiced by members of the royal family and leading political figures. Readers learn that first Lord of the Treasury, the son of Charles Jenkinson, "was offended at the 'just and impartial' character given his father." The partisans "arose in arms at what they considered the gross abuse of their leaders." The royal family "disliked the portrait drawn of King George the Third," and "the Earl of Bute would not be appeased." Reviewers in the British *Quarterly Review* had labeled the book an "'imbecile and immoral work,'" while the *Edinburgh Review* "joined in the hue and cry with still greater virulence, and even more disgusting personal abuse." Poe includes abridged versions of several of the more interesting narrations from the work to illustrate its general character with its "political facts and inferences—attempts at explaining the hidden motives of ministers or their agents—rumors of the day—and remarks upon public events or characters abroad. Although the reviewer seems to relish the details, he admonishes the author and notes that "the Baronet is sadly given to scandal, and is peculiarly *piquant* in the indulgence of his propensity."

"The Posthumous Papers of the Pickwick Club: Containing a Faithful Record of the Perambulations, Perils, Travels, Adventures, and Sporting Transactions of the Corresponding Members. Edited by 'Boz.' Philadelphia: Published by Carey, Lea & Blanchard" Review by Poe that appeared in the November 1836 issue of the SOUTHERN LITERARY MESSENGER. Poe's review of this novel by Charles DICKENS contains the same high level of respect for the English author's talent that he had expressed in an earlier review of *Watkins, Tottle and Other Sketches,* and which he would repeat in reviewing *The Old Curiosity Shop* and *Barnaby Rudge.* Before the review conducts a thorough examination of the incidents in the novel, it praises the "comic power" and "the rich imaginative conception of Mr. Dickens" and asserts that "his general powers as a prose writer are equalled by few." Poe ends the review by quoting the concluding portion of "a vigorous sketch" titled "A Madman's MS."

"Postscript to 'A Reply to Outis'" *See* "A CONTINUATION OF THE VOLUMINOUS HISTORY OF THE LITTLE LONGFELLOW WAR—MR. POE'S FURTHER REPLY TO THE LETTER OF OUTIS."

Power, Mrs. Nicholas (n.d.) Mother of Sarah Helen WHITMAN, with whom Poe drew up a marriage contract in 1848. A woman of strong opinions, she opposed her widowed daughter's marriage to Poe and insisted that Whitman's property be transferred to her before the execution of the marriage contract.

"The Power of Words" Short story. This tale is another of Poe's metaphysical speculations, similar to "THE COLLOQUY OF MONOS AND UNA" and "THE CONVERSATION OF EIROS AND CHARMION."

PUBLISHING AND DRAMATIZATION HISTORY

The story first appeared in the June 1845 issue of the *Democratic Review.* It was reprinted in the October 25, 1845, issue of the *BROADWAY JOURNAL.*

No film has been made of this work to date.

CHARACTERS

AGATHOS, OINOS.

PLOT SYNOPSIS

The story is structured as a dialogue about the creative propensities of divine intelligence in which Oinos, newly arrived from earth, questions Agathos about the nature of creative power and the role of God in creation. Their dialogue takes place as the two "swoop outward from the throne into the starry meadows beyond Orion, where, for pansies and violets, and heart's-ease, are the beds of the triplicate and triple-tinted suns." Oinos begs Agathos to speak "in the earth's familiar tones," as he explains the method of creation and the startling revelation that "the Deity does not create." Agathos relates the example of how the movement of a hand sets off vibrations to the air surrounding. These vibrations, in turn, give "impulse to every particle of the earth's air, which thenceforward, *and for ever,* was actuated by the one movement of the hand." These impulses must then have an effect on "every individual thing that exists *within the universe.*" Questioned by Oinos if impulses or motion, then, are the source of all creation, Agathos gives a qualified positive response and states that the source of all motion (impulse) is thought as he teaches Oinos "the *physical power of words.*" Agathos offers a syllogism to explain creation and concludes that if motion is the source of creation and thought is the source of motion, then thought is the source of creation. As the story ends, Agathos and Oinos hover over a "fair star," the greenest they have seen, which is filled with brilliant flowers and "fierce volcanoes like the passions of a turbulent heart." Agathos reveals that he is the creator of "this wild star—it is now three centuries since with clasped hands, and with streaming eyes, at the feet of my beloved—I spoke it—with a few passionate sentences—into birth."

"Powhatan: A Metrical Romance in Seven Cantos. By Seba Smith. New York, Harper and Brothers" Review by Poe that appeared in the July 1841 issue of *GRAHAM'S MAGAZINE.* Poe begins the review by correcting the error made in notices of the poem, which speak of the author as "Mrs. Seba Smith." He points out the use of the personal pronoun "of the masculine gender" throughout and questions if the error is made because "no gentleman has *read* even so far as the preface of the book. . . . If so, they are decidedly right, too." The review proceeds to denounce the work in the most scathing of terms. After stating that the book is free of typographical errors "from one end to the other," Poe writes that "further than this, in the way of commendation, no man with both brains and conscience should proceed." Calling the poem "a flat affair," the reviewer condemns the author's failure to provide "any artistic *arrangement* of his facts." Halfway through the review, Poe begins to refer to Smith by the name of the protagonist of his epistolary novel *Letters of Major Jack Downing.* The lack of explanation is confusing to the reader, but an explanation for this appears in Poe's entry for Smith in "AUTOGRAPHY." In that work, Poe stated that this poem is "precisely such a one as we might imagine would be written by a veritable Jack Downing; by Jack Downing himself, had this creature of Mr. Smith's fancy been endowed with a real entity. . . . [A]t least one-half of his character actually exists in the bosom of his originator. It was the Jack Downing half that composed 'Powhatan.'"

Pratt, Captain   Character in Poe's short story "THREE SUNDAYS IN A WEEK." He has been absent from England for a year "in foreign travel," having made a journey "round Cape Horn." His assertion that the day after his visit will be Sunday, countered by Captain SMITHERTON's assertion that the day preceding their visit is Sunday, provides the solution to the main predicament of the story—an uncle's demand that his niece may marry only *"when three Sundays come together in a week."*

"A Predicament"   Short story. Although treated as two separate stories, "A Predicament" and "HOW TO WRITE A BLACKWOOD ARTICLE" were originally published together, with "A Predicament" originally titled "The Scythe of Time" and offered as an example of a Blackwood article produced by following the directions in the companion piece. The combined works contain Poe's only use of a female narrator. As a parody of the typical Blackwood tale, the story uses psychological mannerisms to elaborate a great show of learning, and it is centered on a protagonist isolated by a bizarre turn of events.

PUBLISHING AND DRAMATIZATION HISTORY

The story was first published with "How to Write a Blackwood Article" and published under the title "The Psyche Zenobia" in the November 1838 issue of the Baltimore *American Museum.* The stories were presented separately and titled "How to Write a Blackwood Article" and "A Predicament" when they were published in Poe's short-story collection TALES OF THE GROTESQUE AND ARABESQUE in 1840.

The story is preceded by an epigraph taken from John Milton's masque *Comus,* whose theme is the struggle between chaste temperance and sensual pleasure. The line selected is spoken by Comus, the Roman god of sensual pleasure, to a young woman left in the woods by her brothers who go to find food for her: "What chance, good lady, hath bereft you thus?"

No film has been made of the story to date.

CHARACTERS

DIANA (2), POMPEY (2), Signora Psyche ZENOBIA.

PLOT SYNOPSIS

The first title of the story is highly appropriate, for the "huge, glittering, scimitar-like minute-hand" of a clock serves as a scimitar that beheads the narrator, Signora Psyche Zenobia. The story opens as Zenobia walks through the city of Edina with her two faithful companions, her poodle Diana and her servant Pompey. Zenobia views "a Gothic cathedral—vast, venerable, and with a tall steeple" containing a huge clockface, and she feels an intense desire to climb into the peak of the steeple. As she makes her ascent, she ponders in grand philosophical terms the meaning of life and that "upon one such little step in the great staircase of human life how vast a sum of human happiness or misery depends!" Once at the top, accompanied by Diana and Pompey, the signora's curiosity takes over and she "looked about the room for an aperture through which to survey the city." Finding one, she commands Pompey to lift her onto his shoulders, so that she can thrust her head through the opening in the dial-plate. For more than a half hour she enjoys the view, despite the suffering and complaints of Pompey, whom she bullies into silence. Losing track of time, Zenobia is surprised to feel that the exceedingly sharp minute hand is touching her neck, pressing harder and harder into the skin. There follows a slow and methodical description of her gradual decapitation, as the minute hand first buries itself two inches into her neck, then four-and-a-half inches. "At twenty-five minutes past five in the afternoon, precisely," the minute hand completely severs Zenobia's head from her body, but the head and body both remain alive and aware of each other. "Shortly afterward, it [the head] made me a speech, which I could hear but indistinctly without ears." Pompey deserts her while only the bones of Diana remain in a corner after a rat has attacked her. Thus, the headless Zenobia laments, "Dogless, niggerless, headless, what *now* remains for the unhappy Signora Psyche Zenobia? Alas—*nothing!* I have done."

Preface and Introduction to ***The Conchologist's First Book,*** **1839**   Poe's contribution to the scientific manual on conchology, whose complete title is *The Conchologists's First Book: or, A System of Testaceous Malacology,* published in April 1839 by Haswell, Barrington & Haswell and created for use in schools. The book was attacked for having been plagiarized, although Poe contended that, aside from writing the preface and the introduction, he had served merely as editor of the work. The preface, which Poe signed *E. A. P.,* explains the terms "Malacology" and "Conchology" and acknowledges Mr. Thomas WYATT "and his late excellent 'Manual of Conchology.'" The three pages of introduction contain quotations from scientists and are used to introduce 12 pages of engravings of shells, including their parts and hinges. Critics of Poe's time identified much of the work contained in the preface and introduction, including the engravings, as having been closely paraphrased from Captain Thomas Brown's *The Conchologist's Textbook,* published in Glasgow, Scotland, in 1837. The body of *The Conchologist's First Book* is not original; by arrangement with the author, Poe paraphrased Wyatt's *Manual of Conchology*, a more expensive book published unsuccessfully by Harper's. Wyatt paid Poe $50 to popularize the work and to lend his name to it by issuing an edition with Poe's name on the title page and leaving Brown entirely without credit. The arrangement, which helped Wyatt to avoid trouble over copyright, created tensions between Harper's and Poe that six years later made them refuse his request that they issue his collected works.

"The Premature Burial"   Short story. The story begins as an essay, citing a number of supposedly factual burials, but the story recounts only the narrator's delusions. Poe plays upon the public preoccupation in his time with the fear of being buried alive, a fear that was fed by published reports of hungry cadavers and cries heard coming from graves. Nonfiction accounts tell of people leaving instructions to delay their burials and to test their corpses by inflicting pain on their feet in the effort to provoke a reaction. Among ingenious precautions invented in the 19th century to avoid accidental live burial were attaching bells to corpses, installing speaking tubes and air tubes in coffins, and providing a flag a victim could wave in distress.

PUBLISHING AND DRAMATIZATION HISTORY

The story first appeared in the July 31, 1844, issue of the *PHILADELPHIA DOLLAR NEWSPAPER*.

No epigraph precedes the story.

The story was made into a film in 1962. *The Premature Burial* was directed by Roger CORMAN and starred Ray Milland, Hazel Court, Richard Ney, Heather Angel, Alan Napier, and John Dierkes. This adaptation casts Milland as a medical student who has a terrifying phobia of being accidentally entombed. Corman's adaptation includes elements of Poe's short story "BERENICE."

CHARACTERS

Mademoiselle LAFOURCADE, Monsieur RENNELLE, Edward STAPLETON, unnamed narrator.

PLOT SYNOPSIS

Recounted by an unnamed narrator who has for several years "been subject to attacks of the singular disorder which physicians have agreed to term catalepsy," the story opens with several accounts of people buried alive, then rescued from their premature graves. Because the catalepsy seizures render him "senseless and externally motionless . . . while the closest scrutiny, and the most rigorous medical tests, fail to establish any material distinction between the state of

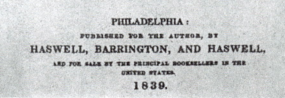

Poe wrote the preface and introduction and lent his name to this scientific manual. (Robert Gregor)

the sufferer and what we conceive of absolute death," he has taken every precaution to avoid being buried alive. He has horrifying fantasies in which he imagines entombment, and he talks "of worms, of tombs, and epitaphs." In his obsession, the narrator makes modifications to the family vault, making arrangements for "the free admission of air and light, and convenient receptacles for food and water, within immediate reach of the coffin." He relates having one seizure while on a gunning expedition aboard a small sloop traveling on the James River in Virginia. He awakens in a very narrow lower berth, and he imagines that the bottom of the berth above him is the lid of a coffin. He believes that strangers "had buried me as a dog—nailed up in some common coffin—and thrust deep, deep, and forever, into some ordinary and nameless grave." After he is awakened by the crew of the sloop, he becomes "a new man, and lived a man's life." He changes his attitude and dismisses "forever my charnel apprehensions, and with them vanished the cataleptic disorder of which, perhaps, they had been less the consequence than the cause."

Preston, James P. (n.d.)   The father of Poe's Richmond classmate, James T. Preston. A colonel in the U.S. Army, he wrote one of the four letters of recommendation that Poe submitted to the Honorable John Henry Eaton, secretary of war, to solicit an appointment to the UNITED STATES MILITARY ACADEMY AT WEST POINT. In the letter, dated May 13, 1829, Preston wrote that Poe had "been born under circumstances of great adversity." He also asserted that he had "undoubted proofs that he is a young gentleman of genius and talents . . . destined to be distinguished."

Preston, Mr.   Character in Poe's short story "WILLIAM WILSON." A fellow commoner with William WILSON at Oxford, Preston is the owner of the chambers in which Wilson meets the wealthy nobleman GLENDENNING and where Wilson also tries to cheat him out of a considerable sum of money in a game of cards.

Price, Addision (1871–1943)   English composer, organist and voice teacher whose published compositions include operas, masses, benediction services, motets, songs, chamber music, and piano pieces. In 1921, he composed the song "Annabel Lee," inspired by Poe's poem of the same name; the song "Bridal Ballad," inspired by Poe's poem of the same name; and "Eldorado," also inspired by Poe's poem of the same name.

Price, Richard (1723–1791)   English nonconformist minister and political philosopher. He is mentioned in "THE DOMAIN OF ARNHEIM" as one of the "perfectionists" whose doctrines are foreshadowed by the narrator's friend ELLISON. In "LIONIZING," the narrator meets "a human-perfectibility man" who quotes Price.

Price, Vincent (1911–1993)   American actor who appeared in more than 100 films. Because of his well-bred manner and formal way of speaking, Price was cast as the gentleman or aristocrat, often sinister and decadent, in such movies as *The Private Lives of Elizabeth and Essex* (1939), *The House of the Seven Gables* (1940), *Shock* (1946), *Dragonwyck* (1946), and *House of Wax* (1953). Despite critical acclaim for his early roles, Price did not attain major audience recognition as an actor and screen presence until he starred in such movies as *The Fly* (1958), *Return of the Fly* (1959), and the Poe cycle of Roger CORMAN. Price appeared in 10 of the 11 Corman-directed films: *The Pit and the Pendulum* (1961), *Tales of Terror* (1962), *The Raven* (1963), *The Masque of the Red Death* (1964), *The Haunted Palace*

(1964), *The Tomb of Ligeia* (1965), *The City Under the Sea* (1965), *The Conqueror Worm* (1968), *The Oblong Box* (1969), and *Cry of the Banshee* (1970).

Priestley, Joseph (1733–1804)   British moral philosopher and chemist who is considered one of the founders of modern chemistry because of his experimental methods. He isolated and described the properties of several gases, and he discovered oxygen and its role in combustion and respiration. He is mentioned in "THE DOMAIN OF ARNHEIM" as one of the "perfectionists" whose doctrines are foreshadowed by the narrator's friend ELLISON. In "LIONIZING," the narrator meets "a human-perfectibility man" who quotes Priestley.

Proffit, Peter   Character and narrator in Poe's short story "THE BUSINESS MAN." He alerts readers at the outset: "I am a business man. I am a methodical man." He prides himself on his "general habits of accuracy and punctuality" and provides readers with a smug self-evaluation of his rise that reveals his egotistical satisfaction at achieving commercial success. The story contains accounts of his eight business "speculations" on the road to success. The reader sees that Proffit uses marginally legal tactics in such businesses as a slum building scheme to drive down real estate prices, insurance fraud, even collecting postage for counterfeit letters. Such activities, coupled with Poe's use of the name Peter Proffit, makes the story a harsh satire on the values of the American businessman.

The Prose Romances of Edgar A. Poe   Collection of Poe's short stories that was published by William H. Graham in 1843. Designed as a cheap edition for the popular market, the collection was to be part of a series that would be completed by further numbers, although only one issue appeared. Priced at 12 and a half cents, the edition included "THE MURDERS IN THE RUE MORGUE" and "THE MAN THAT WAS USED UP." Although two bookstores in Philadelphia sold the work, it had little success and was soon allowed to go out of print.

"The Prose Works of John Milton, With a Biographical Introduction by Rufus Wilmot Griswold. In Two Volumes. Philadelphia: Herman Hooker"   Review by Poe that appeared in the September 27, 1845, issue of the *BROADWAY JOURNAL*. Poe praises Rufus Wilmot GRISWOLD for correcting with this work what he believes to have been an egregious error among Americans, "that no edition of the Prose Works of John Milton has hitherto been issued in America." The review points out, nonetheless, that Griswold has produced two volumes that "contain *nearly* all the prose works of Milton" and he has omitted a treatise entitled "The Christian Doctrine," which he mentions in the introduction as being of doubtful authorship—"a work which [Milton] never would have given to the press himself." Poe counters that Griswold has little authority for this idea and asserts that, despite this assertion, the introduction "is, nevertheless, well written, and well adapted to its purposes. . . . At points, however, it may be thought extravagant or dogmatic." Although the review labels them "trifles," it points out further areas of disagreement with Griswold, particularly in his evaluation of Bacon: "We have no patience with the initial sneer at Bacon, as 'the meanest of mankind.'" Poe also finds that Griswold is too effusive in labeling Milton "the greatest of all human beings," suggesting that "he should have appended the words—'in the opinion, at least, of Dr. Griswold.'"

Prospero, Prince   Character in Poe's short story "THE MASQUE OF THE RED DEATH." After a horrible plague called the Red Death has depopulated half of his kingdom, the "happy and dauntless and sagacious" prince takes a thousand of his friends with him to a secluded rural hideaway, where "the prince had provided all the appliances of pleasure." He believes that he can keep the external world at bay, but his plan fails when he hosts a masked ball and the Red Death appears as a guest, killing the prince and all of his revelers.

Protheroe, Daniel (1866–1934)   Welsh composer whose compositions include songs for men's voices, choral works, music for string quartets, and the *Welsh Symphonic Poem.* In 1929, he wrote "Eldorado," a four-part chorus with piano accompaniment, inspired by Poe's poem of the same name.

Psalemoun   Character mentioned in the final chapter of Poe's novel *THE NARRATIVE OF ARTHUR GORDON PYM.* Also called Tsalemon, he was king of the eight islands visited by the crew of the *Jane Guy* and he lived on the smallest of the islands.

Psyche (1)   A name meaning "soul" that Poe evokes in several works. In mythology, she is a beautiful princess loved by Cupid, the god of love, who hid his identity and carried her away to a secluded castle, where he ordered her to never to look at his face. She disobeyed and looked at him while he slept, thus forcing him to abandon her. After she spent considerable time wandering the world to find him, the two were reunited and Jupiter, the king of the gods, made her immortal. In "THE SPECTACLES," Poe refers to Madame Stephanie LALANDE as having a head that "rivalled in outline that of the Greek Psyche." In "HOW TO WRITE A BLACKWOOD ARTICLE" and "A PREDICAMENT," the main character is named Signora Psyche ZENOBIA.

Psyche (2)   Character in Poe's poem "ULALUME." The speaker states that he wanders "In the ghoul-haunted woodland of Weir" with "my Soul / —Of cypress, with Psyche, my Soul." Psyche leads the speaker to "the door of a tomb," the tomb of his lost love ULALUME whom he had interred in "October, / On *this* very night of last year."

"The Psyche Zenobia"   Original title of Poe's short story "HOW TO WRITE A BLACKWOOD ARTICLE."

Puckler-Muskau, Hermann Ludwig Heinrich, Furst von (1785–1871)   German travel writer and author of the 1833 *Tour in England, Ireland and France,* which served as a source for Poe's "THE DOMAIN OF ARNHEIM." Poe provided a note to explain that the imagined incident in his story had actually occurred in England and "the name of the fortunate heir was Thelluson." He states that he saw an account of the incident in Puckler-Muskau's book, "who makes the sum inherited *ninety millions of pounds.*" The Thelluson case was famous in English law, and the litigation lasted 50 years.

Pundit   Character in Poe's short story "MELLONTA TAUTA." He is a passenger on the hot-air balloon *Skylark.* The name is a Hindu word for a Brahman who is learned in Sanskrit, philosophy, religion, and law. His profound, if erroneous, thoughts appear frequently in the letter that PUNDITA writes to the editor of *GODEY'S MAGAZINE AND LADY'S BOOK,* and he is quoted liberally. He "is the only conversible person on board; and he, poor soul! can speak of nothing but antiquities." He strives at length to convince Pundita "that the ancient Amriccans [sic] *governed themselves!*"

Pundita   Character in Poe's short story "MELLONTA TAUTA." She sends "a long gossiping letter" to the editor of *GODEY'S MAGAZINE AND LADY'S BOOK* and promises to punish the editor for all "impertinences by being as tedious, as discursive, as incoherent, and as unsatisfactory as possible." The letter is conveyed in a bottle that she has corked and thrown into the sea. She is "cooped up" in the hot-air balloon *Skylark* and relates details of a voyage. Pundita is used by Poe to express his pessimistic views of politics. The guarantees of equality for all men that appear in the Declaration of Independence, democratic institutions and rule by the mob come under severe criticism during the course of the voyage, while PUNDIT and Pundita exchange intellectual and pseudoscientific nonsense.

"The Purloined Letter"   Short story. The story is the third and most tightly constructed of Poe's tales of ratiocination. In May 1844, Poe made a list for James Russell LOWELL of works that he believed to be his best compositions. He stated, "The Purloined letter . . . is perhaps the best of my tales of ratiocination" and informed Lowell that it was yet unpublished but in the hands of an editor.

PUBLISHING AND DRAMATIZATION HISTORY

The story first appeared in *The Gift: A Christmas and New Year's Present for 1844*. It was reprinted in the 1845 collection *TALES BY EDGAR A. POE*.

An epigraph attributed to the Roman playwright Seneca precedes the story: *Nil sapientiae odiosius acumine nimio* ("Nothing is more disagreeable to wisdom than too much cunning"). Critics have not found a source in Seneca's writing for the quotation.

The story was very popular in France. Dramatist Victorien Sardou (1831–1908) wrote a play based on the story that was performed with great success on stage at the Gymnase.

CHARACTERS

Minister D——, C. Auguste DUPIN, Monsieur G——, unnamed narrator, unnamed "personage of most exalted station."

PLOT SYNOPSIS

"The Purloined Letter" is a tale of revenge as much as it is a tale that reminds readers of Dupin's highly refined inductive powers. The story opens with the unnamed narrator and Dupin sitting in "profound silence" in Dupin's "little back library," as the narrator is "mentally discussing certain topics which had formed matter for conversation between us at an earlier period of the evening." He refers to their earlier cases that are documented in "THE MURDERS IN THE RUE MORGUE" and "THE MYSTERY OF MARIE ROGÊT." Their reverie is disturbed by the arrival of the prefect of police, Monsieur G——, who has come to consult Dupin for advice about a puzzling case. The Minister D——, "who dares all things, those unbecoming as well as those becoming a man," has stolen an incriminating letter from the royal apartments. He has taken the letter in full sight of the female personage, who could not protest because "the other exalted personage from whom it was her wish to conceal it" has also entered the room. Dupin is even more intrigued by the case because he has had a previous encounter with Minister D—— who "at Vienna once, did me an evil turn, which I told him, quite good-humoredly, that I should remember." The prefect tells Dupin that the police have thoroughly searched the premises where the minister lives, but they have found nothing. They have looked into chair legs, on walls, in books, and in all other possible hiding places. After the prefect tells the story, Dupin's advice is that the police should return to the minister's home and "make a thorough re-search of the premises." Before leaving, the prefect provides Dupin with a thorough description of the letter. A month later, the prefect again visits Dupin, but he has had no further success. He is especially despondent because the reward, the size of which he refuses to identify, has lately doubled. When he tells Dupin that he would gladly pay 50,000 francs to anyone who would aid him in the matter, Dupin tells him "you may as well fill me up a check for the amount mentioned. When you have signed it, I will hand you the letter." The prefect grabs the letter and rushes out, as Dupin explains to the narrator that he visited Minister D——'s and observed the letter arranged in an open rack, but "inside out, re-directed, and resealed." He replaced the letter with his own that contains a few lines guaranteed to reveal him to the minister. Rather than to solve the mystery by searching for the letter, as the police have done, Dupin uses his intellect and enters the mind of the criminal to determine where the criminal would hide the letter.

Pym, Arthur Gordon   Title character in Poe's novel *THE NARRATIVE OF ARTHUR GORDON PYM*. He is the son of "a respectable trader in sea-stores in Nantucket," and his maternal grandfather was "an attorney in good practice." Despite such solid forebears, Arthur is a rebellious youth who runs away to sea by stowing away on a New Bedford whaler. When a mutiny erupts, he tries to suppress it. He then survives a storm that leaves only him and three other survivors. After a series of other difficulties, including enduring cannibalism, Pym and the one other remaining sailor are left drifting toward the South Pole in a canoe. The last sight that Pym reports is a giant human figure with skin white as snow standing guard.

"The Quacks of Helicon: A Satire. By L. A. Wilmer"
Review by Poe that appeared in the August 1841 issue
of *GRAHAM'S MAGAZINE*. The reviewer decries the lack of
satires by American writers and welcomes Wilmer's
book because it is new and well executed. More important, he welcomes the book because "in the universal
corruption amid which we gasp for breath, it is a really
pleasant thing to get even one accidental whiff of the
unadulterated air of truth." Poe does not pretend to be
oblivious to the "many defects" in the poem, and he
notes that "its prevalent blemishes are referrible [*sic*]
chiefly to the leading sin of *imitation*" of such writers as
John Dryden and George Gordon, Lord BYRON. A far
harsher criticism is leveled at the "gross obscenity, the
filth—we can use no gentler name—which disgraces
the 'Quacks of Helicon,'" which Poe asserts "cannot be
the result of innate impurity in the mind of the writer."
Instead, he judges that Wilmer was simply engaging in
"the slavish and indiscriminating imitation of the Swift
and Rochester school." The review states that Wilmer's
inclusion of vulgar material has done the book "an
irreparable injury, without effecting anything whatever
on the score of sarcasm, vigour, or wit." Poe also finds
fault with the title for not being distinctive enough nor
for not confining itself to "*American* quacks, while the
work does." Despite such criticism, Poe finds that this
poem, "even in its mannerism, has imbued itself with
the full spirit of the polish and pungency of Dryden,"
and it has the "far loftier merit of speaking fearlessly
the truth, at an epoch when truth is out of fashion." He
praises Wilmer who shows the courage to review by
name "most of our prominent literati, and treats them,
generally, as they deserve." Poe adds his voice to that of
Wilmer in condemning the literary "cliques" and
"coteries," from whom Poe the author also suffered,
and notes that "we speak of these things in the bitterness of scorn." Even in his approval of Wilmer's attacks,
Poe feels that the work fails to allow for exceptions to
the charges, for "it cannot be gainsaid that the greater
number of those who hold high places in our poetical
literature are absolute nincompoops. . . . [N]either
are we *all* brainless." Poe asserts that Wilmer "as often
tilts at what is true as at what is false," but he feels that
the fearlessness and design of the book will "save it
from that dreadful damnation of 'silent contempt'" to
which he expects editors will consign it.

Quarles Pseudonym used by Poe when he published
"THE RAVEN" in the January 29, 1845, issue of the New
York *EVENING MIRROR*. This first appearance in print of
the poem was accompanied by an introductory paragraph that shows the influence of Nathaniel P. WILLIS
on Poe at the time. The name was also attached to an
anonymous pamphlet that provided a defensive
response to Charles Dickens's criticism of American life
in *American Notes,* but Poe's authorship has never been
ascertained. Poe may have taken the name from that of
François Quarles (1592–1644), an English poet of the
metaphysical school who included in his poems striking
imagery taken from everyday pursuits and interests of
his time.

Quevedo y Villaegas, François Gomez de (1580–1645)
Spanish satirist, moralist, and poet. Poe quoted from
Quevedo's sonnet "Rome in Ruin" in his review "POEMS:
TRANSLATED AND ORIGINAL. BY MRS. E. F. ELLET."

Rachmaninoff, Sergey Vasilyevich (1873–1943) Russian composer, pianist, and conductor. Critics and music aficionados consider him one of the most brilliant pianists of the 20th century, while his own music still enjoys the affection of audiences and listeners. Among his major compositions are the Prelude in C-sharp Minor (1892) for piano, the opera *Aleko* (1893), the Piano Concertos No. 2 in C Minor (1900–01) and No. 3 in D Minor (1909), the Symphony No. 2 in E minor (1906), the symphonic poem *The Isle of the Dead* (1909), *The Liturgy of St. John Chrysotom* (1910) for choir, and 24 piano preludes. After leaving Russia in 1917 and settling in exile in the United States, Rachmaninoff turned primarily to a career as a concert pianist but continued to write, producing such major compositions as the *Variations on a Theme of Corelli* (1934) for piano, the *Rhapsody on a Theme of Paganini* (1936) for piano and orchestra, the Symphony No. 3 in A Minor (1936), the Piano Concerto No. 4 in G Minor (1937). In 1913, Rachmaninoff wrote *Kolokola (The Bells)*, a choral symphony for soprano, tenor, and baritone soloists; choir, and orchestra. The text is a Russian translation by Konstantin Balmont of Poe's poem "THE BELLS."

"The Rambler in North America, 1832–33. By Charles Joseph Latrobe, Author of 'The Alpenstock,' &c. New York: Harper and Brothers" Review by Poe that appeared in the December 1835 issue of the SOUTHERN LITERARY MESSENGER. Written by the son of English missionaries, the book consists of 37 letters that the author sent to his younger brother while traveling with Washington IRVING on "a late tour through the [American] Prairies." Poe expresses approval of Latrobe's approach to his subject for "viewing us, not with a merely English eye, but with the comprehensive glance of a citizen of the world." The review includes a passage from one of the letters in which Latrobe ponders American social and political principles, which Poe believes to be the sole passage that exhibits a "false inference from data undeniably correct." Despite this one point of disagreement, Poe declares this "the best work on America yet published."

Raphael [Raaffaello Sanzio] (1483–1520) Italian Renaissance painter, considered by critics to be one of the greatest artists of all time. Poe refers favorably to him in various works. In "PINAKIDIA," he states that Gray's "image of his bard" in his "Ode to Adversity" "was taken from a picture by Raphael." In "FIFTY SUGGESTIONS," in an entry in which Poe mocks the critics for "painting their faces to look like Macauley," he observes that "some our critics manage to resemble him, at length, as a Massaccian does a Raffaellian Virgin; and, except that the former is feebler and thinner than the other—suggesting the idea of its being the ghost of the other." Poe also makes reference to the painter in "THE DUC DE L'OMELETTE." As "his Satanic Majesty" shows l'Omelette around his chambers, the duke admires the exquisite paintings and thinks with excitement: "And Rafaelle has beheld them! Yes, Rafaelle has been here; for did he not paint the ———? and was he not consequently damned?"

"The Rationale of Verse" Critical essay by Poe conceived as a lecture and first published as "Notes on English Verse" in the March 1843 issue of the *Pioneer*. Poe revised the essay and added material to expand the earlier emphasis upon English verse. The revised and final version of the essay, now titled "The Rationale of Verse," appeared in the October–November 1848 issue of the SOUTHERN LITERARY MESSENGER. Critics consider the essay to be Poe's most complete account of his theory of metrics and poetic form. Poe elaborates in this essay upon topics that are introduced in "THE POETIC PRINCIPLE" and "THE PHILOSOPHY OF COMPOSITION," with the aim of providing a systematic analysis of versification. Poe argues for a formal approach to the composition of a poem, rather than an approach that allows creative whim free rein. For the poet to achieve a true totality of effect, Poe suggests that the poet must turn his attention in composition to the carefully orchestrated use of parallelism, refrain, and repetition. According to Poe, "*Verse* originates in the human enjoyment of equality, fitness. To this enjoyment, also, all the moods of verse—rhythm, metre, stanza, rhyme, alliteration, the *refrain,* and other analogous effects—are to be referred." This rationale of verse states that the human enjoyment of equality, whose "idea embraces those of similarity, proportion, identity, repetition, and adaptation or fitness," is also an important factor in creating verse. "Unpractised ears can appreciate only simple equalities, such as those found in ballad airs. . . . Practised ears, on the other hand, appreciate both equalities at the same instant. . . . One is heard and appreciated from itself: the other is heard by the memory." The essay also provides readers with a lesson in scansion, both the nature of different metres and their uses by specific poets, although Poe finds that when the ancient Greek and Latin verse is "scanned by the Prosodial rules we can, for the most part, make nothing of it whatever." The opposite is true of English verse in which "the more emphatically we dwell on the divisions between the feet, the more distinct is our perception of the kind of rhythm intended."

"The Raven" Poe's most famous poem. The work first appeared in the January 29, 1845, issue of the New York EVENING MIRROR, preceded by the following announcement:

> We are permitted to copy (in advance of publication) from the 2d No. of the American Review, the following remarkable poem by *EDGAR POE*. In our opinion, it is the most effective single example of 'fugitive poetry' ever published in this country; and unsurpassed in English poetry for subtle conception, masterly ingenuity of versification, and consistent, sustaining of imaginative lift and 'pokerishness.' It is one of these 'dainties bred in a book' which we *feed* on. It will stick to the memory of everybody who reads it.

The poem was reprinted a month later in the February 1845 issue of the AMERICAN WHIG REVIEW. The poem made Poe a celebrity during his first nine months living in New York City. To take advantage of the poem's recognition and his own newfound fame, Poe also published THE RAVEN AND OTHER POEMS in 1845. Poe enhanced his fame and aroused discussion of the poem by publishing "THE PHILOSOPHY OF COMPOSITION" in 1846, in which he purports to give an account of how he wrote the poem, from the selection of his theme to the choice of meter and refrain, thus giving further weight to those critics who have viewed Poe as a conscious—rather than solely creative—artist. He claimed to have pondered the poem for years and, so, was able to write the final draft late in 1844 in one sitting. In "The Philosophy of Composition," Poe writes, "I pretend to no originality in either the rhythm or metre of the 'Raven.' . . . [T]he latter is octameter acatalectic alternating with heptameter catalectic and terminating with tetrameter catalectic." The metrical form of the lines was modified from that used by Elizabeth BARRETT (later Browning) in her poem "Lady Geraldine's Courtship," but Poe asserted "what originality the 'Raven' has, is in their [the lines'] *combination into stanza; nothing even remotely approaching this combination has ever been attempted.*" Barrett may have recognized his borrow-

Sir John Tenniel, the original illustrator of Lewis Carroll's Alice's Adventures in Wonderland, *made this engraving for "The Raven" in the* Poetical Works of Edgar Allan Poe *(1858).*

ing, but she was not at first enamored of the poem. She wrote in a letter to the English poet Richard Henry HORNE, dated April 1845, that she found "The Raven" unsettling: "There is certainly a power—but ['The Raven'] does not appear to me the natural expression of a sane intellect in whatever mood." The poem tells a story of a grieving lover visited "upon a midnight dreary" by the ill-omened raven, which the lover in his solitude labels "Prophet! . . . thing of evil!—prophet still, if bird or devil!" The emotional nature of the exchange between the raven and the melancholy speaker develops and changes in the course of the poem, as the speaker is, at first, seemingly amused by the raven's precocity, then angered, and finally driven to despair. While the reader might be drawn by the seeming evil qualities of the bird and its remarkable propensity for appropriately responding "Nevermore" to the speaker's queries, Poe's description of the dramatic action of the poem, revealed in "The Philosophy of Composition," is simple: "A raven, having learned by rote the single word 'Nevermore,' and having escaped from the custody of its owner, is driven at midnight, through the violence of a storm, to seek admission at a window form which a light still gleams—the chamber-window of a student, occupied half in poring over a volume, half in dreaming of a beloved mistress deceased." Many critics, the earliest being James Russell LOWELL in *A Fable for Critics*, have traced Poe's plot of introducing a raven into the life of a nameless narrator to a novel written by Charles DICKENS. In 1841, Poe reviewed Dickens's *Barnaby Rudge* and wrote in his review about the raven that follows Barnaby Rudge even to prison:

> The raven, too, intensely amusing as it is, might have been made, more than we now see it, a portion of the conception of the fantastic Barnaby. Its croakings might have been prophetically heard in the course of the drama. Its character might have performed, in regard to that of the idiot, much the same part as does, in music, the accompaniment in respect to the air. Each might have been distinct. Each might have differed remarkably from each other. Yet between them there might have been wrought an analogical resemblance, and although each might have existed apart, they might have formed together a whole world which would have been imperfect in the absence of either.

In "The Raven," Poe appears to have accomplished what he had suggested that Dickens might have done in *Barnaby Rudge:* to create the narrator and the raven as distinct entities that remain forever bound together in experience.

The Raven and Other Poems   Collection of poems by Poe published in November 1845 by Wiley & Putnam. Poe dedicated the volume to Elizabeth BARRETT, whose *The Drama of Exile and Other Poems* he had reviewed in January in 1845 and after which the two had corresponded. The tribute was gracious, if highly emotive:

> To the Noblest of her Sex—
> To the author of
> The Drama of Exile—
> To Miss Elizabeth Barrett Barrett,
> Of England,
> I Dedicate This Volume
> With the most Enthusiasm Admiration
> And with the most Sincere Esteem.

In an April 1845 letter to Poe in which Barrett acknowledged the introduction and told Poe that "THE RAVEN" had "produced a sensation, a 'fit horror,' here in England. Some of my friends are taken by the fear of it and some by the music. I hear of persons haunted by the 'Nevermore,' and one acquaintance of mine who has the misfortune of possessing a 'bust of Pallas' never can bear to look at it in the twilight." The collection contained the following poems: "The Raven," "THE VALLEY OF UNREST," "BRIDAL BALLAD," "THE SLEEPER," "THE COLISEUM," "LENORE," "Catholic Hymn" (*see* "MORELLA"), "ISRAFEL," "DREAMLAND," "SONNET TO ZANTE," "THE CITY IN THE SEA," "TO ONE IN PARADISE," "EULALIE—A SONG," "TO

Illustration for Poe's "The Raven" by Edouard Manet. (Library of Congress)

F——S O——D," "TO F———," "SONNET—SILENCE," "THE CONQUEROR WORM," and "THE HAUNTED PALACE."

Red Death   Character and menace in Poe's short story "THE MASQUE OF THE RED DEATH." The uninvited guest at the masked ball given by Prince PROSPERO, he is the embodiment of the plague that has decreased the population of Prospero's kingdom by half. At the end of the story he conquerors both Prospero and the revelers, demonstrating that no one can escape him.

Reed, Owen (n.d.)   Composer of *The Masque of the Red Death* (1936), a tone poem for orchestra, with ballet-pantomime, based on Poe's short story of the same name.

"Reminiscences of an Intercourse with Mr. Niebuhr, the Historian, During a Residence with Him in Rome, in the Years 1822 and 1823. By Francis Lieber, Professor of History and Political Economy in South Carolina College. Philadelphia: Carey, Lea & Blanchard" Review by Poe that appeared in the January 1836 issue of the *SOUTHERN LITERARY MESSENGER.* Although

Lieber's book professes to relate his discourses in Rome with German historian Barthold Georg Niebuhr (1776–1831), the major part of the review is devoted to presenting background information on Niebuhr's accomplishment and to delineating Lieber's misadventures in making a then-forbidden direct journey from Greece to Rome. The review contains an account from the book that describes Lieber's first interview with Niebuhr, after finally reaching Rome; the beginning of their two-year sojourn in the Eternal City; and their nine-year correspondence. Despite a loss of many of his papers to the police, Lieber offers what the review calls an invaluable account that enables the reader "to form a more accurate idea of the truly great man . . . than we have hitherto entertained."

Renelle, Monsieur   Character in "THE PREMATURE BURIAL." He is "a banker and a diplomatist of some eminence." After marrying the lovely heiress Mademoiselle Victorine LAFOURCADE, he neglected and "even more positively ill-treated her."

Reni, Guido (1575–1643)   Italian painter of popular religious works and scenes of mythology. In "THE ASSIGNATION," the Byronic stranger asks the unnamed narrator his opinion of the painting *Madonna della Pièta*. The excited narrator cries out, "It is Guido's own! . . . It is Guido's own!—how *could* you have obtained it?—she is undoubtedly in painting what the Venus is in sculpture."

"A Reply to Outis"   *See* "A CONTINUATION OF THE VOLUMINOUS HISTORY OF THE LITTLE LONGFELLOW WAR—MR. POE'S FURTHER REPLY TO THE LETTER OF OUTIS."

"Report of the Committee on Naval Affairs, to Whom Were Referred Memorials From Sundry Citizens of Connecticut Interested in the Whale Fishing, Praying That An Exploring Expedition Be Fitted Out to the Pacific Ocean and South Seas. March 21, 1836"   Review by Poe that appeared in the August 1836 issue of the SOUTHERN LITERARY MESSENGER. Poe asserts that the United States has long required "a more accurate, defined, and available knowledge" of the Pacific Ocean and environs, not only for the sake of increased trade but also because "the Pacific may be termed the training ground, the gymnasium of our national navy." The review expresses high praise for the "hardihood and daring of that branch of our commercial marine employed in its trade" and suggests that their courage and fortitude have been responsible for "our enviable position among the great maritime powers." Poe states that the report under review is based upon information that supports such praise of these "daring men" who have pursued "a dangerous and arduous occupation,

amid the perils and casualties of an intricate navigation, in seas imperfectly known." Judged by the reviewer to be "clear, manly, decided," the report also "enlists our sympathies in the hardships and difficulties they have encountered" and makes a case for increasing "the operations of our commerce in the quarter indicated." Poe also praises Jeremiah REYNOLDS, whose "Address on the Subject of a Surveying and Exploring Expedition to the Pacific Ocean and South Seas" he reviewed in the SOUTHERN LITERARY MESSENGER of January 1837. The address became his major source for THE NARRATIVE OF ARTHUR GORDON PYM. The review ends with Poe's appro-val that Reynolds "has been appointed to the highest civil situation in the expedition; a station which we know him to be exceedingly well qualified to fill."

"Review of Stephens' Arabia Petraea"   Review by Poe that appeared in the October 1837 issue of the *New York Review*. Poe characterized the archaeological monograph and travelogue by John L. Stephens, titled *Incidents of Travel in Egypt, Arabia Petraea and the Holy Land*, as "two volumes of more than ordinary interest—written with a freshness of manner, and evincing a manliness of feeling, both worthy of high consideration." In a lengthy review, Poe described in detail the journey taken by Stephens and the obstacles that he had to overcome in completing that journey. The review compliments Stephens for writing two volumes with "an utter absence of pretension, which will secure them the respect and good-will of all parties." Despite his assertion that "Mr. Stephens writes like a man of good sense and sound feeling," Poe challenges the accuracy of Stephens's account of the crossing of the Red Sea by Moses, and states that "Mr. Stephens is here greatly in error, and has placed himself in direct opposition to all authority on the subject." Poe also corresponded with Charles ANTHON and asked him to translate several Hebrew quotations from the Old Testament that he believed contained inaccurate references.

Reynolds, Jeremiah N. (1799–1858)   American explorer and navigator who lobbied for exploration of the South Pole. Poe lauded his accomplishments in a review of "Report of the Committee on Naval Affairs, to whom were Referred Memorials from Sundry Citizens of Connecticut Interested in the Whale Fishing, Praying that an Exploring Expedition Be Fitted Out to the Pacific Ocean and South Seas." He also reviewed Reynolds's "Address on the Subject of a Surveying and Exploring Expedition to the Pacific Ocean and South Seas" in January 1837 issue of the SOUTHERN LITERARY MESSENGER. Poe used Reynolds's address as his main source in writing THE NARRATIVE OF ARTHUR GORDON PYM, drawing upon the explorer's vast knowledge of the Pacific Ocean. In *Pym,* Poe quotes from the address to provide information about the topography and weather of the Southern Polar region.

"Rhymes of Travel"   Collection of poems written by Bayard Taylor. In "MARGINALIA," published in the April 1849 issue of the SOUTHERN LITERARY MESSENGER, Poe wrote a strong response against "an invidious notice"—an anonymous review—of Taylor's work published in a journal whose name Poe does not identify. Poe vehemently attacks the critic, who "undeservedly, holds himself some position as a poet" and asserts that the reviewer "has never published a poem . . . which could compare . . . with *the worst* of Mr. Taylor's compositions." Poe includes as an example one of Taylor's poems that the critic had copied and derided; Poe praises its evidence of imagination throughout. His concluding comments suggest that Poe feels a kinship with Taylor: "My very soul revolts at *such* efforts . . . to depreciate *such* poems as Mr. Taylor's. *Is* there *no* honor—no chivalry left in the land? Are our most deserving writers to be *forever* sneered down, or hooted down, or damned down with faint praise, by a set of men who possess little other ability than that which assures temporary success to them . . .?"

Richmond, Nancy [Annie] Locke Heywood (1820–1898)
A married woman with whom Poe developed a passionate if platonic relationship. Poe met Annie in October 1847 on a second visit to Lowell, Massachusetts, where he had presented the lecture "THE POETS AND POETRY OF AMERICA" three months earlier. Annie was 11 years younger than Poe and married, but her husband was tolerant of their friendship and allowed Poe to stay in their house on several occasions. By all accounts a sweet and simple person, Annie shared none of Poe's literary ambitions or acumen, yet he seems to have loved her deeply. Poe's poem "FOR ANNIE" first appeared in the April 28, 1849, issue of the *Flag of Our Union* and in the *Home Journal* on the same day. Written after their close friendship ruptured, the tender and melodious poem describes Poe's gratitude in recovering from the severe illness that ensued when he attempted suicide by overdosing on laudanum in November 1848. Poe also wrote "LANDOR'S COTTAGE" in 1849 with Annie in mind. He included in the story an unmistakable description of his love that conveys his reasons for loving Annie, despite her lack of literary knowledge:

> . . . a young woman about twenty-eight years of age—slender, or rather slight, and somewhat above medium height. As she approached, with a certain *modest decision* of step altogether indescribable, I said to myself, "Surely here I have found the perfection of natural, in

contradistinction from artificial grace." The second impression which she made on me, but by far the more vivid of the two, was that of *enthusiasm.* So intense an expression of romance, perhaps I should call it, or of unworldliness, as that which gleamed from her deep-set eyes, had never so sunk into my heart of hearts before. I know not how it is, but this peculiar expression of the eye, wreathing itself occasionally into the lips, is the most powerful, if not absolutely the *sole* spell, which rivets my interest in women. "Romance," provided my readers fully comprehend what I would here imply by the word—"romance" and "womanliness" seem to me convertible terms: and, after all, what man truly loves in woman, is, simply, her womanhood. The eyes of Annie (I heard some one from the interior call her "Annie, darling!") were "spiritual gray"; her hair, a light chestnut: this is all I had time to observe of her.

Until his death, Poe loved the unattainable Annie. Even as he became engaged to marry Elmira ROYSTER Shelton, he wrote to Maria CLEMM on September 5, 1849, "Could we be happier in Richmond or Lowell? For, I suppose we could never be happy at Fordham, and Muddy, I *must* be somewhere where I can see Annie." In the same letter, he writes, "Do not tell me anything about Annie—I cannot bear to hear it now—unless you can tell me that Mr. [Richmond] is dead." After Poe's death, she urged Maria Clemm to live with her. When her husband died in 1873, she legally changed her name from Nancy to Annie.

Richmond Theatre   The site of many stage roles of Poe's mother Elizabeth Arnold Hopkins POE. Built on the site of an academy that burned to the ground in 1802, the brick and frame structure of the theater was also destroyed by fire on December 26, 1811, two and a half weeks after the death of Elizabeth Poe. The theater caught fire from a stage chandelier during the presentation by PLACIDE and company of a play titled *The Bleeding Nun.* Seventy-three people perished in the fire.

Richmond Examiner   Poe served as literary editor in the summer of 1849. He took the post only a year after he had quarreled with John Moncure DANIEL, the editor of the *Examiner,* after Daniel had expressed doubts to a relative of Sarah Helen WHITMAN about Poe's suitability as a spouse.

Ricketts, Mr.   Character in Poe's novel THE NARRATIVE OF ARTHUR GORDON PYM. He is the headmaster of the school that Pym attends from the age of six to the age of 16. Well known "to almost every person who has visited New Bedford," Ricketts is a gentleman with only one arm and "of eccentric manners."

"Rienzi, the Last of the Tribunes. By the Author of 'Eugene Aram,' 'Last Days of Pompeii," &c. &c. Two Volumes in One. Philadelphia: Republished by E. L. Carey and A. Hart" Review by Poe that appeared in the February 1836 issue of the SOUTHERN LITERARY MESSEN-GER. The historical novel written by Edward BULWER-LYTTON receives high praise in the review, as does its author, of whom Poe writes, "We have long learned to reverence the fine intellect of Bulwer. We take up any production of his pen with a positive certainty that, in reading it, the wildest passions of our nature, the most profound of our thoughts, the brightest visions of our fancy, and the most ennobling of our aspirations will, in due turn, be enkindled within us." After comparing Bulwer-Lytton with a number of contemporary writers and finding them wanting, Poe declares him "unap-proached." He then summarizes the current work, which he has declared the writer's "best novel." Assuring readers that "he has adhered with scrupulous fidelity to all the main events in the *public* life of his hero," Poe also relates that Bulwer-Lytton has been scrupulous "in his pictures of the Roman populace, and in those of the Roman nobles of the fourteenth century." Poe writes that the work, while offered as fiction, is "History. We hesitate not to say that it is History in its truest—in its only true, proper, and philosophical garb . . . vitality of Historic Truth." The review relates that the work pres-ents "a profound and lucid exposition" of the nature of government and its relationship to freedom and igno-rance, "Tyranny in the few and Virtue in the many," and that it offers a viable argument for the role of people in determining their governance. The review contains a lengthy extract, chapter five of the sixth book, to sub-stantiate Poe's assertions, and ends with one more reminder of "the exceeding power" of the work.

Riker, Richard (1773–1842) Mentioned in a satiric manner in Poe's short story "MELLONTA TAUTA." Poe speaks of the "aboriginal inhabitants" of New York City, a "tribe of savages infesting the continent at its first dis-covery by Recorder Riker, a knight of the Golden Fleece." In reality, Riker was a New York politician to whom one of Poe's contemporaries, Fitz-Green HAL-LECK, had dedicated a poem, "To the Recorder." Poe designates him "a knight of the Golden Fleece" because of his "fleecing" of the public.

Roberton, Hugh S. (1874–1947) Scottish composer and choral conductor, knighted in 1931 for his musical work. His compositions include nearly 200 part-songs, solo songs, and other works. In 1909 he published "Hear the Tolling of the Bells," for mixed voices, based on the last stanza of Poe's poem "THE BELLS," and "The Sledge Bells," a part-song based on the first stanza of "The Bells." In 1919, Roberton published "Hear the Sledges with the Bells," an unaccompanied part-song

based on the first stanza of "The Bells." In 1914 he composed "Annabel Lee," based on Poe's poem of the same name; it is written for a chorus of men's voices and for mixed voices.

Roberts, Lee S. (1885–1964) American composer whose works include popular ballads, sacred songs, and instrumental pieces. In 1920, Roberts published "To One in Paradise," a song based on Poe's poem of the same name.

Robinson, Miss *See* LEWIS, Sarah Anna "Stella".

Rodman, James E. Character in Poe's unfinished novel THE JOURNAL OF JULIUS RODMAN. He is the person "from whom we obtained the MS., [who] is well known to many readers of this Magazine; and partakes in some degree, of that temperament which embittered the ear-lier portion of the life of his grandfather, Mr. Julius Rodman, the writer of the narrative."

Rodman, Julius Character in Poe's unfinished novel THE JOURNAL OF JULIUS RODMAN. He is an English adven-turer who braves the dangers of the wilderness with a party of companions. Rodman initially begins the adventure as a health cure after he loses his father and his two sisters to smallpox. A melancholy man, he seeks "in the bosom of the wilderness, that peace which his peculiar disposition would not suffer him to enjoy among men."

Rogers, Hartman Character in Poe's novel THE NARRA-TIVE OF ARTHUR GORDON PYM. After the mutiny, he is one of the 13 men remaining aboard the *Grampus* and a member of the cook's gang. He is first mentioned in the narrative on July 5th, and he dies on July 10th, "having been attacked on the eighth with spasms after drinking a glass of grog." He tells one of the other crew members that he believes that he was poisoned.

Rogers, Mary Cecilia (1820–1841) Young woman whose murder and the possible efforts to cover it up inspired Poe's short story "THE MYSTERY OF MARIE ROGÊT." After her father died in a steamboat explosion, 17-year-old Mary took a job as the clerk in John Ander-son's tobacco shop, where her physical attractiveness helped to make repeat customers of the all-male clien-tele. On October 5, 1838, two and a half years before her murder, the New York *Sun* reported that "a Miss Mary Cecilia Rogers" had disappeared from her home and left a suicide note. The following day, another newspaper, the *Times and Commercial Intelligence,* reported that the earlier accounts had been a hoax and that "Miss R. only went on a visit to a friend in Brook-lyn. She is now at home with her mother." She contin-ued to work at the tobacco shop until mid-1839, when her brother gave money to her mother to start a boardinghouse. Mary left the shop and assisted her mother. On July 25, 1841, she told her fiancé, a boarder named Daniel PAYNE, that she was going to visit her aunt and to take her nieces and nephews to church. Three days later, police found her body floating in the Hudson River near Hoboken, New Jersey. Because she had been bound, police concluded that one of the several gangs that roamed the waterfront was responsible for her death. The case took a different turn in November 1842, when Mrs. Frederica Loss, who ran a roadhouse near where Mary's body was found, swore on her deathbed that Mary died during an abortion and that Loss's son had bound the body and thrown it into the river. This version was sensationalized in the papers, but the police refused to accept this solution as well. The case remained unsolved.

Rogêt, Estelle   Character in Poe's story "THE MYSTERY OF MARIE ROGÊT." She is the widowed mother of the murdered Marie ROGÊT and keeps a boardinghouse, assisted by Marie.

Rogêt, Marie   Character in Poe's story "THE MYSTERY OF MARIE ROGÊT." A fictional character based on the real-life Mary Cecilia ROGERS, she works for a perfumer who occupies one of the shops in the Palais Royal. As Poe describes her early in the tall, she is "a sprightly *grisette*," a young woman of the working class, usually a shop assistant, whose "Christian and family name will at once arrest attention from their resemblance to those of the unfortunate 'segar [sic]-girl' [Mary Rogers]."

Rollinat, Joseph-Auguste-Maurice (1846–1903)   French poet and composer whose poetry has been characterized as bizarre and macabre. In 1906, he composed "Le Reve" [A Dream], a song setting of a French translation of Poe's poem of the same name.

"Romance"   Poem written by Poe that first appeared under the title "Preface" in the 1829 poetry collection *AL AARAAF, TAMERLANE, AND MINOR POEMS*, then reprinted under the title "Introduction" in the 1831 *POEMS BY EDGAR A. POE*. Poe titled the poem "Romance" for publication in the February 25, 1843, issue of the *PHILADELPHIA SATURDAY MUSEUM*. Through revisions, Poe pared down the number of stanzas from an original seven to two, and in later versions left out references to "drunkenness of soul" and "the glories of the bowl." The poem portrays romance as a bird "with drowsy head and folded wing . . . far down some shadowy lake" that has been part of the speaker's life since childhood and "Taught me my alphabet to say— / To lisp my very earliest word / while in the wild-wood I did lie." The exotic bird of romance follows the speaker into adulthood, where he finds, "I could not love except where

Death / Was mingling his with Beauty's breath— / Or Hymen, Time, and Destiny / Were stalking between her and me." After "the eternal Condor years / So shook the very Heavens on high, / With tumults they thunder'd by," the speaker no longer has the time for idle considerations or dreams, for "dreams—of those who dream as I, / Aspiringly, are damned and die."

Ronald, Mr. E.   Reference in Poe's novel *THE NARRATIVE OF ARTHUR GORDON PYM*. Arthur Gordon PYM leaves Mr. RICKETTS's school to attend Mr. E. Ronald's academy on the hill. Here Pym meets August BARNARD, the son of a sea captain, who will join him in running off to sea.

Rosa, Salvatore (1615–1673)   Italian painter, etcher, poet, actor, and musician and the epitome of the 19th-century romantic artist. Most of his work is of landscapes near his native Naples. His bold romantic imagination produced wild settings with towering rocky crags and bare, splintered tree trunks. Poe describes in "LANDOR'S COTTAGE" a craggy precipice covered with "wild shrubbery" and trees that are "Salvatorish in character." In "MORNING ON THE WISSAHICCON," Poe writes of "a steep rocky cliff, abutting far into the stream, and presenting much more of the Salvator character than any portion of the shore hitherto passed."

Ross, Mr.   Character in Poe's novel *THE NARRATIVE OF ARTHUR GORDON PYM*. A relative of Arthur Gordon PYM, he lives in New Bedford, Massachusetts, where Pym is "in the habit of spending occasionally two or three weeks at a time." Ross becomes an unwitting accomplice in Pym's plan to run away to sea when Pym and his friend Augustus BARNARD send Pym's father a forged note asking that Pym be allowed to spend a fortnight with Ross's sons, Robert and Emmet.

Rouge-et-Noir, Mr.   A member of the FOLIO CLUB. He admires Lady Morgan, and his "Tale was condemned at the previous monthly meeting." This choice of name for one of the DUNDERHEADS may be a reference to Marie Henri Beyle (1783–1842), who wrote under the pseudonym Stendhal and whose most noted work was *Le rouge et noir (The Red and the Black)*.

Rousseau, Jean-Jacques (1712–1778)   French social and political theorist, philosopher, musician, botanist, and writer. In his 1762 political treatise, *The Social Contract*, Rousseau's defense of the popular will against divine right helped to prepare the ideological background of the French Revolution. Poe quotes from Rousseau's 1761 *Julie, ou la nouvelle Héloïse* in his short story "LOSS OF BREATH," as the narrator states "The road of the passions has led me to true philosophy." At the end of "THE MURDERS IN THE RUE MORGUE," he quotes from the same book, "It is a crochet common to philosophers of all ages to deny what is, and explain what is not," a quotation he repeats in "FIFTY SUGGESTIONS." In his review "OUR AMATEUR POETS, NO. 1—FLACCUS," Poe states that "the utter abandon of the details, reminds us even of Jean Jacques," and in his profile of Charles Fenno HOFFMAN, he compares the expression of an Indian chief in "The Vigil of Faith" as "made to discourse after the manner of Rousseau."

Royce, Edward (1886–1964) American composer whose compositions include orchestral music, songs, and piano pieces. In 1922, Royce published "Evening Star" and "Israfel," songs respectively inspired by Poe's poems of the same name, and "Solace," a song inspired by Poe's poem "TO F———."

Royster, Sarah Elmira (1810–1888) The love of Poe's early life. In 1825, he became secretly engaged to the 15-year-old girl. Elmira's father found Poe an unsuitable choice of son-in-law and intercepted letters from Poe to his daughter. Elmira claimed in later life that she had received none of Poe's letters and did not realize how much she meant to him. In 1827, at the age of 17, she married a successful businessman, Alexander Shelton; but she claimed in later life always to have loved Poe. Soon after Elmira's marriage, Poe wrote the poem "SONG," which is addressed to her. The two met again in Richmond, Virginia, in July 1848, by which time Elmira had been a wealthy widow for four years. A few weeks later, Poe asked Elmira to marry him, but she hesitated because her two children opposed the marriage and she would lose three-quarters of the $100,000 estate left by her husband. Most biographers suggest that the two had reached an "understanding" before Poe left Richmond on September 27, 1849, headed for Baltimore and his death.

Rubadub, Professor Character in Poe's short story "THE UNPARALLELED ADVENTURE OF ONE HANS PFAALL." Satirized for his pedantry, he is the "Vice-President of Rotterdam College of Astronomy" and one of the two people to whom "the aeronaut" in the hot-air balloon drops Hans PFAALL's letter. After reading "this very extraordinary document," the professor "dropped his pipe upon the ground in the extremity of surprise," then ventures to suggest that the odd messenger has disappeared because of "the savage appearance of the burghers of Rotterdam."

Rumgudgeon Character in Poe's short story "THREE SUNDAYS IN A WEEK." He is the grand-uncle of Bobby the narrator and the guardian of KATE, whose marriage he will only agree to *when three Sundays come together in a week!"* The narrator describes him as being "a little,

Sarah Elmira Royster, Poe's first love, whom he met again in later life. (National Archives—Stills Division)

pursy, pompous, passionate, semicircular somebody, with a red nose, a thick skull, a long purse, and a strong sense of his own consequence." He works hard "to earn for himself . . . the character of a curmudgeon," and "To every request, a positive 'No!' was his immediate answer."

"Russia and the Russians; or, a Journey to St. Petersburg and Moscow, Through Courland and Livonia; with Characteristic Sketches of the People. By Leigh Ritchie, Esq. Author of 'Turner's Annual Tour,' 'Schinderhannes,' &c. Philadelphia: E. L. Carey and A. Hart" Review by Poe that appeared in the July 1836 issue of the *SOUTHERN LITERARY MESSENGER*. The review praises the ability of the writer to make Russia and the Russians come alive with "all the spirit and glowing vigor of romance." Poe asserts that Ritchie provides in the travelogue "a brilliant mass of anecdote, narrative, description and sentiment" and finds the book to be "full of every species of entertainment." The review ends with an excerpt of the author's sketch of St. Petersburg to show the vivid nature of Ritchie's writing.

"The Sacred Mountains: By J. T. Headley,—Author of 'Napoleon and His Marshalls,' 'Washington and His Generals, Etc.'" Posthumous review by Poe that appeared in the October 1850 issue of the SOUTHERN LITERARY MESSENGER. The review was published with the following announcement: "From advance sheets of 'The Literati,' a work in press, by the late Edgar A. Poe, we take the following sketches of Headley and Channing—as good specimens of that tomahawk-style of criticism of which the author was so great a master. In the present instances the satire is well-deserved. Neither of these sketches we believe have been in print before." This review focuses on Headley. A review of William Ellery CHANNING's work appears in "OUR AMATEUR POETS, NO. 3." Poe begins his attack early in the review with the statement that "Mr. Headley belongs to that numerous class of authors, who must be read to be understood, and who, for that reason, very seldom are as thoroughly comprehended as they should be." Poe points out the weaknesses in Headley's "design . . . to render more familiar and life-like, some of the scenes of the Bible." He takes issue with the created conversations among biblical figures and asserts that the renderings of incidents from the Old Testament are inaccurate. Despite his contention that "we mean no disparagement to Mr. Headley," Poe proclaims him "the Autocrat of all Quacks."

"Sacred Philosophy of the Seasons, Illustrating the Perfections of God in the Phenomena of the Year. By the Rev. Henry Duncan, D.D., Ruthwell, Scotland. With Important Additions, and Some Modifications to Adapt It To American Readers. By F. W. P. Greenwood. In Four Volumes. Marsh, Capen, Lyon, and Webb, Boston" Review by Poe that appeared in the March 1840 issue of BURTON'S GENTLEMAN'S MAGAZINE. Poe approved of the careful arrangement of topics and the vast amount of information about physical science contained in the work, making it "especially well adapted to those educational purposes for which the volumes are designed." The review digresses into a discussion of the accuracy of several translations from the Hebrew, but Poe soon apologizes for having "been led from our immediate purpose." Poe concludes the review by declaring that the work "is a book of which every one must think well."

Sargent, Epes (1813–1880) Boston dramatist, poet, and editor of *Sargent's Magazine* whose profile appears in "THE LITERATI OF NEW YORK CITY." Poe compares Sargent's *Velasco, A Tragedy*, a drama about the Spanish epic hero El Cid, to the drama *Fashion*, by Anna Cora MOWATT, and finds the two similar in construction, scenic effects, and several other points. This leads to his suggestion that "Mrs. Mowatt received some assistance from Mr. Sargent in the composition of her comedy." In considering the author's prose satire, the review is less kind, and the reviewer asserts, "To those who meddle little with books, some of his satirical papers must appear brilliant."

Sartain, John (1808–1897) Philadelphia engraver who worked with Poe at BURTON'S GENTLEMAN'S MAGAZINE and GRAHAM'S MAGAZINE. In June 1849, after binge drinking and an overnight stay in MOYAMENSING prison, Poe sought refuge in Sartain's studio. The engraver provided Poe, who spoke of wild hallucinations, with rest and meals and cared for him through 10 days of delirium tremens.

Sartain's Union Magazine Publication based in Philadelphia, started by John SARTAIN in January 1849. Poe offered Sartain the final version of "THE RAVEN." The magazine published posthumously Poe's poems "ANNABEL LEE" and "THE BELLS," as well as the essay "THE POETIC PRINCIPLE."

"Satirical Poems" Critical essay by Poe that appeared in the March 15, 1845, issue of the BROADWAY JOURNAL. The essay observes that American journals and newspapers have published some commendable prose satire, but they have been deficient in producing satire in verse: "[We] are scarcely so much satirists, as subjects for satire." Poe acknowledges that recent works have been "intended either for satire or burlesque, on the ground that it is impossible to comprehend them as anything else," but they fail to meet his standards. The essay ponders the reason for this lack and compares it to the wealth of satire in England, which leads to the conclusion that "in America . . . the people who write are the people who read—and thus in satirizing the people we satirize only ourselves, and feel no real sympathy in the satire." Nonetheless, Poe identifies Park

BENJAMIN's "Infactuation" as "full of nerve, point and terseness" and suggests that this is an effort in the direction of producing good satire. He quotes 18 lines verbatim from the poem.

"Saul, A Mystery" *See* "COXE'S SAUL."

Scheherazade Character in Poe's short story "THE THOUSAND-AND-SECOND TALE OF SCHEHERAZADE." Poe presents her as being the original teller of the *Arabian Nights,* and humorously projects her as having pangs of conscience that she did not complete for her husband, the king, the story of Sinbad the sailor. The daughter of the grand vizier (from the Turkish word *vezir* and the Arabic word *wazir,* both meaning a high-ranking executive officer), she insists upon marrying the king despite knowing that he has made a vow to marry each night the most beautiful maiden in his dominion and have her executed the following morning. Scheherazade's plan is to marry the king and then tell him a tale each night, leaving just enough of the story untold at daybreak to tempt him to keep her alive to finish the story the following evening. She succeeds for 1,001 nights, but she makes the mistake of wanting to continue the story even as the king demands that she stop. Scheherazade appears to have lost her touch, because the king is not amused and, instead, condemns her to the original punishment.

Schelling, Friedrich Wilhelm Joseph von (1775–1854) German philosopher and one of the leading exponents of idealism and of the romantic tendency in German philosophy. He is mentioned in "MORELLA" as one of the philosophers whom the narrator discusses with MORELLA. Poe mentions in a disparaging manner in his review "THE POETRY OF RUFUS DAWES" that "there is now much about . . . Schelling" in Dawes's poem "Geraldine."

Schiller, Johann Christoph Friedrich von (1759–1805) German dramatist and poet from whom Poe draws for the epigraphs to several of his stories, some mistakenly attributed. Poe also mentions Schiller in the review "MEMORIALS OF MRS. HEMANS."

Schmitt, Florent (1871–1934) French composer whose works include symphonies, ballets, piano pieces, chamber music, choruses, and songs. In 1909–10, he published *Etude pour le Palais hanté* for the orchestra and for a piano duet, based on Poe's poem "THE HAUNTED PALACE."

Schreker, Franz (1878–1934) Austrian composer whose radical style of composition brought controversy to his opera librettos. In 1912, he published an opera libretto, called *Der rote Tod* (The Masque of the Red Death), inspired by Poe's short story of the same name; however, he never composed music for it.

Scissors Character in Poe's short story "LOSS OF BREATH." He is "the Whig editor" who hears the voices coming from the dungeons of the sepulchre and, instead of acting, republishes "a treatise upon 'the nature and origin of subterranean noises'."

Scott, Cyril (1879–1938) English impressionist composer, poet, and philosopher whose compositions include orchestral and chamber works, piano pieces, songs, and a symphony, as well as poems and works of the occult and mystical subjects. In 1931, he published *The Masque of the Red Death,* a ballet with orchestral accompaniment inspired by Poe's short story of the same name.

Scott, General Winfield (1786–1866) American army officer, born near Petersburg, Virginia. Because of his military successes in the War of 1812 and later on the Canadian frontier, he was brevetted a major general from brigadier general in 1814, as was the fictional General A. B. C. SMITH in Poe's short story "THE MAN THAT WAS USED UP." He was a distant relative of John ALLAN's second wife and was rumored to have helped Poe gain entrance to the UNITED STATES MILITARY ACADEMY AT WEST POINT. In 1848, he assisted Marie Louise SHEW in raising funds to help Poe pay for medical bills.

Scott, Sir Walter (1771–1832) Scottish historical novelist whom Poe admired greatly. Poe admired especially Scott's *The Bride of Lammermoor,* which he used as a standard against which to measure other similar efforts. These efforts often fell far short of the "most pure, perfect, and radiant gem of fictitious literature." In a review, "ELKSWATAWA; OR THE PROPHET OF THE WEST," Poe refers to Scott's writing "mannerisms, [which] until the frequency of their repetition entitled them to such appellation, being well managed and not overdone, were commendable." He suggests that the overuse of such writing mannerisms as occasionally florid language, exotic locale, and heroic characterization has become "a little too much of a good thing" and cautions writers to avoid them. In his review "LIVES OF THE CARDINAL DE RICHELIEU, COUNT OXENSTIERN, COUNT OLIVAREZ, AND CARDINAL MAZARIN," Poe condemns the author G. P. R. James as "an indifferent imitator of the Scotch novelist." Poe provides an anecdote of Scott in his review "MEMORIALS OF MRS. HEMANS, WITH ILLUSTRATIONS OF HER LITERARY CHARACTER FROM HER PRIVATE CORRESPONDENCE." He proclaims Edward BULWER-LYTTON to be "altogether inferior" to Scott in his review "NIGHT AND MORNING: A NOVEL." In his critical essay "THE DRAMA," Poe is "delighted" to find Anna Cora MOWATT "announced as Lucy in 'The Bride of Lammermor,' for our remembrances of this opera were connected only with the music of Bellini and the glowing romance of Scott." To make a point regarding the ineptitude of other critics, he mentions in "MARGINALIA" an anecdote from Scott's "Presbyterian Eloquence," "that ancient fable, not much known," about a singing contest between a nightingale and a cuckoo, and "the ass was chosen umpire." Although the umpire agrees that the song of the nightingale is excellent, he states that "for a good plain song give him the cuckoo." The umpire (ass) represents for Poe the often inept critics who praise the writing that they understand (the "good plain song of the cuckoo") and ignore the "excellent" song of the more refined nightingale because they cannot understand it.

"The Scythe of Time"   *See* "A PREDICAMENT."

"Secret Writing"   *See* CRYPTOGRAPHY.

"Select Orations of Cicero: with an English Commentary, and Historical, Geographical and Legal Indexes. By Charles Anthon, LL.D. Jay—Professor of Ancient Literature in Columbia College, and Rector of the Grammar School. New York: Harper and Brothers" Review by Poe that appeared in the January 1837 issue of the *SOUTHERN LITERARY MESSENGER*. The review opens with praise for Charles ANTHON: "[T]his gentleman has done more for sound scholarship at home, and for our classical reputation abroad, than any other individual in America." After listing Anthon's accomplishments, Poe examines his skills as a critic and commentator, and feels that they "must be regarded with the highest consideration." Praising the simplicity of Anthon's approach, Poe concludes "he has given the world evidence of a comprehensive as well as of an acute and original understanding."

Séverac, Joseph Marie Déodat de (1873–1921) French impressionist composer whose works include operas, incidental music, piano arrangements, songs, chamber music, and symphonic poems. In 1924 he composed the symphonic poem *Un Reve* (A Dream), from the poem of the same name by Poe, translated by the French Symbolist poet and critic Stéphane MALLARMÉ.

Seymour   Character in Poe's novel *THE NARRATIVE OF ARTHUR GORDON PYM*. He is "the black cook" and leads one of the two mutinous factions on board the *Grampus*.

"Shadow—A Parable"   Short story. This tale is one of three by Poe that are placed during a time of plague, the others being "KING PEST" and "THE MASQUE OF THE RED DEATH." The word "shadow" is used in various of

Poe's works to mean fear, darkness, the unknown, ghost, and death.

PUBLISHING AND DRAMATIZATION HISTORY

The tale was first published in the September 1835 issue of the *SOUTHERN LITERARY MESSENGER*.

A line from the "Psalm of David" (Psalm 23) in the Old Testament precedes the story: "Yea! though I walk through the valley of the Shadow." Although most modern readers are accustomed to the King James Version of the psalm, "Yea! though I walk through the valley of the shadow of death. . . ," biblical scholars assert that "valley of the shadow" and "valley of darkness" are also correct as translations of the Hebrew.

The story has not been made into a film to date.

CHARACTERS

OINOS, Shadow, ZOILUS.

PLOT SYNOPSIS

The story is written to those "who are still among the living," but the writer "shall have long since gone . . . into the region of shadows." The narrator, "the Greek Oinos," tells of an experience that occurs in the city of Ptolemais in the plague year 794, when "the peculiar spirit of the skies . . . made itself manifest, not only in the physical orb of the earth, but in the souls, imaginations, and meditations of mankind." A company of seven people has taken refuge in a room with thick walls and a heavy brass door where they drink wine that "reminded us of blood" and try to forget the "dead weight [that] hung upon us." An eighth member of the group, Zoilus, lies dead and enshrouded in the room, "the genius and the demon of the scene." As the revelers try to keep their spirits up, a "vague, and formless, and indefinite" shadowy figure steps out from the "sable draperies" and addresses the group: "I am SHADOW, and my dwelling is near to the Catacombs of Ptolemais." The seven revelers shiver at the sound, for the tones are not of any one being "but of a multitude of beings, and, varying in their cadences from syllable to syllable . . . the well-remembered and familiar accents of many thousand departed friends."

Shakespeare, William (1564–1616)   English poet and dramatist. Poe makes extensive use of Shakespeare's words, phrases, and character names throughout his short stories. In "FOUR BEASTS IN ONE," Poe's narrator addresses onlookers with words taken from *Twelfth Night*: "I see you profit by my advice, and are making the most of your time in inspecting your premises—'in satisfying your eyes / With the memorials and the things of fame / That most renown this city—.'" He then apologizes to readers for having quoted from

Shakespeare, who "will not flourish for seventeen hundred and fifty years to come," because the tale is set in the past. In "THE MASQUE OF THE RED DEATH," the hooded figure who appears in the end acts on the advice that the young prince Hamlet gives to the players in *Hamlet,* as "the figure in question out-Heroded Herod." In the same story, Poe's Prince PROSPERO gathers a large body of people into an abbey to create a safe haven from the reality of the plague-ridden outer world, ruling over his artificial environment much as Shakespeare's duke, Prospero, seeks to do, using his magic on the island paradise in *The Tempest* to keep them from the evil influences of the outside world. A line spoken by Caliban—"the red plague rid you"—in the same play reflects a similar influence on "The Masque of the Red Death." In *THE NARRATIVE OF ARTHUR GORDON PYM,* Augustus BARNARD and Arthur Gordon PYM take their wild nighttime ride in Pym's sailboat named *Ariel,* a name taken from Shakespeare's *Tempest.* In "THE PREMATURE BURIAL," Poe's narrator takes his line "of worms, of tombs, of epitaphs" from *Richard II.* In "X-ING A PARAGRAB," Mr. Touch-and-Go BULLET-HEAD utters the murderous comment made by Richard III in Shakespeare's play of the same name: "So much for Buckingham."

Shapleigh, Bertram (1871–1948) American composer who lived a number of years in Germany and England. His works include orchestral suites, symphonies, choral works, operas, chamber music, pieces for piano and violin, and more than 100 songs. In 1901, he published a collection of five songs based on works by Poe: "Helene, deiner Schonheit Macht" (Helen, Thy Beauty is to Me), based on Poe's poem "TO HELEN"; "Mein Lebenspfad ist rauh und wust" (Beloved! Amid the Earnest Woes), based on Poe's "TO F———"; "Im Dammerlicht, wenn Tag ergluht" (At Morn, at Noon, At Twilight Dim), based on Poe's "HYMN"; "Eldorado," based on Poe's poem of the same name; and "An den Fluss" (Fair River), based on Poe's poem "TO THE RIVER ———." In 1906, Shapleigh published *The Raven,* a cantata for chorus and orchestra, inspired by Poe's poem of the same name.

Shaw, Martin (1875–1937) English composer, conductor, organist, and editor whose compositions include songs and part-songs; ballad operas; church, orchestral, and chamber music; and English carols. In 1921, he published "Annabel Lee," a song inspired by Poe's poem of the same name.

Shea, John Augustus Commissary clerk at the UNITED STATES MILITARY ACADEMY AT WEST POINT. Poe and he became close friends, and Shea later published poetry of his own and had contacts in the literary world. In 1845, he represented Poe in offering "THE RAVEN" to George COLTON for publication in the *AMERICAN WHIG REVIEW.* He also received Poe's changes to the poem before its publication in the February 4, 1845 issue of the *NEW YORK TRIBUNE.*

Shelton, Sarah Elmira Royster *See* ROYSTER, Sarah Elmira.

"Sheppard Lee: Written by Himself. New York: Harper and Brothers" Review by Poe that appeared in the September 1836 issue of the *SOUTHERN LITERARY MESSENGER.* Poe provides a detailed summary of this novel, written by Robert Montgomery BIRD. The plot involves the transmigration of the hero's soul through three bodies, touches on situations that reflect the author's antislavery leanings, and incorporates comments on American manners and morals. The conclusion of the novel reveals that the hero has merely been ill; in that condition, he dreamed that he had died and that his soul had entered three other bodies. The review declares the novel to be "clever, and not altogether unoriginal" and the incidents "well conceived." Poe objects, however, to the author's conception of metapsychosis and the way in which Bird handles the narrative.

Shew, Marie Louise (d. 1877) A medically trained doctor's daughter who served as Virginia CLEMM's nurse in her final days. She was married to a physician when Poe met her, but later divorced her husband and became the object of Poe's attentions. Biographers suggest that Poe might have met Shew in New York City as early as the winter of 1837, a particularly bitter winter during which Poe went to the Northern Dispensary to obtain medicine for a severe cold. Records show that both Shew and Dr. Valentine MOTT worked at the dispensary that winter. After the death of Poe's wife a decade later, Shew noticed unusual symptoms in Poe and reported to Dr. Valentine Mott, then a physician at New York University School of Medicine, that Poe's "pulse beat only ten regular beats, after which it suspended or intermitted." Mott agreed with her conjecture that Poe might have a lesion on one side of the brain and recommended that Poe refrain from all stimulants and tonics—even sedatives—the use of which would intensify hallucinations and lead to greater mental instability.

By all accounts, and from an engraving that remains, Shew was plain in appearance, but her kind heart and desire to help the poor made her appealing to others, including Poe. In 1847, he began his suit, first writing her Valentine poems, then passionate letters declaring his undying love. As he had with others, Poe flattered Shew by dedicating poems to her and

Marie Louise Shew, who nursed the dying Virginia Clemm Poe.
(Edgar Allan Poe Society)

even referring to her in a story. In "TO M. L. S———," written in March 1847, Poe praises Shew, telling her that his "gratitude Nearest resembles worship" and that he "thrills to think / His spirit is communing with an angel's." In "TO MARIE LOUISE," written in March 1848, he confesses that he had once "In the mad pride of intellectuality, / Maintained the 'power of words,'" but that he realizes now the importance of feeling and "where the prospect terminates—*thee* only." Further, critics have determined that Poe speaks of Shew in his description of "the sympathy of a woman, not unwomanly, whose loveliness and love enveloped his existence in the purple atmosphere of Paradise," which appears in the 1847 short story "THE DOMAIN OF ARNHEIM." Biographers have credited Shew for inspiring Poe to write "THE BELLS." In the months after Virginia's death, Poe became emotionally attached to Mrs. Shew and often spent time at her home, which was close to Grace Church in New York. On one evening, Poe claimed that he had to write a poem but was devoid of inspiration. Church bells in the background encouraged his companion to playfully write "The bells, the little silver bells," and Poe finished the stanza.

Shuttleworthy, Barnabas   Character in Poe's short story "THOU ART THE MAN." He is "one of the wealthiest and most respectable citizens" of Rattleborough. He has "a sad habit of swearing" and he is not overly fond of people eating and drinking at his expense. When he goes missing for several days, the citizens suspect foul play. The narrator finds his corpse, engineers it to pop out of the coffin, and throws his voice to accuse the murderer.

"Silence. A Fable"   Short story. Poe subtitled the story "In the manner of the Psychological Autobiographists," and it exhibits the German metaphysics and morbid spiritualism so popular at the time. Critics view the tale as one of Poe's most bewildering, for the narration appears to proceed in an understandable manner until the ending, which leaves the reader with an unsolved mystery. The only clue that Poe has left to the meaning of the ending lies in his poem "SONNET—SILENCE."

Early manuscripts show that Poe originally began the story with a line from his poem "AL AARAAF": "Ours is a world of words: Quiet we call / 'Silence'—which is the merest word of all."

PUBLISHING AND DRAMATIZATION HISTORY

The story first appeared as "Siope—A Fable" in the 1838 *Baltimore Book*, edited by W. H. Carpenter and T. S. Arthur, then was collected with other stories in Poe's *TALES OF THE GROTESQUE AND ARABESQUE*. In the September 6, 1845, issue of the *BROADWAY JOURNAL*, Poe published the story under the title of "Silence—A Fable."

The story is preceded by an epigraph taken from a speech by Apollonius of Rhodes in a fragment of "Homeric Lexicon," a poem by Spartan Alcman (fl. 600 B.C.), who founded the Dorian school of choral lyric poetry, which emphasized simplicity and clarity: "The mountain pinnacles slumber, valleys, crags, and caves silent."

To date, no film has been made of the story.

CHARACTERS

DEMON, unnamed man in a toga, unnamed narrator.

PLOT SYNOPSIS

A demon recounts his unsettling experience on the shores of the river Zaire, where "there is neither quiet nor silence." Rain falls and becomes blood. At the roots of tall, primeval trees, "strange poisonous flowers lie writhing in perturbed slumber." The demon tells of finding a large gray rock into which is carved the word "DESOLATION," and of having watched the actions of a man who stood upon the summit of that rock and "who trembled in the solitude" as the demon created chaos in the world around. The man was "tall and stately in form, and was wrapped up from his shoulders to his feet in the toga of old Rome . . . his features were the features of a deity. . . . his brow was lofty with thought, and his eye wild with care; and in the few furrows upon his cheek I read the fables of sorrow, and weariness, and disgust with mankind, and a longing after solitude." The demon remains hidden and watches the man, then curses everything around so that they are still. The man remains steadfast until the letters in the rock have transformed to "SILENCE," which leads the man to react in terror. The demon finishes his story, then laughs at human frailty, becoming angry when the narrator does not join him in laughing, for "I could not laugh with the Demon, and he cursed me because I could not laugh." The story told by the demon is intended to make a point about the nature of the ancient thinkers, who might have trembled in their solitude but felt terror in silence. The demon becomes upset with the narrator, who expresses his kinship with the ancients in his refusal to laugh.

"Silence—A Sonnet"   Poem by Poe, first published in the January 4, 1840, issue of the Philadelphia *Saturday Courier*. Poe revised the poem and submitted it for publication in the July 26, 1845, issue of the BROADWAY JOURNAL and included it in the collection THE RAVEN AND OTHER POEMS in 1845. The poem states its objective at the beginning: "There is a two-fold *Silence*—sea and shore—Body and Soul." The speaker tells the reader to not fear the silence of the body, the "corporate silence" death, which "human memories and tearless lore, / Render him terrorless." In contrast, that other silence, "his shadow (nameless elf, / Who haunteth the dim regions where hath trod / No foot of man)" is evil. Should the reader encounter that silence, the speaker advises him to "commend thyself to God!" Thus, the death of the body should be accepted as a natural occurrence and considered to mean simply "No more," but the death of the soul dooms one for all eternity.

Simeon the Pharisee   Character in Poe's short story "A TALE OF JERUSALEM." He accompanies the members of the Gizbarim, the subcollectors, or lower-level lackeys in charge of gathering the holy offering, in seeking to obtain the offering for their altar. He belongs to a sect called The Dashers, "that little knot of saints whose manner of dashing and lacerating the feet against the pavement was long a thorn and a reproach to less zealous devotees."

Simms   Character in Poe's novel THE NARRATIVE OF ARTHUR GORDON PYM. One of "the common hands" and a member of the cook's gang after the mutiny, he falls overboard, "being very much in liquor," and drowns. No attempt is made to save him.

Simms, William Gilmore (1806–1870)   American editor and novelist. Poe profiles his signature in two entries in "AUTOGRAPHY," likening both Simms's signature and his poetic style to that of John Pendleton KENNEDY, "although he equals him in no particular, except in his appreciation of the graceful." Of his work, Poe asserts "As a poet, indeed, we like him far better than as a novelist." In an entry in "MARGINALIA," appearing in the December 1844 issue of the *Democratic Review*, Poe wrote, "Mr. Simms has abundant faults—or had;—among which inaccurate English, a proneness to revolting images, and pet phrases, are the most noticeable." Despite these faults, Poe states in the same entry that "he is immeasurably the best writer of fiction in America. He has more vigor, more imagination, more movement and more general capacity than all novelists (save Cooper), combined." Despite such inconsistent review of his work, Simms praised Poe in his review of "THE RAVEN" as "a fantastic and a mystic—a man of dreamy mood and wandering fancies."

Simpson, Adolphus   Character in Poe's short story "THE SPECTACLES." A distant male relative of the narrator, he is a wealthy man who leaves a bequest that requires the inheritor to take his surname, Simpson.

Simpson, Napoleon Bonaparte   *See* Napoleon Bonaparte FROISSART.

Sing, Cheyte   Mentioned in Poe's short story "A TALE OF THE RAGGED MOUNTAINS." The historical reference is to the Rajah of Benares (also known as Chait Singh) who led revolt in 1781 against the ever-increasing demands for money to support the British rule in India. Dr. TEMPLETON was among the British troops fighting the insurrection, and he tells Augustus BEDLOE that his best friend Mr. OLDEB was killed.

Sinivate, Mr. Theodore   Character in Poe's short story "THE MAN THAT WAS USED UP." He is the narrator's "particular friend" whom he believes will give him "something like definite information." Instead, Sinivate "insinuates" information but says nothing directly about General A. B. C. SMITH's injuries, leading the narrator to leave the house "in high dudgeon, with a firm resolve to call my friend, Mr. Sinivate, to a speedy account for his ungentlemanly conduct and ill-breeding."

"Siope—A Fable in the Manner of the Psychological Autobiographists"   *See* "SILENCE—A FABLE."

"Sketches of Conspicuous Living Characters of France. Translated by R. M. Walsh. Lea & Blanchard" Review by Poe that appeared in the April 1841 issue of *GRAHAM'S MAGAZINE*. Poe briefly deals with each of the 15 "men now playing important parts in the great drama of French affairs," and compliments the original author, who published the sketches "in weekly numbers at Paris . . . someone who styles himself '*un homme de rien*' [a man of nothing, i.e., a nobody]—the better to conceal the fact, perhaps, that he is really *un homme de beaucoup*" [a man of importance]. Poe takes the translator to task, however, for "the volume now before us is, in some respects, not very well done." He asserts that the translator has taken "too little care . . . in rendering the French idioms by English equivalents," and that the manuscript contains "a thousand outrageous typographical errors."

"Sketches of History, Life, and Manners in the West. By James Hall. Philadelphia: Harrison Hall" Review by Poe that appeared in the December 1835 issue of the *SOUTHERN LITERARY MESSENGER*. The review briefly describes the content of the work, the object of which is "the sketching of character and life in the West," rather than the furnishing of topographical details, with which similar books have been concerned. Poe reminds readers that Hall had made his name as an author by writing tales and legends—"Wild romance and exciting adventure form its staple"—and editing the *Western Monthly Magazine*. In contrast, the book reviewed is nonfiction. The first volume deals with the government treatment of the Aborigines, the adventures of white settlers of Ohio, and the manners of the French in the Mississippi valley. The second volume deals with the Burr conspiracy and various military operations. Poe promises readers that they will find "in the book a fund both of information and amusement."

"Sketches of Switzerland. By an American, Part Second. Philadelphia: Carey, Lea & Blanchard" Review by Poe that appeared in the December 1835 issue of the *SOUTHERN LITERARY MESSENGER*. Poe asserted that the volumes were "more entertaining upon the whole than those which preceded them" and praises Cooper for looking at Switzerland "with a more instructed eye than the mass of travellers." The review is brief by design, because, Poe observes, "As the book will be universally read it is scarcely necessary to say more."

Skilton, Charles Sanford (1868–1918) American composer, conductor, organist, and critic whose compositions include incidental music; works for the organ, piano, and violin; choral music; and songs. In 1892, he published three songs: "Evening Star" and "To the River ———," inspired by Poe's poems of the same

names, and "Ave Maria," inspired by Poe's poem "HYMN." He published the song "Eldorado," inspired by Poe's poem of the same name, in 1894. In 1895, Skilton wrote *Lenore*, a cantata for baritone solo, vocal quartet, chorus, and orchestra, inspired by Poe's poem of the same name.

"Skimmings; or A Winter At Schloss Hainfeld in Lower Styria. By Captain Basil Hall, Royal Navy, F. R. S. Philadelphia: Replenished By Carey, Lea & Blanchard" Review by Poe that appeared in the October 1836 issue of the *SOUTHERN LITERARY MESSENGER*. Noting that "skimmings" is "hardly better, as a title, than 'Pencilling' or 'Inklings'," Poe calls the use of the term in the title "a little affectation." The work provides a series of anecdotes about the Countess Purgstall, who "had no little influence in the formation of the literary character of Sir Walter Scott." This "elderly Scotch lady" was "an early friend" of the author's father. Poe declares Captain Hall to be "no ordinary writer."

"Slavery in the United States. By J. K. Paulding. New York: Harper and Brothers / The South Vindicated from the Treason and Fanaticism of the Northern Abolitionists. Philadelphia: Published by H. Manly" A joint review of the works that appeared in the April 1836 issue of the *SOUTHERN LITERARY MESSENGER*. The lengthy article begins as a review of the two works, both of which support the tradition of slavery in the South, but it quickly becomes Poe's idealistic defense of the institution of slavery. After a lengthy digression on the "perfectibility of the human nature," "the lawless appetite of the multitude for the property of others," and the issue of "public sentiment," Poe thanks Paulding, "a Northern man . . . for the faithful picture he has drawn of slavery as it appeared to him in his visit to the South." He also praises the author of the second work, which "is more calculated to excite our indignation against the calumnies which have been put forth against us . . . seeking our destruction under the mask of Christian Charity and Brotherly Love." Poe recommends both works and asks leave "to add a few words of our own." In what becomes more than one half of the article, he then paints an idealistic picture of the master and slave relationship as one of emotional codependence in which the sentiments and loyalties between the two "are stronger than they would be under like circumstances between individuals of the white race." Poe maintains that "the habitual use of the word 'my,' used in the language of affectionate appropriation . . . is a term of endearment. That is an easy transition by which he who is taught to call the little negro 'his,' in this sense and *because he loves him,* shall love him *because he is his.*" Taking his sentimental, if unrealistic, argument further, Poe provides the example of the kindly master who "prolongs the life of the aged and decrepid [sic] negro, who has been, for years, a burthen [or] . . . labors to rear the crippled or deformed urchin, who can never be any thing but a burthen." He also writes "of a negress who was invited by a benevolent lady in Philadelphia to leave her mistress." The slave was tempted to try to escape and to accept the "good wages" offered by the lady, until she learned that she would be responsible for her own health and well-being should she become ill. According to Poe's account, the "negress" reacted with shock when the woman answered "no" to her following statement: "And if I am sick or any thing, I am sure you will take care of me, and nurse me, like my good mistress used to do, and bring me something warm and good to comfort me, and tie up my head and fix my pillow." Poe offers a further example to support his assertion of "the moral effect of slavery" in describing the devotion of a pregnant slave who refused to leave the bedside of her dying mistress, despite repeated commands by the master to do so. At the conclusion of the article, Poe berates those who, "in reforming the world address themselves exclusively to the faults of *others,* and the evils of which they know the least, and which least concern themselves." Noting that critics of the institution of slavery are numerous, Poe writes, "Nothing is wanting but manly discussion to convince our own people at least, that in continuing to command the services of their slaves, they violate no law divine or human, and that in the faithful discharge of their reciprocal obligations lies their true duty. . . . society in the South will derive much more of good than of evil from this much abused and partially-considered institution."

"The Sleeper" "Irene" was the title of this poem when it first appeared in the 1831 volume POEMS BY EDGAR A. POE, in which version it contained 74 lines. After numerous revisions in text and structure, the poem was pared down to 60 lines for publication in the May 22, 1841, issue of the Philadelphia *Saturday Chronicle* and in Poe's 1845 collection THE RAVEN AND OTHER POEMS. The poem appears on Poe's list of his best compositions, which he sent to James Russell LOWELL in 1844. The poem explores Poe's favorite theme, the death of a young and beautiful woman and the efforts of a grieving narrator to come to terms with that death. Poe also makes his first exploration of the indefinite nature of the states of life and death. The speaker refers to the lady in the poem in terms that relate to both the living and to the dead, first noting "Soft may the worms about her creep!" then stating "I pray to God that she may lie / Forever with unopened eyes."

Slyass, Mr. Character in Poe's short story "THE LITERARY LIFE OF THINGUM BOB, ESQ." He is "the great Slyass," whose work appears in the *Lollipop,* the magazine for which THINGUM Bob works. Slyass is a writer of renown who "received no less than thirty-seven-and-a-half cents for his inimitable paper on 'Pigs.'" Critics have associated the character with William Cullen BRYANT, whom Poe thought overrated.

Smith, Brevet Brigadier General John A. B. C. Character in Poe's short story "THE MAN THAT WAS USED UP." At their first meeting, Smith strikes the narrator as "remarkable—yes, remarkable . . . six feet in height, and of a presence singularly commanding." The narrator rhapsodizes about the fine appearance of Smith, noting his "richly flowing" hair, "the most brilliantly white of all conceivable teeth," "large and lustrous eyes," and "a pair of shoulders that would have called up a blush of conscious inferiority into the countenance of the marble Apollo." In truth, Smith has been physically decimated by his tremendous feats "during the Bugaboo and Kickapoo campaigns." When the narrator makes a surprise visit to Smith's home, he finds the general's servant POMPEY attending to his needs: screwing on arms and a leg, inserting Smith's teeth, attaching and adjusting his wig. "The manipulations of Pompey" make "a very striking difference" in the appearance of Smith, turning him from "a large and exceedingly odd looking bundle of something" to the stalwart-looking general. This fictional character owes something to General Winfield SCOTT.

Smith, Elizabeth Oakes (1806–1893) Poet and member of the New York City literary set whose salon Poe attended. Poe reviewed "THE POETICAL WRITINGS OF MRS. ELIZABETH OAKES SMITH" in the August 23, 1845, issue of the *BROADWAY JOURNAL.* She held fortnightly gatherings on Sunday nights at her home, and was somewhat feared by many of the literati for her radical support of women's rights. She was married to the political satirist Seba SMITH.

Smith, John Character in Poe's short story "X-ING A PARAGRAB." For many years in "Alexander-the-Great-o-nopolis," he "had there quietly grown fat in editing and publishing the 'Alexander-the-Great-o-nopolis Gazette.'" He aggravates the rival newspaper editor Touch-and-Go BULLET-HEAD by quoting paragraphs from his newspaper and pointing out the overuse of the vowel *o.*

Smith, Leo (1881–1968) British composer, cellist, and writer about music whose compositions include numerous songs, part-songs, and cello pieces. In 1914, he published songs titled "The Sleeper," "To Helen," and "To One in Paradise," inspired by Poe's poems of the same name, and "I Saw Thee On Thy Bridal Day," inspired by Poe's poem "SONG."

Smith, Mrs. Seba   *See* SMITH, Elizabeth Oakes.

Smith, Seba (1792–1868)   American novelist, poet, and political satirist. He wrote *Letters of Major Jack Downing* and *Powhatan: A Metrical Romance in Seven Cantos,* which Poe reviewed in the July 1841 issue of GRAHAM'S MAGAZINE. Although Poe admired *Letters* as "very clever productions; coarse, but full of fun, wit, sarcasm, and sense," he did "not very particularly admire" *Powhatan,* and said so in "AUTOGRAPHY."

Smith, Warren Storey (1885–1958)   American critic, composer, and teacher whose compositions include songs, piano pieces, and orchestral and chamber music. In 1903, he composed the songs "To Helen," inspired by Poe's poem of the same name, and "Thou Was That All To Me, Love," inspired by Poe's poem "TO ONE IN PARADISE."

Smitherton, Captain   Captain in Poe's short story "THREE SUNDAYS IN A WEEK." He has been absent from England for a year "in foreign travel," having made a journey in which he "doubled the Cape of Good Hope." His assertion that the day preceding his visit will be Sunday, countered by Captain PRATT's assertion that the day following their visit is Sunday, provides the solution to the main predicament of the story—an uncle's demand that his niece may marry only *"when three Sundays come together in a week."*

Snap   Character in Poe's short story "THE BUSINESS MAN." He becomes a victim of the assault-and-battery business run by Peter PROFFIT. Antagonized by Proffit into a fight, Snap doubles his fist and knocks Proffit down. Proffit promptly sues him for $500 in damages.

Snobbs, Suky   Name given to Signora Psyche ZENOBIA, a character in Poe's short stories "HOW TO WRITE A BLACKWOOD ARTICLE" and "A PREDICAMENT," by her enemies. In "A Predicament," Zenobia declares, "I am *not* Suky Snobbs."

Snodgrass, Joseph Evans (1813–1880)   Virginia physician and editor. He had reprinted the rumor of Poe's mental derangement and confinement to the Insane Retreat in Utica, New York, in April 1846, in an article titled "The Facts of Poe's Death and Burial" written for *Beadle's Monthly* in 1867. He was called to provide medical assistance by the owner of the tavern in Baltimore outside which Poe was found unconscious only days before his death. A staunch proponent of temperance, Snodgrass attended to Poe, and he later used the example of Poe's final alcoholic stupefaction to provide a lesson in the evils of alcohol use. Once Snodgrass realized that Poe's condition was critical, he placed him at Washington College Hospital, under the care of Dr. John MORAN.

So-and-So, Marquis of   Character in Poe's short story "LIONIZING." He is a guest at a literary salon, but Poe mocks such literary dilettantes by portraying the Marquis "holding the Duchess' poodle" while she sits for her portrait.

"Some Account of Stonehenge, the Giant's Dance, A Druidical Ruin in England"   Essay by Poe that appeared in June 1840 in BURTON'S GENTLEMAN'S QUARTERLY. Poe writes that despite having "excited more surprise and curiosity than any other relic of antiquity in Great Britain," the site is relatively unimpressive when viewed from a distance and "even on a near examination it fails to fulfill the expectations of the stranger who visits it with exaggerated prepossessions." Instead, Poe suggests that visitors should view it "with an artist's eye" and contemplate it with "an intellect stored with antiquarian and historical knowledge." Following these recommendations, Poe methodically describes the layout of the inner and outer circles of the site, citing the number of stones of which Stonehenge originally was composed (129) and the number of stones remaining in 1840 (109). He is careful to list various theories of the origins of Stonehenge, but he shows no favor to any one theory.

Somervell, Sir Arthur (1863–1937)   British composer and educator whose compositions include choruses, song cycles, operettas, symphonic works, a mass, a cantata, and a violin concerto. In 1901 he composed "A Kingdom by the Sea," a song inspired by Poe's "ANNABEL LEE."

"Some Secrets of the Magazine Prison-House"   Article by Poe that appeared in the February 15, 1845, issue of the *BROADWAY JOURNAL.* The focus of the article is the need for an international copyright law, the lack of which prevented authors from collecting money due them by booksellers and sent many writers "into the service of Magazines and Reviews." Although the magazines pay, Poe asks "Why (since they must pay) do they not pay with good grace, and *promptly*?" He provides the example of a starving writer who might die while waiting to receive payment for his work. At the end of the piece, Poe asks two favors of readers: not to think that he writes from any personal experience, and not to apply any of his remarks to any living magazine publisher, for "they are all as remarkable for their generosity and urbanity, as for their intelligence, and appreciation of Genius."

"Some Words with a Mummy"   Short story. This story capitalizes on the craze in Poe's day for ancient Egyptian history and artifacts. Hieroglyphics recently deciphered using the Rosetta Stone, discovered in 1799, had fueled the enthusiasm. Poe also uses the story as a vehicle for criticizing the political and scientific thinking of his day, especially the overly lauded concepts of progress and democracy.

PUBLISHING AND DRAMATIZATION HISTORY

The story was first published in the April 1845 issue of the *American Review* and reprinted without revision in the November 1, 1845, issue of the BROADWAY JOURNAL.

Poe does not append an epigraph to the story.

No film to date has been made of the story.

CHARACTERS

Count ALLAMISTAKEO, Mr. Silk BUCKINGHAM, Mr. GLIDDON, Dr. PONNONNER, unnamed narrator.

PLOT ANALYSIS

The story opens with the narrator being roused from his anticipated rejuvenative sleep on the evening after recovering from a hangover. He receives a hurried note from Dr. Ponnonner, stating that the directors of the City Museum have agreed to allow the doctor to examine a mummy, "to unswathe it and open it, if desirable," which he intends to do "at eleven to-night." The mummy case is placed on a dining table, and the group of characters opens the three protective cases to find the mummy, wrapped in papyrus and bejeweled. Stripping away the papyrus, the group finds "the flesh was in excellent preservation, with no perceptible odor. . . . The skin was hard, smooth, and glossy. The teeth and hair were in good condition." The group examines the body for the usual openings through which internal organs usually were removed before embalming, but they can find none, so they plan a dissection the next day. Not willing to waste the opportunity afforded by so perfectly preserved and intact a body, they decide to experiment with a galvanic battery to see if they can reanimate the corpse. As they apply the wires to an exposed muscle, the mummy's knee rises, connects with Dr. Ponnonner's stomach, and knocks him out of the window. The group rushes out of the room to rescue the doctor.

When the men return, the mummy, whose name is Count Allamistakeo, sits up and admonishes them. A dialogue ensues, "carried on in primitive Egyptian, through the medium . . . of Messieurs Gliddon and Buckingham, as interpreters." The mummy explains that he is of the Scarabaeus, which did not disembowel people before embalming, but instead embalmed people while they were alive so that they could be reanimated in a later time.

The men and the count compare scientific and political achievements in their respective periods, and ancient Egypt proves to be superior in all areas except for one. The doctor asks Allamistakeo, "upon its honor as a gentleman, if the Egyptians had comprehended at any period, the manufacture of either Ponnonner's lozenges [fictitious] or Brandeth's pills [one of the many sometimes dangerous pills, elixirs, powders, and nostrums popular in Poe's time]." The mummy appears defeated and "hung down his head." Unable to deal with "the spectacle of the poor mummy's mortification," the narrator rushes home, where he writes of the night's adventures for his family. He then resolves to "just step over to Ponnonner's and get embalmed for a couple of hundred years." The achievements that the mummy lists are all significant to civilization and have stood the test of time, but to the men present at the museum they are insignificant when compared to a modern lozenge.

"Song" Poem by Poe that appeared in TAMERLANE AND OTHER POEMS, published in 1827. The poem is also known by its first line, "I saw thee on thy bridal day." Critics and biographers assert that the poem is undoubtedly addressed to Poe's lost love Sarah Elmira ROYSTER, because the breaking of their engagement by her father was traumatic and because the poem was written after her marriage to Alexander Barrett Shelton, a man of means and of some social distinction. The four stanzas, each four lines long, contain ballad rhyme (abab) that conveys the sound quality of a song. The first and fourth stanzas are nearly identical to provide the repetition of a song. The speaker addresses the bride, who experiences "a burning blush," despite the happiness all around her, and he knows that blush "was maiden shame" for having abandoned him. The tone of the speaker's words suggest a curse or the unhappy expectation that the bride will regret her choice.

"The Songs of Our Land, and Other Poems. By Mary E. Hewitt. Boston. William D. Ticknor & Co." Review by Poe that appeared in the October 25, 1845, issue of the BROADWAY JOURNAL and was reprinted with revisions in GODEY'S MAGAZINE AND LADY'S BOOK in February 1846. The review lauds the poet's "poetic fervor, classicism of taste, and keen appreciation of the morally as well as the physically beautiful." In the first review, Poe reprints two of the poems and three of the sonnets in their entirety as examples of the superiority of this "most exquisite volume of poems." The second review omits the three sonnets and is more critical of the poet's technique. Poe includes "Alone" in both reviews. In the first, Poe declares that "'Alone' evinces, we think, more of the true poetic inspiration—and undoubtedly more of originality in conception than any other of Mrs. Hewitt's poems." In the second review, he finds significant technical fault, obscuring the merit of the work "first, by its frequent inversions, and secondly, by its rhythmical defects . . . especially the excessive use of difficult consonants." While Poe concluded the initial review "favorably impressed with the book," the second is unenthusiastic: "Mrs. Hewitt has, upon the whole, given indication rather than immediate evidence of poetic power. If not discouraged, she will undoubtedly achieve, hereafter, a very desirable triumph." *See also* Mary Elizabeth HEWITT.

Sonneck, Oscar George Theodore (1873–1928) American musician, musicologist, and foremost researcher in early American music. Sonneck's compositions include songs, string quartets, violin and piano pieces, and other instrumental works. In 1917, he published *Four Poems by Edgar Allan Poe*, for baritone and piano, which included the songs "To Helen," "Eldorado," and "A Dream within a Dream," inspired by Poe's poems of the same names, and "Thou wouldst be loved?" inspired by Poe's poem "TO F——S S. O——D."

"Sonnet—Silence" *See* "SILENCE—A SONNET."

"Sonnet—To Science" Poem by Poe that first appeared in the 1829 *AL AARAAF, TAMERLANE, AND MINOR POEMS*, his second poetry collection. The poem also was published in the October 1830 issue of the Philadelphia *Casket*. Primarily a Romantic protest against scientific rationalism, the poem condemns science for displacing mythology, whose stories of Diana, Hamadryad, and "the gentle Naiad" had nourished the soul. The poem also argues that science has destroyed mysticism and magic, as its "dull realities" displace the Elfin fantasy. Science is a "Vulture" with "piercing eyes," which has "dragged" and "driv'n" figures of mythology that nourish and sustain the creative imagination—just as the speaker has been dragged and driven from "the summer dream beneath the shrubbery." In this defiant protest against cold reason, the scientific spirit and the spirit of poetry stand opposed.

"Sonnet: To Zante" Shakespearean sonnet by Poe that was first published in the January 1837 issue of the *SOUTHERN LITERARY MESSENGER* and later appeared in *THE RAVEN AND OTHER POEMS* in 1845. The roots of this sonnet may actually lie in "AL AARAAF," which was published in 1829, as lines and images from the longer poem echo in the 14-line rhapsody praising the beauties of the island Zante. Critics suggest that the idealized setting of that "Fair isle, . . . How many memories of what radiant hours / At sight of thee and thine at once awake!" that is "No more!" is the home of John ALLAN, from which Poe was exiled, and that the "visions of a maiden that is no more" may actually refer to Sarah Elmira ROYSTER.

Sons of Temperance One of several organizations established in the United States in the early 19th century that worked with evangelical fervor to encourage abstinence from alcoholic beverages. After having several seizures, Poe sought in the summer of 1849 to free himself from the clutches of alcohol. He joined the Shockoe Hill division of the Sons of Temperance in Richmond, where on August 27, 1849, the presiding officer of the chapter, W. J. Glenn, administered the oath of abstinence to Poe. A notice that Poe had joined the Sons of Temperance appeared early in September 1849 in the *Richmond Whig*.

Sophocles (497–405 B.C.) Dramatist during the Greek Golden Age. Poe did not rank Sophocles very high among the ancient dramatists. In "THE ANTIGONE AT PALMO'S," Poe ranked Sophocles's tragedy Antigone as "vastly inferior to any one of the dramas of Aeschylus—and, perhaps, any play of Euripides would have been more acceptable to a modern audience." In "MARGINALIA," which appeared in the August 1845 issue of *GODEY'S MAGAZINE AND LADY'S BOOK*, Poe declared that "EURIPIDES and Sophocles were merely echoes of AESCHYLUS."

Sousa, John Philip (1854–1932) American composer and band leader, known internationally as "the March King." His compositions include approximately 150 marches, 10 comic operas, more than 50 songs, overtures, suites, oratorios, and waltzes, as well as three novels. In 1931 he published "Annabel Lee," a song inspired by Poe's poem of the same name.

Southern Literary Messenger Literary periodical published by Thomas Willis WHITE for which Poe worked as a staff writer, critic, and editor from August 1835 to January 1837. In late September 1835, the *Messenger* fired Poe, whose emotional distress and drinking after Neilson POE attempted to prevent his marriage to Virginia CLEMM had led him to the verge of suicide. After Poe's emotional crisis was resolved in October 1835, White rehired him and in December elevated him to editor. While an editor at the *Messenger*, Poe's time and energy were consumed by journalism and correspondence, leaving him little time for creative work. Before his promotion to editor, Poe published 37 reviews of American and foreign books and periodicals, nine tales (six of them reprints), four poems, and his drama *POLITIAN*. He also supervised the general contents of the magazine and maintained an active correspondence. While publishing criticism in the *Messenger*, Poe helped to build the magazine's readership. His efforts increased the circulation of the *Messenger* from 500 to 3,500 subscribers, and he received a raise from $10 to $15 a week. More important, his association with the magazine gave Poe the opportunity to make a name as a critic.

"The Spectacles" Short story. Critics suggest that the lengthy nature of the story, which continues long after the reader has discovered the central irony, has the air of a work written for payment by the word.

PUBLISHING AND DRAMATIZATION HISTORY

The story was first published in the March 27, 1844 issue of the PHILADELPHIA DOLLAR NEWSPAPER. When the story was reprinted in the March 1845 issue of the BROADWAY JOURNAL, Poe acknowledged the excessive length of the story and wrote that he was "not aware of the great length of 'The Spectacles' until [it was] too late to remedy the evil."

Poe did not append an epigraph to the story.

No film to date has been made of the story.

CHARACTERS

Mademoiselle CROISSART, Monsieur FROISSART, Madame Eugènie LALANDE, Madame Stephanie LALANDE, Mademoiselle MOISSART, Napoleon Bonaparte Simpson, Mr. TALBOT.

PLOT SYNOPSIS

The story relates the experience of a man whose vain refusal to wear spectacles leads him to marry his 82-year-old grandmother. When Napoleon Bonaparte Simpson attends the opera with a friend, he falls in love with the vision of loveliness that he sees in one of the distant boxes. "Being youthful and good-looking," he "resolutely refused" to wear glasses, so he cannot see her in clear focus. Still, the "divine form" of "this queenly apparition" make him fall "deeply, madly, irrevocably in love—and this even before seeing the face of the person beloved." He is charmed by her appearance and falls even more deeply in love after hearing her sing, but he still does not see her clearly. When the two meet, she alludes to an age difference, but does not tell him her age. Rather, she drops a miniature in the grass and promises that it will give him the information he seeks. She also agrees to marry him if he would promise to wear glasses. He promises and, after she leaves, he inspects the back of the miniature while wearing glasses. It reads: "Eugènie Lalande— aged twenty-seven years and seven months." He believes that is her present age. The two marry and he keeps his promise. When he puts on his spectacles, he finds that his wife is a wrinkled, toothless woman of 82. As he rages, she reveals that she is his great-great-

Illustration by F. C. Tilney for "The Spectacles" in Collected Works of Edgar Allan Poe *(1902).*

grandmother and has played a trick on him to cure him of his vanity. She then introduces him to the lovely widow Madame Stephanie LALANDE, with whom she is traveling. Simpson marries Lalande, and the story ends with Simpson's promise that he is "never to be met without SPECTACLES."

Spirit of the Times Philadelphia periodical that published Poe's prospectus for his proposed PENN MAGAZINE in the January 1841 issue. Later, when no other publication would print Poe's response to Thomas Dunn ENGLISH's character attack, Poe paid the paper $10 to print a reply to English in the July 10, 1846 issue.

"Spirits of the Dead" Poem by Poe published in June 1827 in TAMERLANE AND OTHER POEMS under the title "Visit of the Dead." Poe changed the title when the poem was republished in the 1829 AL AARAAF, TAMERLANE, AND MINOR POEMS. The poem relates a dialogue between the spirit of the dead speaker and a visitor to his gravesite. The spirit advises his visitor that "The spirits of the dead, who stood / In life before thee, are again / In death around thee." The spirit advises the visitor not to feel lonely, but to "Be silent in that solitude / Which is not loneliness."

Squibalittle, Mrs. Character in Poe's short story "THE LITERARY LIFE OF THINGUM BOB, ESQ." She is one of the contributors to the *Lollipop* and among those whom THINGUM BOB labels "so rich a galaxy of genius."

Stanard, Jane Stith (1793–1824) The mother of one of Poe's Richmond classmates. She died when Poe was 15, but her memory stayed with him until his own death. In 1848, he wrote Sarah Helen WHITMAN that Jane Stanard was "the first purely ideal love of my soul," and he told Whitman that Stanard was his first "Helen" and the inspiration for his first poem entitled "TO HELEN." To Marie Louise SHEW he declared that the long-dead woman was "the truest, tenderest of this world's most womanly souls, and an angel to my forlorn and darkened nature." Biographers assert that Poe read his early verses to her and that she gave him both helpful criticism and encouragement. She was a beautiful and kind woman whose own hypersensitive nature appealed to the equally hypersensitive Poe. Stanard suffered long periods of melancholia and, in the years that Poe knew her, she gradually became insane. Her death left Poe grief-stricken and provided him with another instance of the death of a beautiful woman, which would become a theme in his fiction.

Stanard, Robert (1814–1857) Poe's classmate in Richmond at William BURKE's school. His mother was Jane STANARD.

"Stanley Thorn. By Henry Cockton, Esq., Author of 'Valentine Vox, the Ventriloquist,' &c., with Numerous Illustrations, Designed by Cruikshank, Leech, &c., and Engraved By Yeager. Lea & Blanchard: Philadelphia" Review by Poe that appeared in the January 1842 issue of *GRAHAM'S MAGAZINE*. Poe begins the review by stating that the novel under review will be attractive "to the uneducated, to those who read little, to the obtuse in intellect." People "who can think but who dislike thinking" and those "who have no brains with which to 'work up' the material" are also potential readers of the novel. In Poe's view, the book demands nothing of the reader and "it is not in the least degree *suggestive*"; thus, he finds it without interest.

Stapleton, Edward Character in Poe's short story "THE PREMATURE BURIAL." His experience in being buried alive is one of the case studies presented at the beginning of the story.

Poe visited Jane Stanard at her house (background) on Capitol Square in Richmond, Virginia. (Edgar Allan Poe Library, Richmond)

Steen, Jan Havickszoon (1626–1679) Dutch painter who is noted for his genre scenes. He painted lively tavern scenes, landscapes, portraits, and religious works. Poe refers to him in a review, "BALLADS AND OTHER POEMS," to support the view that beauty, not truth, is the highest aim of art: "If truth is the highest aim of either Painting or Poesy, then Jan Steen was a greater artist than Angelo." In his review "CHARLES O'MALLEY, THE IRISH DRAGOON," Poe states: "For one Angelo there are five hundred Jan Steens." Poe also mentions Steen in the short story "LIONIZING" as one of the artists discussed by the pretentious Sighor TINTONTINTINO.

Stephens, Ann Sophia (1813–1836) Editor of *Snowden's Lady's Companion* and a historical novelist. In "THE LITERATI OF NEW YORK CITY," Poe declared her writing to be "bold, striking, trenchant," and she "seizes adroitly on salient incidents and presents them with vividness to the eye." He is not fond of her style— "generally turgid"—and he finds her sentences "for the most part too long; we forget their commencements ere we get at their terminations." In "AUTOGRAPHY," Poe states that she has contributed many articles "of merit and popularity" to the journal that she edited and "she has also written much and well, for various other periodicals."

St. Eustache, Jacques Character in Poe's story "THE MYSTERY OF MARIE ROGÊT." He is the boyfriend of the murdered young woman and immediately comes under suspicion for her death.

Stevenson, Andrew (1793–1824) Virginia Congressman. He provided Poe with a letter of recommendation in May 1829 to aid him in gaining admission to the UNITED STATES MILITARY ACADEMY AT WEST POINT.

Stiletto, Don Character in Poe's short story "LIONIZING." He watches as Robert Jones challenges the Elector of BLUDDENNUFF to a duel, and he exclaims *"Dios guarda!'"* ("God protect us!").

Story, Judge Joseph (1779–1845) Poe's review of his eulogy, "JUDGE STORY'S DISCOURSE ON CHIEF-JUSTICE MARSHALL," appeared in the December 1835 issue of the *SOUTHERN LITERARY MESSENGER*. In "AUTOGRAPHY," Poe wrote that "Judge Story, and his various literary and political labors, are too well known to require comment."

"Street Paving" Essay by Poe that appeared in the April 19, 1845, issue of the *BROADWAY JOURNAL*. Poe begins the essay with the fact, "remarkable" to him, that in the last 2,000 years, "the world has been able to make no essential improvements in road-making." He then provides a detailed technical discussion of road-making in ancient Rome, with a thorough explanation of "Macadamizing," the use of "true pavement," and other approaches to road-making. He admits in the essay that all such information is "very school-boyish," but he justifies giving it to readers because it is used in "fairly collating the ancient and modern ideas on the general topic of road-making." Having made a thorough study of the issue, Poe determines that wooden pavements are the road making material of choice and suggests that they should be used to repair the deteriorating road surfaces in New York City.

Stubbs Character in Poe's short story "THE SPECTACLES." He serves as the footman to Mr. TALBOT. Napoleon SIMPSON bothers him continuously for information when he arrives and Talbot is not at home.

Stylus Literary journal that Poe had intended to launch in 1843. The journal was to provide a forum for any and all opinions on "all subjects within its legitimate reach." Thomas CLARKE, the first editor of the *Philadelphia Saturday Evening Post,* joined other backers in early 1843 to provide support for the proposed magazine. He provided Poe with expense money to travel to Washington to secure endorsements and subscriptions of prominent men and government clerks. After

Poe's own cover design for the magazine he hoped to found. (Robert Gregor)

Poe arrived in Washington, Clarke received a letter from another backer, J. E. Dow, informing him that Poe had been drinking too much. Six years later, Edward Howard Norton PATTERSON, after reading announcements of Poe's plans for the *Stylus*, contacted Poe and offered to back the venture. In a letter to Poe dated May 7, 1849, Patterson wrote, "Of this magazine you are to have the entire editorial control." Poe replied with a request of an advance for $50, money that he put toward a trip to Richmond. He made no effort to bring out the *Stylus*.

"A Succession of Sundays" *See* "THREE SUNDAYS IN A WEEK."

Sullivan, Sir Arthur (1842–1900) English composer who won worldwide fame for the series of light operas written with his lyricist partner William Schwenck Gilbert. His compositions include numerous vocal and orchestral works; oratorios and cantatas, incidental music, grand opera, and such light operas as *H.M.S.*

Pinafore, Pirates of Penzance, and *The Mikado.* In 1904, "To One in Paradise," a song for tenor voice with piano inspired by Poe's poem of the same name, was published posthumously.

"The Swiss Heiress; or The Bride of Destiny. Baltimore: Joseph Robinson" Review by Poe that appeared in the October 1836 issue of the SOUTHERN LITERARY MESSENGER. Poe sets the tone for the review with his opening statement that the novel "should be read by all who have nothing better to do." After a detailed summary, during which Poe makes snide remarks as he describes characters or situations, the review concludes with the assurance that "the whole story ends judiciously." Declaring that the novel is "valuable 'work,'" Poe asserts that "in the name of 'fate, fore-knowledge and free will,' we solemnly consign it to the fire."

Sydenham, E. A. (1847–1891) English composer and organist whose works include songs, part-songs, and instrumental pieces. In 1869, he published "Eldorado," a song inspired by Poe's poem of the same name.

"Synopsis of Natural History; Embracing the Natural History of Animals, with Human and General Animal Physiology, Botany, Vegetable Physiology, and Geology, A. Translated From the Latest French Edition of C. Lemmonnier, Professor of Natural History in the Royal College of Charlemagne; With Additions From the Works of Cuvier, Dumaril, Lacepede, Etc., Arranged as a Text Book for Schools. By Thomas Wyatt, A.M., Author of Elements of Botany, a Manual of Conchology, Etc. Thomas Wardle, Philadelphia" Review by Poe that appeared in the July 1839 issue of BURTON'S GENTLEMAN'S QUARTERLY. As the work is a translation, Poe writes, "we need say little more in the way of recommendation than that all the useful spirit of the original has been preserved—and this we say from personal knowledge, and the closest inspection and collation." Poe expresses approval for Wyatt's change of the form of text, which he recommends as a necessary textbook in schools, from "the tabular form of the French publication to one better suiting the purposes of our American schools."

"The System of Doctor Tarr and Professor Fether" Short story. This tale has been read by some critics as a self-parody of "THE FALL OF THE HOUSE OF USHER," because the description of the long approach to the insane asylum is similar in description to the course taken by the visitor to the house of Usher, and the visitors in both stories arrive on horseback. Other critics have viewed the story as Poe's warning of the consequences of allowing slaves the freedom that the abolitionists demanded. The allusion to tarring and feathering also evokes the way in which Southerners often punished abolitionists whom they caught in the South.

PUBLISHING AND DRAMATIZATION HISTORY

The story first appeared in the November 1845 issue of GRAHAM'S MAGAZINE.

Poe did not append an epigraph to the story.

No film to date has been made of the story.

CHARACTERS

Monsieur BOULLARD, Monsieur DE KOCK, Monsieur DESOULIERES, Madame JOYEUSE, Mademoiselle LAPLACE, Monsieur MAILLARD, unnamed narrator.

PLOT SYNOPSIS

The comic story begins with the slow and apprehensive approach of a rather naïve and somewhat slow-witted young man to a private insane asylum, the Maison de Santé [House of Health], simply to satisfy his morbid curiosity. The approach parodies the approach taken by the narrator in "The Fall of the House of Usher," as he rides through "a dense forest. . . . the dank and gloomy wood" and comes upon "a fantastic *chateau*, much dilapidated . . . scarcely tenable through age and neglect." The superintendent of the facility, Monsieur Maillard, greets him at the door. Maillard appears rational, sane, in control, and eminently sociable. He leads the narrator to a lavish feast where people of all ages are dressed in elegant, if ill-fitting clothing, and relates the story of how the former "soothing system" of letting the inmates run free, without restraints, was ineffective. Maillard tells him the inmates had taken over the asylum and that restoring order had been difficult, but that a new system is now in place. As the narrator questions the behavior of some of the people at the feast, Maillard assures him that they are simply eccentric. Soon an uproar draws everyone's attention and what appear to be 10 black orangutans charge into the banquet room. They are actually the asylum guards who the inmates have covered with tar and locked in the basement cells. All of the people, including Maillard, with whom the narrator has spent the previous few hours are the former inmates. The inmates used the system of Dr. Tarr and Professor Fether to take control of the institution.

T., Miss Tabitha   Character in Poe's short story "THE MAN THAT WAS USED UP." She meets the narrator when he sits next to her during the sermon by the Reverend Doctor DRUMMUMMUPP.

Taglioni, Maria (1804–1884)   Italian ballet dancer whom Poe mentions in "MEMOIRS AND LETTERS OF MADAME MALIBRAN": "Human triumph, so far as regards all that is exciting and delicious, never went beyond that which she [Madame Malibran] experienced—or never but in the case of Taglioni."

Talbot, Mr.   Character in Poe's short story "THE SPECTACLES." He accompanies Napoleon Bonapart SIMPSON to the opera and later aids Madame Eugènie LALANDE in tricking Simpson into marrying his own 82-year-old great-great-grandmother.

"A Tale of Jerusalem"   Short story. This story appears to poke fun at Jewish religious dietary laws. Roman soldiers play a practical joke on the Pharisee and the Gizbarim: instead of the sacrificial ram or lamb they expect, they receive "a *hog* of no common size." Critics view the tale as offering a very clever reversal; rather than presenting anti-Semitic criticism or mockery, the Pharisee and the Gizbarim manage to pay back their oppressors and "accidentally" drop a hog on their heads.

PUBLISHING AND DRAMATIZATION HISTORY

The story was first published in the June 9, 1832, issue of the Philadelphia *Saturday Courier,* then revised and reprinted in the September 20, 1845, issue of the *BROADWAY JOURNAL.*

An epigraph from Lucan's *Pharsalia,* act two, lines 375–76, followed by Poe's "translation," precede the story:

> "Intonsos rigidam in frontem ascendre canos / Passus
> erat—"
>
> —Lucan—*De Cantone*

> —a bristly *bore.*
>
> —*Translation.*

Poe replaced the word "descendre" in the original quotation with "ascendre" so that the line no longer reads "He let his uncut gray hair hang down over his stern forehead," but instead "his uncut gray hair stood on end." This retranslation permits Poe his joke of "a bristly *bore* [boar]."

No film to date has been made of the story.

CHARACTERS

ABEL-PHITTIM, BUZI-BEN-LEVI, SIMEON THE PHARISEE.

PLOT SYNOPSIS

The story takes place in Jerusalem on the 10th day of the month of Thammuz, as Pompey and the Roman army control the city. A Pharisee and two Gizbarim negotiate with the Romans for a lamb to use in their religious sacrifice. Although they are grateful, they question if it is avarice or generosity that has changed the minds of the Romans and made them finally provide the lamb for offering. The three stand at the top of the walls of the temple and slowly lower a basket filled with shekels, then wait until the money is counted and their sacrifice is loaded into the same basket. They wait a long while as the Romans count the money, wondering if they will be defrauded, and they rejoice when they feel the tug on the rope, a signal to raise the basket. As they pull the basket up, the three praise the Romans, believing that "the Lord hath softened their hearts to place therein a beast of good weight!" When the contents of the basket are in sight, the trio sees not a fatted calf, lamb, or ram, but a hog: *"it is the unutterable flesh."* They let the basket containing the hog drop on the heads of the Romans below.

"A Tale of the Ragged Mountains"   Short story. This contemplative story deals with two themes that are popular in Poe's work, mesmerism and reincarnation. The story also harks back to Poe's days at the University of Virginia, when he probably walked through the Ragged Mountains soon after the ruptured relationship with Sarah Elmira ROYSTER.

PUBLISHING AND DRAMATIZATION HISTORY

The story first appeared in the April 1844 issue of *GODEY'S MAGAZINE AND LADY'S BOOK* and was reprinted without change in the November 1845 issue of the BROAD-WAY JOURNAL.

Poe does not append an epigraph to the story.

No film to date has been made of the story.

CHARACTERS

Augustus BEDLOE, Mr. OLDEB, Dr. TEMPLETON, unnamed narrator.

PLOT SYNOPSIS

Set in the mountains near Charlottesville, Virginia, the story focuses on Augustus Bedloe, a wealthy young gentleman subject to severe bouts of neuralgia, who has for years been attended to by the 70-year-old physician Dr. Templeton. The two make an arrangement in which Bedloe becomes Templeton's only patient, "in consideration of a liberal annual allowance" for the doctor. The doctor treats his patient with mesmeric techniques (see MESMERISM), and the two have developed so strong a rapport that "the will of the patient succumbed rapidly to that of the physician." Bedloe is also a habitual user of morphine, "which he swallowed in great quantity, and without which he would have found it impossible to exist." One Indian summer morning after breakfast and the usual dose of morphine, Bedloe takes a walk into the Ragged Mountains and enters a chasm that seems "absolutely virgin," as if no other human has ever been in it. He is late returning home, and he has a strange tale to tell Templeton and the narrator when he finally appears.

Bedloe claims that he was transported back in time to the 1780 [sic] Hastings revolt in Benares, India, and killed by an arrow to the right temple. Templeton's response is equally surprising: he first shows Bedloe a watercolor miniature that seems to portray Bedloe, but which the doctor explains is the image of a friend named Oldeb, killed 50 years earlier in the revolt in Benares. The doctor also explains that Bedloe's resemblance to Oldeb drew him to make Bedloe's acquaintance and to become his physician.

A week after the incident, the narrator reads in the newspaper of "the death of AUGUSTUS BEDLO." He died after Dr. Templeton accidentally applied a venomous leech to his right temple while trying to reduce a fever contracted during the excursion into the mountains. The narrator questions the newspaper editor about the misspelling of the last name, observing that "'Bedloe, without the *e*, what is it but Oldeb conversed!'"

"Tales and Sketches. By Miss Sedgwick, Author of 'The Linwoods,' 'Hope Leslie,' &c &c. Philadelphia: Carey, Lea, & Blanchard"   Review by Poe that appeared in the January 1836 issue of the SOUTHERN LITERARY MESSENGER. Poe writes that most of the 11 tales have been published before, and he provides a brief synopsis and critical commentary of each, selecting as the best "The Eldest Sister." The review compliments the author for finally pulling together these writings "which have been so long floating at random before the eye of the world," yet suggests that the timing is not quite right. Because this is Sedgwick's early work, it compares unfavorably with her recently published and reviewed novel *The Linwoods*. Poe ends the review with the warning that "the descent from good to inferior (although the inferior be very far from bad) is most generally detrimental to literary fame."

Tales by Edgar A. Poe   Collection of 12 stories by Poe that was published in 1845 by Wiley & Putnam as part of their Library of American Books series. The collection includes the following stories: "THE BLACK CAT," "THE COLLOQUY OF MONOS AND UNA," "THE CONVERSATION OF EIROS AND CHARMION," "A DESCENT INTO THE MAELSTROM," "THE FALL OF THE HOUSE OF USHER," "THE GOLD-BUG," "LIONIZING," "THE MAN OF THE CROWD," "MESMERIC REVELATION," "THE MURDERS IN THE RUE MORGUE," "THE MYSTERY OF MARIE ROGÊT," and "THE PURLOINED LETTER."

"Tales of the Folio Club: Poe's Introduction"   See "THE FOLIO CLUB."

Tales of the Grotesque and Arabesque   Collection of 25 stories—and the sixth volume of Poe's work—gathered into two volumes that were published in 1839 by the Philadelphia publishing house of Lea & Blanchard. The stories designated "grotesque" were actually satires or comic efforts, while the "arabesques" were serious, imaginative, and poetic, and showed a Middle Eastern influence. Poe dedicated the collection to Judge William DRAYTON, a congressman who had befriended him. Reviews of the book were mixed. An enthusiastic review that appeared in the *Philadelphia Saturday Courier* called the tales "generally wildly imaginative in plot; fanciful in description; . . . indicating the polished writer, possessed of rare and varied learning." The New York EVENING MIRROR asserted that the stories exhibited "a power for vivid description, an opulence of imagination, a fecundity of invention, and a command over the elegances of diction which have seldom been displayed." ALEXANDER'S WEEKLY MESSENGER thought that the tales showed a "playful effusion of a remarkable and powerful intellect." In contrast, the *Boston Nation* called the work "a wild, unmeaning, pointless, aimless set of stories, . . . without anything of elevated fancy or fine humor to redeem them." Volume one of the collection contained the following 14 tales: "BON-BON," "THE DEVIL IN THE BELFRY," "THE DUC DE L'OMELETTE," "THE FALL OF THE HOUSE OF USHER," "HOW TO WRITE A BLACKWOOD ARTICLE," "KING PEST," "LIGEIA," "LIONIZING," "THE MAN THAT WAS USED UP," "MORELLA," "MS. FOUND IN A BOTTLE," "A PREDICAMENT," "SHADOW," and "WILLIAM WILSON." Volume two contained 11 stories: "THE ASSIGNATION," "BERENICE," "THE CONVERSATION OF EIROS AND CHARMION," "FOUR BEASTS IN ONE: THE HOMO-CAMELEOPARD," "LOSS OF BREATH," "METZENGERSTEIN," "MYSTIFICATION," "SILENCE—A FABLE," "A TALE OF JERUSALEM," "THE UNPARALLELED ADVENTURE OF ONE HANS PFAALL," and "WHY THE LITTLE FRENCHMAN WEARS HIS HAND IN A SLING."

"Tales of the Peerage and the Peasantry, Edited by Lady Dacre. New York: Harper & Brothers"   Review by Poe that appeared in the December 1835 issue of the *SOUTHERN LITERARY MESSENGER*. Poe begins the review by chastising Lady Dacre for "this excessive show of modesty, or rather this most unpardonable piece of affectation" in listing herself as the editor on the title page of this republication of her work. In the earlier publication she had claimed authorship and, as Poe points out, despite the identification as editor on the title page, she continues to proclaim herself the author in the preface. The review is enthusiastic in its praise of Lady Dacre, who "is a writer of infinite genius, possessing great felicity of expression, a happy talent for working up a story, and, above all, a far more profound and philosophical knowledge of the hidden springs of the human heart, and a greater skill in availing herself of that knowledge, than *any of her female contemporaries.*" Poe provides a brief synopsis of each of the three stories to show the extent of the author's talents, then includes several passages from the first and longest of the three stories, "Winifred, Countess of Nithsdale," to provide "conclusive evidence of [her] talent and skill." The review ends with the recommendation that the author give more of "*her time* to the exaltation of her literary fame" to attain lasting renown.

"Tale-Writing—Nathaniel Hawthorne.—Twice-Told Tales. By Nathaniel Hawthorne. James Munroe & Co., Boston. 1842.—Mosses From an Old Manse. By Nathaniel Hawthorne. Wiley & Putnam, New York. 1856"   Review by Poe that appeared in the April and May 1842 issues of *GRAHAM'S MAGAZINE*. Although Poe allows that the stories "rivet the attention," he faults Hawthorne for a lack of passion and a tendency to rely on the "abstract ideas of allegory." The rancor of this review might be explained by Poe's negative opinion of the New England writers in general. For more than three years, Hawthorne had been living at the Old Manse in Concord, Massachusetts, Ralph Waldo Emerson's home. In Poe's mind, such a residency aligned Hawthorne with the transcendentalist circle and, more particularly, with such journals as the *Dial* and the *North American Review*, both inimical to Poe and his work. In his review Poe berates Hawthorne for such associations: "Let him mend his pen, get a bottle of visible ink, come out from the Old Manse, cut Mr. Alcott,

hang (if possible) the editor of 'the Dial,' and throw out of the window to the pigs all his odd numbers of the North American Review."

"Tamerlane"   Poem by Poe that first appeared in the 1827 collection *TAMERLANE AND OTHER POEMS*. The poem in its earliest incarnation consisted of 403 lines that Poe pared down to 223 by its publication in the 1827 collection *AL AARAAF, TAMERLANE, AND MINOR POEMS*. Biographers assert that the poem was inspired by Poe's broken love affair with Sarah Elmira ROYSTER, although he places the incident in a distant time, making the great Mongol conqueror Tamerlane suffer the conflict of having sacrificed "the loveliness of loving well" for achieving stature and renown. The poem does not pretend to historical accuracy, as it stresses four main themes in Poe's work: love, beauty, death, and pride. Poe makes his experience that of Tamerlane, with such lines as "We grew in age, and love together, / Roaming the forest and the wild." As the great conqueror Tamerlane ages and nears death, he regrets the love that he wasted and cries out for the love that he rejected while on his quest for "power and pride." In the end, he rethinks his choices and revisits his land "in a peasant's lowly guise," but finds that it is "home no more" and he has only "despair—/ A kingdom for a broken—heart."

Tamerlane and Other Poems. By a Bostonian   Poe's first published collection of poems. It was published anonymously, possibly because Poe did not want John ALLAN to know where he was, an assumption given further credence by Poe's enlistment in the army under the assumed name Edgar A. PERRY the same year. Poe wrote in the preface to the volume that most of the poems were written between 1821 and 1822, "when the author had not completed his fourteenth year." He indicates that they were not originally intended for publication, and "why they are now published concerns no one but himself. Of the smaller pieces very little need be said, they perhaps savour too much of egotism; but they were written by one too young to have any knowledge of the world but from his own breast." Only 50 copies of the collection were published, and few were sold, because Poe had no means of distributing the work. In later years, he said that the collection "was suppressed for private reasons," which means that he ran low on funds. The collection contains "TAMERLANE," "THE LAKE," "VISIT OF THE DEAD," "EVENING STAR," and "A DREAM WITHIN A DREAM."

Tarpaulin, Hugh   Character in Poe's short story "KING PEST." With his shipmate from the *Free and Easy*, he wanders the streets of a plague-ridden city and ducks into a funeral parlor containing KING PEST and his court. Tarpaulin is dunked into the barrel of beer, and his shipmate LEGS rescues him by knocking over the barrel,

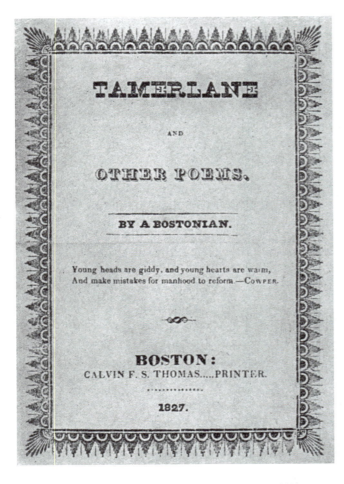

Original jacket of Tamerlane and Other Poems *(1827).*
(Robert Gregor)

creating a "deluge of liquor" that drowns most of the Pest court. Tarpaulin and Legs seize two women and rush away with them, heading for their ship.

Tattle, Mr.   Character in Poe's story "THE MAN THAT WAS USED UP." He plays whist with Mrs. Kathleen O'TRUMP as she explains to the narrator that this is "the age of invention" and speaks of the "horrid affair" and the "terrible wretches those Kickapoos." He does not respond, and his only concern is his game of whist, for which he refuses any hearts.

Taylor, Bayard (1825–1878)   American poet and author of "RHYMES OF TRAVEL" reviewed by Poe. In "MARGINALIA" in the April 1849 issue of the *SOUTHERN LITERARY MESSENGER*, Poe wrote a strong response against "an invidious notice"—an anonymous review—of the work published in a journal whose name Poe does not identify. He vehemently attacks the critic, who "undeservedly, holds, himself, some position as a poet" and

asserts that the reviewer "has never published a poem . . . which could compare . . . with *the worst* of Mr. Taylor's compositions."

Taylor, Cyril (1907–1984)   English clergyman and composer whose compositions include published songs and hymns. In 1930, he published "To Helen," a song inspired by Poe's poem of the same name.

Tchérépnine, Nikolai Nikilaivitch (1873–1937)   Russian composer whose works include songs, chamber music, choral works, orchestral and piano music, and an opera. He wrote *Le Masque de la Mort Rouge*, a ballet inspired by Poe's tale "THE MASQUE OF THE RED DEATH."

"The Tell-Tale Heart"   Short story. Critics have described this tale as the ultimate gothic story, for its mood and its narrator, who is trapped in an old, dark house without the prospect of escape. Some critics have suggested that the narrator might be a woman, for the absence of pronouns fails to indicate either sex. The sense of helpless entrapment escalating into a murderous rage might as easily apply to a woman as to a man.

PUBLISHING AND DRAMATIZATION HISTORY

The story was first published in the January 1843 issue of the Boston *Pioneer.*

Poe appended the following epigraph to the first version of the story, but omitted it in later versions:

> Motto: Art is long and Time is fleeting,
> And our hearts, though stout and brave,
> Still, like muffled drums, are beating
> Funeral marches to the grave.
>
>   —Longfellow, "Psalm of Life"

Critics suggest that the beginning of the "Outis" controversy involving Henry Wadsworth LONGFELLOW the following year made use of the quotation impolitic. (*See* "OUTIS PAPER.")

The Tell-Tale Heart, filmed in 1928, in a version directed by Charles Klein and starring Otto Matiesen and Darvas, is faithful to the details of the story. The 1934 British version, also marketed as *Bucket of Blood*, directed by Brian Desmond Hurst and starring Norman Dryden and Yolande Terrell, is based on the short story but contains numerous additional details to lengthen the feature. The film was remade, once again in Britain, in 1963. This version was directed by Ernest Morris and starred Laurence Payne, Adrienne Corri, Dermot Walsh, and Selma Vaz Dias. In this version, Poe's basic story remains, but a jealous love murder enlivens the plot.

CHARACTERS

Unnamed narrator, unnamed old man, unnamed police officers.

PLOT SYNOPSIS

The story is the monologue of a murderer, the nameless narrator, who reveals having developed "the sense of acute hearing" and who has "heard all the things in the heaven and in the earth. . . . I have heard all things in hell." Having presented these credentials, the narrator than asks how one who has heard all of this can be mad. To further convince the reader of his sanity, the narrator recounts how carefully the crime was committed, then questions how one who has been so methodical and who has planned so carefully could be mistaken for mad: "You fancy me mad. Madmen know nothing." The narrator really has no reason for committing the murder, and he admits as much. As caretaker of an old man, the narrator tends to the old man's needs: "I loved the old man. He had never wronged me. He had never given me insult. For his gold I had no desire." Pressed to justify the murder, the narrator settles on the old man's eye as his reason: "One of his eyes resembled that of a vulture—a pale blue eye, with a film over it. Whenever it fell upon me, my blood ran cold." After methodically working up to the murder, the narrator smothers the old man, dismembers the body, and places the body under the floorboards. The narrator relates these actions, "the wise precautions," as further proof of his sanity. After everything is put away, the police arrive and search the house thoroughly but find nothing. Even though he is safe from discovery, the narrator is driven to confession because he hears clearly the loud beat of a heart, and he believes that the police hear it as well. He jumps from his seat and confesses, because of "the beating of his hideous heart!"

Tem-Pest, Duke Character in Poe's short story "KING PEST." The cadaverous duke is one of the king's relatives decaying in the basement of the mortuary.

Templeton, Doctor Character in Poe's story "A TALE OF THE RAGGED MOUNTAINS." He is a 70-year-old man who causes the death of a patient when he applies a venomous leech to the patient's temple. He uses MESMERISM in his practice and suggests that an old friend has been reincarnated as his patient.

"Ten Thousand a Year. By the Author of 'The Diary of a London Physician.' Carey & Hart, Philadelphia" Review by Poe that appeared in the November 1841 issue of *GRAHAM'S MAGAZINE*. Poe found the novel, a periodical novel written by Dr. Samuel Warren, to be

"'shamefully ill-written.' Its mere English is disgraceful to an L.L.D." The review asserts, "The book is full too of the grossest misusages of language—the most offensive vulgarities of speech and violations of grammar." Poe finds the tone to be "mawkish and inflated," the moralizing is "tedious in the extreme," and "two thirds of the novel might have been omitted with advantage." The review reveals nothing of the plot, stating only that "there is no attempt at plot, but some of the incidents are woefully inadapted and improbable." Poe is equally disdainful of the author's "transparent puerile attempt to throw ridicule upon the ministerial party" by giving them "silly names" that are meant to represent their characteristics.

Teufel Character in "THE DEVIL IN THE BELFRY." His name is German for "devil," used when the large clock strikes 13 and the old men of Vondervotteimittiss cry out "Der Teufel!"

Thayer, Colonel (1785–1872) American soldier, educator, and engineer. He served as superintendent of the UNITED STATES MILITARY ACADEMY AT WEST POINT from 1817 to 1833. After Poe's dismissal from the academy, Poe wrote a letter dated March 10, 1831, to request that Thayer assist him in obtaining "an appointment (if possible) in the Polish army." Colonel Thayer did not reply.

Theology, Theologus Character in Poe's short story "LIONIZING." Among the guests at the dinner given by the Prince of Wales, he is another of the pontificating intellectuals who are more air than substance.

Thingum *See* BOB, Thingum.

Thiodolf, The Icelander and Aslauga's Knight German novel that Poe reviewed in an untitled review in "MARGINALIA" in the December 1846 issue of *GRAHAM'S MAGAZINE*. The work is No. 60 of Wiley & Putnam's Foreign Series of The Library of Choice Reading. The review begins with a statement regarding the cultural inadequacies of the German people and states that the work "could never have been popular out of Germany. It is too simple—too direct—too obvious—too *bald*—not sufficiently complex—to be relished by any people who have thoroughly passed the first (or impulsive) epoch of literary civilization." To explain why literary German remains backward, the reviewer reminds readers that "*during the whole of the middle ages they lived in utter ignorance of the art of writing.*" As a result, the Germans are far behind such literally enlightened nations as France and England. The review expresses even greater contempt for German criticism, as Poe "cannot refrain from laughing all the more heartily, all the more seriously I hear it praised." Of the work under scant consideration in this article, Poe states in the final paragraph, "it's kind can *never* be appreciated by Americans."

This-and-That, Earl of   Character in Poe's short story "LIONIZING." He is paying court to the Duchess of BLESS-MY-SOUL by flirting with her.

Thomas, Calvin Frederick (1808–1876)   Proprietor of a small printing shop in Boston. Poe's first collection of poems, *TAMERLANE AND OTHER POEMS*, was printed by Thomas, who had recently set up his printing business at the age of 19. Because Poe was trying to avoid detection by John ALLAN, it is possible that Thomas never knew Poe's real name nor the value of that early collection.

Thomas, Dr. Creed (1812–1889)   Classmate of Poe's at William Burke's Academy in Richmond, Virginia. He later went to the University of Virginia, as did Poe, and the two probably shared coach rides home for holidays. After Poe's death, Creed recalled the days at Burke's school in an interview: "It was a noticeable fact that he never asked any of his schoolmates to go home with him after school. . . . Poe was never known to enter into this social intercourse. After he left school we saw no more of him until the next day."

Thomas, Frederick William (1806–1866)   Poe's longtime correspondent, as well as a poet, novelist, and newspaper editor. Poe reviewed his novel *Clinton Bradshaw* in December 1835 and included an entry on Thomas in "AUTOGRAPHY." Thomas also wrote *East and West* (1836) and *Howard Pinckney* (1840), and he served as editor of the Cincinnati *Commercial Advertiser*. In his "Autography" entry, Poe wrote that Thomas was "well known as a public lecturer on a variety of topics. His conversational powers are great." Thomas tried to alleviate Poe's financial destitution by using his influence with government officials to obtain for him a post in the Philadelphia Customs House, but Poe was unenthusiastic about the possibility.

Thompson, David (1770–1857)   Canadian surveyor and explorer mentioned in Poe's unfinished novel *THE JOURNAL OF JULIUS RODMAN*. He became an apprentice of Hudson's Bay Company at 14 and later worked with the North West Company, exploring northwest Canada. As background to the Rodman expedition, the narrator relates the expedition undertaken by Thompson in 1810 to cross the continent to the Pacific Ocean. Although most of his people deserted him on the eastern side of the mountains, he crossed the mountain chain and descended the Columbia river "from a point much nearer its source than any white man had done before."

Thompson, John Reuben (1823–1873)   Editor of the *SOUTHERN LITERARY MESSENGER*. He lent Poe money in Richmond on September 26, 1849, when Poe called upon him at the *Messenger*. As Poe left the office, he gave Thompson a small roll of paper containing the poem "ANNABEL LEE," stating as he did so "Here is a little trifle that may be worth something to you."

Thompson, Mr.   Character in Poe's short story "THE MAN THAT WAS USED UP." When Brevet Brigadier General John A. B. C. SMITH first meets the narrator, he does not wait to be introduced before glad-handing and simply speaking out about his own interests, while inaccurately addressing the narrator as "Mr. Thompson," a name that he repeats twice. As the narrator walks away, he says, "Thompson, to be sure, is not my name; but it is needless to say that I left General Smith with a heightened interest in the man."

Thornton, Andrew   Character in Poe's work *THE JOURNAL OF JULIUS RODMAN*. The expedition picks up the Virginian in the woods, and he joins the explorers "upon the instant as soon as we mentioned our design." Julius RODMAN notes that Thornton came "of excellent family, belonging to the Thorntons of the northern part of the State." Readers learn that he has been "rambling around the western country, with no other companion than a large dog." Thornton has no goal and has collected no pelts, nor has he any object in view. Instead, he simply enjoys "the gratification of a roving and adventurous propensity." He entertains members of the expedition with tall tales, with the real task "to depict them to the hearer in sufficiently distinct colors."

Thornton, Philip (n.d.)   Doctor and personal friend of John ALLAN. His name frequently appears in Allan's correspondence, and his bills for medical care appear in Allan family archives.

"Thou Art the Man"   Short story. The tale is a further experiment in the DETECTIVE STORY. In this effort Poe makes his narrator the detective.

PUBLISHING AND DRAMATIZATION HISTORY

The story first appeared in the November 1844 issue of *GODEY'S MAGAZINE AND LADY'S BOOK*.

The title of the story is taken from the Old Testament. The words appear in II Samuel 12:7, in which the prophet Nathan accuses King David of desiring Bathsheba and having her husband killed to achieve that aim: "And Nathan said to David, Thou art the man. Thus saith the Lord God of Israel, I anointed thee king over Israel, and I delivered thee out of the hand of Saul."

No film has made of the story to date.

CHARACTERS

Charles GOODFELLOW, Mr. PENNIFEATHER, Barnabas SHUTTLEWORTHY, unnamed narrator, detective.

PLOT SYNOPSIS

The tale is a detective story in which the narrator is also the detective who solves the mystery. When the wealthiest man in town, Barnabas Shuttleworthy, disappears, everyone suspects foul play. His best friend, Charles Goodfellow, bemoans that he will never receive the shipment of Chateau Margaux, a fine wine, that Shuttleworthy had promised. Fears for the missing man's life are intensified when a bloody waistcoat, bullet, and knife belonging to his nephew Mr. Pennifeather are found. Pennifeather is placed on trial and, based on circumstantial evidence and with no corpse, he is declared *"Guilty of murder in the first degree"* and sentenced to death. The narrator conducts his own investigation, finds the corpse, and sets out to prove that Goodfellow is the murderer. He sends Goodfellow a note that the expected wine will arrive in a few days, then places the corpse in the wine crate and rigs it so that the corpse will spring into the sitting position when the box is opened. When this occurs, the narrator throws his voice to make it seem that the corpse has intoned to Goodfellow, "'Thou art the man!'" The shock leads Goodfellow to confess. Mr. Pennifeather is freed and receives his uncle's estate.

"Thoughts on His Intellectual Character" *See* "LITERARY REMAINS OF THE LATE WILLIAM HAZILY, WITH A NOTICE OF HIS LIFE BY HIS SON, AND THOUGHTS ON HIS GENIUS AND WRITINGS."

"Thoughts on the Religious State of the Country; with Reasons for Preferring Episcopacy. By Rev. Calvin Colton. New York: Harper & Harper" Review by Poe that appeared in the June 1836 issue of the SOUTHERN LITERARY MESSENGER. The review opens by noting that Colton's previous book, *Four Years in Great Britain*, was accepted by the press "with universal approbation. We heard not a dissenting voice. . . . Nor in any private circle, we believe, were the great merits of the work disputed." Poe asserts that the book under review is a "sufficiently well-written performance," but that Colton "excuses himself for apparent inconsistency in now declaring an opinion against the expediency of the practices which were scandalized." Although Poe writes that "all classes of the Christian community who admire perspicuity, liberality, frankness, and unpreju-

diced inquiry" will read the book "with pleasure and profit," he concludes, "in *style* the work appears to us excessively faulty—even uncouth."

"The Thousand-and-Second Tale of Scheherazade" Short story. This story is Poe's addition to the *The Thousand-and-One Nights,* also known as the *Arabian Nights,* but his title includes a serious miscalculation. The original contained one thousand and one *nights,* not *tales*—many of the tales are continued over several nights. Thus, Poe's story should be of the thousand-and-second night.

PUBLISHING AND DRAMATIZATION HISTORY

The story first appeared in the February 1845 issue of GODEY'S MAGAZINE AND LADY'S BOOK, and it was later republished in the October 25, 1845 issue of the BROADWAY JOURNAL.

The story is preceded by an epigraph: "'Truth is stranger than fiction.'—*Old Saying.*"

The story has not been filmed to date.

CHARACTERS

SCHEHERAZADE, unnamed king, unnamed narrator.

PLOT SYNOPSIS

The narrator professes to have uncovered startling information while "in the course of some Oriental investigations" respecting the fate of the vizier's daughter Scheherazade, whom the literary world had supposed lived happily ever after the thousand-and-first night of her tales. Consulting the "'Tellmenow Isitsoornot,'" which "is scarcely known at all, even in Europe; and which has never been quoted . . . by any American," the narrator learns that Scheherazade experienced pangs of conscience after her ordeal was over. She admitted to her sister "a grievous piece of misconduct," that she had withheld the full conclusion of the story of Sinbad the sailor. Despite no show of interest whatsoever from either her sister or the king, Scheherazade begins the sequel and fills it with absurd adventures that gradually irritate the king and lead him to grunt his disapproval. When his wife persists, the king becomes irate and shouts at her, "I can't stand that, and I won't. You have already given me a dreadful headache with your lies. You might as well get up and be throttled." The narrator states that the "Isitsoornot" relates Scheherazade's reaction to her fate: she achieved "great consolation" from knowing that she left much of the story yet untold, and "that the petulance of her brute husband had reaped for him a most righteous reward, in depriving him of many inconceivable adventures."

"Three Sundays in a Week" Short story. This is the most simple love story of Poe's oeuvre, and it has not been held in high regard by critics, but it is the first of Poe's tales to be translated into Spanish. The story was first published in the February 15, 1857, issue of the Madrid-based *El Museo Universal*. Critics have questioned whether the story might have inspired Jules Verne and given him the major premise for his novel *Around the World in Eighty Days* (1873), which is based on the same concept: A day is lost when going westward around the world and a day is gained when going eastward around the world.

PUBLISHING AND DRAMATIZATION HISTORY

The story was first published under the title "A Succession of Sundays" in the November 27, 1841, issue of the Philadelphia *Saturday Evening Post* and republished under the present title in the May 10, 1845, issue of the *BROADWAY JOURNAL*.

No film has been made of the story to date.

CHARACTERS

BOBBY, Doctor Dubble L. DEE, KATE, Captain PRATT, RUMGUDGEON, Captain SMITHERTON.

PLOT SYNOPSIS

This light-hearted love story opens as Bobby asks his uncle Rumgudgeon for permission to marry his daughter Kate. In his imagination, Bobby shakes his fist and has hard words for his uncle: "You hard-hearted, dunder-headed, obstinate, rusty, crusty, musty, fusty, old savage." But such courage is only in his imagination, because "some discrepancy did exist, just then, between what I said and what I had not the courage to say." Instead, Bobby cautiously approaches his uncle and asks him to name a precise date when he and Kate might marry. Thus pressed, Rumgudgeon responds, "you shall have Kate and her plum when three Sundays come together in a week—but not *till* then." The young lovers believe their situation to be hopeless until they hear the conversation of two sea captains who visit Rumgudgeon on a Sunday—one who thinks that the preceding day is Sunday and the other who believes that the following day will be Sunday. Captain Pratt has sailed west around the earth and lost a day, while Captain Smitherton has sailed east around the earth and gained a day. Thus, for Smitherton the previous day was Sunday, for Pratt the next day will be Sunday, and for everyone else the current day is Sunday. As Rumgudgeon must admit, "Three Sundays all in a row!"

Tieck, Johann Ludwig (1773–1853) German writer of fantasy whom Poe mentions in various stories and reviews. In "MEMORIALS OF MRS. HEMANS," he notes that Mrs. Hemans "liked the writings of Novalis and Tieck." In his review "TALE-WRITING—NATHANIEL HAWTHORNE—TWICE TOLD TALES," Poe claims that Hawthorne "is not original in any sense." Instead, he suggests that those who think him original are only those who have not "their acquaintance extending to the German Tieck, whose manner, in *some* of his works, is absolutely identical with that *habitual* to Hawthorne."

Tiger Animal character in Poe's novel THE NARRATIVE OF ARTHUR GORDON PYM. He is Arthur Gordon PYM's dog, and he stows away aboard the *Grampus* without his master's knowledge, leaving Pym to conjecture as to how the animal got there: "for the presence of Tiger I tried in vain to account." Pym relates that he and Tiger, who has been his inseparable companion for seven years, are especially close: "I had an affection far more ardent than common; and never, certainly, did any creature more truly deserve it."

Tintontintino, Signor Character in Poe's short story "LIONIZING." He is from Florence and one of the pretentious guests at the dinner given by the Prince of Wales. A pseudointellectual, he discourses casually about the tendencies of the great painters.

"To ———" (1) ["Wouldst thou be loved? Then let thy heart"] *See* "TO ELIZABETH."

"To ———" (2) ["The bowers whereat, in dreams, I see"] Poem by Poe that first appeared in the 1829 collection AL AARAAF, TAMERLANE, AND MINOR POEMS. The poem later appeared in the September 20, 1845, issue of the *BROADWAY JOURNAL*. The brief, 12-line poem deals with the speaker's loss in which "Thine eyes . . . desolately fall . . . on my funereal mind / Like a starlight on a pall." Yet, even as he must wake he sighs and looks forward to go to sleep again "to dream till day / Of truth that gold can never buy—/ Of the trifles that it may."

"To ———" (3) ["Should my early life seem"] Poem by Poe that first appeared in the 1829 collection AL AARAAF, TAMERLANE, AND MINOR POEMS. The original 40-line poem was shortened to 13 lines for publication in the December 1829 issue of the *Yankee and Boston Literary Gazette*. The poem details the speaker's loss of love and of early hopes that "went gloriously away." The speaker appears to equate parting from his beloved as a sign of one more failure, for he is no longer as young, nor as stoic, nor as proud as he appears to the outside world.

"To ———" (4) ["Sleep on, sleep on, another hour—"] Poem by Poe that appeared in the May 11, 1833 issue of the *BALTIMORE SATURDAY VISITER*. Poe dedicated the poem to an anonymous woman and signed the poem "Tamerlane." The 20-line lyric poem is a lullaby that repeats three times the words "Sleep on, sleep on" as the speaker urges that all is angelic, all is bright, all is like "some fairy dream / But, O, thy spirit, calm, serene, / Must wake to weep."

Toby Character in THE JOURNAL OF JULIUS RODMAN. He is "a negro belonging to Pierre Junot" who had been in the JUNOT family for many years and who "had proved himself to be a faithful negro." Although he is advanced in years, Junot refuses to leave him behind, for he is able-bodied and "still capable of enduring great fatigue." Poe's physical description of Toby shows a racism characteristic of the author's time: "as ugly an old gentleman as ever spoke—having all the peculiar features of his race; the swollen lips, large white protruding eyes, flat nose, long ears, double head, potbelly, and bow legs." The Native Americans whom members of Rodman's expedition meet are "struck with sudden amazement at the sooty appearance of our negro, Toby," and the members of the expedition appease their curiosity completely by sending him ashore "*in naturalibus* [unclothed]" so they might examine him more completely. Toby "took the matter as a very good joke" and allows "the inquisitive savages" to satisfy their curiosity, as they do by "spitting upon their fingers and rubbing the skin of the negro to be sure that it was not painted. The wool on the head elicited repeated shouts of applause, and the bandy legs were the subject of unqualified admiration. A jig dance on the part of our ugly friend brought matters to a climax."

"To Elizabeth" Poem by Poe that appeared in the September 1835 issue of the SOUTHERN LITERARY MESSENGER and reprinted in the August 1839 issue of BURTON'S GENTLEMAN'S MAGAZINE under a different title. Poe first composed the poem for his cousin Elizabeth Rebecca HERRING and actually wrote the poem in her album. Fifteen years later, he made a minor revision to the first line of the poem and addressed it to Frances S. OSGOOD, while retitling it "To F——S S. O——D." The poem was first published under this title in the 1845 collection THE RAVEN AND OTHER POEMS. Only eight lines long, the version addressed to Elizabeth Herring begins with the question "Would'st thou be loved?" and the revision simply rephrases the question to "Thou would'st be loved?" The remaining seven lines are identical to those in the original version, as they urge that to be loved one should be everything "which now thou art / And nothing which thou art not." If the person to whom Poe addresses the poem will follow his advice, then her "gentle ways" and "unassuming beauty" will make "love—a duty."

"To F ———" Poem by Poe that first appeared under this title in the April 1845, issue of the BROADWAY JOURNAL. Dedicated to Frances S. OSGOOD, the poem was also revised to four lines and appeared in the September 6, 1845, issue of the *Broadway Journal* under the title "To Frances." The speaker states that "amid the care—the woes / Crowding my earthly path—" he at least has solace "In dreams of thee" whose memory is "Like some enchanted far-off isle" in the "tumultuous sea of his life." For Poe, Frances Osgood provides a calming influence in his life, "Serenest skies continually / Just o'er that one bright island smile."

"To F——S S. O——D" *See* "TO ELIZABETH."

"To Helen" (1) One of two poems by Poe of this title. The first poem, consisting of 15 lines, was addressed to Jane Stith STANARD and was first published in the 1831 collection POEMS BY EDGAR A. POE, then reprinted in the March 1836 issue of the SOUTHERN LITERARY MESSENGER. He characterizes his "Helen" as possessing sustaining loveliness, peace, serenity, and solace for "The weary, way-worn wanderer." He recalls the glories of antiquity and writes two lines that have since become famous on their own merit: "the glory that was Greece, / And the grandeur that was Rome." From the classical Helen, Poe returns in the last stanza to his very own Helen and refers to the vision that he viewed as a lonely boy who warmed to her kindness and attention: "in that little window-niche / How statue-like I see thee stand."

"To Helen" (2) One of two poems by Poe of this title. The second poem, consisting of 66 lines, was addressed to Sarah Helen WHITMAN and first published in the November 1848 issue of SARTAIN'S UNION MAGAZINE. Poe wrote the poem before he met Whitman. He had seen her three years earlier while visiting Providence in July 1845 to deliver a lecture; although the two did not speak, Poe was captivated by her appearance. She was dressed in white and standing in a rose garden. Poe recalls their first meeting at the outset of the poem: "I saw thee once—once only—years ago: / I must not say *how* many—but *not* many. / It was a July midnight; and from out / A full-orbed moon, that, like thine own soul, soaring." He describes her dressed in white, "half-reclining; while the moon / Fell on the upturn'd faces of the roses." The rest of the poem remains appropriately vague, as Poe had yet to meet his "Helen of a thousand dreams."

"Tomb of Ligeia" *See* "LIGEIA."

"To M. L. S.———" Poem by Poe written to Marie Louise SHEW and published in the March 13, 1847, issue of the *Home Journal*. The poem was a Valentine gift to Shew in which Poe expresses his appreciation for her unselfish assistance and tender ministering to Virginia CLEMM Poe in the final year of her illness. In a single stanza of 18 lines, Poe speaks of "the seraphic glancing" of her eyes and he credits her with "the resurrection of deep-buried faith / In Truth—in Virtue—in Humanity—" as he tells her that he owes her most "whose gratitude / Nearest resembles worship." As Poe writes the lines, he "thrills to think / His spirit is communing with an angel's."

"To My Mother"   Poem by Poe addressed to Maria CLEMM and first published in the July 7, 1849, issue of the *FLAG OF OUR UNION* and reprinted in the annual *Leaflets of Memory for 1850*. The deeply felt and morbid sonnet contains two lines that mention his biological mother, Elizabeth POE, of whom he writes, "My mother—my own mother, who died early / Was but the mother of myself." In contrast, not only has Maria Clemm been kind to him, "but you / Are mother to the one I loved so dearly." She is, to Poe, "more mother unto me" and "dearer than the mother I knew."

"To One in Paradise"   Poem by Poe that was originally included in the first version of Poe's short story "THE ASSIGNATION" that was published under the title of "The Visionary" in the January 1834 issue of *GODEY'S MAGAZINE AND LADY'S BOOK*. The poem also appeared in the 1845 collection *THE RAVEN AND OTHER POEMS*. The poem contains his favorite theme of grieving for the loss of a beautiful woman: "Thou wast that all to me, love, / For which my soul did pine."

Too-Wit   Character in Poe's novel *THE NARRATIVE OF ARTHUR GORDON PYM*. He is a native chieftain who leaps onboard one of the exploratory boats from the *Jane Guy* and seats himself next to Captain GUY. He and his men perceive the ship as a living entity, and he howls and whines in sympathy with the ship when the cook accidentally strikes the deck with an ax and makes "a gash of considerable depth." With his help, the sailors guide the *Jane Guy* safely through the reefs.

"Tortesa, the Usurer: A Play. By N. P. Willis. Samuel Colman, New York"   Review by Poe that appeared in the August 1839 issue of *BURTON'S GENTLEMAN'S MAGAZINE*. Poe also included a discussion of the play in his essay "THE AMERICA DRAMA" that appeared in the August 1845 issue of the *American Whig Review*. Poe determined that that merits of the play lay in "the higher and more difficult dramatic qualities. . . . naturalness, truthfulness, and appropriateness, upon all occasions, of sentiment and language." Although Poe lauds the "refined taste upon every page," he asserts that "the plot is *inconsequential*. . . . The characters, generally, are deficient in prominence—in individuality." Poe also points out a

large number of improbabilities and notes that the plot of "the revulsion of feeling on the part of the usurer is a very antique conception at best." Despite the flaws, Poe concludes by esteeming the play "by far the best American play."

"To the River ———"   Poem by Poe that first appeared in the 1829 collection *AL AARAAF, TAMERLANE, AND MINOR POEMS*. It was reprinted in the August 1839 issue of *BURTON'S GENTLEMAN'S MAGAZINE;* the March 4, 1843, issue of the *PHILADELPHIA SATURDAY MUSEUM,* and the September 1845 issue of the *BROADWAY JOURNAL*. In the 14-line poem, the speaker states that when the beautiful young woman looks into the "labyrinth-like water" of the brook, "then the prettiest of brooks / My pretty self resembles." Her image becomes part of the speaker's heart when she looks at him with "her soul-searching eyes," just as her image becomes part of the brook when she looks into it.

Touch-and-Go Bullet-Head   *See* BULLET-HEAD, Touch-and-Go.

Touch-Me-Not, Royal Highness of   Character in Poe's short story "LIONIZING." He is present in the artist's studio when Robert JONES first appears there, and he is leaning upon the back of the chair in which the Duchess of BLESS-MY-SOUL is seated.

"The Tower of London: A Historical Romance. By W. H. Ainsworth. Author of 'Jack Shepherd.' One Volume. Lea & Blanchard, Philadelphia, 1841"   Review by Poe that appeared in the March 1841 issue of *GRAHAM'S MAGAZINE*. Poe opens the review with the assertion that "it is rarely our lot to review a work more utterly destitute of every ingredient requisite to a good romance." He declared that the novel "is, at once, forced and uninteresting. It is such a novel as sets one involuntarily to nodding." Poe observes that the incidents are dull and the character unrealistic, and he declares this novel to be "a blot on our literature and a curse to our land."

"To Zante"   *See* "SONNET: TO ZANTE."

Tracle, Misthress   Character in Poe's short story "WHY THE LITTLE FRENCHMAN WEARS HIS HAND IN A SLING." She is the "purty widdy" over whom Sir Patrick GRANDISON and Mounseer, the Count A. Goose, Look-aisy MAITER-DI-DAUNS contest.

"Traits of American Life. By Mrs. Sarah J. Hale, Editor of 'The American Ladies' Magazine,' and Author of 'Northwood,' 'Flora's Interpreter,' &c &c. Philadelphia: E. L. Carey, and A. Hart"   Review by Poe that appeared in the December 1835 issue of the *SOUTHERN LITERARY MESSENGER*. Poe writes that the volume is "beautifully printed" and he assures readers that "its neat external appearance is its very least recommendation." He does, however, question the author's assertion in the preface that the sketches and stories in the work "have not entirely the attraction of novelty to plead in their favor—but the author trusts that the sentiments inculcated, and principles illustrated, are such as will bear a reiteration." Although Poe believes that he has read some of the selections earlier, he questions if Sedgwick is indicating that the material is previously published or if she is alluding to the manner of presentation as not exhibiting novelty. Whichever her meaning, Poe declares that all fourteen of the articles "are all written with grace and spirit and form a volume of exceeding interest."

transcendentalism   A movement of philosophical idealism that rejected the emphasis on empirical inquiry of the 18th-century Enlightenment and focused, instead, on the value of the senses and intuition in revealing truth. Most popular in the United States in the 1840s, the movement in New England was influenced by the thought of the German philosopher Immanuel Kant. Transcendental elements appear in the work of Margaret FULLER, Bronson Alcott, Ralph Waldo Emerson, and Henry David Thoreau, all of whom were well read in the works of Johann Gottlieb FICHTE, Johann Wolfgang von Goethe, and Friedrich Wilhelm Joseph von SCHELLING. The New England transcendentalist movement also looked for inspiration to the romanticism of the English poet Samuel Taylor COLERIDGE, whose work and language emphasized observation and induction, and to the moral fervor of the social historian and literary critic Thomas CARLYLE.

The philosophy of New England Transcendentalists was best expressed in Emerson's essay "The Transcendentalist" (1842), which divided human beings into two groups: the materialists and the idealists, or Transcendentalists. Emerson wrote, "The materialist insists on facts, on history, on the force of circumstances and the animal wants of man." In contrast, "the idealist [insists] on the power of Thought and of Will, on inspiration, on miracle, on individual culture."

In 1841, members of the movement, including Nathaniel HAWTHORNE, created the Brook Farm Institute of Agriculture and Education, a social experiment known simply as Brook Farm, as an experience in transcendentalism and communal living. The community existed until 1847, but the experiment failed to truly achieve communal ideals as individual natures prevailed. Hawthorne detailed his experiences on Brook Farm in his novel *The Blithedale Romance* (1852).

Poe rejected the idealism of the movement which, rather than turn to scientific measurement and inquiry to make sense of the world, believed that pure reason in the absence of external evidence would elicit an immediate perception of truth. Unlike the transcendentalists, most of the narrators and characters in Poe's stories and poems cannot trust that their senses are eliciting truths or correctly representing their situations, nor can we as readers. Further, in his preoccupation with scientific advances, Poe appeared to have rejected the idealism that pervaded the thinking of the Transcendentalists. (*See also* "BOSTON AND THE BOSTONIANS. EDITORIAL MISCELLANY," Orestes Augustus BROWNSON, Thomas CARLYLE, Andre-Marie-Jean-Jacques DUPIN, Piero MARONCELLI, "TALE-WRITING.")

Trevanion, Lady Rowena of Tremaine   Character in Poe's short story "LIGEIA." She is the second wife of the narrator, and her appearance contrasts sharply with that of the darkly beautiful LIGEIA, his first wife. The narrator questions the motives of Rowena's family in allowing the marriage: "Where were the souls of the haughty family of the bride, when, through thirst of gold, they permitted to pass the threshold of an apartment so bedecked, a maiden and a daughter so beloved?" Within days, Rowena lives in fear, and the narrator takes pleasure that she "dreaded the fierce moodiness of my temper." At the beginning of the second month of the marriage, Rowena becomes seriously ill and hallucinates. After seeming to recover, she suffers a relapse and becomes even more violently ill than before. She dies three days later. As the narrator watches by the body on the fourth day, he hears a sigh and watches as the cheeks and forehead of the dead woman seem to fill with color. He momentarily believes that he has been too quick in declaring Rowena dead, but the color soon fades and the body remains still. When the corpse opens her eyes, the narrator realizes that Rowena's body has been taken over by the spirit of Ligeia.

Trippetta   Character in Poe's short story "HOP-FROG." A young girl who is "very little less dwarfish" than HOP-FROG, she is a court dancer for the king and the partner of Hop-Frog.

Tsalemon   *See* PSALEMOUN.

Tucker, Nathaniel Beverley (1784–1851)   Court judge, writer, and well-known contributor to the *SOUTHERN LITERARY MESSENGER*. Poe reviewed his novel "GEORGE BALCOMBE" in the January 1837 issue of the *Messenger*. In the "AUTOGRAPHY" entry that appeared in the November 1841 issue of *GRAHAM'S MAGAZINE*, Poe wrote that, as a critic, Tucker "is apt, however, to be led away by personal feelings, and is more given to vituperation for the mere sake of point or pungency than is altogether consonant with his character as a judge." Poe cites as an example Tucker's denunciation in a review of "everything composed by the author of 'The Curiosity Shop,'

[Charles DICKENS] and which prophesied his [Dickens's] immediate downfall." Because Tucker had taken a dislike to Dickens, he allowed this dislike to influence a review of the author's work and foolishly predicted his downfall. The obvious truth is that the opposite occurred in Dickens's career.

Turnip, Miss Tabitha   Character in Poe's short story "HOW TO WRITE A BLACKWOOD ARTICLE." She is a gossip who falsely reports that Signora Psyche ZENOBIA is Suky SNOBBS, and she "propagated that report through sheer envy." Zenobia states that "No one but Tabitha Turnip calls me Suky Snobbs."

Twice-Told Tales *See* "TALE-WRITING—NATHANIEL HAWTHORNE—TWICE-TOLD TALES."

Tyler, Robert (1816–1877)   Son of United States President John Tyler. He was an acquaintance of Poe's friend Frederick William THOMAS, who in 1841 hoped to use this government connection to obtain for Poe a position in the Philadelphia Customs House. The effort was unsuccessful because Poe was unenthusiastic.

Ugo Character in Poe's drama POLITIAN. He is a servant in the household of the Duc di BROGLIO. When JACINTA, a lady's maid, shows off the jewels that she has received from LALAGE, he hints that she has earned them in an immoral manner.

Ugolino (d. 1289) Italian politician mentioned in "THE LITERARY LIFE OF THINGUM BOB, ESQ." His full name is Ugolino della Gherardesca, count of Pisa, whom the poet Dante mentions in canto 33 of the *Inferno*. Ugolino deserted his political party in 1270 and aligned himself with the head of the opposition party, Giovanni Viscounti, then later joined the Florentines to force Pisa to restore his property. A conspiracy arose, and he and his two sons were starved to death in the tower of Gualandi. When Thingum BOB decides to plagiarize the works of ancient authors, he buys a book "which purported to be a translation of one Dante's 'Inferno'" from which he copies "with remarkable neatness a long passage about a man named Ugolino, who had a parcel of brats."

Ulalume Character in Poe's poem "ULALUME." She is the speaker's beloved who died a year before and for whom he continues to grieve deeply. Biographers associate her with Poe's dead wife Virginia CLEMM Poe.

"Ulalume" Poem by Poe published anonymously in the December 1847 issue of the *American Whig Review*. After the first publication, Poe wrote to Nathaniel Parker Willis, who reprinted it in the *Home Journal* with a query as to its author in order to stir up attention. The first version of the poem contained 10 stanzas, but Poe omitted the final stanza in later printings. The poem represents the dual yearnings that speaker feels a year after his love has died. PSYCHE accompanies him on his walk through the gloomy woods "in the lonesome October of my most memorable year," representing the soul and his spiritual side, yet he confesses that he is attracted by Astarte's bediamonded crescent, for "she is warmer than Dian; / she rolls through an ether of sighs— / She revels in a region of sighs." Astarte the moon goddess represents sexuality, fertility, and the possibility of new happiness, but Psyche cautions the speaker, stating, "'Sadly, this star I mistrust— / Her pallor I strangely mistrust." Their wandering leads the speaker to the door of tomb, "a legended tomb," and he asks Psyche to tell him what is written on the door. As she replies, "Ulalume—Ulalume!— / 'T is the vault of thy lost Ulalume!'" the speaker's heart grows "ashen and sober" and he remembers that on this same night a year earlier he had made the same journey. He cries out "I brought a dread burden down here" and questions "of all nights in the year, / Oh, what demon has tempted me here?" As the nine stanzas end, the speaker concedes that he will always be under the spell of the lost Ulalume. The 10 lines of the final stanza of the original poem convey a bitterness and despair that plunges the speaker—already suffering the melancholy grief of the first nine stanzas—into a contemplation of "woodlandish ghouls— / The pitiful, the merciful ghouls" and of "the limbo of lunary souls— / This sinfully scintillant planet / From the Hell of the planetary souls."

Una Character in Poe's short story "THE COLLOQUY OF MONOS AND UNA." Una poses a series of questions to MONOS, newly arrived on the ethereal planet, who describes in painful detail his dying and death, the funeral preparations, the grieving by those left behind, and the bodily sensations remaining after death. He also describes for her the sensations of dying, including the hyperexcitation of his senses and his eerie awareness, as exhibiting more of life than he experienced while fully living. He disparages passion as being "the affliction of an impure nature."

"Undine: A Miniature Romance; From the German of Baron De La Motte Fouqué. Colman's Library of Romance, Edited by Grenville Mellen. Samuel Colman, New York" Review by Poe that appeared in the September 1839 issue of BURTON'S GENTLEMAN'S MAGAZINE. Poe provides a lengthy summary of the translated work and uses the review as a forum in which to point out the flaws of allegory, an "indefensible species of writing—a species whose gross demerits we cannot now pause to examine." He does, however, observe that the "undercurrent of meaning" of the allegory "does not afford the fairest field to the romanticist," but surmises that Fouqué took that route for his novel consciously "and that a personal object alone induced him to choose it." Poe expresses high praise for the novel, which "is a model of models, in regard to the high artistical talent which it evinces." He praises the unity of the novel, which he calls "the finest romance in existence." In the final analysis, Poe asks, "What can be more intensely beautiful than the whole book?"

United States Military Academy at West Point   Military college on the upper Hudson River. Poe received an appointment to West Point in March 1830 and reported to duty as a cadet on June 20, 1830. Despite already having spent two years in the army, Poe seemed immediately unhappy with West Point and sought to leave, but could only do so if thrown out. Poe deliberately failed to carry out his duties. Beginning on January 7, 1831, Poe disobeyed orders of his superiors and refused to attend military formations, recitations, and chapel. On January 28, 1831, Poe was court-martialed and ousted from the academy and the military. The sentence was made effective as of March 6, 1831, in order to allow him to collect sufficient military pay to satisfy debts at the academy, but he was given his release on February 18, 1831.

University of Virginia   *See* JEFFERSON, Thomas.

"The Unparalleled Adventure of One Hans Pfaall"   Short story. Critics consider this story to be one of the first true science-fiction tales. The story also provides entertainment as a hoax that speaks to the fascination with international balloon flight in Poe's time. For the publication of the story in the anticipated 1850 collection of his works edited by Rufus Wilmot GRISWOLD, Poe felt compelled to follow the story with a lengthy explanation of the ways in which this story differs from Richard Adams LOCKE's "Moon-Hoax" and other works that it resembled. In the conclusion of his defense, Poe writes, "In 'Hans Pfaall' the design is original, inasmuch as regards an attempt at *verisimilitude,* the application of scientific principles (so far as the whimsical nature of the subject would permit), to the actual passage between the earth and the moon."

A view, circa 1830, of the United States Military Academy at West Point.   (National Archives—Stills Division)

Poe's room at the University of Virginia. (Edgar Allan Poe Library, Richmond)

PUBLISHING AND DRAMATIZATION HISTORY

The story was first published in the June 1835 issue of the SOUTHERN LITERARY MESSENGER under the title "Hans Pfaall." Poe changed the title to the current one when preparing the story in 1842 for inclusion in a proposed short story collection titled *Phantasy Pieces,* which never saw publication.

The epigraph preceding the story is a four-line excerpt from "Tom O'Bedlam's Song," a "mad song" appearing in the 1661 collection *Wit and Drollery* and reprinted in a chapter entitled "Tom O'Bedlam's" in Isaac D'Israeli's 1832 *Curiosities of Literature.* The term "Tom O'Bedlam" refers to someone who begs for alms on the basis of insanity instead of physical impairment. The term was applied to patients who were released half-cured from St. Mary's of Bethlehem (contracted to

"Bedlam") hospital for the insane in London, after which they would wander the streets and beg, while singing mad songs and wearing outlandish clothing to attract donors. The practice soon inspired various scams, as others began to impersonate these "Tom O'Bedlams" to beg money.

No film to date has been made of the story.

CHARACTERS

GLUCK, Grettel PFAALL, Hans PFAALL, Professor RUBADUB, Mynheer Superbus von UNDERDUK, unnamed aeronaut, unnamed narrator.

PLOT SYNOPSIS

The story opens with the announcement of an event that has caused "a high state of philosophical excitement" in the city of Rotterdam and is expected to keep Europe in an uproar, "all physics in a ferment, all reason and astronomy together by the ears." A hot-air balloon piloted by a little old man appears in the city and drops a scrolled letter sealed with red wax at the feet of the "burgomaster." [sic] The lengthy letter is addressed as follows: *To their Excellencies Von Underduk and Rubadub, President and Vice-President of the States' College of Astronomers, in the city of Rotterdam."* In it is an account of an adventure undertaken by a "humble artizen," Hans Pfaall, with three companions, all of whom had disappeared from the city five years before. The letter describes Pfaall's discovery of a gas 37 times lighter than hydrogen and his experiments in creating a craft to travel to the moon. Among the adventures described in great detail are visits to the North Pole, explosions, crash landings, and trips to the moon. The account is filled with references to scientific devices and procedures, thus adding a learned air and credibility to the story. Pfaall ends his letter with a request that he receive a pardon from the city fathers for "the crime of which I have been guilty in the death of the creditors upon my departure from Rotterdam" in trade for the extensive scientific knowledge that he purports to bring back. The town leaders feel that no pardon is in order, because the aeronaut did not wait for a response and "no one but a man in the moon would undertake a voyage to so vast a distance." Furthermore, Gluck the printer recognized some of the newspapers that were stuck all over the balloon as newspapers of Holland. More damaging, Hans Pfaall and his three companions had been seen only two or three days earlier "in a tippling house in the suburbs, having just returned, with money in their pockets, from a trip beyond the sea."

Unterduk, Mynheer Superbus von   Character in "THE UNPARALLELED ADVENTURE OF ONE HANS PFAALL." He is the burgomaster of Rotterdam. The aeronaut drops the huge letter sealed with red sealing wax at his feet, then unloads a half-dozen bags from the balloon onto the burgomaster, sending him tumbling to the ground. Through it all, however, Unterduk holds fast to the pipe in his mouth, emitting "no less than half a dozen distinct and furious whiffs from his pipe."

"Ups and Downs in the Life of a Distressed Gentleman. By the Author of 'Tales and Sketches, Such as They Are' New York: Leavitt, Lord & Co."   Review by Poe that appeared in the June 1836 issue of the *SOUTHERN LITERARY MESSENGER*. Poe makes his dislike of this novel clear from the beginning of the review: "The book is a public imposition." The negative observations escalate as he provides detailed summaries of each chapter in turn. Poe asserts that the introduction "is by

much the best portion of the work—so much so, indeed, that we fancy it was written by some kind, good-natured friend of the author." The review continues in an ironic tone, pointing out such insignificant details from the novel as "the young gentleman was excessively fond of oysters." After describing "the entire pith and marrow of the book," Poe asserts that "the term flat, is the only general expression which would apply to it. In it is written, we believe, by Col. Stone of the New York Commercial Advertiser, and should have been printed among the quack advertisements in a space corner of his paper."

Usher, Madeline   Character in Poe's short story "THE FALL OF THE HOUSE OF USHER." The twin sister of Roderick USHER, she lives alone with him in the gloomy and dilapidated family mansion, the "House of Usher." While the narrator speaks with her brother, Madeline passes slowly through a remote portion of the apartment without noticing either. The source of her illness "had long baffled the skill of her physicians. A settled apathy, a gradual wasting away of the person, and frequent although transient affectations of a partially cataleptical character, were the unusual diagnosis." Up to the time of the narrator's arrival, she has been ambulatory, but she takes to her bed, succumbing "to the prostrating power of the destroyer." One evening, the narrator is informed by her brother that "that the lady Madeline was no more." She later appears to the narrator and Roderick, with "blood upon her white robes, and the evidence of some bitter struggle upon every portion of her emaciated frame." She stands and stares, then falls forward against her brother and "in her violent and now final death-agonies, bore him to the floor a corpse." The story appears to offer a metaphor for the disintegration of the human mind, with Roderick representing the conscious aspect and Madeline the unconscious. Madeline contrasts with the cerebral Roderick, whose readings have led him into untold areas of the occult.

Usher, Roderick   Character in Poe's short story "THE FALL OF THE HOUSE OF USHER." The twin brother of Madeline USHER, he and the narrator were "boon companions in boyhood," and he appeals to the narrator to visit as "his only personal friend," for he suffers "of acute bodily illness—of a mental disorder which oppressed him." He has a cadaverous appearance, with large and liquid eyes, thin and pallid lips, a nose "of a delicate Hebrew model," and "a finely moulded chin." His skin has "a ghastly pallor" and his hair is wild and uncut, and it "floated rather than fell about the face." He appears to suffer from "a constitutional and family evil. . . . a morbid acuteness of the senses" that allows him to eat only "the most insipid food" and to wear "only garments of certain texture." He cannot stand the smells of any flowers, and "his eyes were tortured by even faint light." When pressed by the narrator, Usher admits that much of his gloomy disposition is due to the severe and long illness of his sister Madeline, his only relative. The narrator and Usher spend many soli-tary hours together, among the "rare and curious" books, some of them on divination and other subjects of the supernatural. Usher dies when his sister rises from her entombment and falls upon him, and he becomes "a corpse, and a victim to the terrors he had anticipated."

V

Valdemar, M. Ernest Character in Poe's short story "THE FACTS IN THE CASE OF M. VALDEMAR." Although he has a Danish last name, he lives in Harlem, New York, and apparently writes and speaks Polish, for he is the author of "the Polish versions of 'Wallenstein' and 'Gargantua'" under the pseudonym of Issachar Marx. Valdemar is also the subject of a mesmeric experiment as he nears death in order to determine if the mesmeric process can forestall death and decomposition. As agreed previously, when his physicians determine that Valdemar has only 24 hours to live, he summons the mesmerist to his bedside. Just as he is about to expire, the mesmerist puts the immobile Valdemar into a trance, a state in which he remains for seven months, during which nurses attend him. Although Valdemar seems technically to be alive, the mesmerist also realizes that to bring Valdemar out of the trance "would be merely to insure his instant, or at least, his speedy dissolution." Sensing that no progress can be made, the narrator decides to awaken Valdemar, whatever the consequences. Valdemar's "hideous voice" intones, "'For God's sake!—quick!—quick!—put me to sleep—or, quick!—waken me!—quick!—*I say to you that I am dead!*'" The doctor awakens him, and the body of M. Valdemar "absolutely rotted away beneath my hands. Upon the bed, before that whole company, there lay a nearly liquid mass of loathsome—of detestable putridity."

Valence Character in Poe's short story "THE MYSTERY OF MARIE ROGÊT." He is an omnibus driver who testifies that he saw Marie Rogêt cross a ferry on the Seine on the Sunday that she disappeared. He claims that she was accompanied by "a young man of dark complexion." To quell doubts, he asserts that he knew Marie and "could not be mistaken in her identity."

"A Valentine" Poem by Poe written expressly for Frances Sargent OSGOOD. Composed on February 13, 1846, as a Valentine's Day gift, the poem was later published in the February 21, 1846, issue of the New York *EVENING MIRROR* under the title "To Her Whose Name Is Written Below." Poe indulged his fascination with puzzles and cryptograms in writing the poem while he manages to convey to readers a message about his feelings for Fanny, with her "luminous eyes, / Bright and expressive as the swan of Leda" and "musical name." The lines reveal her name as one reads the first letter of the first line, the second letter of the second line, the third letter of the third line, and so on.

Valentine, Anne Moore (1787–1850) The sister of Frances ALLAN, she lived with the Allan family for 25 years. When Frances Allen died, Valentine continued to run the Allan household. John ALLAN proposed to her less than a year after her sister's death, but Poe interfered, and his strong objections led Valentine to refuse the proposal. She continued to live in the house after Allan married Louise Patterson. Upon Allan's death, Valentine inherited an annual payment of $300 and "her board and washing."

"The Valley Nis" The original title of the poem "THE VALLEY OF UNREST." The poem first appeared under the title "The Valley Nis" in Poe's 1831 collection *POEMS BY EDGAR A. POE*, published by Elam Bliss.

"The Valley of Unrest" Poem by Poe first published under the title "THE VALLEY NIS" in Poe's 1831 collection *POEMS BY EDGAR A. POE*. The poem appeared in the April 1845 issue of the *American Review* under the current title, as well as in the 1845 poetry collection *THE RAVEN AND OTHER POEMS*. The poem opens with the speaker's question regarding "All things lovely—are not they / Far away—far away?" The speaker seems to exist in a surreal state and expresses confusion about "the valley Nis," although he knows that it means "the valley of unrest" and that it is associated with "Something about Satan's dart— / Something about angel wings— / Much about a broken heart— / All about unhappy things." Once silent and peaceful, "*Now* the *unhappy* shall confess / Nothing there is motionless." The violets are "uneasy," the reedy grass waves over "the old forgotten grave," and the "some lilies wave / All banner-like, above a *grave*." At two points in the poem, Poe speaks to "Helen, like thy human eye / There th' uneasy violets lie" and "Helen, like thy human eye, / Low crouched on Earth, some violets lie." In both instances, the mention of Helen is followed by mention of the grave, which has led critics to believe that this poem must refer to his first "Helen," Jane STANARD. The peace of his childhood had been forever transformed by her death, and now "Eternal dews come down in drops. . . . Eternal dews come down in gems!"

Vanhoveln-Carpé (n.d.) Pseudonym of Myra Kinney-Carpé, an American musician whose compositions consist chiefly of songs and a number of piano pieces. Five songs inspired by Poe's poems were published in 1922: "Grains of the Golden Sand," based on the second stanza of "A DREAM WITHIN A DREAM"; "Thy Naiad Airs," based on the first and second stanzas of "TO HELEN"; "Dream-land," based on the first stanza and part of the third of the poem of the same name; "Eldorado," based on the first and last stanzas of the poem of the same name; and "In Vision," based on the first and second stanzas of the poem "A DREAM."

Vankirk, Mr. Character in Poe's short story "MESMERIC REVELATION." Mr. Vankirk, whose name means "of a church," asks P. to place him into a "mesmeric sleep," during which P. interviews him on a variety of metaphysical topics, including the nature of God, the materiality of deity, and postmortem survival. The interview terminates suddenly when Vankirk dies. P. attempts to bring Vankirk back to life, but Vankirk refuses the effort because while on the "other side" during the trance he has experienced a mesmeric revelation induced by "keenly refined perception." Vankirk chooses to remain in this ideal state of being. He smiles blissfully as he dies, leaving P. frustrated and alarmed without answers regarding the soul's immortality or any control over his subject's condition.

Van Vactor, David (1906–1979) American composer and flutist whose compositions include symphonies, concertos for flute and harp, choral works and songs for flute and woodwind quartet. In 1932, he published *The Masque of the Red Death,* a symphonic prelude for orchestra, inspired by Poe's short story of the same name.

Verplanck, Gulian Crommelin (1786–1870) Orator, politician, and author of addresses and reviews whose profile Poe included in "THE LITERATI OF NEW YORK CITY." Poe praised him as having scholarship that is "more than respectable" and legal acquirements that "are very considerable." As a legislator "he was noted as the most industrious man in that assembly," and his extensive knowledge made him a "walking register or volume of reference." In "AUTOGRAPHY," Poe wrote that Verplanck's writings "all evince the cultivated belles-lettres scholar, and man of intellect and taste."

"The Vicar of Wakefield, A Tale. By Oliver Goldsmith, M.B. Illustrated with Numerous Engravings. With an Account of the Author's Life and Writings. By J. Aikin, **M.D., Author of Select Works of the British Poets. D. Appleton & Co.: New York"** Review by Poe that appeared in the January 1842 issue of GRAHAM'S MAGAZINE. Poe opens the review with praise for the publication, as it is "one of a class which it behoves every editor in the country to encourage, at all times . . . of well-printed, and especially, of well-illustrated works from among the standard fictions of England." He discusses at considerable length the pleasures to be derived from good illustrations, but does not discuss the novel itself. The review also praises the biographical essay provided by the editor, Aiken, which provides all that "need be known of Oliver Goldsmith." Poe finds only one flaw in the work, an error on the first page of the biographical sketch, in which Aikin refers to the masculine Goldsmith with the feminine word form *protégée* instead of *protégé.*

Vidocq, François Eugène (1775–1857) French detective and author of crime books, as well as the founder of the Police de Sureté, the French police force. He served in the military, then committed several crimes and was imprisoned. After his release in 1809, he became an informer for Napoleon, and he was later the first chief of the French police. When he ran into trouble because of his agents, also former prisoners, Vidocq left the police and opened a detective agency. His ghostwritten memoirs were excerpted from September 1838 through May 1839 in BURTON'S GENTLEMAN'S QUARTERLY. Critics have identified two passages among the excerpts as strongly resembling Poe's "THE MURDERS IN THE RUE MORGUE." Poe mentions Vidocq in that story as having been "a good guesser, and a persevering man. But, without educated thought, he erred continually by the very intensity of his investigations. He impaired his vision by holding the object too close." In contrast, Poe's detective, C. Auguste DUPIN, intends "to view it in a sidelong way."

"The Visionary,—A Tale" Title used for Poe's short story "THE ASSIGNATION" when it was first published.

"Visit of the Dead" Original title of Poe's poem "SPIRITS OF THE DEAD."

Vogrich, Max Wilhelm (1852–1916) Austrian composer and pianist, as well as the librettist of his own operas. His compositions include oratorios, symphonies, concertos, choral works, church music, songs, and instrumental pieces. In 1890, he wrote *Annabel Lee,* inspired by Poe's poem of the same name, comprising six duets for soprano and mezzo-soprano.

"Voices of the Night. By Henry Wadsworth Longfellow. John Owen, Cambridge" Review by Poe that appeared in the February 1840 issue of BURTON'S GEN-TLEMAN'S MAGAZINE. Poe begins the review by briefly complimenting Longfellow for being a man of imagination and for having "ability as regards the very loftiest qualities of the soul." He then devotes the greater part of the review to attacking Longfellow's deficiencies and identifying sources from which he plagiarized the poems in the volume. Poe says the poet "is singularly deficient in all those important faculties which give artistic power, and without which never was immortality effected." The review condemns Longfellow for having "no combining or binding force" and "nothing of unity." Although Poe asserts "it is by no means our design to speak of the volume before us in detail," he gives detailed attention to several of the poems, pointing out that Longfellow's "Midnight Mass for the Dying Year" is remarkably similar to Alfred, Lord Tennyson's poem "The Death of the Old Year." The review professes to "have no idea of commenting, at any length, upon this plagiarism," but Poe does castigate Longfellow for the act "which belongs to the most barbarous class of literary robbery."

Voissart, Victor   Character in Poe's short story "THE SPECTACLES." He is the great-grandfather of the narrator.

Volta, Count Alessandro (1745–1827)   Italian physicist known for his pioneering work with electricity; the term *volt*, denoting a unit of electrical measurement, is named for him. In 1800, he developed the "voltaic pile," similar to a battery, that produced a steady stream of electricity. Poe refers to his work in "THE THOUSAND-AND-SECOND TALE OF SCHEHERAZADE" when he has SCHEHERAZADE describe the actions of magicians who "by means of a fluid that nobody ever yet saw, could make the corpses of his friends brandish their arms, kick out their legs, fight, or even get up and dance at his will." In "SOME WORDS WITH A MUMMY," the group of men examining Count ALLAMISTAKEO decide to make "an experiment or two with the Voltaic pile" and to apply electricity to the mummy. In "MARGINALIA," published in the December 1844 issue of the *Democratic Review*, Poe asserts that Charles DICKENS is a man of "higher genius" than Edward BULWER-LYTTON and states that "nothing short of moral Voltaism could have spirited Bulwer into the conception of the concluding passages of the 'Curiosity Shop.'"

Voltaire (François Marie Arouet) (1694–1778)   French philosopher and author. Poe includes him in several stories and in entries in "MARGINALIA." The devil reads a note to BON-BON from someone who "being aged one year and one month" signed his soul away "in consideration of certain mental endowments," and the signature is Arouet, Voltaire's real name. "HOW TO WRITE A BLACKWOOD ARTICLE" refers to Voltaire's 1732 drama *Zaire* when it suggests that alluding to the phrase from the drama, *la tendre Zaire*, will "not only show your knowledge of the language, but your general reading and wit." In "HOP-FROG," the narrator mentions Voltaire's drama *Zadig* as too refined a play for the coarse king to appreciate. In his essay "LITERARY SMALL TALK," Poe criticizes Voltaire's sense of geography, and states, "Voltaire betrays, on many occasions, an almost incredible ignorance of antiquity and its affairs. One of his saddest blunders is that of assigning the Canary Island to the Roman Empire." Poe also refers to Voltaire three times in "PINAKIDIA" and four times in "MARGINALIA," citing references that support his views on rationalism.

Von Jung, Baron Ritzner   Character in Poe's short story "MYSTIFICATION." The Baron Ritzner Von Jung teaches a pompous and sneering duelist a lesson by using his pseudolearning against him. The baron holds only contempt for dueling, but he speaks on the subject "with an ardor, an eloquence, an impressiveness, and an affectionateness of manner, which elicited the warmest enthusiasm from his listeners." When another character challenges his knowledge and the two exchange letters, the baron directs him to consult a passage in Latin that the man cannot read but pretends he can. The passage satisfies him that "the explanation offered was of the fullest, the most honorable, and the most equivocally satisfactory nature," yet this is a second humiliation that the baron has perpetrated on him because the book is nonsense.

von Kempelen   *See* KEMPELEN. Baron Wolfgang von.

"Von Kempelen and His Discovery"   Short story. This story, inspired by the 1848–49 Gold Rush in California, is a satire of the human lust for gold. In a letter to publisher Evert Augustus DUYCKINCK, dated March 8, 1849, Poe wrote of the story:

> I meant it as a kind of 'exercise,' or experiment, in the plausible or verisimilar style. Of course, there is *not one* word of truth in it from beginning to end. I thought that such a style, applied to the gold-excitement, could not fail of effect. My sincere opinion is that nine persons out of ten (even among the best-informed) will *believe* the quiz (provided the design does not leak out before publication) and thus, acting as a sudden, although of course a very temporary check to the gold fever, it will create a *stir* to some purpose.

The story is another of Poe's hoaxes, in addition to "The Balloon-Hoax" and "Mellonta Tauta," although the educated reader will identify the clues that he places throughout, such as von Kempelen's association with Johann Nepomuk Maelzel, whom Poe had exposed as a fraud in his essay "MAELZEL'S CHESS PLAYER"; the falsified reports by actual scientists; the fictionalized locales in Bremen; and the repeated references to the "science" of alchemy.

PUBLISHING AND DRAMATIZATION HISTORY

The story appeared in the April 14, 1849, issue of the FLAG OF OUR UNION, but it did not receive the extent of exposure that Poe had hoped for.

No film to date has been made of the story.

CHARACTERS

Baron Wolfgang von KEMPELEN, Mr. KISSAN, unnamed law officers.

PLOT SYNOPSIS

The story purports to relate the arrest in Bremen of an American chemist named von Kempelen, who has taken ideas contained in the diary of the renowned English chemist and physicist Sir Humphry DAVY regarding the transmutation of lead into gold and made them his own. The inclusion of various reports of the arrest that are attributed to different periodicals is an attempt to bring verisimilitude to the story, as is Poe's description of von Kempelen's physical appearance and family associations. The reports relate that the authorities became suspicious when von Kempelen purchased "a considerable property in Gasperitch Lane" but refused, when questioned, to divulge how he came by the money for the purchase. The police place him under surveillance, follow him to the garret in which he worked, and search the premises, but they find nothing suspicious aside from a huge trunk filled with bits of brass under the bed. The authorities learn later that the substance in the trunk is "gold, in fact, absolutely pure, virgin, without the slightest appreciable alloy!" Despite questioning, von Kempelen refuses to reveal his secret, and "it is more than probable that the matter will remain, for years, *in statu quo*." Speculating that von Kempelen will be forced eventually to reveal the process, people buy lead in anticipation and "In Europe, as yet, the most noticeable results have been a rise of two hundred percent in the price of lead."

Vredenburgh, Peter Character in Poe's novel *THE NARRATIVE OF ARTHUR GORDON PYM*. He is a native of New York, as well as "one of the most valuable hands on board the schooner." On January 10, Arthur Gordon PYM records in his journal that Vredenburgh was lost overboard when his foot slipped while he was going over the bows: "he fell between two cakes of ice, never rising again."

"Wakondah; The Master of Life. A Poem. George L. Curry & Co.: New York"   Review by Poe that appeared in the February 1842 issue of *GRAHAM'S MAGAZINE*. Poe's negative feelings toward the poem, written by the magazine editor Cornelius MATHEWS, are clear from the outset of the review as he questions why Curry & Co. had been "at the trouble of its [the poem's] republication" and states, "We are vexed with these gentlemen for having thrust this affair the second time before us." The reviewer expresses regret at having to review the poem, but vows to speak "*very* distinctly." In short, Poe writes, "'Wakondah,' then, from beginning to end, is trash. With the trivial exceptions which we shall designate, it has *no* merit whatever." To prove his assertions, the reviewer then quotes extensively from the poem, noting, "Were it possible, we would quote the whole poem in support of our opinion." The tone of the review is sarcastic throughout. At one point, after quoting a passage, Poe writes, "Now, Mr. Mathews, we put it to you as to a man of veracity—what *does* it all mean?" As he concludes the review, Poe gives the poet the following advice: "Mr. Mathews, you have clearly mistaken your vocation, and your effusion as little deserves the title of poem, (oh sacred name!) as did the rocks of the royal forest of Fontainebleu that of '*mes déserts*' [my deserts] bestowed upon them by Francis the First." One can only conclude that Poe credits Mathews with the same ignorance or inability to correctly perceive what exists that Francis the First showed in calling rocks his desert.

Walker, Joseph W. (n.d.)   Man who found Poe lying in the street on Wednesday, October 3, 1849. He was a printer with the Baltimore *Sun*. Walker sent a messenger with a note to Dr. Joseph Evans SNODGRASS, whom Poe said he knew, to treat the extremely ill man. His note follows:

> Baltimore City, 3d, 1849.
>
> Dear Sir,—There is a gentleman, rather the worse for wear, at Ryan's 4ᵗʰ ward polls, who goes under the cognomen of Edgar A. Poe, and who appears in great distress, and he says he is acquainted with you, and I assure he is in need of immediate assistance.
>
> Yours in haste,
Jos. W. Walker
>
> To Dr. J. E. Snodgrass

Walthew, Richard (1872–1944)   English composer whose compositions include overtures, piano concertos, cantatas, songs, part-songs, and chamber music. He published two songs inspired by Poe's poems of the same titles: "Annabel Lee" (1887) and "Eldorado" (1896).

Ward, Thomas (1807–1873)   Poet whose talents were derided by Poe in the review "OUR AMATEUR POETS NO. 1—FLACCUS."

"Watkins Tottle, and Other Sketches, Illustrative of Every-Day Life, and Every-Day People. By Boz. Philadelphia: Carey, Lea and Blanchard"   Review by Poe that appeared in the June 1836 issue of the *SOUTHERN LITERARY MESSENGER*. The review lists the names of the sketches contained in the book, noting that "broad humor is . . . the prevailing feature of the volumes," but it also praises "The Black Veil" for being "an act of stirring tragedy, and evincing lofty powers in the writer." Poe never identifies "Boz" as Charles DICKENS, but he does praise highly the author's artistry: "we pause at every sentence, not to dwell upon the sentence, but to obtain a fuller view of the gradually perfecting picture."

Waukerassah, Chief   Character in Poe's unfinished novel *THE JOURNAL OF JULIUS RODMAN*. He is a Minnetaree chief "who behaved with much civility, and was of service to us in many respects." He directs his son MISQUASH to accompany the expedition and to serve as an interpreter.

Weddell, Captain James (1787–1834)   English explorer and navigator. He is the author of *A Voyage Toward the South Pole Performed in the Years 1822–1824*, published in 1825. Poe mentions his 1823 exploration of Antarctica several times in the novel *THE NARRATIVE OF ARTHUR GORDON PYM*.

Weiss, Susan Archer (1822–1917)   Richmond poet who became acquainted with Poe in his later days. She published the essay "The Last Days of Edgar A. Poe" in the March 1878 issue of *Scribner's* magazine, which presents a humane and charitable view of Poe. Her 1907 *Home Life of Poe* provides a detailed view of Poe's final days, but critics question the veracity of what she reports, for she offers little documentation of the events and conversations.

Wertenbaker, William (1797–1882) Secretary to the faculty, librarian, and general factotum at the University of Virginia while Poe attended. One of Wertenbaker's duties was to make sure that students woke up and were dressed on time. In recollections written in 1868, Wertenbaker wrote, "I was myself a member of the last three [Poe's] classes, and can testify that he was tolerably regular in his attendance, and a successful student." In the same recollections, he also recalled Poe's obsessive gambling.

Wetmore, Prosper Montgomery (1798–1876) Both a general and a naval officer of the Port of New York, as well as an author whom Poe profiled in "THE LITERATI OF NEW YORK CITY." In the profile, Poe praises Wetmore's 1830 collection *The Battle of Lexington and other Poems* as "of considerable merit, and one which met a very cordial reception from the press." Poe describes him as having "energy, activity and indefatigability" as well as "unusual influence among his fellow-citizens."

Whipple, Edwin Percy (1819–1886) American literary critic. Throughout "ABOUT CRITICS AND CRITICISM," Poe supports the negative comments he makes with examples from Whipple's writings. He notes that Whipple is lacking in candor and analytical ability and has little discrimination.

White, Thomas Willis (1788–1843) Publisher and founder of the *SOUTHERN LITERARY MESSENGER*. White hired Poe as assistant editor in August 1835, then fired him in late September 1835 when Poe's emotional distress and drinking after his cousin Neilson attempted to prevent his marriage to Virginia CLEMM had led him to the verge of suicide. When the emotional crisis was resolved by October 1835, White rehired Poe and in December elevated him to editor. White fired Poe a second and final time on January 3, 1837 for drinking.

Whitman, John Winslow (d. 1833) Boston lawyer and the husband of Sarah Power WHITMAN. The Whitmans married in 1828 and he died in 1833.

Whitman, Sarah Helen Power (1803–1778) One of Poe's great loves and the inspiration for the second "TO HELEN." Like Poe, she was born on January 19, although six years later, and her belief in mysticism convinced her that they shared a psychic connection. She was widowed at the age of 30 and moved in with her mother and younger sister—a mistake, as her mother was a woman of powerful personality. Whitman conveyed a theatrical presence, dressing in lightly draping silky clothes and dainty slippers, with scarves

Sarah Helen Power Whitman, who was engaged to Poe near the end of his life. (Center for Humanities Research—University of Texas)

streaming lightly as she walked. Her otherworldly appearance was enhanced by the ever-present handkerchief soaked in ether: she had a heart condition, and inhaling the ether soothed her. Three years before they met, Poe had seen Whitman at a party after a lecture he gave in Providence, Rhode Island, but the two had not spoken. Whitman had heard of his admiration for her and had developed a strong liking for his poetry, which led her to compose the playful poem "To Edgar A. Poe" for a Valentine's Day party in 1848, in which she addresses "thou grim and ancient Raven." The two met soon after on September 15, 1848, and wrote a flurry of passionate letters to each other. By December 15, 1848, the two drew up a marriage contract, at the insistence of Whitman's mother, Mrs. Nicholas POWER. By Saturday, December 23, 1848, the relationship was broken off, because Whitman had learned that Poe was still exhibiting an interest in Annie RICHMOND and because reports had circulated that Poe was seen in the bar of a hotel called the Earl House. Poe was devastated by the breech, but pretended that the engagement was only postponed.

Whitman, Walt (1819–1892) American poet and one of the few major writers whom Poe actually met. In November 1845, Whitman visited the office of the *BROADWAY JOURNAL,* which had recently published one of his poems. Poe had just taken control after buying the publication from the publisher John BISCO with a note for $50 endorsed by Horace GREELEY, money which Poe never paid back. Whitman later recalled the meeting in his 1882 book *Specimen Days,* and noted of Poe, "I have a distinct and pleasing remembrance of his looks, voice, manner and matter; very kindly and human, but subdued, perhaps a little jaded." His assessment of Poe changed over the years, but in evaluating Poe's significance in the *Specimen Days,* he acknowledged the "indescribable magnetism about the poet's life and reminiscences, as well as the poems," yet judged him to have been "among the electric lights of imaginative literature, brilliant and dazzling, but with no heat."

Whitworth, Richard Member of the British Parliament. In 1774, he planned to undertake an expedition with Captain Jonathan CARVER to find the source of the Missouri River in Oregon, and convinced the British government to sanction the plan. The expedition never happened, however, because the American Revolutionary War broke out. Whitworth is mentioned in Washington IRVING's "*ASTORIA,*" as well as in Poe's unfinished novel *THE JOURNAL OF JULIUS RODMAN.*

"Why the Little Frenchman Wears His Hand in a Sling" Short story. Poe seems to recall his youth in this story, because the address on the visiting cards of Sir Pathrick O'GRANDISON, "39 Southampton Row, Russell Square, Parish o'Bloomsbury," is the address of the third set of quarters that John ALLAN rented in September 1817 for his family while they lived in London.

PUBLISHING AND DRAMATIZATION HISTORY

The story appeared in the 1840 collection *TALES OF THE GROTESQUE AND ARABESQUE,* and it was first reprinted in the United States in the September 6, 1845, issue of the *BROADWAY JOURNAL.* It was the first of Poe's tales to be pirated in London, appearing in the July 1840 issue of *Bentley's Miscellany.*

No film has to date been made of the story.

CHARACTERS

Mounseer, the Count A. Goose, Look-Aisy, MAITER-DI-DAUNS, Sir Pathrick O'Grandison, Misthress TRACLE.

PLOT ANALYSIS

The story is comic monologue written in a simulated thick Irish brogue and intended to explain why the "little Frenchman" must wear his arm in a sling. It

Illustration by F. C. Tilney for "Why the Little Frenchman Wears His Hand in a Sling" in Collected Works of Edgar Allan Poe *(1902).*

recounts the competition of the Irish "Barronitt" O'Grandison and the French suitor Maiter-di-dauns over the "purty widdy" Misthress Tracle. As the narrator of the story Sir Pathrick O'GRANDISON, Barronitt states in his thick Irish brogue, Maiter-di-dauns is "the little ould furrener Frinchman as lived over the way" from the narrator. The two visit Misthress Tracle, one sitting on each side of her, and each putting an arm around her back to clasp what they believe is her arm on the other side. As they compete with witty remarks, they alternately squeeze what they believe to be her arm and receive a squeeze in return. As the visit continues, each feels confident that he has captured the lady's heart and will, most likely, be chosen by her. After she arises from the "sofy" and leaves them, they realize that they have been squeezing each other's arms. Angered by the ridiculous error, O'Grandison then gives Maiter-di-dauns's arm "a nate little broth of a squaze, as made it all up into a raspberry jam." The result is an injury to the Frenchman, who must wear his left hand in a sling.

"The Wigwam and the Cabin. By William Gilmore Simms. First Series. Wiley & Putnam's Library of American Books. No. IV" Review by Poe that appeared in the January 1846 issue of GODEY'S MAGAZINE AND LADY'S BOOK. This was Poe's second of two different reviews of this work. (*See* "WILEY & PUTNAM'S LIBRARY OF AMERICAN BOOKS. NO. IV. THE WIGWAM AND THE CABIN. BY WILLIAM GILMORE SIMMS.") Poe opens both reviews with a discussion of the writer's earlier work, but in this one he points out the "bad taste" that Simms showed in his anonymously published *Border Beagles,* and which might also be seen in *The Yemasseee, The Partisan,* and "one or two other of the author's earlier works." The "bad taste" to which Poe refers is Simms's "strange propensity for minute details of human and brute suffering, and even indulged at times in more unequivocal obscenities." Poe also finds Simms's English "exceedingly objectionable—verbose, involute, and not unfrequently ungrammatical." He objects to the use of what he calls pet words, "of which we remember at present '*bug,*' '*coil,*' and the compound '*old-time*'." To clarify the title and nature of the collection, Poe quotes from the author's preface, in which Simms writes that in the delineation of the character of the planter, the squatter, the Indian, the negro, the bold and hardy pioneer, and the vigorous yeoman, "I have mostly drawn from living portraits," As in the earlier review, Poe finds the first story in the collection "Murder Will Out" to be the best of the collection, "an admirable tale, nobly conceived, and skilfully carried into execution." In this review Poe does not list the other stories in the collection, nor does he excerpt a passage, as he did in the original version.

Wilckens, Friedrich (1899–1887) Austrian dramatic composer whose works include a criminal-ballet sketch, a symphony, an overture, and a suite for orchestra. In 1928, he wrote the ballet *Don Morte,* inspired by Poe's short story "THE MASQUE OF THE RED DEATH."

"Wiley & Putnam's Library of American Books. No. IV. The Wigwam and the Cabin. By William Gilmore Simms" Review by Poe that appeared in the October 4, 1845, issue of the BROADWAY JOURNAL. This is Poe's first of two different reviews of the work. (*See* "THE WIGWAM AND THE CABIN.") Poe writes that this book is one of the most interesting of the books yet published, as well as "decidedly the most American of the American books." The review praises the collection of tales and takes the opportunity first to discuss Simms's work as a novelist, then to identify briefly the plots of several of the novels before turning to the collection. Poe selects "Murder Will Out" as "the most meritorious" of the stories, and expresses "no hesitation in calling it the best ghost-story we ever read." He adds that "the other tales of the volume are all excellent in their various ways," and provides their titles. The review ends with an excerpted passage from "Murder Will Out," although Poe cautions readers to bear in mind "the absolute impossibility of conveying, by extract, any just conception of a story whose main element is its skilful adaptation of parts."

"William Wilson" Short story. Poe created a semiautobiographical story, to the point that Wilson shares Poe's birthday, and experiences a synthesis of Poe's educational experiences as a nine-year-old in Irvine, Scotland, and in Stoke Newington, outside of London. The descriptions of the school and its haunted surroundings are taken from Poe's memories, as is the name, although not the personality and demeanor, of the character, "the Reverend Dr. BRANSBY." Reverend John BRANSBY, only 33 years old when he taught Poe, expressed irritation in later years regarding the use of his name. Critics have also associated the drinking and gambling that ruin Wilson's life at Eton and Oxford with Poe's dissipations at the University of Virginia. Overall, critics view "William Wilson" as Poe's attempt to come to terms with his own dual nature, to reconcile his self-destructive behavior with the rational need to restrain such behavior.

The German author and critic Thomas Mann identified the story as a classic story of the doppelgänger, the theme of the double that is part of the folklore and storytelling of many different cultures throughout the centuries.

PUBLISHING AND DRAMATIZATION HISTORY

The story first appeared in *The Gift: A Christmas and New Year's Present* for 1840, which appeared in mid-1839, and it was reprinted in the October 1839 issue of BURTON'S GENTLEMAN'S MAGAZINE.

The epigraph that precedes the story is misidentified as an excerpt from *Pharonnida* by the minor English playwright William Chamberlayne (1619–1689): "What say of it? What say CONSCIENCE grim, / That spectre in my path?" This is actually a garbled version of a quotation from Chamberlayne's play *Love's Victory:* "Conscience waits on me like the frightening shades, / Of ghosts when gastly [*sic*] messengers of death."

The story inspired three German films, all called *The Student of Prague* and all based in part on "William Wilson." The 1913 version, directed by Stellan Rye, modifies the story into that of a student who signs away his mirrored reflection to a mysterious man. The 1926 version, directed by Henrik Galeen and starring Conrad Veidt, and the 1935 version, directed by Arthur Robison and starring Anton Walbrook, focus more closely on the theme of the doppelgänger, or double. In 1968, the French filmmakers Roger Vadim and

Louis Malle and the Italian filmmaker Federico Fellini directed Alain Delon, Brigitte Bardot, Jane Fonda, Peter Fonda, and Terence Stamp in a French-Italian production entitled *Spirits of the Dead,* with a freely adapted "William Wilson" as one of the three segments.

CHARACTERS

John Bransby, Lord GLENDINNING, Mr. PRESTON, William Wilson (1), William Wilson (2).

PLOT SYNOPSIS

The story deals with the theme of the double, which has become a popular literary and film device in the form of the "evil twin" whom the "good twin" must vanquish. The story begins as the narrator assumes for readers the name of "William Wilson," for "the page now lying before me need not be sullied with my real appellation." This William Wilson relates his family background, blaming his behavior—"self-willed, addicted to the wildest caprices, and a prey to the most ungovernable passions"—on having inherited the family character. When he is sent away to school, he encounters another student who, "although no relation, bore the same Christian and surname as myself," a fact that does not immediately seem remarkable because his name is "one of those everyday appellations which seem . . . the common property of the mob." The two were also born on the same day, January 19, 1813 (the day, but not the year, of Poe's birth). The second William Wilson begins to compete with the first scholastically and athletically, and he begins an "impertinent and dogged interference with my purposes." The second Wilson also begins to copy the habits of dress, walking, and general manner of the first. The only consolation to the first Wilson is that "the imitation, apparently, was noticed by myself alone." The second Wilson is constantly at the side of the first, calling him to account, stopping him from enjoying his vices, and playing both conscience and guardian angel. He mysteriously appears at significant moments, then disappears before he can be confronted, but he often leaves behind a sign of his presence, such as a cloak of the type that only the two Wilsons wear. From Dr. Bransby's school to Eton, Oxford, and areas of Europe, the second Wilson follows the first, exposing the first for cheating Lord Glendinning at cards in one instance and preventing the seduction of a young and beautiful noblewoman in another. This final interference pushes the first Wilson to violence, and he plunges a sword into the second Wilson. Immediately afterward, he sees a mirror on the wall where none had been before and, looking into it, sees his own reflection covered with blood. As he looks on the floor where the second Wil-

Illustration by F. C. Tilney for "William Wilson" in Collected Works of Edgar Allan Poe *(1902).*

son lies, he sees "Not a thread in all his raiment—not a line in all the marked and singular lineaments of his face which was not, even in the most absolute identity, *mine own!*" He hears Wilson's voice, but "could have fancied that I myself was speaking while he said, *'You have conquered and I yield. Yet, henceforward art thou also dead—dead to the World, to Heaven, and to Hope! In me didst thou exist—and, in my death, see by this image, which is thine own, how utterly thou has murdered thyself.'"*

Willis, Nathaniel Parker (1806–1867)   Editor of the New York EVENING MIRROR and *American Monthly Magazine* who defended Poe's character against the defamation printed by Rufus Wilmot GRISWOLD. Poe reviewed the following works by Willis: "AMERICAN PROSE WRITERS," "DASHES AT LIFE WITH A FREE PENCIL," and "TORTESA, THE USURER." In "THE LITERATI OF NEW YORK CITY," Poe provides a lengthier-than-usual evaluation of Willis's talents and writes, "both as an author and a man, he has made a good deal of noise in the world—at least for an American." Poe attributes Willis's renown to his having "pushed himself" into the world, and attributes his success "one-third to his mental ability and two-thirds to

Nathaniel P. Willis, editor of the New York Evening Mirror.
(Edgar Allan Poe Society)

his physical temperament." Although Poe holds a low opinion of Willis's critical abilities and finds him "remarkably out of his element" in writing the argumentation demanded by newspapers, he finds Willis "as a writer of 'sketches' . . . unequalled."

Wilmer, Lambert A. (1805–1863) Baltimore author and journalist. His dramatic poem *Merlin* was based on Poe's relationship with Sarah Elmira ROYSTER. Poe reviewed his "THE CONFESSIONS OF EMILIA HARRINGTON" in February 1836.

Wilson Character in Poe's novel THE NARRATIVE OF ARTHUR GORDON PYM. After the mutiny, he becomes a member of the mate's party.

Wilson, William *See* "WILLIAM WILSON."

Windenough, Mr. Character in Poe's short story "LOSS OF BREATH." He has sent love letters to another man's wife. He is later mistaken for dead and buried alive, being interred in the same tomb as Mr. LACKOBREATH, where the two first fight then think of a way to escape.

Wolf Dog in Poe's short story "THE GOLD-BUG." He is a Newfoundland retriever belonging to William LEGRAND whose natural action of jumping on his master helps to uncover the secret of the parchment map.

Woodberry, George Edward (1855–1930) Early Poe biographer who tried to correct the misapprehensions about Poe's character created by Rufus Wilmot GRISWOLD. Unlike the biography by John Henry INGRAM, which went too far in ameliorating the past, Woodberry presented a more balanced approach in his 1885 work *The Life of Edgar Allan Poe, Personal and Literary, with His Chief Correspondence with Men of Letters.*

Wormley, Alexander Character in Poe's THE JOURNAL OF JULIUS RODMAN. He is the sixth man that the expedition enlists from the return boat and "a good recruit." A Virginian who once fancied himself a preacher, he had spent some time "going about the country with a long beard and hair, and in his bare feet, haranguing every one he met." When Julius RODMAN meets him, Wormley has turned his fervor to finding gold and "upon the subject he was as entirely mad as any man could well be."

A Wreath of Flowers from New England Poe reviewed this work by Frances Sargent OSGOOD in her entry in "THE LITERATI OF NEW YORK CITY," appearing in the September 1846 issue of *GODEY'S MAGAZINE AND LADY'S BOOK.* Poe wrote that Osgood exhibits "deep feeling and exquisite taste" and that her work had not been as widely circulated as it deserved.

"Writings of Charles Sprague. Now First Collected. Charles S. Francis, New York" Review by Poe that appeared in the May 1841 issue of *GRAHAM'S MAGAZINE.* Poe opens the review by questioning assertions in the "'publisher's preface'" that the author had done "'nothing to promote'" the work, but that he has "'only not forbidden'" it. Poe finds this "unnecessary rigamarole, not to say of superfluous humbug," and suggests that the poet might be guilty of "counterfeit[ing] a modesty which he does not feel." In reviewing the poems, Poe criticizes popular taste, selecting "Shakespeare Ode" as "the best of them. It carries the essential error to the height of its perfection." He observes that public opinion would disagree, and dismisses its importance, writing that "Public opinion, however, is a certain intangible something of which we have no opinion at all."

"Wyandotté, or The Hutted Knoll. A Tale, By the Author of 'The Pathfinder,' 'Deerslayer,' 'Last of the Mohicans,' 'Pioneers,' 'Prairie,' &c., &c. Lea & Blanchard: Philadelphia" Review by Poe that appeared in the November 1843 issue of *GRAHAM'S MAGAZINE.* Poe opens the review by stating that the present work is "precisely similar to the novels enumerated in the title." He notes that, as with the other novels, interest in the novel does not stem from plot but depends upon "first the nature of the theme; secondly, upon a Robinson-Crusoe-like detail in its management; and thirdly, upon the frequently repeated portraiture of the half-civilized Indian." The review then follows these observations with a detailed summary of the novel, and the reviewer points out that "It will be at once seen that there is nothing *original* in this story. . . . it is even excessively commonplace." Although Poe finds the development of the story wanting, he writes, "In the depicting of character, Mr. [James Fenimore] Cooper has been unusually successful." In particular, the review notes that "The negroes are, without exception, admirably drawn. The Indian, Wyandotté, is the great feature of the book."

Wyatt, Cornelius   Character in Poe's short story "THE OBLONG BOX." Wyatt is an artist who has brought aboard the ship an oblong box, six feet long and two-and-half feet wide, that he keeps in his stateroom. Each night the narrator hears in Wyatt's stateroom sounds of the box being pried open and what seems to be sobbing. When the ship is hit by a hurricane and is about to sink, Wyatt refuses to leave without the box. He lashes himself securely to the box with a rope and sinks with it into the stormy waters.

Wyatt, Marian   Character in Poe's short story "THE OBLONG BOX." The sister of the artist Cornelius WYATT and "a very sweet and intelligent girl," she introduces the narrator to the artist's wife when the artist fails to do so.

Wyatt, Mrs.   Character in Poe's short story "THE OBLONG BOX." The real Mrs. Wyatt is dead and lying in the box that is placed in the artist's stateroom. The woman who portrays Mrs. Wyatt in the story is actually the maid of the late woman.

Wyatt, Thomas   Author who paid Poe to co-author "THE CONCHOLOGIST'S FIRST BOOK." The body of *The Conchologist's First Book* is not original, and Poe paraphrased Wyatt's *Manual of Conchology* by arrangement with the author, who had earlier unsuccessfully published the work with Harper's. Wyatt paid Poe $50 to popularize the work and to lend his name to it by issuing an edition with Poe's name on the title page. The arrangement, which helped Wyatt to avoid trouble over copyright, created tensions between Harper's and Poe that made the publisher refuse Poe's request that they issue his collected works six years later.

X

"X-ing a Paragrab"   Short story. This comic tale by Poe has a foundation in reality. Printers in Poe's day who ran out of a given letter while typesetting commonly substituted *x* in its place.

PUBLISHING AND DRAMATIZATION HISTORY

The story first appeared in the May 12, 1849, issue of the *FLAG OF OUR UNION*. No film to date has been made of the story.

CHARACTERS

BOB, the devil, Mr. Touch-and-Go BULLET-HEAD, John SMITH.

PLOT SYNOPSIS

The story mocks literary rivalries as it pits Bullet-Head, the fiery editor and upstart publisher of the *Tea-Pot*, against Smith, the editor of the *Nopolis Gazette*. Smith prints an article that mocks Bullet-Head's overuse of the letter *O*, to which Bullet-Head responds by publishing a paragraph that uses *O* 175 times. When the *Tea-Pot* editor directs his typesetter to ready the paragraph for the next day's paper, the printer's devil finds not one *O* in the print bin. The foreman then directs him to do his best, which he does, and creates a paragraph filled with the letter *X*. When people read their papers, they find the *X*-filled paragraph so annoying that they are ready to ride Bullet-Head out of town on a rail, but he has already vanished from the town, leaving Smith to take their wrath.

Yampoos   Tribe in Poe's novel *THE NARRATIVE OF ARTHUR GORDON PYM*. Their chief TOO-WIT guides the survivors of the *Jane Guy* wreck through treacherous reefs to his village of Yampoos, "the great men of the land." They are "muscular and brawny," with jet black complexions, and thick and long "woolly" hair. Their lips are "thick and clumsy" and, even when they laugh, "the teeth were never disclosed." Only "the men of the canoes" wear skins to cover their bodies, and the rest of the men, women, and children in the village are naked. The homes are extremely primitive and "of the most miserable description imaginable, and unlike those of even the lowest of the savage races with which mankind are acquainted, were of no uniform plan." Some of the Yampoos live in holes dug in the ground, with branches covering the holes, while others simply sleep under skins draped over tree branches.

Yarrington, Martha   The landlady of the boardinghouse where Maria CLEMM, Virginia CLEMM, and Poe lived in Richmond. Poe and Virginia Clemm were married in a public ceremony in her boardinghouse parlor on May 16, 1836. Yarrington helped Maria Clemm to make the wedding cake and to prepare the wedding meal for guests.

A Year in Spain. By a Young American   *See* MACKENZIE, Lieutenant Alexander Slidell.

"The Young Wife's Book; A Manual of Moral, Religious, and Domestic Duties. Philadelphia: Carey, Lea, & Blanchard"   Review by Poe that appeared in the January 1836 issue of the *SOUTHERN LITERARY MESSENGER*. Poe describes the book as "made up of mingled amusement and instruction" and recommends it to both "that particular class of fair friends for whom it is most obviously intended," as well as to "all lovers of good reading." Although the lessons on moral duties, manners, fashion, and like subjects meet with Poe's approval, he finds fault with the manner of publication. Unable to

This illustration, "Sunday Evening at Yarrington's," depicts a common room in the boardinghouse where Poe lived in Richmond, Virginia.

locate information on the title page or in the preface, Poe writes: "[E]very reader, in perusing a book, feels some solicitude to know, for example, who wrote it; or (if this information be not attainable,) at least where it was written—whether in his native country, or in a foreign land—whether it be original or a compilation—whether it be a new publication or a re-publication of old matter—whether we are indebted for it to one author, or to more than one." Of the 73 articles in the book, Poe identifies only 24, leaving him frustrated regarding the sources of those remaining.

Z

Zacchary Mentioned in Poe's short story "MELLONTA TAUTA." Pundita refers to "facsimiles" of newspapers that she has reviewed regarding the past and finds that "*the* great men in those days were one John, a smith, and one Zacchary, a tailor [President Zachary Taylor]."

"Zanoni, A Novel. By the Author of 'Pelham,' 'Rienzi,' &c. Two Volumes. Harper & Brothers" Review by Poe that appeared in the June 1842 issue of GRAHAM'S MAGAZINE. Poe's review of the novel by Edward BULWER-LYTTON begins with reference to an earlier "incomprehensible" effort, a fragment called *Zicci* that was "the jest of the reviewers for years." Of *Zicci*, Poe writes that "its only merit was the novelty of having no merit at all." He identifies the current offering as the same novel under "an altered name." After a lengthy summary of the work, which contains Rosicrucian themes and is set in Naples of the previous century, Poe concludes that "the subject is unfit for prose. It properly belongs to the drama." Poe provides a lengthy list of faults in the novel, then concludes that "There are many fine thoughts in these volumes . . . the book is a valuable addition to our imaginative literature."

Zech, Frederick (1858–1926) American composer, conductor, and pianist whose compositions include piano concertos, violin and cello concertos, sonatas, chamber music, songs, and two operas. In 1902, he published *The Raven*, a symphonic poem inspired by Poe's poem of the same name.

Zenobia, Signora Psyche Character in Poe's short stories "HOW TO WRITE A BLACKWOOD ARTICLE" and "A PREDICAMENT." She is the corresponding secretary to the society named "*Philadelphia, Regular, Exchange, Tea, Total, Young Belles, Lettres, Universal, Experimental, Bibliographical, Association, To, Civilize, Humanity,*" otherwise known as P.R.E.T.T.Y.B.L.U.E.B.A.T.C.H. She joins the society with the goal of introducing "a better style of writing. . . . as good papers now . . . as any to be found even in *Blackwood*." In the first story, she visits William BLACKWOOD in Edinburgh, Scotland, to learn "the exact method of composition" used by the publication. Blackwood's final bit of advice to her in writing the successful Blackwood article is to "get into some immediate difficulty." Zenobia takes his advice seriously, and her successful effort to get into difficulty is recounted in "A Predicament," in which she is beheaded by "the huge, glittering, scimitar-like minute-hand" of a clock mounted on the tower of a Gothic cathedral in Edinburgh.

"Zinzendorff, and Other Poems. By Mrs. L. H. Signourney. New York: Published by Leavitt, Lord & Co., 1836" Review of the poetry collection by Lydia Huntley Signourney that appeared in the January 1836 issue of the SOUTHERN LITERARY MESSENGER. Poe suggests that she has gained fame for her poetry because she has been part of the correct literary clique, "she has trod, however, upon the confines of their circle." More to the point, he states broadly, "no single piece which she has written, and not even her collected works as we behold them in the present volume, and in the one published some years ago, would fairly entitle her to that exalted rank which she actually enjoys." After pointing flaws in her works, Poe finds the poem "Zinzendorff" to be "particularly good—always sweet—occasionally energetic." For the most part, her work is too imitative for his admiration.

Zoubaloff, Jacques-Michel (1886–1954) French composer and painter whose compositions include piano suites and cycles, song settings of poems, and orchestral suites. In 1925, he published "*Tu voudrais etre aimée?*" [Thou wouldst be loved?], a song inspired by Poe's poem "TO F——S S. O——D." That same year, he wrote *Trois Petits Poèmes Musicaux (D'après Edgar Poe)*, piano pieces inspired by three poems written by Poe: "ULALUME," "A DREAM," and "HYMN." In 1927, Zoubaloff published *Politian, Comte de Leicester* (Scenes from *Politian*), a piano score and text inspired by Poe's drama POLITIAN.

APPENDIX I

Edgar Allan Poe: A Timeline

1809

Edgar Poe is born in Boston on January 19.

1810

Rosalie Poe, sister of Edgar, is born in Norfolk, Virginia, on December 20.

1811

Elizabeth Arnold Poe, Edgar's mother, dies in Richmond, Virginia, on December 8.

1812

Poe is baptized on January 7 by the Reverend John Buchanan and christened Edgar Allan Poe, with the Allans as godparents.

Poe's sister Rosalie is baptized on September 3 as Rosalie Mackenzie Poe after her adoption by William and Jane Scott Mackenzie.

1815

John and Frances Allan, with Poe and with Frances's younger sister, Ann Moore Valentine (called Nancy), leave for England aboard the *Lothair* on June 22.

1816

Poe attends the boarding school of the Misses Dubourg in London, where he is known as Master Allan.

1818

Poe attends the Manor House School, run by the Reverend John Bransby in London, where he is known as Edgar Allan.

1820

Poe and the Allan family return to America from England aboard the *Martha* on July 22.

1821

Poe attends the Clarke School run by Joseph Hanson Clarke in Richmond, Virginia.

1822

Poe's cousin and future wife, Virginia Clemm, is born in Baltimore on August 22.

1823

Poe attends the school of William Burke in Richmond.

1824

Poe serves as a lieutenant in the Richmond Junior Volunteers during General Lafayette's visit to Richmond, October 26 through 28.

1825

John Allan inherits a substantial fortune upon the death of his uncle William Galt. He purchases Moldavia, an enormous brick mansion in Richmond, Virginia, to which Poe and the Allan family relocate.

1826

Poe enters the University of Virginia in February. He returns to Richmond in December and learns that Sarah Elmira Royster, his first love, is engaged to Alexander B. Shelton.

1827

Poe and John Allan argue over Poe's gambling debts of $2,000, and Poe leaves the university in March. Poe enlists in the United States Army on May 26 under the name Edgar A. Perry. In November, Poe's troop battery arrives at Fort Moultrie, Sullivan's Island, Charleston, South Carolina.

Poe's first book, *Tamerlane and Minor Poems*, is published in Boston by Calvin F. S. Thomas. The author is noted only as "A Bostonian."

1828

Poe's battery arrives at Fort Monroe, Old Point Comfort, Virginia, on December 15.

1829

Poe is promoted to sergeant major of the regiment of artillery on January 1.

Francis Keeling Allan, Poe's doting foster mother, dies in Richmond on February 28.

Poe is released from the army on April 15, after which he applies for an appointment to West Point.

In December, Poe's second book, *Al Aaraaf, Tamerlane, and Minor Poems,* is published in Baltimore by Hatch & Dunning.

1830

John Allan marries Louisa Gabriella Patterson on October 5.

Poe enters West Point in June.

1831

Poe is court-martialed on February 8 after willfully refusing to attend classes or chapel as part of his plan to leave West Point. On March 6, he is dismissed from military service.

Poe's collection *Poems by Edgar A. Poe* is published in New York by Elam Bliss.

William Henry Leonard Poe, Edgar's older brother, dies of tuberculosis in Baltimore on August 1.

1833

Poe receives his $50 prize from the *Baltimore Saturday Visiter* for "MS. Found in a Bottle" on October 7.

1834

John Allan dies in Richmond, Virginia, on March 27. Poe receives no inheritance.

1835

In March, Poe applies for a position as a teacher in the Baltimore public schools.

Poe's grandmother Elizabeth Cairnes Poe, wife of "General" Poe, dies on July 7.

On September 22, Poe takes out a marriage license for himself and Virginia Clemm. They marry on May 16, 1836.

1836

Poe moves from Baltimore to Richmond and becomes editor of Thomas W. White's *Southern Literary Messenger.*

1837

Poe leaves his position as editor of the *Southern Literary Messenger* in January. In February, Poe moves with his wife, Virginia, and her mother, Maria Clemm, to New York.

1838

Poe and his family move to Philadelphia.

In July, Poe's novel *The Narrative of Arthur Gordon Pym* is published in New York by Harper & Brothers.

1839

The Conchologist's First Book, which Poe coauthored, is published in Philadelphia by Haswell, Barrington & Haswell.

In May, Poe becomes an editor for *Burton's Gentleman's Magazine.*

1840

Poe's two-volume collection *Tales of the Grotesque and Arabesque* is published in Philadelphia by Lea & Blanchard.

In January, the first of four installments of Poe's *Journal of Julius Rodman* appears in *Burton's Gentleman's Magazine.*

On June 6, Poe's prospectus for his proposed magazine *Penn* appears in the *Saturday Evening Post.*

1841

On February 20, the *Saturday Evening Post* announces that Poe will begin as an editor for *Graham's Magazine* in April.

Graham's Magazine publishes Poe's "Murders in the Rue Morgue," the first modern detective story, in April.

1842

Poe and the English author Charles Dickens meet in Philadelphia on March 6 while Dickens is on a tour of America.

In May, Poe leaves *Graham's Magazine,* and Rufus W. Griswold replaces him as editor.

1843

Poe signs an agreement with Thomas Cottrell Clarke on January 31 to proceed with Poe's plans for a magazine, now renamed the *Stylus.*

In March, Poe encourages a friend, F. W. Thomas, to help him to gain a government job as a clerk, a position that would leave him ample time to write; however, Poe fails to obtain a position.

In June, Poe's tale "The Gold-Bug" wins the $100 prize from the Philadelphia *Dollar Newspaper,* which provides him with substantial national attention. On August 8, a theatrical production based on the story and dramatized by Silas S. Steele is performed at the American Theatre in Philadelphia.

Poe's collection *Prose Romances* is published by William H. Graham in Philadelphia.

In July, Poe registers to study law in the office of Henry Beck Hirst, a longtime friend.

In November, Poe delivers his lectures on American poetry in Philadelphia.

1844

Poe and his family move to New York on April 7.

Poe joins the staff of the New York *Evening Mirror* on October 7.

1845

Poe's poem "The Raven" is published in the New York *Evening Mirror,* gaining immediately popularity and bringing Poe praise and fame but earning him only $15.

Poe becomes an editor of the *Broadway Journal* on February 22.

On October 24, Poe becomes the sole owner of the *Broadway Journal,* after signing a note (i.e., an IOU) for $50 with Horace Greeley; Poe never repaid the loan.

On November 19, Poe's collection *The Raven and Other Poems* is published in New York by Wiley & Putnam.

1846

Poe's *Broadway Journal* ceases publication on January 3 because of a lack of funds.

In April, Poe's "The Literati of New York City" appears for the first time in *Godey's Magazine and Lady's Book.*

1847

Virginia Clemm Poe dies of tuberculosis in January in Fordham, New York.

1848

Poe's prose poem "Eureka" is published by George Putnam.

In November, Poe becomes engaged to Sarah Helen Power Whitman, a New England widow and poet.

On December 23, Whitman calls off the engagement when Poe breaks his promise to abstain from drinking.

1849

Poe arrives in Richmond on July 14 on his lecture tour of the South to raise money and support for his proposed magazine, the *Stylus.* While in Richmond, he becomes reacquainted with the now-widowed Sarah Elmira Royster Shelton.

On August 27, Poe signs a pledge with the Sons of Temperance, Shockoe Hill Division, No. 54, promising to abstain completely from drinking alcoholic beverages.

On September 27, Poe leaves Richmond aboard the steamship *Pocahontas.* He arrives in Baltimore on September 28.

On October 3, Poe is found nearly unconscious outside Gunner's Hall, a Baltimore tavern.

On October 8, Poe dies at the Washington College Hospital in Baltimore. He is buried in his grandfather's lot in the Westminster Burying Ground.

The "Ludwig article," Rufus Wilmot Griswold's slanderous obituary of Poe, is published in the *New York Tribune* on October 9, thus distorting Poe's image for more than five decades.

1875

On November 17, the Memorial Grave of Edgar Allan Poe, containing the exhumed remains of Poe and Maria Clemm, is dedicated in Baltimore. Ten years later, the remains of Poe's wife, Virginia, are brought to Baltimore from Fordham, New York, and placed in the Memorial Grave with those of Poe and Virginia's mother, Maria Clemm.

APPENDIX II

Chronology of Poe's Works

"The Happiest Day, the Happiest Hour" (September 15, 1827; poem; first published in the *North American;* reprinted in *Tamerlane and Other Poems* in 1827; reprinted in *Collected Works*)

"Al Aaraaf" (1827; poem; first published in *Tamerlane and Other Poems;* reprinted in 1829 in *Al Aaraaf, Tamerlane, and Minor Poems;* reprinted in *Collected Works*)

"A Dream" (1827; poem; first published in *Tamerlane and Other Poems;* republished in *Al Aaraaf, Tamerlane, and Minor Poems* in 1829; reprinted in *Collected Works*)

"Evening Star" (1827; poem; first published in *Tamerlane and Other Poems;* reprinted in *Collected Works*)

"Imitation" (1827; poem; first published in *Tamerlane and Other Poems;* reprinted in *Collected Works*)

"In Youth I Have Known One with Whom the Earth" (1827; poem; first published in *Tamerlane and Other Poems;* reprinted in *Collected Works*)

"The Lake" (1827; poem; first published in *Tamerlane and Other Poems;* reprinted as "The Lake—To ———" in *Al Aaraaf, Tamerlane, and Minor Poems* in 1829; reprinted in *Collected Works*)

"Song" (1827; poem; first published in *Tamerlane and Other Poems;* reprinted in *Collected Works*)

"Spirits of the Dead" (1827; poem; first published under the title "Visit of the Dead" in *Tamerlane and Other Poems;* retitled and reprinted in *Al Aaraaf, Tamerlane, and Minor Poems* 1829; reprinted in *Collected Works*)

"Tamerlane" (1827; poem; first published in *Tamerlane and Other Poems;* reprinted in *Al Aaraaf, Tamerlane, and Minor Poems* in 1829; reprinted in *Collected Works*)

"To ———" ["The bowers whereat, in dreams, I see"] (1829; poem; first published in *Al Aaraaf, Tamerlane, and Minor Poems;* reprinted in the *Broadway Journal* for September 20, 1845; reprinted in *Collected Works*)

"To ———" ["Should my early life seem"] (1829; poem; first published in *Al Aaraaf, Tamerlane, and Minor Poems;* reprinted in shortened form in the *Yankee and Boston Literary Gazette* for December 1829; reprinted in *Collected Works*)

"To the River ———" (1829; poem; first published in *Al Aaraaf, Tamerlane, and Minor Poems;* reprinted in *Burton's Gentleman's Magazine* for August 1839; reprinted in the *Philadelphia Saturday Museum* for March 4, 1843; and reprinted in the *Broadway Journal* for September 1845; reprinted in *Collected Works*)

Tamerlane and Other Poems (1827; poetry collection published "By a Bostonian.")

Al Aaraaf, Tamerlane, and Minor Poems (December 1829; Poe's second collection of poetry and the first to be published commercially)

"Alone" (1829; poem; first published posthumously in *Scribner's Monthly* in September 1875; reprinted in *Collected Works*)

"An Acrostic" (1829; poem written for Elizabeth Herring; published posthumously in *Collected Works*)

"Fairy Land" (December 1829; poem first titled "Heaven"; first published in *Al Aaraaf, Tamerlane, and Minor Poems;* reprinted in *Collected Works*)

"Romance" (1829; poem; first appeared under the title "Preface" in *Al Aaraaf, Tamerlane, and Minor Poems;* retitled "Introduction" and reprinted in *Poems by Edgar A. Poe;* retitled "Romance" and reprinted in the *Philadelphia Saturday Museum* for February 25, 1843; reprinted in *Collected Works*)

"Sonnet—To Science" (1829; poem; first published in *Al Aaraaf, Tamerlane, and Minor Poems;* reprinted in *Collected Works*)

"The City in the Sea" (1831; poem; first published under the title "The Domed City" in *Poems By Edgar*

A. *Poe;* revised, retitled, and reprinted in the April 1845 issue of the *American Review;* reprinted in *The Raven and Other Poems* in 1845; reprinted in *Collected Works*)

"Israfel" (1831; poem; first appeared in *Poems By Edgar A. Poe;* reprinted in the *Southern Literary Messenger* for August 1836; reprinted in *Collected Works*)

"Lenore" (1831; poem; first published as "A Paean" in *Poems By Edgar A. Poe;* reprinted in the *Pioneer* for February 1843; reprinted in the *Broadway Journal* in August 16, 1845; reprinted in *Collected Works*)

"Letter to B———" (1831; poem; first published in *Poems By Edgar A. Poe* as "Letter to Mr. ———"; reprinted as "Letter to B———" in the *Southern Literary Messenger* for July 1836; reprinted in *Collected Works*)

"The Sleeper" (1831; poem; first published under the title "Irene" in *Poems By Edgar A. Poe;* retitled and reprinted in the *Philadelphia Saturday Courier* for May 22, 1841; reprinted in *The Raven and Other Poems* in 1845; reprinted in *Collected Works*)

"To Helen" (1) (1831; poem; first published in *Poems By Edgar A. Poe;* reprinted in the *Southern Literary Messenger* for March 1836; reprinted in *Collected Works*)

"The Valley of Unrest" (1831; poem; first published under the title "The Valley of Nis" in *Poems By Edgar A. Poe;* retitled and reprinted in the *American Review* of April 1845; reprinted in *The Raven and Other Poems* in 1845; reprinted in *Collected Works*)

Poems By Edgar A. Poe (1831; the third collection of Poe's poems to be published and his second commercial publication)

"Metzengerstein: A Tale In Imitation of the German" (January 14, 1832; short story; first published in the *Philadelphia Saturday Courier;* reprinted in *Collected Works*)

"The Duc de l'Omelette" (March 3, 1832; short story; first published in the *Philadelphia Saturday Courier;* reprinted in *Collected Works*)

"A Tale of Jerusalem" (June 9, 1832; short story; first published in the *Philadelphia Saturday Courier;* reprinted in the *Broadway Journal* for September 20, 1845; reprinted in *Collected Works*)

"Loss of Breath: A Tale à la Blackwood" (November 1832; short story; first published in the *Philadelphia Saturday Courier* with Poe using the pseudonym Lyttleton Barry; retitled and reprinted in the *Southern Literary Messenger* for September 1835; reprinted in *Collected Works*)

"Bon-Bon" (December 1, 1832; short story; first published as "The Bargain Lost" in the *Philadelphia Saturday Courier;* revised and republished in the *Southern Literary Messenger* for August 1835; reprinted in *Collected Works*)

"To ———" ["Sleep on, sleep on, another hour—"] (May 11, 1833; poem; first published in the *Baltimore Saturday Visiter;* reprinted in *Collected Works*)

"The Coliseum" (October 26, 1833; poem; first published in the *Baltimore Sunday Visiter;* reprinted in *Collected Works*)

"MS. Found In a Bottle" (October 19, 1833; short story; first published in the *Baltimore Saturday Visiter;* reprinted in *Collected Works*)

"Assignation, The" (January 1834; short story; first published under the title "The Visionary" in *Godey's Magazine and Lady's Book;* reprinted in *Collected Works*)

"To One in Paradise" (January 1834; poem; first published as part of the short story "The Assignation" in *Godey's Magazine and Lady's Book;* reprinted alone in *The Raven and Other Poems* in 1845; reprinted in *Collected Works*)

"Poems, by William Cullen Bryant. Boston: Russell, Odiorne & Metcalfe. 1834" (January 1835; review; first published in the *Southern Literary Messenger;* reprinted in *Collected Works*)

"Berenice" (March 1835; short story; first published in the *Southern Literary Messenger;* reprinted in *Collected Works*)

"Four Beasts In One: The Homo-Cameleopard" (March 1835; short story; first published in the *Southern Literary Messenger;* reprinted in *Tales of the Grotesque and Arabesque* in 1839; reprinted in *Collected Works*)

"Confessions of a Poet, 2 vols. Carey, Lea & Blanchard" (April 1835; review; first published in the *Southern Literary Messenger;* reprinted in *Collected Works*)

"Morella" (April 1835; short story; first published in the *Southern Literary Messenger;* reprinted in *Burton's Gentleman's Magazine* for November 1839; reprinted in *Collected Works*)

"Horse-Shoe Robinson: A Tale of the Tory Ascendency. By the Author of 'Swallow Barn.' Philadelphia: Carey, Lea & Blanchard" (May 1835; review; first published in the *Southern Literary Messenger;* reprinted in *Collected Works*)

"Journal—By Frances Anne Butler. Philadelphia: Carey, Lea & Blanchard. Presented to the Editor of the Messenger, by Mr. C. Hall" (May 1835; review; first published in the *Southern Literary Messenger;* reprinted in *Collected Works*)

"Lionizing" (May 1835; short story; first published as "Lion-Izing: A Tale" in the *Southern Literary Messenger;* revised and reprinted in *Tales By Edgar A. Poe* in 1845; reprinted in *Collected Works*)

"I Promessi Sposi, or the Betrothed Lovers; a Milanese Story of the Seventeenth Century: as Translated for the Metropolitan, from the Italian of Alessandro Manzoni, by G. W. Featherstonhaugh. Washington:

Stereotyped and Published by Duff Green. 1834. 8vo. pp. 259" (May 1835; review; first published in the *Southern Literary Messenger;* reprinted in *Collected Works*)

"The Infidel; or The Fall of Mexico, a Romance, by the Author of Calavar. Philadelphia: Carey, Lee & Blanchard" (June 1835; review; first published in the *Southern Literary Messenger;* reprinted in *Collected Works*)

"The Unparalleled Adventure of One Hans Pfaall" (June 1835; short story; first published in the *Southern Literary Messenger;* reprinted in *Collected Works*)

"The Conquest of Florida by Hernando De Soto. By Theodore Irving. Philadelphia: Carey, Lea & Blanchard" (July 1835; review; first published in the *Southern Literary Messenger;* reprinted in *Collected Works*)

"The Crayon Miscellany, No.II. Containing Abbotsford and Newstead Abbey. Philadelphia: Carey, Lea & Blanchard. 1835" (July 1835; review; first published in the *Southern Literary Messenger;* reprinted in *Collected Works*)

"Euripides Translated by the Reverend R. Potter, Prebendiary of Norwich. Harper & Brothers, New York. [The Classical Family Library. Numbers XV, XVI, and XVII.]" (September 1835; review; first published in the *Southern Literary Messenger;* reprinted in *Collected Works*)

"Early Naval History of England by Robert Southey, LL.D., Poet Laureate. Philadelphia: Carey, Lea & Blanchard" (September 1835; review; first published in the *Southern Literary Messenger;* reprinted in *Collected Works*)

"King Pest the First. A Tale Containing an Allegory" (September 1835; short story published under the pseudonym Lyttleton Barry; first published in the *Southern Literary Messenger;* reprinted in *Tales of the Grotesque and Arabesque* in 1839; revised for republication in the *Broadway Journal* for October 18, 1845; reprinted in *Collected Works*)

"Mephistopheles In England, or the Confessions of a Prime Minister, 2 vols. Philadelphia: Carey, Lea & Blanchard" (September 1835; review; first published in the *Southern Literary Messenger;* reprinted in *Collected Works*)

"Inaugural Address of the Reverend D. L. Carroll, D. D., President of Hampden Sidney College. Delivered on His Induction into That Office. Published by Request of the Board of Trustees. Richmond: T. W. White, 1835" (December 1835; review; first published in the *Southern Literary Messenger;* reprinted in *Collected Works*)

"Judge Story's Discourse on Chief-Justice Marshall" (December 1835; review; first published in the *Southern Literary Messenger;* reprinted in *Collected Works*)

"The Hawks of Hawk-Hollow; a Tradition of Pennsylvania. By the Author of Calavar and the Infidel. Philadelphia: Carey, Lea & Blanchard" (December 1835; review; first published in the *Southern Literary Messenger;* reprinted in *Collected Works*)

"The Heroine: or Adventures of Cherubina. By Eaton Stannard Barrett, Esq. New Edition. Richmond: Published by P. D. Barnard" (December 1835; review; first published in the *Southern Literary Messenger;* reprinted in *Collected Works*)

"The Crayon Miscellany. By the Author of the Sketch Book No. 3—Containing Legends of the Conquest of Spain. Philadelphia: Carey, Lea & Blanchard" (December 1835; review; first published in the *Southern Literary Messenger;* reprinted in *Collected Works*)

"Binney's Eulogium" (December 1835; review; first published in the *Southern Literary Messenger;* reprinted in *Collected Works*)

"Clinton Bradshaw; or the Adventures of a Lawyer. Philadelphia: Carey, Lea & Blanchard" (December 1835; review; first published in the *Southern Literary Messenger;* reprinted in *Collected Works*)

"Legends of a Log Cabin. By a Western Man. New York: George Dearborn, Publisher" (December 1835; review; first published in the *Southern Literary Messenger;* reprinted in *Collected Works*)

"The Linwoods; or, 'Sixty Years Since' in America. By the Author of 'Hope Leslie,' 'Redwood,' &c. New York: Published by Harper & Brothers" (December 1835; review; first published in the *Southern Literary Messenger;* reprinted in *Collected Works*)

"An Address on Education, as Connected with the Permanence of Our Republican Institutions. Delivered before the Institute of Education of Hampden Sidney College, at Its Anniversary Meeting, September the 24th, 1835, on the Invitation of the Body. By Lucian Minor, Esq., of Louisa. Published by Request of the Institute" (December 1835; review; first published in the *Southern Literary Messenger;* reprinted in *Collected Works*)

"A Life of George Washington, in Latin Prose: By Francis Glass, A.M. of Ohio. Edited by J. N. Reynolds. New York: Published by Harper & Brothers" (December 1835; review; first published in the *Southern Literary Messenger;* reprinted in *Collected Works*)

"Lives of the Necromancers: Or An Account of the Most Eminent Persons in Successive Ages, Who Have Claimed for Themselves, or to Whom Have Been Imputed by Others, the Exercise of Magical Power. By William Godwin, Author of 'Caleb Williams,' &c. New York: Published by Harper &

Brothers" (December 1835; review; first published in the *Southern Literary Messenger;* reprinted in *Collected Works*)

"Memoir of the Reverend John H. Rice, D.D. First Professor of Christian Theology in Union Theological Seminary, Virginia, A. By William Maxwell. Philadelphia: Published by J. Whetham" (December 1835; review; first published in the *Southern Literary Messenger;* reprinted in *Collected Works*)

"Norman Leslie: A Tale of the Present Times. New York: Published by Harper & Brothers" (December 1835; review; first published in the *Southern Literary Messenger;* reprinted in *Collected Works*)

"Nuts to Crack: or Quips, Quirks, Anecdote and Facete of Oxford and Cambridge Scholars. By the Author of Facetiae Cantabrigienses, Etc., Etc., Etc. Philadelphia: E. L. Carey & A. Hart" (December 1835; review; first published in the *Southern Literary Messenger;* reprinted in *Collected Works*)

"Oration on the Life and Character of the Rev. Joseph Caldwell, D.D. Late President of the University of North Carolina, by Walter Andersen, A.M." (December 1835; review; first published in the *Southern Literary Messenger;* reprinted in *Collected Works*)

Politian (December 1835 and January 1836; unfinished drama; excerpts first published in the *Southern Literary Messenger;* printed whole in *The Raven and Other Poems;* reprinted in *Collected Works*)

"The Rambler in North America, 1832–33. By Charles Joseph Latrobe, Author of 'The Alpenstock,' &c. New York: Harper & Brothers" (December 1835; review; first published in the *Southern Literary Messenger;* reprinted in *Collected Works*)

"Shadow—A Parable" (September 1835; short story; first published in the *Southern Literary Messenger;* reprinted in *Collected Works*)

"To Elizabeth" (September 1835; poem; first published in the *Southern Literary Messenger;* reprinted in *Burton's Gentleman's Magazine* for August 1839; reprinted in *Collected Works*)

"Sketches of History, Life, and Manners in the West. By James Hall. Philadelphia: Harrison Hall" (December 1835; review; first published in the *Southern Literary Messenger;* reprinted in *Collected Works*)

"Sketches of Switzerland. By an American, Part Second. Philadelphia: Carey, Lea & Blanchard" (December 1835; review; first published in the *Southern Literary Messenger;* reprinted in *Collected Works*)

"Tales of the Peerage and the Peasantry, Edited by Lady Dacre. New York: Harper & Brothers" (December 1835; review; first published in the *Southern Literary Messenger;* reprinted in *Collected Works*)

"Traits of American Life. By Mrs. Sarah J. Hale, Editor of 'The American Ladies' Magazine,' and Author of 'Northwood,' 'Flora's Interpreter,' &c &c. Philadel-

phia: E. L. Carey, and A. Hart" (December 1835; review; first published in the *Southern Literary Messenger;* reprinted in *Collected Works*)

"Legends of a Log Cabin. By a Western Man. New York: George Dearborn, Publisher" (December 1835; review; first published in the *Southern Literary Messenger*)

"The Christian Florist; Containing the English Botanical Names of Different Plants, with Their Properties Delineated and Explained. Illustrated by Texts From Various Authors. First American From the Second London Edition. Philadelphia: Carey, Lea & Blanchard" (January 1836; review; first published in the *Southern Literary Messenger;* reprinted in *Collected Works*)

"Animal and Vegetable Physiology Considered with Reference to Natural Theology. By Peter Mark Roger, M.D. Secretary to the Royal Society, &C., &C. Two vols. Large octavo. Philadelphia: Published by Carey, Lea, and Blanchard" (January 1836; review; first published in the *Southern Literary Messenger;* reprinted in *Collected Works*)

"The Life and Surprising Adventures of Robinson Crusoe, of York, Mariner: With a Biographical Account of Defoe. Illustrated with Fifty Characteristic Cuts, from Drawings by William Harvey, Esq. and Engraved by Adams. New York: Published by Harper & Brothers" (January 1836; review; first published in the *Southern Literary Messenger;* reprinted in *Collected Works*)

"The Partisan: A Tale of the Revolution. By the Author of 'The Yemassee,' 'Guy Rivers,' &c. New York: Published by Harper & Brothers" (January 1836; review; first published in the *Southern Literary Messenger;* reprinted in *Collected Works*)

"Poems—By Miss H. F. Gould. Third Edition. Boston: Hilliard, Gray & Co. 1835" (January 1836; review; first published in the *Southern Literary Messenger;* reprinted in *Collected Works*)

"Poems; Translated and Original. By Mrs. E. F. Ellet, Philadelphia: Key & Biddle. 1835" (January 1836; review; first published in the *Southern Literary Messenger;* reprinted in *Collected Works*)

"The Poetry of Life. By Sarah Stickney, Author of 'Pictures of Private Life.' Philadelphia: Republished by Carey, Lea & Blanchard" (January 1836; review; first published in the *Southern Literary Messenger;* reprinted in *Collected Works*)

"Reminiscences of an Intercourse with Mr. Niebuhr, the Historian, During a Residence with Him in Rome, in the Years 1822 and 1823. By Francis Lieber, Professor of History and Political Economy in South Carolina College. Philadelphia: Carey, Lea & Blanchard" (January 1836; review; first published in the *Southern Literary Messenger;* reprinted in *Collected Works*)

"Tales and Sketches. By Miss Sedgwick, Author of 'The Linwoods,' 'Hope Leslie,' &c &c. Philadelphia: Carey, Lea & Blanchard" (January 1836; review; first published in the *Southern Literary Messenger;* reprinted in *Collected Works*)

"The Young Wife's Book; A Manual of Moral, Religious, and Domestic Duties. Philadelphia: Carey, Lea & Blanchard" (January 1836; review; first published in the *Southern Literary Messenger;* reprinted in *Collected Works*)

"Zinzendorff, and Other Poems. By Mrs. L. H. Signourney. New York: Published by Leavitt, Lord & Co., 1836" (January 1836; review; first published in the *Southern Literary Messenger;* reprinted in *Collected Works*)

"The American in England. By the Author of 'A Year in Spain.' 2 vols. New York. Harper & Brothers" (February 1836; review; first published in the *Southern Literary Messenger;* reprinted in *Collected Works*)

"Paul Ulric: Or the Adventures of an Enthusiast. New York: Published by Harper & Brothers" (February 1836; review; first published in the *Southern Literary Messenger;* reprinted in *Collected Works*)

"Autography" (February and August 1836; brief articles; first published in the *Southern Literary Messenger;* reprinted in *Collected Works*)

"The Confessions of Emilia Harrington. By Lambert A. Wilmer. Baltimore" (February 1836; review; first published in the *Southern Literary Messenger;* reprinted in *Collected Works*)

"Conti the Discarded: with Other Tales and Fancies, by Henry F. Chorley. 2 vols. New York: Published by Harper & Brothers" (February 1836; review; first published in the *Southern Literary Messenger;* reprinted in *Collected Works*)

"A New and Comprehensive Gazeteer of Virginia, and the District of Columbia: Containing a Copious Collection of Geographical, Statistical, Political, Commercial, Religious, Moral and Miscellaneous Information, Collected and Compiled From the Most Respectable, and Chiefly From Original Sources; by Joseph Martin. To Which Is Added a History of Virginia, From Its First Settlement to the Year 1754: With an Abstract of the Principal Events From That Period to the Independence of Virginia, Written Expressly for the Work, by a Citizen of Virginia. Charlottesville: Published by Joseph Martin. 1835" (February 1836; review; first published in the *Southern Literary Messenger;* reprinted in *Collected Works*)

"Noble Deeds of Woman. 2 vols. Philadelphia: Carey, Lea & Blanchard" (February 1836; review; first published in the *Southern Literary Messenger;* reprinted in *Collected Works*)

"Palestine" (February 1836; essay; first published in the *Southern Literary Messenger;* reprinted in *Collected Works*)

"Rienzi, the Last of the Tribunes. By the Author of 'Eugene Aram,' 'Last Days of Pompeii,' &c. &c. Two Volumes in One. Philadelphia: Republished by E. L. Carey and A. Hart" (February 1836; review; first published in the *Southern Literary Messenger;* reprinted in *Collected Works*)

"Contributions to the Ecclesiastical History of the United States of America—Virginia. A Narrative of Events Connected with the Rise and Progress of the Protestant Episcopal Church in Virginia. To Which Is Added an Appendix, Containing the Journals of the Conventions in Virginia, from the Commencement to the Present Time. By the Reverend Francis L. Hawks, D.D., Rector of St. Thomas's Church, New York. New York: Published by Harper & Brothers" (March 1836; review; first published in the *Southern Literary Messenger;* reprinted in *Collected Works*)

"Georgia Scenes, Characters, Incidents, &c. In the First Half Century of the Republic. By a Native Georgian. Augusta, Georgia" (March 1836; review; first published in the *Southern Literary Messenger;* reprinted in *Collected Works*)

"'Mahmoud.' New York. Published by Harper & Brothers" (March 1836; review; first published in the *Southern Literary Messenger;* reprinted in *Collected Works*)

"Phrenology, and the Moral Influence of Phrenology: Arranged for General Study, and the Purposes of Education, from the First Published Works of Gall and Spurzheim, to the Latest Discoveries of the Present Period. By Mrs. L. Miles. Philadelphia: Carey, Lea & Blanchard" (March 1836; review; first published in the *Southern Literary Messenger;* reprinted in *Collected Works*)

"Report of the Committee on Naval Affairs, to Whom Were Referred Memorials From Sundry Citizens of Connecticut Interested in the Whale Fishing, Praying That An Exploring Expedition Be Fitted Out to the Pacific Ocean and South Seas" (March 21, 1836; review; first published in the *Southern Literary Messenger;* reprinted in *Collected Works*)

"Alnwick Castle with Other Poems. By Fitz-Greene Halleck. New York: George Dearborn" (April 1836; review; first published in the *Southern Literary Messenger;* reprinted in *Collected Works*)

"Bubbles from the Brunnens of Nassau. By An Old Man. New York: Harper & Brothers" (April 1836; review; first published in the *Southern Literary Messenger;* reprinted in *Collected Works*)

"The Culprit Fay, and Other Poems, By Joseph Rodman Drake. New York: George Dearborn" (April 1836; review also known as the Drake-Halleck review; first published in the *Southern Literary Messenger;* reprinted in *Collected Works*)

"Maelzel's Chess-Player" (April 1836; essay; first published in the *Southern Literary Messenger;* reprinted in *Collected Works*)

"Slavery in the United States. By J. K. Paulding. New York: Harper & Brothers/ The South Vindicated from the Treason and Fanaticism of the Northern Abolitionists. Philadelphia: Published by H. Manly" (April 1836; review; first published in the *Southern Literary Messenger;* reprinted in *Collected Works*)

"Didactics—Social, Literary, and Political. By Robert Walsh. Philadelphia: Carey, Lea & Blanchard" (May 1836; review; first published in the *Southern Literary Messenger;* reprinted in *Collected Works*)

"A Life of Washington. By James K. Paulding. New York: Harper & Brothers" (May 1836; review; first published in the *Southern Literary Messenger;* reprinted in *Collected Works*)

"Paris and the Parisians in 1835. By Frances Trollope, Author of 'Domestic Manners of the Americans,' 'The Refugee in America,' &c. New York: Published by Harper & Brothers" (May 1836; review; first published in the *Southern Literary Messenger;* reprinted in *Collected Works*)

"Flora and Thalia; Or Gems of Flowers and Poetry: Being an Alphabetical Arrangement of Flowers, with Appropriate Poetical Illustrations, Embellished with Colored Plates. By a Lady. To Which Is Added a Botanical Description of the Various Parts of a Flower and the Dial of Flowers. Philadelphia: Carey, Lea & Blanchard" (June 1836; review; first published in the *Southern Literary Messenger;* reprinted in *Collected Works*)

"Letters, Conversations, and Recollections of S. T. Coleridge. New York: Harper & Brothers" (June 1836; review; first published in the *Southern Literary Messenger;* reprinted in *Collected Works*)

"Maury's Navigation" (June 1836; review; first published in the *Southern Literary Messenger;* reprinted in *Collected Works*)

"Notices of the War of 1812. By John Armstrong. New York: George Dearborn" (June 1836; review; first published in the *Southern Literary Messenger;* reprinted in *Collected Works*)

"The Pleasant Peregrination Through the Prettiest Parts of Pennsylvania. Performed by Peregrine Prolix. Philadelphia: Grigg & Elliot" (June 1836; review; first published in the *Southern Literary Messenger;* reprinted in *Collected Works*)

"Thoughts on the Religious State of the Country; with Reasons for Preferring Episcopacy. By Rev. Calvin Colton. New York: Harper & Harper" (June 1836; review; first published in the *Southern Literary Messenger;* reprinted in *Collected Works*)

"Ups and Downs in the Life of a Distressed Gentleman. By the Author of 'Tales and Sketches, Such as They Are New York: Leavitt, Lord & Co." (June 1836; review; first published in the *Southern Literary Messenger;* reprinted in *Collected Works*)

"Watkins Tottle, and Other Sketches, Illustrative of Every-Day Life, and Every-Day People. By Boz, Philadelphia: Carey, Lea & Blanchard" (June 1836; review; first published in the *Southern Literary Messenger;* reprinted in *Collected Works*)

"Poe's Reply to His Critics" (July 1836; essay; first published in the *Southern Literary Messenger;* reprinted in *Collected Works*)

"Camperdown; or, News from Our Neighborhood—Being a Series of Sketches, by the Author of 'Our Neighborhood,' &c. Philadelphia: Carey, Lea & Blanchard" (July 1836; review; first published in the *Southern Literary Messenger;* reprinted in *Collected Works*)

"The Doctor, &c. New York: Republished by Harper & Brothers" (July 1836; review; first published in the *Southern Literary Messenger;* reprinted in *Collected Works*)

"England in 1835. Being a Series of Letters Written to Friends in Germany. During a Residence in London and Excursions Into the Provinces. By Frederick Von Raumer, Professor of History at the University of Berlin, Author of the 'History of the Hohenstaufen,' of the 'History of Europe from the End of the Fifteenth Century,' of 'Illustrations of the History of the Sixteenth and Seventeenth Centuries,' &c. &c. Translated from the German by Sarah Austin and H. E. Lloyd. Philadelphia: Carey, Lea & Blanchard" (July 1836; review; first published in the *Southern Literary Messenger;* reprinted in *Collected Works*)

"Erato. By William D. Gallagher. No. 1, Cincinnati, Josiah Drake—No. 11, Cincinnati, Alexander Flash" (July 1836; review; first published in the *Southern Literary Messenger;* reprinted in *Collected Works*)

"Letters to Young Ladies. By Mrs. L. H. Sigourney. Second Edition. Hartford: Published by Wm. Watson" (July 1836; review; first published in the *Southern Literary Messenger;* reprinted in *Collected Works*)

"Life on the Lakes: Being Tales and Sketches Collected During a Trip to the Pictured Rocks of Lake Superior. By the Author of 'Legends of a Log Cabin.' New York: Published by George Dearborn" (July 1836; review; first published in the *Southern Literary Messenger;* reprinted in *Collected Works*)

"Memoirs of an American Lady. With Sketches of Manners and Scenery in America, as They Existed Previous to the Revolution. By the Author of 'Letters from the Mountains.' New York: Published by George Dearborn" (July 1836; review; first published in the *Southern Literary Messenger;* reprinted in *Collected Works*)

"Russia and the Russians; or, a Journey to St. Petersburg and Moscow, Through Courland and Livonia; with Characteristic Sketches of the People. By Leigh Ritchie, Esq. Author of 'Turner's Annual Tour,' 'Schinderhannes,' &c. Philadelphia: E. L. Carey and A. Hart" (July 1836; review; first published in the *Southern Literary Messenger;* reprinted in *Collected Works*)

"Elkswata; or the Prophet of the West. A Tale of the Frontier. New York: Harper & Brothers" (August 1836; review; first published in the *Southern Literary Messenger;* reprinted in *Collected Works*)

"The History of Texas: Or the Emigrants', Farmers', and Politicians' Guide to the Character, Climate, Soil, and Productions of That Country; Geographically Arranged from Personal Observation and Experience. By David B. Edward, Formerly Principal of the Academy, Alexandria, Louisiana; Late Preceptor of Gonzales Seminary, Texas. Cincinnati: J. A. James & Co." (August 1836; review; first published in the *Southern Literary Messenger;* reprinted in *Collected Works*)

"Lafitte: The Pirate of the Gulf. By the Author of the South-West. New York: Harper & Brothers" (August 1836; review; first published in the *Southern Literary Messenger;* reprinted in *Collected Works*)

"Letters Descriptive of the Virginia Springs—The Roads Leading Thereto and the Doings Thereat. Collected, Corrected, Annotated, and Edited by Peregrine Prolix. With a Map of Virginia. Philadelphia: Published by H. S. Tanner" (August 1836; review; first published in the *Southern Literary Messenger;* reprinted in *Collected Works*)

"A New Dictionary of the English Language: By Charles Richardson. London: William Pickering—New York: William Jackson" (August 1836; review; first published in the *Southern Literary Messenger;* reprinted in *Collected Works*)

"The Adventures of a Gentleman in Search of a Horse. By Caveat Emptor, Gent. One, Etc. Philadelphia: Republished by Carey, Lea & Blanchard" (August 1836; review; first published in the *Southern Literary Messenger;* reprinted in *Collected Works*)

"The Book of Gems. The Poets and Artists of Great Britain. Edited by S. C. Hall. London and New York: Saunders & Otley" (August 1836; review; first published in the *Southern Literary Messenger;* reprinted in *Collected Works*)

"The Old World and the New; Or, a Journal of Reflections and Observations Made on a Tour in Europe. By the Reverend Orville Dewey. New York: Harper & Brothers" (August 1836; review; first published in the *Southern Literary Messenger;* reprinted in *Collected Works*)

"Literary Remains of the Late William Hazlitt, with a Notice of his Life by his Son, and Thoughts on his Genius and Writings, By E. L. Bulwer, M. P. and Mr. Sergeant Talfourd, M. P. New York: Saunders & Otley" (September 1836; review; first published in the *Southern Literary Messenger;* reprinted in *Collected Works*)

"Philothea: a Romance. By Mrs. Child, Author of the Mother's Book, &c. Boston: Otis, Broaders & Co. New York: George Dearborn" (September 1836; review; first published in the *Southern Literary Messenger;* reprinted in *Collected Works*)

"Sheppard Lee: Written By Himself. New York: Harper & Brothers" (September 1836; review; first published in the *Southern Literary Messenger;* reprinted in *Collected Works*)

"Address Delivered at the Annual Commencement of Dickinson College, July 21, 1836, by S. A. Roszel" (October 1836; review; first published in the *Southern Literary Messenger;* reprinted in *Collected Works*)

"An Address Delivered before the Students of William and Mary at the Opening of the College on Monday. October 10, 1835. By Thomas R. Dew, President, and Professor of Moral and Political Philosophy. Published by Request of the Students. Richmond: T. W. White" (October 1836; review; first published in the *Southern Literary Messenger;* reprinted in *Collected Works*)

"The American Almanac, and Repository of Useful Knowledge for the Year 1837. Boston: Published by Charles Bowen" (October 1836; review; first published in the *Southern Literary Messenger;* reprinted in *Collected Works*)

"A Dissertation on the Importance of Physical Signs in the Various Diseases of the Abdomen and Thorax. By Robert W. Haxall, M.D. of Richmond, Va. Boston: Perkins and Marvin" (October 1836; review; first published in the *Southern Literary Messenger;* reprinted in *Collected Works*)

"Lives of the Cardinal de Richelieu, Count Oxenstiern, Count Olivarez, and Cardinal Mazarin. By G. P. R. James. Republished by Carey, Lea & Blanchard" (October 1836; review; published in the *Southern Literary Messenger;* reprinted in *Collected Works*)

"Madrid in 1835. Sketches of the Metropolis of Spain and Its Inhabitants, and of Society and Manners in the Peninsula. By a Resident Officer. Two Volumes in One. New York: Saunders & Otley" (October 1836; review; first published in the *Southern Literary Messenger;* reprinted in *Collected Works*)

"Memoirs of Lucian Bonaparte, Prince of Canino. Written by Himself. Translated from the Original Manuscript, Under the Immediate Superintendence of the Author. Part the First, From the Year 1792, to the Year 8 of the Republic" (October 1836; review; first published in the *Southern Literary Messenger;* reprinted in *Collected Works*)

"Memorials of Mrs. Hemans, with Illustrations of Her Literary Character from Her Private Correspondence. By Henry F. Chorley. New York: Saunders & Otley" (October 1836; review; first published in the *Southern Literary Messenger;* reprinted in *Collected Works*)

"A New and Compendious Latin Grammar; With Appropriate Exercises, Analytical and Synthetical. For the Use of Primary Schools, Academies, and Colleges. By Baynard R. Hall, A.M., Principal of the Bedford Classical and Mathematical Academy, and Formerly Professor of the Ancient Languages of the College of Indiana. Philadelphia: Harrison Hall" (October 1836; review; first published in the *Southern Literary Messenger;* reprinted in *Collected Works*)

"Peter Snook" (October 1836; essay; first published in the *Southern Literary Messenger;* reprinted in *Collected Works*)

"Posthumous Memoirs of His Own Time. By Sir N. W. Wraxall, Baronet. Author of 'Memoirs of My Own Time.' Philadelphia: Republished by Carey, Lea & Blanchard" (October 1836; review; first published in the *Southern Literary Messenger;* reprinted in *Collected Works*)

"Skimmings; or A Winter At Schloss Hainfeld in Lower Styria. By Captain Basil Hall, Royal Navy, F.R.S. Philadelphia: Replenished By Carey, Lea & Blanchard" (October 1836; review; first published in the *Southern Literary Messenger;* reprinted in *Collected Works*)

"The Swiss Heiress; or The Bride of Destiny. Baltimore: Joseph Robinson" (October 1836; review; first published in the *Southern Literary Messenger;* reprinted in *Collected Works*)

"The Posthumous Papers of the Pickwick Club: Containing a Faithful Record of the Perambulations, Perils, Travels, Adventures, and Sporting Transactions of the Corresponding Members. Edited by 'Boz.' Philadelphia: Published by Carey, Lea & Blanchard" (November 1836; review; first published in the *Southern Literary Messenger;* reprinted in *Collected Works*)

The Narrative of Arthur Gordon Pym (1836–37; Poe's only novel; first published in serial form in the *Southern Literary Messenger;* republished as a novel in 1838; reprinted in *Collected Works*)

"Life and Literary Remains of L. E. L. By Laman Blanchard. Two Volumes. Lea & Blanchard" (August 1841; review; first published in *Graham's Magazine;* reprinted in *Collected Works*)

"Memoirs and Letters of Madame Malibran. By the Countess de Merlin. With Notices of the Progress of the Musical Drama in England. In Two Volumes. Carey & Hart, Philadelphia." (May 1840; review; first published in *Burton's Gentleman's Magazine;* reprinted in *Collected Works*)

"Address on the Subject of a Surveying and Exploring Expedition to the Pacific Ocean and South Seas. Delivered In the Hall of Representatives on the Evening of April 3, 1836. By J. N. Reynolds. With Correspondence and Documents. New York: Published by Harper & Row" (January 1837; review; first published in the *Southern Literary Messenger;* reprinted in *Collected Works*)

"Astoria; or, Anecdotes of an Enterprise beyond the Rocky Mountains. By Washington Irving. Philadelphia: Carey, Lea & Blanchard" (January 1837; review; first published in the *Southern Literary Messenger;* reprinted in *Collected Works*)

"George Balcombe. A Novel. New York. Harper & Brothers" (January 1837; review; first published in the *Southern Literary Messenger;* reprinted in *Collected Works*)

"Select Orations of Cicero: with an English Commentary, and Historical, Geographical and Legal Indexes. By Charles Anthon, LL.D., Jay—Professor of Ancient Literature in Columbia College, and Rector of the Grammar School. New York: Harper & Brothers" (January 1837; review; first published in the *Southern Literary Messenger;* reprinted in *Collected Works*)

"Sonnet: To Zante" (January 1837; poem; first published in the *Southern Literary Messenger;* reprinted in *The Raven and Other Poems* in 1845; reprinted in *Collected Works*)

"Mystification" (June 1837; short story; first published in the New York *American Monthly Magazine* under the title of "Von Jung, the Mystific"; reprinted under the same name in *Tales of the Grotesque and Arabesque;* retitled and reprinted in the *Broadway Journal* for December 27, 1845; reprinted in *Collected Works*)

"Review of Stephens' Arabia Petraea" (October 1837; review; first published in the *New York Review;* reprinted in *Collected Works*)

"Ligeia" (September 1838; short story; first published in the *Baltimore American Museum;* reprinted with the addition of the poem "The Conqueror Worm" in the *New York World* for February 15, 1845; reprinted in the *Broadway Journal* for September 27, 1845; reprinted in *Collected Works*)

"How to Write a Blackwood Article" (November 1838; short story; first published under the title "The Psyche Zenobia" in the *Baltimore American Museum;* reprinted under the present title in the *Broadway Journal* for July 12, 1845; reprinted in *Collected Works*)

"A Predicament" (November 1838; short story; first published under the title "The Scythe of Time" in the *Baltimore American Museum;* retitled and reprinted in *Tales of the Grotesque and Arabesque* in 1840; reprinted in *Collected Works*)

"Silence—A Fable" (1838; short story; first published as "Siope—A Fable" in the *Baltimore Book;* reprinted as "Siope—A Fable" in *Tales of the Grotesque and Arabesque* in 1840; reprinted under the title "Silence—A Fable" in the *Broadway Journal* for September 6, 1845; reprinted in *Collected Works*)

"Literary Small Talk" (January-February 1839; essay; first published in the *American Museum of Science, Literature and the Arts;* reprinted in *Collected Works*)

"The Haunted Palace" (April 1839; poem; first published in *Baltimore American Museum* and later incorporated into Poe's short story "The Fall of the House of Usher"; reprinted in *Collected Works*)

"Preface and Introduction to 'The Conchologist's First Book,' 1839" (April 1839; essay; first published as part of the scientific manual on conchology, whose complete title is *The Conchologists's First Book: or, A System of Testaceous Malacology;* reprinted in *Collected Works*)

"The Devil in the Belfry" (May 18, 1839; short story; first published in the *Philadelphia Saturday Chronicle and Mirror of the Times;* reprinted in *Collected Works*)

"A Synopsis of Natural History; Embracing the Natural History of Animals, with Human and General Animal Physiology, Botany, Vegetable Physiology, and Geology. Translated From the Latest French Edition of C. Lemmonnier, Professor of Natural History in the Royal College of Charlemagne; With Additions From the Works of Cuvier, Dumaril, Lacepede, Etc., Arranged as a Text Book for Schools. By Thomas Wyatt, A.M., Author of Elements of Botany, a Manual of Conchology, Etc. Thomas Wardle, Philadelphia" (July 1839; review; first published in *Burton's Gentleman's Magazine;* reprinted in *Collected Works*)

"The Man That Was Used Up. A Tale of the Late Bugaboo and Kickapoo Campaign" (August 1839; short story; first published in *Burton's Gentleman's Magazine;* revised and reprinted in *Tales of the Grotesque and Arabesque;* reprinted in *Collected Works*)

"The Fall of the House of Usher" (September 1839; short story; first published in *Burton's Gentleman's Magazine;* reprinted in *Tales By Edgar A. Poe* in 1845; reprinted in *Collected Works*)

"Address Delivered before the Goethean and Diagnothian Societies of Marshall College, at Their Annual Celebration, September 24, 1839. By Joseph O. Chandler" (December 1839; review; first published in *Burton's Gentleman's Magazine;* reprinted in *Collected Works*)

"Hyperion: A Romance. By the Author of 'Outremer.' Two Volumes. Samuel Colman, New York" (October 1839; review; first published in *Burton's Gentleman's Magazine;* reprinted in *Collected Works*)

"The Canons of Good Breeding or the Handbook of the Man of Fashion. By the Author of the 'Laws of Etiquette.' Lea & Blanchard, Philadelphia" (November 1839; review; first published in *Burton's Gentleman's Magazine;* reprinted in *Collected Works*)

"The Conversation of Eiros and Charmion." (December 1839; short story; first published in *Burton's Gentleman's Magazine;* reprinted in *Tales of the Grotesque and Arabesque* in 1839; reprinted in *Collected Works*)

"National Melodies of America. By George P. Morris, Esq." (December 1839; review; first published in *Burton's Gentleman's Magazine* under the title "George P. Morris"; revised and retitled for publication in the *Southern Literary Messenger* for April 1840; reprinted in *Collected Works*)

Tales of the Grotesque and Arabesque (1839; collection of 25 stories in two volumes)

"Tortesa, the Usurer: A Play. By N. P. Willis. Samuel Colman, New York" (August 1845; review; first published in *Burton's Gentleman's Magazine;* reprinted in *Collected Works*)

"Undine: A Miniature Romance; From the German of Baron De La Motte Fouqué. Colman's Library of Romance, Edited by Grenville Mellen. Samuel Colman, New York" (September 1839; review; first published in *Burton's Gentleman's Magazine;* reprinted in *Collected Works*)

"William Wilson" (October 1839; short story; first published in *The Gift: A Christmas and New Year's Present for 1840,* which appeared mid-1839; reprinted in *Burton's Gentleman's Magazine* for October 1839; reprinted in *Collected Works*)

"Alciphron: A Poem. By Thomas Moore, Esq., Author of 'Lalla Rookh,' Etc., Etc. Carey & Hart, Philadelphia." (January 1840; review; first published in *Burton's Gentleman's Magazine;* reprinted in *Collected Works*)

The Journal of Julius Rodman, Being an Account of the First Passage across the Rocky Mountains of North America Ever Achieved by Civilized Man (January–June 1840; unfinished serialized novel; first published in *Burton's Gentleman's Magazine;* reprinted in *Collected Works*)

"Silence—A Sonnet" (January 4, 1840; poem; first published in the *Philadelphia Saturday Courier;* reprinted in the *Broadway Journal* for July 26, 1845; reprinted in *The Raven and Other Poems* in 1845; reprinted in *Collected Works*)

"The Business Man" (February 1840; short story; first published under the title of "Peter Pendulum" in *Burton's Gentleman's Magazine;* retitled and reprinted in the *Broadway Journal* for August 2, 1845; reprinted in *Collected Works*)

"Voices of the Night. By Henry Wadsworth Longfellow. John Owen, Cambridge" (February 1840; review; first published in *Burton's Gentleman's Magazine;* reprinted in *Collected Works*)

"Sacred Philosophy of the Seasons, Illustrating the Perfections of God in the Phenomena of the Year. By the Rev. Henry Duncan, D.D., Ruthwell, Scotland. With Important Additions, and Some Modifications to Adapt It To American Readers. By F. W. P. Greenwood. In Four Volumes. Marsh, Capen, Lyon, & Webb, Boston" (March 1840; review; first published in *Burton's Gentleman's Magazine;* reprinted in *Collected Works*)

"Memoirs and Letters of Madame Malibran. By the Countess de Merlin. With Notices of the Progress of the Musical Drama in England. In Two Volumes. Carey & Hart, Philadelphia" (May 1840; review; first published in *Burton's Gentleman's Magazine;* reprinted in *Collected Works*)

"The Philosophy of Furniture" (May 1840; essay; first published in *Burton's Gentleman's Magazine;* reprinted in *Collected Works*)

"Some Account of Stonehenge, the Giant's Dance, A Druidical Ruin in England" (June 1840; essay; first published in *Burton's Gentleman's Magazine;* reprinted in *Collected Works*)

"The Man of the Crowd" (December 1840; short story; first published in *Atkinson's Casket;* reprinted simultaneously in *Burton's Gentleman's Magazine;* reprinted in *Collected Works*)

"Why the Little Frenchman Wears His Hand in a Sling" (1840; short story collection; first published in *Tales of the Grotesque and Arabesque;* reprinted in the *Broadway Journal* for September 6, 1845; reprinted in *Collected Works*)

"Mercedes of Castile, A Romance, By James Fenimore Cooper. Two Volumes. Lea & Blanchard, 1840" (January 1841; review; first published in *Graham's Magazine;* reprinted in *Collected Works*)

"The Antediluvians, or the World Destroyed: A Narrative Poem, In Ten Books. By James McHenry, M.D., Author of the 'Pleasures of Friendship,' ETC. One Volume. J. B. Lippincott & Co., Philadelphia" (February 1841; review; first published in *Graham's Magazine;* reprinted in *Collected Works*)

"The Tower of London: A Historical Romance. By W. H. Ainsworth. Author of 'Jack Shepherd.' One Volume. Lea & Blanchard, Philadelphia, 1841" (March 1841; review; first published in *Graham's Magazine;* reprinted in *Collected Works*)

"A Descent Into the Maelstrom" (April 1841; short story; first published in *Graham's Magazine;* reprinted in *Collected Works*)

"Barnaby Rudge. By Charles Dickens, (Boz) Author of 'The Old Curiosity Shop,' 'Pickwick,' 'Oliver Twist,' &c, &c. With Numerous Illustrations. By Cattermole, Browne & Sibson. Lea & Blanchard: Philadelphia" (February 1842; review; first published in the *Philadelphia Saturday Evening Post;* reprinted in *Collected Works*)

"The Murders In the Rue Morgue" (April 1841; short story; first published in *Graham's Magazine;* reprinted in *Collected Works*)

"Sketches of Conspicuous Living Characters of France. Translated by R. M. Walsh. Lea & Blanchard" (April 1841; review; first published in *Graham's Magazine;* reprinted in *Collected Works*)

"Some Secrets of the Magazine Prison-House" (February 15, 1845; first published in the *Broadway Journal;* reprinted in *Collected Works*)

"Night and Morning: A Novel. By the Author of 'Pelham,' 'Rienzi,' 'Eugene Aram,' etc. Two Volumes. Republished by Harper & Brothers, New York" (April 1841; review; first published in *Graham's Magazine;* reprinted in *Collected Works*)

"Master Humphrey's Clock. By Charles Dickens. (Boz.) With Ninety-One Illustrations by George Cattermole and Hablot Browne. Philadelphia, Lea and Blanchard; The Old Curiosity Shop, and Other Tales. By Charles Dickens. With Numerous Illustrations by Cattermole and Browne. Philadelphia, Lea & Blanchard" (May 1841; review; first published in *Graham's Magazine;* reprinted in *Collected Works*)

"Writings of Charles Sprague. Now First Collected. Charles S. Francis, New York" (May 1841; review; first published in *Graham's Magazine;* reprinted in *Collected Works*)

"Corse de Leon: Or the Brigand. A Romance, by G. P. R. James. Two Volumes. Harper & Brothers" (June 1841; review; first published in *Graham's Magazine;* reprinted in *Collected Works*)

"Critical and Miscellaneous Essays. By T. Babington Macaulay. Carey & Hart, Philadelphia" (June 1841; first published in *Graham's Magazine;* reprinted in *Collected Works*)

"The Island of the Fay" (June 1841; short story; first published in *Graham's Magazine;* reprinted in *Collected Works*)

"A Few Words on Secret Writing" (July 1841; essay; first published in *Graham's Magazine;* reprinted in *Collected Works*)

"Grammar of the English Language, in a Series of Letters, Addressed to Every American Youth. By Hugh A. Pue. Philadelphia, Published by the Author" (July 1841; first published in *Graham's Magazine;* reprinted in *Collected Works*)

"Powhatan: a Metrical Romance in Seven Cantos. By Seba Smith. New York, Harper & Brothers" (July 1841; review; first published in *Graham's Magazine;* reprinted in *Collected Works*)

"The Biography and Poetical Remains of the Late Margaret Miller Davidson. By Washington Irving. Philadelphia, Lea & Blanchard" (August 1841; review; first published in *Graham's Magazine;* reprinted in *Collected Works*)

"Addendum to 'A Few Words on Secret Writing'" (August 1841; article; first published in *Graham's Magazine;* reprinted in *Collected Works*)

"The Colloquy of Monos and Una" (August 1841; short story; first published in *Graham's Magazine;* reprinted in *Tales By Edgar A. Poe* in 1845; reprinted in *Collected Works*)

"Incidents of Travel in Central America, Etc. By John L. Stephens. Two Volumes. New York, Harper & Brothers" (August 1841; review; first published in *Graham's Magazine;* reprinted in *Collected Works*)

"The Quacks of Helicon: A Satire. By L. A. Wilmer" (August 1841; review; first published in *Graham's Magazine;* reprinted in *Collected Works*)

"Joseph Rushbrook: or, The Poacher. By Captain Marryat, Author of 'Peter Simple,' 'Jacob Faithful,' Etc., Etc. Two Volumes. Philadelphia, Carey & Hart" (September 1841; review; first published in *Graham's Magazine;* reprinted in *Collected Works*)

"Life of Petrarch. By Thomas Campbell, Esq., Author of 'The Pleasures of Hope,' Etc., Complete in One Volume. Philadelphia, Carey & Hart" (September 1841; review; first published in *Graham's Magazine;* reprinted in *Collected Works*)

"Never Bet the Devil Your Head: A Tale With a Moral" (September 1841; short story; first published under the title "Never Bet Your Head: A Moral Tale" in *Graham's Magazine;* retitled and reprinted in the *Broadway Journal* for August 16, 1845; reprinted in *Collected Works*)

"The Pic Nic Papers. By Various Hands. Edited by Charles Dickens, Esq., Author of 'The Pickwick Papers,' etc. Two Volumes. Lea & Blanchard, Philadelphia" (November 1841; review; first published in *Graham's Magazine;* reprinted in *Collected Works*)

"Guy Fawkes; or, The Gunpowder Treason. An Historical Romance. By William Harrison Ainsworth. Author of 'The Tower of London,' 'Jack Sheppard,' Etc. Philadelphia, Lea & Blanchard" (November 1841; review; first published in *Graham's Magazine;* reprinted in *Collected Works*)

"Ten Thousand a Year. By the Author of 'The Diary of a London Physician.' Carey & Hart, Philadelphia" (November 1841; review; first published in *Graham's Magazine;* reprinted in *Collected Works*)

"Three Sundays in a Week" (November 27, 1841; short story; first published under the title "A Succession of Sundays" in the *Philadelphia Saturday Evening Post;* republished under the present title in the *Broadway Journal* for May 10, 1845; reprinted in *Collected Works*)

"A Chapter on Autography" (November and December 1841, January 1842; article series; first published in *Graham's Magazine;* reprinted in *Collected Works*)

"Poetical Remains of the Late Lucretia Maria Davidson. Collected and Arranged By Her Mother, With a Biography By Miss Sedgwick. Lea & Blanchard, Philadelphia" (December 1841; review; first published in *Graham's Magazine;* reprinted in *Collected Works*)

"Stanley Thorn. By Henry Cockton, Esq., Author of 'Valentine Vox, the Ventriloquist,' &c., with Numerous Illustrations, Designed by Cruikshank, Leech, &c., and Engraved By Yeager. Lea & Blanchard: Philadelphia" (January 1842; review; first published in *Graham's Magazine;* reprinted in *Collected Works*)

"The Vicar of Wakefield. A Tale. By Oliver Goldsmith, M.B. Illustrated with Numerous Engravings. With an Account of the Author's Life and Writings. By J. Aikin, M.D., Author of Select Works of the British Poets. D. Appleton & Co.: New York" (January 1842; review; first published in *Graham's Magazine;* reprinted in *Collected Works*)

"A Few Words about Brainard" (February 1842; review; first published in *Graham's Magazine;* reprinted in *Collected Works*)

"Wakondah; The Master of Life. A Poem. George L. Curry & Co.: New York" (February 1842; review; first published in *Graham's Magazine;* reprinted in *Collected Works*)

"The Critical and Miscellaneous Writings of Henry Lord Brougham, to Which Is Prefixed a Sketch of His Character. Two Vols. Lea & Blanchard" (March 1842; review; first published in *Graham's Magazine;* reprinted in *Collected Works*)

"Charles O'Malley, the Irish Dragoon. By Harry Lorrequer. With Forty Illustrations by Phiz. Complete in One Volume. Carey & Hart: Philadelphia" (March 1842; review; first published in *Graham's Magazine;* reprinted in *Collected Works*)

"Ballads and Other Poems. By Henry Wadsworth Longfellow, Author of 'Voices of the Night,' 'Hyperion,' & c. Second Edition. John Owen, Cambridge" (March and April 1842; review; first published in *Graham's Magazine;* reprinted in *Collected Works*)

"Ideals and Other Poems. By Algernon Henry Perkins. Philadelphia" (April 1842; review; first published in *Graham's Magazine;* reprinted in *Collected Works*)

"The Oval Portrait" (April 1842; short story; first published under the title "Life in Death" in *Graham's Magazine;* retitled to "The Oval Portrait" and reprinted in the *Broadway Journal* for April 26, 1845; reprinted in *Collected Works*)

"Tale-Writing—Nathaniel Hawthorne.—Twice-Told Tales. By Nathaniel Hawthorne. James Munroe & Co., Boston. 1842.—Mosses From an Old Manse. By Nathaniel Hawthorne. Wiley & Putnam, New York. 1856" (April and May 1842; review; first published in *Graham's Magazine;* reprinted in *Collected Works*)

"The Masque of the Red Death" (May 1842; short story; first published under the title "The Mask of the Red Death" in *Graham's Magazine;* retitled and reprinted in the *Broadway Journal* for July 19, 1845; reprinted in *Collected Works*)

"The Poets and Poetry of America, with an Historical Introduction. By Rufus Wilmot Griswold. One Vol. Carey & Hart: Philadelphia" (June 1842; review; first published in *Graham's Magazine;* reprinted in *Collected Works*)

"Zanoni, A Novel. By the Author of 'Pelham,' 'Rienzi,' &c. Two Volumes. Harper & Brothers" (June 1842; review; first published in *Graham's Magazine;* reprinted in *Collected Works*)

"The Domain of Arnheim, or the Landscape Garden" (October 1842; short story; first published under the title "The Landscape Garden" in *Snowden's Ladies' Companion;* retitled and reprinted in *Columbian Lady's and Gentleman's Magazine* for March 1847; reprinted in *Collected Works*)

"The Poetry of Rufus Dawes—A Retrospective Criticism" (October 1842; review; first published in *Graham's Magazine;* reprinted in *Collected Works*)

"Mr. Griswold and the Poets" (November 1842; review; first published in the *Boston Miscellany;* reprinted in *Collected Works*)

"The Mystery of Marie Rogêt. A Sequel to 'The Murders In the Rue Morgue'" (November and December 1842, February 1843; short story; first published in serialized form in *Snowden's Ladies' Companion;* reprinted in *Collected Works*)

"The Conqueror Worm" (January 1843; poem; first published in *Graham's Magazine;* reprinted in *The Raven and Other Poems* in 1845; incorporated into the text of the short story "Ligeia" when the story was reprinted in the *Broadway Journal* for September 27, 1845; reprinted in *Collected Works*)

"The Tell-Tale Heart" (January 1843; short story; first published in the *Pioneer;* reprinted in *Collected Works*)

"Our Amateur Poets, No. I.—Flaccus" (March 1843; review; first published in *Graham's Magazine;* reprinted in *Collected Works*)

"The Rationale of Verse" (March 1843; essay; first published under the title "Notes on English Verse" in the *Pioneer;* revised and reprinted under the title "The Rationale of Verse" in the *Southern Literary Messenger* for October–November 1848; reprinted in *Collected Works*)

"The Gold-Bug" (June 21 and 28, 1843; short story; first published in *Philadelphia Dollar Newspaper;* reprinted in *Collected Works*)

"The Black Cat" (August 19, 1843; short story; first published in the *United States Saturday Post;* reprinted in *Collected Works*)

"Our Amateur Poets, No. III. William Ellery Channing" (August 1843; review; first published in *Graham's Magazine;* reprinted in *Collected Works*)

"Our Contributors, No. VIII.—Fitz-Greene Halleck" (September 1843; review; first published in *Graham's Magazine;* reprinted in *Collected Works*)

"Diddling Considered as One of the Exact Sciences" (October 14, 1843; short story; first published under the title "Raising the Wind; or, Diddling Considered as One of the Exact Sciences"; retitled and reprinted in the *Broadway Journal* for September 13, 1845; reprinted in *Collected Works*)

"Wyandotté, or The Hutted Knoll. A Tale, By the Author of 'The Pathfinder,' 'Deerslayer,' 'Last of the Mohicans,' 'Pioneers,' 'Prairie,' &c., &c. Lea & Blanchard: Philadelphia" (November 1843; review; first published in *Graham's Magazine;* reprinted in *Collected Works*)

"The Purloined Letter" (1844; short story; first published in *The Gift: A Christmas and New Year's Present for 1844;* reprinted in *Tales By Edgar A. Poe* in 1845; reprinted in *Collected Works*)

"Orion: An Epic Poem in Three Books. By R. H. Horne. Fourth Edition. Published by J. Miller: London" (March 1844; review; first published in *Graham's Magazine;* reprinted in *Collected Works*)

"Poems by James Russell Lowell. Published by John Owen: Cambridge" (March 1844; review; first published in *Graham's Magazine;* reprinted in *Collected Works*)

"The Spectacles" (March 27, 1844; short story; first published in *Philadelphia Dollar Newspaper;* reprinted in the *Broadway Journal* for March 1845; reprinted in *Collected Works*)

"A Tale of the Ragged Mountains" (April 1844; short story; first published in *Godey's Magazine and Lady's Book;* reprinted in the *Broadway Journal* for November 1845; reprinted in *Collected Works*)

"The Balloon-Hoax" (April 13, 1844; short story; first published as a newspaper article in the *Extra Sun;* reprinted in the *New York Sunday Times* for April 14, 1844; reprinted in *Collected Works*)

"Dream-Land" (June 1844; poem; first published in *Graham's Magazine;* reprinted in the *Broadway Journal* for June 28, 1845; reprinted in *Collected Works*)

"The Premature Burial" (July 31, 1844; short story; first published in the *Philadelphia Dollar Newspaper;* reprinted in *Collected Works*)

"Mesmeric Revelation" (August 1844; short story; first published in *Columbian Magazine;* reprinted in the *Philadelphia Saturday Museum* for August 31, 1844; reprinted in *Collected Works*)

"The Oblong Box" (September 1844; short story; first published in *Godey's Magazine and Lady's Book* for September 1844; reprinted in *Collected Works*)

"The Angel of the Odd" (October 1844; short story; first published in *Columbian Magazine;* reprinted in *Collected Works*)

"Thou Art the Man" (November 1844; short story; first published in *Godey's Magazine and Lady's Book;* reprinted in *Collected Works*)

"Amelia Welby" (December 1844; review; first published in the *Democratic Review;* reprinted in *Collected Works*)

"Byron and Miss Chaworth" (December 1844; essay; first published in *Columbian Magazine;* reprinted in *Collected Works*)

"The Literary Life of Thingum Bob, Esq. Late Editor of the 'Goosetherumfoodle.' by Himself" (December 1844; short story; first published in the *Southern Literary Messenger;* revised and reprinted in the *Broadway Journal* for July 26, 1845; reprinted in *Collected Works*)

"The Elk" (1844; travel essay; first published in the annual *The Opal* for 1844; reprinted in *Collected Works*)

"The Drama of Exile and Other Poems: By Elizabeth Barrett Barrett, Author of 'The Seraphim,' and Other Poems" (January 4 and 11, 1845; review; first published in the *Broadway Journal;* reprinted in *Collected Works*)

"American Prose Writers. No. 2. N. P. Willis. New Views—Imagination—Fancy—Fantasy—Humor—Wit—Sarcasm—The Prose Style of Mr. Willis" (January 18, 1845; review; first published in the *Broadway Journal;* reprinted in *Collected Works*)

"The Raven" (January 29, 1845; poem; first published in the New York *Evening Mirror;* reprinted in *American Whig Review* for February 1845; reprinted in *The Raven and Other Poems* in 1845; reprinted in *Collected Works*)

"The Thousand-and-Second Tale of Scheherazade" (February 1845; short story; first published in *Godey's Magazine and Lady's Book;* reprinted in the *Broadway Journal* for October 25, 1845; reprinted in *Collected Works*)

"A Continuation of the Voluminous History of the Little Longfellow War—Mr. Poe's Further Reply to the Letter of Outis" (March 5, 15, 22, 25, and April 1845; series of articles; first published in the *Broadway Journal;* reprinted in *Collected Works*)

"Satirical Poems" (March 15, 1845; essay; first published in the *Broadway Journal;* reprinted in *Collected Works*)

"Address of the Carriers of the Cincinnati Daily American Republican to Its Patrons, for January, 1845" (March 22, 1845; review; first published in the *Broadway Journal;* reprinted in *Collected Works*)

"Some Words with a Mummy" (April 1845; short story; first published in the *American Review;* reprinted in the *Broadway Journal* for November 1, 1845; reprinted in *Collected Works*)

"Human Magnetism; Its Claim to Dispassionate Inquiry. Being an Attempt to Show the Utility of Its Application for the Relief of Human Suffering. By W. Newnham, Esq., M.R.S.L., Author of the 'Reciprocal Influence of Body and Mind,' Etc. New York: Wiley & Putnam" (April 5, 1845; review; first published in the *Broadway Journal;* reprinted in *Collected Works*)

"Anastatic Printing" (April 12, 1845; essay; first published in the *Broadway Journal;* reprinted in *Collected Works*)

"The Antigone at Palmo's" (April 12, 1845; review; first published in *Broadway Journal;* reprinted in *Collected Works*)

"A Dictionary of Greek and Roman Antiquities. Edited by William Smith, Ph.D., and Illustrated by Numerous Engravings on Wood. Third American Edition, Carefully Revised, and Containing Numerous Additional Articles Relative to the Botany, Mineralogy, and Zoology of the Ancients. By Charles Anthon, LLD. New York: Harper & Brothers" (April 12, 1845; review; first published in the *Broadway Journal;* reprinted in *Collected Works*)

"Achilles' Wrath" (April 18, 1845; essay; first published in the *Broadway Journal;* reprinted in *Collected Works*)

"Street Paving" (April 19, 1845; essay; first published in the *Broadway Journal;* reprinted in *Collected Works*)

"To F———" (April 26, 1845; poem; first published in the *Broadway Journal;* retitled "To Frances," shortened, and reprinted in the *Broadway Journal* for September 6, 1845; reprinted in *Collected Works*)

"Fifty Suggestions" (May and June 1845; collection of brief articles; first published in *Graham's Magazine;* reprinted in *Collected Works*)

"The Pit and the Pendulum" (1843; short story; first published in *The Gift: A Christmas and New Year's Present for 1843;* reprinted with slight revision in the *Broadway Journal* for May 17, 1845; reprinted in *Collected Works*)

"Eleonora" (1842; short story; first published in *The Gift: A Christmas and New Year's Present for 1842;* reprinted in the *Broadway Journal* for May 24, 1845; reprinted in *Collected Works*)

"The Power of Words" (June 1845; short story; first published in the *Democratic Review;* reprinted in the *Broadway Journal* for October 25, 1845; reprinted in *Collected Works*)

"Plato Contra Atheos.—Plato against the Atheists; or the Tenth Book of the Dialogue on Laws, Accompanied with Critical Notes, and Followed by Extended Dissertations on Some of the Main Points of the Platonic Philosophy and Theology Especially as Compared with the Holy Scriptures, by Tayler Lewis,

LL.D., Professor of the Greek Language and Literature, in the University in the City of New York.—New York, Harper & Brothers" (June 21, 1845; review; first published in the *Broadway Journal;* reprinted in *Collected Works*)

"Eulalie—A Song" (July 1845; poem; first published in the *American Review;* reprinted in the *Broadway Journal* for August 9, 1845; reprinted in *The Raven and Other Poems* in 1845; reprinted in *Collected Works*)

"The Imp of the Perverse" (July 1845; short story; first published in *Graham's Magazine;* reprinted in *Collected Works*)

"The Coming of the Mammoth—The Funeral of Time and Other Poems. By Henry B. Hirst, Boston: Philips & Sampson" (July 12, 1845; review; first published in the *Broadway Journal;* reprinted in *Collected Works*)

"The Drama" (1) (July 19, 1845; review; first published in the *Broadway Journal*; reprinted in *Collected Works*)

"The Drama" (2) (July 26, 1845; review; first published in the *Broadway Journal*; reprinted in *Collected Works*)

"A Chaunt of Life and Other Poems, With Sketches and Essays. By Rev. Ralph Hoyt. In Six Parts. Part II. New York: Le Roy & Hoyt" (July 26, 1845; review; first published in the *Broadway Journal;* reprinted in *Collected Works*)

"The American Drama" (August 1845; essay; first published in *American Whig Review;* reprinted in *Collected Works*)

"The Fortune Hunter; or The Adventures of a Man About Town. A Novel of New York Society. By Mrs. Anna Cora Mowatt, Author of Fashion, Etc. New York. William Taylor" (August 2, 1845; review; first published in the *Broadway Journal;* reprinted in *Collected Works*)

"The Lost Pleiad; And Other Poems. By T. H. Chivers, M.D. New York: Edward O. Jenkins" (August 2, 1845; review; first published in the *Broadway Journal;* reprinted in *Collected Works*)

"Editorial Miscellany" (August 9, 1845; brief article; first published in the *Broadway Journal;* reprinted in *Collected Works*)

"Ettore Fieramosca, or the Challenge of Barletta, An Historical Romance of the Times of the Medici, by Massimo D'Azeglio. Translated from the Italian by C. Edwards Lester, U.S. Consul at Genoa, Author of 'The Glory and Shame of England,' Member of the Ateneo Italiano at Florence, Etc. New York: Paine & Burgess" (August 9, 1845; review; first published in the *Broadway Journal;* reprinted in *Collected Works*)

"A Catholic Hymn" (August 16, 1845; poem; first published in the *Broadway Journal;* reprinted in *Collected Works*)

"The Characters of Shakespeare. By William Hazlitt. Wiley & Putnam's Library of Choice Reading. No. XVII" (August 16, 1845; review; first published

in the *Broadway Journal;* reprinted in *Collected Works*)

"Dashes At Life with a Free Pencil. By N. P. Willis. Part III. Loiterings of Travel. New York. J. S. Redfield" (August 23, 1845; first published in the *Broadway Journal;* reprinted in *Collected Works*)

"The Poetical Writings of Mrs. Elizabeth Oakes Smith. First Complete Edition. New York; J. S. Redfield" (August 23, 1845; review; published in the *Broadway Journal*)

"The Indicator and Companion. By Leigh Hunt. Wiley & Putnam's Library of Choice Reading. No. XX. Part II" (August 30, 1845; review; first published in the *Broadway Journal;* reprinted in *Collected Works*)

"Coxe's Saul." (September 6, 1845; review; first published in the *Broadway Journal;* reprinted in *Collected Works*)

"Festus: A Poem by Philip James Bailey, Barrister at Law. First American Edition. Boston: Benjamin P. Mussey. For Sale in New York by Redfield & Company" (September 6, 1845; review; first published in the *Broadway Journal;* reprinted in *Collected Works*)

"Genius and the Character of Burns. By Professor Wilson. Wiley & Putnam's Library of Choice Reading. No. XXI" (September 6, 1845; review; first published in the *Broadway Journal;* reprinted in *Collected Works*)

"Big Abel and the Little Manhattan" (September 27, 1845; review; first published in the *Broadway Journal;* reprinted in *Collected Works*)

"The Prose Works of John Milton, With a Biographical Introduction by Rufus Wilmot Griswold. In Two Volumes. Philadelphia: Herman Hooker" (September 27, 1845; review; first published in the *Broadway Journal;* reprinted in *Collected Works*)

"Wiley & Putnam's Library of American Books. No. IV. The Wigwam and the Cabin. By William Gilmore Simms" (October 4, 1845; review; first published in the *Broadway Journal;* reprinted in *Collected Works*)

"The Broken Vow and Other Poems. By Amanda M. Edmond. Boston: Gould, Kendall & Lincoln" (October 11, 1845; review; first published in the *Broadway Journal;* reprinted in *Collected Works*)

"Historical Sketch; of the Second War between the United States of America and Great Britain, Declared by Act of Congress, the 18th of June, 1812, and Concluded by Peace, the 15th of February, 1815. By Charles J. Ingersoll. In Three Volumes. Vol. I. Embracing the Events of 1812–13. Philadelphia. Lea & Blanchard" (October 11, 1845; review; first published in the *Broadway Journal;* reprinted in *Collected Works*)

"The Songs of Our Land, and Other Poems, by Mary E. Hewitt. Boston. William D. Ticknor & Co." (October 25, 1846; review; first published in the *Broadway Jour-*

nal; reprinted in *Godey's Magazine and Lady's Book* for February 1846; reprinted in *Collected Works*)

"A Chapter of Suggestions" (1845; essay; first published in the annual *The Opal for 1845;* reprinted in *Collected Works*)

The Raven and Other Poems (November 1845; poetry collection)

"The System of Doctor Tarr and Professor Fether" (November 1845; short story; first published in *Graham's Magazine;* reprinted in *Collected Works*)

"Alice Ray: A Romance In Rhyme. By Mrs. Sarah Josepha Hale. Author of 'Northwood' Etc., Etc. Philadelphia" (November 1, 1845; review; first published in the *Broadway Journal;* reprinted in *Collected Works*)

"Boston and the Bostonians. Editorial Miscellany" (November 1 and 22, 1845; two essays; first published in the *Broadway Journal;* reprinted in *Collected Works*)

"America and the American People. By Frederick von Raumer, Professor of History in the University of Berlin, Etc. Etc. Translated from the German by William W. Turner. New York; J. & G. H. Langley" (November 29, 1845; review; first published in the *Broadway Journal;* reprinted in *Collected Works*)

"Brook Farm" (December 13, 1845; review; first published in the *Broadway Journal;* reprinted in *Collected Works*)

"Poems. By Frances S. Osgood. New York: Clark & Austin" (December 13, 1845; review; first published in the *Broadway Journal;* reprinted in *Collected Works*)

"The Facts In the Case of M. Valdemar" (December 1845; short story; first published in the *American Review;* reprinted in the *Broadway Journal* for December 20, 1845; reprinted in *Collected Works*)

Tales By Edgar A. Poe (1845; short story collection)

"The Wigwam and the Cabin. By William Gilmore Simms. First Series. Wiley & Putnam's Library of American Books. No. IV" (January 1846; review; first published in *Godey's Magazine and Lady's Book;* reprinted in *Collected Works*)

"A Valentine" (February 13, 1846; poem written as a Valentine's Day gift for Frances Osgood; first published under the title "To Her Whose Name is Written Below" in the New York *Evening Mirror* for February 21, 1846; reprinted in *Collected Works*)

"The Philosophy of Composition" (April 1846; essay; first published in *Graham's Magazine;* reprinted in *Collected Works*)

"The Literati of New York City" (May–October 1846; series of literary and biographical profiles; first published in *Godey's Magazine and Lady's Book;* reprinted in *Collected Works*)

"The Cask of Amontillado" (November 1846; short story; first published in *Godey's Magazine and Lady's Book;* reprinted in *Collected Works*)

"To M. L. S.———" (March 13, 1847; poem; first published in the *Home Journal;* reprinted in *Collected Works*)

"Ulalume" (December 1847; poem; first published anonymously in the *American Whig Review;* reprinted in *Collected Works*)

"An Enigma" (March 1848; riddle poem; first published in the *Union Magazine of Literature and Art;* reprinted in *Collected Works*)

"Eureka: An Essay on the Material and Spiritual Universe" (1848; scientific essay; reprinted in *Collected Works*)

"The Bells" (May 1848; poem; published posthumously in *Sartain's Union Magazine* for November 1849; reprinted in *Collected Works*)

"The Child of the Sea, and Other Poems. By S. Anna Lewis, Author of 'Records of the Heart,' Etc., Etc." (September 1848; review; first published in the *Southern Literary Messenger;* reprinted in *Collected Works*)

"To Helen" (2) (November 1848; second poem of this title and addressed to Sarah Helen Whitman; first published in *Sartain's Union Magazine;* reprinted in *Collected Works*)

"The Poetic Principle" (December 1848; essay; first published in the *Southern Literary Messenger;* reprinted in *Collected Works*)

"Mellonta Tauta" (February 1849; short story; first published in *Godey's Magazine and Lady's Book;* reprinted in *Collected Works*)

"Hop-Frog" (March 17, 1849; short story; first published in the *Flag of Our Union;* reprinted in *Collected Works*)

"A Dream within a Dream" (March 31, 1849; poem; first published in the *Flag of Our Union;* reprinted in *Collected Works*)

"Von Kempelen and His Discovery" (April 14, 1849; short story; first published in the *Flag of Our Union;* reprinted in *Collected Works*)

"Eldorado" (April 21, 1849; poem; first published in the *Flag of Our Union;* reprinted in *Collected Works*)

"For Annie" (April 28, 1849; poem; first published in the *Flag of Our Union* and in the *Home Journal* on the same day; reprinted in *Collected Works*)

"Annabel Lee" (May 1849; poem; first appeared as part of Poe's obituary in the *New York Tribune* on October 9, 1849; reprinted in the *Southern Literary Messenger* for November 1849; reprinted in *Sartain's Union Magazine* for January 1850; reprinted in *Collected Works*)

"X-ing a Paragrab" (May 12, 1849; short story; first published in the *Flag of Our Union;* reprinted in *Collected Works*)

"Landor's Cottage. A Pendant to 'The Domain of Arnheim'" (June 9, 1849; short story; first published in the *Flag of Our Union;* reprinted in *Collected Works*)

"To My Mother" (July 7, 1849; poem; first published in the *Flag of Our Union;* reprinted in the annual *Leaflets of Memory for 1850;* reprinted in *Collected Works*)

"About Critics and Criticism: By the Late Edgar A. Poe" (1840; essay; published posthumously in *Graham's Magazine* for January 1850; reprinted in *Collected Works*)

"Sacred Mountains, The: By J. T. Headley,—Author of 'Napoleon and His Marshalls,' 'Washington and His Generals, Etc.'" (October 1850; review; first published posthumously in the *Southern Literary Messenger;* reprinted in *Collected Works*)

APPENDIX III

Poe Research Collections

University of California
San Diego Central University Library
Mandeville Department of Special Collections
La Jolla, CA 92093
Telephone: (858) 534-2533

Holdings include first and important editions of his works.

University of Chicago Library
Department of Special Collections
110 E. 57ᵗʰ Street
Chicago, IL 60637
Telephone: (312) 702-8705

Holdings include a collection of first and early editions, including rare works by Edgar Allan Poe and Nathaniel Hawthorne.

Indiana University
Lilly Library
Seventh Street
Bloomington, IN 47405
Telephone: (812) 855-2452

Holdings include first and early editions, as well as manuscripts including correspondence and papers relating to Poe. The library also contains correspondence of Sarah Helen Whitman related to her friendship with Poe.

University of Iowa Libraries
Department of Special Collections
Iowa City, IA 52242
Telephone: (319) 335-5921

Holdings include Poe-related books and articles collected by the late critic Thomas Ollive Mabbott.

Johns Hopkins University
Milton S. Eisenhower Library
Special Collections
John Work Garrett Library
4545 N. Charles Street
Baltimore, MD 21210
Telephone: (410) 516-0341

Holdings include music related to the works of Poe, as catalogued in *Music and Edgar Allan Poe: A Bibliographical Study,* by Mary Garrettson Evans (Baltimore: Johns Hopkins University Press, 1939).

Bronx County Historical Society
Bronx County Research Library
3309 Bainbridge Avenue
Bronx, New York 10467
Telephone: (212) 881-8900

Holdings include catalogued manuscripts, pictures, slides, audiotapes, films, filmstrips. The Society also maintains the Poe Cottage at Fordham, in Poe Park.

Free Library of Philadelphia
Rare Book Department
1901 Vine Street
Philadelphia, PA 19103-1189
Telephone: (215) 686-5416

Holdings include the Colonel Richard Gimble Collection of Edgar Allan Poe, including first editions, manuscripts, autograph letters, reprints, illustrated editions, foreign editions, periodicals and newspapers. The library also contains biographical materials and literary criticism of the time.

Brown University
John Hay Library
20 Prospect Street, Box A
Providence, RI 02912
Telephone: (401) 863-3723

Holdings contains a collection of approximately 500 pieces of correspondence, articles, and notes by Sarah Helen Whitman on a range of subjects, including Poe, spiritualism, American and English literature, and personal matters. The holdings also include correspondence and copies of letters, manuscripts, and reminiscences gathered by Whitman's literary heirs, as well as letters from Maria Clemm to Whitman about Poe.

University of Texas
University of Texas Libraries
Humanities Research Center
Austin, TX 78713-7219
Telephone: (512) 471-9119

Holdings include a comprehensive collection of printed works, 25 manuscripts of poems, stories, and essays; nearly one hundred letters, as well as an extensive body of manuscripts and letters from Poe's friends, relatives, editors, translators, and biographers.

Alderman Library
Manuscripts Department
University of Virginia
Charlottesville, VA 22904
Fax: (804) 924-1431

Holdings include approximately 10,000 pieces of Poe-related material in the Poe-Ingram Collection. Included are letters, manuscripts, photographs, printed matter, biographical source materials collected by Poe biographer John Henry Ingram, including many rarely seen copies and many formerly unknown copies of Poe letters.

Clifton Waller Barrett Library
Special Collections Department
Alderman Library
P.O. Box 400110 University of Virginia
Charlottesville, VA 22904-4110
Fax (804) 924-4968

Holdings include rare editions of Poe's works, many in excellent condition, as well as manuscripts and letters.

The Edgar Allan Poe Library
1914-16 E. Main Street
Richmond, VA 23223
Telephone: (804) 648-5523

Holdings include approximately 10,000 volumes of Poe-related items and manuscripts related to 19th-century American literature.

APPENDIX IV

Selected Bibliography

I. Biographical Works

Allen, Hervey. *The Life and Times of Edgar Allan Poe.* New York: Farrar & Rinehart, Inc., 1934.

Bayless, Joy. *Rufus Wilmot Griswold: Poe's Literary Executor.* Nashville, Tenn.: Vanderbilt University Press, 1943.

Bittner, William. *Poe: A Biography.* Boston: Atlantic Monthly Press, 1962.

Burr, Charles Chauncey. "Character of Edgar A. Poe." *Nineteenth Century* (February 1852): 19–33.

Campbell, Killis. "The Poe-Griswold Controversy." *Publications of the Modern Language Association (PMLA)* 34 (September 1919): 436–464.

Carter, Dr. John F. "Edgar Poe's Last Night in Richmond." *Lippincott's Monthly Magazine* 70 (November 1902): 562–566.

Chase, Lewis. "John Bransby, Poe's Schoolmaster." *Athenaeum* (May 1916): 221–222.

Cohen, B. Bernard and Lucien A. "Poe and Griswold Once More." *American Literature* 34 (March 1962): 97–101.

Davidson, James Wood. "Edgar A. Poe," *Russell's Magazine* 2 (November 1857): 161–173.

Davis, Richard Beale, ed. *Chivers' Life of Poe.* New York: E. P. Dutton & Co., 1952.

Dean, John. "Poe and the Popular Culture of His Day." *Journal of Popular Culture* 10 (1987): 35–40.

Deas, Michael J. *The Portraits and Daguerreotypes of Edgar Allan Poe.* Charlottesville, Va.: University Press of Virginia, 1989.

Didier, Eugene, L. "Life of Poe." *The Life and Poems of Edgar Allan Poe.* New York: W. J. Widdleton, 1877, pp. 19–129.

Didier, Eugene L., "Poe: Real and Reputed," *Godey's Magazine* 128 (April 1894): 452–455.

Dorset, Gerald. *An Aristocrat of the Intellect.* London: Hornsey Printers, 1959.

Dow, Dorothy. *Dark Glory.* New York: Farrar & Rinehart, 1931.

Gerber, Gerald. "Poe's Lyttleton Barry and Isaac D'Israeli's Littleton." *Poe Studies* 14, no. 2 (1981): 32.

Gill, William Fearing. "Edgar A. Poe and His Biographer; A Vindication of Poe from the Aspersions of Rufus W. Griswold." *The Poetical Works of Edgar Allan Poe.* New York: W. J. Widdleton, 1876, pp. 11–36.

Graham, George Rex. "Editor's Table: The Late Edgar Allan Poe." *Graham's Magazine* 36 (March 1850): 224–226. Reprinted in *Edgar Allan Poe: The Critical Heritage,* edited by Ian Walker. London: Routledge & Kegan Paul, 1986, pp. 376–384.

———. "The Genius and Characteristics of the Edgar Allan Poe." *Graham's Magazine* 44 (February 1854): 216–225.

Griswold, Rufus Wilmot. "The Chief Tale Writers of America." *Washington National Intelligencer,* August 30, 1845, p. 2. Reprinted in *Edgar Allan Poe: The Critical Heritage,* edited by Ian Walker. London: Routledge & Kegan Paul, 1986, pp. 182–183.

———. (as "Ludwig"). "Death of Edgar Allan Poe." *New York Tribune,* October 9, 1849, p. 2.

———. "The Late Edgar Allan Poe." *Literary American* 3 (November 10, 1849): 372–373.

———. "Edgar Allan Poe." *International Monthly Magazine* 1 (October 1850): 325–344.

———. "Memoir of the Author." *The Works of the Late Edgar Allan Poe,* 3 vols. New York: J. S. Redfield, 1850–53, III, pp. vii–xxxix. (After the appearance of volume 3 in 1856, this memoir was moved to volume I.)

Griswold, W. M., ed. *Passages from the Correspondence and Other Papers of Rufus W. Griswold.* Cambridge, Mass.: W. M. Griswold, 1898.

Griswold, W. M. "Poe's Moral Nature." *Nation,* LX, May 16, 1895, pp. 381–382.

Haining, Peter, ed. *The Edgar Allan Poe Scrapbook: Articles, Essays, Letters, Anecdotes, Photographs, and Memorabilia About the Legendary American Genius*. New York: Schocken Books, 1978.

Ingram, John H. "Memoir of Poe." *The Works of Edgar Allan Poe*. 4 vols, Edinburgh: Black, 1874–75. Vol. 1, pp. xvii–ci.

———. *Edgar Allan Poe: His Life, Letters and Opinions*. 2 vols. London: John Hogg, 1880.

Ingram, John H. "Memoir of Edgar Allan Poe." *The Complete Poetical Works and Essay on Poetry of Edgar Allan Poe Together with His Narrative of Arthur Gordon Pym*. London: Frederick Warne, 1888, pp. xi–xxxii.

Krutch, Joseph Wood. *Edgar Allan Poe: A Study in Genius*. New York: Alfred A. Knopf, 1926.

Lindsay, Philip. *The Haunted Man: A Portrait of Edgar Allan Poe*. London: Hutchinson, 1953.

Ljungquist, Kent P. and Buford Jones. "William S. Robinson on Griswold, Poe's 'Literary Executioner.'" *Poe Studies: Dark Romanticism* 28 (June/December 1995): 7–8.

Mabbott, Thomas Ollive. "Afterword." *The Collected Works of Edgar Allan Poe: Volume I—Poems*. Cambridge, Mass.: Belknap Press of Harvard University Press, 1969, pp. 571–572.

Mankowitz, Wolf. *The Extraordinary Mr. Poe: A Biography of Edgar Allan Poe*. London: Weidenfeld & Nicolson, 1978.

Miller, John Carl. *Building Poe Biography*. Baton Rouge: Louisiana State University Press, 1977.

———. *John Henry Ingram's Poe Collection at the University of Virginia: A Calendar*. Charlottesville: University Press of Virginia, 1960.

———. "Poe's Biographers Brawl." *American History Illustrated* 11, no. 7 (November 1976); 20–29.

———. *Poe's Helen Remembers*. Charlottesville: University Press of Virginia, 1979.

Moran, Dr. John J. *A Defense of Edgar Allan Poe*. Washington, D.C.: W. F. Boogher, 1885.

Neal, John. "Edgar A. Poe." *Daily Advertiser* (Portland, Maine), April 26, 1850, p. 2.

Neu, Jacob L., "Rufus Wilmot Griswold." *University of Texas Studies in English* no. 5 (1925): 101–165.

Norman, Emma K. "Poe's Knowledge of Latin." *American Literature* 6 (1934): 72–77.

Ostrom, John. "Revised Checklist of the Correspondence of Edgar Allan Poe." *Studies in the American Renaissance* (1981): 169–255.

Pannapacker, William A. "A Question of 'Character': Visual Images and the Nineteenth-Century Construction of Edgar Allan Poe." *Harvard Library Bulletin* 7 (Fall 1996): 9–24.

Peck, George W. "[Review of] The Works of Edgar Allan Poe." *American Whig Review* 11 (March 1850): 301–315.

Phillips, Mary Elizabeth. *Edgar Allan Poe, the Man*. 2 vols. Chicago: John C. Winston, 1926.

Pollin, Burton R. "Frances Sargent Osgood and Saroni's Musical Times: Documents Linking Poe, Osgood and Griswold." *Poe Studies: Dark Romanticism*, 23 (December 1990): 27–36.

Pope-Hennessy, Una. *Edgar Allan Poe: A Critical Biography*. London: Macmillan, 1934. Reprint. New York: Haskell House, 1969.

Porges, Irwin. *Edgar Allan Poe*. New York and Philadelphia: Chilton Books, 1963.

Quinn, Arthur Hobson. *Edgar Allan Poe: A Critical Biography*. New York: D. Appleton-Century Company, 1941.

Reid, Thomas Mayne, "A Dead Man Defended," *Onward* 1 (April 1869): 305–308.

Schulte, Amanda Pogue. *Facts About Poe: Portraits and Daguerreotypes of Edgar Allan Poe*. Charlottesville, Va.: University Press of Virginia, 1926.

Shanks, Edward. *Edgar Allan Poe*. London: Macmillan, 1937.

Sinclair, David. *Edgar Allan Poe*. Totowa, N.J.: Rowman & Littlefield, 1978.

Smith, Charles Alphonso. *Edgar Allan Poe: How to Know Him*. Indianapolis, Ind.: Bobbs-Merrill, 1921.

Stoddard, Richard Henry, "Edgar Allan Poe." *National Magazine* 2 (March 1853): 193–200.

———. "Life of Poe." In *The Works of Edgar Allan Poe*. 6 vols. New York: A. C. Armstrong, 1884, Vol. I.

———. "Memoir of Edgar Allan Poe." *Poems by Edgar Allan Poe*. New York: W. J. Widdleton, 1875, pp. 15–99.

Symons, Julian. *The Tell-Tale Heart: The Life and Works of Edgar Allan Poe*. New York: Harper & Row, 1978.

Thomas, Dwight and David K. Jackson. *The Poe Log: A Documentary Life of Edgar Allan Poe 1809–1849*. Boston: G. K. Hall, 1987.

Thomas, W. Moy. "Edgar Allan Poe." *The Train: A First-Class Magazine* 3 (April 1857): 193–198.

Van Cleef, Augustus. "Poe's Mary." *Harper's Monthly* 78 (March 1889): 634–640.

Wagenknecht, Edward. *Edward Allan Poe: The Man Behind the Legend*. New York: Oxford University Press, 1963.

Walsh, John E., *Plumes in the Dust: The Love Affair of Edgar Allan Poe and Frances Sargent Osgood*. Chicago: Nelson-Hall, 1980.

Weiss, Miriam. "Poe's Catterina." *Mississippi Quarterly* 19 (Winter 1965–66): 29–33.

Whitman, Sarah H. *Edgar Poe and His Critics*. New York: Rudd and Carlton, 1860. Reprinted by Rutgers University Press in 1949, with an introduction by Oral S. Coad.

Winwar, Frances. *The Haunted Palace: The Life of Edgar Allan Poe*. New York: Harper & Row, 1959.

II. General Criticism

Abel, Darrel. "Edgar Poe: A Centennial Estimate." *University of Kansas City Review* 16 (1949): 77–96.

Alexander, Jean, ed. *Affidavits of Genius: Edgar Allan Poe and the French Critics, 1847–1924*. Port Washington, N.Y.: Kennikat Press, 1971.

Allen, Michael. *Poe and the British Magazine Tradition*. New York: Oxford University Press, 1969.

Anderson, Carl L. *Poe in Northlight: The Scandinavian Response to His Life and Works*. Durham, N.C.: Duke University Press, 1973.

Bandy, William T. *The Influence and Reputation of Poe in Europe*. Baltimore, Md.: F. T. Cimino, 1962.

Benson, Adolph B. "Scandinavian References in the Works of Poe." *Journal of English and Germanic Philology* 40 (1941): 73–90.

Bloom, Clive. *Reading Poe, Reading Freud: The Romantic Imagination in Crisis*. New York: St. Martin's Press, 1988.

Bonaparte, Marie. *The Life and Works of Edgar Allan Poe: A Psycho-Analytical Interpretation*. London: Imago, 1949.

Braddy, Haldeen. *Glorious Incense: The Fulfillment of Edgar Allan Poe*. Metuchen, N.J.: Scarecrow Press, 1952.

Cambriare, Celestin Pierre. *The Influence of Edgar Allan Poe in France*. New York: G. E. Stechert, 1927.

Campbell, Killis. *The Mind of Poe and Other Studies*. Cambridge, Mass.: Harvard University Press, 1933.

———. "Miscellaneous Notes on Poe." *Modern Language Notes* 28 (1913): 65–69.

Canny, James R. and Charles F. Heartman. *A Bibliography of the First Printings of the Writings of Edgar Allan Poe*. Hattiesburg, Miss.: The Book Farm, 1943.

Carlson, Eric W., ed. *The Recognition of Edgar Allan Poe*. Ann Arbor, Mich.: University of Michigan, 1966.

Carlson, Thomas C. "The Reception of Edgar Allan Poe in Romania." *Mississippi Quarterly* 38 (1985): 441–446.

Clarke, Graham, ed. *Edgar Allan Poe Critical Assessments, I: Life and Works; II: Poe in the Nineteenth Century; III: Poe the Writer: Poems, Criticism and Short Stories; IV: Poe in the Twentieth Century*. East Sussex, United Kingdom: Helm Information, 1991.

Dameron, J. Lasley and Irby B. Cauthen, Jr. *Edgar Allan Poe: A Bibliography of Criticism, 1827–1967*. Charlottesville: University Press of Virginia, 1974.

Davidson, Edward H. *Poe, a Critical Study*. Cambridge, Mass.: Belknap Press of Harvard University, 1957.

Dayan, Joan. "Amorous Bondage: Poe, Ladies, and Slaves." *American Literature* 66 (1994): 239–273.

Douglas, Ann. *The Feminization of American Culture*. New York: Alfred A. Knopf, 1977.

Englelkirk, John Eugene. *Edgar Allan Poe in Hispanic Literature*. New York: Instituto de las Espanas en los Estados Unidos, 1934. Reprinted by Russell & Russell, 1972.

Fagin, N. Bryllian. *The Histrionic Mr. Poe*. Baltimore: Johns Hopkins University Press, 1949.

Forrest, William M. *Biblical Allusions in Poe*. New York: Macmillan, 1926.

Garrison, Joseph M., Jr. "The Function of Terror in the Work of Edgar Allan Poe." *American Quarterly* 18 (1966): 136–150.

Gimble, Colonel Richard. "Quoth the Raven: An Exhibition of the Work of Edgar Allan Poe." *Yale University Library Gazette* 33 (April 1959): 138–139.

Grossman, John Delaney. *Edgar Allan Poe in Russia: A Study in Legend and Literary Influence*. Wirzburg, Germany: Jal Velag, 1973.

Gunn, James. *Alternate Worlds*. Englewood, N.J.: Prentice-Hall, 1975.

Halliburton, David. *Edgar Allan Poe: A Phenomenological View*. Princeton, N.J.: Princeton University Press, 1973.

Hoffman, Daniel. *Poe Poe Poe Poe Poe Poe Poe*. Garden City, N.Y.: Doubleday & Co., 1972.

Hoffmann, Gerhard. "Edgar Allan Poe and German Literature." In *American-German Literary Interrelations in the Nineteenth Century*. Edited by Christoph Wecker. Munich, Germany: Fink, 1983. 52–104.

Howarth, William L., ed. *Twentieth-Century Interpretations of Poe's Tales*. Englewood Cliffs, N.J.: Prentice-Hall, 1971.

Hyneman, Esther F. *Edgar Allan Poe: An Annotated Bibliography of Books and Articles in English, 1827–1973*. Boston: G. K. Hall, 1974.

Kayser Wolfgang. *The Grotesque in Art and Literature*. New York: McGraw-Hill, 1966.

Kennedy, Gerald. *Poe, Death and the Life of Writing*. New Haven, Conn.: Yale University Press, 1987.

Kesterton, David B., ed. *Critics on Poe*. Coral Gables, Fla.: Miami University Press, 1973.

Ketterer, David. *The Rationale of Deception in Poe*. Baton Rouge: Louisiana State University Press, 1979.

Knapp, Bettina. *Edgar Allan Poe*. New York: Frederick Ungar, 1984.

Lawson, Lewis A. "Poe's Conception of the Grotesque." *Mississippi Quarterly* 19 (1966): 200–205.

Lee, A. Robert. *Edgar Allan Poe: The Design of Order*. Totowa, N.J.: Barnes & Noble, 1987.

Levine, Stuart. *Edgar Poe: Seer and Craftsman*. Deland, Fla.: Everett/Edwards, 1972.

Levy, Maurice. "Poe and the Gothic Tradition." *ESQ: A Journal of the American Renaissance*, 18 (1972): 19–28.

Ljungquist, Kent P. "Uses of the Daemon in Selected Works of Edgar Allan Poe." *Interpretations* 12 (1980): 31–39.

Mainville, Stephen. "Language and the Void: Gothic Landscapes in the Frontiers of Edgar Allan Poe." *Genre* 14 (1981): 347–362.

Matthiessen, F. O. "Poe." *Sewanee Review* 54 (1946): 175–205.

Moldenhauer, Joseph. *A Descriptive Catalogue of Edgar Allan Poe Manuscripts in the Humanities Research Center Library.* Austin, Tex.: Texas University Press, 1973.

Mooney, Stephen L. "Poe's Gothic Wasteland." *Sewanee Review* 70 (1972): 261–283.

Moss, Sidney P. *Poe's Major Crisis: His Libel Suit and New York's Literary World.* Durham, N.C.: Duke University Press, 1970.

Ostrom, John Ward, ed., *The Letters of Edgar Allan Poe.* New York: Gordian Press, Inc, 1966.

Pennzoldt, Peter. *The Supernatural in Fiction.* London: Peter Nevill, 1952.

Phillips, Elizabeth. *Edgar Allan Poe: An American Imagination.* Port Washington, N.Y.: Kennikat Press, 1979.

Pollin, Burton R. "The Living Writers of America: A Manuscript by Edgar Allan Poe." *Studies in the American Renaissance 1991.* Charlottesville: University Press of Virginia, 1991, pp. 151–211.

———. "Music and Edgar Allan Poe: A Second Annotated Checklist." Poe Studies, 15, no. 1 (1982): 7–13.

Quinn, Patrick, ed. *Poetry and Tales.* New York: Library of America, 1978.

Quinn, Arthur H. and Richard H. Hart. *Edgar Allan Poe: Letters and Documents in the Enoch Pratt Free Library.* New York: Scholars' Facsimiles and Reprints, 1941.

Regan, Robert, ed. *Poe: A Collection of Critical Essays.* Englewood Cliffs, N.J.: Prentice-Hall, 1967.

Smith, Ronald. *Poe in the Media: Screen, Songs, and Spoken Word Recordings.* New York: Garland Publishing, 1990.

Stoehr, Taylor. "Unspeakable Horror in Poe." *South Atlantic Quarterly* 78 (1979): 317–332.

Walker, G. A. *Gatherings from Grave Yards.* London: Longman & Co., 1839. Reprinted by Arno Press in 1977.

Wilbur, Richard. "Poe and the Art of Suggestion." *University of Mississippi Studies in English* 3 (1982): 1–13.

Williams, Michael J. *A World of Words: Language and Displacement in the Fiction of Edgar Allan Poe.* Durham, N.C.: Duke University Press, 1988.

III. Tales

Alekna, Richard A. "'The Man That Was Used Up': Further Notes on Poe's Satirical Targets." *Poe Studies* 12 (1979): 36.

Arnold, John. "Poe's 'Lionizing': The Wound the Bawdry." *Literature and Psychology* 17 (1967): 52–54.

Badenhausen, Richard. "Fear and Trembling in the Literature of the Fantastic: Edgar Allan Poe's 'The Black Cat.'" *Studies in Short Fiction* 29 (1992): 486–498.

Baskett, Sam S. "A Damsel with a Dulcimer: An Interpretation of Poe's 'Eleonora.'" *Modern Language Notes* 78 (1958): 332–338.

Bennett, Maurice T. "Edgar Allan Poe and the Literary Tradition of Lunar Speculation." *Science-Fiction Studies* 10 (1983): 137–147.

Benton, Richard. "Is Poe's 'The Assignation' a Hoax?" *Nineteenth Century Fiction* 28 (1963): 193–197.

Bieganowski, Ronald. "The Self-Consuming Narrator in Poe's 'Ligeia' and 'Usher.'" *American Literature* 60 (1988): 175–188.

Bleiler, E. F. "Edgar Allan Poe, 1809–1849." *Supernatural Fiction Writers.* 2 vols. New York: Charles Scribner's, 1985, vol. 2, pp. 697–705.

Blythe, Hal, and Charlie Sweet. "The Reader as Poe's Ultimate Dupe in 'The Purloined Letter.'" *Studies in Short Fiction* 26 (1989): 311–315.

Bronzwaer, W. "Deixis as a Structuring Device in Narrative Discourse: An Analysis of Poe's 'The Murders in the Rue Morgue.'" *English Studies* 56 (1975): 345–359.

Brophy, Brigid. "Detective Fiction: A Modern Myth of Violence?" *Hudson Review* 18 (1965): 11–30.

Brown, Arthur A. "Death and Telling in Poe's 'The Imp of the Pervese.'" *Studies in Short Fiction* 31 (1994): 197–205.

Carson, David L. "Ortolans and Geese: Origin of Poe's 'Duc de L'Omelette.'" *College Language Association Journal* 8 (1965): 277–283.

Carter, Steve. "A Possible Source for 'The Facts in the Case of M. Valdemar,'" *Poe Studies* 12 (1979): 36.

Cassuto, Leonard. "The Coy Reaper: Unmasque-ing the Red Death." *Studies in Short Fiction* 25 (1988): 317–320.

Christie, James W. "Poe's 'Diabolical' Humor: Revisions in 'Bon-Bon'." *Library Chronicle* 41 (1976): 44–45.

Clark, David L. "The Source of Poe's 'The Pit and The Pendulum.'" *Modern Language Notes* 44 (1929): 349–356.

Claudel, Alice M. "What Has Poe's 'Silence—A Fable' to Say?" *Ball State University Forum* 10 (1969): 66–70.

Cleman, John. "Irresistible Impulses: Edgar Allan Poe and the Insanity Defense." *American Literature* 63 (1991): 623–640.

Curran, Robert T. "The Fashionable Thirties: Poe's Satire in 'The Man That Was Used Up.'" *Markham Review* 8 (1978): 14–20.

Dayan, Joan. *Fables of the Mind: An Inquiry into Poe's Fiction.* New York: Oxford University Press, 1987.

———. "The Road to Landor's Cottage: Poe's Landscape of Effect." *University of Mississippi Studies in English* 3 (1982): 136–154.

De Falco, Joseph. "The Sources of Terror in Poe's 'Shadow—A Parable'." *Studies in Short Fiction* 6 (1969): 643–649.

Deniccio, Jerone D. "Fact, Fiction, Fantality: Poe's 'The Thousand-and-Second Tale of Scheherazade.'" *Studies in Short Fiction* 27 (1990): 365–370.

Drabeck, Bernard A. "'Tarr and Fether': Poe and Abolitionism." *American Transcendental Quarterly* 17 (1972): 177–184.

Elbert, Monika M. "'The Man of the Crowd' and the Man Outside the Drowd: Poe's Narrator and the Democratic Reader." *Modern Language Studies* 21, no. 4 (1991): 16–30.

Elmar, Schenkel. "Disease and Vision: Perspectives on Poe's 'The Sphinx.'" *Studies in American Fiction* 13 (1985): 97–102.

Engel, Leonard W. "Victim and Victimizer: Poe's 'The Cask of Amontillado.'" *Interpretations* 15 (1983): 26–30.

Falk, Doris V. "Poe and the Power of Animal Magnetism." *Publications of the Modern Language Association (PMLA)* 84 (1969): 536–546.

Finholt, Richard D. "The Vision at the Brink of the Abyss: 'A Descent into the Maelstrom' in the Light of Poe's Cosmology." *Georgia Review* 27 (1973): 356–366.

Forbes, J. Christopher. "Satire of Irving's *A History of New York* in Poe's 'The Devil in the Belfry.'" *Studies in American Fiction* 10 (1982): 93–100.

Frank, Frederick S. "Polarized Gothic: An Annotated Bibliography of Poe's *Narrative of Arthur Gordon Pym*." *Bulletin of Bibliography* 38 (1981): 117–127.

Fukuchi, Curtis. "Repression and Guilt in Poe's 'Morella.'" *Studies in Short Fiction* 24 (1987): 149–154.

Gargano, James W. "'The Black Cat': Perverseness Reconsidered." *Texas Studies in Literature and Language* 2 (1960): 172–178.

Gerber, Gerald. "Poe's Odd Angel." *Nineteenth Century Fiction* 23 (1968): 88–93.

Glassheim, Eliot. "A Dogged Interpretation of 'Never Bet the Devil Your Head.'" *Poe Newsletter* 2 (October 1969): 44–45.

Goldhurst, William. "The New Revenge Tragedy: Treatments of the Beauchamp Case." *Southern Literary Journal* 22 (1989): 117–127.

———. "Poe's Multiple King Pest: A Source Study." *Tulane Studies in English* 20 (1972): 107–121.

Griffith, Clark. "Poe's 'Ligeia' and the English Romantics." *University of Toronto Quarterly* 24 (1954): 8–25.

Gross, Seymour. "Poe's Revision of 'The Oval Portrait.'" *Modern Language Notes* 74 (1959): 16–20.

Hall, Thomas. "Poe's Use of a Source: Davy's Chemical Researches and 'Von Kempelen and His Discovery.'" *Poe Newsletter* 1 (October 1968): 28.

Harrison, James Albert, ed. *The Complete Works of Edgar Allan Poe*. 17 vols. New York: T. Crowell, 1902.

Hennelly, Mark M. Jr. "Le Grand Captain Kidder and His Bogus Bug." *Studies in Short Fiction* 17 (1980): 77–79.

Hess, Jeffry A. "Sources and Aesthetics of Poe's Landscape Fiction." *American Quarterly* 22 (1970): 177–189.

Hirsch, David H. "'The Duc de L'Omelette' as Anti-Visionary Tale." *Poe Studies* 10 (1978): 36–39.

———. "The Pit and the Apocalypse." *Sewanee Review* 76 (1968): 632–652.

———. "Poe's 'Metzengerstein' as a Tale of the Subconscious." *University of Mississippi Studies in English* 3 (1982): 40–52.

Hoffman, Michael J. "The House of Usher and Negative Romanticism." *Studies in Romanticism* 4 (1965): 158–168.

Hoffman, Stephen K. "Sailing in the Self: Jung, Poe, and 'MS. Found in a Bottle.'" *Tennessee Studies in Literature* 26 (1981): 66–74.

Holsapple, Cortell King. "'The Masque of the Red Death' and *I Promessi Sposi*." *University of Texas Studies in English* 18 (1938): 137–139.

Hubbs, Valentine C. "The Struggle of the Wills in Poe's 'William Wilson.'" *Studies in American Fiction* 1 (1983): 73–79.

Johansen, Ib. "The Madness of the Text: Deconstruction of Narrative Logic in 'Usher,' 'Berenice,' 'Doctor Tarr and Professor Fether.'" *Poe Studies* 22 (1989): 1–9.

Jillson, Willard Rouse. "The Beauchamp-Sharp Tragedy in American Literature." *Kentucky State Historical Society Register* 36 (January 1938): 54–60.

Kehler, Joel R. "New Light on the Genesis and Progress of Poe's Landscape Fiction." *American Literature* 47 (1975): 173–183.

Kennedy, J. Gerald. *The Narrative of Arthur Gordon Pym and the Abyss of Interpretation*. New York: Twayne, 1995.

———. "Poe and Magazine Writing on Premature Burial." *Studies in the American Renaissance* (1977): 165–178.

Kimball, William J. "Poe's *Politian* and the Beauchamp-Sharp Tragedy." *Poe Studies* 4, no. 2, (1971): 25–27.

Kock, Christian. "The Irony of Oxygen in Poe's 'Eiros and Charmion.'" *Studies in Short Fiction* 22 (1985): 317–321.

Lemay, J. A. Leo "Poe's 'The Business Man': Its Contexts and Satire of Franklin's *Autobiography*." *Poe Studies* 15, no. 2 (1982): 29–37.

Lewis, Paul. "Laughing at Fear: Two Versions of the Mock Gothic." *Studies in Short Fiction* 15 (1978): 411–414.

Ljungquist, Kent. "Poe's 'Island of the Fay': The Passing of Fairyland." *Studies in Short Fiction* 14 (1977): 265–271.

Long, David A. "Poe's Political Identity: A Mummy Unswathed." *Poe Studies* 23, no. 1 (1990): 1–22.

Lucas, Mary. "Poe's Theatre: 'King Pest' and 'Hop-Frog.'" *Journal of the Short Story in English* 14 (1990): 25–40.

Mabbott, Thomas Olive, ed. *The Collected Works of Edgar Allan Poe.* Vols. 2 and 3 Tales and Sketches. Cambridge, Mass.: Belknap Press of Harvard University Press, 1978.

Madden, Fred. "Poe's 'The Black Cat' and Freud's 'The Uncanny.'" *Literature & Psychology* 39, nos. 1–2 (1993): 52–62.

Mainville, Stephen. "Language and the Void: Gothic Landscapes in the Frontiers of Edgar Allan Poe." *Genre* 14 (1981): 347–362.

Marrs, Robert L. "'The Fall of the House of Usher': A Checklist of Criticism Since 1960." *Poe Studies* 5 (1972): 23–24.

Martin, Bruce K. "Poe's 'Hop-Frog' and the Retreat from Comedy." *Studies in Short Fiction* 10 (1973): 288–290.

Martin, Terry J. "Detection, Imagination, and the Introduction to 'The Murders in the Rue Morgue.'" *Modern Language Studies* 19 (1989): 31–45.

May, Charles E. *Edgar Allan Poe: A Study of the Short Fiction.* Boston: Twayne, 1991.

May, Leila S. "'Sympathies of a Scarcely Intelligible Nature': The Brother-Sister Bond in Poe's 'The Fall of the House of Usher.'" *Studies in Short Fiction* 30 (1993): 387–396.

Mazurek, Ray. "Art, Ambiguity, and the Artist in Poe's 'The Man in the Crowd.'" *Poe Studies* 12 (1979): 25–28.

McClary, Ben Harris. "Poe's 'Turkish Fig Peddler.'" *Poe Newsletter* 2 (October 1969): 56.

McEntee, Grace. "Remembering Ligeia." *Studies in American Fiction* 20 (1992): 75–83.

McMullen, Bonnie Shannon. "Lifting the Lid on Poe's 'Oblong Box.'" *Studies in American Fiction* 23 (1995): 203–214.

McNeal, Thomas. "Poe's *Zenobia:* An Early Satire on Margaret Fuller." *Modern Language Quarterly* 9 (1950): 215–226.

Michael, John. "Narration and Reflection: The Search for Grounds in Poe's 'The Power of Words' and 'The Domain of Arnheim.'" *Arizona Quarterly* 45 (1989): 1–22.

Miller, F. DeWolfe. "The Basis for Poe's 'The Island of the Fay.'" *American Literature* 14 (1942): 135–140.

Mooney, Stephen Leroy. "The Comic in Poe's Fiction." *American Literature* 33 (1962): 433–441.

———. "Poe's Gothic Wasteland." *Sewanee Review* 70 (1962): 261–283.

Muckley, Peter A. "The Radicalness of These Differences: Reading 'The Purloined Letter.'" *University of Mississippi Studies in English* 8 (1990): 227–242.

Pahl, Dennis. "Rediscovering Byron: Poe's 'The Assignation.'" *Criticism* 26 (1984): 211–299.

Perkins, Leroy, and Joseph A. Dupras. "Mystery and Meaning in Poe's 'X-ing a Paragrab.'" *Studies in Short Fiction* 27 (1990): 489–494.

Person, Leland S., Jr. "Poe's Fiction: Women and the Subversion of Masculine Form." In *Aesthetic Headaches: Women and a Masculine Poetics in Poe, Hawthorne, Melville.* Athens, Ga.: Georgia University Press, 1988. 19–47; 180–182.

Pitcher, Edward W. "Poe's 'The Assignation': a Reconsideration." *Poe Studies* 13 (1980): 1–4.

Pollin, Burton R., ed. *The Collected Writings of Edgar Allan Poe:* (Vol. 1—*The Imaginary Voyages, including The Narrative of Arthur Gordon Pym, The Unparalleled Adventure of One Hans Pfaall and The Journal of Julius Rodman*). Boston: Twayne Publishers, 1981.

———. "Hans Pfaall: A False Variant of the Phallic Fallacy." *Mississippi Quarterly* 31 (1978): 519–527.

———. "Poe's 'Diddling': The Source of Title and Tale." *Southern Literary Journal* 2, no. 1 (1969): 106–111.

———. "Poe's Dr. Ollapod." *American Literature* 42 (1970): 80–82.

———. "Poe's 'Mystification': Its Source in Fay's Norman Leslie." *Mississippi Quarterly* 25 (1972): 111–130.

———. "Poe's 'Shadow' as a Source for His 'The Masque of the Red Death.'" *Studies in Short Fiction* 6 (1968): 104–107.

———. "Poe's 'Some Words with a Mummy' Reconsidered." *Emerson Society Quarterly* 60 (Fall 1970): 60–67.

———. "Politics and History in Poe's 'Mellonta Tauta': Two Allusions Explained." *Studies in Short Fiction* 8 (1971): 627–631.

———. "'The Spectacles' of Poe—Sources and Significance." *American Literature* 37 (1965): 187–190.

Richmond, Lee J. "Edgar Allan Poe's 'Moella': Vampire of Volitoin." *Studies in Short Fiction* 9 (1972): 93–95.

Robinson, E. Arthur. "Cosmic Vision in Poe's 'Eleonora.'" *Poe Studies* 9 (1976): 44–46.

———. "Poe's 'Tell-Tale Heart'." *Nineteenth Century Fiction* 19 (1965): 369–378.

Robinson, Douglas. "Poe's Mini-Apocalypse: 'The Conversation of Eiros and Charmion.'" *Studies in Short Fiction* 19 (1982): 329–337.

———. "Trapped in the Text: 'The Pit and the Pendulum.'" *Journal of the Short Story in English* 7 (1986): 63–75.

Rolt, L. T. C. *The Aeronauts: A History of Ballooning 1783–1903.* New York: Walter, 1966.

Roppolo, Joseph. "Meaning and 'The Masque of the Red Death.'" *Tulane Studies in English* 13 (1963): 59–69.

Rose, Marilyn Gaddis. "'Emmanuele'—'Morella': Gide's Poe Affinities." *Texas Studies in Language and Literature* 5 (1963): 127–137.

Rosenfeld, Alvin. "Description in Poe's 'Landor's Cottage.'" *Studies in Short Fiction* 4 (1967): 264–265.

Rosenszweig, Paul. "'Dust within the Rock': The Phantasm of Meaning in The Narrative of Arthur Gordon Pym." *Studies in the Novel* 14 (1982): 137–151.

Roth, Martin. "The Mysteries of 'The Mystery of Marie Rogêt.'" *Poe Studies* 22, no. 2 (1989): 27–34.

———. "Poe's 'Three Sundays in a Week.'" *Sphinx* 4, no. 4 (1985): 258–267.

Salzberg, Joel. "Preposition and Meaning in Poe's 'The Spectacles.'" *Poe Newsletter* 3, no. 1 (1970): 21.

Scudder, H. H. "Poe's 'Balloon-Hoax.'" *American Literature* 21 (1949): 1799–190.

Sloan, David E. E. "Gothic Romanticism and Rational empiricism in Poe's 'Berenice.'" *American Transcendental Quarterly* 19 (Summer 1973): 19–26.

Soule, George H., Jr. "Byronism in Poe's 'Metzengerstein' and 'William Wilson.'" *Emerson Society Quarterly* 24 (1978): 152–162.

Stern, Madeleine B. "Poe: 'The Mental Temperament' for Phrenologists." *American Literature* 40 (1968): 155–163.

Strepp, Walter. "The Ironic Double in Poe's 'The Cask of Amontillado.'" *Studies in Short Fiction* 13 (1976): 447–453.

Taylor, Walter F. "Israfel in Motley." *Sewanee Review* 42 (1934): 330–340.

Teunissen, John J., and Evelyn J. Hinz. "Poe's 'Journal of Julius Rodman' as Parody." *Nineteenth Century Fiction* 27 (1972): 317–338.

Thompson, Gary R. "Dramatic Irony in 'The Oval Portrait.'" *English Language Notes* 6 (1968): 107–114.

———. "Is Poe's 'A Tale of the Ragged Mountains' a Hoax?" *Studies in Short Fiction* 6 (1969): 454–460.

———. "On the Nose—Further Speculations on the Sources and Meaning of Poe's 'Lionizing.'" *Studies in Short Fiction* 6 (1968): 94–97.

———. *Poe's Fiction: Romantic Irony in the Gothic Tales.* Madison, Wis.: Wisconsin University Press, 1973.

———. "Poe's 'Flawed' Gothic: Absurdist Techniques in 'Metzengerstein' and the Courier Satires." *Emerson Society Quarterly* (supplement) 60 (1970): 35–58.

Tucker, D. "'The Tell-Tale Heart' and the 'Evil Eye.'" *Southern Literary Journal* 13, no. 2 (1981): 92–98.

Vanderbilt, Kermit. "Art and Nature in 'The Masque of the Red Death.'" *Nineteenth-Century Fiction* 22 (1968): 379–389.

Varner, Cornelia. "Notes on Poe's Use of Contemporary Materials in Certain of His Stories." *Journal of English and Germanic Philology* 32 (1933): 77–80.

———. "Poe's 'Tale of Jerusalem' and The Talmud." *American Book Collector* 6 (February 1935), 56–57.

Walsh, John. *Poe, The Detective: The Curious Circumstances Behind "The Mystery of Marie Rogêt."* New Brunswick, N.J.: Rutgers University Press, 1968.

Ware, Tracy. "'A Descent into the Maelstrom': The Status of Scientific Rhetoric in a Perverse Rhetoric." *Studies in Short Fiction* 29 (1992): 77–84.

Weber, Jean-Paul. "Edgar Poe on the Theme of the Clock." *La Nouvelle Revue Française* 68–69 (August–September 1958): 301–311.

Whalen, Terrence. "Poe's 'Diddling' and the Depression: Notes on the Sources of Swindling." *Studies in American Fiction* 23 (1995): 195–201.

Wilkerson, Ronald S. "Poe's 'Balloon-Hoax' Once More." *American Literature* 32 (1960): 313–317.

Williams, Michael. "'The Language of the Cipher': Interpretation in The Gold-Bug." *American Literature* 53 (1982): 646–660.

Wimsatt, William K., Jr. "A Further Note on Poe's 'Balloon-Hoax.'" *American Literature* 22 (1951): 491–492.

Ziolkowski, Theodore. "The Telltale Teeth: Pschodontia to Sociodontia." *Publications of the Modern Language Association (PMLA)* 91 (1976): 9–22.

IV. Poems

Bailey, James O. "The Geography of Poe's 'Dreamland' and 'Ulalume.'" *Studies in Philology,* 45 (1948): 512–523.

Bandy, W. T. "Poe's 'Alone': The First Printing." *Papers of the Bibliographical Society of America* 70 (1976): 405–406.

Bledsoe, Thomas F. "On Poe's 'Valley of Unrest.'" *Modern Language Notes* 61 (1946): 91–92.

Booth, Bradford A. "The Identity of 'Annabel Lee.'" *College English* 7 (October 1945): 17–19.

Broderick, John C. "Poe's Revisions of 'Lenore.'" *American Literature* 35 (1964): 504–510.

Cairns, William B. "Some Notes on Poe's 'Al Aaraaf.'" *Modern Philology* 13 (1915): 35–44.

Campbell, Killis, ed. *The Poems of Edgar Allan Poe.* Boston: Ginn and Company, 1917.

Dedmond, Francis B. "The Word 'Tintinnabulation' and a Source for Poe's 'The Bells.'" *Notes & Queries* 196 (November 24, 1951): 520–521.

De Prospo, R. C. "Poe's Alpha Poem: The Title of 'Al Aaraaf.'" *Poe Studies* 22, no. 2 (1989): 34–39.

Franklin, Rosemary F. "Poe and The Awakening." *Mississippi Quarterly* 47 (1993–1994): 47–57.

Gargano, James W. "Poe's 'To Helen.'" *Modern Language Notes* 75 (1960): 652–653.

Garrison, Joseph M., Jr. "Poe's 'City in the Sea.'" *Poe Studies* 22, no. 2 (1989): 43–44.

Harrison, James Albert, ed. *The Complete Works of Edgar Allan Poe:* Vol. VII—*Poems*. New York: T. Crowell, 1902. Reprinted by AMS Press in 1965.

Hogue, L. Lynn. "Eroticism in Poe's 'For Annie.'" *Poe Symposium, Emerson Society Quarterly* 60 (1970): 85–87.

Kilburn, Patrick. "Poe's 'Evening Star.'" *Explicator* 28 (May 1970): item 76.

Lavin, Audrey. "A Birder's Re-Reading of Poe's 'Romance.'" *University of Mississippi Studies in English* 9 (1991): 199–204.

Ljungquist, Kent. "'The Coliseum': A Dialogue on Ruins." *Poe Studies* no. 16. (1983): 32–33.

Lubbers, Klaus. "Poe's 'The Conqueror Worm.'" *American Literature* 39 (1967): 375–379.

Mabbott, Thomas Olive, ed. *The Collected Works of Edgar Allan Poe*. Vol. 1—*Poems*. Cambridge, Mass.: Belknap Press of Harvard University Press, 1978.

———. "Poe's 'The Sleeper' Again." *American Literature* 21 (1949): 339–340.

Merivale, Patricia. "The Raven and the Bust of Pallas: Classical Artifacts and the Gothic Tale." *PMLA* 89 (1974): 960–966.

Miller, Perry. *The Raven and the Whale*. New York: Harcourt, Brace, 1956.

O'Neill, James. "A Closer Source for the Goths in Poe's 'Letter to B———.'" *Poe Studies* 12 (1979): 19–20.

Person, Leland S., Jr. "Poe's Composition of Philosophy: Reading and Writing 'The Raven.'" *Arizona Quarterly* 46 (1990): 1–15.

Pollin, Burton R. "Poe's 'Eldorado' Viewed as a Song of the West." *Prairie Schooner* 46 (1972): 228–235.

———. "Poe and Frances Osgood, as Linked Through 'Lenore.'" *Mississippi Quarterly* 46 (1993): 185–197.

Postema, James. "Edgar Allan Poe's Control of Readers: Formal Pressures in Poe's Dream Poems." *Essays in Literature* 18 (1991): 68–75.

Reilly, John E. *The Image of Poe in American Poetry*. Baltimore, Md.: Enoch Pratt Free Library, Edgar Allan Poe Society, and the Library of the University of Baltimore, 1976.

Robbins, J. Albert. "A New Manuscript of Poe's 'For Annie.'" *Studies in Bibliography: Papers of the Bibliographical Society of the University of Virginia* 39 (1986): 261–265.

Robinson, David. "'Ulalume': The Ghouls and the Critics." *Poe Studies* 8 (1975): 8–10.

St. Armand, Barton Levi. "Poe's Unnecessary Angel: 'Israfel' Reconsidered." In *Ruined Eden of the Present: Hawthorne, Melville, Poe*. Edited by G. R. Thompson, Virgil L. Lokke, and Chester E. Eisinger. West Lafayette, Ind.: Purdue University Press, 1981. 283–302.

Stovall, Floyd, ed. *The Poems of Edgar Allan Poe*. Charlottesville, Va.: The University of Virginia Press, 1965.

Thomas, J. David. "The Composition of Wilde's *The Harlot House*." *Modern Language Notes* 65 (1950): 485–488.

Thompson, G. R. *Circumscribed Eden of Dreams: Dream Vision and Nightmare in Poe's Early Poetry*. Baltimore, Md.: Edgar Allan Poe Society, 1984.

Thorpe, Dwayne. "Poe's 'City in the Sea': Sources and Interpretation." *American Literature* 51 (1979): 394–399.

Tritt, Michael. "'Ligeia' and 'The Conqueror Worm.'" *Poe Studies* 9 (1976): 21–22.

Wegelin, Oscar. "The Printer of Poe's *Tamerlane*." *New York Historical Society Quarterly Bulletin* 24 (January 1940): 23–25.

Weston, Arthur Harold. "The 'Nicean Barks' of Edgar Allan Poe." *Classical Journal* 29 (1933): 213–215.

Whitty, James, ed. *The Complete Poems of Edgar Allan Poe*. Boston: Houghton Mifflin Company, 1911.

V. Reviews and Essays

Bailey, J. O. "Poe's Palestine." *American Literature* 13 (1941): 44–58.

Brigham, Clarence Saunders. "Edgar Allan Poe's Contributions to Alexander's Weekly Messenger." *Proceedings of the American Antiquarian Society,* new series LII, April 1942, pp. 45–124.

Brooks, Curtis M. "The Cosmic God: Science and the Creative Imagination in *Eureka*." *American Transcendental Quarterly* 26 (1975): 60–68.

Burke, Kenneth. "The Principle of Composition." *Poetry* 99 (October 1961): 46–53.

Cappello, Mary. "'Berenice' and Poe's *Marginalia*: Adversaria of Memory." *New Orleans Review* 17, no. 4 (1990): 54–65.

Colby, Robert A. "Poe's Philosophy of Composition." *University of Kansas City Review* 20 (1954): 211–214.

Foust, R.e. "Aesthetician of Simultaneity: E. A. Poe and Modern Literary Theory." *South Atlantic Review* 46, no. 2 (1981): 17–25.

Harrison, James Albert, ed. *The Complete Works of Edgar Allan Poe*. 17 vols. New York: T. Crowell, 1902.

Hatvary, George Egon. "The Whereabouts of Poe's 'Fifty Suggestions.'" *Poe Studies* 4, no. 2 (December 1971): 47–48.

Irwin, John T. "Handedness and the Self: Poe's Chess Player." *Arizona Quarterly* 45 (1989): 1–28.

Jackson, David Kelly. "Poe Notes: 'Pinakidia' and 'Some Ancient Greek Authors.'" *American Literature* 5 (1933): 258–267.

Mabbott, Thomas Ollive, ed. *The Collected Works of Edgar Allan Poe*. Vols. 2 & 3. Cambridge, Mass.: Belknap Press of Harvard University Press, 1978.

McAndrews, Carleen. "Edgar Allan Poe's Hawthorne Criticism: An Addition." *Nathaniel Hawthorne Review* 18 (1992): 21.

Miller, John Carl, ed. *Marginallia*. Charlottesville, Va.: University of Virginia Press, 1981.

O'Neill, Edward H. "The Poe-Griswold Texts of 'Marginalia.'" *American Literature* 15 (November 1943): 238–250.

Panek, Leroy L. "'Maezel's Chess-Player,' Poe's First Detective Mistake." *American Literature* 48 (1976): 370–372.

Parks, Edd Winfield. *Edgar Allan Poe as Literary Critic.* Athens: Georgia University Press, 1964.

Piacentino, Edward J. "The Poe-Longfellow Plagiarism Controversy: A New Critical Notice in the *Southern Chronicle*." *Mississippi Quarterly* 42 (1989): 173–182.

Pollin, Burton R., ed. *The Collected Writings of Edgar Allan Poe.* Vol. 2, *The Brevities: Pinakidia, Marginalia and Other Works;* Vol. 3, *The Broadway Journal,* Nonfictional Prose, Part I: Text; Vol. 4, *The Broadway Journal,* Nonfictional Prose, Part II: Annotations. New York: Gordian Press, pp. 1985–1986.

Seitz, Don C., ed. *A Chapter on Autography.* New York: Dial Press, 1925.

Sherman, G. W. "Poe and the Panopticon." *Poe Studies* 14, no. 2 (1981): 31.

Thompson, G. Richard, ed. *Essays and Reviews.* New York: Library of America, 1984.

Varner, John Grier. "Poe and Miss Barrett of Wimpole Street." *Four Arts* 2 (January–February 1935): 4–5, 14–15, 17.

Walker, I. M. *Edgar Allan Poe: The Critical Heritage.* London and New York: Routledge & Kegan Paul, 1986.

Welch, Susan. "The Value of Analogical Evidence: Poe's Eureka in the Context of a Scientific Debate." *Modern Language Studies* 21, no. 4 (1991): 3–15.

INDEX

Note: **Boldface** numbers indicate primary discussions of a topic. *Italic* numbers indicate illustrations.